ScottForesman
LITERATURE
AND INTEGRATED STUDIES

Middle School: Grade Six

Middle School: Grade Seven

Middle School: Grade Eight

Forms of Literature

World Literature

American Literature

English Literature

The cover features a detail of Shang Jin's painting *Girl of Yi Nationality* (1993), which appears in full on this page. Born in China in 1947, he frequently depicts members of his country's many ethnic groups, like this Yi girl, whose people live in the uplands of southwestern China and adjacent areas of Laos, Vietnam, and Burma.

ScottForesman
LITERATURE
AND INTEGRATED STUDIES

Grade Seven

Senior Consultants

Alan C. Purves
State University of New York at Albany

Carol Booth Olson
University of California, Irvine

Carlos E. Cortés
University of California, Riverside (Emeritus)

Judith A. Brough
Gettysburg College, Gettysburg

Edward N. Brazee
University of Maine

ScottForesman

Editorial Offices: Glenview, Illinois
Regional Offices: San Jose, California • Tucker, Georgia • Glenview,
Illinois • Oakland, New Jersey • Dallas, Texas

Visit ScottForesman's Home Page at http://www.scottforesman.com

ACKNOWLEDGMENTS

Texts

xxiv "The Dinner Party" by Mona Gardner, copyright © 1942, 1970 by *Saturday Review,* reprinted by permission of Bill Berger Associates, Inc. **6** "A Crush" from *A Couple of Kooks: and Other Stories About Love* by Cynthia Rylant, pages 3–17 Copyright © by Cynthia Rylant. Reprinted by permission of the Publisher, Orchard Books, New York. **13** "Zinnias" from *Small Poems* by Valerie Worth, page 5. Copyright © 1972 by Valerie Worth. Reprinted by permission of Farrar, Straus & Giroux, Inc. **26** "Seventh Grade" from *Baseball in April and Other Stories* by Gary Soto, pages 52–59. Copyright © 1990 by Gary Soto. Reprinted by permission of Harcourt Brace & Company. **35** "Oranges" from *Hey World, Here I Am!* by Jean Little, page 33. "Pure Poetry" by Gerard Malanga from *The Berkshire Anthology,* edited by Gerald Hausman and David Silverstein. Copyright © 1972 by Gerard Malanga. Reprinted by permission of the author. **36** "My Hard Repair Job" from *When I Dance* by James Berry. "The Rebel" from *I Am a Black Woman* by Mari Evans, page 76. Copyright © 1970 by Mari Evans. Reprinted by permission of the author. **40** "Echo and Narcissus" from *The Golden Treasury of Myths and Legends* by Anne Terry White. Copyright © 1959 by Western Publishing Company, Inc. Used by permission. **45** Adapted from "What Is Love" from *Current Health® 1,* Volume 18, No. 6, February 1995, pages 14–16. Copyright © 1995 by Weekly Reader Corporation. Reprinted by permission from Weekly Reader Corporation. All Rights Reserved. **54** "Father's Day" from *Paper Trail* by Michael Dorris, pages 16–19. Copyright © 1994 by Michael Dorris. Reprinted by permission of HarperCollins Publishers, Inc. **60** "A Sea Worry" by Maxine Hong Kingston. Copyright © 1978 by Maxine Hong Kingston. Reprinted by permission of the author. **67** "A Haircut" by I. S. Nakata. **75** "Birdfoot's Grampa" by Joseph Bruchac. Reprinted by permission of Barbara S. Kouts, Literary Agent for Joseph Bruchac. **77** "in the inner city" copyright © 1987 by Lucille Clifton. Reprinted from *Good Woman: Poems and a Memoir 1969–1980,* by Lucille Clifton, with the permission of BOA Editions, Ltd., 92 Park Ave., Brockport, NY 14420. **81** "Key Item" from *Buy Jupiter and Other Stories* by Isaac Asimov. Copyright © 1968 by Mercury Press. Reprinted by permission of Doubleday, a division of Bantam Doubleday Dell Publishing Group, Inc. **90** From "Visual Magic" by David Thomson. Reprinted by permission Penguin Books USA, Inc. All rights reserved. **108** "The Day the Sun Came Out" by Dorothy M. Johnson. Copyright © 1953 by Dorothy M. Johnson. Renewed 1981 by Dorothy M. Johnson. Originally published in *Cosmopolitan,* March 1953, under the title "Too Soon a Woman." Reprinted by permission of McIntosh and Otis, Inc. **116** "Last Cover" by Paul Annixter from *The Best Nature Stories of Paul Annixter,* 1974. **127** "A Letter to God" by Gregorio López y Fuentes, translated by Donald A. Yates from *Great Spanish Short Stories.* Selected and introduced by Angel Flores, pages 244–247. Reprinted by permission of the Estate of Angel Flores and Heather L. Dederick. **130** "Almost Perfect" from *A Light in the Attic* by Shel Silverstein, Copyright © 1981. **134** "Nate 'Tiny' Archibald" from *Champions* by Bill Littlefield, pages 55, 58-64 and 66. Copyright © 1993 by Bill Littlefield. Reprinted by permission of Little, Brown and Company. **145** "The Clever Magistrate" from *The Ch'i-lin Purse: A Collection of Ancient Chinese Stories* by Linda Fang, pages 63–66 and 69–70. Copyright © 1995 by Linda Fang. Reprinted by permission of Farrar, Straus & Giroux, Inc. **151** "Sir Gawain and the Loathly Lady" from *Beauties and Beasts* by Betsy Hearne, pages 131–128. Copyright © 1993 by the Oryx Press. Reprinted by permission of the Oryx Press, 4041 N. Central at Indiana School Rd., Phoenix, AZ 85012 (800) 279–6799. **158** "Greensleeves" (Anonymous) from *The New Guitar Songbook* by Frederick M. Noad, pages 28–29. **164** From "Kusunoki Masashige: The Loyal Samurai" by Ann Woodbury Moore from *Calliope Magazine,* Volume Three, Number Three, January/February 1993 issue: *The Shoguns and Samurai of Japan,* pages 16–19. Copyright © 1993 by Cobblestone Publishing, Inc., 7 School St., Peterborough, N.H. 03458. Reprinted by permission of the publisher. **166** "Haiku" by Matsuo Bashō from *To Walk in Seasons* by William Howard Cohen. Reprinted by permission of Charles E. Tuttle Publishing Company, Inc.

continued on page 736

ISBN: 0-673-29452-8

Copyright © 1997
Scott, Foresman and Company, Glenview, Illinois
All Rights Reserved. Printed in the United States of America.

http://www.sf.aw.com

3 4 5 6 7 8 9 10 DR 03 02 01 00 99 98 97

Senior Consultants

Alan C. Purves
Professor of Education and Humanities, State University of New York at Albany; Director of the Center for Writing and Literacy. Dr. Purves developed the concept and philosophy of the literature lessons for the series, consulted with editors, reviewed tables of contents and lesson manuscript, wrote the Assessment Handbooks, and oversaw the development and writing of the series testing strand.

Carol Booth Olson
Director, California Writing Project, Department of Education, University of California, Irvine. Dr. Olson conceptualized and developed the integrated writing strand of the program, consulted with editors, led a team of teachers in creating literature-based Writing Workshops, and reviewed final manuscript.

Carlos E. Cortés
Professor Emeritus, History, University of California, Riverside. Dr. Cortés designed and developed the multiculturalism strand embedded in each unit of the series and consulted with grade-level editors to implement the concepts.

Judith A. Brough
Chair, Department of Education; Professor of Education; Supervisor of Student Teachers; Gettysburg College, Gettysburg.

Edward N. Brazee
Associate Professor of Education, University of Maine. Founder and Director, Middle Level Education Institute; Founder and Executive Director, Maine Association for Middle Level Education.

Drs. Brough and Brazee advised on middle school philosophy, the needs of the middle school student, and requirements of the middle school curriculum. In addition they reviewed selections, tables of contents, and lessons and developed prototypes and outlines for all middle school unit projects.

Series Consultants

Visual and Media Literacy/Speaking and Listening/Critical Thinking
Harold M. Foster. Professor of English Education and Secondary Education, The University of Akron, Akron. Dr. Foster developed and wrote the Beyond Print features for all levels of the series.

ESL and LEP Strategies
James Cummins. Professor, Modern Language Centre and Curriculum Department, Ontario Institute for Studies in Education, Toronto.

Lily Wong Fillmore. Professor, Graduate School of Education, University of California at Berkeley.

Drs. Cummins and Fillmore advised on the needs of ESL and LEP students, helped develop the Building English Proficiency model for the program, and reviewed strategies and manuscript.

Life Skills/Personal Development
David J. DePalma. Partner, Life Skills Consultants; developmental psychologist.

Charlotte Wright DePalma. Partner, Life Skills Consultants; former high school and university teacher.

Andrea Donnellan White. Partner, Life Skills Consultants; former elementary school teacher.

W. Brent White. Partner, Life Skills Consultants; former middle school teacher.

The Whites and DePalmas conceptualized the Life Skills sequence for the program and wrote pupil book activities as well as the Life Skills book for each middle school grade.

Reviewers and Contributors

Pupil Edition/Teacher Edition
Valerie Aksoy, El Dorado Intermediate School, Concord, California   Sylvia Alchediak, Burney Simmons Elementary School, Plant City, Florida   Doris Ash, Dolan Middle School, Stamford, Connecticut   Camille Barnett, Pioneer Middle School, Cooper City, Florida   Beverly Bradley, W. Mack Lyon Middle School, Overton, Nevada   Candice Bush, O'Callaghan Middle School, Las Vegas, Nevada   Colleen Fleming, Charles Shaw Middle School, Gorham, Maine   Philip Freemer, Hall High School, West Hartford, Connecticut   Ellen Golden, Hammocks Middle School, Miami, Florida   Anita Hartgraves, Martin Middle School, Corpus Christi, Texas   Lea Heyer, Burney Simmons Elementary School, Plant City, Florida   Linda Holland, Medinah Middle School, Roselle, Illinois   Mary Howard, Valley Center Middle School, Valley Center, California   Kathy Jesson, Hammocks Middle School, Miami, Florida   Christina Kenny, Hill Middle School, Long Beach, California   Kathy Knowles, Alamo Junior High School, Midland, Texas   J. Chris Leonard, Southridge Middle School, Fontana, California   Sandra Litogot, O.E. Dunckel Middle School, Farmington Hills, Michigan   Sue Mack, Gregory

Middle School, Naperville, Illinois **Jack Matsumoto,** Edison Regional Gifted Center, Chicago, Illinois **Frances Marie Miller,** Park View Intermediate School, Pasadena, Texas **Cindy Mishlove,** Becker Middle School, Las Vegas, Nevada **Katie Muus,** El Dorado Intermediate School, Concord, California **Virginia Kay Pfautz,** Wyomissing School District, Reading, Pennsylvania **Judith Ruhana,** Nichols Middle School, Evanston, Illinois **Joyce Seigel,** Hammocks Middle School, Miami, Florida **Carol Sheppard,** Pioneer Middle School, Cooper City, Florida **Susan Solomon,** Hammocks Middle School, Miami, Florida **Jennifer Sorrells,** Darnell Cookman Middle School, Jacksonville, Florida **Paula Steenland,** Gompers Middle School, Los Angeles, California **Robert Stewart,** Marshall Junior High School, Plant City, Florida **Jerry Thompson,** Turkey Creek Junior High School, Plant City, Florida **Sue Totz,** Northwood Middle School, Woodstock, Illinois **Karin Warzybok,** Griffiths Middle School, Downey, California **Fran Wood,** Saco Middle School, Saco, Maine **Suzanne Zweig,** Norwood Park Middle School, Chicago, Illinois

Multicultural Review Board

Duane BigEagle, writer and teacher, Tomales, California **Maria Campanario,** Raphael Hernandez School, Stoughton, Massachusetts **Pat Canty,** Beverly Woods Middle School, Charlotte, North Carolina **Jesús Cardona,** John F. Kennedy High School, San Antonio, Texas **Diego Davalos,** Chula Vista High School, Chula Vista, California **Sandra Dickerson,** Milwaukee Public Schools, Milwaukee, Wisconsin **Lucila Dypiangco,** Bell Senior High School, Bell, California **Marion Fleming,** Roselle Junior/Senior High School, Roselle, New York **Gloria Garcia,** Madero Middle School, Chicago, Illinois **Thelma Hernandez,** Edison Junior High School, San Angelo, Texas **Yvonne Hutchinson,** Markham Intermediate School, Los Angeles, California **Narva Jackson,** Roselle Junior/Senior High School, Roselle, New York **May Lee,** Baldwin Senior High School, Baldwin, New York **Dolores Mathews,** Bloomingdale High School, Valrico, Florida **Jack Matsumoto,** Edison Regional Gifted Center, Chicago, Illinois **James Masao Mitsui,** Hazen High School, Renton, Washington **Ed Ramirez,** Wang School, Derry, New Hampshire **Harolene Steele,** Hill Middle School, Winston-Salem, North Carolina **Suthinee Suktrakul,** Norcross High School, Norcross, Georgia **Jerry Tagami,** New Harbor High School, Newport Beach, California **Barbara Wheeler,** Harford County Public Schools, Bel Air, Maryland **Raymond Zamarippa,** Bowie Junior High School, Irving, Texas

Building English Proficiency (ESL/LEP)

Kata Alvidrez, Newton High School, Newton, Iowa **Judy Bebelaar,** International Studies Academy, San Francisco, California **Rebecca Benjamin,** University of New Mexico, Albuquerque, New Mexico **Ioana Cummins,** Toronto, Ontario **Doti Foster,** Lubbock Independent School District, Lubbock, Texas **Bridget Hawthorne,** Oliver Hazard Perry Middle School, Providence, Rhode Island **Sandra Huezo,** Gompers Secondary School, San Diego, California **Nancy Hykel,** Harlandale High School, San Antonio, Texas **Mary Ann Jentel,** Madonna High School for Girls, Chicago, Illinois **Nancy Duke S. Lay,** City College of New York, New York, New York **José Lebrón,** Julia De Burgos Middle School, Philadelphia, Pennsylvania **Mary Linnstaedter,** Nimitz High School, Houston, Texas **Mayra Menéndez,** School Board of Broward County, Fort Lauderdale, Florida **Sharese Tisby,** Waukegan High School, Waukegan, Illinois **Sylvia Velazquez,** Braddock Senior High School, Miami, Florida **Greta Vollmer,** International Studies Academy, San Francisco, California **Shirley Wright,** Longview Independent School District, Longview, Texas **Suzanne Zweig,** Norwood Park School, Chicago, Illinois

Writer's Workshop Prompt Writers

Todd Huck, Rancho Santiago College, Santa Ana, California **Meredith Ritner,** Aliso Viejo Middle School, Aliso Viejo, California **Sharon Schiesl,** Rancho Santa Margarita Middle School, Rancho Santa Margarita, California **Esther Severy,** McFadden Intermediate School, Santa Ana, California

Student Contributors

Justin Behrman   Liz Bonson   Matthew Cleaver   Karen Eckmann   Diana English   Lisa Franklin   Alex Fridell   Laura Gravander   David Ignacio   Anish Karimkuttyil   Mike Kotlarczyk   Aubrey Lambke   Elizabeth Lessner   Justin Magnini   Martin J. Mahoney   Elisabeth Nyden   Emily O'Keefe   Soren Pedersen   Matthew Witvoet   Purnahamsi Yedavalli

CONTENTS

MODEL FOR ACTIVE READING AND DISCUSSION

Mona Gardner   The Dinner Party ◆ short story   xxiv

UNIT 1

RELATIONSHIPS

**THEME OVERVIEW:
TALKING ABOUT RELATIONSHIPS**   **2**

PART ONE: FRIENDS AND FOES

Literature

Cynthia Rylant   6   A Crush ◆ short story
Valerie Worth   13   Zinnias ◆ poem
                    16   WRITING MINI-LESSON   Setting Up Your Working Portfolio
O. Henry   18   After Twenty Years ◆ short story
Gary Soto   26   Seventh Grade ◆ short story
Jean Little   35   Oranges ◆ poem
Gerard Malanga   35   Pure Poetry ◆ poem
Mari Evans   36   The Rebel ◆ poem
James Berry   36   My Hard Repair Job ◆ poem

Exploring the Theme through Folklore

Anne Terry White   40   Echo and Narcissus ◆ Greek myth

Integrated Studies   45   INTERDISCIPLINARY STUDY   The Love Connection
                              What Is Love? ◆ psychology
                              Courtship and Marriage ◆ anthropology
                              Marriage Statistics ◆ mathematics
                         51   READING MINI-LESSON   Skimming the Headings

PART TWO: DIFFERENT POINTS OF VIEW

Literature

Michael Dorris	54	Father's Day ◆ personal essay
Maxine Hong Kingston	60	A Sea Worry ◆ personal essay
I. S. Nakata	67	A Haircut ◆ short story
Joseph Bruchac	75	Birdfoot's Grampa ◆ poem
Walt Whitman	76	When I Heard the Learn'd Astronomer ◆ poem
Lucille Clifton	77	In the Inner City ◆ poem
Isaac Asimov	81	Key Item ◆ short story
	87	**LANGUAGE MINI-LESSON** Choosing the Correct Homophones

Integrated Studies

88	**INTERDISCIPLINARY STUDY** Getting into Focus
	How We See ◆ life science
	Interpreting Visual Evidence by Dr. David Thomson ◆ psychology
92	**READING MINI-LESSON** Taking Notes
93	**WRITING WORKSHOP** Expository Writing
	Assignment Thumbs Up or Thumbs Down?
	Revising Strategy Using Parallel Structure
	Editing Strategy Avoiding Run-on Sentences
99	**BEYOND PRINT** Effective Listening
	He Said, She Said
100	**LOOKING BACK**
	Projects for Collaborative Study
	Read More About Relationships

UNIT 2

CHALLENGES

THEME OVERVIEW:
TALKING ABOUT CHALLENGES 104

PART ONE: CHOICES AND CONSEQUENCES

Literature

Dorothy M. Johnson	108	The Day the Sun Came Out ◆ short story
Paul Annixter	116	Last Cover ◆ short story
Gregorio López y Fuentes	127	A Letter to God ◆ short story
Shel Silverstein	130	Almost Perfect ◆ poem
Bill Littlefield	134	Nate "Tiny" Archibald ◆ biography

Exploring the Theme through Folklore

Linda Fang	145	The Clever Magistrate ◆ Chinese tale
Betsy Hearne	151	Sir Gawain and the Loathly Lady ◆ English legend
Anonymous	158	Greensleeves ◆ traditional song
	161	WRITING MINI-LESSON Arranging Details

Integrated Studies	162	INTERDISCIPLINARY STUDY Doing Battle
		Knights and Samurai ◆ history
		Kusunoki Masashige by Ann Woodbury Moore ◆ history
		Three Haiku ◆ poetry
	167	READING MINI-LESSON Visualizing

ix

Part Two: Finding Your Place

Literature

Anne McCaffrey	170	The Smallest Dragonboy ◆ short story
	184	**LANGUAGE MINI-LESSON** Combining Sentences
Nereida Román	186	Never Fitting In ◆ autobiography
Emily Dickinson	188	I'm Nobody ◆ poem
Kristin Hunter	192	The Scribe ◆ short story
Amiri Baraka	198	SOS ◆ poem
Lillian Morrison	202	The Women's 400 Meters ◆ poem
Jack Anderson	203	Where You Are ◆ poem

Integrated Studies

206   **INTERDISCIPLINARY STUDY**   Help Is on the Way
Scribes ◆ history
Can You Read This? ◆ mathematics
Who Cares? Millions Do by Milton Meltzer and Students
Helping Students by Catherine A. Rolzinski ◆ community service

212   **READING MINI-LESSON**   Using Graphic Aids

213   **WRITING WORKSHOP**   Expository Writing
Assignment   Trying Something New
Revising Strategy   Writing Focused Paragraphs
Editing Strategy   Avoiding Overuse of Commas

219   **BEYOND PRINT**   Visual Literacy
Dishwater or White Water?

220   **LOOKING BACK**
Projects for Collaborative Study
Read More About Challenges

UNIT 3

*J*USTICE

THEME OVERVIEW:
TALKING ABOUT JUSTICE　　224

PART ONE: THE SCENE OF THE CRIME

Literature

Arthur Conan Doyle	228	The Dying Detective ◆ play (dramatized by Michael and Mollie Hardwick)
Carol Ellis	242	The Gun ◆ short story
Shirley Jackson	249	Charles ◆ short story
T. S. Eliot	256	Macavity: The Mystery Cat ◆ poem
Nikki Giovanni	258	Kidnap Poem ◆ poem

Exploring the Theme through Folklore

Anonymous	262	How the Lame Boy Brought Fire from Heaven ◆ African myth
Bernard Evslin	264	Prometheus ◆ Greek myth
	269	**WRITING MINI-LESSON**　Using a Persuasive Tone

Integrated Studies

	270	**INTERDISCIPLINARY STUDY**　Gathering Evidence Determining Guilt ◆ history Genetic Fingerprinting: The Murder with No Body by Anita Larsen ◆ life science The Structure of DNA ◆ life science
	276	**READING MINI-LESSON**　Remembering What You Read

PART TWO: ENCOUNTERS WITH PREJUDICE

Literature

Ray Bradbury	279	All Summer in a Day ◆ short story
Ted Poston	288	The Revolt of the Evil Fairies ◆ short story
Marta Salinas	296	The Scholarship Jacket ◆ short story
Ed J. Vega	301	Translating Grandfather's House ◆ poem
	304	**LANGUAGE MINI-LESSON** Subject and Verb Agreement
Jean Little	306	About Old People ◆ anecdote
E. E. Cummings	309	old age sticks ◆ poem

Integrated Studies

	312	**INTERDISCIPLINARY STUDY** Let's Be Fair
		Prejudice Across the Ages ◆ history
		Brown Eyes Only by Pam Deyell Gingold ◆ sociology
		Three Reasons to Become More Tolerant by Lynn Duvall ◆ sociology
	318	**READING MINI-LESSON** Drawing Conclusions
	319	**WRITING WORKSHOP** Expository Writing
		Assignment Explaining Feelings
		Revising Strategy Concrete and Specific Language
		Editing Strategy Subject and Object Pronouns
	325	**BEYOND PRINT** Effective Speaking
		Helping Margot See the Light
	326	**LOOKING BACK**
		Projects for Collaborative Study
		Read More About Justice

UNIT 4

JOURNEYS

THEME OVERVIEW:
TALKING ABOUT JOURNEYS   330

PART ONE: TRAVELS WITH A TWIST

Literature

Rod Serling	334	The Monsters Are Due on Maple Street ◆ play
Robert Service	349	The Cremation of Sam McGee ◆ poem
Lensey Namioka	356	LAFFF ◆ short story
Ruth Pelz	366	Biddy Mason ◆ biography
Rosemary and Stephen Vincent Benét	369	Western Wagons ◆ poem
Hu Feng	373	The Journey ◆ poem
Gwendolyn Brooks	374	Old Mary ◆ poem
	377	**WRITING MINI-LESSON** Maintaining Your Working Portfolio

Integrated Studies

	378	**INTERDISCIPLINARY STUDY** Winding Roads Three Explorers ◆ geography The Adventures of Marco Polo by Simon Boughton ◆ history
	383	**READING MINI-LESSON** Distinguishing Between Fact and Opinion

PART TWO: THE BRIDGE TO UNDERSTANDING

Literature

Walter Dean Myers	386	Jeremiah's Song ◆ short story
Ashley Bryan	393	Storyteller ◆ poem
Beryl Markham	397	Brothers Are the Same ◆ short story
Jane Yolen	410	Birthday Box ◆ short story
Merrill Markoe	416	The Dog Diaries ◆ essay
Shuntarō Tanikawa	423	On Destiny ◆ poem
Zia Hyder	424	Under This Sky ◆ poem

Exploring the Theme through Folklore

Laurence Yep	429	We Are All One ◆ Chinese folk tale
	434	LANGUAGE MINI-LESSON Adding Punctuation for Clarity

Integrated Studies

	435	INTERDISCIPLINARY STUDY Timeless Tales
		Sundiata Keita: The Legend and the King by Patricia and Fredrick McKissack ◆ history
		The Storytellers ◆ art
	440	READING MINI-LESSON Using Time Order Relationships
	441	WRITING WORKSHOP Narrative Writing
		Assignment Bridging the Gap
		Revising Strategy Dialogue That Reveals Personality
		Editing Strategy Using Commas Correctly
	447	BEYOND PRINT Media Literacy
		A Monster of a Storyboard
	448	LOOKING BACK
		Projects for Collaborative Study
		Reading More About Journeys

UNIT 5

CHANGE

THEME OVERVIEW:
TALKING ABOUT CHANGE   452

PART ONE: TURNING POINTS

Literature

MacKinlay Kantor	456	A Man Who Had No Eyes ◆ short story
Bailey White	462	Turkeys ◆ autobiography
James Herriot	468	Alfred: The Sweet-Shop Cat ◆ narrative nonfiction
Malcolm X with Alex Haley	480	The Autobiography of Malcolm X ◆ autobiography
Mae Jackson	483	i remember ◆ poem
	486	**WRITING MINI-LESSON** Research Technique: Finding Information
Margarita Mondrus Engle	488	Niña ◆ short story

Integrated Studies

	494	**INTERDISCIPLINARY STUDY** Science on the March
		What's in the Blood That Can Make You Sick? ◆ life science
		Breakthroughs in Medicine ◆ science
	499	**READING MINI-LESSON** Recalling Details

PART TWO: NEW DIRECTIONS

Literature

M. E. Kerr   502   The Author ◆ short story

Buson   507   The Reader ◆ poem

510   **LANGUAGE MINI-LESSON**   Consistent Verb Tense

Maya Angelou   512   New Directions ◆ biography

Borden Deal   518   Antaeus ◆ short story

Robert F. Kennedy   530   On the Death of Martin Luther King, Jr. ◆ speech

Samantha Abeel   535   Samantha's Story ◆ autobiography

538   Self Portrait ◆ poem

Exploring the Theme through Folklore

Gayle Ross   542   Rabbit Dances with the People ◆ Cherokee legend

Integrated Studies

546   **INTERDISCIPLINARY STUDY**   From Pen to Printout
Words on the Page ◆ history
A Short History of Punctuation by Polly M. Robertus ◆ language

550   **READING MINI-LESSON**   Comparing and Contrasting

551   **WRITING WORKSHOP**   Narrative Writing
Assignment   Taking New Directions
Revising Strategy   Varied Sentence Structure
Editing Strategy   Clear Pronoun Reference

557   **BEYOND PRINT**   Technology Skills
Wake Things Up with Multimedia

558   **LOOKING BACK**
Projects for Collaborative Study
Read More About Change

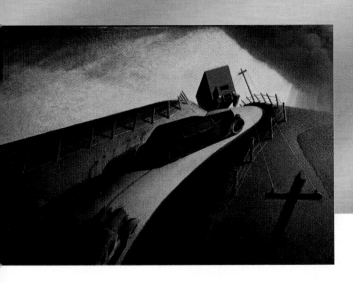

UNIT 6

CONFLICT AND RESOLUTION

**THEME OVERVIEW: TALKING ABOUT
CONFLICT AND RESOLUTION**　　　**562**

PART ONE: YOU'RE INVADING MY SPACE!

Literature

Toni Cade Bambara	566	The War of the Wall ◆ short story
Edwin Markham	573	Outwitted ◆ poem
Roald Dahl	577	The Green Mamba ◆ autobiography
Robert Frost	583	A Minor Bird ◆ poem
Judith Ortiz Cofer	587	Abuela Invents the Zero ◆ short story
Rudyard Kipling	594	Rikki-tikki-tavi ◆ short story
	609	**LANGUAGE MINI-LESSON**　Checking Your Spelling

Integrated Studies

	610	**INTERDISCIPLINARY STUDY**　Guest or Pest?
		Animal and Plant Invaders ◆ earth science
		Mongoose on the Loose by Larry Luxner ◆ science
	615	**READING MINI-LESSON**　Finding Cause-and-Effect Relationships

PART TWO: STANDING YOUR GROUND

Literature

Alfred Brenner   618   Survival ◆ play

Alfred Noyes   640   The Highwayman ◆ poem

Langston Hughes   647   Mother to Son ◆ poem

Alice Walker   648   Women ◆ poem

Juan A. A. Sedillo   652   Gentleman of Rio en Medio ◆ short story

Exploring the Theme through Folklore

Ricardo E. Alegría   658   The Rabbit and the Tiger ◆ Puerto Rican folk tale

   665   **WRITING MINI-LESSON** Preparing Your Presentation Portfolio

Integrated Studies

   666   **INTERDISCIPLINARY STUDY** Women Making Waves
Pursuing Equality ◆ sociology
Fabric of Life by Donna Johnson ◆ anthropology

   670   **READING MINI-LESSON** Summarizing

   671   **WRITING WORKSHOP** Persuasive Writing
Assignment Expressing an Opinion
Revising Strategy Interesting Beginnings
Editing Strategy Distinguishing Between Adjectives and Adverbs

   677   **BEYOND PRINT** Critical Thinking
Yes, We Have No Bananas

   678   **LOOKING BACK**
Projects for Collaborative Study
Read More About Conflict and Resolution

GLOSSARIES, HANDBOOKS, AND INDEXES

Understanding Fiction 682

Understanding Nonfiction.....................684

Understanding Poetry..........................686

Understanding Drama..........................688

Glossary of Literary Terms....................690

Glossary of Vocabulary Words 694

Language and Grammar Handbook...................703

Index of Skills and Strategies 724

Index of Fine Art and Artists...............732

Index of Authors and Titles.................734

Text Acknowledgments........................736

Illustration Acknowledgments................737

GENRE OVERVIEW

Short Stories

The Dinner Party....................................xxiv

A Crush 6

After Twenty Years 18

Seventh Grade......................................26

A Haircut 67

Key Item 81

The Day the Sun Came Out....................108

Last Cover...116

A Letter to God 127

The Smallest Dragonboy 170

The Scribe...192

The Gun 242

Charles..249

All Summer in a Day 279

The Revolt of the Evil Fairies 288

The Scholarship Jacket 296

LAFFF..356

Jeremiah's Song 386

Brothers Are the Same 397

Birthday Box 410

A Man Who Had No Eyes....................456

Niña..488

The Author 502

Antaeus 518

The War of the Wall 566

Abuela Invents the Zero....................587

Rikki-tikki-tavi 594

Gentleman of Río en Medio..................652

Nonfiction

Father's Day 54

A Sea Worry 60

Nate "Tiny" Archibald 134

Never Fitting In 186

About Old People 306

Biddy Mason.....................................366

The Dog Diaries 416

Turkeys...462

Alfred: The Sweet-Shop Cat.................468

The Autobiography of Malcolm X..................480

New Directions...................................512

On the Death of Martin Luther King, Jr 530

Samantha's Story................................535

The Green Mamba 577

Poetry

Zinnias..13

Oranges 35

Pure Poetry 35

The Rebel...36

My Hard Repair Job.............................36

Birdfoot's Grampa...............................75

When I Heard the Learn'd Astronomer.................76

In the Inner City 77

Almost Perfect 130

Greensleeves 158

I'm Nobody 188

SOS 198

The Women's 400 Meters 202

Where You Are 203

Macavity: The Mystery Cat..............................256

Kidnap Poem 258

Translating Grandfather's House 301

old age sticks..309

The Cremation of Sam McGee..........................349

Western Wagons..369

The Journey 373

Old Mary 374

Storyteller 393

On Destiny 423

Under This Sky 424

i remember..483

The Reader 507

Self Portrait 538

Outwitted 573

A Minor Bird..583

The Highwayman..640

Mother to Son..647

Women..648

Drama

The Dying Detective..228

The Monsters Are Due on Maple Street..............334

Survival 618

Folklore

Echo and Narcissus..40

The Clever Magistrate..145

Sir Gawain and the Loathly Lady 151

Greensleeves 158

How the Lame Boy Brought Fire
    from Heaven..262

Prometheus..264

We Are All One..429

Rabbit Dances with the People 542

The Rabbit and the Tiger 658

FEATURE OVERVIEW

Interdisciplinary Studies

The Love Connection..45

Getting into Focus 88

Doing Battle 162

Help Is on the Way 206

Gathering Evidence 270

Let's Be Fair 312

Winding Roads 378

Timeless Tales..435

Science on the March..494

From Pen to Printout 546

Guest or Pest?..610

Women Making Waves 666

Reading Mini-Lesson

Skimming the Headings..51

Taking Notes 92

Visualizing 167

Using Graphic Aids 212

Remembering What You Read 276

Drawing Conclusions..318

Distinguishing Between Fact
    and Opinion..383

Using Time-Order Relationships........................440

Recalling Details 499

Comparing and Contrasting 550

Finding Cause-and-Effect Relationships............615

Summarizing 670

Writing Mini-Lessons

Setting Up Your Working Portfolio........................16

Arranging Details 161

Using a Persuasive Tone 269

Maintaining Your Working Portfolio 377

Research Technique: Finding Information 486

Preparing Your Presentation Portfolio 665

Language Mini-Lessons

Choosing the Correct Homophones.....................87

Combining Sentences 184

Subject and Verb Agreement..............................304

Adding Punctuation for Clarity 434

Consistent Verb Tense.......................................510

Checking Your Spelling.......................................609

Writing Workshops

Indicates workshops found in the Unit Resource Books—Teacher's Resource File

Help! I've Got a Problem (Expository) ....*

Thumbs Up or Thumbs Down?
      (Expository)...93

Examining Choices and Consequences
      (Expository) ....*

Trying Something New (Expository).....................213

Addressing the Judge and Jury (Persuasive)...........*

Explaining Feelings (Expository) 319

Taking an Incredible Journey (Expository)...............*

Bridging the Gap (Narrative) 441

Research Report: Turning Points (Narrative)............*

Taking New Directions (Narrative).......................551

Examining Conflicts (Narrative) ....*

Expressing an Opinion (Persuasive) 671

Beyond Print

He Said, She Said (Effective Listening) 99

Dishwater or White Water?
      (Visual Literacy) 219

Helping Margot See the Light
      (Effective Speaking)....................................325

A Monster of a Storyboard
      (Media Literacy)...447

Wake Things Up with Multimedia
      (Technology Skills).....................................557

Yes, We Have No Bananas
      (Critical Thinking)..677

Model for Active Reading

Good readers are active readers. They jump right into the words and really get involved with what's happening on the page. They picture the characters and setting, and react to the ideas in the story. They question, predict, connect what is happening to their own lives, and in other ways get involved with what they read. The three seventh-grade students pictured on these pages agreed to let us in on their thoughts as they read "The Dinner Party." You might not have the same questions or ideas that they had about this story. However, their ways of responding will help you understand how good readers get actively engaged in what they read.

LISA FRANKLIN Hello. I'm Lisa Franklin and I like some sports, especially soccer. I like to read mysteries, horror stories, and stories about kids my age—teenagers. I usually read at a medium to fast pace.

DAVID IGNACIO My name is David Ignacio. I like to play baseball and soccer and I like to read comic books and science fiction—*Star Trek, the Next Generation*—and books by Michael Crichton. I read at a medium pace because if I read too fast I might not get something that is important.

Purnahamsi Yedavalli (Hamsi)

Hi! My name is Purnahamsi Yedavalli. Everyone calls me Hamsi. I like to read and play sports and talk to my friends. I read a lot—mysteries and books about people's lives to see what they are like. I usually read very quickly because I can understand things pretty fast.

Six Reading Strategies

Following are some of the techniques that good readers use, often without being aware of them.

Question Ask questions that come to mind as you read.

Example: Why doesn't the American join in the argument?

Predict Use what has happened so far to make reasonable guesses about what might happen next.

Example: The servant's eyes widen after being summoned by the hostess. I'll bet he knows there is going to be trouble.

Clarify Clear up confusion and answer questions.

Example: Why does the American ask everyone to sit quietly while he counts? He must know what to do when a cobra is around.

Summarize Review what has happened so far.

Example: This is a gathering of upper-class English people in India. The colonel has very definite views on women.

Evaluate Use your common sense and the evidence in the selection to arrive at sound opinions and valid conclusions.

Example: The colonel's views were proven to be wrong.

Connect Compare the text with something in your own experience, with another text, or with ideas within the text.

Example: There are men today who would agree with the colonel, but I haven't come across many.

THE DINNER

▲ *Dinner at Haddo House* was painted by Alfred Edward Emslie in the early 1900s. Imagine that the two people in the foreground are discussing women's rights. What do you think each might be saying?

PARTY

MONA GARDNER

The country is India. A colonial official and his wife are giving a large dinner party. They are seated with their guests—army officers and government attachés and their wives, and a visiting American naturalist—in their spacious dining room, which has a bare marble floor, open rafters, and wide glass doors opening onto a veranda.

A spirited discussion springs up between a young girl who insists that women have outgrown the jumping-on-a-chair-at-the-sight-of-a-mouse era and a colonel who says that they haven't.

"A woman's unfailing reaction in any crisis," the colonel says, "is to scream. And while a man may feel like it, he has that ounce more of nerve control than a woman has. And that last ounce is what counts."

The American does not join in the argument but watches the other guests. As he looks, he sees a strange expression come over the face of the hostess. She is staring straight ahead, her muscles contracting slightly. With a slight gesture she summons the servant standing behind her chair and whispers to him. The servant's eyes widen, and he quickly leaves the room.

Of the guests, none except the American notices this or sees the servant place a bowl of milk on the veranda just outside the open doors.

The American comes to with a start. In India, milk in a bowl means only one thing—bait for a snake. He realizes there must be a cobra in the room. He looks up at the rafters—the likeliest place—but they are bare. Three corners of the room are empty, and in the fourth the servants are waiting to serve the next course. There is only one place left—under the table.

His first impulse is to jump back and warn the others, but he knows the commotion would frighten the cobra into striking. He speaks quickly, the tone of his voice so arresting that it sobers everyone.

"I want to know just what control everyone at this table has. I will

LISA I think this might be a story about people planning a dinner party. But something is going to happen when all the people get there. (predict)

DAVID Looks like there will be a lot of conversation; probably different people talking about different ideas or topics. (evaluate)

HAMSI I think people will be eating together and something strange will happen to upset the party. (predict)

LISA I don't like this colonel. He has sexist ideas about women. (connect)

HAMSI Maybe back then women were *expected to* scream and jump on chairs. These days women wouldn't react this way. (clarify, connect)

HAMSI The naturalist isn't taking sides. Why? Because he's an American? (question, clarify)

DAVID Why is the hostess making this face? What is going on here? Is she upset about the conversation? (question)

HAMSI Is there a mouse or something like that under the table? (predict)

DAVID How does he know so much about cobras? Oh, he's a naturalist—he's got inside info. (clarify)

HAMSI The fact that he is a naturalist is important here. He knows something about why they are putting out the milk. (evaluate)

count three hundred—that's five minutes—and not one of you is to move a muscle. Those who move will forfeit fifty rupees. Ready!"

The twenty people sit like stone images while he counts. He is saying ". . . two hundred and eighty . . ." when, out of the corner of his eye, he sees the cobra emerge and make for the bowl of milk. Screams ring out as he jumps to slam the veranda doors safely shut.

"You were right, Colonel!" the host exclaims. "A man has just shown us an example of perfect control."

"Just a minute," the American says, turning to the hostess. "Mrs. Wynnes, how did you know that cobra was in the room?"

A faint smile lights up the woman's face as she replies: "Because it was crawling across my foot."

DAVID   The author fooled me. I had no idea it was a snake. (summarize)

LISA   Great ending! Mrs. Wynnes proved the colonel wrong. (evaluate)

Discussion After Reading

Once they've finished a selection, active readers reflect and respond in a variety of ways. After a general discussion, these students answered the kinds of questions that you will find following the other selections in this book.

General Comments

HAMSI   It is important that this is a *young* woman arguing with the colonel—she is not set in the past—when women were expected to be weak and fearful.

LISA   It seems to me that women were less valued at that time in this place.

HAMSI   This is a society where men are considered very important.

DAVID   The setting was important, I think.

HAMSI   Not very many places would it be common for a snake to come gliding into your dining room.

LISA   Yes, and a man's attitude might be different toward women in America because things were changing here; women were fighting for their rights.

DAVID   You know, *anyone* would scream, (in this situation). The American knew what to do because he was a naturalist. And they all thought *he* was brave. But she was even braver. It was on her foot!

LISA   I felt proud when she reacted as she did.

HAMSI   Yes, she knows about snakes and knows that screaming is the wrong thing to do. She sounds so natural when she says, "It was crawling on my foot."

Based on his past behavior, what do you think the colonel will say to Mrs. Wynnes after her revelation?

LISA   He will probably act as though nothing unusual happened. He seems like the kind of man who would hate to admit he was wrong.

HAMSI   No, he'll probably say, "She is an exception. Most women would scream and panic."

DAVID   Or he might change his opinion and congratulate her.

HAMSI   Yes, he might change. Maybe he said what he did because he didn't know any better. Now he does.

DAVID   Sometimes people criticize others because they don't want to show their true feelings—so they cover up by talking big.

Why is it important that the author let the reader know the American is a naturalist?

DAVID   An everyday guy wouldn't know anything about snakes, so he wouldn't know what to do with the others in the situation.

LISA   Sure, he would probably jump up and scream just like anyone else.

HAMSI   So he *has* to be a naturalist for his actions to seem real. *And* we see a lot of what is going on through his eyes.

What examples of irony can you find in the story?

HAMSI   It is ironic that the colonel says men would stay calm and women would scream—and then Mrs. Wynnes does just the opposite.

DAVID   It's kind of ironic that an American would know so much about an Indian snake (even if he is a naturalist).

Relationships

Friends and Foes
Part One, pages 4–51

Different Points of View
Part Two, pages 52–101

Talking About
RELATIONSHIPS

You probably have many important relationships, full of love, laughter, and closeness. And you've probably begun to realize that anger and tears play a part in relationships too. Some people seem to be friends from the moment they meet, while others find when they care for someone they end up getting hurt. Why do some relationships thrive while others fail miserably? No one knows for sure, but whatever we do, connecting with people is an important part of life.

Notice how the comments from students across the country match the ideas in the literature you will be reading.

> **Talk about it when you're mad instead of ignoring the problem.**
>
> Angela – Fort Worth, Texas

In the awful quarrel we had, my temper burnt our friendship to cinders.

from "My Hard Repair Job"
by James Berry, page 36

"Friends and family offer valuable support when we need it."

Marcus – Oakland, CA

...ever optimistic, my aunt was the one who pitched a baseball with me early summer evenings, who took me horseback riding, who sat by my bed when I was ill.

from "Father's Day" by Michael Dorris, page 56

"My parents and I are really close."

Ian – Orlando, FL

This summer my son body surfs. ... I hope that by September he will have had enough of the ocean.

from "A Sea Worry" by Maxine Hong Kingston, page 61

"I will never get married or have kids; it's too hard."

Julie – Holland, MI

As far as anyone knew, Dolores had never been in love nor had anyone ever been in love with her.

from "A Crush" by Cynthia Rylant, page 8

Part One

Friends and Foes

If asked what you value most in life, what would you say? Chances are that good friends would be high on your list. Making good friends can be difficult. Keeping them is, at times, even harder.

Multicultural Connection **Communication** involves expressing a variety of ideas and emotions through words and actions. This often means attempting to communicate with people who come from very different backgrounds. As you read the selections that follow, look for what happens when communication ripens into friendship or even love—or when it breaks down and friends become foes.

Literature

Cynthia Rylant	**A Crush** ◆ short story	6
Valerie Worth	**Zinnias** ◆ poem	13
	Writing Mini-Lesson ◆ Setting Up Your Working Portfolio	16
O. Henry	**After Twenty Years** ◆ short story	18
Gary Soto	**Seventh Grade** ◆ short story	26
Jean Little	**Oranges** ◆ poem	35
Gerard Malanga	**Pure Poetry** ◆ poem	35
Mari Evans	**The Rebel** ◆ poem	36
James Berry	**My Hard Repair Job** ◆ poem	36
Anne Terry White	**Echo and Narcissus** ◆ Greek myth	40

Interdisciplinary Study The Love Connection

What Is Love? ◆ psychology	45
Courtship and Marriage ◆ anthropology	47
Marriage Statistics ◆ mathematics	50
Reading Mini-Lesson ◆ Skimming the Headings	51

Before Reading

A Crush

by Cynthia Rylant

Cynthia Rylant
born 1954

Cynthia Rylant grew up in a small West Virginia town, much like the one she writes about in "A Crush." As a child she could hardly wait to leave, but as an adult Rylant has often revisited the town and its people in her writing. "I had many heroes," Rylant says. "First was a pock-faced man named Tom who visited my grandparents. Then my Uncle Joe who went to Vietnam." As in this story, Rylant enjoys writing about people who don't stand out in the usual ways, but whose lives shine with value and beauty.

Building Background

Unexpected Heroes What does the word hero mean to you? Chances are you thought of a knight in shining armor or the firefighter who rescues a child from a burning building. Not every story has a hero who is brave, wise, or good-looking. Different characters, such as Forrest Gump with his slow wit and off-beat personality, can star in highly interesting stories. What stories, plays, or movies can you think of with such unusual heroes?

Getting into the Story

Writer's Notebook The title of the story, "A Crush," explains simply what the story is about—a sudden, strong, attraction to someone. Have you ever had a crush? In your notebook write about how it felt and what you did. If you've never had a crush, imagine the feelings or write about a friend who had one.

Reading Tip

Visualization Setting is an important story element in "A Crush." Visualizing, or picturing it in your mind's eye, will help you understand the setting better. The author of "A Crush" provides details you can use to create that picture. Below is a word web with details that you will find in the opening part of the story. Copy the web and as you read add other details that the author provides to help you visualize the small town setting of the story.

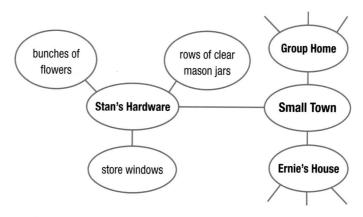

CYNTHIA RYLANT

When the windows of Stan's Hardware started filling up with flowers, everyone in town knew something had happened. Excess[1] flowers usually mean death, but since these were all real flowers bearing the aroma of nature instead of floral preservative, and since they stood bunched in clear mason jars instead of impaled[2] on styrofoam crosses, everyone knew nobody had died. So they all figured somebody had a crush and kept quiet.

There wasn't really a Stan of Stan's Hardware. Dick Wilcox was the owner, and since he'd never liked his own name, he gave his store half the name of his childhood

---

1. **excess** (ek′ses), *adj.* too much or too many; extra.
2. **impale** (im pāl′), *v.* pierce with something pointed; fasten.

▲ *The Young Sailor II* was painted in 1906 by the French Impressionist painter Henri Matisse.
Body language is a form of **communication**. What does this young man's pose seem to express?

hero, Stan Laurel[3] in the movies. Dick had been married for twenty-seven years. Once, his wife Helen had dropped a German chocolate cake on his head at a Lion's Club[4] dance, so Dick and Helen were not likely candidates for the honest expression of the flowers in those clear mason jars lining the windows of Stan's Hardware, and speculation[5] had to move on to Dolores.

PREDICT: Who do you think Dolores is? What will she be like?

Dolores was the assistant manager at Stan's and had worked there for twenty years, since high school. She knew the store like a mother knows her baby, so Dick—who had trouble keeping up with things like prices and new brands of drywall[6] compound—tried to keep himself busy in the back and give Dolores the run of the floor. This worked fine because the carpenters and plumbers and painters in town trusted Dolores and took her advice to heart. They also liked her tattoo.

Dolores was the only woman in town with a tattoo. On the days she went sleeveless, one could see it on the taut brown skin of her upper arm: "Howl at the Moon." The picture was of a baying coyote which must have been a dark gray in its early days but which had faded to the color of the spackling paste Dolores stocked in the third aisle. Nobody had gotten out of Dolores the true story behind the tattoo. Some of the men who came in liked to show off their own, and they'd roll up their sleeves or pull open their shirts, exhibiting bald eagles and rattlesnakes and Confederate flags, and they'd try to coax out of Dolores the history of her coyote. All of the men had gotten their tattoos when they were in the service, drunk on weekend leave and full of the spitfire of young soldiers. Dolores had never been in the service and she'd never seen weekend leave and there

wasn't a tattoo parlor anywhere near. They couldn't figure why or where any half-sober woman would have a howling coyote ground into the soft skin of her upper arm. But Dolores wasn't telling.

That the flowers in Stan's front window had anything to do with Dolores seemed completely improbable.[7] As far as anyone knew, Dolores had never been in love nor had anyone ever been in love with her. Some believed it was the tattoo, of course, or the fine dark hair coating Dolores's upper lip which kept suitors away. Some felt it was because Dolores was just more of a man than most men in town, and fellows couldn't figure out how to court someone who knew more about the carburetor of a car or the back side of a washing machine than they did. Others thought Dolores simply didn't want love. This was a popular theory among the women in town who sold Avon and Mary Kay cosmetics. Whenever one of them ran into the hardware for a package of light bulbs or some batteries, she would mentally pluck every one of the black hairs above Dolores's lip. Then she'd wash that grease out of Dolores's hair, give her a good blunt cut, dress her in a decent silk-blend blouse with a nice Liz Claiborne skirt from the Sports line, and, finally, tone down that swarthy,[8] longshoreman[9] look of Dolores's with a concealing beige foundation,[10] some frosted peach lipstick, and a good gray liner for the eyes.

---

3. **Stan Laurel,** one partner in the comedy team of Laurel and Hardy, popular in the 1940's.
4. **Lion's Club,** a group of business and professional people whose goal is to serve the community.
5. **speculation** (spek′yə lā′shən), *n.* a guessing; conjecture.
6. **drywall,** large panels used for building walls.
7. **improbable** (im prob′ə bəl), *adj.* unlikely.
8. **swarthy** (swôr′ŦHē), *adj.* having a dark skin.
9. **longshoreman,** a person who works loading and unloading ships in port.
10. **foundation,** a cosmetic applied to the face as a base for other make-up.

Dolores simply didn't want love, the Avon lady would think as she walked back to her car carrying her little bag of batteries. If she did, she'd fix herself up.

The man who was in love with Dolores and who brought her zinnias and cornflowers and nasturtiums and marigolds and asters and four o'clocks in clear mason jars did not know any of this. He did not know that men showed Dolores their tattoos. He did not know that Dolores understood how to use and to sell a belt sander. He did not know that Dolores needed some concealing beige foundation so she could get someone to love her. The man who brought flowers to Dolores on Wednesdays when the hardware opened its doors at 7:00 a.m. didn't care who Dolores had ever been or what anyone had ever thought of her. He loved her and he wanted to bring her flowers.

QUESTION: What questions do you have about the man who loves Dolores? Jot down your questions in your Writer's Notebook.

Ernie had lived in this town all of his life and had never before met Dolores. He was thirty-three years old, and for thirty-one of those years he had lived at home with his mother in a small, dark house on the edge of town near Beckwith's Orchards. Ernie had been a beautiful baby, with a shock of shining black hair and large blue eyes and a round, wise face. But as he had grown, it had become clearer and clearer that though he was indeed a perfectly beautiful child, his mind had not developed with the same perfection. Ernie would not be able to speak in sentences until he was six years old. He would not be able to count the apples in a bowl until he was eight. By the time he was ten, he could sing a simple song. At age twelve, he understood what a joke was. And when he was twenty, something he saw on television made him cry.

*E*rnie's mother kept him in the house with her because it was easier, so Ernie knew nothing of the world except this house. They lived, the two of them, in tiny dark rooms always illuminated by the glow of a television set, Ernie's bags of Oreos and Nutter Butters littering the floor, his baseball cards scattered across the sofa, his heavy winter coat thrown over the arm of a chair so he could wear it whenever he wanted, and his box of Burpee seed packages sitting in the middle of the kitchen table.

These Ernie cherished.[11] The seeds had been delivered to his home by mistake. One day a woman wearing a brown uniform had pulled up in a brown truck, walked quickly to the front porch of Ernie's house, set a box down, and with a couple of toots of her horn, driven off again. Ernie had watched her through the curtains, and when she was gone, had ventured onto the porch and shyly, cautiously, picked up the box. His mother checked it when he carried it inside. The box didn't have their name on it but the brown truck was gone, so whatever was in the box was theirs to keep. Ernie pulled off the heavy tape, his fingers trembling, and found inside the box more little packages of seeds than he could count. He lifted them out, one by one, and examined the beautiful photographs of flowers on each. His mother was not interested, had returned to the television, but Ernie sat down at the kitchen table and quietly looked at each package for a long time, his fingers running across the slick paper and outlining the shapes of zinnias and cornflowers and nasturtiums and marigolds and asters and four o'clocks, his eyes drawing up their colors.

Two months later Ernie's mother died. A neighbor found her at the mailbox beside the road. People from the county courthouse

---

11. **cherish** (cher′ish), *v.* hold dear; treat with affection.

▲ *Good Friends–Zinnias & Asters* was painted by Don Ricks. Why do you suppose the artist calls these two kinds of flowers good friends?

came out to get Ernie, and as they ushered[12] him from the home he would never see again, he picked up the box of seed packages from his kitchen table and passed through the doorway.

Eventually Ernie was moved to a large white house near the main street of town. This house was called a group home, because in it lived a group of people who, like Ernie, could not live on their own. There were six of them. Each had his own room. When Ernie was shown the room that would be his, he put the box of Burpee seeds—which he had kept with him since his mother's death—on the little table beside the bed and then he sat down on the bed and cried.

Ernie cried every day for nearly a month. And then he stopped. He dried his tears and he learned how to bake refrigerator biscuits and how to dust mop and what to do if the indoor plants looked brown.

_____

12. **usher** (ush′ər), *v.* guide; escort.

Ernie loved watering the indoor plants and it was this pleasure which finally drew him outside. One of the young men who worked at the group home—a college student named Jack—grew a large garden in the back of the house. It was full of tomato vines and the large yellow blossoms of healthy squash. During his first summer at the house, Ernie would stand at the kitchen window, watching Jack and sometimes a resident of the home move among the vegetables. Ernie was curious, but too afraid to go into the garden.

Love is such a mystery . . . it can hardly be spoken of.

*T*hen one day when Ernie was watching through the window, he noticed that Jack was ripping open several slick little packages and emptying them into the ground. Ernie panicked and ran to his room. But the box of Burpee seeds was still there on his table, untouched. He grabbed it, slid it under his bed, then went back through the house and out into the garden as if he had done this every day of his life.

He stood beside Jack, watching him empty seed packages into the soft black soil, and as the packages were emptied, Ernie asked for them, holding out his hand, his eyes on the photographs of red radishes and purple eggplant. Jack handed the empty packages over with a smile and with that gesture became Ernie's first friend.

Jack tried to explain to Ernie that the seeds would grow into vegetables but Ernie could not believe this until he saw it come true. And when it did, he looked all the more intently at the packages of zinnias and cornflowers and the rest hidden beneath his bed. He thought more deeply about them but he could not carry them to the garden. He could

not let the garden have his seeds.

That was the first year in the large white house.

The second year, Ernie saw Dolores, and after that he thought of nothing else but her and of the photographs of flowers beneath his bed.

Jack had decided to take Ernie downtown for breakfast every Wednesday morning to ease him into the world outside that of the group home. They left very early, at 5:45 a.m., so there would be few people and almost no traffic to frighten Ernie and make him beg for his room. Jack and Ernie drove to the Big Boy restaurant which sat across the street from Stan's Hardware. There they ate eggs and bacon and French toast among those whose work demanded rising before the sun: bus drivers, policemen, nurses, mill workers. Their first time in the Big Boy, Ernie was too nervous to eat. The second time, he could eat but he couldn't look up. The third time, he not only ate everything on his plate, but he lifted his head and he looked out the window of the Big Boy restaurant toward Stan's Hardware across the street. There he saw a dark-haired woman in jeans and a black T-shirt unlocking the front door of the building, and that was the moment Ernie started loving Dolores and thinking about giving up his seeds to the soft black soil of Jack's garden.

Love is such a mystery, and when it strikes the heart of one as mysterious as Ernie himself, it can hardly be spoken of. Ernie could not explain to Jack why he went directly to his room later that morning, pulled the box of Burpee seeds from under his bed, then grabbed Jack's hand in the kitchen and walked with him to the garden where Ernie had come to believe things would grow. Ernie handed the packets of seeds one by one to

Jack, who stood in silent admiration of the lovely photographs before asking Ernie several times, "Are you sure you want to plant these?" Ernie was sure. It didn't take him very long, and when the seeds all lay under the moist black earth, Ernie carried his empty packages inside the house and spent the rest of the day spreading them across his bed in different arrangements.

$\mathcal{T}$hat was in June. For the next several Wednesdays at 7:00 a.m. Ernie watched every movement of the dark-haired woman behind the lighted windows of Stan's Hardware. Jack watched Ernie watch Dolores, and discreetly[13] said nothing.

When Ernie's flowers began growing in July, Ernie spent most of his time in the garden. He would watch the garden for hours, as if he expected it suddenly to move or to impress him with a quick trick. The fragile green stems of his flowers stood uncertainly in the soil, like baby colts on their first legs, but the young plants performed no magic for Ernie's eyes. They saved their shows for the middle of the night and next day surprised Ernie with tender small blooms in all the colors the photographs had promised.

The flowers grew fast and hardy, and one early Wednesday morning when they looked as big and bright as their pictures on the empty packages, Ernie pulled a glass canning jar off a dusty shelf in the basement of his house. He washed the jar, half filled it with water, then carried it to the garden where he placed in it one of every kind of flower he had grown. He met Jack at the car and rode off to the Big Boy with the jar of flowers held tight between his small hands. Jack told him it was a beautiful bouquet.

When they reached the door of the Big Boy, Ernie stopped and pulled at Jack's arm, pointing to the building across the street. "OK," Jack said, and he led Ernie to the front door of Stan's Hardware. It was 6:00 a.m. and the building was still dark. Ernie set the clear mason jar full of flowers under the sign that read "Closed," then he smiled at Jack and followed him back across the street to get breakfast.

When Dolores arrived at seven and picked up the jar of zinnias and cornflowers and nasturtiums and marigolds and asters and four o'clocks, Ernie and Jack were watching her from a booth in the Big Boy. Each had a wide smile on his face as Dolores put her nose to the flowers. Ernie giggled. They watched the lights of the hardware store come up and saw Dolores place the clear mason jar on the ledge of the front window. They drove home still smiling.

All the rest of that summer Ernie left a jar of flowers every Wednesday morning at the front door of Stan's Hardware. Neither Dick Wilcox nor Dolores could figure out why the flowers kept coming, and each of them assumed somebody had a crush on the other. But the flowers had an effect on them anyway. Dick started spending more time out on the floor making conversation with the customers, while Dolores stopped wearing T-shirts to work and instead wore crisp white blouses with the sleeves rolled back off her wrists. Occasionally she put on a bracelet.

By summer's end Jack and Ernie had become very good friends, and when the flowers in the garden behind their house began to wither, and Ernie's face began to grow gray as he watched them, Jack brought home one bright day in late September a great long box. Ernie followed Jack as he carried it down to the basement and watched as Jack pulled a long glass tube from the box and attached this tube to the wall above a table. When Jack plugged in the tube's electric cord, a soft lavender light washed the room.

"Sunshine," said Jack.

---

13. **discreetly** (dis krēt′lē), *adv.* in a way that shows good judgment; cautiously.

Then he went back to his car for a smaller box. He carried this down to the basement where Ernie still stood staring at the strange light. Jack handed Ernie the small box, and when Ernie opened it he found more little packages of seeds than he could count, with new kinds of photographs on the slick paper.

"Violets," Jack said, pointing to one of them.

Then he and Ernie went outside to get some dirt.

Zinnias

Valerie Worth

Zinnias, stout and stiff,
Stand no nonsense: their colors
Stare, their leaves
Grow straight out, their petals
5 Jut like clipped cardboard,
Round, in neat flat rings.

Even cut and bunched,
Arranged to please us
In the house, in water, they
10 Will hardly wilt—I know
Someone like zinnias; I wish
I were like zinnias.

After Reading

Making Connections

1. If you were given the job of continuing this story for a TV script, what would you have happen next?

2. 🐾 **Communication** between Ernie and Dolores consists only of his flowers. Do you think Ernie wants to meet Dolores and have a closer relationship with her? Explain.

3. Why doesn't the author ever have Dolores and Ernie meet?

4. The author chooses a small town for the **setting** of this story. How might the story be different if it were set in a city?

5. Compare the **character** of Ernie to heroes you have met in other stories. Which qualities do they have in common, and which are different?

6. Ernie's act of kindness changes people around him. In what ways have you or others you know made changes in your community?

7. Do you know any people like Ernie? How do you feel about them? Has this story changed your attitude in any way?

Literary Focus: Characterization Through Detail

The characters in this story say and do very little, so you must look at the details the author uses for important clues to **characterization**. The author describes "the fine dark hair coating Dolores's upper lip" and her knowledge of carburetors. From these details you might conclude that Dolores is not overly concerned about her appearance and is good at mechanics. What other inferences, or conclusions, can you make?

Read through the story quickly again to look for other details about characters. Ask yourself: "What conclusions can I draw about the character from these details?" You may find it helpful to organize your ideas about characters on a reasoning frame like the one below.

Detail: She knows about carburetors and backs of washing machines.

Detail:

Detail:

Conclusion about (character's name):

Vocabulary Study

Find the word that is not related in meaning to the other words in the set and write its letter on your paper.

excess
impale
speculation
improbable
swarthy
cherish
usher
discreetly

1. **a.** guess   **b.** fact   **c.** speculation   **d.** hunch
2. **a.** improbable **b.** likely   **c.** certain   **d.** sure
3. **a.** love   **b.** cherish   **c.** loath   **d.** value
4. **a.** loudly   **b.** obnoxiously   **c.** rudely   **d.** discreetly
5. **a.** swarthy   **b.** fair   **c.** pale   **d.** white
6. **a.** hate   **b.** disdain   **c.** dislike   **d.** cherish
7. **a.** pierce   **b.** impale   **c.** mend   **d.** puncture
8. **a.** discreetly **b.** cautiously   **c.** honestly   **d.** quietly
9. **a.** escort   **b.** usher   **c.** brush   **d.** accompany
10. **a.** excess   **b.** abundance   **c.** express   **d.** extra

Expressing Your Ideas

Writing Choices

Take a Second Look Before you read the selection, you wrote in your notebook about your experience with a crush. Write a **compare and contrast essay** describing the differences and similarities between your crush and Ernie's.

Thanks a Lot If you worked at the hardware store, you might think the flowers were for you. How could you say "thanks" if you didn't even know who they were from? Write a **thank you note** you might leave for your unknown admirer.

Flower Power Ernie learned to plant flowers by watching how Jack did it. Jack probably learned by reading the directions on the package. Imagine you work for the Blooming World seed company, and your job is to write the **instructions** for planting flower seeds. You can use a real or an imaginary flower.

Other Options

Crush Collage Work in a small group to create a **collage** representing "A Crush." You may use pictures cut from old magazines or small objects that can be glued or stapled to paper. Look for things that remind you of the characters, setting, ideas, or feelings described in the story. Discuss with your group why you chose each object and be prepared to explain your choices to the rest of the class.

Tattoos-R-You The howling coyote on Dolores's upper arm gives us insight into her personality. If you were to design a **tattoo** for Ernie, or for another fictional character you have read about, what would you choose? Tattoos usually are forever, so take some time to consider what pictures and slogans might best represent the character. Then use those symbols to design the tattoo.

Writing Mini-Lesson

Setting Up Your Working Portfolio

What Is a Working Portfolio? A working portfolio is a collection of the writing you do throughout the school year. Think of your working portfolio as a road map. It can show you and others where you've been and where you're heading as a writer. Later in the year, you'll create a presentation portfolio to display pieces you're proud of.

How to Get Started

Start by setting some writing goals. What do you like to write? What kind of writing do you like least? Where do you think you need to work the hardest? Write two or three goals you'd like to reach this year in your writing. Keep them in the front of your portfolio.

Then decide what to use for your working portfolio. You might try a three-ring binder, an expandable folder, or a report folder. You, your group, or your teacher might have other ideas. You may want to decorate the cover of your portfolio. You could draw, use a photograph, or make a collage. What do you think would be a good image for the cover of your portfolio?

What to Put in Your Working Portfolio

- Working drafts of your writing including lists, charts, other planning pieces, and first drafts

- Final drafts of your writing, including pieces that have been revised and edited, as a record of your completed work

- Other completed assignments that are not pieces of writing, such as videotapes or audiotapes

- Self-evaluations in which you examine ways you've improved and ways you can still improve as a writer

- Reflections in which you consider how the writing you've done has helped you grow as a student and as a person

Before Reading

After Twenty Years

by O. Henry

O. Henry
1862–1910

Born William Sydney Porter, O. Henry spent more of his North Carolina childhood reading and watching the people around him than in school. He worked for a time in Texas, first on a ranch and then as a bank clerk in Austin, where he was unjustly accused in 1896 of stealing money. He fled to Honduras but was later imprisoned for three years when he returned to Austin to see his dying wife. After prison O. Henry settled in New York City, where with his keen eye and ironic sense of humor he wrote about what he knew best: ordinary people, the streets of New York City, and the West.

Building Background

Walking a Beat The automobile was first used for police work in Akron, Ohio, in 1899. Before that, police patrolled neighborhoods on foot. A police officer's territory was called a beat, and each officer got to know the local residents and businesses well. The standard police weapon at the turn of the century was a nightstick, or short club. Guns were not essential since the police, also called officers of the peace, could expect to discourage law-breakers and keep order just by being in the neighborhood.

Getting into the Story

Writer's Notebook The story is about two friends who plan to meet again for the first time in twenty years. Have you ever lost touch with a friend when one of you moved away? Imagine what that person would be like today. In your notebook, write about an imaginary reunion you and your friend might have. What might be the same about your friend? What might have changed? Use a chart like the one below to organize your thoughts before you begin.

Friend: Sam	
Same	**Different**
Blue eyes	Learned to play piano
Two sisters	Grew four inches

Reading Tip

Use Context for Older Vocabulary Language has changed some in the century since this story was written. Some words common then have disappeared from everyday use. Others seem old-fashioned. Don't let unfamiliar words in this story stop you in your tracks. When you read a word such as "nigh" or "adown," try to get the meaning from context. Read the surrounding sentence and paragraph for clues, and then use what you have learned to figure out the meaning.

After TWENTY Years

O. Henry

The policeman on the beat moved up the avenue impressively. The impressiveness was <u>habitual</u>[1] and not for show, for spectators were few. The time was barely 10 o'clock at night, but chilly gusts of wind with a taste of rain in them had well nigh depeopled the streets.

Trying doors as he went, twirling his club with many intricate and artful movements,

---

1. **habitual** (hə bich′ü əl), *adj.* done by habit; usual; customary.

▲ *The City from Greenwich Village,* by John Sloan, was painted in 1922. What is the mood of this painting?

turning now and then to cast his watchful eye adown the pacific[2] thoroughfare, the officer, with his stalwart[3] form and slight swagger, made a fine picture of a guardian of the peace. The vicinity was one that kept early hours. Now and then you might see the lights of a cigar store or of an all-night lunch counter; but the majority of the doors belonged to business places that had long since been closed.

When about midway of a certain block the policeman suddenly slowed his walk. In the doorway of a darkened hardware store a man leaned, with an unlighted cigar in his mouth. As the policeman walked up to him the man spoke up quickly.

"It's all right, officer," he said, reassuringly. "I'm just waiting for a friend. It's an appointment made twenty years ago. Sounds a little funny to you, doesn't it? Well, I'll explain if you'd like to make certain it's all straight. About that long ago there used to be a restaurant where this store stands—'Big Joe' Brady's restaurant."

"Until five years ago," said the policeman. "It was torn down then."

The man in the doorway struck a match and lit his cigar. The light showed a pale, square-jawed face with keen eyes, and a little white scar near his right eyebrow. His scarfpin[4] was a large diamond, oddly set.

"Twenty years ago to-night," said the man, "I dined here at 'Big Joe' Brady's with Jimmy Wells, my best chum, and the finest chap in the world. He and I were raised here in New York, just like two brothers, together. I was eighteen and Jimmy was twenty. The next morning I was to start for the West to make my fortune. You couldn't have dragged Jimmy out of New York; he thought it was the only place on earth. Well, we agreed that night that

The light showed a pale, square-jawed face with keen eyes, and a little white scar . . .

we would meet here again exactly twenty years from that date and time, no matter what our conditions might be or from what distance we might have to come. We figured that in twenty years each of us ought to have our destiny worked out and our fortunes made, whatever they were going to be."

"It sounds pretty interesting," said the policeman. "Rather a long time beween meets, though, it seems to me. Haven't you heard from your friend since you left?"

"Well, yes, for a time we corresponded," said the other. "But after a year or two we lost track of each other. You see, the West is a pretty big proposition, and I kept hustling around over it pretty lively. But I know Jimmy will meet me here if he's alive, for he always was the truest, stanchest[5] old chap in the world. He'll never forget. I came a thousand miles to stand in this door to-night, and it's worth it if my old partner turns up."

The waiting man pulled out a handsome watch, the lids[6] of it set with small diamonds.

"Three minutes to ten," he announced. "It was exactly ten o'clock when we parted here at the restaurant door."

"Did pretty well out West didn't you?" asked the policeman.

"You bet! I hope Jimmy has done half as

---

2. **pacific** (pə sif′ik), *adj.* peaceful; calm; quiet.
3. **stalwart** (stôl′wərt), *adj.* strongly built; sturdy.
4. **scarfpin** (skärf′pin′), pin used to fasten a scarf around the neck.
5. **stanchest** (stônch′əst), *adj.* most loyal (also spelled *staunchest*).
6. **lid,** moveable cover. At the turn of the century, a man's pocket watch often had two lids. One protected the glass of the timepiece. The second opened to reveal the metal back, which often bore an inscription.

▲ *Portrait of Vlaminck* is an oil painting on canvas by André Derain, which was painted in 1905.

well. He was a kind of plodder,[7] though, good fellow as he was. I've had to compete with some of the sharpest wits going to get my pile. A man gets in a groove in New York. It takes the West to put a razor-edge on him."

The policeman twirled his club and took a step or two.

"I'll be on my way. Hope your friend comes around all right. Going to call time on him sharp?"

"I should say not!" said the other. "I'll give him half an hour at least. If Jimmy is alive on earth he'll be here by that time. So long, officer."

"Good-night, sir," said the policeman, passing on along his beat, trying doors as he went.

There was now a fine, cold drizzle falling, and the wind had risen from its uncertain puffs into a steady blow. The few foot passengers astir in that quarter hurried

---

7. **plodder** (plod′ər), *n.* person who works hard, but slowly.

dismally and silently along with coat collars turned high and pocketed hands. And in the door of the hardware store the man who had come a thousand miles to fill an appointment, uncertain almost to absurdity,[8] with the friend of his youth, smoked his cigar and waited.

About twenty minutes he waited, and then a tall man in a long overcoat, with collar turned up to his ears, hurried across from the opposite side of the street. He went directly to the waiting man.

"Is that you, Bob?" he asked, doubtfully.

"Is that you, Jimmy Wells?" cried the man in the door.

"Bless my heart!" exclaimed the new arrival, grasping both the other's hands with his own. "It's Bob, sure as fate. I was certain I'd find you here if you were still in existence. Well, well, well!—twenty years is a long time. The old restaurant's gone, Bob; I wish it had lasted, so we could have had another dinner there. How has the West treated you, old man?"

"Bully; it has given me everything I asked it for. You've changed lots, Jimmy. I never thought you were so tall by two or three inches."

"Oh, I grew a bit after I was twenty."

"Doing well in New York, Jimmy?"

"Moderately. I have a position in one of the city departments. Come on, Bob; we'll go around to a place I know of, and have a good long talk about old times."

The two men started up the street, arm in arm. The man from the West, his egotism[9] enlarged by success, was beginning to outline the history of his career. The other, submerged in his overcoat, listened with interest.

At the corner stood a drug store, brilliant

"Twenty years is a long time, but not long enough to change a man's nose from a Roman to a pug."

with electric lights. When they came into this glare each of them turned simultaneously[10] to gaze upon the other's face.

The man from the West stopped suddenly and released his arm.

"You're not Jimmy Wells," he snapped. "Twenty years is a long time, but not long enough to change a man's nose from a Roman to a pug."[11]

"It sometimes changes a good man into a bad one," said the tall man. "You've been under arrest for ten minutes, 'Silky' Bob. Chicago thinks you may have dropped over our way and wires us she wants to have a chat with you. Going quietly, are you? That's sensible. Now, before we go to the station here's a note I was asked to hand to you. You may read it here at the window. It's from Patrolman Wells."

The man from the West unfolded the little piece of paper handed him. His hand was steady when he began to read, but it trembled a little by the time he had finished. The note was rather short.

Bob: I was at the appointed place on time. When you struck the match to light your cigar I saw it was the face of the man wanted in Chicago. Somehow I couldn't do it myself, so I went around and got a plain clothes man to do the job.

Jimmy

---

8. **absurdity** (ab sėr′də tē), *n.* something unreasonable or ridiculous.
9. **egotism** (ē′gə tiz′əm), *n.* habit of thinking too highly of oneself; conceit.
10. **simultaneously** (sī′məl tā′nē əs lē), *adv.* happening at the same time.
11. **Roman to a pug,** two distinct types of noses: a pug nose is shorter and flatter, while a Roman nose has a prominent bridge.

After Reading

Making Connections

1. Do you think Jimmy Wells was right not to arrest his friend himself? Why or why not?

2. Why do you think Silky Bob decided to travel 1,000 miles to keep his appointment with Jimmy?

3. O. Henry's **plots** often end with a twist. When did you figure out who Jimmy Wells was?

4. Why did O. Henry keep the patrolman's identity a secret until the end?

5. What details and descriptions does O. Henry use to build **suspense** in this story?

6. Imagine a **dialogue** between Jimmy Wells and a police officer of today. Write their discussion.

Literary Focus: Plot

The plan or story in a piece of literature is its **plot**. You can outline a story's plot by identifying the main character's problem and listing the events that lead to its solution. In this story, Bob explains his problem to the patrolman: "I'm just waiting for a friend. It's an appointment made twenty years ago." You want to read the rest of the story to find out if his friend will keep the appointment. Were you surprised at the end? The irony, or unexpected outcome of this plot, makes it interesting. Go over the story again to identify the plot elements. Use a chart like the one below to help you organize your thoughts.

Title: "After Twenty Years"
Setting: New York City street, about 1900
Characters: Bob, Jimmy Wells, the plain clothes man

Problem: Will Jimmy keep the appointment made with Bob 20 years ago?

▼

Event: Policeman stops to talk with Bob, who waits in doorway where restaurant once stood.

▼

Event: (Add additional event boxes as needed.)

▼

Solution:

Vocabulary Study

Decide if the following pairs of words are synonyms or antonyms. Write the correct answer on your paper.

habitual
pacific
stalwart
stanchest
plodder
absurdity
egotism
simultaneously

1. habitual—customary
2. stalwart—frail
3. plodder—racer
4. quiet—pacific
5. meekness—egotism
6. stanchest—most loyal
7. absurdity—reasonableness
8. pacific—disturbed
9. egotism—selfishness
10. simultaneously—together

Expressing Your Ideas

Writing Choices

Extra! Extra! Imagine you are a reporter, and write a **news story** detailing the capture of Silky Bob. Be sure to include answers to six basic news questions: Who? Did what? When? Where? Why? and How? Top your story off with an eye-catching headline.

True Confessions What would Bob and Jimmy have told each other about their lives if they had gotten together again for dinner? Write out a **dialogue** the two men might have had.

Turn the Tables How might the story have differed if Bob had recognized Jimmy when they first met? Write a **story** ending that fits this new plot twist.

Other Options

Wanted, Dead or Alive Presumably Jimmy Wells recognized Silky Bob through a "wanted" poster he saw at police head-quarters. Work with a classmate to create the **poster** that tipped him off. Look back through the story to include all of Silky Bob's distinctive features. Your poster should use both pictures and descriptive words to put Bob behind bars!

Sing Out Write "The Ballad of Silky Bob." A **ballad** is a poem that tells a story in simple verse. For an example of a ballad, see "The Highwayman" in Unit 6, Part Two. Write Bob's story in three or four rhyming stanzas. Then write a refrain to go after each stanza. Ballads are often sung. You can set your ballad to a tune you already know or make up your own.

Before Reading

Seventh Grade

by Gary Soto

Gary Soto
born 1952

In *Baseball in April,* a short story collection that includes "Seventh Grade," Gary Soto draws on his experiences growing up in Fresno, California, to write about the lives of Mexican American teenagers. A sprinkling of Spanish reflects the Mexican heritage of Soto's characters. Their problems are, however, familar to all teenagers.

Building Background

Fascinating Fresno The story "Seventh Grade" takes place in a school in Fresno, a thriving hub city in California's astonishingly fertile San Joaquin Valley. Fresno County processes, sells, and ships some 200 agricultural products, more agricultural products than any other county in the United States. Spanish-speaking people have lived in the Valley since the mid-1800s. In the Fresno area Spanish is as common as English, but the setting is typical of urban America.

Getting into the Story

Discussion The boys in "Seventh Grade" want to make good impressions on girls, but they're not sure how to do it. Have you ever tried to make an impression on someone? In a small group, discuss things you've done to impress people.

Reading Tip

Foreign Words The French and Spanish words sprinkled throughout this story add interest and a light-hearted touch. You may be able to figure out from context what some of the words mean. The chart that follows will help you with the others.

Spanish	English	French	English
raza-style (rä′sä)	in the style of Mexican Americans	bonjour (boN zhür′)	hello
saludo de vato (sä lü′dō dā vä′tō)	special greeting between Mexican Americans	très bien (tre bē eN′)	very good
ese (ā′sä)	familiar form of address between Mexican Americans	parlez-vous francais (pär′lā vü′ fräN sā′)	do you speak French
		le bateau est sur l'eau (le ba tō′ e syr lō)	the boat is on the water

This lithograph by Keith Haring was created in 1985. It is untitled.
What **communication** about friends and foes do you think the artist might have had in mind? What title would you suggest?

Seventh Grade

Gary Soto

On the first day of school, Victor stood in the line half an hour before he came to a wobbly card table. He was handed a packet of papers and a computer card on which he listed his one elective,[1] French. He already spoke Spanish and English, but he thought some day he might travel to France, where it was cool; not like Fresno, where summer days reached 110 degrees in the shade. There were rivers in France, and huge churches, and fair-skinned people everywhere, the way there were brown people all around Victor.

Besides, Teresa, a girl he had liked since they were in catechism classes at Saint Theresa's, was taking French, too. With any luck they would be in the same class. Teresa is going to be my girl this year, he promised himself as he left the gym full of students in their new fall clothes. She was cute. And good at math, too, Victor thought as he walked down the hall to his homeroom. He ran into his friend, Michael Torres, by the water fountain that never turned off.

They shook hands, *raza*-style, and jerked their heads at one another in a *saludo de vato.* "How come you're making a face?" asked Victor.

"I ain't making a face, *ese.* This *is* my face." Michael said his face had changed during the summer. He had read a *GQ* magazine that his older

---

1. **elective** (i lek′tiv), *n.* subject or course of study that may be taken, but is not required.

brother had borrowed from the Book Mobile and noticed that the male models all had the same look on their faces. They would stand, one arm around a beautiful woman, and *scowl*.[2] They would sit at a pool, their rippled stomachs dark with shadow, and *scowl*. They would sit at dinner tables, cool drinks in their hands, and *scowl*.

"I think it works," Michael said. He scowled and let his upper lip quiver.[3] His teeth showed along with the ferocity[4] of his soul. "Belinda Reyes walked by a while ago and looked at me," he said.

Victor didn't say anything, though he thought his friend looked pretty strange. They talked about recent movies, baseball, their parents, and the horrors of picking grapes in order to buy their fall clothes. Picking grapes was like living in Siberia, except hot and more boring.

"What classes are you taking?" Michael said, scowling.

"French. How 'bout you?"

"Spanish. I ain't so good at it, even if I'm Mexican."

"I'm not either, but I'm better at it than math, that's for sure."

A tinny, three-beat bell propelled students to their homerooms. The two friends socked each other in the arm and went their ways, Victor thinking, man, that's weird. Michael thinks making a face makes him handsome.

On the way to his homeroom, Victor tried a scowl. He felt foolish, until out of the corner of his eye he saw a girl looking at him. Umm, he thought, maybe it does work. He scowled with greater conviction.[5]

In homeroom, roll was taken, emergency cards were passed out, and they were given a bulletin to take home to their parents. The principal, Mr. Belton, spoke over the crackling loudspeaker, welcoming the students to a new year, new experiences, and new friendships. The students squirmed in their chairs and ignored him. They were anxious to go to first period. Victor sat calmly, thinking of Teresa, who sat two rows away, reading a paperback novel. This would be his lucky year. She was in his homeroom, and would probably be in his English and math classes. And, of course, French.

The bell rang for first period, and the students herded noisily through the door. Only Teresa lingered,[6] talking with the homeroom teacher.

"So you think I should talk to Mrs. Gaines?" she asked the teacher. "She would know about ballet?"

"She would be a good bet," the teacher said. Then added, "Or the gym teacher, Mrs. Garza."

Victor lingered, keeping his head down and staring at his desk. He wanted to leave when she did so he could bump into her and say something clever.

He watched her on the sly. As she turned to leave, he stood up and hurried to the door, where he managed to catch her eye. She smiled and said, "Hi, Victor."

He smiled back and said, "Yeah, that's me." His brown face blushed. Why hadn't he said, "Hi, Teresa," or "How was your summer?" or something nice?

As Teresa walked down the hall, Victor walked the other way, looking back, admiring how gracefully she walked, one foot in front of the other. So much for being in the same

> He scowled . . . . His teeth showed along with the ferocity of his soul.

---

2. **scowl** (skoul), *v.* look angry or sullen by lowering the eyebrows; frown.
3. **quiver** (kwiv′ər), *v.* shake with a slight but rapid motion; shiver; tremble.
4. **ferocity** (fə ros′ə tē), *n.* savage cruelty; fierceness.
5. **conviction** (kən vik′shən), *n.* firmness of belief.
6. **linger** (ling′gər), *v.* stay, as if unwilling to leave.

class, he thought. As he trudged[7] to English, he practiced scowling.

In English they reviewed the parts of speech. Mr. Lucas, a portly[8] man, waddled down the aisle, asking, "What is a noun?"

"A person, place, or thing," said the class in unison.

"Yes, now somebody give me an example of a person—you, Victor Rodriguez."

"Teresa," Victor said automatically. Some of the girls giggled. They knew he had a crush on Teresa. He felt himself blushing again.

"Correct," Mr. Lucas said. "Now provide me with a place."

Mr. Lucas called on a freckled kid who answered, "Teresa's house with a kitchen full of big brothers."

After English, Victor had math, his weakest subject. He sat in the back by the window, hoping that he would not be called on. Victor understood most of the problems, but some of the stuff looked like the teacher made it up as she went along. It was confusing, like the inside of a watch.

After math he had a fifteen-minute break, then social studies, and, finally, lunch. He bought a tuna casserole with buttered rolls, some fruit cocktail, and milk. He sat with Michael, who practiced scowling between bites.

Girls walked by and looked at him.

"See what I mean, Vic?" Michael scowled. "They love it."

"Yeah, I guess so."

They ate slowly, Victor scanning the horizon for a glimpse of Teresa. He didn't see her. She must have brought lunch, he thought, and is eating outside. Victor scraped his plate and left Michael, who was busy scowling at a girl two tables away.

The small, triangle-shaped campus bustled with students talking about their new classes. Everyone was in a sunny mood. Victor hurried to the bag lunch area, where he sat down and opened his math book. He moved his lips as if he were reading, but his mind was some-

where else. He raised his eyes slowly and looked around. No Teresa.

He lowered his eyes, pretending to study, then looked slowly to the left. No Teresa. He turned a page in the book and stared at some math problems that scared him because he knew he would have to do them eventually. He looked to the right. Still no sign of her. He stretched out lazily in an attempt to disguise his snooping.

Then he saw her. She was sitting with a girlfriend under a plum tree. Victor moved to a table near her and daydreamed about taking her to a movie. When the bell sounded, Teresa looked up, and their eyes met. She smiled sweetly and gathered her books. Her next class was French, same as Victor's.

They were among the last students to arrive in class, so all the good desks in the back had already been taken. Victor was forced to sit near the front, a few desks away from Teresa, while Mr. Bueller wrote French words on the chalkboard. The bell rang, and Mr. Bueller wiped his hands, turned to the class, and said, *"Bonjour."*

"Bonjour," braved a few students.

"Bonjour," Victor whispered. He wondered if Teresa heard him.

Mr. Bueller said that if the students studied hard, at the end of the year they could go to France and be understood by the populace.

One kid raised his hand and asked, "What's 'populace'?"

"The people, the people of France."

Mr. Bueller asked if anyone knew French. Victor raised his hand, wanting to impress Teresa. The teacher beamed and said, *"Très bien. Parlez-vous français?"*

Victor didn't know what to say. The teacher wet his lips and asked something else in

---

7. **trudge** (truj), *v.* walk wearily or with effort.
8. **portly** (pôrt′lē), *adj.* having a large body; overweight.

French. The room grew silent. Victor felt all eyes staring at him. He tried to bluff[9] his way out by making noises that sounded French.

"La me vave me con le grandma," he said uncertainly.

Mr. Bueller, wrinkling his face in curiosity, asked him to speak up.

Great rosebushes of red bloomed on Victor's cheeks. A river of nervous sweat ran down his palms. He felt awful. Teresa sat a few desks away, no doubt thinking he was a fool. Without looking at Mr. Bueller, Victor mumbled, "Frenchie oh wewe gee in September."

Mr. Bueller asked Victor to repeat what he said.

"Frenchie oh wewe gee in September," Victor repeated.

Mr. Bueller understood that the boy didn't know French and turned away. He walked to the blackboard and pointed to the words on the board with his steel-edged ruler.

"*Le bateau,*" he sang.

"*Le bateau,*" the students repeated.

"*Le bateau est sur l'eau,*" he sang.

"*Le bateau est sur l'eau.*"

Victor was too weak from failure to join the class. He stared at the board and wished he had taken Spanish, not French. Better yet, he wished he could start his life over. He had never been so embarrassed. He bit his thumb until he tore off a sliver of skin.

The bell sounded for fifth period, and Victor shot out of the room, avoiding the stares of the other kids, but had to return for his math book. He looked sheepishly[10] at the teacher, who was erasing the board, then widened his eyes in terror at Teresa who stood in front of him. "I didn't know you knew French," she said. "That was good."

Mr. Bueller looked at Victor, and Victor looked back. Oh please, don't say anything, Victor pleaded with his eyes. I'll wash your car, mow your lawn, walk your dog—anything! I'll be your best student, and I'll clean your erasers after school.

Mr. Bueller shuffled through the papers on his desk. He smiled and hummed as he sat down to work. He remembered his college years when he dated a girlfriend in borrowed cars. She thought he was rich because each time he picked her up he had a different car. It was fun until he had spent all his money on her and had to write home to his parents because he was broke.

Victor couldn't stand to look at Teresa. He was sweaty with shame. "Yeah, well, I picked up a few things from movies and books and stuff like that." They left the class together. Teresa asked him if he would help her with her French.

"Sure, anytime," Victor said.

"I won't be bothering you, will I?"

"Oh no, I like being bothered."

"*Bonjour,*" Teresa said, leaving him outside her next class. She smiled and pushed wisps of hair from her face.

"Yeah, right, *bonjour*," Victor said. He turned and headed to his class. The rosebushes of shame on his face became bouquets of love. Teresa is a great girl, he thought. And Mr. Bueller is a good guy.

He raced to metal shop. After metal shop there was biology, and after biology a long sprint to the public library, where he checked out three French textbooks.

He was going to like seventh grade.

> He bit his thumb until he tore off a sliver of skin.

---

9. **bluff** (bluf), *v.* fool by pretending confidence.
10. **sheepishly** (shē′pish lē), *adv.* in an awkwardly bashful or embarrassed manner.

After Reading

Making Connections

1. What was your favorite scene in "Seventh Grade"? What made it enjoyable for you?

2. If you had been a friend of Victor's in French class, how would you have reacted to his bluff? Explain.

3. What do you think Teresa's **point of view** of the incident in French class was?

4. Why does the author choose not to reveal what Teresa is thinking until the end of the story?

5. What would happen if a student tried an outrageous bluff in a class at your school? Explain.

6. At the end of the story, the author states that Victor "was going to like seventh grade." Do you agree? Explain your answer.

7. **Communication** of our feelings toward others is often difficult. How can you show someone that you really care for them without saying so directly?

Literary Focus: Point of View

You can figure out **point of view** in a story by asking yourself, "Who is telling this story?" In "Seventh Grade" a narrator writes about another person, When a narrator tells a story about someone else, the author is using **third-person point of view**. As you read the story what pronouns did you see used over and over again? Did you answer *he* and *his*? These are both third-person pronouns that indicate third-person point of view.

In some stories the narrator knows the thoughts and feelings of every character. In a small group discuss how the story would have changed if the narrator had revealed Michael's or Teresa's thoughts, too. How might it have changed if Victor had told his own story?

Vocabulary Study

On your paper write the letter of the correct ending.

elective
scowl
quiver
ferocity
conviction
linger
trudge
portly
bluff
sheepishly

1. As an **elective** Victor chose **a.** a sandwich for lunch. **b.** a French class. **c.** a trip to France.

2. Ordinarily a person will **scowl** when **a.** his team wins a game. **b.** trying to attract someone. **c.** having an argument.

3. You would expect someone's lip to **quiver** when **a.** they've been sunburned. **b.** they're scowling. **c.** they're about to cry.

4. To show his **ferocity** Michael **a.** bared his teeth. **b.** registered for math. **c.** ducked behind a pillar.

5. Victor scowled with greater **conviction** because he **a.** found it would attract girls. **b.** thought it might attract girls. **c.** felt foolish.

6. A student will **trudge** to her next class because she **a.** feels excited by her success. **b.** is in a hurry. **c.** failed an exam.

7. We might assume that Victor's **portly** English teacher likes **a.** to sing. **b.** to eat. **c.** to sail.

8. Victor may **linger** in the lunch area because **a.** he wants to talk to a girl. **b.** he has to be home soon. **c.** he has other places to go.

9. Victor looked **sheepishly** at his French teacher because he was **a.** embarrassed. **b.** confused. **c.** terrified.

10. Victor's **bluff** showed that **a.** he really knew French. **b.** he was a truthful person. **c.** he was faking.

Expressing Your Ideas ───────

Writing Choices

Looking Back Think about the discussion about impressing other people that you had before you read the story. Were there any similarities between what was said then and the story? Write a **comparison**.

Guide to Grade 7 Work with a partner to create a **pamphlet** titled "How to Get Along in Seventh Grade." Begin by brainstorming the important dos and don'ts; then list them in the pamphlet along with suggestions for putting them into practice.

Other Options

Post It With a partner turn the ideas in your pamphlet, or in another pair's pamphlet, on "How to Get Along in Seventh Grade" into a **poster**. Illustrations for dos and don'ts might include art, photos, cartoons, and so on.

How to Be Cool First impressions can be important. **Draw** a seventh-grade student who would be certain to impress the opposite sex with the right haircut, clothing, shoes, and so on. Label each item and tell why it would impress others.

Before Reading

Oranges by Jean Little
Pure Poetry by Gerard Malanga

The Rebel by Mari Evans
My Hard Repair Job by James Berry

Building Background

What Makes a Poem What do you expect from a poem? Lines of about equal length? Lines ending with words that rhyme with another line? Poems don't all fit a particular description, but they do use common poetic techniques. Poems use words sparingly, often making one word or phrase do double duty with two or more meanings. The sounds and rhythms of the words are selected to give the meaning a boost. Some poets come up with more unusual techniques, such as using the way a poem looks on the page to add meaning. With or without rhyme, with long lines or short, all poetry tries to express the poet's thoughts and feelings in an imaginative way.

Getting into the Story

What Keeps a Friendship	What Ruins a Friendship
loyalty	angry words
sharing	jealousy
liking the same things	stubbornness

Discussion The four poems that follow are about friendships—what makes them tick and what makes them stop. With a partner, talk about good friendships you currently have or have had in the past. Can you agree on the qualities that good friendships have? Why do good friendships sometimes end? What causes them to fail? How might they be saved? It might help to organize your thoughts on a chart like the one here. Make two copies so that you and your partner can refer to it as you read the poems.

Reading Tip

Understanding Poetry How you read a poem can make it easier or more difficult to understand. Always begin with the title, which is part of the poem and often a good clue to its meaning. Don't let the shape of a poem on the page trip you up. Most poems are written in full sentences, even if they don't look that way at first. Try skipping line breaks and use natural stopping points, such as commas and periods. This tip works especially well when you read the poem aloud. Hearing the poem will make you more of sentences as well as any unusual ways the poet uses so

Jean Little
born 1932

Canadian author Jean Little has published many stories and poems for young people. Nearly blind herself, she writes with sensitivity about disabilities, death, and friendship. Kate and Emily, the two characters featured in the poem "Oranges," also are each the subject of short stories exploring their individual personalities and their friendship.

Gerard Malanga
born 1943

Gerard Malanga wears many hats. In addition to his unusual poetic technique, he has expressed his creativity as a photographer, cinematographer, and actor. He continues to write and work as a curator in a New York photography gallery.

James Berry
born 1924

As a teacher in England, James Berry noticed a need for children's books that reflected different backgrounds, so he began to write about his childhood in Jamaica. Whether he writes about friendship or the life and folklore of the Caribbean, Berry bases his writing largely on personal experience. In some poems he even tries to recreate the sounds of Caribbean English. "It's so important to me to use authentic voices," Berry says.

Mari Evans

Mari Evans published her first short story in a school newspaper in fourth grade. Greatly encouraged by her father to write, she soon took poet Langston Hughes as a model. "My father inspired a belief in myself and my ability to produce," Evans said. As a writer, teacher, and television show host, Evans has worked for civil rights and social justice. Her writing includes poetry, prose, and drama for both young people and adults.

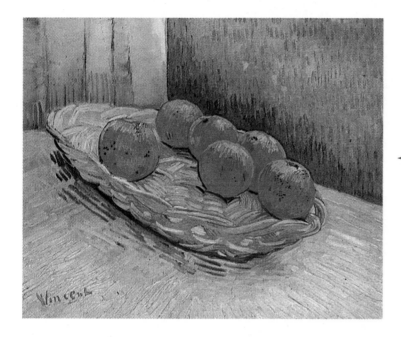

◄ *Still Life: Basket with Six Oranges* was painted by Vincent Van Gogh in 1888.

Oranges

Jean Little

I peel oranges neatly.
The sections come apart cleanly, perfectly, in my hands.

When Emily peels an orange, she tears holes in it.
Juice squirts in all directions.

5 "Kate," she says, "I don't know how you do it!"

Emily is my best friend.
I hope she never learns how to peel oranges.

Pure Poetry

Gerard Malanga

~~i keep crossing out words lines whole passages~~
~~until nothing is left~~
~~except~~ you

Haitian Funeral Procession, by Ellis Wilson, was painted in the 1950s.
👣 The **communication** of sympathy at the loss of a loved one is common among all cultures. What words of support would you offer to the people in the painting?

The Rebel

Mari Evans

When I
die
I'm sure
I will have a
5 Big Funeral

Curiosity
seekers

coming to see
if I
10 am really
Dead

or just
trying to make
Trouble

My Hard Repair Job

James Berry

In the awful quarrel
we had, my temper burnt
our friendship to cinders.
How can I make it whole again?

5 This way, that way,
that time, this time,
I pick up the burnt bits,
trying to change them back.

After Reading

Making Connections

1. Which of these poems would you recommend to a friend? Why?

2. Which of these four poems could you relate to most? Why?

3. 👣 **Communication** has obviously broken down between the narrator of "My Hard Repair Job" and a person he values. What advice would you like to give to the narrator?

4. Refer to the friendship chart that you made before reading the poems. What would you now like to add to, or drop from, it?

5. Gerard Malanga uses an unusual technique in "Pure Poetry." How would you recite this poem? Why would you do it that way?

6. James Berry suggests that a lost friendship is like a fire burnt out. How would you **symbolize** lost friendship? Explain.

7. Why do you think Mari Evans chooses to capitalize certain words in "The Rebel?"

8. Poetry may express in a short space the ideas a story takes much longer to express. Which poem do you think best expresses the ideas from one or more of the stories you've read thus far? Explain.

9. Kate, the narrator in Jean Little's poem, uses an orange to describe her friendship with Emily. What fruit might you choose to describe one of your friendships? Explain.

Literary Focus: Figurative Language

You can often discover more than one meaning in a poem by paying attention to the poet's use of figurative language. **Figurative language** has a meaning beyond its usual, everyday definition. For example, Jean Little uses peeling oranges as a metaphor, or comparison between two unlike things, to express something about personality and friendship. What does the orange metaphor tell you about the two people? When the poet writes in "My Hard Repair Job" that "my temper burnt/ our friendship to cinders," to what does he compare an angry outburst?

It may help you to identify the figurative language in a poem if you choose several important images from the poem and look for connections between them. For instance you might use a sequence chart, such as the one that follows, to identify and organize important images in "My Hard Repair Job."

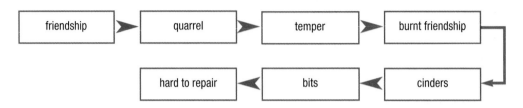

friendship → quarrel → temper → burnt friendship → cinders → bits → hard to repair

Expressing Your Ideas

Writing Choices

Like Night and Day? Choose any two of the four poems and write a short **essay** telling how they are alike and how they are different. Be sure to use quotations or examples from the poems to support your statements.

Ol' Buddy, Ol' Pal Think about a good friendship you currently have or about one you have lost. Then write a **poem** about it. It may help to begin by rereading the poems "Oranges" and "My Hard Repair Job." Think about how your own experiences are similar or different. You can choose to model your poem on these examples by selecting your own metaphor for friendship or lost friendship, or you may use your creativity to write a different kind of friendship poem.

Who? You! Use Gerard Malanga's technique to write a **poem** in the style of "Pure Poetry." Be sure it ends with a pronoun: *you, me, her, him, us,* or *them*.

Other Options

Find Fine Art Find a work of art that you feel matches one of the poems. Tell your classmates in an **oral presentation** why you picked that particular work of art and how it reflects the content of the poem.

Body Language Select one of the poems to **pantomime**. Other students should guess which poem's ideas you are silently acting out.

Team Up to Compose Work in groups of four to six to create a **collaborative song** on the subject of friends or foes. One person makes up and sings the words and music for the first line, a second person the following line, and so on. Practice your song and then sing it to the class.

Before Reading

Echo and Narcissus

a Greek myth retold by Anne Terry White

Anne Terry White
1896-1980

Born in the Ukraine, a country bordering Russia, Anne Terry White came to live in the United States when she was eight years old. Her career as a leading author of a variety of materials for young people came out of her desire to help her two young daughters appreciate the world's great literature. Among her writings are many retellings of traditional European and Asian stories, fables, myths, and legends.

Building Background

It's Greek to Me Why does thunder rumble and lightning flash in the skies? Without scientific explanations these natural events would be frightening. Since ancient peoples didn't have any scientific answers, they created stories, or myths, to explain the mysteries of nature and ease their fears. The ancient Greeks told stories of powerful beings such as Zeus, king of the gods and ruler of the skies, and his wife, Hera, goddess of marriage. They believed that these gods could control nature and human beings. Nymphs, such as Echo, and other minor gods had lesser powers. Mortals, or ordinary people, like Narcissus, could love and even marry gods. Unlike gods, however, mortals could not live forever.

Getting into the Story

Discussion Myths did more than help the Greeks conquer their fears of the natural world. Myths were also a form of entertainment. Can you recall a favorite story read to you as a young child? What was it about? Why did you like it? You may have found it funny or exciting, yet at the same time you may have learned something from it. Discuss your favorite childhood stories with the class. How did they help you better understand your world?

Reading Tip

Greek Myths Live On Gods, goddesses, important mortals, and places from Greek mythology have lent their names to many familiar words in modern English. For example, Echo is a wood nymph that you will meet in the myth "Echo and Narcissus." Today, her name stands for sounds that repeat. You can hear echoes when a sound you make bounces back from a hillside or canyon wall.

The name Narcissus gave birth to the English words *narcissism, narcissist,* and *narcissistic.* What do you think these words mean? Check your responses in a dictionary.

From the title of the story you are about to read, what do you predict it might be about?

Echo and

adapted by Anne Terry White

Of all the mountain nymphs,[1] none was more charming than Echo. But she had one fault. She talked too much. It was chatter, chatter all day long, and no matter what the subject, Echo always had the last word.

Now one day when Zeus was enjoying the company of the nymphs, Hera suddenly appeared. All hurried to get away except Echo, who, to distract[2] the goddess, started to talk. She kept Hera amused so long that the nymphs made their escape. But Hera was furious when she found out how she had been deceived.

"You shall never get the chance to do it again," she told Echo. "That amusing tongue of yours shall lose its power. From now on it will never be able to start chattering, nor do anything except the one thing you are so fond of—reply. Yes, indeed, you shall have the last word, Echo. But that is all you will have! Never will you be able to speak *first!*"

Soon after this, Echo found out just how bad her punishment was. She fell in love, and, as luck would have it, with a young hunter who could not love anybody but himself. Narcissus was an exceptionally[3] handsome

Echo and Narcissus, seen at left and right, by Alice and Martin Provensen, was probably painted in 1959.

Narcissus

youth. But he was as cold as he was handsome.

Poor Echo trailed all over the mountains after Narcissus. How she longed to speak to him and win his love by gentle words! Alas, she had not the power!

Then one day while Narcissus was hunting, it happened that he became separated from his companions.

"Who's here?" he shouted.

"Here!" Echo replied.

Narcissus looked around. He could see no one.

"Come!" he called.

Echo immediately answered, "Come!"

Narcissus waited, but when no one came, he called again: "Why do you keep away from me?"

"Away from me!" Echo called back.

"Let us meet!" Narcissus said.

"Let us meet!" the nymph agreed with all her heart. She ran to the spot, arms upraised and ready to throw around his neck.

Narcissus started back. "Do not touch me!" he cried. "I would rather die than that you should have me!"

"Have me!" Echo pleaded.

But in vain. The young man strode off,

---

1. nymph (nimf), *n.* maiden goddess of nature in Greek and Roman myths, who lived in seas, woods, or mountains.
2. distract (dis trakt′), *v.* to draw away the attention.
3. exceptionally (ek sep′shən əl lē), *adv.* unusually.

leaving the nymph to hide her blushes in the thick woods.

From that time on, Echo would never show herself. Caves and mountain cliffs became her home. Her body wasted away with grief and longing until all her flesh was gone. Her bones changed into rocks. And nothing was left of her but her voice, with which she still replies to anyone who calls.

Cruel Narcissus! Echo was not the only being whose heart he broke. But at last he got what he deserved. A maiden whom he had spurned[4] asked the goddess of vengeance[5] to take her part.

"Oh, may the time come," the girl prayed, "when Narcissus may feel what it is to love and get no love in return!"

And the avenging goddess heard. . . .

There was a sparkling spring in the hills, to which for some reason shepherds never drove their flocks. Neither did mountain goats nor any beasts of the forest ever drink from it. Fresh green grass grew all around, and rocks sheltered the spring from the sun. The water in the pool was as clear as polished silver. Not a dead branch, not a dead leaf polluted it.

To this pool one day Narcissus came, worn out with hunting, hot and thirsty. He stooped down to drink—and saw his lovely image in the water.

"It is the water-spirit," he thought, for he had never seen his own reflection before. Enchanted, he knelt down to look and could not take his gaze away. He bent close to place a kiss upon the parted lips, and stretched out his arms to clasp the lovely being. At his touch the image dissolved into a thousand ripples. But even as he watched, it came back as clear as before.

"Beautiful being," Narcissus said, "why do you flee from me? Surely my face cannot displease you, for every nymph of the mountains is in love with me, and you yourself look as if you are not indifferent.[6] Your smile answers mine. When I stretch out my arms to you, you do the same."

Tears of longing rolled down his cheeks and splashed into the silver pool. At once the image fled again.

"Stay, oh, stay!" he pleaded. "If I may not touch you, let me at least gaze upon you!"

He was unable to tear himself away. Day after day he hung over the water, feasting his eyes on his own reflection. Love, which he had so often scorned,[7] now so consumed[8] him that he lost his color and was no more than a waxy image of himself. All he could do was sigh, "Alas! Alas!" And Echo answered him, "Alas!"

At last Narcissus faded away altogether and passed from the upper world. But even as his shade was being ferried to the regions of the dead, it looked down into the river Styx[9] to catch a last beloved reflection. The nymphs who had given their hearts to him heaped wood into a funeral pile[10] and would have burned his body, as the custom was. But his remains were nowhere to be found. Only a wax-white flower with a purple heart stood in the place where he had knelt and sighed. And to this flower the grieving maidens gave his name—Narcissus.

---

4. **spurn** (spėrn), *v.* refuse with anger and disgust.
5. **vengeance**(ven′jəns), *n.* punishment in return for a wrong; revenge.
6. **indifferent** (in dif′ər ənt), *adj.* uncaring; showing no interest.
7. **scorn** (skôrn), *v.* look down upon; despise.
8. **consume** (kən süm′), *v.* use up; spend.
9. **Styx** (stiks), in Greek myths, a river that crosses into the land of the dead. Souls were ferried across it to the underworld.
10. **funeral pile** (fyü′nər əl pīl), heap of wood on which a dead body is burned, often also called a *funeral pyre.*

After Reading

Making Connections

1. If you had to spend the day with either Echo or Narcissus, which one would it be and how would you get through the day?

2. Narcissus is described as being "as cold as he was handsome." Write a similar description of Echo.

3. The actions of characters in Greek myths often explain human nature as well as the natural world. Write down three common human behaviors that you found described in this myth. Support your answers with examples.

4. Because Narcissus was so self-centered, he "faded away altogether." Do you agree that self-centered people fade away? If so, explain. If not, how would you describe the effects of being self-centered?

Literary Focus: Personification

As a young child you probably made your stuffed animals and other toys come alive by talking for them. Many of the stories you read and saw on television also had talking animals. This is called **personification**, the use of human traits in representing animals, objects, events, or even ideas.

Myths often contain personification. In this myth Echo is presented as a nymph who looks and behaves like a person, but she is also a personification of a natural event, an echo. What traits does the nymph Echo have in common with a real echo?

A diagram like the one below can help you compare an object, event, or idea with its personification.

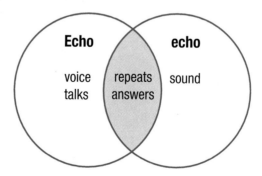

Echo — voice, talks | repeats, answers | echo — sound

Vocabulary Study

On your paper write the word from the list that best completes each sentence.

consume
nymph
distract
scorn
exceptionally
spurn
indifferent
vengeance

1. The mountain ____ Echo liked to frolic through the mountains and woods.

2. Her constant chattering tended to ____ and anger Hera.

3. Hera's ____ took away Echo's power of speech.

4. Narcissus was ____ selfish.

5. He loved himself but would ____ Echo.

6. To ____ Echo's attentions, he refused to let her touch him.

7. Narcissus was ____ to everyone but himself.

8. His own reflection tended to ____ him from all else.

9. Narcissus's love for his own reflection seemed to ____ him.

10. Being ____ handsome led to Narcissus's downfall.

Expressing Your Ideas

Writing Choices

Make a Myth Myths are attempts to explain what we encounter in nature. Choose any natural object or event and write a **myth** about how it came to be or why it behaves as it does. You can use the actions of gods and goddesses in your explanation, or you can create another setting for your myth.

Other Viewpoints The same story may change dramatically when told from another point of view. This myth portrays Echo as talkative and flighty and Narcissus as egotistical and withdrawn. Is this how they view themselves? Imagine you are either Echo or Narcissus and write your **autobiography**. For a convincing self-portrait, remember to use what you learned about them in the myth and what you know about the way people act.

Other Options

Comic Echoes Work with a partner to turn this myth into a **comic strip, action comic,** or **picture book**. Discuss which scenes are most important to the story and then illustrate each scene you have chosen. Check to see that your illustrations tell a connected story. Add dialogue balloons or captions to your pictures.

Tune In Imagine hearing this myth read on a tape or over the radio with appropriate background music. What **music** best represents Echo? What kind of music does Narcissus bring to mind? Find examples of music that could be appropriate for each character. If possible, record the story using the background music you have chosen.

Friends and Foes

The Love Connection

Psychology Connection

There are lots of kinds of love, and there is room for it all. There is friendship, love for family, romantic love, and even love for humankind. The more the world is filled with love, the less room there is for hate — the more friends, the fewer foes.

What Is LOVE?

Ask a couple of your friends what they love—go ahead, ask them. Ice cream? Horseback riding? What about you— what do you love? Going shopping with your older sister? Chocolate layer cake?

Now ask your friends whom they love. Their parents, their brother or sister (sometimes)? What about you—whom do you love?

We use the word love in a lot of different ways. We love things; we love people. But what does it *mean* to say we love something or someone? It means all kinds of different feelings.

Don't You Love It?

When you think about the things you love or the stuff you really love to do, you probably mean you like it more than any similar thing. If you say you love chocolate ice cream, you probably like it more than any other ice cream flavor, or maybe any other dessert. If you love your new jeans, you probably like them more than your other clothes. How do you decide you love something? The stuff you love makes you feel good.

The same is true with *doing* something you love. You may like the way it feels to catch a ball square in your glove, or how you feel like you're flying when you run fast.

Working hard is sometimes part of doing the things we love. Shaquille O'Neal loves to play basketball, but he also knows he has to practice a lot to stay good at it. If you love playing the piano, you might not always like practicing every day, but you know it's part of learning to play well. So you stick with it.

Loving Others

Hard work and sticking with it are also part of loving the people around us. Sometimes you have fights with your brother or sister even though you love them. Sometimes your mom or dad make you mad or hurt your feelings even though they love you. When we love other people, we have to learn to forgive them, understand them, and make up.

That is what loving people is all about. You may not always agree with them, but you trust them. You know that deep down these people care about you. They help you, take care of you, and listen to you, and you do the same for them. You can feel comfortable together.

We don't love everyone the same, of course, even in our own families. You may feel closer to one of your brothers than another one; you may even be closer to your mom than your dad. That's OK because everybody loves in different ways. As you get older, you may get closer to your sister, or you may do more things with your dad and get to know him better. Relationships can change.

Not only do people love people differently, they show it differently. Couples who are married may show they love each other by hugging and kissing, saying they love each other, listening to each other, or doing things together. Brothers and sisters may show it by helping each other, spending time together, and talking about everyday stuff.

Even whole families show love in different ways. Parents usually show love toward their children the same way that their parents showed love toward them when they were growing up. Some families outwardly show more affection—touching, kissing, hugging—while others show love by doing things for each other.

Friends Who Care

Do you have a good friend? You probably do. Do you love him or her? You might not say that, but you probably do spend a lot of time together. You probably can talk to this friend differently from the way you talk to other friends, and you may like more of the same things.

Having a friend to care about you makes you feel good in a different way than the people in your family do. Learning how to be and stay a good friend, however, can take just as much work, especially as you grow older and your interests change.

It's Up to You!

How we show love is something each of us does differently. It makes us as unique as the way we look and how we think. But it doesn't really matter whom we love or what we love, but *that* we love. It's the best feeling around.

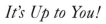

Responding

1. Think about a friend that you have known for a long time. Write one paragraph that describes your relationship when you first met. Write another paragraph that describes your relationship now. How has it changed?

2. Love is not always easy. It can bring frustration or hurt. It requires effort. Write the phrase *Love is. . . .* Complete the statement with as detailed an explanation as you can give.

Anthropology Connection

The words *love* and *relationship* bring to mind romance and marriage. Romance is as old and as universal as humanity. However, the rituals of courtship and marriage have changed with time and take on different forms in every culture.

Courtship
and
Marriage

French artist Antoine Watteau creates a romantic vision of courtship in his painting, *Love Song*. His is a world of warmth, song, flowers, velvet, and lace. There is no room for discord in Watteau's eighteenth-century woodland setting. ▼

▲ A Somalian man courts a young woman. Once married, according to traditional custom, the woman would live with her husband's clan, or extended family. The man might also take as many as three additional wives.

▲ A late eighteenth-century romance glows in Kitagawa Utamaro's *The Courtesan Ajeraki and Her Gallant*. Utamaro captures the luxury of rich silks and formal dress in his painting of upper-class Japanese courtship.

▲ Roy Lichtenstein's *The Ring*, 1962, depicts a modern ritual with origins in ancient Egypt and Rome. In Rome, rings were sometimes exchanged to seal a contract. Today, an engagement ring shows a couple's commitment to marry.

Italian artist Lorenzo Lotto painted his *Bridal Couple: Messer Marsilio and His Wife* in the sixteenth century. Lotto gives us more than what a camera might capture in a modern wedding photograph. Not only do we see the bride and groom, but a smiling angel as well. We can believe that this couple will have a happy and blessed life together. ▼

An Aztec artist shows in great detail a wedding between two high-ranking families. Sixteenth-century Tenochtitlán (tā nōch′tē– tlän′), the capital of the Aztecs, rose from an island in a lake. Palaces and ornate temples built on pyramids proved its wealth. There a wedding was cause for elaborate celebration. ▼

Harlem photographer James van der Zee captures more than the image of the bride and groom in his wedding portrait. Like Italian artist Lotto, van der Zee hints at future happiness and fulfillment. While Lotto's angel blesses a bride and groom, van der Zee's double exposure catches a glimpse of domestic life to come.

Many Muslim, Hindu, and Sikh brides have elaborate designs painted on their hands and feet on their wedding day. Patterns are created with a powder that stains the skin red. The powder is made from crushed leaves. ▼

This modern Japanese bride is wearing a traditional kimono. The groom wears a kimono also, called a *haori hakama*. Most Japanese wedding ceremonies take place at a shrine or chapel. ▼

As this couple demonstrates, romantic love is not for the young only. Respect, care, and commitment will nourish a relationship through the years and allow love to thrive. ▼

▲ The Jewish wedding ceremony takes place under a huppah, a canopy representing the couple's future home. At the end of the ceremony, the groom steps on and breaks a glass. Symbolizing the destruction of the Jewish Temple in Jerusalem, this ritual reminds the couple that a marriage can also break if it is not cherished.

Responding

1. What common threads join these people, from ancient times to today, and from all over the world?

2. Ask your parents about their courtship. Was it different from dating today?

Mathematics Connection
Statistics can show trends, but they do not make predictions. You are an individual and you will create your own destiny. Just for fun, check out where family members who have made their love connections fit on these charts.

Marriage Statistics

Median *Age* at First Marriage

Year	Males	Females
1900	25.9	21.9
1910	25.1	21.6
1920	24.6	21.2
1930	24.3	21.3
1940	24.3	21.5
1950	22.8	20.3
1960	22.8	20.3
1970	23.2	20.8
1980	24.7	22.0
1990	26.1	23.9

Sources: U.S. Bureau of the Census, *The Statistical History of the U.S.* (1976), and *Marital Status and Living Arrangements:* March 1993 (1994)

Top 10 *States* with the Most Weddings

1. California
2. Texas
3. New York
4. Florida
5. Nevada
6. Ohio
7. Illinois
8. Virginia
9. Tennessee
10. Pennsylvania

Source: National Center for Health Statistics, 1994

Top 5 *Months* for Weddings in the U.S.

1. June
2. August
3/4. May and October (a tie)
5. September

Source: National Center for Health Statistics, 1994

Wedding *Anniversary* Gifts

Anniversary	Traditional	Modern
1st	Paper	Clocks
2nd	Cotton	China
3rd	Leather	Crystal, Glass
4th	Linen, Silk	Appliances
5th	Wood	Silverware
25th	Silver	Sterling Silver
50th	Gold	Gold
60th	Diamond	Diamond

Responding

1. Ask your parents and grandparents the following questions.
• In what year were you married?
• How old were you when you married?
• In what month were you married?
• In what state were you married?

2. How are their marriage statistics similar to or different from the statistics given for age, state, and month?

Reading Mini-Lesson

Skimming the Headings

Big, Bold Heads Point the Way

If you had read only the title and headings for "What Is Love?" on page 45, you would have been able to get some of the main ideas without reading a single sentence. You would have seen:

What Is Love?	Don't You Love It?	Loving Others
Friends Who Care	It's Up to You	

Skimming the headings as your first reading step gives you a rough outline of the purpose of the article before you begin to read it. That way, you start out with a better understanding than you would if you hadn't "warmed up" first. You will read faster, understand better, and remember more of what you read if you keep in mind this brief outline. Like signs along a highway, headings tell you what to expect. They help you find your way through unfamiliar territory.

As further preparation for reading new articles, try this. Make a two-column chart. List the headings from any unfamiliar reading of your choice in the left column. In the right column, write what each heading makes you think of. If the heading is a question, give an answer to that question. For each heading write down whatever first pops into your mind. After you have read the article look at your chart. How accurate was it in predicting what the article would be about?

Activity Options

1. Another way to approach an unfamiliar reading is to make a meaning web for each heading in a selection. Choose a new selection and work with a small group. Write each heading in a circle and have members of the group suggest ideas they associate with the heading. Then read the selection and compare its content with your ideas. A sample meaning web is shown at the left.

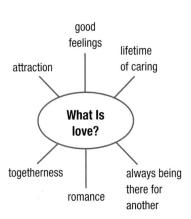

2. Find and read an article that does not have headings. Write brief headings that you think would help a reader get the main ideas of the article. To see if you have been successful, ask a classmate to read just the headings. If you've done a good job, your classmate should be able to predict some of the ideas in the article.

Part Two

Different Points of View

All of us have our own ways of making sense of the world. Our beliefs and opinions can seem so right that it's hard to imagine how anyone could disagree with us. People, however, have different points of view on just about *everything*. Disagreement stirs things up. It can make us angry, move us to cry or laugh, or even prompt us to look at things in a new way.

Multicultural Connection Identifying with a **group** involves the feeling of belonging based on shared connections. Within any group there will be varying points of view, which may strain relationships. Sometimes misunderstandings may arise because of the ways one group views or is viewed by another. The following selections show how people may see things very differently.

Literature

Michael Dorris	**Father's Day** ◆ personal essay	54
Maxine Hong Kingston	**A Sea Worry** ◆ personal essay	60
I. S. Nakata	**A Haircut** ◆ short story	67
Joseph Bruchac	**Birdfoot's Grampa** ◆ poem	75
Walt Whitman	**When I Heard the Learn'd Astronomer** ◆ poem	76
Lucille Clifton	**In the Inner City** ◆ poem	77
Isaac Asimov	**Key Item** ◆ short story	81
	Language Mini-Lesson ◆ Choosing the Correct Homophones	87

Interdisciplinary Study Getting into Focus

How We See ◆ life science 88

Interpreting Visual Evidence by Dr. David Thomson ◆ psychology 90

Reading Mini-Lesson ◆ Taking Notes 92

Writing Workshop Expository Writing

Thumbs Up or Thumbs Down? 93

Beyond Print Effective Listening

He Said, She Said 99

Before Reading

Father's Day

by Michael Dorris

Michael Dorris
born 1945

Michael Dorris grew up an only child with no father. His "parents" were six strong women—his mother, two grandmothers, and three aunts. He recalls being a "very lonely kid." His good friends included books and a librarian who gave him prizes for reading. One aunt lent him her library card to check out books for adults. "I have always read constantly," Dorris says. In college, his writing got some "very nasty" reviews in the school paper. He quit writing stories for nearly ten years. Writing, Dorris admits, is not easy but it *is* his pleasure. His advice to other aspiring writers is to write every day, try many kinds of writing, and *don't* be discouraged by bad reviews.

Building Background

Terms of War In the essay "Father's Day" you will find World War II terms seldom heard today. For example, a *gold star* was given to parents who lost a son or daughter in the war. *Dog tags* were metal identification tags worn by members of the armed services. The author mentions that he was not *drafted*—made to serve in the military during the Vietnam War. He was exempted under code *A-IV,* which excused draft-age men who had completed military service or who were the only surviving son in a family.

Getting into the Essay

Writer's Notebook In his essay, Michael Dorris describes and celebrates someone who was a powerful influence in his life. In your notebook, tell about a relative who has played an important part in your life. What has that person said and done that has had special meaning for you?

Reading Tip

Challenging Vocabulary Michael Dorris's writing is very honest and straightforward, even if some of the words are new to you. When you come to an unfamiliar word, notice how it is used. What other words in the passage are clues to its meaning? For example, notice how this sentence reveals the meaning of *periphery: "Unless dragged to center stage, she stands at the periphery in snapshots."* You may find it helpful to create a chart like the one below, writing down words you don't know. Write in what you think they mean as well as the meanings you find in a dictionary. For fun, "grade" your *infer-ability*: **E** = Excellent; **G** = Good try; **O** = Oops.

New Word	Inferred Meaning	Dictionary Meaning	My Score
periphery	edge	outside boundary	E
_____	_____	_____	___
_____	_____	_____	___

MICHAEL DORRIS

My father, a career army officer, was twenty-seven when he was killed, and as a result, I can't help but take war personally. Over the years his image has coalesced[1] for me as an amalgam of familiar anecdotes:[2] a dashing mixed-blood man from the Northwest who, improbably, could do the rumba;[3] a soldier who regularly had his uniform altered by a tailor so that it would fit better; a date, according to my mother, who "knew how to order" in a restaurant; the person whom, in certain lights and to some people, I resemble. He is a compromise of his quirkier[4] qualities, indistinct, better remembered for his death—my grandmother still wears a gold star on her best coat—than for his brief life.

---

1. **coalesce** (kō′ə les′), *v.* unite, grow together.
2. **anecdote** (an′ik dōt), *n.* a short, often humorous, retelling of events.
3. **rumba,** a lively dance from Cuba.
4. **quirkier** (kwėr′kē ər), *adj.* more peculiar; offbeat.

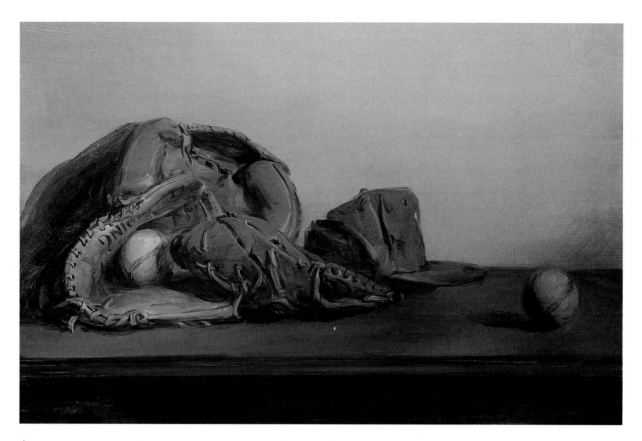

▲ Thomas Torak's painting *After the Game* is a loving treatment of well-worn baseball equipment of the kind the narrator and his aunt probably used. This type of painting is called a still life. Can you see why?

From the perspective of the present, my father was a bit player[5] on the edges of the movie frame, the one who didn't make it back, whose fatality added anonymous[6] atmosphere and a sense of mayhem[7] to the plot. His grave, in a military cemetery near Tacoma, is located by graph paper like a small town on a map: E-9. He's frozen in age, a kid in a T-shirt, a pair of dog tags stored in a box in my closet. His willingness to die for his country may have contributed in some small part to the fall of the Nazis,[8] but more in the way of a pawn exchanged for its counterpart, a pair of lives eliminated with the result that there were two fewer people to engage in combat. I was a few months old the last time he saw me, and a single photograph of me in his arms is the only hard evidence that we ever met.

The fact of my father's death exempted me, under the classification "sole surviving son" (A-IV), from being drafted during the Vietnam War, but it also obliged me to empathize with the child of every serviceperson killed in an armed engagement. "Glory" is an inadequate substitute, a pale abstraction,[9]

5. **bit player,** a minor character in a movie.
6. anonymous (ə non′ə məs), *adj.* nameless; unknown.
7. mayhem (mā′hem), *n.* senseless damage.
8. **Nazis,** Hitler's political forces in Germany that started World War II.
9. abstraction (ab strak′shən), *n.* not representing an actual object or thing; idea.

compared to the enduring,[10] baffling blankness of a missing parent.

There was a children's book in the 1950s—perhaps it still exists—titled *The Happy Family*, and it was a piece of work.[11] Dad toiled at the office, Mom baked in the kitchen, and brother and sister always had neighborhood friends sleeping over. The prototype of "Leave It to Beaver" and "Father Knows Best,"[12] this little text reflects a midcentury standard, a brightly illustrated reproach to my own unorthodox household, but luckily that wasn't the way I heard it. As read to me by my Aunt Marion—her acid delivery was laced with sarcasm[13] and punctuated with many a sidelong glance—it turned into hilarious irony.[14]

Compassionate and generous, irreverent,[15] simultaneously opinionated and openminded, iron-willed and ever optimistic, my aunt was the one who pitched a baseball with me in the early summer evenings, who took me horseback riding, who sat by my bed when I was ill. A fierce, lifelong Democrat—a precinct captain even—she helped me find my first jobs and arranged among her friends at work for my escorts to the father-son dinners that closed each sports season. When the time came, she prevailed upon the elderly man next door to teach me how to shave.

"Daddy" Tingle, as he was known to his own children and grandchildren, was a man of many talents. He could spit tobacco juice over the low roof of his garage, gum a sharpened mumbly-peg[16] twig from the ground even without his false teeth, and produce, from the Bourbon Stockyards where he worked, the jewel-like cornea of a cow's eye—but he wasn't much of a shaver. After his instruction, neither am I.

Aunt Marion, on the other hand, was a font of information and influence. When I was fifteen, on a series of tempestuous Sunday mornings at a deserted River Road park, she gave me lessons in how to drive a stick shift. A great believer in the efficacy of the *World Book Encyclopedia*—the major literary purchase of my childhood—she insisted that I confirm any vague belief by looking it up. To the then-popular tune of "You, You, You," she counted my laps in the Crescent Hill pool while I practiced for a life-saving certificate. Operating on the assumption that anything out of the ordinary was probably good for me, she once offered to mortgage the house so that I could afford to go to Mali[17] as a volunteer participant in Operation Crossroads Africa. She paid for my first Smith-Corona typewriter in thirty-six $4-a-week installments.

For over sixty years Aunt Marion was never without steady employment: telegraph operator for Western Union, budget officer for the city of Louisville, "new girl" at a small savings and loan (when, after twenty-five years in a patronage job,[18] the Democrats lost the mayor's race), executive secretary for a nationally renowned attorney.

Being Aunt Marion, she didn't and doesn't give herself much credit. Unless dragged to center stage, she stands at the periphery in snapshots, minimizes her contributions. Every June for forty years I've sent her a Father's Day card.

---

10. **enduring** (en dủr′ing), *adj.* lasting.
11. **piece of work,** a phrase that expresses contempt for someone or something.
12. **"Leave It to Beaver," "Father Knows Best,"** TV shows that portrayed "perfect" families.
13. **sarcasm** (sar′kaz′əm), *n.* mocking humor; ridicule.
14. **irony** (ī′rə nē), *n.* an unexpected twist.
15. **irreverent** (i rev′ər ənt), *adj.* disrespectful.
16. **mumbly-peg** (also called mumblety peg), a game played with a small knife, in which players take turns throwing it into the ground. Perhaps, in the story, a twig was substituted for a knife.
17. **Mali,** a country in West Africa.
18. **patronage job,** a government job given as a reward for supporting a successful political campaign.

After Reading

Making Connections

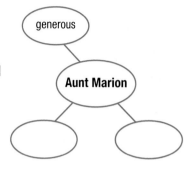

1. Make a web with Aunt Marion in the center. Add the words you think best describe her.

2. Do you think "Father's Day" is a good title for this essay? If so, why? If not, what title might be more fitting?

3. Does this essay strike you as mainly about growing up in the 1950s, or could someone in the 1990s have a similar childhood? Explain.

4. How would this essay be different if it were told from Aunt Marion's **point of view?**

5. How would you describe the author's attitude toward war? Find a sentence that reveals his **point of view.**

6. Reread the description you wrote in your Writer's Notebook. How does the person you wrote about compare or contrast to Aunt Marion?

7. 🐾 A **group** sometimes can help fill the vacancy left by an absent parent. What groups or organizations do you know about that relate to young people who may need additional parenting? Tell about what they do.

Literary Focus: Characterization Through Description

You can describe characters in various ways. Two good ways are to *tell* and *show* what a character is like. For example, Dorris *tells* readers that "Daddy" Tingle was "a man of many talents." Then he goes on to *show* how "Daddy" Tingle was talented. One talent was his ability to "spit tobacco juice over the low roof of his garage."

Go back to the web you began for Aunt Marion. Choose one of the words you think describes her character especially well. Around that word, add details from the story that show why the word is true.

Continue building on your description web. You may want to change some of your describing words or add new ones as you revisit the essay. As you work around the web, you will sharpen your "writer's eye" for detail.

Vocabulary Study

Write the letter of the word that is not related in meaning to the other words in the set.

coalesce
anecdote
quirkier
anonymous
mayhem
abstraction
enduring
sarcasm
irony
irreverent

1. **a.** unknown   **b.** anonymous   **c.** unusual   **d.** nameless
2. **a.** story   **b.** anecdote   **c.** account   **d.** cure
3. **a.** quirkier   **b.** weirder   **c.** odder   **d.** faster
4. **a.** coalesce   **b.** blend   **c.** crumble   **d.** combine
5. **a.** lie   **b.** ruin   **c.** mayhem   **d.** damage
6. **a.** abstraction   **b.** mistake   **c.** idea   **d.** concept
7. **a.** disrespectful   **b.** pointless   **c.** rude   **d.** irreverent
8. **a.** remaining   **b.** enduring   **c.** boring   **d.** lasting
9. **a.** smile   **b.** ridicule   **c.** sarcasm   **d.** taunt
10. **a.** irony   **b.** opposite   **c.** surprise   **d.** metal

Expressing Your Ideas

Writing Choices

It All Adds Up Write a brief **character sketch** of either the man or the woman in the picture above. Decide which trait you think best describes your impressions of the person. Read the sketch to your classmates to see if they can guess the character trait you had in mind.

Kip = Kind, Irreverent, Playful Write the letters of your first name in a vertical line down the left side of a piece of paper. Now write words that **describe** you that start with each of the letters.

Other Options

In the Mind's Eye Draw or find **pictures** you think look like the author's father, Aunt Marion, his grandmother, and "Daddy" Tingle. You could arrange them as if in a family album to share with the class.

Updating the Good Old Days With a small group of classmates, watch reruns of TV shows from the 1950s, such as "Leave It to Beaver." In a **skit,** re-enact a scene from one of the 1950s shows just as it was. Then put on an updated version of the same scene for the 1990s. Discuss the differences.

Photo Opportunity As a class, everyone should bring in a photograph, either personal or from a magazine. No one must see the photo except the owner. In turn, each person vividly **describes** his or her photograph to the class. All photos are then put in a box. People pull out photos and name the owner based on descriptions.

Before Reading

A Sea Worry

by Maxine Hong Kingston

Maxine Hong Kingston
born 1940

Kingston "flunked kindergarten" because she did not talk at school for any reason. At home she spoke Chinese and listened eagerly to her mother "talk story." Kingston says, "I come from a tradition of storytellers." As a child in California, she helped in the family laundry. In summer when the temperature in the laundry reached 111° Fahrenheit, one of her parents would call time out for a ghost story to give everyone some chills up their backs. For several years, Kingston lived in Hawaii with her husband and son Joseph, the surfer she writes about in "A Sea Worry." Joseph, she reports, is no longer a "surfing addict." However, he stays near the sea he loves as a musician on a cruise ship.

Building Background

Surf's Up! Does your favorite sport have something to do with where you live? In Hawaii, which is known for sandy beaches and majestic waves, surfing is a passion. Whenever the waves are breaking just right, devout surfers flock to the shore. They feel that surfing gives their lives a purpose, and may even be worth risking death. When young surfers can't resist the pull of the hazardous sea, you can guess what emotion it stirs in a surfer's mother.

Getting into the Essay

Writer's Notebook "A Sea Worry" reveals a lot about the appeal of surfing. In your notebook, write about a sport or other favorite activity that has a hold on you. What makes this activity so appealing?

Reading Tip

Jargon Surfing, like other special activities, has its own **jargon,** or special vocabulary. Just as skiers have many words for kinds of snow, surfers have many descriptions of waves—*tube, pipe line,* and *mirror tube,* for example. Make a chart like the one below to illustrate the surfing terms in the essay. After you have read the selection, draw a picture of what you think each wave would look like.

Surfing Term	Meaning	Illustration
tube	the tunnel formed by a curling wave: the most pleasurable wave formation for surfing	
pipe line	a very long, spacious tube	

A surfer rides a wave in Hawaii in this photograph by Vince Cavatio. Can you see why this wave might be called a "pipeline"?

A SEA Worry

Maxine Hong Kingston

This summer my son body-surfs.[1] He says it's his "job" and rises each morning at 5:30 to catch the bus to Sandy Beach.[2] I hope that by September he will have had enough of the ocean. Tall waves throw surfers against the shallow bottom. Undertows have snatched them away. Sharks prowl Sandy's. Joseph told me that once he got out of the water because he saw an enormous shark. "Did you tell the lifeguard?" I asked. "No." "Why not?" "I didn't want to spoil the surfing." The ocean pulls at the boys, who turn into surfing addicts. At sunset you can see the surfers waiting for the last golden wave.

"Why do you go surfing so often?" I ask my students.

"It feels so good," they say. "Inside the tube, I can't describe it. There are no words for it."

"You can describe it," I scold, and I am very angry. "Everything can be described. Find the words for it, you lazy boy. Why don't you go home and read?" I am afraid that the boys give themselves up to the ocean's mindlessness.

When the waves are up, surfers all over Hawaii don't do their homework. They cut school. They know how the surf is breaking at any moment because every fifteen minutes the reports come over the radio; in fact, one of my former students is the surf reporter.

Some boys leave for mainland colleges, and write their parents heartrending letters. They beg to come home for Thanksgiving. "If I can just touch the ocean," they write from Missouri and Kansas, "I'll last for the rest of the semester." Some come home for Christmas and don't go back.

Even when the assignment is about something else, the students write about surfing. They try to describe what it is to be inside the wave as it curls over them, making a tube or "chamber" or "green room" or "pipeline" or "time warp." They write about the silence, the peace, "no hassles," the feeling of being

---

1. **body-surf,** to ride the waves without a board.
2. **Sandy Beach,** one of the most famous body-surfing places in Hawaii.

Eddie Aikau's memorial on Waimea Bay, Hawaii, was photographed by Joli. ➤

reborn as they shoot out the end. They've written about the perfect wave. Their writing is full of clichés. "The endless summer," they say. "Unreal."

Surfing is like a religion. Among the martyrs[3] are George Helm, Kimo Mitchell, and Eddie Aikau. Helm and Mitchell were lost at sea riding their surfboards from Kaho'olawe,[4] where they had gone to protest the Navy's bombing of that island. Eddie Aikau was a champion surfer and lifeguard. A storm had capsized the *Hokule'a*, the ship that traced the route that the Polynesian ancestors sailed from Tahiti, and Eddie Aikau had set out on his board to get help.

Since the ocean captivates[5] our son, we decided to go with him to Sandy's.

We got up before dawn, picked up his friend, Marty, and drove out of Honolulu. Almost all the traffic was going in the opposite direction, the freeway coned[6] to make more lanes into the city. We came to a place where raw mountains rose on our left and the sea fell on our right, smashing against the cliffs. The strip of cliff pulverized[7] into sand is Sandy's. "Dangerous Current Exist," said the ungrammatical sign.

Earll and I sat on the shore with our blankets and thermos of coffee. Joseph and Marty put on their fins and stood at the edge of the sea for a moment, touching the water with their fingers and crossing their hearts before going in. There were fifteen boys out there, all about the same age, fourteen to twenty, all with the same kind of lean v-shaped build, most of them with black hair that made their wet heads look like sea lions. It was hard to tell whether our kid was one of those who popped up after a big wave. A few had surfboards, which are against the rules at a body-surfing beach, but the lifeguard wasn't on duty that day.

As they watched for the next wave, the boys turned toward the ocean. They gazed slightly upward; I thought of altar boys before a great god. When a good wave arrived, they turned, faced shore, and came shooting in, some taking the wave to the right and some to the left, their bodies fish-like, one arm out in front, the hand and fingers pointed before them, like a swordfish's beak. A few held credit card trays, and some slid in on trays from MacDonald's.

---

3. **martyr** (mär′tər), *n.* person who dies for a belief or cause.
4. **Kaho'olawe,** smallest of the main Hawaiian islands.
5. **captivate** (kap′tə vāt), *v.* charm; fascinate.
6. **coned,** a verb the author created from the noun *cone* to describe how extra lanes are created by placing traffic cones at intervals on the highway.
7. **pulverize** (pul′və rīz), *v.* break into pieces; grind into dust.

"That is no country for middle-aged women," I said. We had on bathing suits underneath our clothes in case we felt moved to participate. There were no older men either.

Even from the shore, we could see inside the tubes. Sometimes, when they came at an angle, we saw into them a long way. When the wave dug into the sand, it formed a brown tube or a golden one. The magic ones, though, were made out of just water, green and turquoise rooms, translucent[8] walls and ceilings. I saw one that was powder-blue, perfect, thin; the sun filled it with sky blue and white light. The best thing, the kids say, is when you are in the middle of the tube, and there is water all around you but you're dry.

The waves came in sets; the boys passed up the smaller ones. Inside a big one, you could see their bodies hanging upright, knees bent, duckfeet fins paddling, bodies dangling there in the wave.

Once in a while, we heard a boy yell, "Aawhoo!" "Poon-tah!" "Aaroo!" And then we noticed how rare a human voice was here; the surfers did not talk, but silently, silently rode the waves.

Since Joseph and Marty were considerate of us, they stopped after two hours, and we took them out for breakfast. We kept asking them how it felt, so they would not lose language.

"Like a stairwell in an apartment building," said Joseph, which I liked immensely. He hasn't been in very many apartment buildings, so had to reach a bit to get the simile. "I saw somebody I knew coming toward me in the tube, and I shouted, 'Jeff. Hey, Jeff,' and my voice echoed like a stairwell in an apartment building. Jeff and I came straight at each other—mirror tube."

"Are there ever girls out there?" Earll asked.

"There's a few who come out at about eleven," said Marty.

"How old are they?"

"About twenty."

"Why do you cross your heart with water?"

"So the ocean doesn't kill us."

I described the powder-blue tube I had seen. "That part of Sandy's is called Chambers," they said.

I have gotten some surfing magazines, the ones kids steal from the school library, to see if the professionals try to describe the tube.

Bradford Baker writes:

> . . . Round and pregnant in Emptiness
> I slide,
> Laughing,
> into the sun,
> into the night.

Frank Miller calls the surfer

> . . . mother's fumbling
> curly-haired
> tubey-laired
> son.

"Ooh, offshores—" writes Reno Abbellira, "where wind and wave most often form that terminal rendezvous of love—when the wave can reveal her deepest longings, her crest caressed, cannily covered to form those peeling concavities we know, perhaps a bit irreverently, as tubes. Here we strive to spend every second—enclosed, encased, sometimes fatefully entombed, and hopefully, gleefully ejected—Whoosh!"

"An iridescent[9] ride through the entrails of God," says Gary L. Crandall.

I am relieved that the surfers keep asking one another for descriptions. I also find some comfort in the stream of commuter traffic, cars filled with men over twenty, passing Sandy Beach on their way to work.

---

8. translucent (tran slü′snt), *adj.* letting light through without being completely clear.
9. iridescent (ir′ə des′nt), *adj.* colorful; showing colors that change.

After Reading

Making Connections

1. Pick out your favorite passage from this selection to read aloud. Explain your choice.

2. Chart the differences and similarities between surfing and the sport or activity you wrote about in your notebook. You can use a Venn diagram to record your ideas.

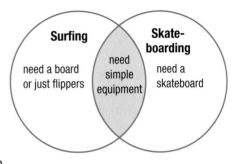

3. How do you think the author would react if her son told her that he decided to quit surfing?

4. In "A Sea Worry" Maxine Hong Kingston writes as a mother, a teacher, and an author. Find examples in the essay of these three **points of view.**

5. Does the author's attitude toward surfing change from the beginning to the end of the essay? Explain your opinion.

6. Find some details in the essay that help you imagine what surfing is like. Explain how these details bring surfing to life for you.

7. Think of an activity popular with young people in your community that adults may consider a waste of time. Brainstorm some attributes of the activity that might get critical adults to see things differently.

Literary Focus: Simile

You can use a **simile**—a comparison between two unlike things, using the words *like* or *as*—to describe something. For example, the author writes, "Surfing is like a religion." She uses *religion*—something familiar to most people—to describe a quality of *surfing*—something outside many readers' experience. The simile helps readers understand the importance of surfing to surfers.

With a partner, find other similes in the essay. Discuss what each one explains about the key thing being compared or described. You can record the similes and their effects on a chart like this:

Simile	What the Simile Explains
Surfing is like a religion.	It tells how surfers feel. It shows how the writer sees it.

Vocabulary Study

On your paper write the letter of the situation that best demonstrates the meaning of each vocabulary word below.

martyr
captivate
pulverize
translucent
iridescent

1. **pulverize**   **a.** The crashing waves turn the rocks to sand. **b.** The dry sand absorbs the breakers. **c.** Strong tides pull the surfer back into the sea.

2. **martyr**   **a.** The surfer was prepared to kill for his sport. **b.** The surfer died in an effort to save the beaches. **c.** The surfer's parents feared for their child's life.

3. **iridescent**   **a.** A surfer fails to warn others about a shark. **b.** High tides leave the land flooded. **c.** The foaming surf brings a spray of rainbow bubbles.

4. **translucent**   **a.** Each surfer stood on the edge of the sea. **b.** A surfer's outline could be seen inside the rolling wave. **c.** The rock wall blocked our view of the surfer's ride.

5. **captivate**   **a.** A fishing boat drags a shark from the sea in a net. **b.** The sea lures the surfer to Sandy Beach day after day. **c.** The surfers advise their families not to worry.

Expressing Your Ideas

Writing Choices

Look at It This Way Write a **persuasive paragraph** about surfing as if you were Maxine Hong Kingston's son or one of her students. Your purpose is to get critical adults to see the good points of surfing.

I Slide, Laughing . . . Use ideas from the story and your own imagination (or surfing experience) to write a **poem** about surfing. Imagine yourself as a surfer riding the waves. See if you can invent fresh similes to describe the experience.

Surf City You are a features editor for a respected surfing magazine. Make a **list** of five stories you will assign to your team of reporters for upcoming issues.

Other Options

Help Wanted With a classmate, dramatize an **interview** between a surfer and a potential employer. First, decide on a job. What questions would the employer ask? What aspects of surfing are good training for the job?

Surfin' USA Plan a **presentation** of surfing music for the class. Check your local library and private collections for recordings.

Heroes All Get together in small groups and plan to **research** a famous surfer, such as Duke Kahanamoku or Eddie Aikau. A good source is the book *Surfing: The Ultimate Pleasure* by Leonard Lueras. Share your research in an **oral presentation.**

A Haircut

by I. S. Nakata

Building Background

Mistaken Identification In this story, a case of mistaken identification has elements of dark humor. Here are some facts to let you in on the narrator's inside joke: *Nippon* is the Japanese word for Japan, thus *Nipponese* means Japanese. In World War II, Japan bombed Pearl Harbor, a U.S. naval base in Hawaii. In reaction, the U.S. government moved Americans of Japanese descent to *relocation camps*—fenced areas where they were forced to stay until the end of the war.

Getting into the Story

Discussion Often, people assume things about others based on groups they belong to. Discuss with your class ways in which people sometimes make assumptions about others. Has anyone ever "grouped" you and jumped to a wrong conclusion? Have you ever made a wrong assumption about someone for similar reasons? Share your thoughts on the pros and cons of using categories in our attempts to understand others. You might want to draw boxes like the ones below in which to note assumptions you have observed.

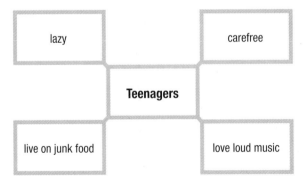

lazy		carefree
	Teenagers	
live on junk food		love loud music

Reading Tip

Words—Faulty and Funny In this story two strangers reveal pre-formed ideas about each other by the words they use. As you read "A Haircut," look for words and situations that point to things being other than what they seem.

A Haircut

I. S. Nakata

People have trouble deciding what I am. Indians have mistaken me for one of their own; in Chinatown I am often presented with a Chinese menu; and once even a Japanese kid asked me if I was Korean. My ancestors are full-blooded Japanese, but I have had to get used to people thinking I'm something else.

Like that time I went to the barber college on North Clark Street for my cut-rate haircut. It's a place where student-barbers get on-the-job training, and that's where I met this guy.

Tall, his face weather-beaten, he looked like a construction worker in his neatly-pressed army-surplus woolen shirt and khaki pants.

He was last in line, and he kept staring at me as I walked in. I just stared back.

Finally he smiled and said with a southern drawl straight out of Alabama, "Say, I know now, you're Indian, ain't you?"

I looked into the long mirror that covered most of the opposite wall. "No," I told the guy, "I'm not an Indian." I shook my black hair to make the denial more emphatic.

"Not an Indian?" Alabama said. "I would have sworn you were."

"I'm not."

Alabama shook his head and said, "You can't fool me. I've been all over the country. Seen all kinds of Indians. Cherokees in the Carolinas and Georgia and Alabama, Navajos in New Mexico and Arizona, Winnebagos[1] in Wisconsin, and even some Shastas once in the mountains of California. I know you're some kind of Indian."

I shook my head, crossed my arms in front of my chest, and took a deep breath. "No."

"Cherokee?"

"No, not Cherokee."

"Not Sioux, are you?"

"Never been in North or South Dakota," I said.

"I AM NOT RUNNING AWAY FROM THE POLICE," I told him.

"Winnebago?"

I didn't answer. I knew a lot about the Winnebagos. After World War II at an army post just outside Paris, I had met a Winnebago Indian from Black River Falls, Wisconsin. Jameson, I think his name was. A medic.[2] And in the week or so that we were at the army post we spent a lot of time talking and eating. Every night we would go and buy a couple of long loaves of bread fresh from the baker's oven, and we would eat and talk for hours. He made me promise to visit him when I got back to the States.

"That's God's country—where the Winnebagos live," I told Alabama. "Plenty of hunting and fishing, especially for muskellunge."[3]

"Muskellunge, huh?" Alabama said. He looked impressed.

"Yeah, muskellunge. Most people call them muskies. Good eating, too. Salted, fried, or broiled in the ashes of hickory wood."

"Wish you was there, huh, Chief?"

"Yeah, nice place," I said.

"So, you're a Winnebago?" he said with a happy nod.

"I never said that. I am not a Winnebago." I said flatly, stiffening.

"Now, now, Chief. don't get me wrong," he said. "I'm your friend. Yes, sir, I'm truly your friend. I've worked with Indians and helped lots of them working for Standard Oil. The reason I thought you were Winnebago is because you know so much about them."

"I don't know so much."

"You do. You sure do, Chief." He looked slyly around and then lowered his voice. "You running away from there, Chief? Maybe from the police?"

"I AM NOT RUNNING AWAY FROM THE POLICE," I told him.

"OK, Chief," he said quickly. "I didn't mean no harm, you know that."

For a long time Alabama didn't say anything. Some of the guys ahead of us moved up in line and we moved along, too. Soon Alabama had a choice of sitting or standing. He sat down on the bench and slid over to make room for me. Then he began again.

"So you're not a Winnebago, huh?"

I didn't answer him.

"Crow?"

"No, I am not a Crow," I said very sharply, although I had nothing against that tribe.

He rubbed his chin with his left hand and thought hard. "Arapaho?"

I shook my head.

"Navajo, then?"

I smiled. The Navajos were a tribe that I'd be proud to be part of. Great weavers, great in handicrafts, and among the best when it came

---

1. **Winnebago,** an American Indian tribe who call themselves Hochangara (or HoChunk), meaning people of the early, or first, speech.
2. medic (med′ik), *n.* a person in the armed forces who gives first-aid to soldiers.
3. **muskellunge** (mus′kə lunj), a large, slender freshwater fish of North America.

▲ *Barber Shop* was painted in 1988 by Robert Cottingham. ☙ Symbols such as the
barber pole pictured here provide a sense of **group** identity to those who understand
their meaning.

to farming. I'd once gone to an art school in Kansas City with Custer Begay—a Navajo and a fine artist. I started thinking about Custer and his beautiful drawings of Indians on horseback. Then I remembered some of the great times we'd had and I began to laugh.

"A man should be proud of what he is."

Alabama slapped his knee and said, "You're a Navajo! From Arizona."

This guy would not give up!

"Well," I said with a sigh, "I *was* once on a reservation[4] in Arizona."

I really had been, too. I'd been sent to Arizona to live in a relocation camp for Japanese-Americans during World War II, before I volunteered for the army.

Alabama's eyes lit up. "I knew it! You couldn't fool me. What reservation was it, Chief?"

"Poston, Arizona," I said, remembering the wartime internment[5] camp. "On the Colorado River."

"I mean," Alabama moaned, "what tribe was it?"

"Nipponese. We were scattered a bit until Uncle Sam gathered us up and put us all together again."

Alabama nodded a couple of times. "Well, I sure do think that was the best thing to do, having the government look after you all. Nipponese, eh? That must be a very small tribe. Never heard of it, Chief."

I had enjoyed my joke, Alabama wanted me to be something else, but I wasn't going to be anyone else but myself.

"A Nipponese is a Japanese. I am Japanese." I spoke slowly, feeling a little self-conscious[6] as I wondered what I am supposed to be when I proclaim myself to the beholder.

Alabama stroked his stubbly chin and looked puzzled. "Jap,[7] eh? Wouldn't think it to look at you. You could pass for Indian any day."

"Japanese," I said.

"Sure, sure, Jap-a-nees. Japanese. But you were born in the USA, weren't you? You can't talk American like that without you being born here."

"I was born in Hawaii."

"Well, you're American like the rest of us, then. A man should be proud of what he is. Ain't you?"

Did I sense a threatening tone in his voice?

"I am pleased that I am who I am, Alabama," I told him. "It's good to be alive."

"Sure is, all right," he said. "But you're wrong about me. I don't come from Alabama."

"No?"

"No sir." He stood up because it was finally his turn to get a haircut. "I'm from Georgia," he said in a loud voice, "and right proud of it."

"Sorry I made the mistake," I told him. Then I shrugged. For the life of me I couldn't see what difference it made if he came from Georgia or Alabama.

---

4. **reservation** (rez′ər vā′shən), *n.* land set aside by the government for a special purpose: *an Indian reservation.*

5. **internment** (in tėrn′mənt), *n.* a confining; a restricting within a place, usually during wartime.

6. **self-conscious** (self′kon′shəs), *adj.* embarrassed; shy.

7. **Jap,** an insulting slang word for *Japanese.*

After Reading

Making Connections

1. Do you think "Alabama" and "Chief" could become friends? Explain.

2. List some positive and negative **character traits** "Alabama" exhibits. Find passages from the story that illustrate the traits you have identified. You can jot down your choices on a chart like the one at the right.

Alabama	
+	−
friendly	prejudiced

3. What better questions might "Alabama" have asked to find out what kind of person the narrator is?

4. 🖐 Why do you think it was so important to Alabama to find out what **group** the narrator came from?

5. How does the author make the words the two characters say to each other seem like a real-life conversation?

6. Do you see the two characters' **points of view** as mostly alike or mostly different? Explain.

7. Would "Alabama's" attitudes make him fit in or stand out in your community?

Literary Focus: Irony

A contrast between what you may expect or think should happen and what actually happens is **irony**. Writers use irony for various purposes:

- to produce humor
- to surprise readers
- to comment on human behavior

Reread the last paragraph of "A Haircut." Ask yourself: *Why is this ironic? What effect does the irony have on me? What comment, if any, is the writer making about human behavior?*

Find a partner and brainstorm an ending for the story that is not ironic. Perform your new ending for classmates. Discuss *why* your ending is not ironic. Share your thoughts on which ending is better.

Vocabulary Study

Write the letter of the word pair that best expresses a relationship similar to that expressed in the original pair.

medic
reservation
internment
self-conscious

1. **JAIL : INTERNMENT :: a.** Wisconsin : state **b.** hair : beard **c.** school : education **d.** health care : doctor

2. **MEDIC : FIRST AID :: a.** barber : barbershop **b.** chief: leader **c.** police officer : suspect **d.** barber : haircut

3. **RESERVATION : PROPERTY :: a.** earth : sky **b.** hill : valley **c.** tree : leaves **d.** city : town

4. **INTERNMENT : FREEDOM :: a.** joy : happiness **b.** teasing : joke **c.** prison : liberty **d.** pride : shame

5. **SELF-CONSCIOUS : HUMILIATED :: a.** sad : happy **b.** annoyed : enraged **c.** friendly : harmless **d.** right : wrong

Expressing Your Ideas

Writing Choices

A Quick Haircut Write a **summary** of the story "A Haircut" in as few words as possible. Compare the longest and shortest summaries. Does the shortest one do the job as well as the longest one?

The Fairest of Them All Write a **character sketch** of someone you know who treats others fairly. Choose a person who does not prejudge others by their appearance, age, ethnic or social group, and so on. In what ways does the person demonstrate an unbiased and open mind?

Words of Advice A proverb is a short saying intended to help people lead their lives. Write a short **proverb** that would benefit the men in "A Haircut."

Other Options

I M GR8T Work on your own or with a partner. List some things that each character in "A Haircut" seems proud of. Use your ideas to **design** a vanity license plate for both of them. Display your plates and be ready to answer questions other classmates may have about them.

Last Seen Wearing . . . Suppose the two characters vanished after meeting. In a small group, create a missing-person **profile** for each. Use what you know about their personalities to imagine how each dressed. How did their haircuts look? Where might each go to eat? What foods would each order? Draw sketches of them. Add written description as needed.

Japanese American Internment In a small group, do a **research report** on the internment of Japanese Americans during World War II. Consider these questions: In what years did it occur? Why did it occur? How many people were involved?

Before Reading

Birdfoot's Grampa by Joseph Bruchac

When I Heard the Learn'd Astronomer by Walt Whitman

In the Inner City by Lucille Clifton

"This place is awesome!"

"This is like being in jail."

"I feel at home here."

"Let's go! I'm bored."

Building Background

My Kind of Place Imagine being in a place you really like. Is it indoors or outdoors? Is it in the city or in the country? What is its effect on you? Each of the poems you are about to read tells about an environment that has special meaning for the poet or someone in the poem. Some of the feelings expressed in these poems may remind you of how you feel about your favorite place.

Getting into the Poems

Discussion The places in these poems are seen from different points of view. Find someone in your class whose favorite place is very different from yours. Tell one another three or four reasons why your place is special to you. Then explain to the entire class how the other person feels about his or her place, and why. As you read each of the poems, think about the different way each poet describes the environment.

Reading Tip

Reading a Poem Reading poetry can be especially rewarding because the language is rich—every word carries meaning. Here's a method you can use with these poems to get the meaning.

First, read the poem just to get the sense of it.

Second, read the poem again to see how the poet uses language. How do the words express different points of view?

You can organize your ideas after each reading on a chart like the one at the left.

key words

"title" main/general ideas

first point of view

second point of view

Joseph Bruchac
born 1942

A well-known storyteller who lives in upstate New York, Bruchac writes about being Native American and about the "beautiful and all-too-fragile world of human life and living things." Bruchac, whose Abenaki name is Sozap, follows the old ways as much as possible. He has taught English literature in West Africa, African literature in American colleges, and creative writing in American prisons.

Walt Whitman
1819–1892

Whitman grew up in a poor family, and his education ended early in his teens. He once remarked that his early friendships with the merchants, sailors, farmers, and fishermen of Brooklyn were ". . . my best experiences and deepest lessons in human nature." He blazed the way to a new, freer kind of poetry. Yet during his lifetime, he got many harsh reviews. "Whitman," wrote Robert Louis Stevenson, is like a "shaggy dog . . . baying at the moon." Whitman is now known as one of most celebrated and original American poets.

Lucille Clifton
born 1936

Clifton was born in Depew, New York, and moved with her family to the "big city" of Buffalo, New York, when she was about six. The new house, she recalls, "smelled like new days." She spent two years at Fredonia State Teachers College near Buffalo, New York, where she met her future husband. As a writer and mother of six, Clifton once said, "I never do all the things you're supposed to, like write at a set time every day. And I can't write if it's quiet."

BIRDFOOT'S GRAMPA

Joseph Bruchac

The old man
  must have stopped our car
  two dozen times to climb out
  and gather into his hands
5 the small toads blinded
  by our lights and leaping,
  live drops of rain.

The rain was falling,
  a mist about his white hair
10 and I kept saying
  you can't save them all
  accept it, get back in
  we've got places to go.

But, leathery hands full
15 of wet brown life
  knee deep in the summer
  roadside grass,
  he just smiled and said
  they have places to go to
20 *too*

(from *Entering Onondaga* Cold Mountain Press, 1978)

Dream of the Frog is a bronze sculpture by Steve Kestrel. How does the sculptor's portrayal of the frog support Birdfoot's Grampa's feelings about toads?

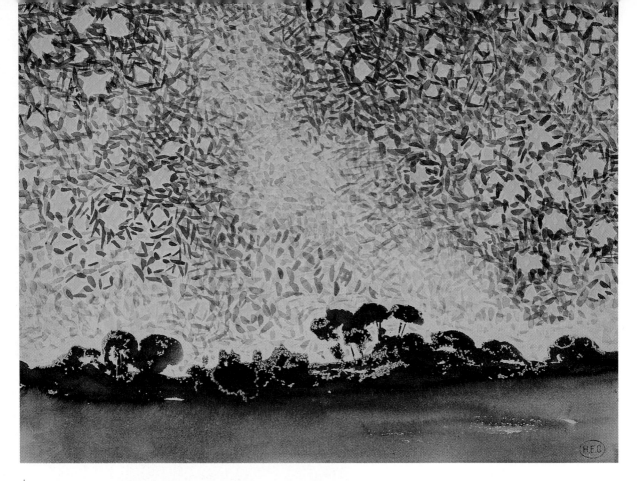

▲ *Landscape with Stars* is a watercolor by Henri Edmond Cross. How does this painting reflect Whitman's point of view?

When I Heard
the Learn'd Astronomer

Walt Whitman

When I heard the learn'd astronomer,
When the proofs, the figures, were ranged in columns before me,
When I was shown the charts and diagrams, to add, divide, and measure them,
When I sitting heard the astronomer where he lectured with much applause in the lecture-room,
5 How soon unaccountable I became tired and sick,
Till rising and gliding out I wander'd off by myself,
In the mystical moist night-air, and from time to time,
Look'd up in perfect silence at the stars.

In the Inner City

Lucille Clifton

in the inner city
or
like we call it
home
5 we think a lot about uptown
and the silent nights
and the houses straight as
dead men
and the pastel lights
10 and we hang on to our no place
happy to be alive
and in the inner city
or
like we call it
15 home

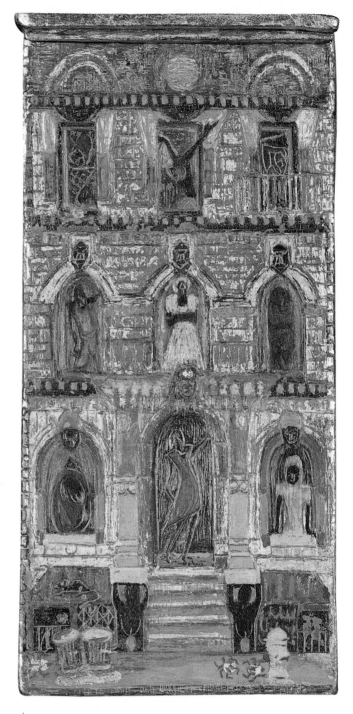

▲ *Welcome to My Ghetto Land,* painted by Jean Lacy in 1986, is mixed media on wood panel. 🐾 How does this artwork support the strong sense of **group** identity expressed in the poem?

After Reading

Making Connections

1. In all, these three poems express six different points of view. Which are most and least like your own? Identify and list the points of view. Then **classify** them on a chart like the one below.

Viewpoints Most Like Mine	Viewpoints Least Like Mine
Grampa—respects living things	Birdfoot—in a big hurry

2. What words or phrases in these poems do you find particularly meaningful? Why?

3. Reread "Birdfoot's Grampa." Then close your eyes. What **images** come to mind?

4. Walt Whitman repeats the word *when* at the beginning of the first four lines of "When I Heard the Learn'd Astronomer." Why do you think he does that?

5. Why do you think Lucille Clifton uses no **punctuation** or **capitalization** in her poem?

6. Suppose your town is preparing a time capsule. Which one of these poems would you include in the time capsule to help people in the distant future understand our world today? Explain your choice.

Literary Focus: Repetition in Poetry

Writers repeat certain words and phrases in a poem for various reasons. For example, **repetition** may emphasize an idea or high-light a point of view. Lucille Clifton begins and ends her poem with the same phrase. What can you conclude about the speaker's point of view from this repetition?

In a small group, go back to the poems and find other examples of repeated words and phrases. Discuss the purposes for the repetitions. You might want to jot down your ideas on a chart like this:

Repeated Words and Phrases	Purposes of the Repetition
In the inner city/or like we call it/home	It stresses the speaker's view that the inner city is home, not "no place."

Expressing Your Ideas

Writing Choices

Dear Poet, . . . Write a **letter** to one of the poets about your response to his or her poem. Some points you might consider are how the poem relates to your experience, how you agree (or disagree) with the poem's message, or what stands out for you in the poem.

Humph! Imagine you are the astronomer in Walt Whitman's poem. Write a **poem** about the same event from the astronomer's point of view.

In the Style of . . . Choose one of the poems and try to write a **poem** of your own in the same style. Choose a different subject but try to use the poet's style. You might want to use the painting below for inspiration.

Other Options

Picture This Choose one of these poems you think would make a good coffee-table book. Draw a **picture** for the book cover that captures an important aspect of the poem. You might prefer to draw a series of pictures for the text that will appear on each page of the book.

Once Upon a Time . . . Each of these poems contains a key element of a good story—conflicting points of view. Use one of the poems as material to tell a **story**. As a storyteller, you can make whatever changes you feel are necessary to add interest.

Poetry Reading Choose your favorite poem and give an oral presentation of it to the class. You may choose to read your poem with a partner.

▲ French artist Paul Gauguin left his life as a Paris banker and escaped to the island of Tahiti. He painted this scene, called *The Three Huts,* in 1889.

Before Reading

Key Item

by Isaac Asimov

Isaac Asimov
1920–1992
Born in Russia, Asimov and his parents immigrated to the United States. As a youth, he worked in their candy store after school. It was not the candy he found most tempting, however, it was the science-fiction magazines they sold. "I was hooked," Asimov said. At eighteen, he took his first science-fiction story to a publisher. The editor rejected the story, telling Asimov he was a superb storyteller who couldn't write. The editor's remarks gave Asimov the determination to learn how to write. And did he write! Over the years he wrote over 400 books—fiction and nonfiction, funny and serious. His choice of topics ranged from Shakespeare to the Bible to technology and science. Asimov also taught chemistry.

Building Background

This science-fiction story is set in the 1950s. At the time, one of the largest computers in the United States was called the UNIVAC (Universal Automatic Computer). By today's standards, the UNIVAC system was huge. It had more than 80,000 vacuum tubes and took up an entire room. It did scientific calculations, from forecasting weather to predicting presidential elections. Magnetic tape and high-speed drums stored over six million words—about one-seventh as many words as a notebook-sized computer can hold in its memory today. The UNIVAC was a real-life model of the computer you will read about in "Key Item." For a picture of UNIVAC, see page 85.

Getting into the Story

Writer's Notebook Have you ever talked to a computer as if it were human? The computer in this story, like other computers, speaks, calculates, holds data in its memory, and so on. Jot down what you see as some of the similarities and differences between computers and people.

Reading Tip

Problem Solving In "Key Item" a problem-solving computer gives humans a problem to solve. The characters in the story use various thinking strategies to find the solution, such as ruling out what is *not* the problem. As you read, look for other problem-solving strategies. You can note your findings on a chart.

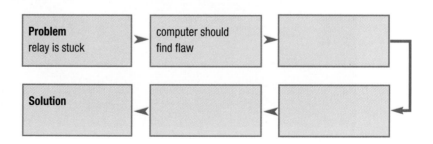

Problem relay is stuck	→	computer should find flaw	→	
Solution	←		←	

KEY

ISAAC ASIMOV

Jack Weaver came out of the vitals of Multivac looking utterly worn and disgusted.

From the stool, where the other maintained his own stolid[1] watch, Todd Nemerson said, "Nothing?"

"Nothing," said Weaver. "Nothing, nothing, nothing. No one can find anything wrong with it."

"Except that it won't work, you mean."

"You're no help sitting there!"

"I'm thinking."

"Thinking!"

Nemerson stirred impatiently on his stool. "Why not? There are six teams of computer technologists roaming around in the corridors of Multivac. They haven't come up with anything in three days. Can't you spare one person to think?"

"It's not a matter of thinking. We've got to look. Somewhere a relay is stuck."

"It's not that simple, Jack!"

---

1. **stolid** (stol′id), *adj.* without excitement; unemotional.

ITEM

"Who says it's simple? You know how many million relays we have there?"

"That doesn't matter. If it were just a relay, Multivac would have alternate circuits, devices for locating the flaw, and facilities to repair or replace the ailing part. The trouble is, Multivac won't only not answer the original question, it won't tell us what's wrong with it. —And meanwhile, there'll be panic in every city if we don't do something. The world's economy depends on Multivac, and everyone knows that."

"I know it, too. But what's there to do?"

"I told you, *think*. There must be something we're missing completely. Look, Jack, there isn't a computer bigwig[2] in a hundred years who hasn't devoted himself to making Multivac more complicated. It can do so much now—it can even talk and listen. It's practically as complex as the human brain. We can't understand the human brain, so why would we understand Multivac?"

"Aw, come on. Next you'll be saying Multivac is human."

"Why not?" Nemerson grew absorbed and seemed to sink into himself. "Now that you mention it, why not? Could we tell if Multivac passed the thin dividing line where it stopped being a machine and started being human? *Is* there a dividing line, for that matter? If the brain is just more complex than Multivac, and we keep making Multivac more complex, isn't there a point where . . ." He mumbled down into silence.

Weaver said impatiently, "What are you driving at? Suppose Multivac were human. How would that help us find out why it isn't working?"

"For a human reason, maybe. Suppose *you* were asked the most probable price of wheat next summer and didn't answer. Why wouldn't you answer?"

"Because I wouldn't know. But Multivac would know! We've given it all the factors. It can analyze futures in weather, politics, and economics. We know it can. It's done it before."

"All right. Suppose I asked the question and you knew the answer but didn't tell me. Why not?"

Weaver snarled. "Because I had a brain tumor. Because I had been knocked out. In other words, because my machinery was out of order. That's just what we're trying to find out about Multivac. We're looking for the place where its machinery is out of order, for the key item."

"Only you haven't found it." Nemerson got off his stool. "Listen, ask me the question Multivac stalled on."

"How? Shall I run the tape through you?"

"Come on, Jack. Give me the talk that goes along with it. You do talk to Multivac, don't you?"

"I've got to. Therapy.[3]

Nemerson nodded. "Yes, that's the story. Therapy. That's the official story. We talk to it in order to pretend it's a human being so that we don't get neurotic[4] over having a machine know so much more than we do. We turn a frightening metal monster into a protective father image."

"If you want to put it that way."

"Well, it's wrong and you know it. A computer as complex as Multivac *must* talk and listen to be efficient. Just putting in and taking out coded dots isn't sufficient. At a certain level of complexity, Multivac must be made to seem human because—it *is* human. Come on, Jack, ask me the question. I want to see my reaction to it."

Jack Weaver flushed. "This is silly."

---

2. **bigwig,** an informal word meaning an *important person.*

3. **therapy** (ther′ə pē), *n.* treatment of a disease or mental disorder.

4. **neurotic** (nù rot′ik), *adj.* suffering from an emotional disorder, such as depression.

▲ *Computer Cosmology,* by Colleen Browning, was painted in 1980. Discuss the perspective in this painting. Are we looking down, sideways, or up into the scene?

"Come on, will you?"

It was a measure of Weaver's depression and desperation that he acceded. Half sullenly,[5] he pretended to be feeding the program into Multivac, speaking as he did so in his usual manner. He commented on the latest information concerning farm unrest, talked about the new equations describing jet-stream contortions, lectured on the solar constant.

```
"All right, now. Work
that out and give us the
       answer pronto."
```

He began stiffly enough, but warmed to this task out of long habit, and when the last of the program was slammed home, he almost closed contact with a physical snap at Todd.

He ended briskly, "All right, now. Work that out and give us the answer pronto."

For a moment, having done, Jack Weaver stood there, nostrils flaring, as though he was feeling once more the excitement of throwing into action the most gigantic and glorious machine ever put together by the mind and hands of man.

Then he remembered and muttered, "All right. That's it."

Nemerson said, "At least I know now why *I* wouldn't answer, so let's try that on Multivac. Look, clear Multivac; make sure the investigators have their paws off it. Then run the program into it and let me do the talking. Just once."

Weaver shrugged and turned to Multivac's control wall, filled with its somber,[6] unwinking dials and lights. Slowly he cleared it. One by one he ordered the teams away.

Then, with a deep breath, he began once more feeding the program into Multivac. It was the twelfth time all told, the dozenth time. Somewhere a distant news commentator would spread the word that they were trying again. All over the world a Multivac-dependent people would be holding its collective breath.

Nemerson talked as Weaver fed the data silently. He talked diffidently, trying to remember what it was that Weaver had said, but waiting for the moment when the key item might be added.

Weaver was done and now a note of tension was in Nemerson's voice. He said, "All right, now, Multivac. Work that out and give us the answer."

He paused and added the key item. He said *"Please!"* And all over Multivac, the valves and relays went joyously to work.

---

5. **sullenly** (sul′ən lē), *adv.* silently, due to bad feeling, such as anger.

6. **somber** (som′bər), *adj.* gloomy, dark, dismal.

After Reading

Making Connections

1. The word "please" is the key item that gets Multivac to function. What is the "key item" that motivates you?

2. What problem-solving strategy do you think enabled Nemerson to succeed with Multivac where other technicians failed?

3. What words or phrases did the author use that enable you to visualize the **setting** for this story?

4. "Key Item" is set in the 1950s. What changes would have to be made to set the story in the present?

5. Authors write stories for various purposes, such as to entertain, pose questions, or deliver a message. What **purpose** do you think motivated Asimov to write "Key Item"?

6. Refer back to your Writer's Notebook entry. How do your views of humans and computers compare to the **plot** of this story?

7. Our dependency on computers continues to grow. How might a major computer breakdown affect life in your community?

Literary Focus: Setting

The **setting** is the time and place in which events in a story happen. A setting can be described in exact detail or it can be suggested as shown in "Key Item." Early in the story you read about ". . . six teams of computer technologists roaming around in the corridors of Multivac." From those details, you know the setting is inside Multivac, a computer the size of a building.

What other clues can you find to the setting of the story? How do you imagine Multivac looks inside? You may want to draw your impressions of the setting.

◄ Dr. J. Presper Eckert leans on the console of a UNIVAC computer while newsman Walter Cronkite reads the results of the 1952 presidential election. Asimov probably assumed that computers would get larger as they were required to process more information.

Vocabulary Study

A. Create a word map like the one below for the word *somber.* Include at least one more synonym, one more antonym, and another example of something you would describe as somber.

stolid
therapy
neurotic
sullenly
somber

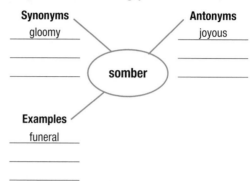

Synonyms
gloomy
_____
_____

somber

Antonyms
joyous
_____
_____

Examples
funeral
_____
_____

B. Make word maps for the vocabulary words *stolid, therapy, neurotic,* and *sullenly.* Share your best one with classmates.

Expressing Your Ideas

Writing Choices

Key Items In a small group, write an **instruction manual** that tells a teacher how to get your class to go "joyously to work." You might also add a chapter with tips to students on how to get top performance from a teacher.

A Collective Sigh of Relief Imagine working for the Multivac Corporation. Your job is to inform and reassure the public about the operations of Multivac. Write a **press release** to explain Multivac's recent problem. Include whatever details you think will restore people's confidence in Multivac.

Future World Write a short **analysis** of what you think computers will be able to do for us in the future.

Other Options

The Pros and Cons Form two teams to **debate** the effects of computers on our lives. One team argues that computers are a positive influence. The other team argues that computers are a negative influence. Present your debate to the class to see how many classmates each team can sway to its point of view.

Vac Man Computers have become a major form of entertainment, from arcades to living rooms. On your own, or with a small group, **invent** a computer game based on ideas from the story about Multivac.

Personification Plus In "Key Item" the computer Multivac is made to seem human. In a small group, think of another object that you could humanize. Make a list of its human characteristics and then create a **model** of it. Share your creation with the class.

Language Mini-Lesson

Choosing the Correct Homophone

Recognizing Homophones A galloping heard? The principle's office? Some crazy misunderstandings can happen when homophones—words that sound alike but have different spellings and meanings—get confused. For example, what misunderstanding might come up if the wrong homophone were used in the sentence, *The tie complemented his suit?* How is the meaning of *compliment* different?

Spelling Strategy To use homophones correctly, you first need to know what each homophone means. What is the difference in meaning between *heard* and *herd? straight* and *strait?* If you're not sure which homophone to use, look them both up in the dictionary.

Even if you know the meanings of the words, you might make careless errors if you don't think about the meanings as you write. For example, you probably know that *they're* means "they are," but if you don't think about it, you might use *there* or *their* instead. Other commonly confused homophones to watch for include *it's/its, to/too/two,* and *you're/your.*

Activity Options

1. Make up some outrageous sentences using homophones. Brainstorm a list of homophone pairs and then write sentences in which you purposely confuse them. Trade with a partner and see if you can make sense out of each other's sentences. Then, choose a few favorites to illustrate.

2. Write several pairs of homophones or use your list from the first activity. Get together with a partner and write a limerick using as many homophone pairs as you can. Write more than one limerick if you like.

3. Write a short skit about waking up in the morning. Use the following pairs of homophones in your skit: feat-feet; week-weak; way-weigh; threw-through; plain-plane; and great-grate.

Life Science Connection
How do we get our lives into focus?
We see with our eyes. We interpret
and understand what we see with
our brains.

How we see

Vision: The Eyes Have It

The human eye works much like a camera—a motion-picture camera, at that. For most people, the visual system is made up of not one camera but two, both of which send images to the "darkroom" where they are made into one image. Within its range, the human eye is capable of more accurate and sensitive performance than most cameras. However, it has more working parts that can break down and these parts are not easy to replace or repair.

Study the detailed drawing of the eye on this page. First, notice the cornea. This protective window covers the exposed surface of the eyeball. A thin film of fluid bathes the cornea and keeps it clean. Besides protecting the eye, the cornea bends incoming light rays toward the lens.

How much light does the eye need in order to see something? The amount depends on several things, such as whether the day is cloudy or bright, or whether we are doing close work or just looking out the window. The iris, the colored part of the eye just in front of the lens, regulates the amount of light entering the eye at any one time. The iris contracts and expands the pupil, the round opening in the center of the eye. In bright light, the pupil gets smaller. In dark-

ness, it gets larger. Only the amount of light needed reaches the lens.

The lens of the eye focuses light on the retina. The retina has layers of tissue that pick up signals through memory cells, called rods and cones.

The signals from cones and rods come together in one main cable, the optic nerve. The optic nerve sends the nerve impulses on to the part of the brain that handles seeing. When no light energy can get through to the brain because of diseased or damaged eyes, the individual is blind.

Human Eye Structure

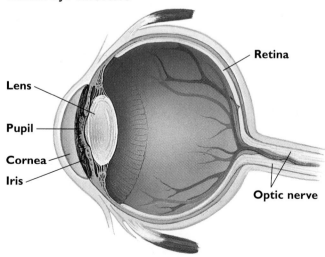

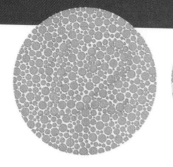
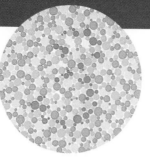
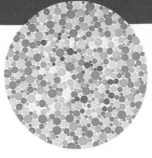

The patterns at the left are used to test for color-blindness. If you have normal color vision, you will be able to see in the circles from left to right, the numbers 12, 3, and 57.

Vision and the Brain

The most important part of the visual process takes place in the brain. The brain takes the scrambled impressions the eye has received and decodes them. For example, the pattern of light that falls on the retina makes an image that is upside down. But in the brain, the pattern is somehow perceived in its real position. Still, what we see would not mean much if the brain didn't compare the picture with what is already in its data bank of past images. The image we see has meaning only because we've experienced similar images before. To a new baby, the world is something of a blur of shapes, forms and colors. The infant organizes these into meaningful patterns as he or she grows older.

Finally, the part of the brain that handles sight passes along the information it receives to the parts of the brain that direct action. These messages tell us to duck when an object is thrown at us, or to walk around a pile of rubble that is in our path.

Color Vision

Color vision is handled by the cones in the retina. Each of about eight million cones picks out wavelengths of light that make up only one primary color—red or blue or yellow. These primary colors are thought to be mixed to form the hundreds of colors of the spectrum.

In each color that we see, three aspects are perceived. The first is the hue. This is the family of color. The hue is the color's quality of being red, or blue-green, or some other color. The second aspect is the color's brightness. This refers to the lightness or darkness of the color. The third aspect of a color is its saturation—the purity of the hue. This has to do with the amount of gray we see mixed with the pure color.

Suppose, for example, you were looking at something painted a pure, bright, orange color. Its hue would be halfway between red and yellow, because that's what orange is. Its brightness would show it as neither light orange nor dark orange. Its high color saturation would show no gray. Lighter, darker, or grayer mixtures of any combination of hues make many colors possible.

Certain people can't see differences among colors. These people are color-blind. Some people are totally color-blind; they see everything in shades of gray. People with red-green color-blindness see only blue and yellow hues along with grays. Those with the blue-yellow type see green and red and shades of gray.

Responding

1. Take a poll in your class. How many students are color-blind? Determine what percentage have red-green color-blindness, blue-yellow color-blindness, and total color-blindness.

2. With other classmates, make a bulletin board display that teaches the three aspects of color: hue, brightness, and saturation. First, choose three different colors as your models. Then, use magazine pictures to demonstrate variations in the three aspects of each color.

Psychology Connection

There may be more than one way to look at something. What do you see first when you look at each of these images? Look again. Do you now have another point of view?

Interpreting
visual
evidence

By Dr. David Thomson

The Vegetable Gardener

This picture looks perfectly normal: a dark green bowl, filled with different vegetables and nuts. But the title of the picture is *The Vegetable Gardener,* not *A Bowl of Vegetables.* Turn the book upside down and you will see why. ➤

◄ **What do you see here?**
A young girl, or an old woman? Or both? (Clues: The girl's ear is one of the old woman's eyes. Her neck band is the old woman's mouth.)

⋀ Magic Eye

To see the animal in the picture, bring the picture very close to your face. Look through the picture without focusing on it as you slowly draw it away to your usual reading distance. Keep staring without refocusing and try not to blink. Suddenly, hidden images will appear and you will see the animal.

◄ Moving Picture

Hold the book up at arm's length and look at this picture of a parrot and its cage. Still looking at the picture, bring the book closer and closer to your eyes. If you bring the book close enough, the parrot will appear to be in its cage.

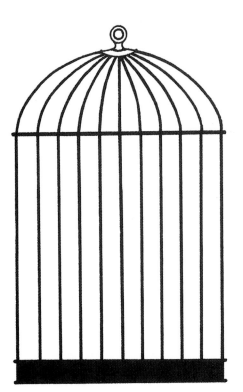

Responding

1. Look at the pictures on these two pages. Write what image you saw first in each picture. What did you see next? Compare your list with a classmate's list.

2. Find an unusual painting or other piece of art in this or another of your textbooks. Compare your interpretation of the art with the interpretation of two classmates.

Reading Mini-Lesson

Taking Notes

You've just read about how your point of view influences what you see. Now let's consider how your note-taking helps determine what you remember.

Taking notes is a very important study skill. Of course, taking notes from your reading is more difficult than just copying them from the board, but it is also more meaningful. When you take reading notes, *you* must select the most important information, *you* must decide what form to use to organize the information, *you* must THINK—and this helps you remember what you've read.

An outline is the most common way of taking notes while reading. To make an outline, look for the main points and add the details that are important to understanding what you are reading. For example, "How We See" on pages 88–89 has three main parts. At the left is one possible way to begin an outline. It shows the first main part and important points to remember under that heading.

Taking careful notes and saving and organizing them will help you in two ways: You will better understand the information, and you will find that your notes are a big help when you need to review.

I. Vision: The Eyes Have It
   A. Human eye compared to a camera
   B. Cornea
      1. Protects the eye
      2. Bends light rays toward the lens
   C. Lens focuses light rays
   D. Iris controls light coming into eye
      1. Iris is colored part of eye
      2. It contracts and expands the pupil
   E. Retina picks up signals
      1. Rods and cones
      2. Signals come together in optic nerve
   F. Optic nerve sends impulses to brain
II. Vision and the Brain
   A. (and so on)

Activity Options

1. The last two parts of "How We See" are not completed in the outline started at the left. Focus on the last two sections of the reading, titled *Vision and the Brain* and *Color Vision,* and complete the outline.

2. One effective way to take notes is to sketch a graphic of some kind. The drawing on page 88 shows you the eye's structure. Copy or trace the diagram in the middle of a sheet of paper. Then draw a line from the name of each part to a blank space where you will have room to write. In the blank spaces write the function or purpose of each part of the eye.

3. Practice taking notes while doing a reading assignment in a science, social studies, or other textbook. Choose the method of taking notes that you prefer and apply it as you study the assigned material.

Writing Workshop

Thumbs Up or Thumbs Down?

Assignment In the selections, seeing things from different points of view sometimes leads characters to new insights. Work with a partner to analyze a book, movie, or TV show and compare your points of view. See the Writer's Blueprint for details.

WRITER'S BLUEPRINT

Product	A critical review
Purpose	To analyze a book, story, movie, or TV show from two points of view
Audience	People who might read the book or story, or see the movie or TV show
Specs	To write a successful essay, you should:

❑ Work with a partner and choose a book, movie, or TV show that you both know. Then decide together on three elements of the book or movie to analyze such as plot, character, setting, or believability.

❑ Independently, you will each write a critical essay in which you review the work in terms of the three elements.

❑ Begin by stating your overall opinion of the book, movie, or TV show.

❑ Go on to support your opinion with specific details and examples of each element.

❑ Conclude by summarizing the main points you made about each of the three elements and telling whether you recommend the book, movie, or TV show. Use parallel structure in your summaries to add clarity and smoothness to your writing.

❑ Exchange and read each other's essays. Then discuss the similarities and differences between your points of view.

❑ Follow the rules for grammar, usage, spelling, and mechanics. Avoid comma splices that result in run-on sentences.

Choose a work to analyze. With your partner make a list of movies and books you have both seen or read recently. Examine elements in the ones you find most interesting. These elements might be plot, setting, characters, believability, or mood. Decide which movie or book you want to write about. Discuss the elements each of you will examine in your papers.

OR . . .
If you're having trouble coming up with books or movies you've both seen, look through the book-shelves in the library or your classroom for book titles. Skim the movie list-ings in the newspaper for movie titles.

Create a chart. Working separately, create a chart for your chosen movie, book, story, or TV show. Be sure to include your opinions about each element of this work that you examine.

Selection	Element	My Opinion	Reasons for my opinion
The True Confessions of Charlotte Doyle	Setting	Believable	Information about sailing terms. Information about how sailors told time.
	Character	Strong	Traveled alone. Stuck to her beliefs even when it was dangerous.

Try a quickwrite. For a few minutes, jot down details from your book, story, TV show, or movie that illustrate your opinions about each element you chose to analyze. In a critical essay it is very impor-tant to support your opinions with details. Here is part of one stu-dent's quickwrite on *The True Confessions of Charlotte Doyle.*

> *The True Confessions of Charlotte Doyle* had an interesting setting, strong main character, and a believable story. I've never read a book set on a ship before, and it was interesting to learn the terms used on ships and that sailors used bells to tell time. Charlotte was a strong character. She decided what was right and stuck to her opinion.

STUDENT MODEL

Plan your essay. Use your quickwrite and your chart to help you pull together your opinions and the details to support them. Create webs for each element to connect your opinions and the details. Here is a web for the setting of *The True Confessions of Charlotte Doyle*.

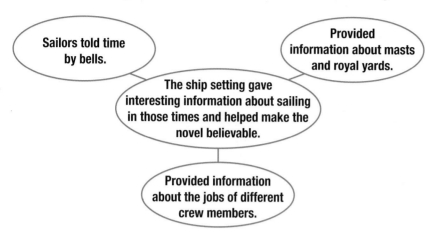

Sailors told time by bells.

Provided information about masts and royal yards.

The ship setting gave interesting information about sailing in those times and helped make the novel believable.

Provided information about the jobs of different crew members.

 STEP **2** DRAFTING

Before you write, review the Writer's Blueprint and the work you did in the Prewriting steps. You might want to look ahead to the Revising Strategy on parallel structure before you begin writing. Using parallel structure will help clarify your writing.

As you draft, don't worry about mistakes in spelling and punctuation. Just concentrate on getting your ideas on paper. Here are some ideas for getting started.

- Tell which movie, book, or TV show you chose and explain your choice.

- State your overall impression of the movie, book, or TV show.

Work with your partner to review your drafts and your summary paragraphs before you revise them.

✔ Have we followed the specs in the Writer's Blueprint?

✔ Have we made our opinions clear and supported them with details?

✔ Have we detailed the similarities and differences in our points of view in our summary paragraphs?

✔ Have we used parallel structure in our sentences to clearly express our ideas?

Revising Strategy

Using Parallel Structure

Sentences should be clear, smooth, and concise. One way to accomplish this is to make items of equal importance in a sentence balanced. This is called parallel structure. In this pair of sentences the second is parallel because *movie* is modified by three adjectives.

The movie was **fast-paced, believable,** and **the actors did a good job.**

The movie was **fast-paced, believable,** and **well-acted.**

In the Literary Source, Michael Dorris uses parallel structure to describe his father. Each part begins with a noun followed by a description beginning with "who." Notice how the writer of the passage below made a sentence parallel.

LITERARY SOURCE

". . . a dashing mixed-blood man from the Northwest who, improbably, could do the rumba; a soldier who regularly had his uniform altered by a tailor so that it would fit better; a date, according to my mother, who 'knew how to order' in a restaurant . . ."
from "Father's Day" by Michael Dorris

In conclusion, I really enjoyed reading this book. Three of the reasons for liking it were the realistic characters, the interesting setting, and ~~it was believable~~. *the believability* ⊂

STUDENT MODEL

4 EDITING

Ask a partner to review your revised draft before you edit. When you edit, watch for errors in grammar, usage, spelling, and mechanics. Make sure you haven't written any run-on sentences.

Editing Strategy

FOR REFERENCE . . .
More rules for avoiding run-on sentences are listed in the *Language and Grammar Handbook.*

Avoiding Run-on Sentences

When you edit your paper, check to see that you have not included run-on sentences. Run-on sentences happen when you join two or more sentences without the proper punctuation between them. Read these example sentences.

The movie was popular we stood in line for tickets.

The book was gripping, I read it in one night.

The first example has no punctuation between sentences. The second example has only a comma joining two sentences.

Tips for Correcting Run-on Sentences

- Separate the two sentences with a period.

  The book was gripping. I read it in one night.

- If the ideas are closely related, join them with a comma and a conjunction such as *and, but,* or *so* or with a semi-colon.

  The movie was popular, and we stood in line for tickets.

  The movie was popular; we stood in line for tickets.

Notice how the writer of the draft below corrected a run-on.

> This book was believable. It took place in 1832, everything was
> ∧ *(and*
> as it would be in those days. Since Charlotte was a girl, she had many
>
> people follow her around to make sure she was okay.

STUDENT MODEL

STEP 5 PRESENTING

Here are a few ideas for presenting your essay.

- Using your summary of both essays, present a program similar to that on television featuring movie critics. When you and your partner present your reviews, you should each take on the role of a critic and discuss your own point of view. Before you present, each of you should decide if you'll give your book, movie, or TV show a "thumbs up" or "thumbs down."

- If you have access to a computer printer, set your essays up as newspaper or magazine reviews. Check a newspaper or magazine for correct format. Display your reviews for the class to read.

STEP 6 LOOKING BACK

Self-evaluate. What grade would you give your paper? Look back at the Writer's Blueprint and evaluate yourself on each point, from 6 (superior) down to 1 (weak).

Reflect. Think about what you learned from writing your essay as you write answers to these questions.

✔ How has your essay improved your understanding of the book, story, TV show, or movie?

✔ Now that you have read and heard your partner's opinion of the work that you selected, would you change the way you presented your opinions? How?

For Your Working Portfolio: Add your essay, your summary paragraph, and your reflection responses to your working portfolio.

Beyond Print

He Said, She Said

Sometimes people just don't listen to you, do they? Have you ever been told that you said something mean about someone and you never said it at all? Or have you heard rumors about your liking someone when you never said a thing about that person? Wouldn't it be a better world if people listened more carefully?

Listening Tips

Think as you listen. Look in the speaker's eyes. Relate what the speaker says to your own experience.

Give the speaker feedback. Repeat the speaker's words as you understood them until he or she agrees you've got them right.

Try to make a vivid mental image. When the speaker tells you about something, try to picture it in your mind.

Activity

It's time to play a game that will help you avoid the problems encountered by poor listening.

Here are the rules:

1. Get into groups of five.

2. Create a written list of five things about yourself. You may want to include some of the following information in this list:

name of a good friend	favorite TV show	favorite foods
something you value	a book you like	favorite sport
favorite sports team	favorite music	your hero

3. Whisper your list of five things to a person in your group.

4. That person whispers your list to the next person, and so on.

5. The last person to receive the list tells everything he or she heard.

6. Check off each correct item the person names.

7. After each person in each group has had a turn, tally the scores. The group with the most correct items wins the game.

Five Things About Me

1. I love horses.

2. My favorite book is Hatchet.

3. My favorite sport is soccer.

4. I like to watch old movies.

5. I always

Projects for Collaborative Study

Theme Connection

Friends in Deed Did you ever wonder why certain people are friends with certain other people? Is it because they are alike or because they are different? Talk to a good friend (not a classmate) about your relationship. Make a list of your likenesses and differences. Do you like your likenesses as well as your differences? Which do you value more?

In an open forum, everyone shares what they have learned about their friendships. Keep track of your findings, and chart them in a graph with these two headings:

Friends with Stimulating Similarities

and

Friends with Dynamic Differences

Literature Connection

The Characters Have It You've just read a number of selections in which strong **characterization** plays a vital role. This may have been accomplished through **dialogue**—characters talking to one another—or **monologue**—characters thinking or talking to themselves. More often than not, characterization occurs when an author gives us bits of information showing what the character is about.

■ As a group, find examples in one of the selections that illustrate how the author **shows** what a character is like without telling. Find effective dialogue too.

Life Skills Connection

A Friendly Opportunity You are traveling on a field trip to Washington, D. C. When you arrive, you are asked to pick a roommate who will be your "buddy" on all outings. How will you choose?

■ As a class, write your answers to these questions on the board:

• What qualities do you want most in a friend?

• What are the differences between an acquaintance, a friend, and a best friend?

■ Now, answer these questions yourself:

• How do you know when you are someone's friend?

• What do you do to make friends with people you like?

Multicultural Connection

Let's Talk People who speak many different languages come from countries around the world to live in the United States. Often they settle in neighborhoods with others of the same background. They find that **communication** in their first language is not only a possibility but a rich reality. Find out more about it.

• Research a community with many people from the same background. What language is spoken? What businesses and social organizations are found?

• Create charts and graphs that show these findings.

Read More About Relationships

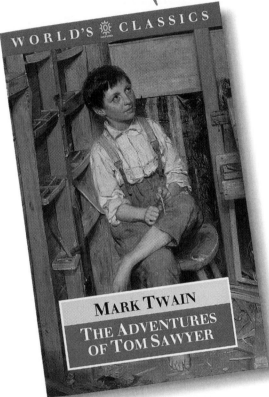

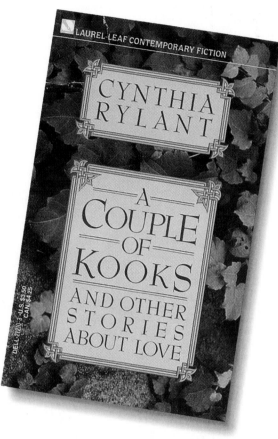

The Adventures of Tom Sawyer (1876) by Mark Twain. In this American classic, Twain created a character whose fun-loving ways and sense of adventure have endeared him to readers for generations.

A Couple of Kooks (1994) by Cynthia Rylant. If you enjoyed reading "A Crush," you will delight in this collection of short stories about characters you would want to have as friends.

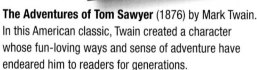

More Good Books

Local News (1993) by Gary Soto. This collection of short stories is brimming with the energy of a Mexican American neighborhood and the joys and sorrows of young life.

The Yearling (1938) by Marjorie Kinnan Rawlings. Jody Baxter is a lonely boy living in the Florida scrub. He finds a fawn and convinces his parents to let him keep it.

The Friends (1973) by Rosa Guy. Phyllisia has moved from the West Indies to Harlem. Her classmates are very hostile towards her. Only Edith, a ragged outcast, befriends her.

Tristan and Iseult (1971) by Rosemary Sutcliff. Iseult is princess of Ireland. Tristan is the brave young man who loves her. This novel, full of daring deeds and high adventure, is based on an old Celtic legend.

Nothing But the Truth (1991) by Avi. Philip decides to hum during the national anthem, disobeying a school rule. His parents take his side and conflict ensues—involving the community and national news media.

Challenges

Choices and Consequences
Part One, pages 106–167

Finding Your Place
Part Two, pages 168–221

Talking About
CHALLENGES

Challenges come in many forms at many different times in your life. A challenge may involve a goal you set for yourself—a race you want to win, a talent you want to enhance—or a situation that is thrust upon you—expectations of parents and teachers or pressure from friends. How you handle each of these challenges is the biggest challenge of all. Just remember to be true to yourself, do your best, and keep trying. The rest should fall into place.

Read each of the comments from students and compare them to the quotations from the literature you will be reading.

"**Being a girl in a sport that is mostly boys is really challenging.**"

Michelle—Lexington, KY

I don't see why people make such a big deal about a girl playing boys' games. . . . To me all sports are for everybody.

from "Never Fitting In" by Nereida Román, page 186

"Sometimes I feel pressured, but it's not too hard to say no."

Sam–Moab, UT

Beterli flushed and took a step forward, hand half-raised. Keevan stood his ground, but if Beterli advanced one more step, he would call the wing-second. No one fought on the Hatching Ground. Surely Beterli knew that much.

from "The Smallest Dragonboy" by Anne McCaffrey, page 174

"The things I want are sometimes hard for other people to understand."

Pak–Stanford, CT

. . . Colin threatened to break the family tradition with his leaning toward art. . .

from "Last Cover" by Paul Annixter, page 119

"What will we learn from our challenges—and how difficult will they be?"

LaVonne–Fargo, MN

Bang! they're off careening down the lanes, each chased by her own bright tiger.

from "The Women's 400 Meters" by Lillian Morrison, page 202

 When I have a hard time dealing with something, I ask my mom for help and the pressure is off me.

Sarah–Boise, ID

Part One

Choices and Consequences

You are the master of your fate. It may not seem so when your mom yells at you to take out the garbage, but think of the hundreds of choices you make every day. Chocolate or vanilla? Do your homework or ride your bike? Every decision changes your future in some way, and while most are pretty small, a few will change your life forever.

Multicultural Connection **Change** creates challenges. The characters in these stories face challenges, make choices both big and small, and live out the consequences. A person's cultural background may influence the way he or she reacts to challenges. How do the people in these stories draw upon their backgrounds as they deal with change?

Literature

Dorothy M. Johnson   **The Day the Sun Came Out** ◆ short story 108

Paul Annixter   **Last Cover** ◆ short story 116

Gregorio López
    y Fuentes   **A Letter to God** ◆ short story 127

Shel Silverstein   **Almost Perfect** ◆ poem 130

Bill Littlefield   **Nate "Tiny" Archibald** ◆ biography 134

Linda Fang   **The Clever Magistrate** ◆ Chinese tale 145

Betsy Hearne   **Sir Gawain and the Loathly Lady**
           ◆ English legend 151

Anonymous   **Greensleeves** ◆ traditional song 158

    Writing Mini-Lesson ◆ Arranging Details .161

Interdisciplinary Study   Doing Battle

Knights and Samurai ◆ history 162

Kusunoki Masashige by Ann Woodbury Moore ◆ history 164

Three Haiku ◆ poems 166

    Reading Mini-Lesson ◆ Visualizing 167

Before Reading

The Day the Sun Came Out

by Dorothy M. Johnson

Dorothy M. Johnson
1905–1984

Johnson was a journalist, publisher, and teacher, but is best known as a writer of short stories about the American West. As in "The Day the Sun Came Out," her stories often dealt with themes showing the courage and strength of ordinary people. She strove for historical accuracy in all her work. For her sensitive, realistic portrayal of Native Americans, she was made an honorary member of the Blackfeet Indian tribe in Montana. Several of her stories, such as "A Man Called Horse," have been made into motion pictures.

Building Background

The Move West Westward movement of European settlers began soon after the first colonists arrived on the Atlantic shores of North America. The Louisiana Purchase in 1803 provided a staggering amount of new land to settle, and as Native Americans were driven from their lands, settlers quickly followed, believing it was their destiny to take over the entire continent. Glowing reports from those who had gone before stirred the imaginations of those left behind and thousands more set out on the westward trails. By the 1830s and 1840s, the most determined settlers had already pushed through vast, largely unsettled regions as far as California and Oregon.

Getting into the Story

Writer's Notebook "I'm doing this for your own good." Have you ever heard those words at a time when you were angry about what the speaker was doing? In "The Day the Sun Came Out," the narrator gets furious because of something someone does for his own good. Write in your notebook about a time someone did something you disliked "for your own good." How did you react? When did you realize it was the right thing to do? Did your feelings change afterward?

Reading Tip

Author's Language An author may use words and expressions from a particular time and place to re-create a mood. At the beginning of this story, a family is nearly out of food and in despair. The author helps readers feel this mood of poverty and hopelessness by using the same language poor farmers moving West in the mid-1800s used. "I ain't going back," one character says. "We're prid'near out of food," says another.

As you read the story, make a list of words and expressions from the time the story takes place. How do they help set the mood for the story? Look for the point when the mood of the story changes. How does the language change at that point?

THE DAY THE

Dorothy M. Johnson

We left the home place behind, mile by slow mile. We were heading for the mountains, across the prairie where the wind blew forever.

At first there were four of us with the one-horse wagon and its skimpy load. Pa and I walked because I was a big boy of eleven. My two little sisters walked until they got tired. Then they had to be boosted up in the wagon bed.

That was no covered Conestoga,[1] like Pa's folks came West in. It was just an old farm wagon, drawn by one tired horse. It creaked and rumbled westward to the mountains, toward the little woods town where Pa thought he had an old uncle who owned a little two-bit[2] sawmill.

Two weeks we had been moving when we picked up Mary. She had run away from some-

---

1. **Conestoga** (kon′ə stō′gə), a covered wagon with broad wheels used by American pioneers to travel west.
2. **two-bit,** cheap or worthless; comes from two bits, a slang expression for a quarter of a dollar.

◄ *Woman Holding a Basket* is a sculpture by George Lundeen. Compare this young woman to Mary as you read.

SUN CAME OUT

where that she wouldn't tell. Pa didn't want her along. But she stood up to him with no fear in her voice.

"I'd rather go with a family and look after kids," she said, "but I ain't going back. If you won't take me, I'll travel with any wagon that will."

Pa scowled at her, and wide blue eyes stared back.

"How old are you?" he demanded.

"Twenty," she said. "There's teamsters[3] come this way sometimes. I'd rather go with you folks. But I won't go back."

"We're prid'near[4] out of food," my father told her. "We're clean out of money. I got all I can handle without taking anybody else." He turned away as if he hated the sight of her. "You'll have to walk," he said.

So she went along with us. She looked after the little girls, but Pa wouldn't talk to her.

EVALUATE: Do you think Pa's decision to take Mary along was a good one?

On the prairie, the wind blew. But in the mountains, there was rain. When we stopped at little timber claims along the way, the homesteaders said it had rained all summer. Crops among the blackened stumps were rotted and spoiled. There was no cheer any-where. The people we talked to were past worrying. They were scared and desperate.

So was Pa. He traveled twice as far each day as the wagon. He ranged through the woods with his rifle. But he never saw game. He had been depending on killing a deer. But we never got any deer meat except as a grudging[5] gift from the homesteaders.

He brought in a porcupine once. And that was fat meat and good. Mary roasted it in chunks over the fire, half crying with the smoke. Pa and I rigged up the tarp sheet for a shelter to keep the rain from putting the fire clean out.

The porcupine was long gone, except for some of the tried-out fat[6] that Mary had saved, when we came to an old, empty cabin. Pa said we'd have to stop. The horse was wore out. It couldn't pull any more up those hills in the mountains.

At the cabin, at least there was a place to stay. We had a few potatoes left and some cornmeal. There was a creek that probably had fish in it, if a person could catch them. Pa tried it for half a day before he gave up. To

---

3. **teamster,** person who hauls things on wagons pulled by teams of horses.
4. **prid'near** (prid nēr'), pretty near, or nearly.
5. grudging (gruj'ing), *adj.* given unwillingly.
6. **tried-out fat,** fat melted from meat.

The Day the Sun Came Out   **109**

this day I don't care for fishing. I remember my father's sunken eyes in his sad face.

He took Mary and me outside the cabin to talk. Rain dripped on us from branches overhead.

"I think I know where we are," he said. "I figure to get to old John's and back in about four days. There'll be food in the town. They'll let me have some whether old John's still there or not."

He looked at me. "You do like she tells you," he warned. It was the first time he had admitted Mary was on earth since we picked her up two weeks before.

"You're my pardner," he said to me, "but it might be she's got more brains. You mind what she says."

He burst out with bitterness. "There ain't anything good left in the world. Or people to care if you live or die. But I'll get food in the town and come back with it."

He took a deep breath and added, "If you get too all-fired hungry, butcher the horse. It'll be better than starvin'."

He kissed the little girls good-bye. Then he plodded off through the woods with one blanket and the rifle.

The cabin was moldy[7] and had no floor. We kept a fire going under a hole in the roof, so it was full of blinding smoke, but we had to keep the fire so as to dry out the wood.

The third night, we lost the horse. A bear scared him. We heard the racket. Mary and I ran out. But we couldn't see anything in the pitch-dark.

In gray daylight I went looking for him. I must have walked fifteen miles. It seemed like I had to have that horse at the cabin when Pa came or he'd whip me. I got plumb lost two or three times. I thought maybe I was going to die there alone and nobody would ever know it. But I found the way back to the clearing.

That was the fourth day. And Pa didn't come. That was the day we ate up the last of the grub.

The fifth day, Mary went looking for the horse. My sisters cried. They huddled in a blanket by the fire, because they were scared and hungry.

I never did get dried out, always having to bring in more damp wood and going out to yell to see if Mary would hear me and not get lost. But I couldn't cry like the little girls did, because I was a big boy, eleven years old.

It was near dark when there was an answer to my yelling. Mary came into the clearing.

Mary didn't have the horse. We never saw hide nor hair of that old horse again. But she was carrying something big and white that looked like a pumpkin with no color to it.

She didn't say anything, just looked around and saw Pa wasn't there yet, at the end of the fifth day.

"What's that thing?" my sister Elizabeth demanded.

"Mushroom," Mary answered. "I bet it hefts ten pounds."

"What are you going to do with it now?" I said. "Play football here?"

"Eat it—maybe," she said, putting it in a corner. Her wet hair hung over her shoulders. She huddled by the fire.

My sister Sarah began to cry again. "I'm hungry!" she kept saying.

"Mushrooms ain't good eating," I said. "They can kill you."

"Maybe," Mary answered. "Maybe they can, I don't set up to know all about everything, like some people."

PREDICT: What will Mary do with the mushroom?

"What's that mark on your shoulder?" I asked her. "You tore your dress on the brush."

---

7. moldy (mōl′dē), *adj.* old and decaying; musty.

"What do you think it is?" she said. Her head was bowed in the smoke.

"Looks like scars," I guessed.

"'Tis scars. They whipped me, them I used to live with. Now mind your own business. I want to think."

Elizabeth cried, "Why don't Pa come back?"

"He's coming," Mary promised. "Can't come in the dark. Your pa'll take care of you soon's he can."

She got up and looked around in the grub box.

"Nothing there but empty dishes," I growled. "If there was anything, we'd know it."

Mary stood up. She was holding the can with the porcupine grease.

"I'm going to have something to eat," she said coolly. "You kids can't have any yet. And I don't want any crying, mind."

It was a cruel thing, what she did then. She sliced that big, solid mushroom and heated grease in the pan.

The smell of it brought the little girls out of their bed. But she told them to go back in so fierce a voice that they obeyed. They cried to break your heart.

I didn't cry, I watched, hating her.

I endured[8] the smell of the mushroom frying as long as I could. Then I said, "Give me some."

"Tomorrow," Mary answered. "Tomorrow, maybe. But not tonight." She turned to me with a sharp command: "Don't bother me! Just leave me be."

She knelt there by the fire and finished frying the slice of mushroom.

If I'd had Pa's rifle, I'd have been willing to kill her right then and there.

She didn't eat right away. She looked at the brown, fried slice for a while and said, "By tomorrow morning, I guess you can tell whether you want any."

The girls stared at her as she ate. Sarah was chewing on an old leather glove.

When Mary crawled into the quilts with them, they moved away as far as they could get.

I was so scared that my stomach heaved, empty as it was.

Mary didn't stay in the quilt long. She took a drink out of the water bucket and sat down by the fire and looked through the smoke at me.

And so would you sit up. If it might be your last night on earth. . . .

She said in a low voice, "I don't know how it will be if it's poison. Just do the best you can with the girls. Because your pa will come back, you know. . . . You better go to bed. I'm going to sit up."

And so would you sit up. If it might be your last night on earth and the pain of death might seize you at any moment, you would sit up by the smoky fire, wide-awake, remembering whatever you had to remember, savoring[9] life.

We sat in silence after the girls had gone to sleep. Once I asked, "How long does it take?"

"I never heard," she answered. "Don't think about it."

I slept after a while, with my chin on my chest.

Mary's moving around brought me wide-awake. The black of night was fading.

"I guess it's all right," Mary said. "I'd be able to tell by now, wouldn't I?"

I answered gruffly, "I don't know."

Mary stood in the doorway for a while, looking out at the dripping world as if she found it beautiful. Then she fried slices of the mushroom while the little girls danced with anxiety.

---

8. **endure** (en dùr′), *v.* put up with; withstand.

9. **savor** (sā′vər), *v.* enjoy very much.

▲ *Morning Mist* was painted by Mort Künstler in 1981. 🐾 For people who left established towns to cross the prairie, life in the wilderness was a big **change**. What new hardships and rewards might they have experienced?

We feasted, we three, my sisters and I, until Mary ruled, "That'll hold you," and would not cook any more. She didn't touch any of the mushroom herself.

That was a strange day in the moldy cabin. Mary laughed and was gay. She told stories. And we played "Who's Got the Thimble?" with a pine cone.

In the afternoon we heard a shout. My sisters screamed and I ran ahead of them across the clearing.

The rain had stopped. My father came plunging out of the woods leading a pack horse—and well I remember the treasures of food in that pack.

He glanced at us anxiously as he tore the ropes that bound the pack.

"Where's the other one?" he demanded.

Mary came out of the cabin then, walking sedately.[10] As she came toward us, the sun began to shine.

My stepmother was a wonderful woman.

_____

10. **sedately** (si dāt′lē), *adv.* calmly; seriously.

After Reading

Making Connections

1. What color do you think best represents this story? Why? Would that color change at any point?

2. 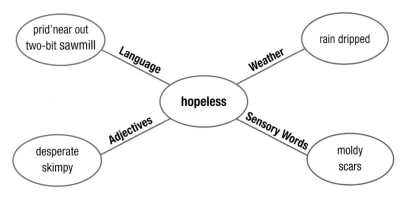 **Change** sometimes creates harsh challenges. Could you have faced the challenge and made the choice that Mary did in order to save others? Explain.

3. Why do you think the author chose to spell words such as *pardner* and *starvin'* as the characters would have pronounced them?

4. How does weather help to create **mood** in this story?

5. The author chose a title about weather. What does the sun **symbolize?**

6. In this story Mary was prepared to face severe consequences to save the children. What other stories can you recall from literature or from real life in which people risk their lives to help others?

Literary Focus: Mood

You understand the **mood**, or atmosphere, of a story when you identify the feeling it gives you. In this story many elements work together to create mood. The language of the poverty-stricken pioneers, the bad weather, adjectives that describe neediness and hardship, and descriptive details such as the moldy cabin combine to create a mood. What adjective would you use to describe that mood? What else in the story contributes to the mood?

Reread the story to find examples of how the author creates mood. Ask yourself: Why has the author chosen these words and details? How do they help create the mood? Using a web like the one below, as you read, can help you organize your ideas about mood.

prid'near out two-bit sawmill — Language — Weather — rain dripped

hopeless

desperate skimpy — Adjectives — Sensory Words — moldy scars

Vocabulary Study

On your paper write the letter of the word that is *not* related in meaning to the other words in the set.

grudging
moldy
endure
savor
sedately

1. **a.** quit   **b.** stop   **c.** endure   **d.** leave
2. **a.** sedately   **b.** calmly   **c.** seriously   **d.** musically
3. **a.** damp   **b.** sweet   **c.** stale   **d.** moldy
4. **a.** grudging   **b.** generous   **c.** plentiful   **d.** kind
5. **a.** savor   **b.** deny   **c.** enjoy   **d.** appreciate

Expressing Your Ideas

Writing Choices

Nobody Understands Me! When Mary eats the mushroom alone, her good intentions are misunderstood. Use the notes from your notebook to write an **essay** about a time someone misunderstood your actions or words. Explain what you really meant or thought and what the other person understood. How did you feel? Why do you think the misunderstanding occurred? Did it get cleared up?

What's the Message? Is there a moral to this story? Write a **proverb** that sums up in a single sentence any lesson to be learned. Remember, a good proverb will be short, to the point, and stated in a way that's easy to remember. Examples of well-known proverbs follow: "A stitch in time saves nine." "Haste makes waste." "Neither a borrower nor a lender be." "Curiosity killed the cat."

Delicious Meal or Fatal Mistake? Research the various kinds of poisonous mushrooms and their effects on people who mistakenly eat them. Write a **report** to share with the class.

Other Options

Westward Ho! Work in a small group. Look back at the story to see what kinds of supplies the family took on its trip west. Then brainstorm items that were available in pioneer days that you would take on a trip west in a Conestoga wagon. Make and **illustrate** a final supply **list,** including quantities.

On Sale Today Would anyone you know fry mushrooms in tried-out porcupine fat? They probably would if advertising convinced them that it would be healthy and delicious. Work with a partner to create an **advertising campaign** for porcupine grease. A successful campaign will tell why, how, and when to use it. You can choose among ads for newspapers, magazines, radio, TV, or billboards.

Tee Time Create T-shirt **designs** and **slogans** for one or more of the major characters in the story. Choose a specific moment in the story that each shirt represents. Present your designs to the class and explain what part of the story each illustrates.

Before Reading

Last Cover

by Paul Annixter

Paul Annixter
born 1894

During his long career as a writer, Howard Allison Sturtzel published many short stories and novels under the pen name Paul Annixter. As a teenager, economic hardship forced him to leave home and ride the rails, stopping where he could find work as a farm-hand or day laborer. Later, young Howard lived alone on a timber claim in northern Minnesota, where for more than a year, he hunted and cut wood for a living. These early experiences provided material for "Last Cover" and other realistic stories about animals, facing the elements, and being alone.

Building Background

Food or Friend? From buying those tiny cans of fancy cat food to getting their dogs' teeth cleaned, American pet owners treat their animals well. And who hasn't heard of someone leaving a few thousand dollars to a parakeet in a will? Yet some of these same pet owners think nothing of ordering a steak or wearing leather shoes. Many stories, such as the one you are about to read, explore our relationship with animals and our conflicting attitudes towards them.

Getting into the Story

Discussion In "Last Cover" two very different brothers share a special love for a pet. With a small group discuss how you are different from your brothers and sisters or other people you live with. How do the differences affect your relationships? Are they more or less important to you than the similarities?

Reading Tip

Time Shifts The simplest way to tell a story is from beginning to end. Many stories, however, begin somewhere in the middle, jump back to fill in details, and then continue on. The author of "Last Cover" uses references to time to alert you to the unusual sequence in this story. By keeping track of clues such as "three weeks before," "it was late February," or "one afternoon a year and a half before," you can tell when story events happened. It may help to record events on a time line such as the one below.

When:	1½ years ago	3 weeks ago	late Feb.
What:	fox arrives	fox leaves	search for fox

LAST COVER

PAUL ANNIXTER

I'm not sure I can tell you what you want to know about my brother; but everything about the pet fox is important, so I'll tell all that from the beginning.

It goes back to a winter afternoon after I'd hunted the woods all day for a sign of our lost pet. I remember the way my mother looked up as I came into the kitchen. Without my speaking, she knew what had happened. For six hours I had walked, reading signs, looking for a delicate print in the damp soil or even a hair that might have told of a red fox passing that way—but I had found nothing.

"Did you go up in the foothills?" Mom asked.

I nodded. My face was stiff from held-back tears. My brother, Colin, who was going on twelve, got it all from one look at me and went into a heartbroken, almost silent, crying.

Three weeks before, Bandit, the pet fox Colin and I had raised from a tiny kit, had disappeared, and not even a rumor had been heard of him since.

"He'd have had to go off soon anyway," Mom comforted. "A big, lolloping fellow like him, he's got to live his life same as us. But he may come back. That fox set a lot of store by you boys in spite of his wild ways."

▲ These two country boys, painted by Connie Hayes, look very much at home in this setting. 🐾 How would their appearance **change** if they were standing on a city sidewalk?

"He set a lot of store by our food, anyway," Father said. He sat in a chair by the kitchen window mending a piece of harness. "We'll be seeing a lot more of that fellow, never fear. That fox learned to pine for table scraps and young chickens. He was getting to be an egg thief, too, and he's not likely to forget that."

"That was only pranking[1] when he was little," Colin said desperately.

From the first, the tame fox had made tension in the family. It was Father who said we'd better name him Bandit, after he'd made away with his first young chicken.

"Maybe you know," Father said shortly. "But when an animal turns to egg sucking he's usually incurable.[2] He'd better not come pranking around my chicken run again."

---

1. **prank,** play pranks, or mischievous tricks.
2. incurable (in kyùr′ə bəl), *adj.* not capable of being cured or healed.

It was late February, and I remember the bleak, dead cold that had set in, cold that was a rare thing for our Carolina hills. Flocks of sparrows and snowbirds had appeared to peck hungrily at all that the pigs and chickens didn't eat.

"This one's a killer," Father would say of a morning, looking out at the whitened barn roof. "This one will make the shoats[3] squeal."

A fire snapped all day in our cookstove and another in the stone fireplace in the living room, but still the farmhouse was never warm. The leafless woods were bleak and empty, and I spoke of that to Father when I came back from my search.

"It's always a sad time in the woods when the seven sleepers are under cover," he said.

"What sleepers are they?" I asked. Father was full of woods lore.

"Why, all the animals that have got sense enough to hole up and stay hid in weather like this. Let's see, how was it the old rhyme named them?

Surly bear and sooty bat,
Brown chuck and masked coon,
Chippy-munk and sly skunk,
And all the mouses
'Cept in men's houses.

"And man would have joined them and made it eight, Granther Yeary always said, if he'd had a little more sense."

"I was wondering if the red fox mightn't make it eight," Mom said.

Father shook his head. "Late winter's a high time for foxes. Time when they're out deviling, not sleeping."

My chest felt hollow. I wanted to cry like Colin over our lost fox, but at fourteen a boy doesn't cry. Colin had squatted down on the floor and got out his small hammer and nails to start another new frame for a new picture. Maybe then he'd make a drawing for the frame and be able to forget his misery. It had been that way with him since he was five.

I thought of the new dress Mom had brought home a few days before in a heavy cardboard box. That box cover would be fine for Colin to draw on. I spoke of it, and Mom's glance thanked me as she went to get it. She and I worried a lot about Colin. He was small for his age, delicate and blond, his hair much lighter and softer than mine, his eyes deep and wide and blue. He was often sick, and I knew the fear Mom had that he might be predestined.[4] I'm just ordinary, like Father. I'm the sort of stuff that can take it—tough and strong—but Colin was always sort of special.

Mom lighted the lamp. Colin began cutting his white cardboard carefully, fitting it into his frame. Father's sharp glance turned on him now and again.

"There goes the boy making another frame before there's a picture for it," he said. "It's too much like cutting out a man's suit for a fellow that's say, twelve years old. Who knows whether he'll grow into it?"

Mom was into him then, quick. "Not a single frame of Colin's has ever gone to waste. The boy has real talent, Sumter, and it's time you realized it."

"Of course he has," Father said. "All kids have 'em. But they get over 'em."

"It isn't the pox we're talking of," Mom sniffed.

"In a way it is. Ever since you started talking up Colin's art, I've had an invalid for help around the place."

Father wasn't as hard as he made out, I knew, but he had to hold a balance against all Mom's frothing. For him the thing was the land and all that pertained[5] to it. I was following in Father's footsteps, true to form, but

---

3. **shoat** (shōt), a young pig that no longer nurses.
4. **predestined** (prē des′tənd), *adj.* having one's fate determined beforehand. (In this case, Colin's mother may be worried that he is predestined to die young.)
5. **pertain** (pər tān′), *v.* have to do with; be related.

Colin threatened to break the family tradition with his leaning toward art, with Mom "aiding and abetting him," as Father liked to put it. For the past two years she had had dreams of my brother becoming a real artist and going away to the city to study.

I haven't the words to tell you what the fox meant to us.

It wasn't that Father had no understanding of such things. I could remember, through the years, Colin lying on his stomach in the front room making pencil sketches, and how a good drawing would catch Father's eye halfway across the room, and how he would sometimes gather up two or three of them to study, frowning and muttering, one hand in his beard, while a great pride rose in Colin, and in me too. Most of Colin's drawings were of the woods and wild things, and there Father was a master critic. He made out to scorn what seemed to him a passive[6] "white-livered" interpretation of nature through brush and pencil instead of rod and rifle.

At supper that night Colin could scarcely eat. Ever since he'd been able to walk, my brother had had a growing love of wild things, but Bandit had been like his very own, a gift of the woods. One afternoon a year and a half before, Father and Laban Small had been running a vixen[7] through the hills with their dogs. With the last of her strength the she-fox had made for her den, not far from our house. The dogs had overtaken her and killed her just before she reached it. When Father and Laban came up, they'd found Colin crouched nearby holding her cub in his arms.

Father had been for killing the cub, which was still too young to shift for itself, but Colin's grief had brought Mom into it. We'd taken the young fox into the kitchen, all of us, except Father, gone a bit silly over the little thing. Colin had held it in his arms and fed it warm milk from a spoon.

"Watch out with all your soft ways," Father had warned, standing in the doorway. "You'll make too much of him. Remember, you can't make a dog out of a fox. Half of that little critter has to love, but the other half is a wild hunter. You boys will mean a whole lot to him while he's kit, but there'll come a day when you won't mean a thing to him and he'll leave you shorn."

For two weeks after that Colin had nursed the cub, weaning it from milk to bits of meat. For a year they were always together. The cub grew fast. It was soon following Colin and me about the barnyard. It turned out to be a patch fox, with a saddle of darker fur across its shoulders.

I haven't the words to tell you what the fox meant to us. It was far more wonderful owning him than owning any dog. There was something rare and secret like the spirit of the woods about him, and back of his calm, straw-gold eyes was the sense of a brain the equal of a man's. The fox became Colin's whole life.

Each day, going and coming from school, Colin and I took long side trips through the woods, looking for Bandit. Wild things' memories were short, we knew; we'd have to find him soon or the old bond would be broken.

Ever since I was ten I'd been allowed to hunt with Father, so I was good at reading signs. But, in a way, Colin knew more about the woods and wild things than Father or me. What came to me from long observation, Colin seemed to know by instinct.

It was Colin who felt out, like an Indian,

---

6. **passive** (pas′iv), *adj.* not active; being inactive.

7. **vixen,** a female fox.

▲ Swedish painter Bruno Liljefors painted foxes with the same sensitivity that Colin showed for them. If this fox could speak, what do you think it would say?

the stretch of woods where Bandit had his den, who found the first slim, small fox-print in the damp earth. And then, on an afternoon in March, we saw him. I remember the day well, racing clouds, the wind rattling the tops of the pine trees and swaying the Spanish moss.[8] Bandit had just come out of a clump of laurel; in the maze of leaves behind him we caught a glimpse of a slim red vixen, so we knew he had found a mate. She melted from sight like a shadow, but Bandit turned to

watch us, his mouth open, his tongue lolling as he smiled his old foxy smile. On his thin chops, I saw a telltale chicken feather.

Colin moved silently forward, his movements so quiet and casual he seemed to be standing still. He called Bandit's name, and the fox held his ground, drawn to us with all his senses. For a few moments he let Colin

_____

8. **Spanish moss,** a mosslike plant that grows on certain trees, hanging from branches in gray streamers.

actually put an arm about him. It was then I knew that he loved us still, for all of Father's warnings. He really loved us back, with a fierce, secret love no tame thing ever gave. But the urge of his life just then was toward his new mate. Suddenly, he whirled about and disappeared in the laurels.

Colin looked at me with glowing eyes. "We haven't really lost him, Stan. When he gets through with his spring sparking he may come back. But we've got to show ourselves to him a lot, so he won't forget."

"It's a go," I said.

"Promise not to say a word to Father," Colin said, and I agreed. For I knew by the chicken feather that Bandit had been up to no good.

A week later the woods were budding and the thickets were rustling with all manner of wild things scurrying on the love scent. Colin managed to get a glimpse of Bandit every few days. He couldn't get close though, for the spring running was a lot more important to a fox than any human beings were.

Every now and then Colin got out his framed box cover and looked at it, but he never drew anything on it; he never even picked up his pencil. I remember wondering if what Father had said about framing a picture before you had one had spoiled something for him.

I was helping Father with the planting now, but Colin managed to be in the woods every day. By degrees he learned Bandit's range, where he drank and rested and where he was likely to be according to the time of day. One day he told me how he had petted Bandit again, and how they had walked together a long way in the woods. All this time we had kept his secret from Father.

As summer came on, Bandit began to live up to the prediction Father had made. Accustomed to human beings he moved without fear about the scattered farms of the region, raiding barns and hen runs that other foxes wouldn't have dared go near. And he taught his wild mate to do the same. Almost every night they got into some poultry house, and by late June Bandit was not only killing chickens and ducks but feeding on eggs and young chicks whenever he got the chance.

Stories of his doings came to us from many sources, for he was still easily recognized by the dark patch on his shoulders. Many a farmer took a shot at him as he fled and some of them set out on his trail with dogs, but they always returned home without even sighting him. Bandit was familiar with all the dogs in the region, and he knew a hundred tricks to confound[9] them. He got a reputation that year beyond that of any fox our hills had known. His confidence grew, and he gave up wild hunting altogether and lived entirely off the poultry farmers. By September the hill farmers banded together to hunt him down.

It was Father who brought home that news one night. All time-honored rules of the fox chase were to be broken in this hunt; if the dogs couldn't bring Bandit down, he was to be shot on sight. I was stricken and furious. I remember the misery of Colin's face in the lamplight. Father, who took pride in all the ritual[10] of the hunt, had refused to be a party to such an affair, though in justice he could do nothing but sanction[11] any sort of hunt, for Bandit, as old Sam Wetherwax put it, had been "purely getting in the Lord's hair."

The hunt began next morning, and it was the biggest turnout our hills had known. There were at least twenty mounted men in the party and as many dogs. Father and I were working in the lower field as they passed along the river road. Most of the hunters carried rifles, and they looked ugly.

Twice during the morning I went up to the house to find Colin, but he was nowhere

9. **confound** (kon found'), *v.* confuse; mix up.
10. **ritual** (rich'ü əl), ceremony.
11. **sanction** (sangk'shən), approve or allow.

around. As we worked, Father and I could follow the progress of the hunt by the distant hound music on the breeze. We could tell just where the hunters first caught sight of the fox and where Bandit was leading the dogs during the first hour. We knew as well as if we'd seen it how Bandit roused another fox along Turkey Branch and forced it to run for him, and how the dogs swept after it for twenty minutes before they sensed their mistake.

Noon came, and Colin had not come in to eat. After dinner Father didn't go back to the field. He moped about, listening to the hound talk. He didn't like what was on any more than I did, and now and again I caught his smile of satisfaction when we heard the broken, angry notes of the hunting horn, telling that the dogs had lost the trail or had run another fox.

I was restless and I went up into the hills in midafternoon. I ranged the woods for miles, thinking all the time of Colin. Time lost all meaning for me, and the short day was nearing an end, when I heard the horn talking again, telling that the fox had put over another trick. All day he had deviled the dogs and mocked the hunters. This new trick and the coming night would work to save him. I was wildly glad, as I moved down toward Turkey Branch and stood listening for a time by the deep, shaded pool where for years we boys had gone swimming, sailed boats, and dreamed summer dreams.

Suddenly, out of the corner of my eye, I saw the sharp ears and thin, pointed mask of a fox—in the water almost beneath me. It was Bandit, craftily submerged[12] there, all but his head, resting in the cool water of the pool and the shadow of the two big beeches that spread above it. He must have run forty miles or more since morning. And he must have hidden in this place before. His knowing, crafty mask blended perfectly with the shadows and a mass of drift and branches that had collected by the bank of the pool. He was so still that a pair of thrushes flew up from the spot as I came up, not knowing he was there.

Bandit's bright, harried[13] eyes were looking right at me. But I did not look at him direct. Some woods instinct, swifter than thought, kept me from it. So he and I met as in another world, indirectly, with feeling but without sign or greeting.

There was magic in it, as if by will we wove a web of protection about the fox, . . .

Suddenly I saw that Colin was standing almost beside me. Silently as a water snake, he had come out of the bushes and stood there. Our eyes met, and a quick and secret smile passed between us. It was a rare moment in which I really "met" my brother, when something of his essence[14] flowed into me and I knew all of him. I've never lost it since.

My eyes still turned from the fox, my heart pounding. I moved quietly away, and Colin moved with me. We whistled softly as we went, pretending to busy ourselves along the bank of the stream. There was magic in it, as if by will we wove a web of protection about the fox, a ring-pass-not that none might penetrate.[15] It was so, too, we felt, in the brain of Bandit, and that doubled the charm. To us he was still our little pet that we had carried

12. **submerge** (səb mėrj′), v. cover with water.
13. **harried** (har′ēd), adj. worried.
14. **essence** (es′ns), that which makes a thing what it is.
15. **penetrate** (pen′ə trāt), v. enter into or pass through.

about in our arms on countless summer afternoons.

Two hundred yards upstream, we stopped beside slim, fresh tracks in the mud where Bandit had entered the branch. The tracks angled upstream. But in the water the wily creature had turned down.

We climbed the far bank to wait, and Colin told me how Bandit's secret had been his secret ever since an afternoon three months before, when he'd watched the fox swim downstream to hide in the deep pool. Today he'd waited on the bank, feeling that Bandit, hard pressed by the dogs, might again seek the pool for sanctuary.

We looked back once as we turned homeward. He still had not moved. We didn't know until later that he was killed that same night by a chance hunter, as he crept out from his hiding place.

That evening Colin worked a long time on his framed boxcover that had lain about the house untouched all summer. He kept at it all the next day too. I had never seen him work so hard. I seemed to sense in the air the feeling he was putting into it, how he was *believing* his picture into being. It was evening before he finished it. Without a word he handed it to Father. Mom and I went and looked over his shoulder.

It was a delicate and intricate[16] pencil drawing of the deep branch pool, and there was Bandit's head and watching, fear-filled eyes hiding there amid the leaves and shadows, woven craftily into the maze of twigs and branches, as if by nature's art itself. Hardly a fox there at all, but the place where he was—or should have been. I recognized it instantly, but Mom gave a sort of incredulous[17] sniff.

"I'll declare," she said, "it's mazy as a puzzle. It just looks like a lot of sticks and leaves to me."

Long minutes of study passed before Father's eye picked out the picture's secret, as few men's could have done. I laid that to Father's being a born hunter. That was a picture that might have been done especially for him. In fact, I guess it was.

Finally he turned to Colin with his deep, slow smile. "So that's how Bandit fooled them all," he said. He sat holding the picture with a sort of tenderness for a long time, while we glowed in the warmth of the shared secret. That was Colin's moment. Colin's art stopped being a pox to Father right there. And later, when the time came for Colin to go to art school, it was Father who was his solid backer.

---

16. intricate (in′trə kit), *adj.* with many twists or turns; entangled or complicated.
17. incredulous (in krej′ə ləs), *adj.* not ready to believe; doubting.

After Reading

Making Connections

1. With which character did you sympathize most? Explain.

2. How do you think Stan and Colin differ from each other? Use a diagram such as the one below to compare and contrast the two boys. Qualities that belong only to Stan go in one circle, those that belong only to Colin go in the other. Place shared qualities in the overlapping space in the middle.

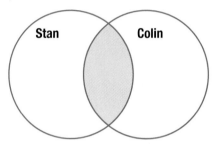

3. Early in the story the boys choose to keep a wild pet even though their father warns them against it. List the consequences of that choice for Stan and Colin, for their parents, for the community, and for the fox.

4. ☝ Show through examples the **changes** in Father's attitude toward Colin during the story.

5. How would this story differ if told from Father's **point of view?**

6. Is hunting the best way to control wild animal populations? Why or why not? If not, what are some alternatives?

7. Do you think wild animals have rights? If so, what are they?

Literary Focus: Flashback

An author may begin a story at an interesting moment and then fill in background information with a **flashback.** Flashbacks interrupt with a scene that occurred earlier. You can recognize flashbacks by looking for time words that signal an earlier event. In this story the flashback begins, "One afternoon a year and a half before. . . ."

Refer to the time line that you created as you read, or skim back over the story, paying attention to the order of events. Ask yourself: Why does the author begin the story after the fox disappears instead of when the boys find it? How else could the author have presented the information in the flashback? How would the story change if the flashback were left out entirely?

Vocabulary Study

Write *S* for synonym or *A* for antonym on your paper to show how these word pairs are related.

incurable
predestined
pertain
passive
confound
submerge
harried
penetrate
intricate
incredulous

1. predestined—fated
2. passive—active
3. confound—confuse
4. harried—calm
5. penetrate—pierce
6. incredulous—unbelieving
7. intricate—simple
8. incurable—curable
9. pertain—belong
10. submerge—sink

Expressing Your Ideas _____

Writing Choices

Respectfully Yours In this story, Stan respects and admires Colin's talents, even though the two brothers are very different. Write a **personal narrative** about someone you respect and admire who is not at all like you. Explain how you are different, what you admire about the other person, and why.

Petition Power Imagine that the fox hunt in this story were about to happen in your community and that you object to it. Write a **petition** to stop the fox hunt. You will need a statement that says what you are protesting, why, and what you want done about it. Have those in class who agree sign the petition.

Wild and Woolly Wild foxes do not make good pets for the reasons given in this story. Is there a wild animal you'd like to keep for a pet? Research that animal to determine whether or not it would make a good pet. Write a **report** on what you find out.

Other Options

Frame It In the story Colin finds comfort in making frames and drawing pictures to put in them. Use wood, cardboard, craft sticks, or other materials to create a **frame** and then **draw** a picture that you think might be like those Colin created.

Take a Vote If you had been a farmer in Stan's community, how would you have handled the fox problem? Hold a **town meeting** in your class to discuss it. You will need to appoint or elect a chairperson to conduct the meeting and a secretary to record it.

What Do You Think? Find out what your classmates think about hunting, land owner's rights, and animal rights by conducting a **survey.** Draw up five to eight questions that can be answered yes or no. Be as specific as possible in each question. Then poll your classmates on their opinions and tabulate the results to present to the class.

Before Reading

A Letter to God by Gregorio López y Fuentes
Almost Perfect by Shel Silverstein

Gregorio López y Fuentes
1895–1966

Born in an old hacienda in the state of Veracruz, López based much of his writing on the drama and folklore of the country people who shared his Mexican homeland. As in this selection, he often wrote about his neighbors with sympathy and humor.

Shel Silverstein
born 1932

"I would hope that people, no matter what age, would find something to identify with in my books," Silverstein says. He started to write and draw as a young teenager because he wasn't good at sports or popular with girls. He has worked as a cartoonist, folk singer, songwriter, and playwright.

Building Background

Universal Themes The story "A Letter to God" is about a Mexican farmer. The poem that follows it is about an American woman. The cultural differences between the two selections add interest. The similarities between the two main characters, however, are more striking than the differences. Both share traits, or characteristics, that are common to human beings everywhere.

Getting into the Selections

Writer's Notebook The two main characters in these selections have a certain outlook that colors their lives. In your notebook describe how you usually see the world. Do you see it from the bright or the dark side? Can you recall a time you had to make the best out of a bad situation? How did you handle it? Did your choice affect the outcome?

Reading Tip

Comparison and Contrast Looking for similarities and differences in selections will help you better understand the readings and form opinions about them. Use a chart such as the one below to compare and contrast Lencho from "A Letter to God" and Mary Hume from "Almost Perfect." Add other traits as you read.

Trait	Lencho	Mary
Seeks perfection	✔	✔
Stubborn		

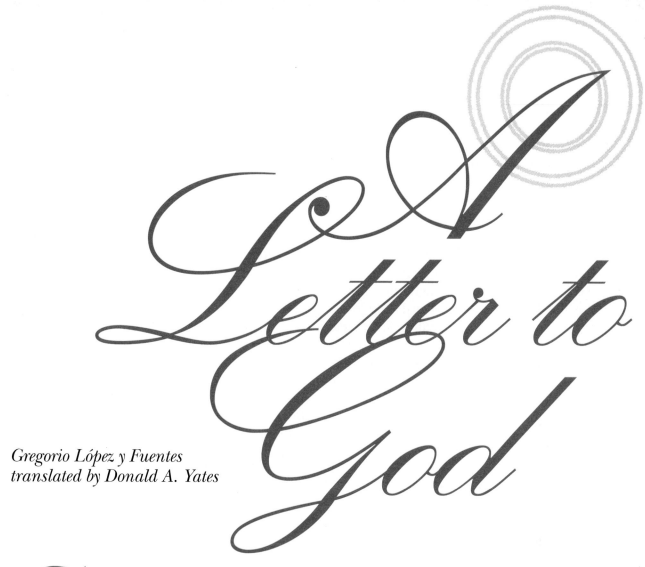

A Letter to God

Gregorio López y Fuentes
translated by Donald A. Yates

The house—the only one in the entire valley—sat on the crest of a low hill. From this height one could see the river and, next to the corral, the field of ripe corn dotted with the kidney bean flowers that always promised a good harvest.

The only thing the earth needed was a rainfall, or at least a shower. Throughout the morning Lencho—who knew his fields intimately[1]—had done nothing else but scan the sky toward the northeast.

"Now we're really going to get some water, woman."

The woman, who was preparing supper, replied:

"Yes, God willing."

The oldest boys were working in the field, while the smaller ones were playing near the house, until the woman called to them all:

"Come for dinner. . . ."

It was during the meal that, just as Lencho had predicted, big drops of rain began to fall. In the northeast huge mountains of clouds could be seen approaching. The air was fresh and sweet.

The man went out to look for something in the corral for no other reason than to allow himself the pleasure of feeling the rain on his body, and when he returned he exclaimed:

"Those aren't raindrops falling from the

---

1. **intimately** (in′tə mit lē), *adv.* closely; very well.

sky, they're new coins. The big drops are ten-*centavo*[2] pieces and the little ones are fives. . . ."

With a satisfied expression he regarded the field of ripe corn with its kidney bean flowers, draped in a curtain of rain. But suddenly a strong wind began to blow and together with the rain very large hailstones began to fall. These truly did resemble new silver coins. The boys, exposing themselves to the rain, ran out to collect the frozen pearls.

"It's really getting bad now," exclaimed the man, mortified.[3] "I hope it passes quickly."

It did not pass quickly. For an hour the hail rained on the house, the garden, the hillside, the cornfield, on the whole valley. The field was white, as if covered with salt. Not a leaf remained on the trees. The corn was totally destroyed. The flowers were gone from the kidney bean plants. Lencho's soul was filled with sadness. When the storm had passed, he stood in the middle of the field and said to his sons:

"A plague[4] of locusts would have left more than this. . . . The hail has left nothing: this year we will have no corn or beans. . . ."

That night was a sorrowful one:

"All our work, for nothing!"

"There's no one who can help us!"

"We'll all go hungry this year. . . ."

But in the hearts of all who lived in that solitary[5] house in the middle of the valley, there was a single hope: help from God.

"Don't be so upset, even though this seems like a total loss. Remember, no one dies of hunger!"

"That's what they say: no one dies of hunger. . . ."

All through the night, Lencho thought only of his one hope: the help of God, whose eyes, as he had been instructed, see everything, even what is deep in one's conscience.

Lencho was an ox of a man, working like an animal in the fields, but still he knew how to write. The following Sunday, at daybreak, after having convinced himself that there is a protecting spirit, he began to write a letter which he himself would carry to town and place in the mail.

It was nothing less than a letter to God.

"God," he wrote, "if you don't help me, my family and I will go hungry this year. I need a hundred *pesos*[6] in order to resow the field and to live until the crop comes, because the hailstorm. . . ."

He wrote "To God" on the envelope, put the letter inside and, still troubled, went to town. At the post office he placed a stamp on the letter and dropped it into the mailbox.

One of the employees, who was a postman and also helped at the post office, went to his boss laughing heartily and showed him the letter to God. Never in his career as a postman had he known that address. The postmaster—a fat, amiable[7] fellow—also broke out laughing, but almost immediately he turned serious and, tapping the letter on his desk, commented:

"What faith! I wish I had the faith of the man who wrote this letter. To believe the way he believes. To hope with the confidence that he knows how to hope with. Starting up a correspondence with God!"

So, in order not to disillusion[8] that prodigy[9] of faith, revealed by a letter that could not be delivered, the postmaster came up with an idea: answer the letter. But when he opened it, it was evident that to answer it he needed something more than good will,

---

2. **centavo** (sen tä′vō), a coin used in some Latin American countries.
3. **mortified** (môr′tə fīd), *adj.* ashamed; humiliated.
4. **plague** (plāg), *n.* widespread trouble or calamity.
5. **solitary** (sol′ə ter′ē), *adj.* away from people; lonely.
6. **peso** (pā′sō), a unit of money in some Latin American countries.
7. **amiable** (ā′mē ə bəl), *adj.* pleasant; agreeable.
8. **disillusion** (dis′i lü′zhən), *v.* set free from false ideas; disenchant.
9. **prodigy** (prod′ə jē), *n.* marvel or wonder.

Campesino con Yunta de Bueyes (*Farmer with Yoked Oxen*) is a wood carving by Mardonio Magana, sculpted in 1928. What does this simple sculpture reveal about the farmer?

ink and paper. But he stuck to his resolution:[10] he asked for money from his employee, he himself gave part of his salary, and several friends of his were obliged to give something "for an act of charity."

It was impossible for him to gather together the hundred *pesos* requested by Lencho, so he was able to send the farmer only a little more than half. He put the bills in an envelope addressed to Lencho and with them a letter containing only a single word as a signature: GOD.

The following Sunday Lencho came a bit earlier than usual to ask if there was a letter for him. It was the postman himself who handed the letter to him, while the postmaster, experiencing the contentment of a man who has performed a good deed, looked on from the doorway of his office.

Lencho showed not the slightest surprise on seeing the bills—such was his confidence—but he became angry when he counted the money . . . God could not have made a mistake, nor could he have denied Lencho what he had requested!

Immediately, Lencho went up to the window to ask for paper and ink. On the public writing table, he started in to write, with much wrinkling of his brow, caused by the effort he had to make to express his ideas. When he finished, he went to the window to buy a stamp which he licked and then affixed[11] to the envelope with a blow of his fist.

The moment that the letter fell into the mailbox, the postmaster went to open it. It said:

"God: of the money that I asked for, only seventy *pesos* reached me. Send me the rest, since I need it very much. But don't send it to me through the mail, because the post office employees are a bunch of crooks. Lencho."

---

10. **resolution** (rez′ə lü′shən), *n.* something decided on.
11. **affix** (ə fiks′), *v.* stick on; fasten; attach.

Almost Perfect

Shel Silverstein

"Almost perfect . . . but not quite."
Those were the words of Mary Hume
At her seventh birthday party,
Looking 'round the ribboned room.
5 "This tablecloth is *pink* not *white*—
Almost perfect . . . but not quite."

"Almost perfect . . . but not quite."
Those were the words of grown-up Mary
Talking about her handsome beau,[1]
10 The one she wasn't gonna marry.
"Squeezes me a bit too tight—
Almost perfect . . . but not quite."

"Almost perfect . . . but not quite."
Those were the words of ol' Miss Hume
15 Teaching in the seventh grade,
Grading papers in the gloom
Late at night up in her room.
"They never cross their t's just right—
Almost perfect . . . but not quite."

20 Ninety-eight the day she died
Complainin' 'bout the spotless floor.
People shook their heads and sighed,
"Guess that she'll like heaven more."
Up went her soul on feathered wings,
25 Out the door, up out of sight.
Another voice from heaven came—
"Almost perfect . . . but not quite."

---

1. **beau** (bō), *n.* a young man courting a young woman.

After Reading

Making Connections

1. If Lencho and Mary Hume were your neighbors, which would you get along with better? Why?

2. Give Lencho and Mary grades on their report cards in citizenship and study skills. Choose at least five areas to grade, such as "stays on task," "works well with others," or "class participation."

3. Why do you think the author waits until the end of the story to reveal certain things about Lencho's **character?**

4. The author writes that Lencho "regarded the field. . . draped in a curtain of rain." Explain what this **metaphor** describes.

5. Look back over the poem and pick out a repeated phrase. Why does the author use it over and over? How does **repetition** affect the message of the poem?

6. What do you think would happen next in the story if the postmaster decided to confront Lencho with the truth?

7. Compare your view of the world to those of the main characters in the story and poem. Are you more or less demanding? Which approach is more likely to help one get along in the world?

Literary Focus: Irony

You can appreciate the **irony** in these selections if you compare a logical prediction of how they will end with the actual outcome. In "A Letter to God," the events, dialogue, and character descriptions lead you to believe that Lencho will be thrilled when he receives his money. How does he actually feel? The irony, or unexpected twist, at the end reveals something about Lencho's character. How does it change the mood of the story?

In his poem "Almost Perfect," Shel Silverstein uses irony to create humor in a similar way. How would you expect a person to feel on arriving in heaven? How do you think Mary Hume feels? How does her reception by "another voice from heaven" affect the mood of the poem?

Vocabulary Study

Write the letter of the most likely answer on your paper.

intimately
mortified
plague
solitary
amiable
disillusion
prodigy
resolution
affix
beau

1. Who would you expect to converse **intimately? a.** a husband and wife **b.** a bank teller and customer **c.** a student and principal.

2. You might eat a **solitary** meal if you were **a.** with friends. **b.** dieting to lose weight. **c.** at home alone.

3. If your uncle is **amiable,** he might **a.** buy you an ice cream cone. **b.** forget your birthday. **c.** have few friends.

4. Making a **resolution** might help you **a.** find a lost item. **b.** break a bad habit. **c.** guess the number of beans in a jar.

5. You would be **mortified** if **a.** you won a card game. **b.** you ripped the seat of your pants. **c.** your favorite TV star called on the phone.

6. You would be a **prodigy** if you **a.** placed third in the 50-yard dash. **b.** failed to lift the heaviest weight at the Olympics. **c.** composed a symphony at the age of eight.

7. What would you **affix? a.** a sticker **b.** an apple pie **c.** a shoelace

8. You might look for a **beau a.** at a store ribbon counter. **b.** at a community dance. **c.** in your best friend's closet.

9. Which of the following might **disillusion** you? **a.** going to see a good movie **b.** finding that a friend lied **c.** passing your final math exam

10. If your community experienced a **plague,** it would cause **a.** great hardship. **b.** great joy. **c.** great relief.

Expressing Your Ideas

Writing Choices

Genre Swap Why do authors choose a particular genre, or kind of writing? See if you can rewrite Lencho's story as a **poem** or describe Mary's problem in a **short story.**

Eyes on Irony Choose a favorite or well-known story and use irony to rewrite the ending. Begin just before the point where you will make changes.

Other Options

Raise Your Voices Work with a small group to practice "Almost Perfect" as a **choral reading.** Assign solo and group parts and add actions and sound effects. Put on your choral reading for the class.

Illustrate an Image Look through "A Letter to God" and choose a favorite metaphor or other image. **Draw** the image as you imagine it in the story.

Before Reading

Nate "Tiny" Archibald

by Bill Littlefield

Bill Littlefield
born 1948

When he's not commenting on sports for National Public Radio or hosting his show, "Only a Game," Bill Littlefield teaches English and writing courses at Curry College in Massachusetts. *Champions,* his book for young adults, portrays ten notable athletes who led interesting and productive lives outside of their sports careers. Littlefield notes, "*Champions* in this title has a rather wider meaning than someone who wins a gold medal or pitches the final game of the World Series." He decided to include Tiny Archibald's story because of the new challenges the basketball player took on when his sports career ended.

Building Background

The Game of Basketball The first basketball game was played more than one hundred years ago when a gym teacher hooked a peach basket to the balconies at either end of a gym and invited students to shoot balls into it. Hundreds of people sometimes played in one game. Today, basketball teams have five members: two forwards to shoot baskets and catch rebounds, a center, often positioned near the basket, and two guards who take the ball down the court and set up plays.

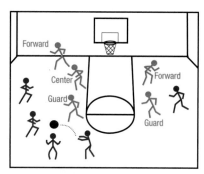

Getting into the Selection

Writer's Notebook "Nate 'Tiny' Archibald" is a true story about a man who was determined to succeed at basketball despite setbacks. In your notebook write about a time you wanted (or still want) to do something so badly you wouldn't give up. What did you want? What problems did you encounter? How did you feel about the outcome? As you read, look for times Tiny Archibald could have given up, but didn't.

Reading Tip

Basketball Jargon Like every sport, basketball has specialized words, or **jargon**, that describe the playing positions, court, plays, and other aspects of the game. When you come across sports jargon in a story, first try using context clues. When you read that Tiny was practicing basketball and "popped jump shots," you may not understand exactly what he was doing, but you know from the context it's some kind of basketball play. If this is enough information, you could keep going. Sometimes context does not explain enough, and you need to look up a word or phrase. Look for the word first in a regular dictionary, then in a sports dictionary or reference book.

Nate "Tiny" Archibald

Bill Littlefield

A lot of men who played on the same teams as Nate "Tiny" Archibald will tell you that he never said much. That's a peculiar quality in a game much given to woofing, trash-talking, and one-upsmanship by mouth, but Tiny never seemed to have time for that segment of basketball. He was too busy cutting by men who were ten inches taller than he was, or stealing the ball, or popping it in from thirty feet as the buzzer sounded. And even when the season was over there was no leisure for talk. Because then it was time to go back to the playgrounds and teach the game to everyone who was willing to work all day long to learn it.

Like countless city kids, Tiny Archibald grew up dreaming of playing pro basketball. It's a low-percentage dream. There are so few jobs in the National Basketball Association,

◄ This contemporary photograph by E. H. Wallop uses an interesting perspective. Why do you think the picture was shot this way rather than straight-on or looking up at the players?

and so many hungry applicants. Even boys who grow up in ghettos where the schools are third rate have a far better chance to become doctors or lawyers than they do to compete in the NBA. And even the ones who make it to the pros often have careers that last only a few years.

He'd practice dribbling ... so that he didn't have to notice the garbage and wrecked cars in the streets.

But the logic of numbers couldn't compete with the glamour of the dream for the young Archibald, who early on inherited the nickname "Tiny" from his father. Tiny wanted to play the game he loved against the very best. And he coupled his dream with a dedication that few of his fellow ballplayers could match. Even his mother was astonished by Tiny's determination and by the way it drove his concentration on the game. "It's just as though he was in a cave, and all that was in the cave was a basketball and a hoop," she told John Devaney, who wrote a book about Tiny years later.

In his cave, Tiny was focused and safe. As a little boy in the South Bronx, he played basketball each day after school. If the gym was open, he played indoors as long as there were ten guys there to make up two teams. After everybody else went home, Tiny stayed around and popped jump shots by himself until the janitor told him it was time to lock up. Then he went outside and fired away at the basket on the asphalt court outside. The rim was bent and somebody had stolen the net, but it was still a basket. Tiny would practice until it was too dark to see whether his shots were going in or not. Then he'd dribble the ball he'd borrowed from the coach all the way home. He'd practice dribbling behind his back and between his legs, moves that required concentration enough so that he

didn't have to notice the garbage and wrecked cars in the streets. With a basketball in his hands, he could pretend not to hear the youngsters who were calling to him to come over and share the wine they were drinking or the drugs they wanted him to try. The street life of the South Bronx had no place in Tiny Archibald's cave.

Early in his high school career, though, there came a point where dedication to basketball and an insatiable[1] appetite to practice the game seemed to have carried Archibald as far as they could. He came home from school one evening to learn that his father had departed the premises, which meant that even the spotty income he'd been providing was gone. There wasn't much room for economizing.[2] Already Tiny and his three brothers were crowded into one room. His mother and Tiny's three sisters shared the other one.

Tiny had never been much of a student, and when his father deserted the family, the little interest Tiny'd had in academics vanished entirely. At the end of the semester, he'd flunked so many courses that he was no longer eligible to play basketball. When he learned that he'd lose his spot on the team until his grades improved, he went to his coach, Floyd Lane, and told him he was quitting.

"What? Because of the grades?" Lane asked. "Don't be a jerk. Hit the books. Get the grades back up. There'll be a place for you when you do."

"Nah," Tiny told him. "I'm quittin' school, too. I gotta find a job, help support my family."

Floyd Lane had heard that song before, but it broke his heart to hear it from Tiny. "What are you gonna do?" he barked. "Wait tables? You gonna wash dishes?"

---

1. **insatiable** (in sā′shə bəl), *adj.* not able to be satisfied.
2. **economize** (i kon′ə mīz), *v.* cut down expenses.

"Whatever I can find," Tiny said with a shrug.

"I'll tell you what you can find," Lane said. "You can find a whole lot better job if you pay attention to what you gotta do here at school, then get yourself back on this basketball team. We'll get some college coaches in here lookin' you fellas over, handing out some scholarships, and you won't be here to show 'em what you can do if you're elbow deep in suds somewhere."

"I don't know . . ." Tiny muttered.

"Listen to me," Lane demanded. "You remember the day you first tried out for the team?"

"Me and about nine thousand other guys, all of 'em good players." Tiny smiled.

"Sure," said Lane. "And I told you to drive to the basket, show me how you drive, and you did, and I said it was all wrong."

"Yeah," Tiny said. "You said I was out of control."

"And you did it again, and again after that. And I said, 'No! No! No!' And the next thing I know, you're going right out of the building."

"I almost didn't come back," Tiny said.

"But you *did* come back, didn't you? And then you remember that day that summer I had those fellas from the Knicks in here? You didn't much like that, either."

"I couldn't see how I'd ever play against guys like that," Tiny said. "I could play against the best on the playgrounds, but those guys looked like they were ten feet tall."

"And you wondered what all you were workin' at then, didn't you? And I told you then. And I'm tellin' you again now. Maybe you'll make it to the NBA, and maybe you won't. It's not impossible. There's fellas six foot or so, just like you, who have made it before. But you leave this team and this school, you won't make it ever. And if you stay, if you tough this out, you may get a chance to go to college on a basketball scholarship. You take advantage of that, and even if you don't

ever play a day as a pro, you'll have *something.* You'll have a college degree. And you'll have a better job than dishwasher and a lot more ways to help your family, too."

Tiny Archibald had never been much of a talker, but that day, fortunately for him, he was a good listener. He took Floyd Lane's advice. He survived a semester without basketball and improved his grades. Then he rejoined the team. And when Don Haskins, then the basketball coach at Texas Western University (now the University of Texas at El Paso) stopped by to see whether his old pal Floyd Lane had any players worth recruiting, Tiny Archibald was the one who caught his eye.

Because he never grew to be taller than six feet one, Tiny Archibald should have been at a serious disadvantage in a game dominated by giant centers and wide-body forwards—a game in which even the guards were often six four or six five. But he compensated[3] by developing the ability to make everyone on his team a better player. This is a curious talent shared by some of basketball's best players: the Isiah Thomases,[4] Larry Birds,[5] and Magic Johnsons.[6] Their passes are so precise they make the players who catch them look as if they are exactly where they are supposed to be. They expect so much from their teammates that their teammates find themselves delivering more than they knew they had. Tiny Archibald made himself that kind of player in college at Texas Western University. Perhaps because he'd worked for all those hours in the gym

---

3. **compensate** (kom′pən sāt), *v.* balance; make up for.
4. **Isiah Thomas,** a star guard for the Detroit Pistons.
5. **Larry Bird,** a 6 foot 9 inch player who helped propel the Boston Celtics into championships in the early 1980s.
6. **Magic Johnson,** a Los Angeles Laker star who retired in 1991 when he learned he was infected with the virus that causes AIDS.

Nate "Tiny" Archibald   **137**

and on the playgrounds at home, he discovered that he had developed the remarkable knack of doing whatever his team needed done. He could score when he had to, and led his conference[7] in scoring. But he could get the ball to his teammates as well as any guard in the country, and he ran the team with confidence and imagination.

Bob Cousy, formerly a brilliant guard with the Celtics and coach of the Cincinnati Royals during Tiny's senior year in college, had heard plenty about the Texas Western guard. Though he'd never seen Tiny play, Cousy chose him in the second round of the 1970 NBA draft. A few weeks after the draft, Coach Cousy was in New York on business and called Tiny, who was visiting his family in the Bronx. How would Tiny like to stop by Cousy's hotel room so the coach could get a look at him?

"Sure," Tiny said.

"I knew he was little, but I didn't know he was that little."

A while later Cousy heard a knock at his door. When he opened it, his jaw dropped a foot. "Geez," he told his coaching staff when he'd returned to Cincinnati, "I knew he was little, but I didn't know he was *that* little. Or that skinny. Or that baby-faced. I thought he was the bellhop."

Bob Cousy wasn't the only man who had trouble believing Tiny Archibald really belonged in the NBA, at least at the outset. The first time Tiny's team came into New York's Madison Square Garden to play the Knicks, Tiny didn't arrive with his teammates. He'd stopped off to visit his brothers and sisters, and he came downtown to the Garden by himself. The usher at the players' gate wouldn't let him in, figuring he was just a teenager trying to see the game for free.

"I play for the Royals, sir," Tiny told him,

but the guard just smiled. "Sure, kid. And I'm the shortstop for the Yankees."

Eventually Tiny got the guard to call Coach Cousy in the locker room, or he might have missed his first chance to play in front of folks from his hometown. "Yeah, he's one of my guys," Cousy told the astonished guard, "but I don't blame you for wondering about it. We haven't even got a uniform that fits him yet. His number's stuffed halfway down into his pants."

Tiny Archibald's first few years in the NBA were remarkable on a number of counts. Bob Cousy asked him to "quarterback"[8] the team in his rookie season, and he did the job so well that many were surprised when Tiny was left off the All-Star team. During his second season he *was* an All-Star, though the Royals did not accomplish much as a team. The club's move to Kansas City–Omaha didn't improve it either, but Tiny kept soaring. During the 1972–73 season, he became the only player ever to lead the NBA in both scoring and assists,[9] averaging thirty-four points and eleven assists per game. That year the *Sporting News* voted him Pro Basketball Player of the Year.

During those heady times, lots of things changed for Tiny. He had money to help his family, just as Floyd Lane had predicted he would one day. And it was a good thing. Two of Tiny's brothers had begun using drugs. He sent them money to come to Kansas City and join him, figuring that they'd never make it if they stayed in the South Bronx. Meanwhile Tiny himself commuted back to New York

---

7. **conference** (kon′fər əns), association of athletic teams.
8. **quarterback** (kwôr′tər bak′), call the signals and select plays.
9. **assist**, a basketball play that directly helps a teammate to score.

Nate Archibald demonstrates why he led the NBA in both scoring and assists as he eyes the basket and goes for the score. This photograph of the Celtics star was taken by Jerry Wachter.

wo years later, Tiny led the Kings to their first playoff appearance, and though the team lost early in the so-called "second season," Tiny was proud of the progress the Kings had made. But NBA basketball, like all the professional sports, is a business without much room for loyalty or sentiment.[10] Before the 1976–77 season, Tiny was traded to the New York Nets. A year later he was playing for Buffalo, and a year after that a multiplayer deal took him to the Boston Celtics. None of the three teams were enjoying good seasons in those years, and Tiny Archibald began to wonder if he'd ever experience the thrill of playing for a champion. He'd set records, played in several All-Star games, and been voted Player of the Year, but he'd never helped his team to an NBA championship. In fact, he'd never been close.

His chance came in the 1980–81 season. That year the Celtics, a team that had fallen apart in the late seventies, flanked Tiny with Larry Bird, Robert Parish, and rookie star Kevin McHale. Coach Bill Fitch convinced this group that it could be a contender,[11] and during the regular season the Celts won sixty-two of their eighty-two games. At thirty-two, which is past middle age for an NBA player, Tiny was reborn. He'd lost large parts of two previous years to injuries, but this time around he not only made the All-Star team for the sixth time but he was voted the game's most valuable player. Now there were no more awards to win—save a championship ring—and as the playoffs began, Tiny Archibald found himself concentrating on that goal so hard it hurt.

Tiny scored twenty-seven points and assisted on seven more buckets[12] against the

each spring, as soon as the NBA season was over. "I think every black man who gets out of the ghetto has an obligation to the kids on the block," he told those who wondered why he never took the summers off. He set up playground leagues and funded clinics. He brought NBA players into New York for exhibitions. He sponsored tournaments and set up educational programs. Of the kids he was trying to help he simply said, "If I can get them playing basketball all day, all they're going to feel like doing at night is going home and sleeping."

---

10. **sentiment** (sen′tə mənt), *n.* feeling, especially refined or tender feeling.
11. **contender** (kən tend′ər), *n.* one who takes part in a major contest; competitor.
12. **bucket,** basketball jargon for a basket.

Chicago Bulls in game one of the opening round. The Bulls never recovered. In round two, the Celtics met the Philadelphia 76ers, the club that had knocked them from the playoffs the previous year. The 76ers shocked Boston by winning two of the first three games of the series, and game four nearly ended Tiny Archibald's championship hopes. Down two points with eight seconds to go in the game, Archibald got control of a loose ball but elected not to call time-out. Instead he pushed the ball upcourt and made a bad pass, which Bobby Jones of the 76ers intercepted. With one play that he'd have given anything to call back, Tiny had handed Philadelphia a three-games-to-one advantage—a lead that a team that good was almost impossibly unlikely to lose. If the 76ers finished Boston off with one more win, it wouldn't matter that Tiny had turned in a great season, or that he'd been the MVP[13] in the All-Star game. This time around he'd be remembered as the goat who tossed away the playoffs with a bad decision and a worse pass.

The only person in Boston happier than Archibald himself might have been his wife.

But the Celtics came back. Tiny and his teammates whittled his goat's horns to nothing. In game five Archibald popped in twenty-three points and earned seven assists. With the game still in doubt in the closing seconds, he made the three-point play that clinched[14] a 111–109 win. In game six he calmly sunk two foul shots to put the Celts ahead to stay at 96–95. Game seven ended with a single point separating the two teams, but it was the Celtics who'd won.

Six games later, in a series that couldn't help but be anticlimactic, Boston had dumped the Houston Rockets for the NBA championship, and Tiny Archibald had his ring. The only person in Boston happier than Archibald himself might have been his wife. "He finally has his championship," she said with visible relief. "That's all he's talked about. Now we can get our lives together."

If Tiny's life came together then, it almost came apart a few years later when his NBA career ended. Leaving the game is tough for any pro athlete, and for Tiny Archibald it was agonizing. At first he had no idea how to fill all the hours that basketball had demanded of him since his childhood. "I'd been playing and practicing so long that I didn't know anything else," he told *Sports Illustrated*'s Franz Lidz. "I almost never came out of that twilight." The off-season wasn't the problem, of course. In the summer, Tiny could pull on his cutoff shorts, lace up his high-tops, and shoot hoops with the playground kids. Wherever his NBA career had taken him, his support for the programs he'd begun in Harlem had never waned.[15] But what would he do when the pro basketball season began?

It turned out that he just had to look a little harder for more folks to help. And his search led him in an unlikely direction. In high school and college, Tiny had characterized himself as an athlete rather than a scholar, but at Texas Western he'd begun to think that teaching might be something he'd be good at. Now, without the grind of basketball to interfere with academics, Tiny decided to pursue that possibility more formally. He enrolled in a master's program in adult education and human resource development at Fordham University, and he liked

---

13. **MVP,** abbreviated form of Most Valuable Player, awarded yearly by vote to one basketball player in the league.
14. **clinch** (klinch), *v.* fix firmly; settle decisively.
15. **wane** (wān), *v.* decline in strength or intensity; lessen.

▲ Nate Archibald was photographed by Claudio Edinger with a basketball team at the Harlem Armory Shelter. 🐾 Here Archibald works to combat the street culture of the homeless. How is he uniquely qualified to bring **change** to their lives?

the atmosphere of higher education so much that he eventually began work in a Ph.D. program in the same field.

Then, perhaps because the plight[16] of the homeless in New York and elsewhere was so much in the news at the time, it occurred to Tiny that maybe the kids on the playground weren't the only ones who could benefit from his encouragement and his example. He signed on as the recreation director for the Harlem Armory Shelter. He began calling

businesses and corporations, urging and cajoling[17] them to donate money and equipment to the shelter. Tiny wouldn't call the work a big deal. "I'm just trying to save people from the streets that I was saved from by basketball," he has said. And he had some fun at his work. One night he convinced the New Jersey Nets to part with half a dozen tickets, which he gave to six residents of the shelter. After making sure they were all wearing coats and ties, Tiny drove the men to the game and brought them into the locker room to meet the Nets. One of the players pulled Tiny aside and asked him, "Who are they? Lawyers?"

Eventually, within a few years of his retirement, the transition was complete. Tiny Archibald, All-Star point guard and playground legend, had become Nathaniel ("Nate," "Tiny") Archibald, recreation director, doctoral candidate, Harlem schools drug counselor, all-around friend to those who need one most.

In 1991, Tiny Archibald was elected to membership in the Basketball Hall of Fame. That honor insured his achievements as a basketball player would be preserved for future fans to appreciate. But Archibald's work in the schools and the shelters of New York has insured that admiration for him won't be limited to basketball fans. Those fortunate enough to have seen him play will remember him as a quick, canny,[18] hard-working guard. Those fortunate enough to have known him will remember him as a warm, unselfish, and giving man.

---

16. **plight** (plīt), *n.* a bad or hopeless situation.
17. **cajole** (kə jōl′), *v.* coax; persuade.
18. **canny** (kan′ē), *adj.* shrewd or cautious in dealing with others.

After Reading

Making Connections

1. ☝ The **changes** in Tiny Archibald's life often came from choices he made. Which changes do you think resulted in his greatest accomplishments—those made on or off the basketball court? Explain.

2. Make an illustration showing the inside of Tiny's basketball locker. What important personal items do you think he'd keep there?

3. Is Tiny Archibald's life an inspiration to you? Why or why not?

4. The author uses **slang** like "fellas" and "workin'" in the conversation between Tiny and his high school coach. What does this show about Tiny? What effect does it have on the story?

5. The author assumes readers know basketball **jargon.** How would the story change if the author avoided those terms?

6. How does this story fit the theme "choices and consequences"?

7. When Tiny was not playing pro basketball he was helping kids in his community learn to play. What kind of community service could you become involved in that would use your talents?

Literary Focus: Tone

You can determine the **tone**, or author's attitude, in a biography by looking at the words and details the author chooses to describe the person he or she is writing about. In one paragraph about Tiny, the author uses the words "talent," "remarkable," "confidence," and "imagination." You can conclude from these complimentary words that the tone of this part of the biography is admiring.

What other words might you choose to describe the tone? Look back through the story for more clues to the author's attitude toward Tiny. Does the tone change at all? When you consider tone, a map like the one below can help you organize your thoughts.

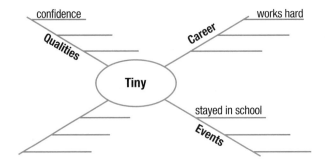

Vocabulary Study

On your paper write the word from the list that is most clearly related to the content of the sentence.

insatiable
economize
compensate
sentiment
contender
clinch
wane
plight
cajole
canny

1. Because his family had very little money, Tiny and his brother shared one room.

2. Tiny made up for his lack of height by developing skills that made his teammates better players.

3. Tiny Archibald had an overwhelming need to practice basketball constantly.

4. In the closing seconds of a game, Tiny sank a basket that won the championship.

5. Tiny found that professional basketball players are traded to other teams without much regard for their feelings.

6. Throughout his career Tiny didn't allow his interest in helping others to lessen.

7. In the 1980–1981 season, Tiny helped the Boston Celtics become real competitors for the championship.

8. Tiny is remembered as a cautious and clever basketball guard.

9. After he retired from basketball, the awful situation of homeless people attracted Tiny's attention.

10. When corporations didn't want to contribute to a shelter for the homeless, he coaxed them until they agreed.

Expressing Your Ideas

Writing Choices

Dear Sir Without his high school coach, Tiny might have spent his life washing dishes. What might Tiny now say to Floyd Lane? Imagine you are Tiny and write a **letter** to Lane.

Objective: Job! Look over the biography and note all of Tiny's accomplishments. Write a **resume** he might have used to apply for a job when he graduated with his doctorate from the university.

Other Options

My Hero Read another chapter of Bill Littlefield's book *Champions,* or a similar book about sports heroes. Relate the story to your class in an **oral report.**

Pros and Cons College basketball players sometimes leave school before graduation to become professional basketball players. Is this a good decision for them to make? In a small group, **debate** the pros and cons of this choice.

Before Reading

The Clever Magistrate

a Chinese tale retold by Linda Fang

Linda Fang
born 1944

Fang (fong) began her career as a professional storyteller by accident when she asked why no one told Chinese stories on a program at the TV station where she worked. The producer asked her to volunteer. This story is based on a legend about a real county magistrate who lived in the fourteenth century. Fang says she really likes the story because of its message: Always be fair. "Storytelling is for everybody," she says. "You can even find more stories for adults than for children. It's very important because you can bring about understanding between people." Linda Fang is the co-founder of the Washington Storytellers Association.

Building Background

Ancient Chinese Law In 221 B.C. seven Chinese states were united under the **Ch'in dynasty** into an empire that was the beginning of modern China. The Ch'in dynasty removed the many nobles who ruled small areas around their castles and set up counties divided into smaller areas called prefectures instead. Governors and magistrates were selected to govern these areas. They held the power to apply and enforce the "rule of law" throughout the land. Rule of law was a new idea in China. Under it, everyone should be treated equally, without regard to who they were, rich or poor. The Ch'in dynasty ruled only 15 years, but the way of governing it set up has had lasting effects for 2,000 years.

Getting into the Story

Discussion In "The Clever Magistrate," a judge settles a dispute in a fair, if unexpected, way. Work in a small group. Recall an argument or conflict that occurred between students on the playground or in school. You may have been involved in the argument, seen it happen, or tried to help. Explain to your group what the argument was about and how it was settled. Did the people involved need help to settle it? With your group discuss whether the argument was settled fairly. If not, how might it have been handled better?

Reading Tip

Folk tales Stories passed along by oral tradition, or by storytelling, are called **folk tales**. They usually involve simple conflicts that have obvious solutions where good triumphs over evil or right over wrong. Often the solution teaches some kind of lesson, as when Cinderella proves it is better to be humble and kind than vain and mean.

As you read, look for the lesson in "The Clever Magistrate" by first summarizing the main points. Upon looking over your summary, what lesson would you say the story teaches? Do you agree with the lesson?

The Clever Magistrate

retold by Linda Fang

One cold winter day, a farmer was carrying two buckets of spoiled food from a restaurant to his pigsty. As he was passing a coat shop, he accidentally spilled some of the slop on the ground. Sour cabbage, rotten eggs, and fish bones scattered all over the ground. Ugh! Ugh! What a smell!

The shopkeeper, who happened to be standing inside the door, saw this and was furious. He rushed out, grabbed the man, and shouted, "You dirty beggar! Look what you've done in front of my shop! It will be impossible to get rid of the smell! How are you going to pay for the damage?"

"I am so sorry," said the farmer. "I will clean it up right away. As for the damage, all I have is this coin." He took out a coin and handed it to the shopkeeper.

The shopkeeper snatched the coin, put it between his teeth, and bit down on it. The metal was soft, which proved that it contained silver. He thrust it into his pocket

This doll, representing a hired mourner, was crafted in the early twentieth century by an unknown Chinese artist. Compare this simple peasant's coat with the elegant robe of the provincial official on page 147. ➤

and said, "All right, I will take it. But you still need to clean up the mess."

"Let me go and get some rags and a mop," said the farmer. "I will be right back."

"No," said the shopkeeper. "I want you to clean it up right away. It smells so bad that I am going to be sick. Take off your coat and wipe up the mess."

"Please don't ask me to do that!" cried the farmer. "This is the only quilted coat I have, and if I use it to wipe up the mess, it will be ruined. I won't be able to wear it anymore."

"That's your problem, not mine!" said the shopkeeper. "In fact, the coat you are wearing is no better than rags. If you don't do what I say, I am going to take you to court."

The farmer pleaded with him to reconsider, but the shopkeeper would not relent.[1] Just then they heard, "Make way for the magistrate![2] Make way for the magistrate!"

The county magistrate was coming down the road in his sedan chair.[3] When he saw the commotion, he ordered his guards to put down the chair and bring the two men before him.

"What is the matter?" he asked.

The shopkeeper quickly replied, "*Ta-jen,*[4] this man made a mess in front of my shop. He gave me a coin to pay for the damage, but when I asked him to wipe up the mess, he wouldn't do it."

The magistrate stepped down from his chair and went over to look at the mess. Sour cabbage, rotten eggs, and fish bones were scattered all over the place. Ugh! Ugh! What a smell!

"Why don't you clean up the mess?" asked the magistrate.

"He wants me to wipe up the mess with my coat," said the farmer. "It will be ruined if I do so. And this is the only coat I have."

"Is that what you want?" the magistrate asked the shopkeeper.

"Yes, that is exactly what I want."

"And you will not settle for less?"

"No, I will not settle for anything less."

"Well," said the magistrate to the farmer, "if that is what he wants, you'd better do it."

"*Ta-jen,* have mercy! I can't do that!" cried the farmer. "Without the coat I will freeze to death."

"I am sorry," said the magistrate. "But that doesn't change anything. If you don't do it, I will have to put you in jail."

"That is not just!" cried the farmer.

"Hmm . . ." said the magistrate. He looked angry.

"*Ouh! Ouh! Ouh!*" cried the guards. "*Ouh! Ouh! Ouh!*" They looked threatening.

The farmer realized that there was no way out. Reluctantly, he used his coat to clean up the mess. Sour cabbage, rotten eggs, and fish bones. Ugh! Ugh! What a smell! He threw the coat into one of his buckets and stood shivering in front of the magistrate.

The shopkeeper laughed. "Ha, ha, ha!"

"Well," said the magistrate to the shopkeeper, "are you satisfied now?"

"Yes, *Ta-jen,* I am completely satisfied."

"No more complaints?"

"No more complaints!" said the shopkeeper.

"Case closed," said the magistrate.

"Case closed."

"But his case against you is now open."

"What!" said the shopkeeper, stunned.

"Well, you see, he is now freezing without a coat. In such weather he could catch a cold. Is that not possible?" asked the magistrate.

"Yes, *Ta-jen.*"

"His cold could develop into pneumonia.[5] Is that not possible?"

---

1. relent (ri lent´), *v.* become less harsh; be more merciful.
2. magistrate (maj´ə strāt), *n.* a government official who has power to apply and enforce the law.
3. sedan chair (si dan´), a covered chair for one person, carried on poles by two bearers.
4. Ta-jen (tä jen´), Your Excellency; Your Honor.
5. pneumonia (nŭ mō´nyə), a serious lung disease.

▲ *Portrait of a Provincial Treasurer, Lu Ming,* a watercolor on silk, was painted in the eighteenth century by an unknown artist. How might a poor farmer respond to a magistrate dressed in such rich attire?

"Yes, *Ta-jen.*"

"Then he could die. His family could sue you for murder, and if you are convicted, you would be put to death. Isn't that almost inevitable?"[6]

"Yes, *Ta-jen.*"

"Well, I don't think you can afford that, can you?"

"Oh, no, *Ta-jen.* I cannot afford that. What shall I do?"

"Well, it would be better to settle this out of court."

"Yes, yes, we'd better settle this out of court. But how?"

"We should get him a coat so he won't catch a cold."

"But where can we get one?"

"Right here, from your coat shop."

The shopkeeper looked as if he had swallowed a fly alive. He yelled at the farmer, "Go get a coat and be gone!"

The farmer went into the shop, picked out a very cheap coat, and came out. The magistrate stopped him.

"You poor thing!" he said. "Look at the coat you've got. It is so thin. You could still catch a cold, isn't that so?"

"Yes, *Ta-jen.*"

"You might get pneumonia, isn't that so?"

"Yes, *Ta-jen.*"

"You might even die, isn't that so?"

"Yes, *Ta-jen.*"

"And then your family could come and harass[7] this nice gentleman. I know all your tricks!" The magistrate turned to one of his guards. "Go into the shop and get him the warmest coat you can find."

So the guard went into the shop and picked out the warmest coat he could find for the farmer. As you might guess, the warmest coat happened to be the most expensive.

When the farmer left, the magistrate smiled at the shopkeeper. "Well, what do you think about the way I settled this case? Didn't I handle it very well?"

"Yes, *Ta-jen,*" the shopkeeper said glumly.[8] "There is no question about that."

"I am glad I was able to take care of this case," said the magistrate. "You have to watch out for these troublemakers. Next time, if you have a case like this, don't try to settle it yourself. Be sure to let me handle it for you."

---

6. **inevitable** (in evʹə tə bəl), *adj.* sure to happen.

7. **harass** (harʹəs), *v.* trouble by repeated attacks; disturb or torment.

8. **glumly** (glumʹlē), *adv.* with bad humor; dismally.

After Reading

Making Connections

1. Which of the characters in the story would you choose to invite to dinner? Why? Describe what you think the evening would be like.

2. Do you think the magistrate handled the situation well? Explain.

3. Compare and contrast the **characters** of the shopkeeper and the farmer. Use examples from the dialogue to support your answer.

4. Find examples in the **dialogue** that show how the magistrate manipulates, or tricks, the shopkeeper into agreeing he should give the farmer a coat.

5. List several phrases that are repeated throughout the story. Why do you think the author uses this **repetition?**

6. The Chinese magistrates were appointed to safeguard the "rule of law," or apply justice equally for all people. What safeguards does our legal system have that ensure equal treatment under the law?

7. How are arguments or conflicts between students resolved at your school? What are the consequences of inappropriate behavior? Does the system work well? How would you improve it?

Literary Focus: Dialogue

Since very little action occurs in this tale, you must pay attention to **dialogue** to understand the plot and the lesson it teaches. For instance, the magistrate uses his dialogue with the shopkeeper to lead him into a logical trap. "No more complaints!" and "Case closed," the shopkeeper echoes happily. The magistrate's next words introduce an interesting plot twist by opening the farmer's case.

Reread the dialogue to pick up other clues that help you understand the story. Ask yourself: What does this dialogue tell me about the plot and the relationships among the characters? Listing bits of dialogue and why they are important may help organize your ideas.

Dialogue	Importance
"But his case against you is now open."	advances the action; shows magistrate's impartiality

Vocabulary Study

On your paper write the word from the list that best completes the meaning of the sentence.

relent
magistrate
inevitable
harass
glumly

1. A poor peasant accidentally knocked over a fruit vendor's cart. The fruit vendor began to ____ him, demanding he pick up the fruit and pay several silver coins in damages.

2. The peasant explained he had no money, but the vendor would not ____.

3. The peasant was nearly in tears. It seemed ____ that he would have to pay.

4. ____, the peasant began to gather the fruit.

5. Just at that moment, the ____ appeared in his sedan chair. "What is the problem?" he asked.

Expressing Your Ideas

Writing Choices

A Day in the Life . . . The problem between the shopkeeper and the farmer was only one small incident in a busy day for the magistrate. Imagine you are the magistrate and write a **diary entry** describing what you do on any typical day. You may choose the day of this story or any other day.

Legal Eagles How can a situation like that between the shopkeeper and farmer be prevented in the future? Write a new **law** to cover such cases. Make sure it protects the guilty person but does justice for the injured party at the same time.

"Yes, Dear!" What do you think the shopkeeper told his wife after he got home? Think about what you know about the character of the shopkeeper from the story. Then write a **dialogue** that might have occurred between the couple the evening after the story took place.

Other Options

Roving Reporter A reporter's job is to be objective, or to listen to all sides of the story and present the facts. Work with a group of four. One person is a reporter who **interviews** the three main characters in the story. The other three people in the group play the three characters who respond to the interviewer's questions. After practicing, you might want to audiotape or videotape your interviews and play them for the class.

Dress Up Imagine that you are a theatrical costume designer. **Design** and sketch costumes for each of the three main characters. Research dress in ancient China to inspire your creations.

Sum It Up Work with a partner to find another folk tale or fairy tale that you like. **Summarize** the tale for your classmates, stating at the end what lesson, if any, you think the story teaches.

Before Reading

Sir Gawain and the Loathly Lady

an English legend retold by Betsy Hearne

Betsy Hearne
born 1942

Hearne has enjoyed fairy tales since she was a child, especially those like "Beauty and the Beast." This tale of King Arthur has a similar theme, she points out, except that the roles are reversed. Here, the knight is a beauty and the lady a beast. "It's also partly about the fact that in many cases women have not had choices, and that each person should have control," Hearne says. Besides writing, Hearne teaches children's literature, folklore, and storytelling in the Graduate School of Library and Information Science at the University of Illinois Urbana-Champaign.

Building Background

The Code of Chivalry Although no one is really sure whether or not a real man named Arthur ever ruled England, stories about this king and his Knights of the Round Table have been popular since the Middle Ages. In the early tales Arthur's knights were perfect examples of **chivalry.** Brave, honest, kind, and fair to their enemies, under the code of chivalry they also protected and respected women. That respect was part of the tradition of **courtly love,** a pure love sung about by troubadours, wandering singers who roamed from castle to castle earning their living by entertaining lords and ladies. Legends such as the one you are about to read make the Middle Ages seem romantic. What do you think life was really like back then?

Getting into the Story

Writer's Notebook In "Sir Gawain and the Loathly Lady," two men set out to answer the question, "What do women most desire?" What would you answer if someone asked what you most desire? Consider what you want out of life above and beyond money and possessions. Then answer the question in your notebook. Be sure to explain why you want whatever you choose. As you read, compare your answer to the answer given in the story.

Reading Tip

Archaic English This story came from a long English poem written in the Middle Ages. To keep the flavor of the original, it uses some **archaic,** or out-dated, language. The chart lists and defines some of these words and phrases from the story. Look for others you may add.

Archaic English	Meanings
well met	greeting: glad to meet you
nay	no
with great heat	quickly; with great anger
tidings	information
alas	exclamation of sorrow or grief
tarry	stay; wait

SIR GAWAIN AND the LOATHLY LADY

retold by
BETSY HEARNE

Now if you listen awhile I will tell you a tale of Arthur the King and how an adventure once befell him.

Of all kings and all knights, King Arthur bore away the honor wherever he went. In all his country there was nothing but chivalry,[1] and knights were loved by the people.

One day in spring King Arthur was hunting in Ingleswood with all his lords beside him. Suddenly a deer ran by in the distance and the king took up chase, calling back to his knights, "Hold you still every man, I will chase this one myself!" He took his arrows and bow and stooped low like a woodsman to stalk the deer. But every time he came near the animal, it leapt away into the forest. So King Arthur went a while after the deer, and no knight went with him, until at last he let fly an arrow and killed the deer. He had raised a bugle to his lips to summon the knights when he heard a voice behind him.

"Well met, King Arthur!"

Though he had not heard anyone approach, the king turned to see a strange knight, fully armed, standing only a few yards away.

"You have done me wrong many a year and given away my northern lands," said the strange knight. "I have your life in my hands—what will you do now, King Alone?"

"Sir Knight, what is your name?" asked the king.

"My name is Gromer Somer Joure."

"Sir Gromer, think carefully," said the king. "To slay me here, unarmed as I am, will get you no honor. All knights will refuse you wherever you go. Calm yourself—come to Carlyle and I shall mend all that is amiss."[2]

"Nay," said Sir Gromer, "by heaven, King! You shall not escape when I have you at advantage. If I let you go with only a warning, later you'll defy me, of that I'm sure."

"Spare my life, Sir Gromer, and I shall grant you whatever is in my power to give. It is

---

1. **chivalry** (shiv′əl rē), *n.* knightly qualities, such as bravery, honor, courtesy, and respect for women.
2. **amiss** (ə mis′), *adj.* wrong.

This portrait is from a medieval manuscript known as the Capodilista Codex. Such knights wore the heavy weapons of warfare from 1100–1300. To what might they compare today?

shameful to slay me here, with nothing but my hunting gear, and you armed for battle."

"All your talking will not help you, King, for I want neither land nor gold, truly." Sir Gromer smiled. "Still . . . if you will promise to meet me here, in the same fashion, on a day I will choose . . . "

"Yes," said the king quickly. "Here is my promise."

"Listen and hear me out. First you will swear upon my sword to meet me here without fail, on this day one year from now. Of all your knights none shall come with you. You must tell me at your coming what thing women most desire—and if you do not bring the answer to my riddle, you will lose your head. What say you, King?"

"I agree, though it is a hateful bargain," said the king. "Now let me go. I promise you as I am the true king, to come again at this day one year from now and bring you your answer."

The knight laughed, "Now go your way, King Arthur. You do not yet know your sorrow. Yet stay a moment—do not think of playing false—for by Mary[3] I think you would betray me."

"Nay," said King Arthur. "You will never find me an untrue knight. Farewell, Sir Knight, and evil met. I will come in a year's time, though I may not escape." The king began to blow his bugle for his knights to find him. Sir Gromer turned his horse and was gone as quickly as he had come, so that the lords found their king alone with the slain deer.

"We will return to Carlyle," said the king. "I do not like this hunting."

The lords knew by his countenance[4] that the king had met with some disturbance, but no one knew of his encounter. They wondered at the king's heavy step and sad look, until at last Sir Gawain said to the king, "Sire, I marvel[5] at you. What thing do you sorrow for?"

"I'll tell you, gentle Gawain," said Arthur. "In the forest as I pursued the deer, I met with a knight in full armor, and he charged me I should not escape him. I must keep my word to him or else I am foresworn."[6]

"Fear not my lord. I am not a man that would dishonor you."

"He threatened me, and would have slain[7] me with great heat, but I spoke with him since I had no weapons."

"What happened then?" said Gawain.

"He made me swear to meet him there in one year's time, alone and unarmed. On that day I must tell him what women desire most, or I shall lose my life. If I fail in my answer, I know that I will be slain without mercy."

"Sire, make good cheer," said Gawain. "Make your horse ready to ride into strange country, and everywhere you meet either man or woman, ask of them the answer to the riddle. I will ride another way, and every man and woman's answer I will write in a book."

"That is well advised, Gawain," said the king. They made preparations to leave immediately, and when both were ready, Gawain rode one way and the king another—each one asked every man and woman they found what women most desire.

Some said they loved beautiful clothes; some said they loved to be praised; some said they loved a handsome man; some said one, some said another. Gawain had so many answers that he made a great book to hold them, and after many months of traveling he came back to court again. The king was there already with his book, and each looked over the other's work. But no answer seemed right.

"By God," said the king, "I am afraid. I will

---

3. **by Mary,** an oath taken on the Virgin Mary.
4. **countenance** (koun′tə nəns), *n.* facial expression.
5. **marvel** (mär′vəl), *v.* be filled with wonder; be astonished.
6. **foresworn** (fôr swôrn′), untrue to one's sworn word or promise; made a liar.
7. **slain** (slān), *v.* killed.

Grotesque Old Woman was painted by an unknown artist in 1520. What is your reaction to such a "loathly lady"?

"What do you want with me, lady?" said the king, taken aback by the lady's boldness.

"Sir, I would like to speak with you. You will die if I do not save you, I know it very well."

"What do you mean, my lady, tell me," stammered the king. "What is your desire, why is my life in your hand? Tell me, and I shall give you all you ask."

"You must grant me a knight to wed," said the lady slowly. "His name is Sir Gawain. I will make this bargain: if your life is saved another way, you need not grant my desire. If my answer saves your life, grant me Sir Gawain as my husband. Choose now, for you must soon meet your enemy."

"By Mary," said the king, "I cannot grant you Sir Gawain. That lies with him alone—he is not mine to give. I can only take the choice to Sir Gawain."

"Well," she said. "Then go home again and speak to Sir Gawain. For though I am foul, yet am I merry, and through me he may save your life or ensure[10] your death."

"Alas!" cried the king. "That I should cause Gawain to wed you, for he will not say no. I know not what I should do."

"Sir King, you will get no more from me. When you come again with your answer I will meet you here."

"What is your name, I pray you tell me?"

"Sir King, I am the Dame Ragnell, that never yet betrayed a man."

"Then farewell, Dame Ragnell," said the king.

Thus they departed, and the king returned to Carlyle again with a heavy heart. The first man he met was Sir Gawain. "Sire, how did you fare?" asked the knight.

"Never so ill," said the king. "I fear I will die at Sir Gromer's hand."

seek a little more in Ingleswood Forest. I have but one month to my set day, and I may find some good tidings."[8]

"Do as you think best," said Gawain, "but whatever you do, remember that it is good to have spring again."

King Arthur rode forth on that day, into Ingleswood, and there he met with a lady. King Arthur marveled at her, for she was the ugliest creature that he had ever seen. Her face seemed almost like that of an animal, with a pushed-in nose and a few yellowing tusks for teeth. Her figure was twisted and deformed, with a hunched back and shoulders a yard broad. No tongue could tell the foulness of that lady. But she rode gaily on a palfrey[9] set with gold and precious stones, and when she spoke her voice was sweet and soft.

"I am glad that I have met with you, King Arthur," she said. "Speak with me, for your life is in my hand. I know of your situation, and I warn you that you will not find your answer if I do not tell you."

---

8. **tidings** (tī′dingz), news; information.
9. **palfrey** (pôl′frē), a gentle riding horse.
10. ensure (en shùr′), *v.* make sure or certain.

"Nay," said Gawain. "I would rather die myself I love you so."

"Gawain, I met today with the foulest lady that I ever saw. She said she would save my life, but first she would have you for her husband."

"Is this all?" asked Gawain. "Then I shall wed her and wed her again! Though she were a fiend,[11] though she were as foul as Beelzebub,[12] her I shall marry. For you are my king and I am your friend—it is my part to save your life, or else I am a false knight and a great coward. If she were the most loathsome[13] woman that ever a man might see, for your love I would spare nothing."

"Thank you Gawain," said King Arthur then. "Of all knights that I have found, you are the finest. You have saved my life, and my love will not stray from you, as I am king in this land."

The day soon came when the king was to meet the Dame Ragnell and bear his answer to Sir Gromer. Gawain rode with him to the edge of Ingleswood Forest, but there the king said, "Sir Gawain, farewell. I must go west, and you must go no further."

"God speed you on your journey. I wish I rode your way," said Gawain.

The king had ridden but a mile or so more when he met the Dame Ragnell. "Ah, Sir King, you are welcome here bearing your answer."

"Now," said the king, "since it can be no other way, tell me your answer, save my life, and Gawain shall you wed; so he has promised. Tell me in all haste. Have done, I may not tarry."

"Sire," said the Dame Ragnell, "now you will know what women desire most, high and low. Some men say we desire to be fair, or to wed, or to remain fresh and young, or to have flattery from men. But there is one thing that is every woman's fantasy: we desire of men, above all other things, to have sovereignty,[14] for then all is ours. Therefore go on your way,

Sir King, and tell that knight what I have said to you. He will be angry and curse the woman who told you, for his labor is lost. Go forth—you will not be harmed."

The king rode forth in great haste until he came to the set place and met with Sir Gromer.

"Come, come, Sir King," said the knight sternly. "Now let me have your answer, for I am ready."

The king pulled out the two books for Sir Gromer to see. "Sir, I dare say the right one is there."

Sir Gromer looked over them, every one, and said at last, "Nay, nay, Sir King, you are a dead man."

"Wait, Sir Gromer," said the king. "I have one more answer to give."

"Say it," said Sir Gromer, "or so God help me you shall bleed."

"Now," said the king, "here is my answer and that is all—above all things, women desire sovereignty, for that is their liking and their greatest desire; to rule over any man. This they told me."

Sir Gromer was silent a moment with rage, but then he cried out, "And she that told you, Sir Arthur, I pray to God I might see her burn in a fire, for that was my sister, Dame Ragnell. God give her shame—I have lost much labor. Go where you like, King Arthur, for you are spared. Alas that I ever saw this day, for I know that you will be my enemy and hunt me down."

"No," said King Arthur, "you will never find me an attacker. Farewell." King Arthur turned his horse into the forest again. Soon he met with the Dame Ragnell, in the same

---

11. **fiend** (fēnd), *n.* an evil spirit, devil or demon.
12. **Beelzebub** (bē el′zə bub), the Devil; Satan.
13. **loathsome** (lōтн′səm), *adj.* making one feel sick; disgusting.
14. **sovereignty** (sov′rən tē), *n.* complete control over one's own life.

Sir Gawain and the Loathly Lady **155**

place as before. "Sir King," she said. "I am glad you have sped well. I told you how it would be, and now since I and none other have saved your life, Gawain must wed me."

"I will not fail in my promise," said the king. "If you will be ruled by my council, you shall have your will."

"No, Sir King, I will not be ruled," said the Lady. "I know what you are thinking. Ride before, and I will follow to your court. Think how I have saved your life and do not disagree with me, for if you do you will be shamed."

The king was ashamed to bring the loathly lady openly to the court, but forth she rode till they came to Carlyle. All the country wondered when she came, for they had never seen so foul a creature, but she would spare no one the sight of her. Into the hall she went, saying, "Arthur, King, fetch in Sir Gawain, before all the knights, so that you may troth[15] us together. Set forth Gawain my love, for I will not wait."

Sir Gawain stepped forward then, and said, "Sir, I am ready to fulfill the promise I made to you."

"God have mercy," said the Dame Ragnell when she saw Gawain. "For your sake I wish I were a fair woman, for you are of such good will." Then Sir Gawain wooed her as he was a true knight, and Dame Ragnell was happy.

"Alas!" said the Queen Guinevere, and all the ladies in her bower.[16] "Alas!" said both king and knights, that the beautiful Gawain should wed such a foul and horrible woman.

She would be wedded in no other way than this—openly, with announcements in every town and village, and she had all the ladies of the land come to Carlyle for the feast. The queen begged Dame Ragnell to be married in the early morning, as privately as possible. "Nay," said the lady. "By heaven I will not no matter what you say. I will be wedded openly, as the king promised. I will not go to the church until high-mass time,[17] and I will dine in the open hall, in the midst of all the court."

At the wedding feast there were lords and ladies from all estates, and Dame Ragnell was arrayed in the richest manner—richer even than Queen Guinevere. But all her rich clothes could not hide her foulness. When the feasting began, only Dame Ragnell ate heartily, while the knights and squires sat like stones. After the wedding feast, Sir Gawain and the Lady Ragnell retired to the wedding chamber that had been prepared for them.

"Ah, Gawain," said the lady. "Since we are wed, show me your courtesy and come to bed. If I were fair you would be joyous—yet for Arthur's sake kiss me at least."

Sir Gawain turned to the lady, but in her place was the loveliest woman that he had ever seen.

"By God, what are you?" cried Gawain.

"Sir, I am your wife, surely. Why are you so unkind?"

"Lady, I am sorry," said Gawain. "I beg your pardon, my fair madam. For now you are a beautiful lady, and today you were the foulest woman that ever I saw. It is well, my lady, to have you thus." And he took her in his arms and kissed her with great joy.

"Sir," she said, "you have half-broken the spell on me. Thus shall you have me, but my beauty will not hold. You may have me fair by night and foul by day, or else have me fair by day, and by night ugly once again. You must choose."

"Alas!" said Gawain, "The choice is too hard—to have you fair on nights and no more, that would grieve my heart and shame me. Yet if I desire to have you fair by day and foul by night I could not rest. I know not in the world

---

15. **troth** (trôth), bind by a promise to marry.
16. **bower** (bou′ər), a shaded place formed by trees or shrubs growing on a lattice.
17. **high-mass time,** the hour when a formal, Roman Catholic church service is held each morning.

Il Ramoscello (*The Little Branch*), painted in 1865 by Dante Gabriel Rossetti, reflects ideal feminine beauty of the kind described in the story. ➤

what I should say, but do as you wish. The choice is in your hands."

"Thank you, courteous[18] Gawain," said the lady. "Of all earthly knights you are blessed, for now I am truly loved. You shall have me fair both day and night, and ever while I live as fair. For I was shaped by witchcraft by my stepmother, God have mercy on her. By enchantment[19] I was to be the foulest creature, till the best knight of England had wedded me and had given me the sovereignty of all his body and goods. Kiss me, Sir Gawain—be glad and make good cheer, for we are well." The two rejoiced together and thanked God for their fortune.

King Arthur came himself to call them to breakfast the next day, wondering why Gawain stayed so late with his loathly bride. Sir Gawain rose, taking the hand of his lady, and opened the door to greet the king.

The Dame Ragnell stood by the fire, with pale lovely skin and red hair spilling down to her knees. "Lo," said Gawain to the king, "this is my wife the Dame Ragnell, who once saved your life." And Gawain told the king the story of the lady's enchantment.

"My love shall she have, for she has been so kind," said the king. And the queen said, "You have my love forever, Lady, for you have saved my Lord Arthur." And from then on, at every great feast, that lady was the fairest, and all his life Gawain loved the Lady Ragnell.

Thus ends the adventure of King Arthur and of the wedding of Sir Gawain.

---

18. **courteous** (kėr′tē əs), *adj.* thoughtful of others; polite; full of courtly manners.
19. **enchantment** (en chant′mənt), the use of magic spells.

Greensleeves

Anonymous

After Reading

Making Connections

1. Imagine you are the casting director for a movie version of this story. Who would you cast in the four major roles? Why?

2. ☀ Sir Gawain resists any **change** in his loyalty to his king. He faces, however, great change in his own life by marrying the loathsome lady. Would you have made the same choice?

3. Guinevere wanted the loathsome Dame Ragnell to have a quiet wedding. Do you think she was right? Why or why not?

4. How does Sir Gawain act according to the code of chivalry? Find examples of his behavior from the story. Then use a **character trait** web like the one below to organize your ideas.

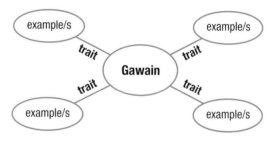

5. Choose a short section of the story that uses the elegant, archaic language of the Middle Ages and rewrite it in modern English.

6. How is the **plot** of this story similar to the well-known folk tale "Beauty and the Beast"? How is it different? Can you think of other stories or movies with similar themes?

7. Do you have a Sir Gawain in your life—a person, either male or female, who will sacrifice for you? Describe that person.

8. Do you know a Dame Ragnell, a person who some people find unattractive but who is actually beautiful? Describe that person.

Literary Focus: Diction

Diction, or the words and phrases an author chooses, can help strengthen the setting of a story. "Sir Gawain and the Loathly Lady," contains many archaic words and phrases such as "nay" or "well met." The word order in sentences such as "What say you, King?" also gives the story an old-fashioned feel.

Pay special attention to the elegant and archaic language of this story as you read it over again. Ask yourself: How does the diction add to the atmosphere of the story? How would the story change if it were retold in modern English?

Vocabulary Study

Write the letter of the word that is **not** related in meaning to the other words in the set.

chivalry
amiss
countenance
marvel
slain
ensure
fiend
loathsome
sovereignty
courteous

1. **a.** face **b.** countenance **c.** elbow **d.** expression
2. **a.** fiend **b.** demon **c.** devil **d.** palfrey
3. **a.** hated **b.** slain **c.** disliked **d.** detested
4. **a.** marvel **b.** laugh **c.** chuckle **d.** giggle
5. **a.** kindness **b.** chivalry **c.** courtesy **d.** jealousy
6. **a.** ensure **b.** enchant **c.** charm **d.** bewitch
7. **a.** ugly **b.** disgusting **c.** bewildered **d.** loathsome
8. **a.** control **b.** sovereignty **c.** quality **d.** power
9. **a.** improper **b.** superb **c.** wrong **d.** amiss
10. **a.** courteous **b.** conceited **c.** rude **d.** obnoxious

Expressing Your Ideas

Writing Choices

Only Skin Deep? What would Dame Ragnell say if she were asked to write a **how-to manual** on beauty and manners? Imagine you are the loathsome lady. Choose what you would like to write—an introduction to the manual or one page on any topic that might appear in it.

Your Life, Alas! Use the kind of language found in this story to write a **personal narrative** about an event from your life. Include archaic words and phrases from the story or from other stories or movies set in the Middle Ages. Try to imitate the kind of sentence structure in this selection.

Underneath the Armor In your library find books with pictures of life in the Middle Ages. Study these for information about daily life then. Write an account of a typical day and use the pictures as illustrations as you give an **oral report** to the class.

Other Options

Lords and Ladies of the Court Choose a scene from the story that involves several people, such as the hunting party, Arthur leading Dame Ragnell into the castle, or the wedding feast. Work in a group to form a **tableau** of this scene. Assign roles and decide what positions to assume.

Buy Now and Save What products might Dame Ragnell or Sir Gawain endorse on TV? Choose either of these people or any other character from the story. Select a product the person might like to endorse; then create a **TV** or **magazine ad** showing their endorsement.

Comic Concerns Work with several classmates to create a **comic book** version of "Sir Gawain and the Loathly Lady." If possible, share your book with other classes or arrange to put it in the school library.

Writing Mini-Lesson

Arranging Details

Consider different arrangements. The way a writer arranges details can affect the reader's ability to understand what is being said or sympathize with it. There are several ways to arrange details.

- Chronological—Begin with details about the first event in an episode and end with details about the last event.

- Order of importance—Make a big splash by beginning with the most important detail and then ending with the least important detail. Or, begin with the least important and work your way up to the most important.

- Spatial—Describe the details of a setting in the order you would encounter them if you moved through it.

Writing Strategy To choose an order for your details, think about the purpose of your writing and what you would like readers to notice. Then, try outlining your details in several different orders. Decide which one emphasizes the parts that you want readers to notice the most.

Activity Options

1. Write a paragraph describing how you begin your day, using one of the arrangements described above. Then trade with a partner and rewrite your partner's paragraph using a different order. Discuss the results.

2. In groups of three, have each person write a paragraph describing the scene in your classroom, using a different arrangement for the details. Share your descriptions with each other and discuss how they compare.

3. Review the literature to see how the details in each of the selections are arranged. Make a chart to record the different orders you find. Do some stories use more than one arrangement? Can you find arrangements that are not listed above?

Choices and Consequences

Doing Battle

Knights

History Connection

Every choice we make has a consequence. A kindness can make someone feel good. An unselfish act might save a life. Doing battle for justice can make the world a better place.

This knight's armor is made of steel plates fastened together by leather straps and rivets. His velvet brigandine, or jacket, is lined with steel plates. This suit of armor weighs 41 pounds. ➤

Religion, Honor, Courtesy—these were important concerns to the European knights of the Middle Ages. Best known for their metal suits of armor, knights were driven by a code of honor. They fought battles to defend the honor of their church, their king, or their land. In his training to become a knight, a young man learned to honor and protect women. He learned music and hunting, often using a trained hawk. He received religious instruction and training in warfare and horsemanship. A knight was prepared to defend honor whenever and wherever he was needed.

◀ Half-brothers Peter I and Henry battled for the right to the throne of Castile (Spain) at Najera in 1367. With the aid of the French, Henry II was crowned in 1369.

and SAMURAI

Samurai fight during the Heiji Insurrection of 1159. This was one of the first samurai battles.

In the twelfth century, the power of the Japanese emperor was crumbling. It was then that the samurai warriors took their place in Japanese society. The samurai were bonded together by a strong sense of loyalty to their chiefs, or shoguns, who were the new ruling powers. *Bushido,* "the way of the warrior," strictly dictated the behavior of all samurai. Loyalty and sacrifice anchored the code. No sacrifice, not even death, was too great for a samurai in the service of his shogun.

Pictured here is a decorated dress version of the *yoroi,* the traditional samurai armor. Very strong and waterproof, it was made of many rows of lacquered armor plates laced together with leather or silk cords. The face mask of molded sheet metal covered with stenciled leather was made to protect the face and frighten the enemy.

Responding

1. What similarities can you see between the codes of behavior of knights and samurai?

2. What groups in your school or community include a code of honor?

163

History Connection
Loyalty was the heart of the *bushido* code. A model samurai, Kusunoki Masashige fully embraced the challenge of the code. Another samurai, Matsuo Munefusa, traded his sword for ink and brush when he became a poet.

KUSUNOKI

THE LOYAL SAMURAI

by Ann Woodbury Moore

The most noble samurai of Japanese history, Kusunoki Masashige is revered for his loyalty, courage, and unselfishness. In the early twentieth century, all Japanese elementary school students learned a song describing his farewell to his son. His story inspired the suicide pilots known as kamikaze during World War II. A bronze statue of him stands outside the Imperial Palace in Tokyo, and a museum and shrine mark the spot where he died. Since documented historical facts about Kusunoki are scarce, most of the tales about him have been taken from the Taiheiki, a fourteenth-century romanticized historical account of the samurai wars.

Kusunoki was born around 1294. He studied military strategy at a monastery near Nara and became so skilled a warrior that his teachers, fearful of his power, tried to murder him. The clever samurai easily escaped and later became chieftain of a province near Kyoto, Japan's imperial capital.

In the 1330s, Kusunoki joined Emperor Go-Daigo in his bid to defeat the military shogunate dictator at Kamakura and return the controlling power to the emperor. Aided by dissatisfied warriors and monk-soldiers, Kusunoki defended the fortified encampments of Akasaka (1331) and Chihaya (1332) against the shogun's armies.

AFTER HOURS OF FIERCE FIGHTING AT MINATOGAWA, KUSUNOKI'S SOLDIERS WERE CUT OFF AND VIRTUALLY WIPED OUT.

The wooden fortresses, built atop hills, were surrounded by thick forests. Booby traps, such as enormous logs suspended along the hillsides by ropes—which were cut as soon as the enemy climbed on the logs—were used effectively. Kusunoki's defense of Chihaya is considered one of the most brilliant sieges in Japanese history. One of his tactics included

MASASHIGE

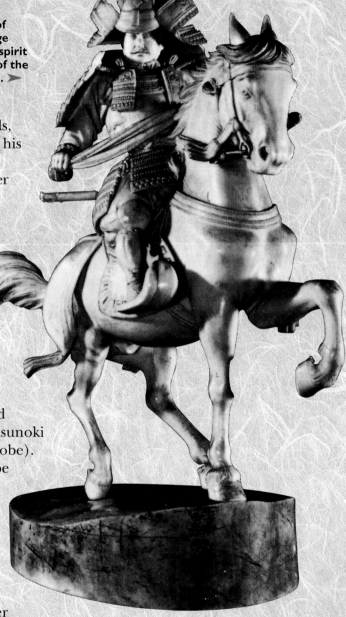

This ivory statue of Kusunoki Masashige captures the bold spirit and fierce loyalty of the legendary samurai. ➤

dropping heavy rocks onto the enemy's shields, then shooting the soldiers with arrows. Once, his troops poured boiling water on the attackers, causing the soldiers to flee in terror. On another occasion, Kusunoki patiently waited for the enemy to move closer, then cut down huge trees to crush them. When the attackers dropped a bridge across a gully, Kusunoki's men pumped oil onto it and set it afire. The bridge burned through and collapsed, sending the soldiers on it to the bottom of the chasm.

In 1336, Ashikaga Takauji, one of Go-Daigo's generals, revolted and led an army toward Kyoto. Kusonoki let Ashikaga temporarily reoccupy Kyoto. But Go-Daigo did not agree with this maneuver and ordered Kusunoki to join an army at Minatogawa (present-day Kobe). Kusonoki knew the result of this plan would be almost certain defeat, but he obeyed. Before leaving, he presented his ten-year-old son, Masatsura, with a sword and urged him to continue the fight when he was grown.

After hours of fierce fighting at Minato-gawa, Kusunoki's soldiers were cut off and virtually wiped out. He and his brother retreated to a nearby farmhouse, where, rather than be captured by the enemy, they ran each other through with their swords. Masatsura followed in his father's footsteps and died in battle twelve years later.

In the late seventeenth century, Matsuo Munefusa decided to leave his life as a samurai and become a poet. Known by his pseudonym, Matsuo Basho, he became a master writer of haiku.

Haiku is a short poem that often refers to nature. There are seventeen syllables and three lines in a haiku poem. The first and third lines have five syllables, and the second has seven. Although brief and simple, haiku is meant to challenge the reader to think.

haiku

On the wide seashore
a stray blossom and the shells
make one drifting sand.

— **Matsuo Basho**

The stone gods vanished —
only the dead leaves kneeling
on this temple stoop.

— **Matsuo Basho**

A weightless balloon
slips from the hand of a child —
the wandering moon.

—**Ann Atwood**

Responding

1. Why do you think Kusunoki took part in the Battle of Minatogawa, even though defeat was certain?

2. How do you feel about Kusunoki's decision to fight in the Battle of Minatogawa? Is honor and loyalty worth dying for? Explain your answer.

3. Write a haiku poem. Illustrate it if you wish and then share it with the class.

Reading Mini-Lesson

Visualizing

Picture this: You are going to a basketball game at a rival school. On the way you get lost and ask for directions to the gymnasium. A helpful bystander tells you, "After the second traffic light—well, maybe it's the third light—anyway, there's a gas station on the left—you take a left and then a quick right . . ." In your head you can follow the first two or three moves, but the directions soon become a jumble.

The person then begins to draw a crude map. Suddenly, the route becomes clear to you. It even seems to be clearer to the person giving the directions. The map takes on more and more details. The map shown here would be easy to follow because you can see the whole route at once and then follow directions one step at a time. Now you can visualize how you're going to get there.

Visualizing is also an important skill when you're trying to find your path through a reading. You might have to make your own map. Use clues or details to sketch a mental picture of the setting.

The fourth paragraph of the selection about Kusunoki Masashige on page 164 contains many visual details and a number of events. For you to understand the events, you need to be able to visualize the setting. Look at the clues provided by the descriptions: "wooden fortresses, built atop hills, were surrounded by thick forests," "enormous logs suspended along hillsides," "huge trees," "a gully," "chasm." Can you visualize this setting? If you can, you will be able to *see* and really understand the events that took place there.

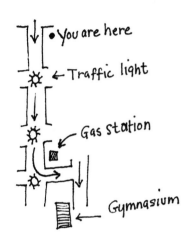

Activity Options

1. Kusunoki's travels led him to a number of places. Using a world atlas as a reference, make a map that will help you visualize the path that he took, beginning with where he studied military strategy and ending with the location where he died.

2. The simplest things to visualize in this story are the fortified encampments where the battles took place. With a small group of classmates, make a drawing or a model to illustrate what the wooden fortresses built atop hills looked like and how the booby traps worked to fend off attackers.

Part Two

Finding Your Place

Have you ever wondered about your place in the world? Do you sometimes dream of where you want to be in life? When you find your place will you know it? What if you're in it right now? The most exciting, challenging, and surprising adventure in life can be finding your place. It's the pursuit all humans have in common and it's different for everyone.

 **Multicultural Connection** **Individuality** involves figuring out just who you are and where you fit in. This may mean conforming to group expectations or it may mean challenging group pressures. The following stories and poems explore some ways people discover where they belong. How do the characters maintain their individuality while finding a place in the group?

Literature

Anne McCaffrey	**The Smallest Dragonboy** ◆ short story	170
	Language Mini-Lesson ◆ Combining Sentences	184
Nereida Román	**Never Fitting In** ◆ autobiography	186
Emily Dickinson	**I'm Nobody** ◆ poem	188
Kristin Hunter	**The Scribe** ◆ short story	192
Amiri Baraka	**SOS** ◆ poem	198
Lillian Morrison	**The Women's 400 Meters** ◆ poem	202
Jack Anderson	**Where You Are** ◆ poem	203

Interdisciplinary Study Help Is on the Way

Scribes ◆ history 206

Can You Read This? ◆ mathematics 209

Who Cares? Millions Do by Milton Meltzer; Students Helping
  Students by Catherine A. Rolzinski ◆ community service 210

  Reading Mini-Lesson ◆ Using Graphic Aids 212

Writing Workshop Expository Writing

Trying Something New 213

Beyond Print Looking at Images

Dishwater or White Water? 219

Before Reading

The Smallest Dragonboy

by Anne McCaffrey

Anne McCaffrey
born 1926

Often called the "Dragon Lady," Anne McCaffrey has won many writing awards, including the Hugo—one of the highest honors for science fiction. At Dragonhold, her home in Ireland, she writes stories about fantastic winged dragons. Many of her most heroic characters are women and children who struggle to find their place, as McCaffrey did growing up in Massachusetts. "When I was a very young girl," she recalls, "I promised myself fervently (usually after I'd lost another battle with one of my brothers) that I would become a famous author." Often her stories center on the idea that if you want something, you will get it with enough effort and determination.

Building Background

Making a Good Impression In this science-fiction story, you enter the magical, hazardous world of Pern, a planet of volcanic rock formations called *weyrs.* Pern is threatened by the evil Thread, which carries *spores* (tiny cells) from the Red Star, a wandering planet. Spores that land on Pern feed on living matter. Flying dragons who can *go between* (fly through time and space) and communicate with their riders by *telepathy* (mental power) blast the Thread with their fiery breath.

The birth of new dragons is an important event on Pern. As soon as a dragon hatches from its large egg, it chooses its own rider—a worthy boy who *Impresses* (bonds with) the dragon. The dragon and dragonrider become lifelong partners.

Getting into the Story

Writer's Notebook On the planet Pern, one character deals with a situation many people on Earth often face—namely, the feeling of not fitting in. Have you ever felt left out because you were too big, too small, or just too *something?* What did you do about it? How did things turn out? Write about it in your notebook.

Reading Tip

Characters, Places, and Terms to Know Pern has its own unique vocabulary. The chart below explains some of the words in the story.

Keevan	main character; smallest candidate to be a dragonrider	**F'nor** and **L'vel**	experienced dragonriders
Beterli	oldest candidate to be a dragonrider	**Lessa**	the chief weyrwoman
Mende	Keevan's foster mother	**weyr**	community of dragonriders
K'last	a dragonrider and Keevan's father	**weyrleader**	the leader of a weyr
F'lar	the chief dragonrider and weyrleader	**wingsecond**	an officer in a weyr
pinions	a dragon's transparent wings	**turn**	a year

The Smallest

Anne McCaffrey

lthough Keevan lengthened his walking stride as far as his legs would stretch, he couldn't quite keep up with the other candidates. He knew he would be teased again.

Just as he knew many other things that his foster mother told him he ought not to know, Keevan knew that Beterli, the most senior of the boys, set that spanking[1] pace just to embarrass him, the smallest dragonboy. Keevan would arrive, tail fork-end of the group, breathless, chest heaving, and maybe get a stern look from the instructing wingsecond.

Dragonriders, even if they were still only hopeful candidates for the glowing eggs which were hardening on the hot sands of the Hatching Ground cavern, were expected to be punctual and prepared. Sloth[2] was not tolerated[3] by the Weyrleader of Benden Weyr. A good record was especially important now. It was very near hatching time, when the baby dragons would crack their mottled shells, and stagger forth to choose their lifetime companions. The very thought of that glorious

---

1. **spanking,** quick and vigorous.
2. **sloth** (slôth), laziness; unwillingness to work.
3. tolerate (tol′ə rāt′), v. permit; put up with.

Weyrworld, by Michael Whelan, was painted in 1991. How does the artist's vision of Keevan's planet differ from Earth? ➤

Dragonboy

moment made Keevan's breath catch in his throat. To be chosen—to be a dragonrider! To sit astride the neck of a winged beast with jeweled eyes: to be his friend, in telepathic communion with him for life; to be his companion in good times and fighting extremes; to fly effortlessly over the lands of Pern! Or, thrillingly, *between* to any point anywhere on the world! Flying *between* was done on dragonback or not at all, and it was dangerous.

Keevan glanced upward, past the black mouths of the weyr caves in which grown dragons and their chosen riders lived, toward the Star Stones that crowned the ridge of the old volcano that was Benden Weyr. On the height, the blue watch dragon, his rider mounted on his neck, stretched the great transparent pinions that carried him on the winds of Pern to fight the evil Thread that fell at certain times from the skies. The many-faceted rainbow jewels of his eyes glistened fleetingly in the greeny sun. He folded his great wings to his back, and the watch pair resumed their statuelike pose of alertness.

hen the enticing⁴ view was obscured⁵ as Keevan passed into the Hatching Ground cavern. The sands underfoot were hot, even through heavy wher-hide boots. How the bootmaker had protested having to sew so small! Keevan was forced to wonder why being small was reprehensible.⁶ People were always calling him "babe" and shooing him away as being "too small" or "too young" for this or that. Keevan was constantly working, twice as hard as any other boy his age, to prove himself capable. What if his muscles weren't as big as Beterli's? They were just as hard. And if he couldn't overpower anyone in a wrestling match, he could outdistance everyone in a footrace.

"Maybe if you run fast enough," Beterli had jeered on the occasion when Keevan had been goaded to boast of his swiftness, "you could catch a dragon. That's the only way you'll make a dragonrider!"

"You just wait and see, Beterli, you just wait," Keevan had replied. He would have liked to wipe the contemptuous⁷ smile from Beterli's face, but the guy didn't fight fair even when a wingsecond was watching. "No one knows what Impresses a dragon!"

"They've got to be able to *find* you first, babe!"

SUMMARIZE: What is Keevan's goal and what are his obstacles?

Yes, being the smallest candidate was not an enviable position. It was therefore imperative that Keevan Impress a dragon in his first hatching. That would wipe the smile off every face in the cavern and accord him the respect due any dragonrider, even the smallest one.

Besides, no one knew exactly what Impressed the baby dragons as they struggled from their shells in search of their lifetime partners.

"I like to believe that dragons see into a man's heart," Keevan's foster mother, Mende, told him. "If they find goodness, honesty, a flexible mind, patience, courage—and you've got that in quantity, dear Keevan—that's what dragons look for. I've seen many a well-grown lad left standing on the sands, Hatching Day, in favor of someone not so strong or tall or handsome. And if my memory serves me"— which it usually did: Mende knew every word of every Harper's tale worth telling, although Keevan did not interrupt her to say so—"I

---

4. **enticing,** arousing desire or hope; tempting.
5. **obscure** (əb skyùr′), *v.* hide from view; dim.
6. **reprehensible** (rep′ri hen′sə bəl), *adj.* deserving blame; hateful.
7. **contemptuous** (kən temp′chü əs), *adj.* scornful or mocking.

don't believe that F'lar, our Weyrleader, was all that tall when bronze Mnementh chose him. And Mnementh was the only bronze dragon of that hatching."

Dreams of Impressing a bronze were beyond Keevan's boldest reflections, although that goal dominated the thoughts of every other hopeful candidate. Green dragons were small and fast and more numerous. There was more prestige to Impressing a blue or brown than a green. Being practical, Keevan seldom dreamed as high as a big fighting brown, like Canth, F'nor's fine fellow, the biggest brown on all Pern. But to fly a bronze? Bronzes were almost as big as the queen, and only they took the air when a queen flew at mating time. A bronze rider could aspire to become Weyrleader! Well, Keevan would console himself, brown riders could aspire to become wingseconds, and that wasn't bad. He'd even settle for a green dragon: they were small, but so was he. No matter! He simply had to Impress a dragon his first time in the Hatching Ground. Then no one in the Weyr would taunt him anymore for being so small.

Shells, Keevan thought now, but the sands are hot!

"Impression time is <u>imminent</u>,[8] candidates," the wingsecond was saying as everyone crowded respectfully close to him. "See the extent of the striations on this promising egg." The stretch marks *were* larger than yesterday.

Everyone leaned forward and nodded thoughtfully. That particular egg was the one Beterli had marked as his own, and no other candidate dared, on pain of being beaten by Beterli at his first opportunity, to approach it. The egg was marked by a large yellowish splotch in the shape of a dragon backwinging to land, talons outstretched to grasp rock. Everyone knew that bronze eggs bore distinctive markings. And naturally, Beterli, who'd

been presented at eight Impressions already and was the biggest of the candidates, had chosen it.

"I'd say that the great opening day is almost upon us," the wingsecond went on, and then his face assumed a grave expression. "As we well know, there are only forty eggs and seventy-two candidates. Some of you may be disappointed on the great day. That doesn't necessarily mean you aren't dragonrider material, just that *the* dragon for you hasn't been shelled. You'll have other hatchings, and it's no disgrace to be left behind an Impression or two. Or more."

Keevan was positive that the wingsecond's eyes rested on Beterli, who'd been stood off at so many Impressions already. Keevan tried to squinch down so the wingsecond wouldn't notice him. Keevan had been reminded too often that he was eligible to be a candidate by one day only. He, of all the hopefuls, was most likely to be left standing on the great day. One more reason why he simply had to Impress at his first hatching.

"Now move about among the eggs," the wingsecond said. "Touch them. We don't know that it does any good, but it certainly doesn't do any harm."

Some of the boys laughed nervously, but everyone immediately began to circulate among the eggs. Beterli stepped up officiously to "his" egg, daring anyone to come near it. Keevan smiled, because he had already touched it—every inspection day, when the others were leaving the Hatching Ground and no one could see him crouch to stroke it.

Keevan had an egg he concentrated on, too, one drawn slightly to the far side of the others. The shell had a soft greenish-blue tinge with a faint creamy swirl design. The consensus[9] was that this egg contained a mere green, so Keevan was rarely bothered by rivals.

---

8. **imminent** (im'ə nənt), *adj.* about to happen soon.
9. **consensus** (kən sen'səs), general opinion.

A steady gaze and a commanding pose reveal the **individuality** of this young person, illustrated by Walter Velez. Do you think this youngster might one day be a dragonrider?

could get run down that way in the mad scramble. Oh, I forget, you can run fast, can't you?"

"You'd better make sure a dragon sees *you*, this time, Beterli," Keevan replied. "You're almost overage, aren't you?"

Beterli flushed and took a step forward, hand half-raised. Keevan stood his ground, but if Beterli advanced one more step, he would call the wingsecond. No one fought on the Hatching Ground. Surely Beterli knew that much.

Fortunately, at that moment, the wingsecond called the boys together and led them from the Hatching Ground to start on evening chores. There were "glows" to be replenished in the main kitchen caverns and sleeping cubicles, the major hallways, and the queen's apartment. Firestone sacks had to be filled against Thread attack, and black rock brought to the kitchen hearths. The boys fell to their chores, tantalized[10] by the odors of roasting meat. The population of the Weyr began to assemble for the evening meal, and the dragonriders came in from the Feeding Ground on their sweep checks.

It was the time of day Keevan liked best: once the chores were done but before dinner was served, a fellow could often get close enough to the dragonriders to hear their talk. Tonight, Keevan's father, K'last, was at the main dragonrider table. It puzzled Keevan how his father, a brown rider and a tall man, could *be* his father—because he, Keevan, was so small. It obviously puzzled K'last, too, when he deigned to notice his small son: "In a few more Turns, you'll be as tall as I am—or taller!"

K'last was pouring Benden wine all around the table. The dragonriders were relaxing. There'd be no Thread attack for three more days, and they'd be in the mood to tell tall tales, better than Harper yarns, about impossible

He was somewhat perturbed then to see Beterli wandering over to him.

"I don't know why you're allowed in this Impression, Keevan. There are enough of us without a babe," Beterli said, shaking his head.

"I'm of age," Keevan kept his voice level, telling himself not to be bothered by mere words.

"Yah!" Beterli made a show of standing on his toetips. "You can't even see over an egg; Hatching Day, you better get in front or the dragons won't see you at all. 'Course, you

---

10. **tantalize** (tan′tl īz), *v.* tease or torment with something desired.

maneuvers they'd done a-dragonback. When Thread attack was closer, their talk would change to a discussion of tactics of evasion, of going *between,* how long to suspend there until the burning but fragile Thread would freeze and crack and fall harmlessly off dragon and man. They would dispute the exact moment to feed firestone to the dragon so he'd have the best flame ready to sear Thread midair and render it harmless to ground—and man—below. There was such a lot to know and understand about being a dragonrider that sometimes Keevan was overwhelmed. How would he ever be able to remember everything he ought to know at the right moment? He couldn't dare ask such a question; this would only have given additional weight to the notion that he was too young yet to be a dragonrider.

SUMMARIZE: What is a dragonrider's job and what know-how does the job require?

"Having older candidates makes good sense," L'vel was saying, as Keevan settled down near the table. "Why waste four to five years of a dragon's fighting prime until his rider grows up enough to stand the rigors?" L'vel had Impressed a blue of Ramoth's first clutch. Most of the candidates thought L'vel was marvelous because he spoke up in front of the older riders, who awed them. "That was well enough in the Interval when you didn't need to mount the full Weyr complement[11] to fight Thread. But not now. Not with more eligible candidates than ever. Let the babes wait."

"Any boy who is over twelve Turns has the right to stand in the Hatching Ground," K'last replied, a slight smile on his face. He never argued or got angry. Keevan wished he were more like his father. And oh, how he wished he were a brown rider! "Only a dragon—each particular dragon—knows what he wants in a

rider. We certainly can't tell. Time and again the theorists," K'last's smile deepened as his eyes swept those at the table, "are surprised by dragon choice. *They* never seem to make mistakes, however."

"Now, K'last, just look at the roster this Impression. Seventy-two boys and only forty eggs. Drop off the twelve youngest, and there's still a good field for the hatchlings to choose from. Shells! There are a couple of weyrlings unable to see over a wher egg much less a dragon! And years before they can ride Thread."

"True enough, but the Weyr is scarcely under fighting strength, and if the youngest Impress, they'll be old enough to fight when the oldest of our current dragons go *between* from senility."

"Half the Weyr-bred lads have already been through several Impressions," one of the bronze riders said then. "I'd say drop some of *them* off this time. Give the untried a chance."

"There's nothing wrong in presenting a clutch with as wide a choice as possible," said the Weyrleader, who had joined the table with Lessa, the Weyrwoman.

"Has there ever been a case," she said, smiling in her odd way at the riders, "where a hatchling didn't choose?"

Her suggestion was almost heretical[12] and drew astonished gasps from everyone, including the boys.

F'lar laughed. "You say the most outrageous things, Lessa."

"Well, *has* there ever been a case where a dragon didn't choose?"

"Can't say as I recall one," K'last replied.

"Then we continue in this tradition," Lessa said firmly, as if that ended the matter.

But it didn't. The argument ranged from

---

11. **complement,** the number required to complete or fill something.
12. **heretical** (hə ret′ə kəl), having an opinion opposed to that accepted by authorities.

one table to the other all through dinner, with some favoring a weeding out of the candidates to the most likely, lopping off those who were very young or who had had multiple opportunities to Impress. All the candidates were in a swivet,[13] though such a departure from tradition would be to the advantage of many. As the evening progressed, more riders were favoring eliminating the youngest and those who'd passed four or more Impressions unchosen. Keevan felt he could bear such a dictum only if Beterli were also eliminated. But this seemed less likely than that Keevan would be turfed out,[14] since the Weyr's need was for fighting dragons and riders.

By the time the evening meal was over, no decision had been reached, although the Weyrleader had promised to give the matter due consideration.

e might have slept on the problem, but few of the candidates did. Tempers were uncertain in the sleeping caverns next morning as the boys were routed out of their beds to carry water and black rock and cover the "glows." Twice Mende had to call Keevan to order for clumsiness.

"Whatever is the matter with you, boy?" she demanded in exasperation when he tipped black rock short of the bin and sooted up the hearth.

"They're going to keep me from this Impression."

"What?" Mende stared at him. "Who?"

"You heard them talking at dinner last night. They're going to turf the babes from the hatching."

Mende regarded him a moment longer before touching his arm gently. "There's lots of talk around a supper table, Keevan. And it cools as soon as the supper. I've heard the same nonsense before every hatching, but nothing is ever changed."

"There's always a first time," Keevan answered, copying one of her own phrases.

"That'll be enough of that, Keevan. Finish your job. If the clutch does hatch today, we'll need full rock bins for the feast, and you won't be around to do the filling. All my fosterlings make dragonriders."

"The first time?" Keevan was bold enough to ask as he scooted off with the rockbarrow.

Perhaps, Keevan thought later, if he hadn't been on that chore just when Beterli was also fetching black rock, things might have turned out differently. But he had dutifully trundled the barrow to the outdoor bunker for another load just as Beterli arrived on a similar errand.

"Heard the news, babe?" Beterli asked. He was grinning from ear to ear, and he put an unnecessary emphasis on the final insulting word.

"The eggs are cracking?" Keevan all but dropped the loaded shovel. Several anxieties flicked through his mind then: he was black with rock dust—would he have time to wash before donning the white tunic of candidacy? And if the eggs were hatching, why hadn't the candidates been recalled by the wingsecond?

"Naw! Guess again!" Beterli was much too pleased with himself.

With a sinking heart, Keevan knew what the news must be, and he could only stare with intense desolation at the older boy.

"C'mon! Guess, babe!"

"I've no time for guessing games," Keevan managed to say with indifference. He began to shovel black rock into the barrow as fast as he could.

"I said, guess." Beterli grabbed the shovel.

"And I said I have no time for guessing games."

Beterli wrenched the shovel from Keevan's hands. "Guess!"

---

13. **swivet,** a state of high agitation or upset.
14. **turfed out,** British slang for kicked out; expelled from a desirable position.

"I'll have that shovel back, Beterli." Keevan straightened up, but he didn't come to Beterli's bulky shoulder. From somewhere, other boys appeared, some with barrows, some mysteriously alerted to the prospect of a confrontation[15] among their numbers.

"Babes don't give orders to candidates around here, babe!"

Someone sniggered and Keevan, incredulous, knew that he must've been dropped from the candidacy.

He yanked the shovel from Beterli's loosened grasp. Snarling, the older boy tried to regain possession, but Keevan clung with all his strength to the handle, dragged back and forth as the stronger boy jerked the shovel about.

With a sudden, unexpected movement, Beterli rammed the handle into Keevan's chest, knocking him over the barrow handles. Keevan felt a sharp, painful jab behind his left ear, an unbearable pain in his left shin, and then a painless nothingness.

Mende's angry voice roused him, and startled, he tried to throw back the covers, thinking he'd overslept. But he couldn't move, so firmly was he tucked into his bed. And then the constriction of a bandage on his head and the dull sickishness in his leg brought back recent occurrences.

"Hatching?" he cried.

"No, lovey," Mende said in a kind voice. Her hand was cool and gentle on his forehead. "Though there's some as won't be at any hatching again." Her voice took on a stern edge.

Keevan looked beyond her to see the Weyrwoman, who was frowning with irritation.

"Keevan, will you tell me what occurred at the black-rock bunker?" asked Lessa in an even voice.

He remembered Beterli now and the quarrel over the shovel and . . . what had Mende said about some not being at any hatching? Much as he hated Beterli, he couldn't bring himself to tattle on Beterli and force him out of candidacy.

"Come, lad," and a note of impatience crept into the Weyrwoman's voice. "I merely want to know what happened from you, too. Mende said she sent you for black rock. Beterli—and every Weyrling in the cavern—seems to have been on the same errand. What happened?"

CONNECT: If you were Keevan, what would you say to Lessa?

"Beterli took my shovel. I hadn't finished with it."

"There's more than one shovel. What did he *say* to you?"

"He'd heard the news."

"What news?" The Weyrwoman was suddenly amused.

"That . . . that . . . there'd been changes."

"Is that what he said?"

"Not exactly."

"What did he say? C'mon, lad, I've heard from everyone else, you know."

"He said for me to guess the news."

"And you fell for that old gag?" The Weyrwoman's irritation returned.

"Consider all the talk last night at supper, Lessa," Mende said. "Of course the boy would think he'd been eliminated."

"In effect, he is, with a broken skull and leg." Lessa touched his arm in a rare gesture of sympathy. "Be that as it may, Keevan, you'll have other Impressions. Beterli will not. There are certain rules that must be observed by all candidates, and his conduct proves him unacceptable to the Weyr."

She smiled at Mende and then left.

"I'm still a candidate?" Keevan asked urgently.

---

15. **confrontation** (kon′frən tā′shən), *n.* face-to-face standoff or opposition.

"Well, you are and you aren't, lovey," his foster mother said. "Is the numbweed working?" she asked, and when he nodded, she said, "You just rest. I'll bring you some nice broth."

At any other time in his life, Keevan would have relished such cosseting,[16] but now he just lay there worrying. Beterli had been dismissed. Would the others think it was his fault? But everyone was there! Beterli provoked that fight. His worry increased, because although he heard excited comings and goings in the passageway, no one tweaked back the curtain across the sleeping alcove he shared with five other boys. Surely one of them would have to come in sometime. No, they were all avoiding him. And something else was wrong. Only he didn't know what.

Mende returned with broth and beachberry bread.

"Why doesn't anyone come see me, Mende? I haven't done anything wrong, have I? I didn't ask to have Beterli turfed out."

Mende soothed him, saying everyone was busy with noontime chores and no one was angry with him. They were giving him a chance to rest in quiet. The numbweed made him drowsy, and her words were fair enough. He permitted his fears to dissipate.[17] Until he heard a hum. Actually, he felt it first, in the broken shin bone and his sore head. The hum began to grow. Two things registered suddenly in Keevan's groggy mind: the only white candidate's robe still on the pegs in the chamber was his; and the dragons hummed when a clutch was being laid or being hatched. Impression! And he was flat abed.

Bitter, bitter disappointment turned the warm broth sour in his belly. Even the small voice telling him that he'd have other opportunities failed to alleviate[18] his crushing depression. *This* was the Impression that mattered! This was his chance to show *everyone*,

from Mende to K'last to L'vel and even the Weyrleader that he, Keevan, was worthy of being a dragonrider.

He twisted in bed, fighting against the tears that threatened to choke him. Dragonmen don't cry! Dragonmen learn to live with pain.

Pain? The leg didn't actually pain him as he rolled about on his bedding. His head felt sort of stiff from the tightness of the bandage. He sat up, an effort in itself since the numbweed made exertion difficult. He touched the splinted leg; the knee was unhampered. He had no feeling in his bone, really. He swung himself carefully to the side of his bed and stood slowly. The room wanted to swim about him. He closed his eyes, which made the dizziness worse, and he had to clutch the wall.

Gingerly, he took a step. The broken leg dragged. It hurt in spite of the numbweed, but what was pain to a dragonman?

No one had said he couldn't go to the Impression. "You are and you aren't," were Mende's exact words.

Clinging to the wall, he jerked off his bedshirt. Stretching his arm to the utmost, he jerked his white candidate's tunic from the peg. Jamming first one arm and then the other into the holes, he pulled it over his head. Too bad about the belt. He couldn't wait. He hobbled to the door, hung on to the curtain to steady himself. The weight on his leg was unwieldy. He wouldn't get very far without something to lean on. Down by the bathing pool was one of the long crooknecked poles used to retrieve clothes from the hot washing troughs. But it was down there, and he was on the level above. And there was no one nearby to come to his aid: everyone would be in the Hatching Ground right now, eagerly waiting for the first egg to crack.

---

16. **cosset** (kos′it), treat as a pet; pamper.
17. **dissipate,** disappear; dispel.
18. **alleviate** (ə lē′vē āt), *v.* relieve; lessen.

A *Destiny's Road,* by Michael Whelan, was painted in 1991. How does the artist communicate the rugged **individuality** of those who want to be dragonriders?

The humming increased in volume and tempo, an urgency to which Keevan responded, knowing that his time was all too limited if he was to join the ranks of the hopeful boys standing around the cracking eggs. But if he hurried down the ramp, he'd fall flat on his face.

He could, of course, go flat on his rear end, the way crawling children did. He sat down, sending a jarring stab of pain through his leg and up to the wound on the back of his head. Gritting his teeth and blinking away tears, Keevan scrabbled down the ramp. He had to wait a moment at the bottom to catch his breath. He got to one knee, the injured leg straight out in front of him. Somehow, he managed to push himself erect, though the room seemed about to tip over his ears. It wasn't far to the crooked stick, but it seemed an age before he had it in his hand.

Then the humming stopped!

Keevan cried out and began to hobble frantically across the cavern, out to the bowl of the Weyr. Never had the distance between living caverns and the Hatching Ground seemed so great. Never had the Weyr been so breathlessly silent. It was as if the multitude of people and dragons watching the hatching held every breath in suspense. Not even the wind muttered down the steep sides of the

The Smallest Dragonboy   **179**

bowl. The only sounds to break the stillness were Keevan's ragged gasps and the thump-thud of his stick on the hard-packed ground. Sometimes he had to hop twice on his good leg to maintain his balance. Twice he fell into the sand and had to pull himself up on the stick, his white tunic no longer spotless. Once he jarred himself so badly he couldn't get up immediately.

hen he heard the first exhalation of the crowd, the oohs, the muted cheer, the susurrus[19] of excited whispers. An egg had cracked, and the dragon had chosen his rider. Desperation increased Keevan's hobble. Would he never reach the arching mouth of the Hatching Ground?

Another cheer and an excited spate of applause spurred Keevan to greater effort. If he didn't get there in moments, there'd be no unpaired hatchling left. Then he was actually staggering to the Hatching Ground, the sands hot on his bare feet.

No one noticed his entrance or his halting progress. And Keevan could see nothing but the backs of the white-robed candidates, seventy of them ringing the area around the eggs. Then one side would surge forward or back and there'd be a cheer. Another dragon had been Impressed. Suddenly a large gap appeared in the white human wall, and Keevan had his first sight of the eggs. There didn't seem to be *any* left uncracked, and he could see the lucky boys standing beside wobble-legged dragons. He could hear the unmistakable plaintive crooning of hatchlings and their squawks of protest as they'd fall awkwardly in the sand.

Suddenly he wished that he hadn't left his bed, that he'd stayed away from the Hatching Ground. Now everyone would see his ignominious[20] failure. So he scrambled as desperately to reach the shadowy walls of the Hatching Ground as he had struggled to cross the bowl. He mustn't be seen.

PREDICT: Keevan has finally made it to the Hatching Ground. What do you think will happen?

He didn't notice, therefore, that the shifting group of boys remaining had begun to drift in his direction. The hard pace he had set himself and his cruel disappointment took their double toll of Keevan. He tripped and collapsed sobbing to the warm sands. He didn't see the consternation[21] in the watching Weyrfolk above the Hatching Ground, nor did he hear the excited whispers of speculation. He didn't know that the Weyrleader and Weyrwoman had dropped to the arena and were making their way toward the knot of boys slowly moving in the direction of the entrance.

"Never seen anything like it," the Weyrleader was saying. "Only thirty-nine riders chosen. And the bronze trying to leave the Hatching Ground without making Impression."

"A case in point of what I said last night," the Weyrwoman replied, "where a hatchling makes no choice because the right boy isn't there."

"There's only Beterli and K'last's young one missing. And there's a full wing of likely boys to choose from . . ."

"None acceptable, apparently. Where is the creature going? He's not heading for the entrance after all. Oh, what have we there, in the shadows?"

Keevan heard with dismay the sound of voices nearing him. He tried to burrow into

---

19. **susurrus** (sù sėr′əs), soft whispering.
20. **ignominious** (ig′nə min′ē əs), shameful, disgraceful.
21. **consternation** (kon′stər nā′shən), *n.* great dismay.

the sand. The mere thought of how he would be teased and taunted now was unbearable.

Don't worry! Please don't worry! The thought was urgent, but not his own.

Someone kicked sand over Keevan and butted roughly against him.

"Go away. Leave me alone!" he cried.

Why? was the injured-sounding question inserted into his mind. There was no voice, no tone, but the question was there, perfectly clear, in his head.

Incredulous, Keevan lifted his head and stared into the glowing jeweled eyes of a small bronze dragon. His wings were wet, the tips drooping in the sand. And he sagged in the middle on his unsteady legs, although he was making a great effort to keep erect.

Keevan dragged himself to his knees, oblivious[22] of the pain in his leg. He wasn't even aware that he was ringed by the boys passed over, while thirty-one pairs of resentful eyes watched him Impress the dragon. The Weyrmen looked on amused and surprised at the draconic choice, which could not be forced. Could not be questioned. Could not be changed.

Why? asked the dragon again. *Don't you like me?* His eyes whirled with anxiety, and his tone was so piteous that Keevan staggered forward and threw his arms around the dragon's neck, stroking his eye ridges, patting the damp, soft hide, opening the fragile-looking wings to dry them, and wordlessly assuring the hatchling over and over again that he was the most perfect, most beautiful, most beloved dragon in the Weyr, in all the Weyrs of Pern.

"What's his name, K'van?" asked Lessa, smiling warmly at the new dragonrider. K'van stared up at her for a long moment. Lessa would know as soon as he did. Lessa was the only person who could "receive" from all dragons, not only her own Ramoth. Then he gave her a radiant smile, recognizing the traditional shortening of his name that raised him forever to the rank of dragonrider.

My name is Heth, the dragon thought mildly, then hiccuped in sudden urgency. *I'm hungry.*

"Dragons are born hungry," said Lessa, laughing. "F'lar, give the boy a hand. He can barely manage his own legs, much less a dragon's."

K'van remembered his stick and drew himself up. "We'll be just fine, thank you."

"You may be the smallest dragonrider ever, young K'van," F'lar said, "but you're one of the bravest!"

And Heth agreed! Pride and joy so leaped in both chests that K'van wondered if his heart would burst right out of his body. He looped an arm around Heth's neck and the pair, the smallest dragonboy and the hatchling who wouldn't choose anybody else, walked out of the Hatching Ground together forever.

---

22. **oblivious** (ə bliv′ē əs), *adj.* paying no attention; unaware.

After Reading

Making Connections

1. Do you think Beterli deserved to be banned from all future Impressions? Explain your **point of view.**

2. Choose a passage you particularly like from the story and read it aloud to the class. Tell why the part you selected appeals to you.

3. Name a **character trait** of Keevan you especially admire. Find one or more places in the story that show this quality.

4. Often, science-fiction characters are good people or evil people, not well-rounded beings with both good and bad traits. Do you think Keevan and Beterli fit that pattern? Explain.

5. At what point in the story did you guess Keevan would Impress a dragon? What part, if any, of the outcome surprised you?

6. Both Keevan and Beterli struggle to find their place. What place do you expect these two characters to have on Pern as adults?

7. How is this science-fiction story *like* and *unlike* another type of fiction you know, such as a western or a survival story? You can use a Venn diagram like the one at the right to note your ideas.

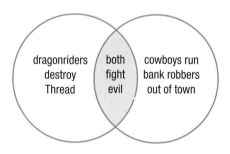

dragonriders destroy Thread | both fight evil | cowboys run bank robbers out of town

Literary Focus: Plot

A story is made up of a series of events we call the **plot.** At some point in a story, usually near the end, there is a **climax,** or turning point—the most exciting moment in the story. This decisive event leads the story to its conclusion.

With a partner, find the climax in "The Smallest Dragonboy." What changes occur or conclusion results from the climax? You can note your ideas on a diagram like the one at the right.

Climax

Change #1 Keevan is knocked unconscious.

Change #2

Change #3

Conclusion

Vocabulary Study

Decide if the following pairs are synonyms or antonyms. Make an answer sheet and write *S* for synonym or *A* for antonym.

tolerate
obscure
reprehensible
contemptuous
imminent
tantalize
confrontation
alleviate
consternation
oblivious

1. obscure—clear
2. oblivious—aware
3. contemptuous—mocking
4. consternation—confidence
5. reprehensible—blameworthy
6. tolerate—permit
7. confrontation—opposition
8. imminent—delayed
9. tantalize—torment
10. alleviate—worsen

Expressing Your Ideas

Writing Choices

Out of This World With a small group, collaborate on a **science-fiction story** set on another planet (real or imaginary). After your team plans the setting, characters, and plot, you might divide the events among group members to write.

Dear Diary, . . . Take the part of one of these characters—Mende, Beterli, or Keevan. Write a series of **diary entries** describing events in the story. Another option is to write three entries about the same event in the diaries of Mende, Beterli, and Keevan.

Heth, Do You Read Me? Heth sends thought messages to Keevan. Write a **speech** in which Keevan mentally introduces himself to Heth.

Other Options

Suited to a T Keevan and Beterli have very distinct and different personalities. **Design** a T-shirt for each character. Include symbols, words, or sayings that express important aspects of each one's character.

A Place in the Story Work on your own or with a partner to create a **diorama** or **mural** of the Hatching Grounds of Pern. Before you begin, go back to the story for details about the setting. Jot them down or make rough sketches of what you envision.

Fighting for a Place Imagine you are Beterli's lawyer. Present a **speech** in which you try to convince F'lar the Weyrleader to give Beterli another chance to be a dragonrider.

Language Mini-Lesson

Combining Sentences

Simple sentences such as *John and Sue drove to Los Angeles* are important in writing, but a whole string of them can result in dull and repetitive writing. To keep your writing focused and interesting, combine related ideas into compound and complex sentences.

Sentence-Combining Strategies

Here are two ways to combine simple sentences that have related ideas.

John bathed the dog. The dog shook water on John.

Compound Sentence: Use a comma and a coordinating conjunction such as *and, but,* and *or* to combine simple sentences with similar ideas into a compound sentence.

John bathed the dog, and the dog shook water on him.

Complex Sentence: Use a subordinating conjunction such as *after, because, since,* or *when* to join simple sentences with similar ideas into a complex sentence.

When John bathed the dog, she shook water on him.

Activity Options

1. Work with a partner to combine the following simple sentences.
   Jeff and April planned a birthday party. The party was to be a surprise. The party was for Jeff and April's friend Anne. Jeff and April are the ones who got the surprise. Anne left town on the day of the party.

2. Work with a partner or group to write a radio commercial persuading consumers to use Power Glue, a new product on the market. Use only complex sentences. After the commercial is written, have one group member present it to the class.

3. Imagine that you have some chores to do around the house that you really don't want to do. Think of a funny reason why you can't do these jobs and write down what you would say to get out of the work. Use compound and complex sentences. Then read your explanation aloud to a partner or to the class.

Before Reading

Never Fitting In by Nereida Román

I'm Nobody by Emily Dickinson

Nereida Román
born 1976

As a high-school student, Román belonged to a group called *Las Mujeres Hispanas* (Latina Women).The group met to read and talk about the writings of famous Hispanic women. During that time, Román wrote "Never Fitting In."

Emily Dickinson
1830–1886

Seven of her poems were published in Dickinson's lifetime. Late at night, alone, she wrote nearly 1,800 more on whatever paper was at hand. After she died, her poems found their place among our literary treasures.

Building Background

Two Worlds, One Goal The authors of these selections—an autobiography and a poem—focus on finding their special place. Yet they come from very different times and situations. Nereida Román is a young writer growing up in the 1990s in New York City—a big, culturally diverse place with up-to-the-minute attitudes. Román writes about her experiences at her school in *El Barrio,* the Hispanic community.

Emily Dickinson grew up in a quiet Massachusetts village in the 1800s. In her strict, slow-paced world, people rode in horse-drawn carriages, and household duties filled a woman's days. Respectable people were those who worked hard, put mind before feeling, practiced self-restraint, and showed devotion to God and family.

Getting into the Selections

Writer's Notebook The next two selections are about people being who they are. Have you ever tried to please others by *not* being yourself? In your notebook, write what you like about being you no matter what others think.

To get started, write your name in a circle. Around the circle jot down words and phrases about yourself. When something pops up that you particularly like, begin writing.

energetic . . . *people say I'm h-y-p-e-r, but I'm just high energy. If you say "let's race," I say "go!" One time. . .*

Reading Tip

Well-Formed Opinions Nereida Román and Emily Dickinson know their own minds and say what they think. As you read, ask yourself if you agree with their opinions. Responding to others' opinions can make you more clear about your own.

NEVER FITTING IN

Nereida Román

As you may have guessed, my name is Nereida Román. If you don't think that you can pronounce it, you're not alone. Almost nobody can. It's a strange name to go with a strange person, as you will probably notice when you read what I've written.

I'm thirteen and in the eighth grade. No, I wasn't skipped. I started school early. I think that was one of the dumbest things I ever did. It means I could probably graduate from high school when I'm sixteen.

I'm strange! I've always done things differently. For example, all the girls in school are into boys, music and more boys. I don't like boys. Well, I like them a little, but they're not as important to me as they are to some of the other girls.

I've been the kind of person that never fits in right, but the thing that has bothered me the most is being called a "tomboy." After that comes, of course, being called a "nerd" (which, because of my age and grade, seems to be the truth). And if kids have nothing else to bother me about, they bother me about my hair. It never seems to stay in the right place.

I don't see why people make such a big deal about a girl playing "boys' games." I don't even see why people say that most sports are boys' sports. To me all sports are for everybody. But people never think of it from my point of view. I don't think that there is anything wrong with a girl playing football, basketball or any other sport.

Everybody makes fun of me. "Tomboy, why don't you act like a girl?" they say to me. I don't understand what they want me to act like. Girls don't act a certain way. If I want to play sports, I think that it's my business. Even if other people don't think that it is acceptable, I think they should mind their own business.

I was on the school basketball team. I was the only girl on the team. During the entire season I only got one pass. From the beginning of the season all the way to the end, I was never accepted by any other member of the team. I was really bothered at first. I was so bothered that I quit the team, but I noticed then that when I was on the team, I was having a lot of fun, more than I ever thought. So I joined the team again, but I still don't fit in

▲ Elsie Benally created *Women's Basketball Team* from sun-dried clay, paint, wool, and cardboard. Would you like to join them for a little four-on-four?

right. They still bother me to this day, but I don't pay much attention to them anymore.

'm not too sure why I turned out to be a tomboy, but I think it had something to do with my having lived among boys, five older than me and one younger. I didn't have an older sister or live with any other girls. My mother raised me, my two brothers, and the other four boys as equals. I played almost every sport you can think of when I was younger, and I still do now. I always thought that there was nothing wrong with having fun my way but, of course, nobody agrees with me.

I'm not the only tomboy in my family, but I'm the first. Sometimes I think that some of my cousins have followed my example. I hope they don't have the same problems that I, and probably all the tomboys in the world, have had. I'm not sure if my cousins look up to me, or if they just like sports. I never told them that it's okay to be different, but every now and then, they tell me.

▲ *Mink Pond,* by Winslow Homer, was painted in 1891. Why do you think Winslow Homer and Emily Dickinson both featured the image of a frog in their work? What meaning does the frog convey in the painting and in the poem?

I'M NOBODY

Emily Dickinson

I'm nobody! Who are you?
Are you nobody, too?
Then there's a pair of us—don't tell!
They'd banish us, you know.

5 How dreary to be somebody!
How public, like a frog
To tell your name the livelong day
To an admiring bog.

After Reading

Making Connections

1. Draw silhouettes of Nereida Román's and Emily Dickinson's heads. Write words and phrases in each outline to show what you think would be on their minds.

I've never fitted in!

What a joy to be on one's own!

2. Nereida Román is determined to maintain her **individuality,** yet she feels she is "strange." What do you think?

3. Compare points made by Román with those made by Dickinson. How are their challenges alike? How are they different?

4. Nereida Román isn't sure if her cousins look up to her, or if they just like sports. What do you think? Why?

5. Emily Dickinson sometimes worried about being "different" from other people. In this poem, does she seem worried? Find one or more phrases in the poem that support your answer.

6. Do you think Román could relate to Dickinson's poem? Why or why not?

7. Look back at the notes you made for your notebook entry. Draw a similar web for Nereida Román. Add as many elements of her personality as you can.

8. What opportunities are available for young women trying to find their place in sports after completing high school?

Literary Focus: Tone

In a piece of writing, the author's attitude toward the subject is called **tone.** Like a tone of voice in speaking, tone in writing expresses feeling—surprise, amusement, impatience, pride, and so on. Tone can also affect the meaning of words.

Reread the second stanza of the poem "I'm Nobody" with this question in mind: *What is Dickinson's attitude toward being a "somebody"?* How would you describe her tone? What words, images, or comparisons are the clues?

Vocabulary Study

Vocabulary Template Look at the template below, which focuses on the word *dreary*. Next, create a template of your own using the word *banish* from "I'm Nobody."

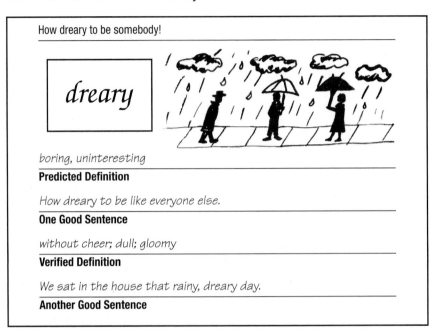

How dreary to be somebody!

dreary

boring, uninteresting
Predicted Definition

How dreary to be like everyone else.
One Good Sentence

without cheer; dull; gloomy
Verified Definition

We sat in the house that rainy, dreary day.
Another Good Sentence

Expressing Your Ideas ⎯⎯⎯⎯⎯⎯⎯

Writing Choices

My Place Recall how Nereida Román finds her place on the boys' basketball team. Write an **autobiographical sketch** about finding your own place. You may want to use your Before Reading web for ideas.

Tell Me This Reflect on what Román and Dickinson say about finding a place. What else would you like to know about their experiences? Write down **questions** you would ask these authors if you could.

Looking Ahead Do some **research** on a career in which you might be interested. Look for information on the skills and education needed, and the job availability.

Other Options

She Scored How Many Goals? Román's teammates don't quite accept her. In a small group, create a **questionnaire** that investigates classmates' attitudes about girls and boys on the same sports teams. Show the results on a **graph.**

A Room of Her Own Use your imagination and what you know about Román or Dickinson and **draw a picture** of her room. Go back to the selections for ideas on what would make a room the right place for the author. Explain your drawing to the class.

The Scribe

by Kristin Hunter

Kristin Hunter
born 1935

An avid reader by the age of five, Kristen Hunter doesn't remember a time when she didn't want to be a writer. As an only child surrounded mostly by grownups, she filled lonely hours making up fantasies and reading books. That, she feels, was the best possible training for her writing career. After writing two books for adults, an editor suggested she write for children—an "outlandish" idea Hunter first thought. Then one day a group of young people singing on the street captured her interest and imagination. Those street singers inspired her first novel for teens, *The Soul Brothers and Sister Lou.*

Building Background

A Legacy of Slavery Slave owners of the 1800s thought educated slaves were hard to control, so it became a crime in the South to teach *any* black person to read. When slavery ended, a huge number of blacks were set free unable to read and write. Such a sweeping obstacle takes generations to overcome.

The price of *not* having an education is high—especially if you lack skills in reading, writing, and math. Check cashing businesses, also called currency exchanges, serve people who don't trust or understand banks. Such stores charge up to 6% of the amount of the check or money order, plus a service fee.

Getting into the Story

Discussion Imagine yourself in this situation: You are baby-sitting a child who needs a dose of medicine while you're in charge. You don't know exactly *what, when,* or *how much.* Fortunately, the mom wrote you a note. Unfortunately, you can't read!

Does that scene seem farfetched to you? Many Americans—young and old—struggle with **illiteracy.** Even though they are intelligent, they can't read a label or jot down a phone message.

In a group, brainstorm examples of how people depend on reading and writing. Organize your ideas on a chart.

Things to Read and Write	Why It Is Important
Mrs. Jones leaves a note when I baby-sit.	It tells me how to reach her in an emergency.

Reading Tip

Understanding Motivation Throughout this story, the main character takes bold and unusual steps in his neighborhood. A radical action, however, can make perfect sense when you know the reasons behind it. As you read, look for what motivates a young boy to interrupt business-as-usual.

The Scribe

Kristin Hunter

W e been living in the apartment over the Silver Dollar Check Cashing Service five years. But I never had any reason to go in there till two days ago, when Mom had to go to the Wash-a-Mat and asked me to get some change.

And man! Are those people who come in there in some bad shape.

Old man Silver and old man Dollar, who own the place, have signs tacked up everywhere:

NO LOUNGING, NO LOITERING
THIS IS **NOT** A WAITING ROOM
and
MINIMUM CHECK CASHING FEE, 50¢
and
LETTERS ADDRESSED, 50¢
and
LETTERS READ, 75¢
and
LETTERS WRITTEN, ONE DOLLAR

The Block by Romare Bearden was created in 1971 from cut and pasted paper on board. How does James express his **individuality** in a crowded inner city environment like the one portrayed here? ➤

And everybody who comes in there to cash a check gets their picture taken like they're some kind of criminal.

After I got my change, I stood around for a while digging the action. First comes an old lady with some kind of long form to fill out. The mean old man behind the counter points to the "One Dollar" sign. She nods. So he starts to fill it out for her.

"Name?"

"Muskogee Marie Lawson."

"SPELL it!" he hollers.

"M, m, u, s—well, I don't exactly know, sir."

"I'll put down 'Marie,' then. Age?"

"Sixty-three my last birthday."

"Date of birth?"

"March twenty-third"—a pause—"I think, 1900."

"Look, Marie," he says, which makes me mad, hearing him first-name a dignified[1] old gray-haired lady like that, "if you'd been born in 1900, you'd be seventy-two. Either I put that down, or I put 1910."

"Whatever you think best, sir," she says timidly.[2]

---

1. **dignified** (dig′nə fīd), *adj.* having self-respect or pride.
2. **timidly** (tim′id lē), *adv.* shyly; fearfully.

He sighs, rolls his eyes to the ceiling, and bangs his fist on the form angrily. Then he fills out the rest.

"One dollar," he says when he's finished. She pays like she's grateful to him for taking the trouble.

Next is a man with a cane, a veteran who has to let the government know he moved. He wants old man Silver to do this for him, but he doesn't want him to know he can't do it himself.

"My eyes are kind of bad, sir, will you fill this thing out for me? Tell them I moved from 121 South 15th Street to 203 North Decatur Street."

Old man Silver doesn't blink an eye. Just fills out the form, and charges the crippled man a dollar.

And it goes on like that. People who can't read or write or count their change. People who don't know how to pay their gas bills, don't know how to fill out forms, don't know how to address envelopes. And old man Silver and old man Dollar cleaning up on all of them. It's pitiful. It's disgusting. Makes me so mad I want to yell.

And I do, but mostly at Mom. "Mom, did you know there are hundreds of people in this city who can't read and write?"

Mom isn't upset. She's a wise woman. "Of course, James," she says. "A lot of older people around here haven't had your advantages. They came from down South, and they had to quit school very young to go to work.

"In the old days, nobody cared whether our people got an education. They were only interested in getting the crops in." She sighed. "Sometimes I think they *still* don't care. If we hadn't gotten you into that good school, you might not be able to read so well either. A lot of boys and girls your age can't, you know."

"But that's awful!" I say. "How do they expect us to make it in a big city? You can't even cross the streets if you can't read the WALK and DON'T WALK signs."

"It's hard," Mom says, "but the important thing to remember is it's no disgrace. There was a time in history when nobody could read or write except a special class of people."

And Mom takes down her Bible. She has three Bible study certificates and is always giving me lessons from Bible history. I don't exactly go for all the stuff she believes in, but sometimes it *is* interesting.

"In ancient times," she says, "no one could read or write except a special class of people known as *scribes*. It was their job to write down the laws given by the rabbis and the judges. No one else could do it.

"Jesus criticized the scribes," she goes on, "because they were so proud of themselves. But he needed them to write down his teachings."

"Man," I said when she finished, "that's something."

My mind was working double-time. I'm the best reader and writer in our class. Also it was summertime. I had nothing much to do except go to the park or hang around the library and read till my eyeballs were ready to fall out, and I was tired of doing both.

So the next morning, after my parents went to work, I took Mom's card table and a folding chair down to the sidewalk. I lettered a sign with a Magic Marker, and I was in business. My sign said:

Public SCRIBE
All Services FREE

I set my table up in front of the Silver Dollar and waited for business. Only one thing bothered me. If the people couldn't read, how would they know what I was there for?

But five minutes had hardly passed when an old lady stopped and asked me to read her grandson's letter. She explained that she had just broken her glasses. I knew she was fibbing, but I kept quiet.

I read the grandson's letter. It said he was having a fine time in California, but was a little short. He would send her some money as soon as he made another payday. I handed the letter back to her.

"Thank you, son," she said, and gave me a quarter.

I handed that back to her too.

The word got around. By noontime I had a whole crowd of customers around my table. I was kept busy writing letters, addressing envelopes, filling out forms, and explaining official-looking letters that scared people half to death.

I didn't blame them. The language in some of those letters—"Establish whether your disability[3] is one-fourth, one-third, one-half, or total, and substantiate[4] in paragraph 3(b) below"—would upset anybody. I mean, why can't the government write English like everybody else?

Only one long shadow fell across my table. The shadow of a tall, heavy, blue-eyed cop.

Most of my customers were old, but there were a few young ones too. Like the girl who had gotten a letter about her baby from the Health Service and didn't know what "immunization"[5] meant.

At noontime one old lady brought me some iced tea and a peach, and another gave me some fried chicken wings. I was really having a good time, when the shade of all the people standing around me suddenly vanished. The sun hit me like a ton of hot bricks.

Only one long shadow fell across my table. The shadow of a tall, heavy, blue-eyed cop. In our neighborhood, when they see a cop, people scatter. That was why the back of my neck was burning.

"What are you trying to do here, sonny?" the cop asks.

"Help people out," I tell him calmly, though my knees are knocking together under the table.

"Well, you know," he says, "Mr. Silver and Mr. Dollar have been in business a long time on this corner. They are very respected men in this neighborhood. Are you trying to run them out of business?"

"I'm not charging anybody," I pointed out.

"That," the cop says, "is exactly what they don't like. Mr. Silver says he is glad to have some help with the letter-writing. Mr. Dollar says it's only a nuisance[6] to them anyway and takes up too much time. But if you don't charge for your services, it's unfair competition."

Well, why not? I thought. After all, I could use a little profit.

"All right," I tell him. "I'll charge a quarter."

"Then it is my duty to warn you," the cop says, "that it's against the law to conduct a business without a license.[7] The first time you accept a fee, I'll close you up and run you off this corner."

He really had me there. What did I know about licenses? I'm only thirteen, after all. Suddenly I didn't feel like the big black businessman anymore. I felt like a little kid who wanted to holler for his mother. But she was at work, and so was Daddy.

"I'll leave," I said, and did, with all the cool I could muster. But inside I was burning up, and not from the sun.

---

3. **disability** (dis′ə bil′ə tē), *n.* lack of ability or power to do or act.
4. **substantiate** (səb stan′shē āt), prove.
5. **immunization** (im′yə nī zā′shən), *n.* protection from disease.
6. **nuisance** (nü′sns), *n.* something that annoys or troubles.
7. **license** (lī′sns), *n.* a card or paper that shows permission by law.

Seated Negress, by Robert Vickrey, was painted in 1954. How does the artist convey his respect for this woman's dignity and **individuality**?

One little old lady hollered, "You big bully!" and shook her umbrella at the cop. But the rest of those people were so beaten-down they didn't say anything. Just shuffled back on inside to give Mr. Silver and Mr. Dollar their hard-earned money like they always did.

I was so mad I didn't know what to do with myself that afternoon. I couldn't watch TV. It was all soap operas anyway, and they seemed dumber than ever. The library didn't appeal to me either. It's not air-conditioned, and the day was hot and muggy.

Finally I went to the park and threw stones at the swans in the lake. I was careful not to hit them, but they made good targets because they were so fat and white. Then after a while the sun got lower. I kind of cooled off and came to my senses. They were just big, dumb, beautiful birds, and not my enemies. I threw them some crumbs from my sandwich and went home.

"Daddy," I asked that night, "how come you and Mom never cash checks downstairs in the Silver Dollar?"

"Because," he said, "we have an account at the bank, where they cash our checks free."

"Well, why doesn't everybody do that?" I wanted to know.

"Because some people want all their money right away," he said. "The bank insists that you leave them a minimum[8] balance."

"How much?" I asked him.

"Only five dollars."

"But that five dollars still belongs to you after you leave it there?"

"Sure," he says. "And if it's in a savings account, it earns interest."[9]

"So why can't people see they lose money when they *pay* to have their checks cashed?"

"A lot of *our* people," Mom said, "are scared

---

8. **minimum** (min′ə məm), *adj.* lowest amount allowed.
9. **interest** (in′tər ist), *n.* money paid for the use of money, a percentage of the amount saved.

of banks, period. Some of them remember the Depression,[10] when all the banks closed and the people couldn't get their money out. And others think banks are only for white people. They think they'll be insulted, or maybe even arrested, if they go in there."

Wow. The more I learned, the more pitiful it was. "Are there any black people working at our bank?"

"There didn't used to be," Mom said, "but now they have Mr. Lovejoy and Mrs. Adams. You know Mrs. Adams, she's nice. She has a daughter your age."

"Hmmm," I said, and shut up before my folks started to wonder why I was asking all those questions.

The next morning, when the Silver Dollar opened, I was right there. I hung around near the door, pretending to read a copy of *Jet* magazine.

"Psst," I said to each person who came in. "I know where you can cash checks *free*."

It wasn't easy convincing them. A man with a wine bottle in a paper bag blinked his red eyes at me like he didn't believe he had heard right. A carpenter with tools hanging all around his belt said he was on his lunch hour and didn't have time. And a big fat lady with two shopping bags pushed past me and almost knocked me down, she was in such a hurry to give Mr. Silver and Mr. Dollar her money.

But finally I had a little group who were interested. It wasn't much. Just three people. Two men—one young, one old—and the little old lady who'd asked me to read her the letter from California. Seemed the grandson had made his payday and sent her a money order.

"How far is this place?" asked the young man.

"Not far. Just six blocks," I told him.

"Aw shoot. I ain't walking all that way just to save fifty cents."

So then I only had two. I was careful not to tell them where we were going. When we finally got to the Establishment Trust National Bank, I said, "This is the place."

"I ain't goin' in there," said the old man. "No, sir. Not me. You ain't gettin' me in *there*." And he walked away quickly, going back in the direction we had come.

To tell the truth, the bank did look kind of scary. It was a big building with tall white marble pillars.[11] A lot of Brink's armored trucks and Cadillacs were parked out front. Uniformed guards walked back and forth inside with guns. It might as well have had a "Colored Keep Out" sign.

Whereas the Silver Dollar is small and dark and funky and dirty. It has trash on the floors and tape across the broken windows. People going in there feel right at home.

I looked at the little old lady. She smiled back bravely.

"Well, we've come this far, son," she said. "Let's not turn back now."

So I took her inside. Fortunately Mrs. Adams' window was near the front.

"Hi, James," she said.

"I've brought you a customer," I told her.

Mrs. Adams took the old lady to a desk to fill out some forms. They were gone a long time, but finally they came back.

"Now, when you have more business with the bank, Mrs. Franklin, just bring it to me," Mrs. Adams said.

"I'll do that," the old lady said. She held out her shiny new bankbook.[12] "Son, do me a favor and read that to me."

"Mrs. Minnie Franklin," I read aloud. "July 9, 1972. Thirty-seven dollars."

---

10. **the Depression,** the disastrous economic collapse in the United States and other countries in the 1930s. The Great Depression caused severe widespread poverty.

11. **pillar** (pil′ər), *n.* slender column used as support or ornament for a building.

12. **bankbook** (bangk′bŭk′), *n.* a book in which a record of a person's account at a bank is kept.

"That sounds real nice," Mrs. Franklin said. "I guess now I have a bankbook, I'll have to get me some glasses."

Mrs. Adams winked at me over the old lady's head, and I winked back.

"Do you want me to walk you home?" I asked Mrs. Franklin.

"No thank you, son," she said. "I can cross streets by myself all right. I know red from green."

And then she winked at both of us, letting us know she knew what was happening.

"Son," she went on, "don't ever be afraid to try a thing just because you've never done it before. I took a bus up here from Alabama by myself forty-four years ago. I ain't thought once about going back. But I've stayed too long in one neighborhood since I've been in this city. Now I think I'll go out and take a look at *this* part of town."

Then she was gone. But she had really started me thinking. If an old lady like that wasn't afraid to go in a bank and open an account for the first time in her life, why should *I* be afraid to go up to City Hall and apply for a license?

Wonder how much they charge you to be a scribe?

Another Voice

SOS

Amiri Baraka

Calling black people

Calling all black people, man woman child

Wherever you are, calling you, urgent, come in

Black People, come in, wherever you are, urgent, calling

you, calling all black people

calling all black people, come in, black people, come

on in.

After Reading

Making Connections

1. Could you be friends with James? Why or why not?

2. Compare what you know about banking with James's experience.

3. James and the Silver Dollar Check Cashing Service both offer to help people who can't read or write. What **motivates** them? How do you know?

4. James refers to the owners of the check cashing service as "Mr. Silver" and "Mr. Dollar." Why do you think the author has him use those **symbolic names?**

5. Sometimes people are afraid to do something for the first time. Find examples of this in the story, then discuss whether these people eventually "find their place."

6. Compare the narrator's courage to the courage of Mrs. Franklin.

7. How is the poem "SOS" similar to the story "The Scribe"?

8. If James came to your neighborhood, what might he see as a problem? How could a young person help solve it?

Literary Focus: Theme

One way to determine the **theme,** or central meaning, of a story is to ask yourself these questions:

- What happened to the main character?

- Does he or she change during the story?

- What does he or she learn?

- Are there key phrases or sentences that say something important about life?

You can go back to the story to answer these questions. Use your answers to determine the main idea that holds the story together. Then, write a sentence that states the theme of the story.

Not all readers will see the theme exactly the same way. In a small group, share your theme statements and the reasons for your conclusions.

Vocabulary Study

Decide if the vocabulary words in the list are used correctly in these sentences. On a separate piece of paper, write *C* for correct or *I* for incorrect.

dignified
timidly
disability
immunization
nuisance
license
minimum
interest
pillar
bankbook

1. Not being able to read and write is a **disability.**

2. Imagine all you would miss if you couldn't read a daily **nuisance.**

3. Reading skills are a good **immunization** for success in the future.

4. When she was sixteen years old she got her first driver's **license.**

5. I took out my **bankbook** and began reading about the origin of the piggy bank.

6. What is the **minimum** amount I can deposit in this bank?

7. My savings account earns **interest.**

8. Of course, a bank **pillar** can answer most of your banking questions.

9. Being illiterate can cause people to act **timidly** in banks.

10. The kind man thanked me in a polite, **dignified** way.

Expressing Your Ideas

Writing Choices

To the Rescue Think of another problem the people in James's neighborhood are likely to face. Consider what James might do about it. Then write a **new scene** for the story.

A Letter from California The narrator briefly summarizes a letter an old lady receives from her grandson. Write the **letter** her grandson sent, adding details to go with the main points of the message.

Radio WLIT Work with a small group to write a **script** for a radio play based on a scene from "The Scribe." Read the play for the class, using your voices and sound effects to bring the scene to life.

Other Options

Words to Go Advertising helps business. Create a **poster** or **leaflet** for James's Scribe Services. Consider ways to inform people who have trouble reading. Include a logo, or symbol, for his business.

Bank on This Did you know banks compete for customers? Research the rules for savings accounts in two or more banks. Decide which one is better than the others. Share your findings with the class in an **oral report.** Use visual aids, such as graphs or charts.

A Friendly Bank James admits the local bank looks scary. Do an **architectural drawing** of a bank lobby that would make people in his neighborhood feel at ease.

Before Reading

The Women's 400 Meters by Lillian Morrison
Where You Are by Jack Anderson

Lillian Morrison
born 1917

Lillian Morrison calls her poetry *kinetic,* meaning it captures bodies in motion. Among her favorite subjects are athletes—baseball players, boxers, and runners to name a few. For several years, Morrison was a librarian at the New York Public Library.

Jack Anderson
born 1935

Drama critic, Shakespearean actor, dance historian, truck driver—Jack Anderson's life, like his poetry, has been full of variety. Anderson's poetry often shows his keen sense of place, as seen in "Where You Are."

Building Background

Poetry in Motion A pen and a video camera may seem nothing alike, but a pen in the hand of a poet can produce "movies." In the next two poems, you may even feel as though *you* are in the movie. Both poets create scenes with images you can *see, hear,* and almost *touch.* Then they use action words to set the scene in motion. In one of the poems, the heart of the action involves you!

Getting into the Poems

Writer's Notebook Do you know—*really* know—where you are right now? To see if you do, read the boxed paragraph and do what it says.

> **Do not take your eyes from this page. When you finish reading this paragraph, close your eyes. Do *not* look around first. With your eyes shut, picture where you are right now and what's happening around you. After about a minute, open your eyes and read on.**

How well did you observe your surroundings before the experiment? Are you noticing things now you didn't before?

In your notebook, write down where you are right now and what's going on around you.

Reading Tip

Vivid Images Poetry has the power to pull you into its world. Part of the fun of reading a good poem is going along for the ride . . . or walk . . . or run. As you read, see if you can put yourself in the scene.

▲ The speed and intensity of a track meet is captured in this photograph by Pablo Rivera.

The Women's 400 Meters[1]

Lillian Morrison

Skittish,[2]
they flex[3] knees, drum heels and
shiver at the starting line

waiting the gun
5 to pour them over the stretch
like a breaking wave.

Bang! they're off
careening[4] down the lanes,
each chased by her own bright tiger.

---

1. **400 Meters,** a traditional track-and-field race that is 400 meters (about a quarter of a mile) long.
2. **skittish** (skit′ish), *adj.* apt to jump, start, or run.
3. **flex** (fleks), *v.* bend.
4. **careen** (kə rēn′), *v.* rush headlong with a swaying motion.

Where You Are Jack Anderson

This is where you are.
Please note.
You are reading a poem
Beginning, "This is where you are."
5 Now get up
And walk three times around the room,
Then drink from a faucet
(If you can find a faucet).
Do not use a glass.
10 Stick your mouth directly
Into the stream of water.
Feel the water,
Its coldness, its wetness.
If there is no faucet near you
15 Or if the water is not potable,[1]
Observe the sky
And whatever may fill it
(in the margin you may write
The names of three things
20 You see in the sky)
And try to decide
Whether our present condition
Is best described
As peace or war.

25 What is the difference
Between this and "this"?
Please take note
Of where you are.
Did you really walk around the room
30 As requested?
Have you written anything in the margin?
Are you sitting, standing,
Or reclining?[2]
You are reading a poem
35 Which will end,
"Of all this is."
But you are not there yet.
You are here.
You are getting there.
40 Now explain precisely[3]
What the point
Of all this is.

---

1. **potable,** suitable for drinking; drinkable.
2. **recline** (ri klīn′), *v.* lean back; lie down.
3. **precisely** (pri sīs′lē), *adv.* exactly, definitely.

◄ Rene Magritte's *Le Faux Miroir (The False Mirror)* was painted in 1935. Both the artist and the poet "Observe the sky/And whatever may fill it." How do you think their observations differ or are alike?

After Reading

Making Connections

1. Which poem did you enjoy more? Find a classmate who chose the other poem and share the reasons for your opinions.

2. Which poem do you consider more active. Why?

3. Follow these instructions in "Where You Are" and discuss your answer.
   > (. . . write
   > The names of three things
   > You see in the sky)
   > And try to decide
   > Whether our present condition
   > Is best described
   > As peace or war.

4. Find a word or phrase you consider important in either poem and explain your choice.

5. After reading "Where You Are," do you have an idea as to what the poet thinks is "the point of all this"? What do you think it is?

6. Do you think the athletes in "The Women's 400 Meters" would like to be cheerleaders? Why or why not?

7. 🐾 The **individuality** of an athlete's efforts inspires Lillian Morrison to write poetry. What kind of people would you like to write poetry about and why?

Literary Focus: Setting

These two poems contain few details about the **setting**—the time and place where the action occurs. Instead, you must infer the setting from clues—such as the title and the activity described.

Draw or describe in writing the settings you envisioned as you read these poems. What words or phrases were your clues? You can organize your responses on a chart like the one below. Share your impressions with classmates. Discuss similarities and differences in the ways you envisioned the settings.

Title	Setting I Envision	Clues to the Setting
"The Women's 400 Meters"		
"Where You Are"		

Vocabulary Study

skittish
flex
careen
recline
precisely

In a group of five, pantomime the five vocabulary words at the left (in any order) for the class. Classmates write down the word they think each member is pantomiming. Remember, no talking!

Expressing Your Ideas

Writing Choices

What Am I Doing Here? You find yourself in the scene above. How did you get there? What do you see when you look out the window? What do you see when you look around the room? Write a **detailed description** that will enable the reader to see what you see.

Log in a Poem Look back at what you wrote in your Writer's Notebook. Write a short **analysis** of the reasons you think you were asked to do this writing and whether you found it interesting or helpful.

What I Like Reflect on your answer to After Reading question 7. Use your ideas to write a **song, ballad,** or **haiku.** Consider what the activity and its participants symbolize for you.

Other Options

And They're Off! Have you ever felt you were actually seeing a sports event you heard on the radio? Imagine you are a sports announcer and give a play-by-play **description** of the women's 400 meters race. Use words from the poem and whatever additions you need to make it realistic.

Grandstand Chat Pretend you and a classmate are Morrison and Anderson at a sports event together. Improvise a **conversation.** First, decide on the event you're watching— such as a player at bat or making a free throw. Go back to the poems for ideas about what each would notice. Then make up your chat as you go.

Poetry Charades Form teams to **pantomime** these and other poems familiar to classmates. Write the titles of the poems on slips of paper. Teams take turns drawing a slip of paper and silently performing the poem. The other team tries to guess the title within an agreed time limit.

Finding Your Place

Help Is on the Way

SCRIBES

History Connection

Scribes have found their place in societies all over the world— from ancient times to the present. Whenever people have needed someone to copy books, to read letters, to record history, they have turned to scribes for help.

I n ancient societies, scribes were held in high esteem. Before the invention of the printing press, they recorded all government documents. They copied books. Since most people did not read or write, scribes also kept libraries and preserved treasured manuscripts.

◄ **This figurine from sixth-century B.C. Greece shows a scribe at work.**

This eighth-century Chinese scribe recorded the religious teachings of Buddha. ▼

◄ **Egyptian scribes in a field write with reed pens on papyrus. They are measuring and recording a harvest in fifteenth-century B.C. Thebes.**

St. Jerome is shown working in his study. Many scribes of the Middle Ages spent their lives copying the Bible.

These late fourth-century scribes wrote Arabic script from right to left. The number of manuscripts copied greatly increased three centuries later with the spread of Islam.

Interdisciplinary Study **207**

A public typist, or modern day scribe, works in Mexico City. Because not all people can read and write, there is still a need for public scribes today. ➤

◄ Christine de Pisan (1364–1430) is shown in her study writing an original manuscript. Although most women of her time did not receive an education, women of the upper class did read and write.

Responding

1. Ancient scribes used a variety of inks and pens. What tools do you think a modern day scribe might use?

2. Think about the service scribes from ancient times provided for their communities. Name some jobs that serve some of the same functions today.

Mathematics Connection

Surveys to determine the percentage of literate people throughout the world provide a wide range of results. Although the number of people who can read and write has increased greatly since ancient times, the world is far from 100 percent literate and the need for scribes continues.

Can You Read This?

The definition of *literacy* differs from one country to another, but usually it means a reading and writing level that suits the nation's labor needs. A high or low literacy rate points to a country's economic development. It is also a measure of its public school system.

The 10 Most Schooled Countries

Country	Average Years of Schooling
United States	12.4
Canada	12.2
Norway	12.1
France	12.0
Australia	12.0
United Kingdom	11.7
Germany	11.6
Switzerland	11.6
Austria	11.4
Sweden	11.4

Source: Human Development Report 1994, *UN Development Program*

Literacy Rates of the World's Most Populous Nations As Determined by the United Nations

Nation	Population (In millions of people, 1994)	Literacy Rate (Male/Female)
China	1,192	92/68
India	912	64/35
United States	261	99
Indonesia	200	91/77
Brazil	155	84/81
Russia	148	NA
Pakistan	126	49/22
Japan	125	99
Bangladesh	117	49/23
Nigeria	98	63/41

Sources: The United Nations Human Development Report, 1993, 1994

Various standards are used for determining literacy. According to United Nations figures, the United States is 99% literate. The literacy rate in this case is the percentage of persons over age 15 who can read and write a short statement about their lives. Still other figures show that 20% of U.S. citizens are *functionally illiterate*. They can not read or write well enough to fill out forms, write short letters, or qualify for most jobs. This handicap puts them at a disadvantage socially and economically.

Responding

1. Figure the range of male and female literacy rates for all countries in the graph where the information is listed. To find the range, subtract the lowest figure from the highest figure.

2. Study the United Nations literacy chart. What might be a reason for the difference between male and female literacy rates?

Community Service

Many people, young and old, find literacy a challenge. Some may not have had the opportunity for an education. Others may be struggling to learn a new language. Whatever the cause, you can help others meet the challenge. By volunteering your time, you can make a difference.

Who Cares?

Aa Bb Cc Dd Ee Ff

Who Cares? Millions Do. . .
by Milton Meltzer

There are adults in the United States who can't read well enough to fill out forms, read letters children bring home from school, or take telephone messages, to name just a few of the tasks that define modern life. They lack the skills to cope successfully as worker, parent, and citizen.

Why has this happened? There's no one answer, no single cause to be blamed. Many didn't get the individual help they needed when in school. Many had to quit school early to earn a living. Others came to this country from foreign lands and never got the chance to learn to read and write.

The nonreaders are everywhere, in every community large or small. But so are the people who want to help them.

Students Helping Students
by Catherine A. Rolzinski

The Valued Youth Partnership Program (VYP) in San Antonio, Texas, addresses the school dropout problem through a prevention method of cross-age tutoring. Not only do the children in the elementary grades benefit from the tutoring, but the middle school tutors receive many benefits in return.

Antonio Olivares Elementary School, pre-kindergarten through fifth grade, and Kazen Middle School, sixth, seventh, and

eighth grades, are in the same neighborhood. Kazen students walk over to Antonio Olivares Elementary School and tutor Mondays through Fridays. The tutors themselves attend training sessions on Fridays.

My tutor helps me study and read. If I have problems with definitions he can help me. I learn more, so I can be whatever I want to be. I am learning the words I need for what I want to be when I grow up.

Nicholas, third grader

I help them learn and I learn myself. Some of the things I didn't understand in the third grade, I am really learning now.

Oscar, Nicholas's tutor

He helps me with my spelling and makes me feel comfortable.

Christine, third-grade student

I come over second period and help them learn spelling, math and reading. I like teaching them. It's easier than I thought and fun. If you like kids, you want them to learn. I feel like a brother.

Albert, Christine's seventh-grade tutor

I like it because I can help other kids, and I can learn new things. I do this during second period. I like getting paid for teaching in this class.

Veronica, age 13, tutor to Darlene and Marielle

I'm going to be a tutor when I'm older.

Darlene, age six, first-grade student

She helps me and I like her.

Marielle, age seven, first-grade student

In different ways I've heard the tutors tell me, "Now I know why teachers tell me what they tell me. Now I know how teachers feel."

First grade teacher

Responding

Can you accept a challenge? Make a promise to yourself. Sometime in the next week help someone with a reading or writing task. You might choose to help a classmate with homework or read a story to your pre-school brother or sister every night. Report back to your class. What did you do to help? How did it make you feel?

211

Reading Mini-Lesson

Using Graphic Aids

Graphs, charts, and maps are aids to understanding that present information so that you can *see* it, rather than just read it. A graphic aid such as a chart, for example, can show you at a glance a number of statistics that would take many paragraphs to list and explain. A graph can illustrate a relationship that would be difficult to picture from data given as a list or explained in sentences. A map can give you an eagle's-eye view of an area.

Graphic aids are particularly useful for making comparisons, for showing change, and for showing relationships. Your social studies book probably has graphs, charts, and maps in every chapter. When you work in science labs, you often need to make charts or graphs to organize the data from your observations. Your geography and science books probably contain maps and charts that show climate and landforms.

"The 10 Most Schooled Countries" graphic on page 209 allows easy comparison of average years of schooling. Countries are ranked top to bottom from most years to least. You could also show all or part of this information with a graph. If we wanted to compare years of schooling for just the United States, Australia, and Sweden, we could show it with a graph as at the left.

The "Literacy Rates" chart on page 209 ranks nations by population in the center column from largest to smallest. The column at the right gives you literacy rates for males and females in each country. What two countries have the lowest literacy rates? What two countries do not separate the rates for males and females? Note that figures for Russia are N(ot) A(vailable).

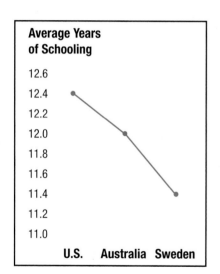

Average Years of Schooling

12.6
12.4
12.2
12.0
11.8
11.6
11.4
11.2
11.0

U.S.   Australia   Sweden

Activity Options

1. Use data from the Literacy Rates chart on page 209 to make a graph that shows the literacy rates of females in China, India, Indonesia, Brazil, Pakistan, Bangladesh, and Nigeria.

2. Use your graph to answer these questions about female literacy rates: Which two nations listed on your chart have the highest rates of female literacy? Which two have the lowest rates?

Writing Workshop

Trying Something New

Assignment As Mrs. Franklin advises in "The Scribe," " . . . don't ever be afraid to try a thing just because you've never done it before." Explain how you might follow Mrs. Franklin's advice. See the Writer's Blueprint for details.

WRITER'S BLUEPRINT

Product   An essay
Purpose   To speculate about something new you'd like to try
Audience   Your family or friends
Specs   To write a successful essay, you should:

❑ Begin by explaining what you'd like to do and why.
❑ Go on to identify obstacles you might face and the personal qualities you would need to handle them.
❑ Consider how you think you'll feel at different times during this experience.
❑ End by exploring how you might change by trying something you've never done before.
❑ Write focused paragraphs that each include a main idea with supporting details.
❑ Follow the rules for grammar, usage, spelling, and mechanics. Avoid using unnecessary commas.

The instructions that follow are designed to help you write a successful essay.

 **STEP 1 PREWRITING**

Brainstorm a list of new experiences that you'd like to try. Ask others about challenging experiences they've had. Think about experiences you would like to have related to school, sports, travel, stories

OR . . .
Draw three pictures showing different things you have never experienced but would like to try. Choose one of the pictures as the topic of your essay.

you've read, or hobbies. Then, choose the experience that is most interesting or important to you.

Create a staircase of details about your experience. Close your eyes and visualize yourself completing your experience. Create a staircase in which each step represents one part of your chosen experience. Be sure to include obstacles that you might face along the way. Add details that describe each part on each step of your staircase.

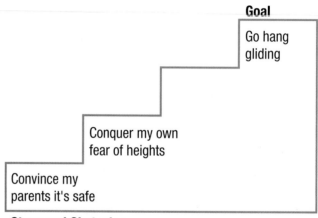

Goal
Go hang gliding

Conquer my own fear of heights

Convince my parents it's safe

Steps and Obstacles

Try a quickwrite. Using the descriptions from your staircase, write about your experience for a few minutes. At this point don't worry about grammar, punctuation, or spelling. Just get your ideas down on paper. Here is part of one student's quickwrite.

○ Foreign travel—see new culture first hand, eat different food, see

new places. better than just reading about it or t.v. Never been outside U.S.

○ Countries: Philippines- Russia- Mexico- Germany—probably would fly there.

Would need to learn a new language, hire interpreter?

STUDENT MODEL

Ask yourself: *Have I thought about all the steps necessary to complete my chosen experience?* Look at your staircase and your quickwrite. If you feel that something is missing, show your staircase to a partner. Discuss what steps he or she would expect to see.

Plan your essay using your quickwrite, staircase, and other notes. At this point, refine each step in your staircase into a storyboard. Draw the key steps in the experience you've chosen, and arrange the drawings in chronological order.

STEP  DRAFTING

Before you write, think about building paragraphs that are focused on a main idea with supporting details. Refer to the Revising Strategy on focused paragraphs before starting. Here are some tips that might help you get started.

- Tell a story to explain why you are interested in the experience.

- Start by quoting Mrs. Franklin, " . . . don't ever be afraid to try a thing just because you've never done it before." Explain how your essay will relate to these words.

- Start with an exciting description of the new experience.

STEP 3 REVISING

Ask a partner for comments on your draft before you revise it.

✔ Have I explained the new experience and told why I want to try it?

✔ Do I identify possible obstacles I might encounter and think of ways to overcome them?

✔ Do I consider my feelings about the experience and how it might change me?

✔ Are all my paragraphs focused on a main idea with supporting details?

> **COMPUTER TIP**
> If you're writing your essay on a computer, save details that are unrelated to a particular paragraph on the clipboard. You might find a better place to paste them into your essay.

Revising Strategy

Writing Focused Paragraphs

For a paragraph to be focused, it needs to be about one main idea. All the details and sentences in the paragraph should help develop that main idea. Follow these points to develop focused paragraphs.

- Find a main idea on which to focus.

- List details about the main idea.

- Use these details to develop sentences that support the main idea.

Notice in the Literary Source how Nereida Román uses details to stay focused on the main idea that she's different from other girls at school.

Notice how the writer of the following paragraph revised it based on a comment from a partner.

LITERARY SOURCE

"I'm strange! I've always done things differently. For example, all the girls in school are into boys, music and more boys. I don't like boys. Well, I like them a little, but they're not as important to me as they are to some of the other girls."

from "Never Fitting In" by Nereida Román

A major setback to foreign travel is foreign language. I only know English and a little French, so I couldn't talk to someone from China. This problem is difficult to overcome, but definitely not impossible. I could take courses in the appropriate language, but that probably wouldn't be enough. I would most likely need to hire an interpreter, and even then it would be difficult. ~~I'd also need to save up a lot of money before I could travel abroad. I'd probably have to fly and airline tickets are expensive.~~ Despite ~~these~~ *this* rather tall obstacle, I believe I would be able to persevere and make this a positive experience.

STUDENT MODEL

Ask a partner to review your revision before you edit. Watch for errors in grammar, usage, spelling, and mechanics. Avoid overusing commas.

Editing Strategy

FOR REFERENCE . . .
More rules on correct use of commas are listed in the Language and Grammar Handbook.

Avoiding Overuse of Commas

Modern writers use commas when needed to signal pauses in sentences. Using too many commas makes your sentences choppy or confusing. Follow these rules for using commas.

- Don't use a comma to separate a subject and verb.

  Faulty: One challenge, would be learning to use the scuba gear.
  Revised: One challenge would be learning to use the scuba gear.

- Don't use a comma with words or phrases joined by coordinating conjunctions, unless you're joining independent clauses.

  Faulty: If I could learn to speak French, I would feel proud and excited, and would go to France as soon as possible.
  Revised: If I could learn to speak French, I would feel proud and excited and would go to France as soon as possible.

- Don't use a comma before the first or after the last item in a series.

  Faulty: I would learn to cook, lasagna, pizza, and tamales, before I tried desserts.
  Revised: I would learn to cook lasagna, pizza, and tamales before I tried desserts.

Notice how the writer of the draft below corrects comma overuse.

> There are many places in the world I'd love to see, including, China, Mexico, Russia, and the Philippines. I think visiting a foreign country could benefit me in many ways. It would allow me to experience a different culture, and environment, and to see new things.

STUDENT MODEL

5 PRESENTING

Here are two ideas for presenting your essay.

- Get together with a group and read your essays aloud. Then allow time after each reading to discuss parts of the essay that were especially good.

- Work with a group to design a poster of the new experiences you would like to have. Present your poster orally to the class and then display it in the classroom.

STEP **6** LOOKING BACK

Self-evaluate. What grade would you give your essay? Look back at the Writer's Blueprint and evaluate yourself on each point, from 6 (superior) down to 1 (weak).

Reflect. Think about what you learned from writing your essay as you write answers to these questions:

✔ Will you really try the experience you described in your essay? Why or why not?

✔ What did you learn about yourself and your personal qualities as you considered the experience you want to try and the obstacles you would face?

For Your Working Portfolio: Add your essay and your reflection responses to your working portfolio.

Beyond Print

Dishwater or White Water?

Have you seen any of the old adventure movies made in the forties and fifties on TV? What did the men do in those movies? They fought the bad guys, piloted the planes, and protected the women. The women cooked the meals, raised the babies, and waited at home.

Times have changed. In the film *The River Wild,* Meryl Streep isn't exactly cooking. Streep plays the traditional role of mother/home-maker, but she also portrays an expert white-water rafter, better than the men she meets in the movie. Welcome to the nineties—where the images of women say "We can do anything men can do!"

Activity

You are on the marketing team for this movie. You've been given two pictures to use in the advertising campaign. One of the pictures shows Streep holding her son close to her while water splashes on them. The other is the picture at the left above. Your boss sends you the following:

Memo: To Marketing Personnel

From: Gloria Dawn, VP Marketing

Choose one of these pictures for our campaign. Answer the following questions (and be prepared to defend your ideas **verbally** at tomorrow's meeting).

- Which picture represents the image of women most people will find acceptable? Why?
- What does each picture say about women?
- Is the picture of Streep holding her son too old-fashioned? Why?
- Is the picture of Streep all alone off-putting? Why?
- Are people ready for the image of women shown here?
- Which picture may harm the movie? Why?
- Which image will sell the movie? Why?

Tips on Your Verbal Presentation

1. *Make an outline:* Write down key points to answer each question.

2. *Consider both sides:* People feel strongly about this topic. Stand by your decision but be sensitive to the opinions of those who disagree. Include fair rebuttals.

3. *Practice your answers:* Pretend you are making your pitch to the boss. Be brief. Select the best information.

4. *Be convincing and honest:* Look your boss in the eyes. Be sincere and committed.

Projects for Collaborative Study

Theme Connection

Lend a Helping Hand Every young person faces the challenge of making the right choices as he or she struggles to carve out a place in life. For those in your community who face overwhelming challenges or who get into difficulties, what kind of help is available? Work in a group to research community organizations that provide assistance of various kinds to young people.

■ Brainstorm the types of help young people might need. Assign specific research topics to pairs of group members, such as physical and mental health, juvenile delinquency, financial need, substance abuse, and so on.

■ Prepare an attractive brochure that describes the resources that you uncover. Be sure to include organization phone numbers and addresses. Make the brochure available to students in your school.

Literature Connection

Life's Little Ironies In several of the selections in this unit, there is an ironic twist, an unexpected outcome. Sir Gawain gallantly marries a loathsome woman only to have her turn into a beauty; Keevan is chosen to be a defender of his planet when he can barely stand.

With a small group of classmates, brainstorm ideas for plots that contain **irony.** You may want to reread the discussion of irony on page 131. Use your best plot idea to create a skit that you perform for your class.

Life Skills Connection

Decisions, Decisions Every day you make an incredible number of decisions. Think about all the choices you've made since yesterday. In which areas of your life (food, homework, friends, sports, clothes, activities, family duties, and so on) did you make these choices? Were these decisions easy or difficult, fun or stressful?

You can reduce stress and increase your chances for feeling happy with effective decision making. Even if you aren't sure at the time, you usually can look back at a decision and determine whether your choice worked well or not.

■ Make a list of your best and worst decisions. What did you learn from each? What were the results?

■ As a class, discuss what you can learn from both positive and negative experiences.

👣 Multicultural Connection

Finding one's place in society may involve conflict between the individual and groups. In expressing her **individuality,** Nereida Román is called both "tomboy" and "nerd." Cultural ideas about what is appropriate for males or females are slow to **change.** How accepting are you and your classmates of those who don't fit your expectations?

As a class, take a poll to find out what kinds of individual differences you find hard to accept. Discuss the consequences to others of these dislikes or prejudices. What steps might help overcome them?

Read More About Challenges

Eyes of Darkness (1985) by Jamake Highwater. This novel highlights the challenges encountered by a young Native American man as, caught between the world of his forebearers and the white world, he struggles to find his place.

Dicey's Song (1982) by Cynthia Voight. When her mother enters a mental institution, Dicey faces the challenge of adjusting to a new place and a new role in life as she helps her grandmother bring up her siblings.

More Good Books

Missing Pieces (1995) by Norma Fox Mazer. Jessie Wells takes on a challenging task when she sets out to find and get to know the father who abandoned her and her mother when Jessie was a baby.

Cool Salsa: Bilingual Poems on Growing Up Latino in the United States (1994) edited by Lori M. Carlson. This collection of poems celebrates the glory and the pain of growing up in the United States as a Latino American teenager.

Redwall (1987) by Brian Jacques. An unlikely hero, a monastery mouse, will draw you into his fantastic adventures as he defends Redwall Abbey against a greedy horde of rats.

New World (1995) by Gillian Cross. Fourteen-year-olds Miriam and Stuart encounter some terrifying challenges in cyberspace as they participate in trials of a new virtual-reality game.

The Moves Make the Man (1984) by Bruce Brooks. Jerome knows all the moves needed to excel in basketball and in human relations. His friend Bix concentrates only on athletics.

Justice

The Scene of the Crime
Part One, pages 226–276

Encounters with Prejudice
Part Two, pages 277–327

Talking About
JUSTICE

Fairness and justice are very important words to people and nations alike. Without justice wrongs would go unpunished and rights would not be rewarded. Without justice we would never know where we stand —from which team gets the throw-in for a foul on the soccer field to the appropriate punishment for forgetting the assigned homework. Being fair means taking into consideration not only your rights and happiness but the rights and happiness of those around you.

Think about the words of the students from across the country. Compare them to the quotations from the selections you are about to read.

I recognized the voices: Mr. Schmidt, my history teacher, and Mr. Boone, my math teacher. They seemed to be arguing about me.

from "The Scholarship Jacket" by Marta Salinas, page 298

Derek felt his face get hot, but he asked, "What gun?"

from "The Gun" by Carol Ellis, page 243

. . . strangely enough most of the Good Fairies usually turned out to be extremely light in complexion, . . .

from "The Revolt of the Evil Fairies" by Ted Poston, page 290

"I like teachers who are fair to all of us!"

Morgan—Oak Park, IL

"Gun control is a really important issue."

David—York, NE

"How do we make sure people get justice in America?"

Wei Chen—New York, NY

225

Part One

The Scene of the Crime

What's a crime? What isn't a crime? Can you commit a crime and not even know it? When is breaking the law the only way to get justice? These are some of the questions the following selections raise. In some, you must follow a trail of clues to solve the mystery. Others take you right to the scene of a crime in progress.

🐾 Multicultural Connection **Communication** involves expressing feelings and thoughts not only through what we say but also what we do. Sometimes we need to look beyond words to learn what is really being communicated both within and across cultural groups. How are the characters in these selections forced to look beyond words to understand what's really going on at the scene of the crime?

Literature

Arthur Conan Doyle **The Dying Detective** ◆ play 228
    (dramatized by Michael and Mollie Hardwick)

Carol Ellis   **The Gun** ◆ short story 242

Shirley Jackson   **Charles** ◆ short story 249

T. S. Eliot   **Macavity: The Mystery Cat** ◆ poem 256

Nikki Giovanni   **Kidnap Poem** ◆ poem .258

Anonymous   **How the Lame Boy Brought Fire from Heaven**
             ◆ African myth 262

Bernard Evslin   **Prometheus** ◆ Greek myth 264

    Writing Mini-Lesson ◆ Using a Persuasive Tone 269

Interdisciplinary Study Gathering Evidence

Determining Guilt ◆ history 270

Genetic Fingerprinting: The Murder with No Body
    by Anita Larsen ◆ life science 272

The Structure of DNA ◆ life science 274

    Reading Mini-Lesson ◆ Remembering What You Read 276

Before Reading

The Dying Detective

by Arthur Conan Doyle, dramatized by Michael and Mollie Hardwick

Arthur Conan Doyle
1859-1930

Arthur Conan Doyle sailed off in 1882 at the age of twenty to see the world. He traveled from Africa to the Arctic as a surgeon on a whaling ship. Evidence of his life as doctor and world traveler shows up in the adventures of his scientific detective, Sherlock Holmes. In fact, Doyle delivered Holmes to the world in detective stories he wrote while waiting for patients who didn't show up. His mysteries soon brought him fame, fans, and money.

Michael Hardwick and Mollie Hardwick
Married since 1961, these English authors became free-lance playwrights in 1963. They have turned many Sherlock Holmes mysteries into dramas for movies, radio, and TV. Michael Hardwick is an authority on Sherlock Holmes.

Building Background

His Style Rings a Bell Who is this famous fellow, with his deerstalker cap, magnifying glass, and curving pipe? Does "Elementary, my dear Watson," give you a clue? If you guessed **Sherlock Holmes,** you've solved the mystery! Holmes is so familiar to people through stories, plays, movies, and TV shows that he has come to almost seem real. In a way he is. Conan Doyle—the writer who invented Holmes—based his masterful detective on Dr. Joseph Bell, a specialist in criminal psychology and a surgeon of remarkable skill.

Getting into the Play

Writer's Notebook Have you ever sensed that someone or something was not quite what it appeared to be . . . and then discovered you were right? A word for that sense is *intuition*—a quality that makes a good detective. Of course, a skilled crime-solver also uses solid clues and facts to solve a case.

Consider what you know about detectives. In your notebook, list some qualities you think a detective needs.

Reading Tip

Stage Directions Some of the most important words in a play aren't the ones that are spoken. They're the **stage directions** that tell you *how* to speak the words. On the chart below are several stage directions you'll see in *The Dying Detective*. Try saying the line, *"Yes, yes. I know"* using some of them.

Stage Direction	Make Your Voice Sound	Stage Direction	Make Your Voice Sound
harshly	without kindness	*grimly*	stern and full of dread
beseeching	pleading	*drowsily*	sleepy
startled	amazed and surprised	*snarling*	growling
deliberately	careful, thoughtful	*triumphantly*	victorious, like a winner

The Dying Detective

Arthur Conan Doyle
dramatized by Michael and Mollie Hardwick

CHARACTERS, in order of appearance

MRS. HUDSON

DR. WATSON

SHERLOCK HOLMES

CULVERTON SMITH "A great yellow face, coarse-grained and greasy, with heavy double chin, and two sullen, menacing grey eyes which glared at me from under tufted and sandy brows . . . "

INSPECTOR MORTON Middle-aged, tough, dressed in plain clothes.

PLACE

SCENE ONE: Sherlock Holmes's bedroom, afternoon

SCENE TWO: The same, dusk

SCENE THREE: The same, evening

SCENE ONE

SHERLOCK HOLMES's *bedroom at 221B Baker Street. The essential features are: a bed with a large wooden head, placed crosswise on the stage, the head a foot or two from one side wall; a small table near the bed-head, on the audience's side, on which stand a carafe*[1] *of water and a glass, and a tiny metal or ivory box; a window in the back wall, the curtains parted; and, under the window, a table or chest of drawers, on which stand a green wine bottle, some wine-glasses, a biscuit-barrel, and a lamp. Of course there may be further lamps and any amount of furnishing and clutter:* HOLMES's *bedroom was adorned with pictures of celebrated criminals and littered with everything from tobacco pipes to revolver cartridges.*

There is daylight outside the window. SHERLOCK HOLMES *lies in the bed on his back, tucked up to the chin and evidently asleep. He is very pale.* MRS. HUDSON *enters followed by* DR. WATSON, *who is wearing his coat and hat and carrying his small medical bag.* MRS. HUDSON *pauses for a moment.*

---

1. **carafe** (kə raf′), a glass bottle for holding water or other liquid.

Sherlock Holmes's apartment has been re-created in San Francisco, California. Notice the deerstalker cap and cloak, which are symbols of the famous detective.

MRS. HUDSON. He's asleep, sir.

(They approach the bed. WATSON *comes round to the audience's side and looks down at* HOLMES *for a moment. He shakes his head gravely, then he and* MRS. HUDSON *move away beyond the foot of the bed.* WATSON *takes off his hat and coat as they talk and she takes them from him.)*

WATSON. This is dreadful, Mrs. Hudson. He was perfectly hale and hearty when I went away only three days ago.

MRS. HUDSON. I know, sir. Oh, Dr. Watson, sir, I'm glad you've come back. If anyone can save Mr. Holmes, I'm sure you can.

WATSON. I shall have to know what is the matter with him first. Mrs. Hudson, please tell me, as quickly as you can, how it all came about.

MRS. HUDSON. Yes, sir. Mr. Holmes has been working lately on some case down near the river—Rotherhithe, I think.

WATSON. Yes, yes. I know.

MRS. HUDSON. Well, you know what he is for coming in at all hours. I was just taking my lamp to go to my bed on Wednesday night when I heard a faint knocking at the street door. I . . . I found Mr. Holmes there. He could hardly stand. Just muttered to me to help him up to his bed here, and he's barely spoken since.

WATSON. Dear me!

MRS. HUDSON. Won't take food or drink. Just lies there, sleeping or staring in a wild sort of way.

WATSON. But, goodness gracious, Mrs. Hudson, why did you not send for another doctor in my absence?

MRS. HUDSON. Oh, I told him straightaway I was going to do that, sir. But he got so agitated[2]—almost shouted that he wouldn't allow any doctor on the premises. You know how masterful he is, Dr. Watson.

WATSON. Indeed. But you could have telegraphed for me.

(MRS. HUDSON *appears embarrassed.*)

MRS. HUDSON. Well, sir . . .

WATSON. But you didn't. Why, Mrs. Hudson?

MRS. HUDSON. Sir, I don't like to tell you, but . . . well, Mr. Holmes said he wouldn't even have you to see him.

WATSON. What? This is monstrous! I, his oldest friend and . . .

(HOLMES *groans and stirs slightly.*)

Ssh! He's waking. You go along, Mrs. Hudson, and leave this to me. Whether he likes it or not, I shall ensure that everything possible is done.

MRS. HUDSON. Thank you, sir. You'll ring if I can be of help.

(*She exits with* WATSON'*s things.* HOLMES *groans again and flings out an arm restlessly.* WATSON *comes to the audience's side of the bed and sits on it.*)

WATSON. Holmes? It's I—Watson.

HOLMES (*sighs*). Ahh! Well, Watson? We . . . we seem to have fallen on evil days.

WATSON. My dear fellow!

(*He moves to reach for* HOLMES'*s pulse.*)

HOLMES (*urgently*). No, no! Keep back!

WATSON. Eh?

HOLMES. Mustn't come near.

WATSON. Now, look here, Holmes . . . !

HOLMES. If you come near . . . order you out of the house.

WATSON (*defiantly*). Hah!

HOLMES. For your own sake, Watson. Contracted . . . a coolie disease—from Sumatra.[3] Very little known, except that most deadly. Contagious[4] by touch. So . . . must keep away.

WATSON. Utter rubbish, Holmes! Mrs. Hudson tells me she helped you to your bed. There's nothing the matter with her.

HOLMES. Period of . . . incubation.[5] Only dangerous after two or three days. Deadly by now.

WATSON. Good heavens, do you suppose such a consideration weighs with me? Even if I weren't a doctor, d'you think it would stop me doing my duty to an old friend? Now, let's have a good look at you.

(*He moves forward again.*)

HOLMES (*harshly*). I tell you to keep back!

WATSON. See here, Holmes . . .

HOLMES. If you will stay where you are, I will talk to you. If you will not, you can get out.

WATSON. Holmes! (*Recovering*) Holmes, you aren't yourself. You're sick and as helpless as a child. Whether you like it or not, I'm going to examine you and treat you.

---

2. **agitated** (aj′ə tāt′id), *adj.* upset, disturbed.
3. **Sumatra** (sù mä′trə), an island in Indonesia, which lies on the equator in the Indian Ocean.
4. **contagious** (kən tā′jəs), *adj.* spreading by contact; catching.
5. **incubation** (ing′kyə bā′shən, in′kyə bā′shən), *n.* stage of a disease from the time of infection until the first symptoms appear.

HOLMES (*sneering*). If I'm to be forced to have a doctor, let him at least be someone I've some confidence in.

WATSON. Oh! You . . . After all these years, Holmes, you haven't . . . confidence in me?

HOLMES. In your friendship, Watson—yes. But facts are facts. As a medical man you're a mere general practitioner, of limited experience and mediocre qualifications.

WATSON. Well . . . ! Well, really!

HOLMES. It is painful to say such things, but you leave me no choice.

WATSON (*coldly*). Thank you. I'll tell you this, Holmes. Such a remark, coming from you, merely serves to tell me what state your nerves are in. Still, if you insist that you have no confidence in me, I will not intrude my services. But what I shall do is to summon Sir Jasper Meek or Penrose Fisher, or any of the other best men in London.

HOLMES (*groans*). My . . . dear Watson. You mean well. But do you suppose they—any of them—know of the Tapanuli[6] Fever?

WATSON. The Tap . . . ?

HOLMES. What do you yourself know of the Black Formosa Corruption?

WATSON. Tapanuli Fever? Black Formosa Corruption? I've never heard of either of 'em.

HOLMES. Nor have your colleagues. There are many problems of disease, many pathological[7] possibilities, peculiar to the East. So I've learned during some of my recent researches. It was in the course of one of them that I contracted this complaint. I assure you, Watson, you can do nothing.

WATSON. Can't I? I happen to know, Holmes, that the greatest living authority on tropical disease, Dr. Ainstree, is in London just now.

HOLMES (*beseeching*). Watson!

WATSON. All remonstrance[8] is useless. I am going this instant to fetch him. (*He gets up.*)

HOLMES (*a great cry*). No!

WATSON. Eh? Holmes . . . my dear fellow . . .

HOLMES. Watson, in the name of our old friendship, do as I ask.

WATSON. But . . .

HOLMES. You have only my own good at heart. Of course, I know that. You . . . you shall have your way. Only . . . give me time to . . . to collect my strength. What is the time now?

(*WATSON sits and consults his watch.*)

WATSON. Four o'clock.

HOLMES. Then at six you can go.

WATSON. This is insanity!

HOLMES. Only two hours, Watson. I promise you may go then.

WATSON. Hang it, this is urgent, man!

HOLMES. I will see no one before six. I will not be examined. I shall resist!

WATSON (*sighing*). Oh, have it your own way, then. But I insist on staying with you in the meantime. You need an eye keeping on you, Holmes.

HOLMES. Very well, Watson. And now I must sleep. I feel exhausted. (*Drowsily*) I wonder how a battery feels when it pours electricity into a non-conductor?

WATSON. Eh?

HOLMES (*yawning*). At six, Watson, we resume our conversation.

(*He lies back and closes his eyes.* WATSON *makes as though to move, but thinks better of it. He sits still, watching* HOLMES. *A slow black-out.*)

SCENE TWO

The stage lights up again, though more dimly than before, to disclose the same scene. Twilight is apparent through the window. HOLMES *lies motionless.*

---

6. **Tapanuli** (tăp′ə nŭ′lē), a tiny atoll east of Indonesia in the South Pacific Ocean.
7. **pathological,** concerned with diseases.
8. **remonstrance,** a protest or complaint.

WATSON *sits as before, though with his head sagging, half-asleep. His chin drops suddenly and he wakes with a jerk. He glances round, sees the twilight outside, and consults his watch. He yawns, flexes his arms, then proceeds to glance idly about him. His attention is caught by the little box on the bedside table. Stealthily, he reaches over and picks it up.*

HOLMES (*very loudly and urgently*). No! No, Watson, no!

WATSON (*startled*). Eh? What?

HOLMES. Put it down! Down this instant! Do as I say, Watson!

WATSON. Oh! All right, then. (*Putting the box down*) Look here, Holmes, I really think . . .

HOLMES. I hate to have my things touched. You know perfectly well I do.

WATSON. Holmes . . . !

HOLMES. You fidget me beyond endurance. You, a doctor—you're enough to drive a patient into an asylum!

WATSON. Really!

HOLMES. Now, for heaven's sake, sit still, and let me have my rest.

WATSON. Holmes, it is almost six o'clock, and I refuse to delay another instant.

(*He gets up determinedly.*)

HOLMES. Really? Watson, have you any change in your pocket?

WATSON. Yes.

HOLMES. Any silver?

WATSON (*fishing out his change*). A good deal.

HOLMES. How many half-crowns?

WATSON. Er, five.

HOLMES (*sighing*). Ah, too few, too few. However, such as they are, you can put them in your watch-pocket—and all the rest of your money in your left trouser-pocket. It will balance you so much better like that.

WATSON. Balance . . . ? Holmes, you're raving! This has gone too far . . . !

HOLMES. You will now light that lamp by the window, Watson, but you will be very careful that not for one instant shall it be more than at half flame.

WATSON. Oh, very well.

(WATSON *goes to the lamp and strikes a match.*)

HOLMES. I implore[9] you to be careful.

WATSON (*as though humoring him*). Yes, Holmes.

(*He lights the lamp, carefully keeping the flame low. He moves to draw the curtains.*)

HOLMES. No, you need not draw curtains.

(WATSON *leaves them and comes back round the bed.*)

WATSON. Well, thank heaven for that.

HOLMES. His name is Mr. Culverton Smith, of 13 Lower Burke Street.

WATSON (*staring*). Eh?

HOLMES. Well, go on, man. You could hardly wait to fetch someone before.

WATSON. Yes, but . . . Culverton Smith? I've never heard the name!

HOLMES. Possibly not. It may surprise you to know that the one man who knows everything about this disease is not a medical man. He's a planter.

WATSON. A planter!

HOLMES. His plantation is far from medical aid. An outbreak of this disease there caused him to study it intensely. He's a very methodical[10] man, and I asked you not to go before six because I knew you wouldn't find him in his study till then.

WATSON. Holmes, I . . . I never heard such a . . . !

HOLMES. You will tell him exactly how you have left me. A dying man.

WATSON. No, Holmes!

HOLMES. At any rate, delirious.[11] Yes, not

---

9. **implore** (im plôr′), *v.* beg earnestly for.
10. **methodical** (mə thod′ə kəl), *adj.* done in an orderly manner.
11. **delirious** (di lir′ē əs), *adj.* out of one's senses for a time.

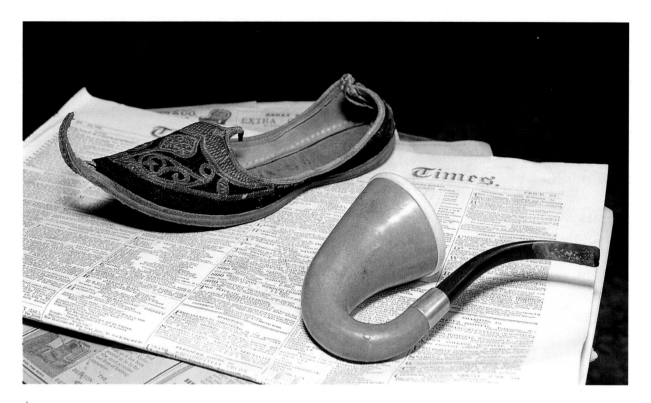

A pipe rests near a Persian slipper like the one in which Holmes kept tobacco. He often studied the *London Times* for clues.

dying, delirious. *(Chuckles)* No, I really can't think why the whole ocean bed isn't one solid mass of oysters.

WATSON. Oysters?

HOLMES. They're so prolific,[12] you know.

WATSON. Great Heavens! Now, Holmes, you just lie quiet, and . . .

HOLMES. Strange how the mind controls the brain. Er, what was I saying, Watson?

WATSON. You were . . .

HOLMES. Ah, I remember. Culverton Smith. My life depends on him, Watson. But you will have to plead with him to come. There is no good feeling between us. He has . . . a grudge. I rely on you to soften him. Beg, Watson. Pray. But get him here by any means.

WATSON. Very well. I'll bring him in a cab, if I have to carry him down to it.

HOLMES. You will do nothing of the sort. You will persuade him to come—and then return before him. *(Deliberately)* Make any excuse so as not to come with him. Don't forget that, Watson. You won't fail me. You never did fail me.

WATSON. That's all very well, Holmes, but . . .

HOLMES *(interrupting).* Then, shall the world be overrun by oysters? No doubt there are natural enemies which limit their increase. And yet . . . No, horrible, horrible!

WATSON *(grimly).* I'm going, Holmes. Say no more, I'm going!

(He hurries out. HOLMES *remains propped up for a moment, staring after* WATSON, *then sinks back into a sleeping posture as the stage blacks out.)*

---

12. **prolific** (prə lif′ik), *adj.* producing many offspring.

SCENE THREE

The stage lights up on the same scene. HOLMES *lies still. It is now quite dark outside. After a moment* WATSON *bustles in, pulling off his coat. He pauses to hand it to* MRS. HUDSON, *who is behind him.*

WATSON. Thank you, Mrs. Hudson. A gentleman will be calling very shortly. Kindly show him up here immediately.

MRS. HUDSON. Yes, sir. (*She exits.* WATSON *approaches the bed.*)

HOLMES (*drowsily*). Watson?

WATSON. Yes, Holmes. How are you feeling?

HOLMES. Much the same, I fear. Is Culverton Smith coming?

WATSON. Should be here any minute. It took me some minutes to find a cab, and I almost expected him to have got here first.

HOLMES. Well done, my dear Watson.

WATSON. I must say, Holmes, I'm only doing this to humor you. Frankly, I didn't take to your planter friend at all.

HOLMES. Oh? How so?

WATSON. Rudeness itself. He almost showed me the door before I could give him your message. It wasn't until I mentioned the name, Sherlock Holmes . . .

HOLMES. Ah!

WATSON. Quite changed him—but I wouldn't say it was for the better.

HOLMES. Tell me what he said.

WATSON. Said you'd had some business dealings together, and that he respected your character and talents. Described you as an amateur of crime, in the way that he regards himself as an amateur of disease.

HOLMES. Quite typical—and surely, quite fair?

WATSON. Quite fair—if he hadn't put such sarcasm into saying it. No, Holmes, you said he bears you some grudge. Mark my words, as soon as he has left this house I insist upon calling a recognized specialist.

HOLMES. My dear Watson, you are the best of messengers. Thank you again.

WATSON. Not at all. Holmes, Holmes—let me help you without any of this nonsense. The whole of Great Britain will condemn me otherwise. Why, my cabmen both enquired anxiously after you; and so did Inspector Morton . . .

HOLMES. Morton?

WATSON. Of the Yard. He was passing our door just now as I came in. Seemed extemely concerned.

HOLMES. Scotland Yard[13] concerned for me? How very touching! And now, Watson, you may disappear from the scene.

WATSON. Disappear! I shall do no such thing. I wish to be present when this Culverton Smith arrives. I wish to hear every word of this so-called medical expert's opinion.

HOLMES (*turning his head*). Yes, of course. Then I think you will just find room behind the head of the bed.

WATSON. What? Hide?

HOLMES. I have reason to suppose that his opinion will be much more frank and valuable if he imagines he is alone with me.

(*We hear the murmur of* MRS. HUDSON'S *and* CULVERTON SMITH'S *voices offstage.*)

Listen! I hear him coming. Get behind the bed, Watson, and do not budge, whatever happens. *Whatever* happens, you understand?

WATSON. Oh, all right, Holmes. Anything to please you. But I don't like this. Not at all.

(*He goes behind the bed-head and conceals himself.* MRS. HUDSON *enters, looks round the room and then at* HOLMES. SMITH *enters behind her.*)

MRS. HUDSON (*to* SMITH). Oh, Dr. Watson must have let himself out. No doubt he'll be back directly, sir.

SMITH. No matter, my good woman. (MRS. HUDSON *bristles at this form of address.*) You

---

13. **Scotland Yard,** the Criminal Investigation Department of London's police headquarters.

may leave me alone with your master.

MRS. HUDSON. As you wish—*sir.*

(She sweeps out. SMITH *advances slowly to the bed and stands at the foot, staring at the recumbent[14]* HOLMES.*)*

SMITH *(almost to himself).* So, Holmes. It has come to this, then.

*(*HOLMES *stirs.* SMITH *chuckles and leans his arms on the bed-foot and his chin on them, continuing to watch* HOLMES.*)*

HOLMES *(weakly).* Watson? Who . . . ? Smith? Smith, is that you?

*(*SMITH *chuckles.)*

HOLMES. I . . . I hardly dared hope you would come.

SMITH. I should imagine not. And yet, you see, I'm here. Coals of fire,[15] Holmes—coals of fire!

HOLMES. Noble of you . . .

SMITH. Yes, isn't it?

HOLMES. I appreciate your special knowledge.

SMITH. Then you're the only man in London who does. Do you know what is the matter with you?

HOLMES. The same as young Victor—your cousin.

SMITH. Ah, then you recognize the symptoms. Well, then, it's a bad look-out for you. Victor was a strong, hearty young fellow—but a dead man on the fourth day. As you said at the time, it *was* rather surprising that he should contract an out-of-the-way Asiatic disease in the heart of London—a disease of which *I* have made very special study. *(Chuckles)* And now, you, Holmes. Singular coincidence, eh? Or are you going to start making accusations once again—about cause and effect, and so on.

HOLMES. I . . . I knew you caused Victor Savage's death.

*(*SMITH *comes round the bed.)*

SMITH *(snarling).* Did you? Well, proving it is a different matter, Holmes. But what sort of

The artist Walter Paget illustrated a scene from the original story. Here Holmes leaves his bed to lock the door—preventing Watson from bringing help. How does Holmes prevent Watson from leaving in the play?

a game is this, then—spreading lying reports about me one moment, then crawling to me for help the next?

HOLMES *(gasping).* Give . . . give me water. For . . . pity's sake, Smith. Water!

*(*SMITH *hesitates momentarily, then goes to the table and pours a glass from the carafe.)*

SMITH. You're precious near your end, my friend, but I don't want you to go till I've had a word with you.

---

14. **recumbent,** lying down, reclining.

15. **coals of fire,** a biblical reference from Proverbs 25: 21–22, "If your enemy is hungry, give him bread to eat; and if he is thirsty, give him water to drink; for you will heap coals of fire on his head, and the Lord will reward you."

(He holds out the glass to HOLMES *who struggles up feebly to take it and drinks.)*

HOLMES *(gulping water).* Ah! Thank . . . thank you. Please . . . do what you can for me. Only cure me, and I promise to forget.

SMITH. Forget what?

HOLMES. About Victor Savage's death. You as good as admitted just now that you had done it. I swear I will forget it.

SMITH *(laughs).* Forget it, remember it—do as you like. I don't see you in any witness-box, Holmes. Quite another shape of box, I assure you. But you must hear first how it came about.

HOLMES. Working amongst Chinese sailors. Down at the docks.

SMITH. Proud of your brains, aren't you? Think yourself smart? Well, you've met a smarter one this time.

*(*HOLMES *falls back, groaning loudly.)*

Getting painful, is it?

*(*HOLMES *cries out, writhing*[16] *in agony.)*

SMITH. That's the way. Takes you as cramp, I fancy?

HOLMES. Cramp! Cramp!

SMITH. Well, you can still hear me. Now, can't you just remember any unusual incident— just about the time your symptoms began?

HOLMES. I . . . can't think. My mind is gone! Help me, Smith!

SMITH. Did nothing come to you through the post, for instance?

HOLMES. Post? Post?

SMITH. Yes. A little box, perhaps?

*(*HOLMES *emits a shuddering groan.)*

SMITH *(closer; deadly).* Listen! You *shall* hear me! Don't you remember a box—a little ivory box? *(He sees it on the table and holds it up.)* Yes, here it is on your bedside table. It came on Wednesday. You opened it—do you remember?

HOLMES. Box? Opened? Yes, yes! There was . . . sharp spring inside. Pricked my finger. Some sort of joke . . .

SMITH. It was no joke, Holmes. You fool! Who asked you to cross my path? If you'd only left me alone I would never have hurt you.

HOLMES. Box! Yes! Pricked finger. Poison!

SMITH *(triumphantly).* So you do remember. Good, good! I'm glad indeed. Well, the box leaves this room in my pocket, and there's your last shred of evidence gone. *(He pockets it.)* But you have the truth now, Holmes. You can die knowing that I killed you. You knew too much about what happened to Victor Savage, so you must share his fate. Yes, Holmes, you are very near your end now. I think I shall sit here and watch you die.

(He sits on the bed.)

HOLMES *(almost a whisper)* The shadows . . . falling. Getting . . . so dark. I can't see. Smith! Smith, are you there? The light . . . for charity's sake, turn up the light!

*(*SMITH *laughs, gets up and goes to the light.)*

SMITH. Entering the valley of the shadow, eh, Holmes? Yes, I'll turn up the light for you. I can watch your face more plainly, then.

(He turns the flame up full.)

There! Now, is there any *further* service I can render you?

HOLMES *(in a clear, strong voice).* A match and my pipe, if you please.

(He sits bolt upright, SMITH *spins round to see him.)*

SMITH. Eh? What the devil's the meaning of this?

HOLMES *(cheerfully).* The best way of successfully acting a part is to *be* it. I give you my word that for three days I have neither tasted food nor drink until you were good enough to pour me out that glass of water. But it's the tobacco I find most irksome.[17]

---

16. **writhe** (rīŧн), *v.* twist and turn in pain or discomfort.
17. **irksome** (ėrk′səm), *adj.* annoying; tiresome.

(We hear the thud of footsteps running upstairs offstage.)

Hello, hello! Do I hear the step of a friend.

(INSPECTOR MORTON hurries in.)

MORTON. Mr. Holmes?

HOLMES. Inspector Morton, this is your man.

SMITH. What is the meaning of . . . ?

MORTON. Culverton Smith, I arrest you on the charge of the murder of one Victor Savage, and I must warn you that anything you say . . .

SMITH. You've got nothing on me! It's all a trick! A pack of lies!

(He makes to escape. MORTON restrains him.)

MORTON. Keep still, or you'll get yourself hurt!

SMITH. Get off me!

MORTON. Hold your hands out!

(They struggle. MORTON gets out handcuffs and claps them on SMITH's wrists.)

That'll do.

HOLMES. By the way, Inspector, you might add the attempted murder of one Sherlock Holmes to that charge. Oh, and you'll find a small box in the pocket of your prisoner's coat. Pray, leave it on the table, here. Handle it gingerly, though. It may play its part at his trial.

(MORTON retrieves the box and places it on the table.)

SMITH. Trial! You'll be the one in the dock,[18] Holmes. Inspector, he asked me to come here. He was ill, and I was sorry for him, so I came. Now he'll pretend I've said anything he cares to invent that will corroborate[19] his insane suspicions. Well, you can lie as you like, Holmes. My word's as good as yours.

HOLMES. Good heavens! I'd completely forgotten him!

MORTON. Forgotten who, sir?

HOLMES. Watson, my dear fellow! Do come out!

(WATSON emerges with cramped groans.)

I owe you a thousand apologies. To think that I should have overlooked you!

WATSON. It's all right, Holmes. Would have come out before, only you said, whatever happened, I wasn't to budge.

SMITH. What's all this about?

HOLMES. I needn't introduce you to my witness, my friend Dr. Watson. I understand you met somewhere earlier in the evening.

SMITH. You . . . you mean you had all this planned?

HOLMES. Of course. To the last detail. I think I may say it worked very well—with your assistance, of course.

SMITH. Mine?

HOLMES. You saved an invalid trouble by giving my signal to Inspector Morton, waiting outside. You turned up the lamp.

(SMITH and WATSON are equally flabbergasted.)

MORTON. I'd better take him along now, sir. *(To SMITH)* Come on.

(He bundles SMITH roughly towards the door.)

We'll see you down at the Yard tomorrow, perhaps, Mr. Holmes?

HOLMES. Very well, Inspector. And many thanks.

WATSON. Goodbye, Inspector.

(MORTON exits with SMITH.)

WATSON *(chuckles).* Well, Holmes?

HOLMES. Well, Watson, there's a bottle of claret over there—it is uncorked—and some biscuits in the barrel. If you'll be so kind, I'm badly in need of both.

WATSON. Certainly. You know, Holmes, all this seems a pretty, well, elaborate way to go about catching that fellow. I mean, taking in Mrs. Hudson—*and me*—like that. Scared us half to death.

---

18. **dock,** the place where a suspect stands or sits in a court of law.

19. **corroborate** (kə rob′ə rāt′), support, confirm.

HOLMES. It was very essential that I should make Mrs. Hudson believe in my condition. She was to convey it to you, and you to him.

WATSON. Well . . .

HOLMES. Pray do not be offended, my good Watson. You must admit that among your *many* talents, dissimulation[20] scarcely finds a place. If you'd shared my secret, you would never have been able to impress Smith with the urgent necessity of coming to me. It was the vital point of the whole scheme. I knew his vindictive[21] nature, and I was certain he would come to gloat over his handiwork.

(WATSON *returns with the bottle, glasses and barrel.*)

WATSON. But . . . but your appearance, Holmes. Your face! You really do look ghastly.

HOLMES. Three days of absolute fast does not improve one's beauty, Watson. However, as you know, my habits are irregular, and such a feat means less to me than to most men. For the rest, there is nothing that a sponge won't cure. Vaseline to produce the glistening forehead; belladonna[22] for the watering of the eyes; rouge over the cheekbones and crust of beeswax round one's lips . . .

WATSON (*chuckling*). And that babbling oysters!

(*He begins pouring the wine.*)

HOLMES. Yes. I've sometimes thought of writing a monograph on the subject of malingering.[23]

WATSON. But why wouldn't you let me near you? There was no risk of infection.

HOLMES. Whatever I may have said to the contrary in the grip of delirium, do you imagine that I have no respect for your medical talents? Could I imagine that you would be deceived by a dying man with no rise of pulse or temperature? At four yards' distance I *could* deceive you.

(WATSON *reaches for the box.*)

WATSON. This box, then . . .

HOLMES. No, Watson! I wouldn't touch it. You can just see, if you look at it sideways, where the sharp spring emerges as you open it. I dare say it was by some such device that poor young Savage was done to death. He stood between that monster and an inheritance, you know.

WATSON. Then it's true, Holmes! You . . . you might have been killed, too!

HOLMES. As you know, my correspondence is a varied one. I am somewhat on my guard against any packages which reach me. But I saw that by pretending he had succeeded in his design I might be enabled to surprise a confession from him. That pretense I think I may claim to have carried out with the thoroughness of a true artist.

WATSON. (*warmly*). You certainly did, Holmes. Er, a biscuit?

(*He holds out the barrel.*)

HOLMES. On second thoughts, Watson, no thank you. Let us preserve our appetite. By the time I have shaved and dressed, I fancy it will just be nice time for something nutritious at our little place in the Strand.

(*They raise their glasses to one another and drink. The curtain falls.*)

---

20. **dissimulation** (di sim⁄yə lā′shən), hiding the truth; pretending.
21. **vindictive** (vin dik′tiv), *adj.* wanting revenge; spiteful.
22. **belladonna,** a drug made from a poisonous plant.
23. **monograph on . . . malingering,** a scholarly article about pretending to be sick in order to avoid work.

After Reading

Making Connections

1. If you were cast in this play, which character would you like to play—Holmes or Smith? Why?

2. Holmes proves to be trickier than Smith. Do you think using deception to bring a villain to justice is an acceptable practice? Why or why not?

3. Look back at your Writer's Notebook. Which of the **characteristics** of a good detective you listed match those exhibited by Holmes? Can you find any you hadn't thought of?

4. Find clues in the **plot** that Sherlock Holmes is not really sick.

5. What makes it possible for you to envision the scene of the crime even though the **setting** of the story is in Holmes's apartment?

6. Sherlock Holmes and Culverton Smith are both very crafty. Do you think Smith would make a good detective? Could Holmes be a successful criminal? Use a chart like the one below.

Sherlock Holmes	Why is he a good detective?	Could he be a successful criminal?
Culverton Smith	Why is he a successful criminal?	Could he be a good detective?

7. Do you think a detective could catch a criminal today with a stunt similar to the one Holmes pulled on Smith? Why or why not?

Literary Focus: Stock Characters

Have you ever wondered why Batman needs Robin? Certain kinds of stories call for **stock characters,** such as the trusty sidekick in a heroic adventure or the wicked criminal in a detective story. Usually, a stock character shows just a few simple traits, which help set the plot of a story in motion. For example, how does the way Culverton Smith behaves heighten the drama of *The Dying Detective?*

Dr. Watson is one of the most famous stock characters in literature. Like many sidekicks, he acts as the hero's **foil,** someone who makes another appear better by contrast. Watson's well-meaning but less than brilliant observations make Holmes's powers of deduction seem even more impressive. How do you think Watson compares with Robin or another fictional pal you know? How does Culverton Smith compare to The Joker or another dramatic villain?

Vocabulary Study

Write the letter of the word or phrase that best completes the sentence.

agitated
contagious
incubation
implore
methodical
delirious
prolific
writhe
irksome
vindictive

1. Due to the period of **incubation** for Tapanuli Fever, Mrs. Hudson could get sick **a.** immediately on contact. **b.** several days after contact. **c.** a week before contact.

2. When Holmes must **implore** Watson to be careful, you know the mission ahead is **a.** dangerous. **b.** amusing. **c.** routine.

3. A **methodical** criminal is **a.** wild. **b.** armed. **c.** precise.

4. When answering the reporter's **irksome** questions, she **a.** smiled. **b.** frowned. **c.** laughed.

5. You would not expect an **agitated** suspect to **a.** talk fast. **b.** sweat. **c.** fall asleep.

6. Watson knew his patient was **delirious** when he **a.** sneezed and coughed. **b.** talked nonsense. **c.** stopped eating.

7. A **vindictive** crook will most likely try to **a.** pay for his wrong doing. **b.** get a fair trial. **c.** get back at his enemies.

8. Watson is most apt to get a **contagious** disease from **a.** bumping his head on the headboard. **b.** caring for a sneezing patient. **c.** spraining his ankle.

9. The suspect began to **writhe** because he **a.** was sick and in pain. **b.** felt hopeful about his release. **c.** wanted to mail a letter.

10. Conan Doyle, a **prolific** author, wrote **a.** many stories. **b.** very few stories. **c.** expensive stories.

Expressing Your Ideas

Writing Choices

Move Over Webster! Use the story and your imagination to write **definitions** for these terms from the play: *biscuit barrel, Tapanuli Fever,* and *Sherlockian Complaint.*

Making Headlines Sherlock Holmes solves the case. Write a **newspaper report** telling how Holmes caught Culverton Smith. Make up a sensational headline.

Other Options

Get Set Imagine you are the set designer for this play. Create a **diorama** or **scale drawing** of the stage. Go back to the play—including the stage directions—for details.

Take Two With a partner, do two different **readings** of Scene Two. First read the script as the stage directions suggest. Then try new interpretations. Compare the two different readings.

The Gun

Carol Ellis

Carol Ellis
born 1945

The author of more than thirty books for young adults, Carol Ellis is now busy working on a new series about vampires. Her first thriller series, called *Zodiac Chillers,* has recently been released. Born in Texas, she now lives in New York State with her husband and their son.

Building Background

In the Crossfire The Second Amendment to the United States Constitution says: A well regulated militia being necessary to the security of a free state, the right of the people to keep and bear arms shall not be infringed.

Today the right to keep and bear arms lies in the crossfire of a heated controversy over gun control. Some people feel the best defense against crime is their right to own and carry a gun. Others say guns cause more crime. Recently, after a long and stormy debate, Congress passed a bill making guns harder to get. "Too tough!" say some people. "Make it tougher!" say others. The American Medical Association calls firearms a public health emergency with a simple cure—ban all handguns. Do you think this would solve the problem?

Getting into the Story

Discussion Decisions involving a gun are central to the story you are about to read. What do you think you would do if you found a gun? In a small group, brainstorm some good and bad choices a person in that situation could make. Together, decide where to write each idea on a line labeled as shown below.

good choice   bad choice

Reading Tip

Getting Inside a Character's Head In "The Gun," you go through an experience with the main character while it's happening. Early in the story, you will see text written in italics, *like this.* The italicized words and phrases are the thoughts of the main character, Derek. As you read, notice what you find out about Derek and his situation by knowing what's going through his mind.

THE GUN

CAROL ELLIS

"He runs!" Derek said, dribbling the basketball down the cracked cement of the empty school yard. "He jumps!" Quick and agile,[1] he side-stepped his friend Jerry and leaped into the air. "He shoots, and—" he watched as the ball dropped through the hoop, then finished his commentary[2] with a grin "—nothing but net!"

"Nothing, but trouble, you mean." Jerry grabbed the ball and tucked it under his arm. "Look over there."

Turning, Derek saw two men coming through the gate of the school yard. It was a drizzly March day and both of them wore trench coats. Their faces were calm, and they walked casually, like maybe they were out for a stroll. But Derek knew they weren't. Even before the taller one reached into his pocket, he knew they were cops.

It was about the gun, Derek thought. It had to be. He felt panicky for a second, and had to remind himself that he'd thrown it away.

"Derek Robinson?" the tall one said.

"Yeah?"

---

1. **agile** (aj′əl), *adj.* moving with ease; nimble.
2. **commentary** (kom′ən ter′ē), *n.* series of comments or remarks.

◄ What was your initial reaction to this photograph by Peter Poulides? Why do you think he positioned the gun so that it is aimed directly at the viewer?

Reed stayed on his feet, looking around.

Kramer came right to the point. "It's about the gun, Derek."

Derek felt his face get hot, but he asked, "What gun?"

Kramer sighed. "The one you were flashing around in school yesterday."

His eyes on the building across the street, Reed said, "And before that, the one Max Cooper saw you stuffing under your jacket."

Max Cooper owned the deli that Derek passed every day on his way to school. *Great,* Derek thought. *The guy had seen him.*

"Plenty of people saw you with it," Kramer said. "And we'll find it, Derek, you can count on that. So do yourself a favor and cooperate."

"OK . . . OK," Derek said. "I had a gun."

"Right. Where'd you get it?"

"I found it. In a lot." Derek shook his head, remembering the fear and excitement he'd felt when he saw it. "I couldn't believe it. A .38, just lying there!"

"You knew the caliber[3]?" Kramer raised an eyebrow. "Where'd you learn about guns?"

"Where do you think? It's not the first gun I've seen in this neighborhood."

"Just the first one you found lying in a vacant lot."

"Yeah."

"Detectives Kramer and Reed." His hand came all the way out of his pocket and he flashed his badge. "Can we talk to you for a minute? We have a few questions."

"What about?"

"Why don't you step into our office?" Reed motioned to a bench on the other side of the school yard.

Derek's heart sped up. *Definitely the gun,* he thought. With a quick glance at Jerry, he followed the officers across the yard and sat down on the bench. Kramer sat next to him.

---

3. **caliber** (kalʹə bər), *n.* inside diameter of the barrel of a gun.

Kramer raised his eyebrow again. "So you took it to school?"

"Yeah. Look," Derek said, sitting up straighter on the hard bench. "It was dumb, OK? I know it. That's why I got rid of it. I dumped it on my way home, right back where I found it."

"Where's this lot?" Reed asked, getting out a notebook.

"Does the usual stuff include holding up a hardware store . . . ?"

"Corner of Fourth and Cooper," Derek said. "Nothing there but weeds. That's where I picked it up and that's where I put it back. All you have to do is look and you'll find it."

"We'll find it, all right," Kramer said. "But let's back up a little. You still had the gun with you after school. That's what . . . three, three-thirty?"

Derek nodded. "Three."

"So you left school. Then what'd you do?"

"Shot some hoops. Had some pizza," Derek said. "The usual stuff."

Reed slipped the notebook back in his pocket. "Does the usual stuff include holding up a hardware store at four-thirty?" His voice was quiet, almost conversational.[4] But his eyes were as gray and chilly as the sky.

Derek's face got hot again and his heart started hammering. He wanted to stand but he was afraid his legs might shake. "That's crazy!" He wanted to sound cool, but he knew he sounded scared. "I never held up any hardware store! That's crazy," he said again.

"Seventeen or eighteen. Brown hair." Kramer was reading from a little notepad. "About five-eleven, approximately a hundred and fifty pounds. Wearing jeans and a hooded, black-and-red Bulls jacket." He stopped and eyed Derek's jacket. "Black-and-white high-tops." He glanced down at Derek's

shoes, then closed the notepad. "And carrying a .38 caliber revolver."

"It fits pretty well," Reed commented quietly. "Don't you think, Derek?"

Derek knew he didn't have any reason to be so scared, but when he spoke, his voice shook. He couldn't help it. "Yeah, it fits. But it wasn't me. I had nothing to do with any robbery."

"Maybe you didn't," Kramer admitted. "So let's go back over what you did after school, OK?"

"I told you." Derek looked at Jerry standing on the other side of the yard, shooting hoops and missing them all because he was keeping one eye on the little gathering by the bench. Suddenly, Derek's fear left him. When he spoke again, his voice was strong and confident because he was telling the truth. "We left school at three," he said. "We shot a few hoops, then we had some pizza."

"We?"

"Me and Jerry." Derek nodded towards his friend. "We had some pizza at Luigi's, you can ask Jerry. That was about four." He stood up now, knowing that his knees wouldn't quiver like an old man's. "And then we went down by the train tracks."

There was a pause as the two detectives eyed each other. Then Reed asked, "With the gun?" His voice was quieter than ever.

Derek nodded.

"And what were you doing there?"

"Shooting at tin cans," Derek said. He hadn't told them before because he didn't want to admit any more about the gun than he had to. But it didn't matter now. They were after a hold-up guy; they wouldn't care about a little target practice. Especially since Derek didn't have the gun anymore.

"Let's see if I've got this straight," Kramer

---

4. **conversational** (kon′vər sā′shə nəl), *adj.* talking in a friendly, easy way.

Sly's Eye was painted by Colleen Browning in 1977. Try to imagine the thoughts of the woman riding this train. ➤

Colleen Browning, "Sly's Eye," 1977. Oil, 45 ¾ x 56 ½ in. Art and Law 1986. ©1986 West Publishing Corp., Eagan, MN

said. "You left Luigi's and went to the train tracks and shot at tin cans with the .38 you found."

"Yeah, it was about four-thirty, quarter to five," Derek said.

"Did you shoot at anything besides tin cans?"

"Bottles and cans. That's all."

"Weren't you afraid somebody would hear the gunshots?" Kramer asked.

Derek shook his head. "We waited for the trains to pass through."

Kramer nodded. "Very clever. Did Jerry fire the gun, too?'

"No. Only me."

"And then what?" Reed asked.

"When the gun was empty, we split. Jerry went home and so did I," Derek told him. "And I threw the gun back in the lot where I found it." He shoved his hands in his pockets. "Look, ask Jerry. He was with me at Luigi's. Plenty of other people saw me there, too. And Jerry was with me at the tracks."

"About four-thirty, quarter to five?" Kramer asked.

"Yeah."

As Kramer got up from the bench and headed over to Jerry, Derek took a deep breath and let it out. He might still be in trouble about the gun. But no way could they pin the robbery on him. He hadn't done it and he'd just proved it.

When Kramer came back, he nodded at Reed. "It checks out," he said.

Derek let out a sigh of relief. "OK if I go now?"

"I don't think so," Reed said.

"But I told you what happened and you said it checked out!" Derek cried. "I didn't rob anyone!"

"No, we know you didn't," Reed said.

"So?"

"So at four-forty yesterday afternoon, a stray bullet from a .38 caliber revolver smashed through the window of the D train and into the head of a young woman." Reed looked at Derek with cold eyes. "You didn't rob anyone, Derek," he said. "You killed someone."

After Reading

Making Connections

1. Now that you've read the story, think again about what you would do if you found a gun. Has your answer changed from your Before Reading response? Explain.

2. In your opinion, what was Derek's biggest mistake?

3. Write two questions you would like to ask Derek. Exchange questions with a classmate and answer each other's questions orally.

4. Are any of the choices Derek made about the gun he found similar to choices you charted before reading? If so, in what way?

5. Would you call the shooting in this story a crime or an accident? Explain.

6. Suggest one adjective for Derek and one for Jerry, to **characterize** the kind of person each is. What in the story leads you to your conclusions?

7. Do you think the scene of the crime, or **setting,** in this story is in any way the cause of the crime? Why or why not?

8. What do you think would be the appropriate form of justice for someone like Derek?

Literary Focus: Interior Monologue and Dialogue

In this story, you get to "read" Derek's mind because the author uses **interior monologue**—talk that goes on inside a character's head. (**Interior** means *inside*; **monologue** means *speaking alone*.) Interior monologue can give you information about a character and events that you may not learn from dialogue—talk between two or more characters.

For example, when Derek first sees two detectives at the schoolyard, <u>he thinks</u> to himself, "*It was about the gun, . . .*" When the detectives ask if they can talk to him, <u>he says</u>, "What about?" His words plus his thoughts tell us that he may have done something he doesn't want to admit.

With a partner, find another example of what Derek is thinking while talking with the detectives. Discuss what his interior monologue and dialogue together tell you. Make a chart.

What Derek Thinks	What Derek Says	What the Reader Learns
It was about the gun.	What about?	He's hiding something.

Vocabulary Study

Write the word from the list at the left that is most clearly related to the situation conveyed in each sentence. One word is used twice.

agile
commentary
caliber
conversational

1. Derek struggled to sound friendly and casual under questioning.

2. The officer was surprised by how gracefully the boy moved.

3. Remarks continuously ran through Derek's mind about what was happening to him.

4. The size of the bullet led detectives to the gun Derek found.

5. Jerry dribbled and shot the basketball in one fluid movement.

Expressing Your Ideas

Writing Choices

You're Under Arrest Detectives Kramer and Reed trick Derek into making a confession. Write a **comparison/contrast essay** in which you analyze the way Kramer and Reed operate as compared to another detective, such as Sherlock Holmes.

Crime and Punishment In the scene below, a law-breaker of the 1800s is being punished in a pillory. Investigate this form of punishment and the types of crimes it was used to punish. Then write a **report** on the subject.

Other Options

Pros and Cons Reread the words of the second amendment as they appear on page 241. Consider what these words mean to you. Form opposing teams—one supporting gun control and the other in favor of free access to firearms—and stage a **formal debate.** Let your classmates decide which team is more persuasive.

Testing Public Opinion Gun control is one of the most hotly debated topics in our country. With a small group, create a **questionnaire** to find out where your class stands. Chart the survey results on a large **graph** for the classroom.

A National Health Problem The American Medical Association reports that guns are now the second leading cause of death among people ages 15 through 24 years. With a small group, design a **public service TV ad** to educate people about our national firearm epidemic. Include a solution for the problem.

Before Reading

Charles

by Shirley Jackson

Shirley Jackson
1919–1965

"I can't persuade myself that writing is honest work," Shirley Jackson once said. "It's great fun and I love it." Jackson became famous for hair-raising horror tales as well as comical stories about family life, like the one you are about to read. Her oldest child was the model for "Charles." Jackson lived with her husband and four children in a large, old house known for lots of noisy activity and laughter. She wrote at the end of the day, after washing and mending clothes, cooking, doing dishes, and tucking her children in for the night. She said that writing gave her a chance to sit down. Often a story took shape in her mind before she began writing it. It pleased her to see a story grow. She died in 1965 at forty-five years of age.

Building Background

Taught to the Tune of a Hickory Stick Spanking, shaking, forced exercise, detention in uncomfortable spaces . . . these are forms of corporal (physical) punishment some schools have used to keep order. At one time, **corporal punishment** was considered necessary to raise good children. Today many people believe that physical punishment does not work as a form of discipline and, in fact, that it encourages violence.

Corporal punishment is outlawed in schools in many countries—England, France, Germany, Spain, China, and Russia, to name a few. Today, a bill before the United States Congress asks that funds be cut to public schools using corporal punishment. If you were in Congress, how would you vote?

Getting into the Story

Writer's Notebook "Charles" tells about a boy's first weeks in kindergarten. Think back to your early school days. Do you recall your first impressions? Was there a classroom "outlaw"? What behaviors were "crimes" in kindergarten. In your notebook, write about your early classroom recollections.

Reading Tip

Comical Contrasts Have you ever known someone to hold an opinion of a person that doesn't change, no matter what the person does? In this story, the contrast between a mother's perception of her child and the child's actual behavior creates a comical contrast. As you read, compare the boy Laurie's actions with what his mother thinks about him.

Charles

SHIRLEY JACKSON

The day my son Laurie started kindergarten he renounced corduroy overalls with bibs and began wearing blue jeans with a belt. I watched him go off the first morning with the older girl next door, seeing clearly that an era of my life was ended, my sweet-voiced nursery-school tot replaced by a long-trousered, swaggering character who forgot to stop at the corner and wave goodbye to me.

He came home the same way, the front door slamming open, his hat on the floor, and the voice suddenly become raucous[1] shouting, "Isn't anybody *here?*"

At lunch he spoke insolently[2] to his father, spilled his baby sister's milk, and remarked that his teacher said we were not to take the name of the Lord in vain.

"How *was* school today?" I asked, elaborately[3] casual.

"All right," he said.

"Did you learn anything?" his father asked.

Laurie regarded his father coldly. "I didn't learn nothing," he said.

"Anything," I said. "Didn't learn anything."

"The teacher spanked a boy, though," Laurie said, addressing his bread and butter. "For being fresh," he added, with his mouth full.

"What did he do?" I asked. "Who was it?"

Laurie thought. "It was Charles," he said. "He was fresh. The teacher spanked him and made him stand in a corner. He was awfully fresh."

"What did he do?" I asked again, but Laurie slid off his chair, took a cookie, and left, while his father was still saying, "See here, young man."

The next day Laurie remarked at lunch, as soon as he sat down, "Well, Charles was bad again today." He grinned enormously and said, "Today Charles hit the teacher."

"Good heavens," I said, mindful of the Lord's name. "I suppose he got spanked again?"

"He sure did," Laurie said. "Look up," he said to his father.

"What?" his father said, looking up.

"Look down," Laurie said. "Look at my thumb. Gee, you're dumb." He began to laugh insanely.

---

1. **raucous** (rô′kəs), *adj.* harsh-sounding; hoarse.
2. **insolently** (in′sə lənt lē), *adv.* rudely; disrespectfully.
3. **elaborately** (i lab′ər it lē), *adv.* very carefully.

"Why did Charles hit the teacher?" I asked quickly.

"Because she tried to make him color with red crayons," Laurie said. "Charles wanted to color with green crayons so he hit the teacher and she spanked him and said nobody play with Charles but everybody did."

The third day—it was Wednesday of the first week—Charles bounced a see-saw on the head of a little girl and made her bleed, and the teacher made him stay inside all during recess. Thursday Charles had to stand in a corner during story-time because he kept pounding his feet on the floor. Friday Charles was deprived[4] of blackboard privileges because he threw chalk.

On Saturday I remarked to my husband, "Do you think kindergarten is too unsettling[5] for Laurie? All this toughness and bad grammar, and this Charles boy sounds like such a bad influence."

"It'll be all right," my husband said reassuringly. "Bound to be people like Charles in the world. Might as well meet them now as later."

On Monday Laurie came home late, full of news. "Charles," he shouted as he came up the hill; I was waiting anxiously on the front steps. "Charles," Laurie yelled all the way up the hill. "Charles was bad again."

"Come right in," I said, as soon as he came close enough. "Lunch is waiting."

"You know what Charles did?" he demanded, following me through the door. "Charles yelled so in school they sent a boy in from first grade to tell the teacher she had to make Charles keep quiet, and so Charles had to stay after school. And so all the children stayed to watch him."

"What did he do?" I asked.

"He just sat there," Laurie said, climbing into his chair at the table. "Hi, Pop, y'old dust mop."

"Charles had to stay after school today," I told my husband. "Everyone stayed with him."

"What does this Charles look like?" my husband asked Laurie. "What's his other name?"

"He's bigger than me," Laurie said. "And he doesn't have any rubbers[6] and he doesn't even wear a jacket."

Monday night was the first Parent-Teachers meeting, and only the fact that the baby had a cold kept me from going; I wanted passionately to meet Charles's mother. On Tuesday Laurie remarked suddenly, "Our teacher had a friend come to see her in school today."

"Charles's mother?" my husband and I asked simultaneously.[7]

"Naaah," Laurie said scornfully. "It was a man who came and made us do exercises, we had to touch our toes. Look." He climbed down from his chair and squatted down and touched his toes. "Like this," he said. He got solemnly[8] back into his chair and said, picking up his fork, "Charles didn't even *do* exercises."

"That's fine," I said heartily. "Didn't Charles want to do exercises?"

"Naaah," Laurie said. "Charles was so fresh to the teacher's friend he wasn't *let* do exercises."

"Fresh again?" I said.

"He kicked the teacher's friend," Laurie said. "The teacher's friend told Charles to touch his toes like I just did and Charles kicked him."

"What are they going to do about Charles, do you suppose?" Laurie's father asked him.

Laurie shrugged elaborately. "Throw him out of school, I guess," he said.

---

4. deprive (di prīv′), *v.* take away by force.
5. unsettling (un set′ling), *adj.* disturbing.
6. **rubbers,** low-cut rubber overshoes used in rain.
7. **simultaneously** (sī′məl tā′nē əs lē), at the same time; together.
8. solemnly (sol′əm lē), *adv.* gloomily; seriously.

▲ Children's jackets hang in a coatroom in Jeffry W. Myers's 1995 photograph. Does this image bring back kindergarten memories?

Wednesday and Thursday were routine; Charles yelled during story hour and hit a boy in the stomach and made him cry. On Friday Charles stayed after school again and so did all the other children.

With the third week of kindergarten Charles was an institution in our family; the baby was being a Charles when she cried all afternoon; Laurie did a Charles when he filled his wagon full of mud and pulled it through the kitchen; even my husband, when he caught his elbow in the telephone cord and pulled telephone, ashtray, and a bowl of flowers off the table, said, after the first minute, "Looks like Charles."

During the third and fourth weeks it looked like a reformation[9] in Charles; Laurie reported grimly at lunch on Thursday of the third week, "Charles was so good today the teacher gave him an apple."

"What?" I said, and my husband added warily, "You mean Charles?"

"Charles," Laurie said. "He gave the crayons around and he picked up the books afterward and the teacher said he was her helper."

"What happened?" I asked incredulously.[10]

"He was her helper, that's all," Laurie said, and shrugged.

"Can this be true, about Charles?" I asked my husband that night. "Can something like this happen?"

"Wait and see," my husband said cynically.[11] "When you've got a Charles to deal with, this may mean he's only plotting."

He seemed to be wrong. For over a week Charles was the teacher's helper; each day he handed things out and he picked things up; no one had to stay after school.

"The PTA meeting's next week again," I told my husband one evening. "I'm going to find Charles's mother there."

"Ask her what happened to Charles," my husband said. "I'd like to know."

"I'd like to know myself," I said.

On Friday of that week things were back to normal. "You know what Charles did today?" Laurie demanded at the lunch table, in a

---

9. reformation (ref′ər mā′shən), *n*. a change for the better.
10. incredulously (in krej′ə ləs lē), *adv.* doubting; not able to believe.
11. cynically (sin′ik lē), *adv.* showing doubt about the goodness or sincerity of others.

▲ *Young Peter* was painted by contemporary artist Henriette Wyeth. 🐾 If **communication** with this boy were possible, what do you think he would say to you?

voice slightly awed. "He told a little girl to say a word and she said it and the teacher washed her mouth out with soap and Charles laughed."

"What word?" his father asked unwisely, and Laurie said, "I'll have to whisper it to you, it's so bad." He got down off his chair and went around to his father. His father bent his head down and Laurie whispered joyfully. His father's eyes widened.

"Did Charles tell the little girl to say *that?*" he asked respectfully.

"She said it *twice,*" Laurie said. "Charles told her to say it *twice.*"

"What happened to Charles?" my husband asked.

"Nothing," Laurie said. "He was passing out the crayons."

Monday morning Charles abandoned the little girl and said the evil word himself three or four times, getting his mouth washed out with soap each time. He also threw chalk.

My husband came to the door with me that evening as I set out for the PTA meeting. "Invite her over for a cup of tea after the meeting," he said. "I want to get a look at her."

"If only she's there," I said prayerfully.

"She'll be there," my husband said. "I don't see how they could hold a PTA meeting without Charles's mother."

At the meeting I sat restlessly, scanning each comfortable matronly face, trying to determine which one hid the secret of Charles. None of them looked to me haggard[12] enough. No one stood up in the meeting and apologized for the way her son had been acting. No one mentioned Charles.

After the meeting I identified and sought out Laurie's kindergarten teacher. She had a plate with a cup of tea and a piece of chocolate cake; I had a plate with a cup of tea and a piece of marshmallow cake. We maneuvered up to one another cautiously, and smiled.

"I've been so anxious to meet you," I said. "I'm Laurie's mother."

"We're all so interested in Laurie," she said.

"Well, he certainly likes kindergarten," I said. "He talks about it all the time."

"We had a little trouble adjusting, the first week or so," she said primly, "but now he's a fine little helper. With occasional lapses, of course.

"Laurie usually adjusts very quickly," I said. "I suppose this time it's Charles's influence."

"Charles?"

"Yes," I said, laughing, "you must have your hands full in that kindergarten, with Charles."

"Charles?" she said. "We don't have any Charles in the kindergarten."

---

12. **haggard** (hag′ərd), *adj.* looking worn from pain or worry.

After Reading

Making Connections

1. Does Laurie remind you of yourself or anyone you knew when you were five years old? Why or why not?

2. How does Laurie's kindergarten experience compare with the events you wrote about in your Writer's Notebook?

3. Imagine you are Laurie's teacher. Make a report card like the one at the right, giving the grades you feel he deserves. Explain your decisions under Teacher's Comments.

Report Card for Laurie	
Behavior	**Grade**
Social skills	____
Communication skills	____
Imagination	____
Adjustment	____
Teacher's Comments:	
_____	
_____	
_____	

(E=Excellent; F=Fair; N=Needs Improvement)

4. Imagine you are Laurie's mom. What will you say to Laurie's father when you get home from the meeting?

5. At what point in the **plot** did you suspect Laurie and Charles were the same boy? Discuss the clues the author gave you.

6. 👣 In her **communication** with Laurie's mother, his teacher says, "We are all so interested in Laurie." What do you think she is really saying?

7. The teacher spanked Laurie. Do you think spanking is an effective way to correct misbehavior? Why or why not?

8. If Laurie were your child, how would you want the teacher to handle him?

Literary Focus: Inference

One thing we know for sure—Charles is Laurie . . . or do we? The author never actually says Charles and Laurie are the same boy. Instead, she leads us to make that **inference**, or draw that conclusion. At the end, the teacher confirms our suspicions by what she *doesn't* say about Charles—*"We don't have any Charles in the kindergarten."*

In a small group, discuss why it is reasonable to conclude that Charles and Laurie are the same boy. Go back to the story and list several clues to Charles's identity. You can start your list with the clues group members pointed out when they answered question number 5 above.

Vocabulary Study

On your paper, write the letter of the word most nearly *opposite* in meaning to the capitalized word.

raucous
insolently
elaborately
deprive
unsettling
solemnly
reformation
incredulously
cynically
haggard

1. INCREDULOUSLY: **a.** doubtfully **b.** acceptingly **c.** clumsily **d.** suspiciously

2. INSOLENTLY: **a.** rudely **b.** disrespectfully **c.** sadly **d.** politely

3. ELABORATELY: **a.** casually **b.** very carefully **c.** constantly **d.** rarely

4. DEPRIVE: **a.** take **b.** give **c.** withhold **d.** deny

5. RAUCOUS: **a.** hoarse **b.** harsh **c.** soothing **d.** rough

6. UNSETTLING: **a.** boring **b.** disturbing **c.** comforting **d.** troubling

7. SOLEMNLY: **a.** gloomily **b.** seriously **c.** dangerously **d.** cheerfully

8. CYNICALLY: **a.** suspiciously **b.** cleverly **c.** doubtfully **d.** trustingly

9. REFORMATION: **a.** disaster **b.** improvement **c.** creation **d.** change

10. HAGGARD: **a.** worn out **b.** exhausted **c.** refreshed **d.** injured

Expressing Your Ideas

Writing Choices

Laurie's Future Write a **description** of Laurie as an adult. Use ideas from the story and your imagination to predict his occupation, what kind of parent he'll be, and so on.

My Past "Charles" is a story from Jackson's humorous book, *Life Among the Savages.* She called it "a disrespectful memoir of my children." Write a brief **memoir,** or autobiographical incident, based on your own childhood or early school experience.

What Next? Write another **chapter** about Laurie's adventures in kindergarten. For instance, what might happen with Laurie on a field trip to a fire station or a farm?

Other Options

Our Laurie Is Charles? Sometimes it's hard to believe that a parent and a teacher are talking about the same child. In a group of three, perform a **skit** in which Laurie's parents and his teacher talk about him.

Our Pride and Joy Work with a partner to create Laurie's **baby book** from infancy through kindergarten. Contents may include pictures, anecdotes, and keepsakes.

Rules of Order It is always a good idea to have rules to live by in the classroom. As a class, create a list of five to ten **class rules** that everyone agrees upon.

Before Reading

Macavity: The Mystery Cat by T. S. Eliot

Kidnap Poem by Nikki Giovanni

T. S. Eliot
1888–1965

Thomas Sterns Eliot grew up in Missouri. In 1914, he sailed to London. There, he taught school and edited a magazine before becoming a writer. He won the Nobel Prize for literature in 1948. His book *Old Possum's Book of Practical Cats* became the musical *Cats*.

Nikki Giovanni
born 1943

Giovanni calls poetry her "way of capturing a moment." She sees herself as a person always changing and growing. Born in Tennessee, she spent her childhood in Ohio.

Building Background

Tell-tale Style Imagine you are a detective trying to trace a lost poem to its author. The author has left no fingerprints. Luckily, for you, poems are like fingerprints—no two are exactly alike. The following two poems take you to "crime" scenes in very different ways. "Macavity: The Mystery Cat" carries you along with lots of **rhythm** and **rhyme.** The regular beat, sound-alike words, and repeated verse may remind you of a traditional folk song.

"Kidnap Poem" takes you on a "crime spree," breaking rules of punctuation and grammar. There are no commas to slow you down, no periods to make you stop. Nouns turn into verbs, and verbs do things they can't do—or can they? As for capital crimes . . . guilty again. This poem uses capitalization only once.

Getting into the Poems

Discussion Some people (often adults) are afraid of poetry. They think it's full of meanings they won't understand. Others (often children) just like a poem for its sound, beat, and story—even if it's an incredible criminal cat called "the Hidden Paw."

In a small group, brainstorm what you liked about two or three childhood poems. You can jot down ideas on a web.

After brainstorming a few moments, compose a statement together that tells what you like best about this kind of poetry.

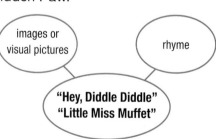

Reading Tip

Finding the Story These poems tell stories in different ways. "Macavity: The Mystery Cat" is a typical tale with lots of details about the main characters and the places where events occur. "Kidnap Poem" uses words that bring pictures to mind and suggest a story. Your imagination fills in the details. As you read, ask yourself how these poems fit the theme "Scene of the Crime."

Macavity: The Mystery Cat

T. S. Eliot

Macavity's a Mystery Cat: he's called the Hidden Paw—
For he's the master criminal who can defy[1] the Law.
He's the bafflement of Scotland Yard, the Flying Squad's despair:[2]
For when they reach the scene of crime—*Macavity's not there!*

5 Macavity, Macavity, there's no one like Macavity,
He's broken every human law, he breaks the law of gravity.
His powers of levitation would make a fakir stare,[3]
And when you reach the scene of crime—*Macavity's not there!*
You may seek him in the basement, you may look up in the air—
10 But I tell you once and once again, *Macavity's not there!*

Macavity's a ginger cat, he's very tall and thin;
You would know him if you saw him, for his eyes are sunken in.
His brow is deeply lined with thought, his head is highly domed;
His coat is dusty from neglect, his whiskers are uncombed.
15 He sways his head from side to side, with movements like a snake;
And when you think he's half asleep, he's always wide awake.

Macavity, Macavity, there's no one like Macavity,
For he's a fiend[4] in feline shape, a monster of depravity.[5]
You may meet him in a by-street, you may see him in the square—
20 But when a crime's discovered, then *Macavity's not there!*

He's outwardly respectable. (They say he cheats at cards.)
And his footprints are not found in any file of Scotland Yard's.
And when the larder's looted, or the jewel-case is rifled,[6]
Or when the milk is missing, or another Peke's[7] been stifled,[8]
25 Or the greenhouse glass is broken, and the trellis past repair—
Ay, there's the wonder of the thing! *Macavity's not there!*

---

1. **defy** (di fī′), *v.* resist or stand against authority.
2. **Scotland Yard . . . Flying Squad's despair** (di sper′), *n.* Scotland Yard is the police headquarters in London; the Flying Squad is a criminal investigation team. They feel without hope (*despair*) because they can't catch Macavity.
3. **levitation . . . a fakir,** Macavity's ability to float in the air (*levitate*) would surprise even a Moslem or Hindu holy person (*fakir*), who are said to possess such powers.
4. **fiend** (fēnd), an evil spirit; demon.
5. **depravity** (di prav′ə tē), bad or wicked conduct; corruption.
6. **rifle** (rīf′əl), *v.* search and rob; steal.
7. **Peke,** a small, silky dog with a broad, flat face; Pekingese.
8. **stifle** (stī′fəl), smother.

◄ Marc Rosenthal painted this snarling cat. Does it fit your image of Macavity?

And when the Foreign Office finds a Treaty's gone astray,
Or the Admiralty loses some plans and drawings by the way,
There may be a scrap of paper in the hall or on the stair—
30 But it's useless to investigate—*Macavity's not there!*
And when the loss has been disclosed, the Secret Service say:
"It *must* have been Macavity!"—but he's a mile away.
You'll be sure to find him resting, or a-licking of his thumbs,
Or engaged in doing complicated long division sums.

35 Macavity, Macavity, there's no one like Macavity,
There never was a cat of such deceitfulness and suavity.[9]
He always has an alibi,[10] and one or two to spare:
At whatever time the deed took place—MACAVITY WASN'T THERE!
And they say that all the Cats whose wicked deeds are widely known
40 (I might mention Mungojerrie, I might mention Griddlebone[11])
Are nothing more than agents for the Cat who all the time
Just controls their operations: the Napoleon of Crime!

---

9. **suavity** (swä′və tē), smooth politeness.
10. alibi (al′ə bī), *n.* a claim that a person was somewhere else when a crime occurred.
11. **Mungojerrie . . . Griddlebone,** characters in Eliot's book *Old Possum's Book of Practical Cats.*

Kidnap Poem

Nikki Giovanni

ever been kidnapped
by a poet
if i were a poet
i'd kidnap you

5 put you in my phrases
and meter you to jones beach
or maybe coney island[1]
or maybe just to my house

lyric you in lilacs
10 dash you in the rain
alliterate[2] the beach
to complement[3] my sea

play the lyre for you
ode you with my love song
15 anything to win you
wrap you in the red Black green[4]
show you off to mama

yeah if i were
a poet i'd kid
20 nap you

Peggy Tagel's 1993 creation of a dancing couple is very fluid and colorful. What kind of music do you think is playing?

---

1. **jones beach . . . coney island,** Jones Beach is a beach for swimmers on Long Island, New York. Coney Island, no longer an island, is an amusement area in New York City.
2. **alliterate** (ə lit′ə rāt), *v.* write something using words that start with the same letter or sound.
3. **complement** (kom′plə mənt), to complete or make perfect.
4. **red Black green,** the colors of the flag adopted by African Americans in mid 1970. Green stands for the earth; red for the blood shed; and black for racial identity.

After Reading

Making Connections

1. Draw symbols to represent each poem. Tell how you made your choices.

2. Who do you think "you" is in each of these poems? Explain.

3. Go back to the statement you helped to compose before reading these poems. How close do these poems come to your favorite kind of poetry?

4. Find examples of these literary techniques in the poems:
   - **alliteration:** repeated consonant sounds at the beginnings of words or within words, such as *sways, side, snake, asleep*
   - **personification:** making animals and objects seem human
   - **repetition:** repeated use of sounds, words, phrases or sentences

5. Name one of the scenes of the crime in "Kidnap Poem" and tell what the poet intends to do there.

6. Why do you think Giovanni capitalized the word Black? (Hint: The footnote on page 258 may suggest an answer.)

7. Stanza 5 of "Macavity" names four misdeeds (not counting cheating at cards). Would those acts be crimes if committed in our human society? Why or why not?

Literary Focus: Poems That Rhyme/Poems That Don't

When we think of *poetry,* we often think of **rhyme**—two or more words that end with the same sound, as in "Macavity: The Mystery Cat."

> *Macavity, Macavity, there's no one like **Macavity**,*
> *For he's a fiend in feline shape, a monster of **depravity**.*

Look for other examples of rhyme in "Macavity: The Mystery Cat." Then go to the nonrhyming "Kidnap Poem" and jot down features of poetry it contains, such as **repetition** and **alliteration**. What do the two poems have in common? You might note your ideas on a Venn diagram.

Macavity: The Mystery Cat — lines end in rhyme / both poems use alliteration / Kidnap Poem — lines don't rhyme

Vocabulary Study

Choose the vocabulary word at the left that completes the rhyme in each of the stanzas below. The rhyme must make sense.

defy
despair
rifle
alibi
alliterate

1. I'm innocent. I do not lie.
   I have the perfect ____.

2. Gather gaily at the gate—
   A perfect phrase to ____.

3. The truth of this you can't deny,
   When you disobey, then you ____.

4. Watching the balloon fly off in the air
   Left the poor child in great ____.

5. Believe me, this is no trifle
   When through my private things you ____.

Expressing Your Ideas _____

Writing Choices

Story Found in Poem Both poems contain events that would make good stories. Write a **short story** based on events or ideas from either poem.

Case of the Missing Stanza Would you like the adventures of Macavity or the kidnapping poet to continue? Write one more **stanza** for either selection. Put it where you think it belongs in the poem.

"Distinctive" Cat Needs Home If innocent kittens have trouble finding homes, what about Macavity? Write a **newspaper ad** to find him a home. The challenge is to make his faults sound like fine qualities.

Other Options

Wanted: Fed and Alive! "Outlaws" like those in these two poems make life interesting. Create a **wanted poster** for either one. Draw a picture of the suspect, list the "crimes," tell where the suspect was last seen, and specify the reward for leads.

Hear Ye, Hear Ye With a group, put on a **mock trial** for Macavity. Refer to the poem for the crimes committed and the evidence available. You'll need Macavity (if you can find him), two lawyers, a judge, witnesses, and a jury.

Poet Fest Find T. S. Eliot's *Old Possum's Book of Practical Cats* or poems by Nikki Giovanni. Individually or in a small group, choose an assortment of poems you especially like and present them to the class in a **poetry reading.** If you wish, choose appropriate music for each poem.

Before Reading

How the Lame Boy Brought Fire from Heaven an African myth
Prometheus a Greek myth retold by Bernard Evslin

Bernard Evslin
1922-1993

The Greek myth "Prometheus" has been told and retold by many people throughout the ages. Bernard Evslin's accounts of the deeds and squabbles among ancient Greek heroes and gods are among the liveliest and most humorous. Evslin brings gods and superhuman characters to life as thinking, feeling beings who behave a lot like we do.

The author of the African myth "The Lame Boy" is unknown, which is typical of the storytelling tradition. No one knows who first told the ancient myths or exactly how they began. They were passed along by word of mouth for hundreds of generations before writing was invented. Like any good story, they got more colorful and exciting with retelling.

Building Background

Myth Making Does your family have some favorite stories they tell again and again? Such stories contain family history, values, concerns, and answers to questions. Storytellers—like you and your family—pass the stories on to the next generation, along with their own additions and variations. That's how **folk tales** and **myths** begin and grow.

In ancient times, before people had scientific answers for their questions about nature, they invented stories to explain the world. The myths you are about to read tell about the origin of fire.

Getting into the Myths

Writer's Notebook These myths tell about the importance and danger of fire to humanity. List in your notebook some ways that fire is a benefit to people as well as a cause of destruction. Draw on your own experience and stories you've read.

Reading Tip

Who's Who Use this chart to keep track of characters in the stories.

African Mythology

Obassi Osaw (o bäs′sē ō′sô)	creator who kept fire away from humans
Etim'Ne (e′tim′ne)	chief who wanted his people to have fire
Lame Boy	servant who obeyed Etim'Ne
Akpan Obassi	messenger and the son of Obassi Osaw

Greek Mythology

Titans	family of giants who ruled the world
Prometheus (prə mē′ thē əs)	Titan who wanted humans to have fire
Zeus (züs)	ruling god who kept fire away from humans
Fates	three goddesses who determined humans' lives
Hephaestus (hi fes′təs)	the lame god of skillful metalwork
Heracles (her′ə klēz′)	a very strong hero, also known as Hercules

This strong, bronze figure is from Benin, Africa. What kind of **communication** do you think he is meant to give? ➤

How the Lame Boy Brought Fire from Heaven

In the beginning of the world, Obassi Osaw made everything but he did not give fire to the people who were on Earth.

Etim'Ne said to the Lame Boy: "What is the use of Obassi Osaw sending us here without any fire? Go therefore and ask him to give us some." So the Lame Boy set out.

Obassi Osaw was very angry when he got the message, and sent the boy back quickly to Earth to reprove[1] Etim for what he had asked. In those days the Lame Boy had not become lame, but could walk like other people.

When Etim'Ne heard that he had angered Obassi Osaw, he set out himself for the latter's

---

1. **reprove** (ri prüv′), *v.* scold; find fault with.

town and said: "Please forgive me for what I did yesterday. It was by accident." Obassi would not pardon him, though he stayed for three days begging forgiveness. Then he went home.

When Etim reached his town, the boy laughed at him. "Are you a chief," said he, "yet could get no fire? I myself will go and bring it to you. If they will give me none, I will steal it."

That very day the lad set out. He reached the house of Obassi Osaw at evening time and found the people preparing food. He helped with the work, and when Obassi began to eat, knelt down till the meal was ended.

The master saw that the boy was useful and did not drive him out of the house. After he had served for several days, Obassi called to him and said: "Go to the house of my wives and ask them to send me a lamp."

The boy gladly did as he was bidden, for it was in the house of the wives that fire was kept. He touched nothing, but waited until the lamp was given him, then brought it back with all speed. Once, after he had stayed for many days among the servants, Obassi sent him again, and this time one of the wives said: "You can light the lamp at the fire." She went into her house and left him alone.

The boy took a brand[2] and lighted the lamp; then he wrapped the brand in plantain[3] leaves and tied it up in his cloth, carried the lamp to his master, and said: "I wish to go out for a certain purpose." Obassi answered: "You can go."

The boy went to the bush outside the town where some dry wood was lying. He laid the brand amongst the dry wood, and blew till it caught alight. Then he covered it with plantain stems and leaves to hide the smoke, and went back to the house. Obassi asked: "Why have you been so long?" And the lad answered: "I did not feel well."

That night when all the people were sleeping, the thief tied his clothes together and crept to the end of town where the fire was hidden. He found it burning and took a glowing brand and some firewood and set out homeward.

When Earth was reached once more, the lad went to Etim and said: "Here is the fire which I promised to bring you. Send for some wood, and I will show you what we must do."

So the first fire was made on Earth. Obassi Osaw looked down from his house in the sky and saw the smoke rising. He said to his eldest son Akpan Obassi: "Go, ask the boy if it is he who has stolen the fire."

Akpan came down to Earth and asked as his father had bidden him. The lad confessed: "I was the one who stole the fire. The reason why I hid it was because I feared."

Akpan replied: "I bring you a message. Up till now you have been able to walk. From today you will not be able to do so anymore."

That is the reason why the Lame Boy cannot walk. He it was who first brought fire to Earth from Obassi's home in the sky.

---

2. **brand,** a piece of burning wood.
3. plantain (plan′tən), *n.* a plant with large leaves, similar to a banana plant.

Prometheus

retold by Bernard Evslin

Prometheus was a young Titan, no great admirer of Zeus. Although he knew the great lord of the sky hated explicit[1] questions, he did not hesitate to beard him when there was something he wanted to know.

One morning he came to Zeus and said, "O Thunderer, I do not understand your design. You have caused the race of man to appear on earth, but you keep him in ignorance and darkness."

"Perhaps you had better leave the race of man to me," said Zeus. "What you call ignorance is innocence. What you call darkness is the shadow of my decree. Man is happy now. And he is so framed that he will remain happy unless someone persuades him that he is unhappy. Let us not speak of this again."

But Prometheus said, "Look at him. Look below. He crouches in caves. He is at the mercy of beast and weather. He eats his meat raw. If you mean something by this, enlighten me with your wisdom. Tell me why you refuse to give man the gift of fire."

Zeus answered, "Do you not know, Prometheus, that every gift brings a penalty? This is the way the Fates weave destiny—by which gods also must abide. Man does not have fire, true, nor the crafts which fire teaches. On the other hand, he does not know disease, warfare, old age, or that inward pest called worry. He is happy, I say, happy without fire. And so he shall remain."

"Happy as beasts are happy," said Prometheus. "Of what use to make a separate race called man and endow[2] him with little

---

1. **explicit** (ek splis′it), *adj.* outspoken, frank; not reserved.
2. **endow** (en dou′), *v.* to give at birth some special ability or talent.

Prometheus Carrying Fire, by Jan Cossiers, was painted in the middle 1700s. It now hangs in the Prado in Madrid.

"Would not fire, and the graces he can put on with fire, make him more interesting?"

"More interesting perhaps, but infinitely[5] more dangerous. For there is this in man too: a vaunting pride that needs little sustenance[6] to make it swell to giant size. Improve his lot, and he will forget that which makes him pleasing—his sense of worship, his humility. He will grow big and poisoned with pride and fancy himself a god, and before we know it, we shall see him storming Olympus.[7] Enough, Prometheus! I have been patient with you, but do not try me too far. Go now and trouble me no more with your speculations."

Prometheus was not satisfied. All that night he lay awake making plans. Then he left his couch at dawn and, standing tiptoe on Olympus, stretched his arm to the eastern horizon where the first faint flames of the sun were flickering. In his hand he held a reed filled with a dry fiber; he thrust it into the sunrise until a spark smoldered. Then he put the reed in his tunic and came down from the mountain.

At first men were frightened by the gift. It was so hot, so quick; it bit sharply when you touched it, and for pure spite, made the shadows dance.

fur, some wit, and a curious charm of unpredictability? If he must live like this, why separate him from the beasts at all?"

"He has another quality," said Zeus, "the capacity for worship. An aptitude[3] for admiring our power, being puzzled by our riddles and amazed by our caprice.[4] That is why he was made."

3. aptitude (ap′tə tüd), *n.* talent, natural ability.
4. caprice, a sudden change of mind without reason.
5. infinitely (in′fə nit lē), *adv.* extremely; vastly.
6. sustenance (sus′tə nəns), *n.* support; aid.
7. Olympus, Mount Olympus was the center of the earth and the home of the gods according to Greek mythology.

They thanked Prometheus and asked him to take it away. But he took the haunch[8] of a newly killed deer and held it over the fire. And when the meat began to sear and sputter, filling the cave with its rich smells, the people felt themselves melting with hunger and flung themselves on the meat and devoured it greedily, burning their tongues.

"This that I have brought you is called 'fire,'" Prometheus said. "It is an ill-natured spirit, a little brother of the sun, but if you handle it carefully, it can change your whole life. It is very greedy; you must feed it twigs, but only until it becomes a proper size. Then you must stop, or it will eat everything in sight—and you too. If it escapes, use this magic: water. It fears the water spirit, and if you touch it with water, it will fly away until you need it again."

He left the fire burning in the first cave, with children staring at it wide-eyed, and then went to every cave in the land.

Then one day Zeus looked down from the mountain and was amazed. Everything had changed. Man had come out of his cave. Zeus saw woodsmen's huts, farmhouses, villages, walled towns, even a castle or two. He saw men cooking their food, carrying torches to light their way at night. He saw forges blazing, men beating out ploughs, keels, swords, spears. They were making ships and raising white wings of sails and daring to use the fury of the winds for their journeys. They were wearing helmets, riding out in chariots to do battle, like the gods themselves.

Zeus was full of rage. He seized his largest thunderbolt. "So they want fire," he said to

> "It is an ill-natured spirit, a little brother of the sun. . . ."

himself. "I'll give them fire—more than they can use. I'll turn their miserable little ball of earth into a cinder." But then another thought came to him, and he lowered his arm. "No," he said to himself, "I shall have vengeance[9]—and entertainment too. Let them destroy themselves with their new skills. This will make a long, twisted game, interesting to watch. I'll attend to them later. My first business is with Prometheus."

He called his giant guards and had them seize Prometheus, drag him off to the Caucasus,[10] and there bind him to a mountain peak with great chains specially forged by Hephaestus—chains which even a Titan in agony could not break. And when the friend of man was bound to the mountain, Zeus sent two vultures to hover[11] about him forever, tearing at his belly and eating his liver.

Men knew a terrible thing was happening on the mountain, but they did not know what. But the wind shrieked like a giant in torment and sometimes like fierce birds.

Many centuries he lay there—until another hero was born brave enough to defy the gods. He climbed to the peak in the Caucasus and struck the shackles from Prometheus and killed the vultures. His name was Heracles.

---

8. **haunch,** the hip and leg of an animal.
9. **vengeance,** punishment in return for a wrong; revenge.
10. **Caucasus,** a mountain range in Southeastern Europe, extending from the Black Sea to the Caspian Sea.
11. **hover** (huv′ər), *v.* hang fluttering or suspended in air.

After Reading

Making Connections

1. Wherever you go on earth, stealing is a crime. Do you think it was justified in these stories? Explain.

2. In your notebook, add any ideas about fire that came to you during reading. Do you think stealing it was worth the two characters' sacrifices? Why or why not?

3. These storytellers use **images** to make vivid pictures for their audience. What images stand out for you?

4. Compare the motives and methods of Prometheus and the Lame Boy for stealing fire. You can organize your ideas on a chart like the one below.

	Prometheus	**The Lame Boy**
Motive		
Method		

5. Do you think either character had regrets about what he did? What in the story leads you to your conclusion?

6. 👆 **Communication** between Prometheus and Zeus is rather one-sided. Reflect on their argument about giving fire to humankind. What do you think of the way Zeus responds to Prometheus?

7. Zeus asks Prometheus, "Do you not know . . . that every gift brings a penalty?" Name a gift of nature other than fire and explain how it is both a benefit and a penalty.

Literary Focus: Theme

We know these stories about how we got fire aren't factual, so what's the point? That's another way of asking, "What's the **theme?**" These two myths share a **universal theme**—a central idea that holds true for humankind everywhere, for all time. Underlying these colorful tales of daring crimes is the matter of justice versus law, the individual against a powerful system. The question seems to be, "What can the little guy do against injustice?"

Working with a partner or on your own, write a sentence that you feel explains the meaning of these two myths. In your statement, try to use at least three of these words: *justice* (or *just*), *law, humankind, benefit.* Share your statements with the class.

Vocabulary Study

Write the letter of the word that is *not* related in meaning to the other words in the set.

reprove
plantain
explicit
endow
aptitude
infinitely
sustenance
hover

1. **a.** explicit   **b.** clear   **c.** definite   **d.** blurry
2. **a.** talent   **b.** disability   **c.** skill   **d.** aptitude
3. **a.** endlessly   **b.** infinitely   **c.** rarely   **d.** continually
4. **a.** sustenance   **b.** support   **c.** aid   **d.** lack
5. **a.** descend   **b.** flutter   **c.** hover   **d.** fly
6. **a.** scold   **b.** approve   **c.** blame   **d.** reprove
7. **a.** palm   **b.** plantain   **c.** ant   **d.** grass
8. **a.** give   **b.** steal   **c.** endow   **d.** provide
9. **a.** reprove   **b.** praise   **c.** criticize   **d.** scold
10. **a.** help   **b.** sustenance   **c.** grudge   **d.** aid

Expressing Your Ideas

Writing Choices

Modern Mythology Write a modern-day **myth** about a gift to humankind that can bring both benefit and destruction to the world. Your myth might also explain the origin of the gift.

Fearless Leaders In an **essay,** compare the two creators, Zeus and Obassi Osaw. How do they treat the people they rule? Tell how they compare or contrast with a modern-day ruler you know about.

Burning Issues Write a **science report** on any aspect of fire that interests you. For example, you could research spontaneous combustion, how a spark plug works, how firefighters put out a fire, or first-aid treatments for burns.

Other Options

Playing with Fire Invent a **board game** based on one or both of the myths. You might want to study other board games for ideas about design, rules, and strategies. Be creative in using "found materials." Ask classmates to play the game and offer suggestions for improvement.

On Stage With a small group, write and produce a **play** based on one of the myths. Put together costumes, create a set, and invent dialogue based on the story. Make programs, listing characters, actors, and stage crew. Present your play to your class or, if possible, to elementary school students.

Some Hot Tips Give an **oral presentation** to the class on how to use fire safely. For example, you might show how to build a campfire, cook over it, tend it, and put it out.

Writing Mini-Lesson

Using a Persuasive Tone

Choosing an Appropriate Tone In persuasive writing, tone can convey your support for a particular position. But your tone should match your purpose and your audience. Notice how the tone differs in the following examples. Which one is appropriate for use in a trial?

1. Even though some people thought they saw Mr. Brown at the scene of the crime, it isn't clear what happened. Also, they found the diamonds in his car. I guess he did it, but maybe not.

2. Mr. Brown is definitely guilty. Everyone saw him at the scene of the crime, and he had a ton of stolen property at his house. I know he did it.

3. Several eyewitnesses have testified that Mr. Brown was at the scene of the crime. In addition, the stolen diamonds were found in his possession. This evidence strongly suggests that Mr. Brown is guilty.

Writing Strategy To use tone persuasively, keep the following hints in mind:

- Make your position clear and be firm—don't hedge.

- Give logical reasons instead of using overstatements and generalizations.

- Avoid phrases such as *I think* or *In my opinion*—let your evidence do the talking.

Activity Options

1. Watch television court dramas. What tone do the lawyers use to present their cases? Take notes on word choice, imagery, and intonation.

2. Write a paragraph arguing for a community improvement, such as a new park or a shopping mall. Trade with a partner and rewrite each other's paragraphs using more or less force.

3. Find ads that use a forceful tone and share them in class. Do they persuade you? Why or Why not?

The Scene of the Crime

Gathering Evidence

Determining

History Connection

Determining the guilt of an accused person was not always the precise science it is today. Once, trial by ordeal, torturing the accused to extract a "confession," was used to convict the suspected criminal. Today, objective scientific analysis of clues gathered at the scene of the crime often carry the weight in court. Justice, while not perfect, usually does prevail.

For centuries, trial by ordeal was the accepted procedure used to "help the criminal remember his crime" and confess to it. Although an almost foolproof way to extract a confession, these methods were useless in determining true guilt.

In this example of trial by ordeal, a man is tied and left in the desert. ▼

POLICE LINE DO NOT CROSS POL

CE LINE DO NOT CRO

▲ A torture wheel was frequently used during the Spanish Inquisition to obtain confessions of heresy.

◄ A form of trial by ordeal, well known in medieval Germany and England, was walking over glowing plowshares. It was thought that the innocent would not be harmed by the ordeal.

Guilt

Every person's fingerprints are different. Because of this, investigators may use fingerprints found on objects to identify people who have touched the objects. Fingerprints are classified into three main types: the arch, the loop, and the whorl. ▼

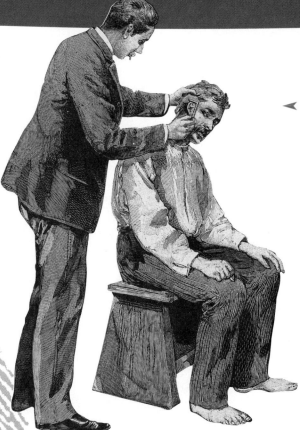

◄ In 1882 Alphonse Bertillon developed a system of precise measurements of the head, body, and limbs of criminals. Bertillon claimed that the odds of any two people having the exact same set of measurements were 286,435,456 to one. The complicated Bertillon system of measurements was eventually replaced by fingerprinting.

CROSS POLICE LINE DO NOT CROS.
POLICE LINE DO N

◄ The lie detector, or polygraph, test was first used in the United States in 1921. It records blood pressure, pulse, and respiration rate, all of which commonly vary in certain ways when an individual is telling the truth or a lie. Because of their inexact nature, the results of this test are rarely allowed as evidence in court.

◄ A lab technician of today tests physical evidence found on a pair of blue jeans.

Responding

Do you think that the use of scientific tests of physical evidence can ever replace the role of the jury in the American court system? Give reasons for your answer.

Life Science Connection

Convict a murderer without the victim's body? It had never been done before. Science and technology broke new ground in the Helen McCourt case. As a result of recent scientific discoveries, a killer who probably would have otherwise escaped punishment was brought to justice.

GENETIC FINGERPRINTING:

The Murder with No Body

By Anita Larsen

ON FEBRUARY 9, 1988, twenty-two-year-old Helen McCourt finished work, then took the bus home to Billinge, Merseyside, in England. Her usual pattern was to walk the 300 yards from her bus stop to her home. But that day, McCourt never arrived home.

Police were sure that foul play was involved but were unable to find Helen's body. Without her body, police couldn't prove anything— even that there *had* been a murder.

In the course of their investigation, police came upon the name Ian Simms in Helen's diary. Three weeks later, Helen's blood-stained clothes were found in a plastic garbage bag. In a dump three miles away, police found more blood-stained clothing. The clothes belonged to Simms. This pointed to a strong suspicion that Simms had something to do with McCourt's disappearance.

But police were still stymied. Without Helen's body, they couldn't prove that the clothes were hers. And if they couldn't prove that, they had no case to take to court.

Without Helen's body, they couldn't prove that the clothes were hers. . . . Enter forensic science.

Enter forensic science.

Dr. John Moore recalled work done by Dr. Alec Jeffreys of the University of Leicester in 1984. Dr. Jeffreys is not a forensic scientist. He is a geneticist, someone who specializes in the biology of heredity. His work focuses on *d*eoxyribo*n*ucleic *a*cid, a chemical compound called DNA, for short.

DNA is the molecule of heredity; it provides the blueprint that directs the development and maintenance of everyone's bodies. Offspring inherit about half of their DNA from their mother, and about half from their father. DNA appears in the nucleus of every cell in our bodies except red blood cells, which have no nucleus.

Most of these nucleated cells contain 23 pairs of *chromosomes*. These chromosomes are bundles of DNA and contain *genes*. Genes determine the unique characteristics of every living thing.

Dr. Jeffreys had devised a way to visually identify

▲ Technicians analyze autoradiographs (DNA maps) of blood samples.

DNA. And a DNA print of biological clues left at a crime scene can often be as unique as a fingerprint.

Collection and analyses of biological clues at a crime scene is a clean, high-tech process. But it begins in the chaos of violence. Consider an example: A murderer attacks a victim. The victim struggles, wounding the attacker. If enough nucleated white cells of the wounded killer's blood are left on the victim's shirt, investigators can obtain a sample.

The DNA print taken from the biological evidence at a crime scene can be compared to one taken from a suspect. That can result in a match as clear-cut as the match of two fingerprints.

On the other hand, failing to find a match between these two DNA prints can prove that the suspect is innocent.

In the Helen McCourt murder case, Dr. Moore applied this scientific breakthrough to solve the case. Helen was missing, presumed dead. But her parents were still living and could provide blood samples.

If investigators could match Helen's parents' DNA prints with a DNA print from the stains on Simms's clothing, it would prove that those bloodstains were Helen's. That would mean they could prove that Simms was very seriously implicated in Helen's death.

The DNA prints did, in fact, establish beyond all doubt that the blood on Simms's clothing was Helen's. Largely on the basis of this evidence, Simms was arrested, tried, convicted, and sentenced to life imprisonment on March 14, 1989.

Responding
Research current newspapers and magazines to find an article about a case in which genetic fingerprinting played an important role in determining guilt. Summarize the article for the class.

Advances in science have changed the American legal system. Gathering evidence at the scene of the crime now must be done with especially great care, so that accurate scientific tests can be run. For example, DNA tests performed on blood samples can prove the guilt or innocence of the accused. In the end, many feel, justice is better served.

The Structure of DNA

Deep in the animated network of the cell nucleus lies the molecule of heredity—DNA. Its twin spirals are built from four interlocking chemical bases—adenine paired with thymine and cytosine paired with guanine. Code messages, genes, are stored along a chromosome in sequences of these chemical bases. Genes define the unique characteristics of each living thing. It is here, for example, that butterflies are given their wing patterns and people are assigned eye color.

Scientists have been challenged by the inner workings of DNA since 1944, when American researcher Oswald Avery defined its role in transferring hereditary characteristics. James D. Watson and Francis Crick described the spiral structure of DNA in 1953. In 1984 Alec Jeffreys, a geneticist in Leicester, England, devised a way to visually identify DNA found between the genes. In certain regions the DNA patterns vary distinctively from person to person except in cases of identical twins. Jeffreys's method of identification, known as DNA fingerprinting (simplified in the painting at the right), has become a valuable technique for investigating crimes in which biological clues are left behind. Now, in some jurisdictions, suspects can be linked to a crime by evidence that incriminates them to their very molecules.

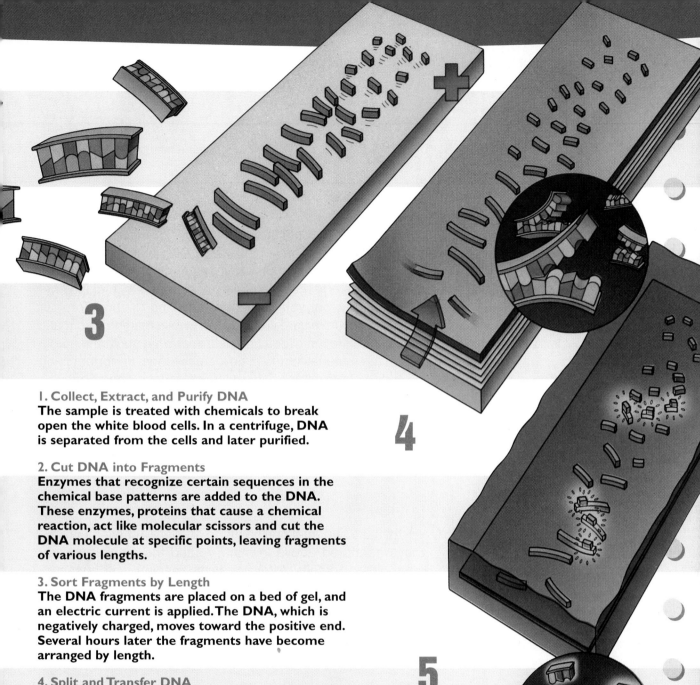

1. Collect, Extract, and Purify DNA
The sample is treated with chemicals to break open the white blood cells. In a centrifuge, **DNA** is separated from the cells and later purified.

2. Cut DNA into Fragments
Enzymes that recognize certain sequences in the chemical base patterns are added to the **DNA**. These enzymes, proteins that cause a chemical reaction, act like molecular scissors and cut the **DNA** molecule at specific points, leaving fragments of various lengths.

3. Sort Fragments by Length
The **DNA** fragments are placed on a bed of gel, and an electric current is applied. The **DNA**, which is negatively charged, moves toward the positive end. Several hours later the fragments have become arranged by length.

4. Split and Transfer DNA
Alkaline chemicals are introduced to split the **DNA** fragments apart. At the same time, a nylon sheet is placed over the gel and covered with layers of paper. Blotting draws the fragments onto the nylon where they are later fixed in place.

5. Attach Radioactive Probes
The nylon sheet is immersed in a bath, and radioactive probes—synthetic **DNA** segments of known sequence—are added. The probes target a specific base sequence and bond to it. X-ray film is then exposed to the nylon sheet. Two dark bands develop at the probe sites. These are the end result, a **DNA** fingerprint of the evidence, which is then compared with prints of all suspects.

Responding
Do further research on the structure of chromosomes. Make a model chromosome and display it with those of other students in your classroom.

Reading Mini-Lesson

Remembering What You Read

What do you remember about the article "Genetic Fingerprinting: The Murder with No Body" on pages 272–273? Did you keep your concentration as you read it? It is easy to let your mind wander.

Reading without remembering is like fishing without catching anything—time goes by, but you don't have anything to show for your efforts. One way to make sure you stay alert while reading is to make a mental outline of the main idea and details of what you are reading.

First, skim the material for the main idea, the most important thing about the topic. The topic of this article is "genetic fingerprinting," and the main idea can be stated: *Genetic fingerprinting can identify individuals in criminal investigations.* Using this main idea to focus your mind, you can add a mental list of details, such as *done by geneticists,* as you read. Unless the reading is very short, don't try to get every detail. Focus on subtopics or groups of details.

Activity Options

Title:_____

Main Idea:_____

Details:_____
_____

Main Idea:_____

Details:_____
_____

Main Idea:_____

Details:_____
_____

1. Try to make a mental outline of the article. With the main idea that was stated above in mind, reread the article and add subtopics or details. After you finish reading, see how successful you were. Close your book and try to write your mental outline from memory, using a form like the one shown at the left. Don't be discouraged if, on this first try, you find you forgot some important details. As with everything else, you'll improve with practice.

2. Most of your textbook chapters will be organized in sections of main ideas and details. Choose a section from your science or your social studies textbook and make a mental outline, as described above, as you read. Again, close the book and try to write down your outline. Did you do better this time?

3. Work with a partner. Each of you should find an article and read it using the mental-outline techniques you have learned. Then, from memory, take turns telling each other the main points and adding as many significant details as you can.

Part Two

Encounters with Prejudice

Never judge a book by its cover, the old saying goes. It's not always so easy to be as open-minded in judging people. The clothes someone wears, the color of their skin, their sex, their age—all of these aspects of a person are like the cover of a book. If for some reason we don't like what we see when we first meet someone, it can be hard for us to see the real material inside.

 Multicultural Connection **Interactions** sometimes involve dealing with prejudices or misunderstandings that may result when persons of different backgrounds or appearances interact. What types of intergroup misunderstandings occur in these selections?

Literature

Ray Bradbury	**All Summer in a Day** ◆ short story	279
Ted Poston	**The Revolt of the Evil Fairies** ◆ short story	288
Marta Salinas	**The Scholarship Jacket** ◆ short story	296
Ed J. Vega	**Translating Grandfather's House** ◆ poem	301
	Language Mini-Lesson ◆ Subject and Verb Agreement	304
Jean Little	**About Old People** ◆ anecdote	306
E. E. Cummings	**old age sticks** ◆ poem	309

Interdisciplinary Study Let's Be Fair

Prejudice Across the Ages ◆ history 312

Brown Eyes Only by Pam Deyell Gingold ◆ sociology 314

Three Reasons to Become More Tolerant by Lynn Duvall

◆ sociology 316

Reading Mini-Lesson ◆ Drawing Conclusions 318

Writing Workshop Expository Writing

Explaining Feelings 319

Beyond Print Effective Speaking

Helping Margot See the Light 325

Before Reading

All Summer in a Day

by Ray Bradbury

Ray Bradbury
born 1920

A very imaginative childhood provided Bradbury with a wealth of material for his writing. When he was twelve years old, he decided to write at least four hours a day every day. Keeping up that practice has allowed him to write more than 500 short stories, plays, poems, and scripts during his long career. Bradbury uses a science fiction setting in much of his work, but, as in "All Summer in a Day," he is more interested in explaining human character and problems than in technology or science. "If you're too good a scientist, you're not a good writer," he claims.

Building Background

Fact and Fantasy When you gaze at the night sky from Earth, it's natural to wonder what is—or could be—out there. Writers and scientists go about answering that question in different ways. Where science fiction writers imagine a colony of space travelers or a hostile environment full of aliens, scientists might find a planet on which

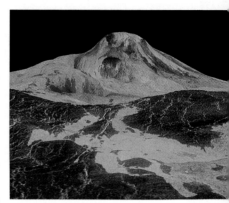

nothing could survive. When the *Magellan* spacecraft probed Venus in 1990, it confirmed that Venus has a stifling atmosphere with thick layers of carbon dioxide and a barren surface so hot the rocks glow faintly red (see the image made by *Magellan's* cloud piercing radar). That's the scientific answer to what Venus is really like. In the imaginative story that follows, the author pictures somewhat different conditions on the planet.

Getting into the Story

Writer's Notebook In this selection, a group of Earthlings must adjust to life on Venus. Sometimes just changing schools or moving a few miles can make it seem as though you're on a different planet. In your notebook write about a time you had to leave the old and familiar to move on. What were you feeling? What did you miss? How did you try to comfort yourself?

Reading Tip

Visualization Since science fiction presents an imaginary world, it is often helpful to visualize, or draw mental pictures, of the setting and events. Science fiction writers usually provide lots of description to spark your **visualization.** Close your eyes and picture "a thousand forests . . . crushed under the rain," and rain like "the endless shaking down of clear bead necklaces upon the roof." As you read, jot down other descriptions that help you create vivid pictures of the story's setting and events in your mind.

ALL *Summer* IN A DAY

Ray Bradbury

"Ready?"

"Ready."

"Now?"

"Soon."

"Do the scientists really know? Will it happen today, will it?"

"Look, look; see for yourself!"

The children pressed to each other like so many roses, so many weeds, intermixed, peering out for a look at the hidden sun.

It rained.

It had been raining for seven years; thousands upon thousands of days compounded[1] and filled from one end to the other with rain, with the drum and gush of water, with the sweet crystal fall of showers and the concussion[2] of storms so heavy they were tidal waves come over the islands. A thousand forests had been crushed under the rain and grown up a thousand times to be crushed again. And this was the way life was forever on the planet Venus, and this was the schoolroom of the children of the rocket men and women who had come to a raining world to set up civilization and live out their lives.

"It's stopping, it's stopping!"

"Yes, yes!"

Margot stood apart from them, from these children who could never remember a time when there wasn't rain and rain and rain. They were all nine years old, and if there had been a day, seven years ago, when the sun came out for an hour and showed its face to the stunned world, they could not recall. Sometimes, at night, she heard them stir, in remembrance,[3] and she knew they were

---

1. **compound** (kom pound′), *v.* add to; increase; multiply.
2. **concussion** (kən kush′ən), a sudden, violent shaking.
3. **remembrance** (ri mem′brəns), *n.* memory.

A Robert Vickrey painted *The Magic Carpet* in 1965. What do you suppose the title means?

dreaming and remembering gold or a yellow crayon or a coin large enough to buy the world with. She knew they thought they remembered a warmness, like a blushing in the face, in the body, in the arms and legs and trembling hands. But then they always awoke to the tatting drum, the endless shaking down of clear bead necklaces upon the roof, the walk, the gardens, the forests, and their dreams were gone.

All day yesterday they had read in class about the sun. About how like a lemon it was, and how hot. And they had written small stories or essays or poems about it:

> *I think the sun is a flower*
> *That blooms for just one hour.*

That was Margot's poem, read in a quiet voice in the still classroom while the rain was falling outside.

"Aw, you didn't write that!" protested one of the boys.

"I did," said Margot. "I *did.*"

"William!" said the teacher.

But that was yesterday. Now, the rain was slackening,[4] and the children were crushed in the great thick windows.

"Where's teacher?"

"She'll be back."

"She'd better hurry; we'll miss it!"

They turned on themselves, like a feverish wheel, all tumbling spokes.

Margot stood alone. She was a very frail[5]

---

4. **slacken** (slak′ən), *v.* become slower or less active.
5. **frail** (frāl), *adj.* slender and not very strong; weak.

girl who looked as if she had been lost in the rain for years and the rain had washed out the blue from her eyes and the red from her mouth and the yellow from her hair. She was an old photograph dusted from an album, whitened away, and if she spoke at all, her voice would be a ghost. Now she stood, separate, staring at the rain and the loud, wet world beyond the huge glass.

"What're *you* looking at?" said William.

Margot said nothing.

"Speak when you're spoken to." He gave her a shove. But she did not move; rather, she let herself be moved only by him and nothing else.

They edged away from her; they would not look at her. She felt them go away. And this was because she would play no games with them in the echoing tunnels of the underground city. If they tagged her and ran, she stood blinking after them and did not follow. When the class sang songs about happiness and life and games, her lips barely moved. Only when they sang about the sun and the summer did her lips move as she watched the drenched windows.

And then, of course, the biggest crime of all was that she had come here only five years ago from Earth, and she remembered the sun and the way the sun was and the sky was when she was four in Ohio. And they, they had been on Venus all their lives, and they had been only two years old when last the sun came out and had long since forgotten the color and heat of it and the way it really was. But Margot remembered.

"It's like a penny," she said once, eyes closed.

"No, it's not!" the children cried.

"It's like a fire," she said, "in the stove."

"You're lying; you don't remember!" cried the children.

THE CHILDREN HATED HER FOR ALL THESE REASONS . . . .

But she remembered and stood quietly apart from all of them and watched the patterning windows. And once, a month ago, she had refused to shower in the school shower rooms, had clutched her hands to her ears and over her head, screaming that the water mustn't touch her head. So after that, dimly, dimly, she sensed it, she was different, and they knew her difference and kept away.

There was talk that her father and mother were taking her back to Earth next year; it seemed vital to her that they do so, though it would mean the loss of thousands of dollars to her family. And so the children hated her for all these reasons of big and little consequence.[6] They hated her pale snow face, her waiting silence, her thinness, and her possible future.

"Get away!" The boy gave her another push. "What're you waiting for?"

PREDICT: How do you think Margot's argument with the children will end?

Then, for the first time, she turned and looked at him. And what she was waiting for was in her eyes.

"Well, don't wait around here!" cried the boy savagely. "You won't see nothing!"

Her lips moved.

"Nothing!" he cried. "It was all a joke, wasn't it?" He turned to the other children. "Nothing's happening today. *Is* it?"

They all blinked at him and then, understanding, laughed and shook their heads. "Nothing, nothing!"

"Oh, but," Margot whispered, her eyes helpless. "But this is the day, the scientists

---

6. **consequence** (kon′sə kwens), *n.* importance.

predict, they say, they *know*, the sun . . ."

"All a joke!" said the boy, and seized her roughly. "Hey, everyone, let's put her in a closet before teacher comes!"

"No," said Margot, falling back.

They surged[7] about her, caught her up and bore her, protesting, and then pleading, and then crying, back into a tunnel, a room, a closet, where they slammed and locked the door. They stood looking at the door and saw it tremble from her beating and throwing herself against it. They heard her muffled cries. Then, smiling, they turned and went out and back down the tunnel, just as the teacher arrived.

"Ready, children?" She glanced at her watch.

"Yes!" said everyone.

"Are we all here?"

"Yes!"

The rain slackened still more.

They crowded to the huge door.

The rain stopped.

It was as if, in the midst of a film concerning an avalanche, a tornado, a hurricane, a volcanic eruption, something had, first, gone wrong with the sound apparatus,[8] thus muffling and finally cutting off all noise, all of the blasts and repercussions[9] and thunders, and then, second, ripped the film from the projector and inserted in its place a peaceful tropical slide which did not move or tremor. The world ground to a standstill. The silence was so immense and unbelievable that you felt your ears had been stuffed or you had lost your hearing altogether. The children put their hands to their ears. They stood apart. The door slid back and the smell of the silent, waiting world came in to them.

The sun came out.

It was the color of flaming bronze, and it

was very large. And the sky around it was a blazing blue tile color. And the jungle burned with sunlight as the children, released from their spell, rushed out, yelling, into the springtime.

"Now, don't go too far," called the teacher after them. "You've only two hours, you know. You wouldn't want to get caught out!"

But they were running and turning their faces up to the sky and feeling the sun on their cheeks like a warm iron; they were taking off their jackets and letting the sun burn their arms.

"Oh, it's better than the sun lamps, isn't it?"

"Much, much better!"

They stopped running and stood in the great jungle that covered Venus, that grew and never stopped growing, tumultuously,[10] even as you watched it. It was a nest of octopi, clustering up great arms of fleshlike weed, wavering, flowering in this brief spring. It was the color of rubber and ash, this jungle, from the many years without sun. It was the color of stones and white cheeses and ink, and it was the color of the moon.

The children lay out, laughing, on the jungle mattress and heard it sigh and squeak under them, resilient[11] and alive. They ran among the trees, they slipped and fell, they pushed each other, they played hide-and-seek and tag, but most of all they squinted at the sun until tears ran down their faces, they put their hands up to that yellowness and that amazing blueness and they breathed of the

---

7. **surge** (sėrj), *v.* move like waves; rise up excitedly.

8. **apparatus** (ap′ə rat′əs), *n.* equipment or machinery needed for a specific use.

9. **repercussion** (rē′pər kush′ən), *n.* sound flung back; echo.

10. **tumultuously** (tü mul′chü əs lē), *adv.* in a disorderly way.

11. **resilient** (ri zil′ē ənt), *adj.* springing back.

Charles E. Burchfield (1893–1967), *Fantasy of Heat*, 1952–1958, watercolor on paper, 40 x 30 inches. Private Collection.
Photograph courtesy of the Charles Burchfield Archives, Burchfield-Penney Art Center, Buffalo State College, Buffalo, New York.

▲ Can you feel the warmth of the sun in this Charles Burchfield watercolor titled *Fantasy of Heat?*

fresh, fresh air and listened and listened to the silence which suspended them in a blessed sea of no sound and no motion. They looked at everything and savored everything. Then, wildly, like animals escaped from their caves, they ran and ran in shouting circles. They ran for an hour and did not stop running.

And then—

In the midst of their running, one of the girls wailed.

Everyone stopped.

The girl, standing in the open, held out her hand.

"Oh, look, look," she said, trembling.

They came slowly to look at her opened palm.

In the center of it, cupped and huge, was a single raindrop.

She began to cry, looking at it.

They glanced quietly at the sky.

"Oh. Oh."

A few cold drops fell on their noses and their cheeks and their mouths. The sun faded behind a stir of mist. A wind blew cool around them. They turned and started to walk back toward the underground house, their hands at their sides, their smiles vanishing away.

A boom of thunder startled them and like leaves before a new hurricane, they tumbled upon each other and ran. Lightning struck ten miles away, five miles away, a mile, a half mile. The sky darkened into midnight in a flash.

They stood in the doorway of the underground for a moment until it was raining hard. Then they closed the door and heard the gigantic sound of the rain falling in tons and avalanches, everywhere and forever.

"Will it be seven more years?"

"Yes. Seven."

Then one of them gave a little cry.

"Margot!"

"What?"

"She's still in the closet where we locked her."

"Margot."

They stood as if someone had driven them, like so many stakes, into the floor. They looked at each other and then looked away. They glanced out at the world that was raining now and raining and raining steadily. They could not meet each other's glances. Their faces were solemn and pale. They looked at their hands and feet, their faces down.

"Margot."

CONNECT: Have the children's feelings toward Margot changed? Explain.

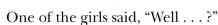

One of the girls said, "Well . . . ?"

No one moved.

"Go on," whispered the girl.

They walked slowly down the hall in the sound of cold rain. They turned through the doorway to the room in the sound of the storm and thunder, lightning on their faces, blue and terrible. They walked over to the closet door slowly and stood by it.

Behind the closet door was only silence.

They unlocked the door, even more slowly, and let Margot out.

After Reading

Making Connections

1. What scenes from the story stand out most in your mind?

2. What do you think the children saw when they opened the closet at the end of the story?

3. 🐾 What is the first clue in the **interactions** between the children that tells you they dislike Margot?

4. Do you think the children will treat Margot differently after what they did to her? Why or why not?

5. How does the author appeal to your sense of smell, taste, sight, touch, or hearing? Support your answer with examples from the story.

6. Were your experiences in adjusting to new places that you wrote about in your notebook at all similar to Margot's? Explain.

7. Margot might have adjusted better to Venus if the children had liked her. Name a few things you might do to help new students adjust to your school.

8. How is this story similar to or different from the **plots** of other science fiction stories you may have read?

Literary Focus: Metaphor and Simile

In this story the sun is described as "like a lemon" and also is compared to "a flower." The first comparison is a **simile** and the second is a **metaphor.** Similes are easy to spot. They compare two unlike things using the words of comparison *like* or *as.* Metaphors compare unlike things without using any words of comparison, as when Margot writes, "I think the sun is a flower." Ray Bradbury frequently enriches his writing with metaphors and similes, as in the metaphor where Margot compares the sun to "gold or a yellow crayon or a coin large enough to buy the world." The metaphors and similes in this story help you, the reader, to better visualize the setting and understand the events. Look for other similes and metaphors in the story. Using a chart like the one below will help you classify the similes and metaphors you find.

Quotation	Simile (like, as)	Metaphor
like so many roses, so many weeds	✓	
the sweet crystal fall of showers		✓

Vocabulary Study

On your paper write the letter of the word pair that best expresses a relationship like that expressed in the original pair.

compound
remembrance
slacken
frail
consequence
surge
apparatus
repercussion
tumultuously
resilient

1. **COMBINE : COMPOUND :: a.** shatter : break **b.** accept : reject **c.** lengthen : shorten **d.** walk : run

2. **NOISILY : TUMULTUOUSLY :: a.** quietly : loudly **b.** loosely : tightly **c.** jokingly : seriously **d.** happily : ecstatically

3. **CONSEQUENCE : IMPORTANCE :: a.** cookie : dough **b.** car : automobile **c.** words : book **d.** pencil : paper

4. **SURGE : WAVE :: a.** like : food **b.** pounce : cat **c.** vegetable : garden **d.** chair : room

5. **FRAIL : STRONG :: a.** weak : wobbly **b.** wet : dry **c.** hard : tough **d.** cold : icy

6. **SLACKEN : TIGHTEN :: a.** iron : flatten **b.** look : see **c.** push : pull **d.** hear : listen

7. **CAMERA : APPARATUS :: a.** goat : cow **b.** art : crayon **c.** carrot : vegetable **d.** magazine : newspaper

8. **SPRINGY : RESILIENT :: a.** yellow : gold **b.** true : false **c.** lucky : unfortunate **d.** cute : ugly

9. **REMEMBRANCE : REMEMBER :: a.** like : unlikely **b.** sight : see **c.** appearance : disappear **d.** renewal : newer

10. **REPERCUSSION : ECHO :: a.** tot : baby **b.** friend : foe **c.** bird : fly **d.** truck : train

Expressing Your Ideas

Writing Choices

I Wanna Go Back! If you were Margot, how would you convince your parents to take you back to Earth? Write a **dialogue** that might occur between Margot and her parents.

Locked-Up Thoughts What was Margot thinking in the closet? Get into her head, and write an **interior monologue** of her thoughts and emotions while in the closet.

Other Options

It's a Jungle Out There What did the children see when they went out in the sun? Make a **detailed illustration** of the environment they encountered. Use your imagination, but also include images from the story.

Map It Out Look back through the story for clues about where the children's city and their school were located in relation to the jungle. Create a **map** with a **legend** of this area.

Before Reading

The Revolt of the Evil Fairies

by Ted Poston

Ted Poston
1906–1974

Born Theodore Roosevelt Augustus Major Poston, Ted Poston grew up working on his father's small newspaper in Hopkinsville, Kentucky. After college he decided to make journalism his career. He went to New York City, where he landed a job as city hall reporter for the *New York Post*. Later, Poston won many journalistic awards for his work covering race relations and the civil rights movement. He also published about twenty short stories, including this story based on his life at Booker T. Washington Colored Grammar School in Hopkinsville.

Building Background

Segregation The Civil War gave U.S. slaves their freedom, but the Jim Crow laws passed afterward in the South took some of it back. These laws provided that black Americans remain segregated, or separated from whites, in public places such as hotels, restaurants, and buses. Most schools also were segregated. Northern blacks did not face as much segregation by law, but were often forced by prejudice and poverty into separate neighborhoods. In 1954, a Supreme Court order declared it illegal to segregate schools. Today, segregation in many other areas is illegal. Do you notice any kinds of segregation that occur anyway? Why do you think this happens?

Getting into the Story

Discussion Discrimination and prejudice can exist within as well as across races or ethnic groups. At such times education and ability may not be the first consideration. Have you ever been involved in a situation where someone was chosen for an honor or to participate in some event for reasons other than their abilities? Discuss the outcome of such a situation with your classmates. Was such unfair treatment just accepted or did resentment and conflict result?

Reading Tip

Language Choices Prejudice may cause those who dislike someone or something for no particular reason to use insulting language. Those insults can range from nasty comments to nicknames that put down everyone of a certain race or nationality. As you read through this story, you may find some rude or offensive language. Remember that the author carefully chose those words. Your job as a reader is to understand why the author chose to use such language, and how that language helps get across the main idea.

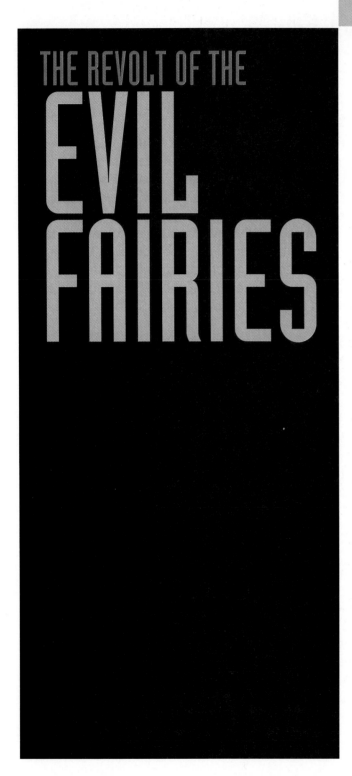

THE REVOLT OF THE EVIL FAIRIES

TED POSTON

THE GRAND DRAMATIC OFFERING of the Booker T. Washington Colored Grammar School was the biggest event of the year in our social life in Hopkinsville, Kentucky. It was the one occasion on which they let us use the old Cooper Opera House, and even some of the white folks came out yearly to applaud our presentation. The first two rows of the orchestra were always reserved for our white friends, and our leading colored citizens sat right behind them—with an empty row intervening, of course.

Mr. Ed Smith, our local undertaker, invariably[1] occupied a box to the left of the house and wore his cutaway coat and striped breeches.[2] This distinctive[3] garb was usually reserved for those rare occasions when he officiated at the funerals of our most prominent colored citizens. Mr. Thaddeus Long, our colored mailman, once rented a tuxedo and bought a box too. But nobody paid him much mind. We knew he was just showing off.

The title of our play never varied. It was always Prince Charming and the Sleeping Beauty, but no two presentations were ever the same. Miss H. Belle LaPrade, our sixth-grade teacher, rewrote the script every season, and it was never like anything you read in the storybooks.

---

1. **invariably** (in ver′ē ə blē), *adv.* without change or exception.
2. **cutaway coat and striped breeches,** daytime formal wear for men, similar to a tuxedo.
3. **distinctive** (dis tingk′tiv), *adj.* different from others; special.

A 🖌 Jacob Lawrence painted *Vaudeville* in 1951. Of the vaudeville experience, Lawrence once said, "We would go there to see the comedians, the chorus lines, the dance, performance. . . ." What is your interpretation of the **interaction** going on in this painting?

The Revolt of the Evil Fairies   **289**

the script every season, and it was never like anything you read in the storybooks.

Miss LaPrade called it "a modern morality play[4] of conflict between the forces of good and evil." And the forces of evil, of course, always came off second best.

The Booker T. Washington Colored Grammar School was in a state of ferment[5] from Christmas until February, for this was the period when parts were assigned. First there was the selection of the Good Fairies and the Evil Fairies. This was very important, because the Good Fairies wore white costumes and the Evil Fairies black. And strangely enough most of the Good Fairies usually turned out to be extremely light in complexion, with straight hair and white folks' features. On rare occasions a darkskinned girl might be lucky enough to be a Good Fairy, but not one with a speaking part.

There never was any doubt about Prince Charming and the Sleeping Beauty. They were always lightskinned. And though nobody ever discussed those things openly, it was an accepted fact that a lack of pigmentation[6] was a decided advantage in the Prince Charming and Sleeping Beauty sweepstakes.

And therein lay my personal tragedy. I made the best grades in my class, I was the leading debater, and the scion[7] of a respected family in the community. But I could never be Prince Charming, because I was black.

In fact, every year when they started casting our grand dramatic offering my family started pricing black cheesecloth at Franklin's Department Store. For they knew that I would be leading the forces of darkness and skulking[8] back in the shadows—waiting to be vanquished[9] in the third act. Mamma had experience with this sort of thing. All my brothers had finished Booker T. before me.

Not that I was alone in my disappointment. Many of my classmates felt it too. I probably just took it more to heart. Rat Joiner, for instance, could rationalize[10] the situation. Rat was not only black; he lived on Billy Goat Hill.[11] But Rat summed it up like this:

"If you black, you black."

I should have been able to regard the matter calmly too. For our grand dramatic offering was only a reflection of our daily community life in Hopkinsville. The yallers[12] had the best of everything. They held most of the teaching jobs in Booker T. Washington Colored Grammar School. They were the Negro doctors, the lawyers, the insurance men. They even had a "Blue Vein Society," and if your dark skin obscured your throbbing pulse you were hardly a member of the elite.

Yet I was inconsolable[13] the first time they turned me down for Prince Charming. That was the year they picked Roger Jackson. Roger was not only dumb; he stuttered. But he was light enough to pass for white, and that was apparently sufficient.

In all fairness, however, it must be admitted that Roger had other qualifications. His father owned the only colored saloon in town and was quite a power in local politics. In fact, Mr. Clinton Jackson had a lot to say about just who taught in the Booker T. Washington Colored Grammar School. So it was understandable that Roger should have been picked for Prince Charming.

My real heartbreak, however, came the

---

4. **morality play** (mə ral′ə tē), a type of play in which each character represents a quality such as truth, beauty, or ignorance.
5. ferment (fèr′ment), n. excitement or unrest.
6. **pigmentation** (pig′mən tā′shən), skin coloring.
7. scion (sī′ən), descendant or child.
8. skulk (skulk), v. hide in a cowardly way.
9. vanquish (vang′kwish), v. conquer; defeat.
10. rationalize (rash′ə nə līz), v. to find an explanation or excuse for.
11. **Billy Goat Hill,** a poor neighborhood in town.
12. yaller (yal′ər), a "yellow," or a light-skinned black.
13. inconsolable (in′kən sō′lə bəl), adj. brokenhearted.

kindergarten. She had soft light hair, bluish-gray eyes, and a dimple which stayed in her left cheek whether she was smiling or not.

Of course Sarah never encouraged me much. She never answered any of my fervent[14] love letters, and Rat was very scornful of my one-sided love affairs. "As long as she don't call you a black baboon," he sneered, "you'll keep on hanging around."

After Sarah was chosen for Sleeping Beauty, I went out for the Prince Charming role with all my heart. If I had declaimed[15] boldly in previous contests, I was matchless now. If I had bothered Mamma with rehearsals at home before, I pestered her to death this time. Yes, and I purloined[16] my sister's can of Palmer's Skin Success.[17]

I knew the Prince's role from start to finish, having played the Head Evil Fairy opposite it for two seasons. And Prince Charming was one character whose lines Miss LaPrade never varied much in her many versions. But although I never admitted it, even to myself, I knew I was doomed from the start. They gave the part to Leonardius Wright. Leonardius, of course, was yaller.

The teachers sensed my resentment. They were almost apologetic. They pointed out that I had been such a splendid Head Evil Fairy for two seasons that it would be a crime to let anybody else try the role. They reminded me that Mamma wouldn't have to buy any more cheesecloth because I could use my same old costume. They insisted that the Head Evil Fairy was even more important than Prince Charming because he was the one who cast the spell on Sleeping Beauty. So what could I do but accept?

I had never liked Leonardius Wright. He was a goody-goody, and even Mamma was always throwing him up to me. But, above all, he too was in love with Sarah Williams. And now he got a chance to kiss Sarah every day in rehearsing the awakening scene.

▲ *Grand Performance* is a lively scene painted in 1993 by Jacob Lawrence. Born in 1917 in New Jersey, Lawrence created this piece at age 76. Can you identify the various kinds of performers?

Well, the show must go on, even for little black boys. So I threw my soul into my part and made the Head Evil Fairy a character to be remembered. When I drew back from the couch of Sleeping Beauty and slunk away into the shadows at the approach of Prince Charming, my facial expression was indeed something to behold. When I was vanquished by the shining sword of Prince Charming in

---

14. **fervent** (fėr′vənt), *adj.* showing great warmth of feeling; very eager and serious.
15. **declaim** (di klām′), *v.* recite in public.
16. **purloin** (pər loin′), steal.
17. **Palmer's Skin Success,** an old-fashioned product to lighten dark skin.

The Revolt of the Evil Fairies   **291**

the last act, I was a little hammy perhaps—but terrific!

The attendance at our grand dramatic offering that year was the best in its history. Even the white folks overflowed the two rows reserved for them, and a few were forced to sit in the intervening one. This created a delicate situation, but everybody tactfully ignored it.

When the curtain went up on the last act, the audience was in fine fettle.[18] Everything had gone well for me too—except for one spot in the second act. That was where Leonardius unexpectedly rapped me over the head with his sword as I slunk off into the shadows. That was not in the script, but Miss LaPrade quieted me down by saying it made a nice touch anyway. Rat said Leonardius did it on purpose.

The third act went on smoothly, though, until we came to the vanquishing scene. That was where I slunk from the shadows for the last time and challenged Prince Charming to mortal combat. The hero reached for his shining sword—a bit unsportsmanlike, I always thought, since Miss LaPrade consistently left the Head Evil Fairy unarmed—and then it happened!

Later I protested loudly—but in vain— that it was a case of self-defense. I pointed out that Leonardius had a mean look in his eye. I cited the impromptu[19] rapping he had given my head in the second act. But nobody would listen. They just wouldn't believe that Leonardius really intended to brain me when he reached for his sword.

Anyway, he didn't succeed. For the minute I saw that evil gleam in his eye—or was it my own?—I cut loose with a right to the chin, and Prince Charming dropped his shining sword and staggered back. His astonishment lasted only a minute, though, for he lowered his head and came charging in, fists flailing. There was nothing yellow about Leonardius but his skin.

The audience thought the scrap was something new Miss LaPrade had written in. They might have kept on thinking so if Miss LaPrade hadn't been screaming so hysterically from the sidelines. And if Rat Joiner hadn't decided that this was as good a time as any to settle old scores. So he turned around and took a sock at the male Good Fairy nearest him.

When the curtain rang down, the forces of Good and Evil were locked in combat. And Sleeping Beauty was wide awake and streaking for the wings.

They rang the curtain back up fifteen minutes later, and we finished the play. I lay down and expired according to specifications but Prince Charming will probably remember my sneering corpse to his dying day. They wouldn't let me appear in the grand dramatic offering at all the next year. But I didn't care. I couldn't have been Prince Charming anyway.

---

18. **in fine fettle,** in good spirits.
19. impromptu (im promp′tü), *adj.* without preparation; offhand.

After Reading

Making Connections

1. What advice would you give to the narrator about dealing with **interactions** involving prejudice in the future?

2. Would you have been as persistent as the narrator in trying out for the part of Prince Charming?

3. Although about a serious subject, this story contains considerable **humor.** Which parts of the story did you think were funniest?

4. In your discussion before reading the story, you talked about instances in which people were unfairly selected for honors. Were these situations similar in any way to those in the story? Explain.

5. List several ways described in the story in which prejudice affects the narrator, his family, and friends.

6. Write a one-sentence **summary** that explains why the narrator attacks Leonardius. Use a diagram to organize your thoughts.

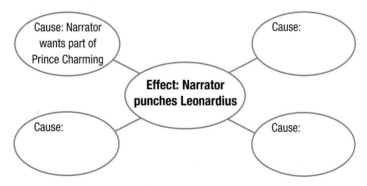

7. In this play, the roles were assigned according to how the children looked. What would be a fairer way to assign parts in a play?

Literary Focus: Point of View

The narrator of this story writes from a **first-person point of view**—that is, he uses the words *I* and *we* to describe events that happened to him personally. When you read in the story, "But I could never be Prince Charming, because I was black," you are getting the narrator's opinion, or point of view. In a first-person story, you get only the narrator's thoughts and feelings.

An **autobiography** is the story of a real person's life, written by the person who lived it. All autobiography is written from a first-person point of view. Authors of fiction use first-person point of view to help readers feel that they are in the middle of the action.

Vocabulary Study

On your paper write the letter of the word that is not related in meaning to the other words in the set.

invariably	
distinctive	
ferment	
skulk	
vanquish	
rationalize	
inconsolable	
fervent	
declaim	
impromptu	

1. **a.** speak   **b.** recite   **c.** declaim   **d.** investigate
2. **a.** distinctive   **b.** reliable   **c.** special   **d.** unusual
3. **a.** leap   **b.** jump   **c.** skulk   **d.** bound
4. **a.** conquer   **b.** win   **c.** vanquish   **d.** consider
5. **a.** rationalize   **b.** advertise   **c.** publicize   **d.** announce
6. **a.** quiet   **b.** unrest   **c.** ferment   **d.** uproar
7. **a.** inconsolable   **b.** heartbroken   **c.** angelic   **d.** upset
8. **a.** fervent   **b.** easygoing   **c.** unhurried   **d.** calm
9. **a.** offhand   **b.** intricate   **c.** unrehearsed   **d.** impromptu
10. **a.** briskly   **b.** rapidly   **c.** swiftly   **d.** invariably

Expressing Your Ideas

Writing Choices

Opinion, Please What did you think of this version of Sleeping Beauty? Play drama critic and write a **review** of the production. Explain what parts you liked and didn't like, and give advice to anyone who may be considering going to see it.

Stopping Segregation The narrator in this story faced a kind of segregation that workers in the civil rights movement of the 1950s and 1960s fought to end. Read about the civil rights movement; then write a one-page **research report**. Topics you might write about include desegregation, Rosa Parks, and voter registration.

Play It Again Look over the story to see how the play "Prince Charming and the Sleeping Beauty" differs from the fairy tale version of the story. Work with a group to write a **script** for the play. Think about how you would produce the play at your school.

Other Options

Dress It Up How do you think the evil fairies looked in their black cheesecloth? Design **costumes** and **scenery** for the play. If possible, work with the students writing a script for the play. Help them use your ideas in their production.

Publicity Crew Think about this play's most dramatic image. Is it the evil fairies? The lovely Sleeping Beauty? Prince Charming? Use your ideas to design a **poster** advertising the play. Your poster should attract interest and contain information on the time, the place, and the price of tickets.

The Pros and Cons Select a civil rights or desegregation issue, such as whether or not students should be bused to schools outside their neighborhoods to achieve integrated classes. With a group, **debate** the issue in front of your classmates. Have them vote on which side gave the best argument.

Before Reading

The Scholarship Jacket by Marta Salinas
Translating Grandfather's House by Ed J. Vega

Marta Salinas

Salinas's stories have appeared in the *Los Angeles Herald Examiner* and in *California Living.* In her writing Salinas shows her concern for bilingual students who are punished for speaking Spanish and who often are not given the opportunities afforded to those whose native language is English. Such students often face economic problems along with the difficulties of overcoming stereotypes.

Ed J. Vega

Vega's poem "Translating Grandfather's House" appears in a poetry collection titled *Cool Salsa: Bilingual Poems on Growing Up Latino in the United States* edited by Lori M. Carlson.

Building Background

Ethnic Heritage Your ethnic heritage is an unchanging part of you. The color of your skin, hair, and eyes, and the shape of your features give others information at a glance. That information may lead them to guess things about your family background that may or may not be true. A guess about you or your family based on prejudice can surprise you or hurt your feelings, but what you do about it is your choice.

Getting into the Selections

Writer's Notebook Just like the characters in the story and poem that follow, most of us are concerned about how other people see us. Often we have little control over how others form their opinions of us. Which of the following qualities do you most want others to consider when they judge you: appearance, achievement in school, athletic ability, family, personal qualities (honesty, kindness, and so on)? In your notebook, rank these in order of importance to you. Add other categories that you feel are important.

Reading Tip

Predictions Thinking ahead to what might happen next as you read a story helps focus your attention and sets a purpose for reading. A good guess, or **prediction,** is based on what has already happened in the story, as well as what you know from experience. As you read on after making a prediction, ask yourself whether or not your guess was on target. Use a chart like the one below to help you keep track of your predictions.

Prediction	Reason	Outcome	
		Right	Wrong
Narrator (or someone close to her) wants scholarship jacket.	subject of first paragraph described in detail	✓	

▲ Look at the composition of this 1927 drawing by Diego Rivera. Notice how the artist arranged the subject. Why do you think he did this?

THE SCHOLARSHIP JACKET

MARTA SALINAS

he small Texas school that I attended carried out a tradition every year during the eighth grade graduation; a beautiful gold and green jacket, the school colors, was awarded to the class valedictorian,[1] the student who had maintained the highest grades for eight years. The scholarship[2] jacket had a big gold S on the left front side and the winner's name was written in gold letters on the pocket.

My oldest sister Rosie had won the jacket a few years back and I fully expected to win also. I was fourteen and in the eighth grade. I had been a straight A student since the first grade, and the last year I had looked forward to owning that jacket. My father was a farm laborer who couldn't earn enough money to feed eight children, so when I was six I was given to my grandparents to raise. We couldn't participate in sports at school because there were registration fees, uniform costs, and trips out of town; so even though we were quite agile[3] and athletic, there would never be a sports school jacket for us. This one, the scholarship jacket, was our only chance.

In May, close to graduation, spring fever struck, and no one paid any attention in class; instead we stared out the windows and at each other, wanting to speed up the last few weeks of school. I despaired every time I looked in the

---

1. **valedictorian** (val′ə dik tôr′ē ən), *n.* student with the best grades who gives the farewell speech at graduation.
2. **scholarship** (skol′ər ship), *n.* showing knowledge gained through study.
3. **agile** (aj′əl), moving quickly and easily.

mirror. Pencil thin, not a curve anywhere, I was called "Beanpole" and "String Bean" and I knew that's what I looked like. A flat chest, no hips, and a brain, that's what I had. That really isn't much for a fourteen-year-old to work with, I thought, as I absentmindedly wandered from my history class to the gym. Another hour of sweating in basketball and displaying my toothpick legs was coming up. Then I remembered my P.E. shorts were still in a bag under my desk where I'd forgotten them. I had to walk all the way back and get them. Coach Thompson was a real bear if anyone wasn't dressed for P.E. She had said I was a good forward and once she even tried to talk Grandma into letting me join the team. Grandma, of course, said no.

I decided I wasn't going to make it any easier for him so I looked him straight in the eye.

I was almost back at my classroom's door when I heard angry voices and arguing. I stopped. I didn't mean to eavesdrop; I just hesitated, not knowing what to do. I needed those shorts and I was going to be late, but I didn't want to interrupt an argument between my teachers. I recognized the voices: Mr. Schmidt, my history teacher, and Mr. Boone, my math teacher. They seemed to be arguing about me. I couldn't believe it. I still remember the shock that rooted me flat against the wall as if I were trying to blend in with the graffiti[4] written there.

"I refuse to do it! I don't care who her father is, her grades don't even begin to compare to Martha's. I won't lie or falsify records. Martha has a straight A plus average and you know it." That was Mr. Schmidt and he sounded very angry. Mr. Boone's voice sounded calm and quiet.

"Look, Joann's father is not only on the Board, he owns the only store in town; we could say it was a close tie and—"

The pounding in my ears drowned out the rest of the words, only a word here and there filtered through. ". . . Martha is Mexican . . . resign . . . won't do it . . . ." Mr. Schmidt came rushing out, and luckily for me went down the opposite way toward the auditorium, so he didn't see me. Shaking, I waited a few minutes and then went in and grabbed my bag and fled from the room. Mr. Boone looked up when I came in but didn't say anything. To this day I don't remember if I got in trouble in P.E. for being late or how I made it through the rest of the afternoon. I went home very sad and cried into my pillow that night so Grandmother wouldn't hear me. It seemed a cruel coincidence[5] that I had overheard that conversation.

The next day when the principal called me into his office, I knew what it would be about. He looked uncomfortable and unhappy. I decided I wasn't going to make it any easier for him so I looked him straight in the eye. He looked away and fidgeted with the papers on his desk.

"Martha," he said, "there's been a change in policy this year regarding the scholarship jacket. As you know, it has always been free." He cleared his throat and continued. "This year the Board decided to charge fifteen dollars—which still won't cover the complete cost of the jacket."

I stared at him in shock and a small sound of dismay escaped my throat. I hadn't expected this. He still avoided looking in my eyes.

"So if you are unable to pay the fifteen dollars for the jacket, it will be given to the next one in line."

---

4. **graffiti** (grə fē′tē), *n.* drawings or writings scratched or scribbled, usually on a wall.
5. **coincidence** (kō in′sə dəns), *n.* two things that occur by chance at the same time.

Standing with all the dignity I could muster, I said, "I'll speak to my grandfather about it, sir, and let you know tomorrow." I cried on the walk home from the bus stop. The dirt road was a quarter of a mile from the highway, so by the time I got home, my eyes were red and puffy.

"Where's Grandpa?" I asked Grandma, looking down at the floor so she wouldn't ask me why I'd been crying. She was sewing on a quilt and didn't look up.

"I think he's out back working in the bean field."

I went outside and looked out at the fields. There he was. I could see him walking between the rows, his body bent over the little plants, hoe in hand. I walked slowly out to him, trying to think how I could best ask him for the money. There was a cool breeze blowing and a sweet smell of mesquite[6] in the air, but I didn't appreciate it. I kicked at a dirt clod. I wanted that jacket so much. It was more than just being a valedictorian and giving a little thank you speech for the jacket on graduation night. It represented eight years of hard work and expectation.[7] I knew I had to be honest with Grandpa; it was my only chance. He saw me and looked up.

He waited for me to speak. I cleared my throat nervously and clasped my hands behind my back so he wouldn't see them shaking. "Grandpa, I have a big favor to ask you," I said in Spanish, the only language he knew. He still waited silently. I tried again. "Grandpa, this year the principal said the scholarship jacket is not going to be free. It's going to cost fifteen dollars and I have to take the money in tomorrow, otherwise it'll be given to someone else." The last words came out in an eager rush. Grandpa straightened up tiredly and leaned his chin on the hoe handle. He looked out over the field that was filled with the tiny green bean plants. I waited, desperately hoping he'd say I could have the money.

He turned to me and asked quietly, "What does a scholarship jacket mean?"

I answered quickly; maybe there was a chance. "It means you've earned it by having the highest grades for eight years and that's why they're giving it to you." Too late I realized the significance of my words. Grandpa knew that I understood it was not a matter of money. It wasn't that. He went back to hoeing the weeds that sprang up between the delicate little bean plants. It was a time consuming job; sometimes the small shoots were right next to each other. Finally he spoke again.

"Then if you pay for it, Marta, it's not a scholarship jacket, is it? Tell your principal I will not pay the fifteen dollars."

I walked back to the house and locked myself in the bathroom for a long time. I was angry with Grandfather even though I knew he was right, and I was angry with the Board, whoever they were. Why did they have to change the rules just when it was my turn to win the jacket?

It was a very sad and withdrawn girl who dragged into the principal's office the next day. This time he did look me in the eyes.

"What did your grandfather say?"

I sat very straight in my chair.

"He said to tell you he won't pay the fifteen dollars."

The principal muttered something I couldn't understand under his breath, and walked over to the window. He stood looking out at something outside. He looked bigger than usual when he stood up; he was a tall gaunt[8] man with gray hair, and I watched the back of his head while I waited for him to speak.

---

6. **mesquite** (me skēt′), *n.* a common tree or shrub of the pea family found in the southwestern United States and Mexico.

7. **expectation** (ek′spek tā′shən), *n.* anticipation; something expected.

8. **gaunt** (gônt), *adj.* thin and bony, with hollow eyes.

"Why?" he finally asked. "Your grandfather has the money. Doesn't he own a small bean farm?"

I looked at him, forcing my eyes to stay dry. "He said if I had to pay for it, then it wouldn't be a scholarship jacket," I said and stood up to leave. "I guess you'll just have to give it to Joann." I hadn't meant to say that; it had just slipped out. I was almost to the door when he stopped me.

I was afraid I was going to be sick. I didn't need any sympathy speeches.

"Martha—wait."

I turned and looked at him, waiting. What did he want now? I could feel my heart pounding. Something bitter and vile[9] tasting was coming up in my mouth; I was afraid I was going to be sick. I didn't need any sympathy speeches. He sighed loudly and went back to his big desk. He looked at me, biting his lip, as if thinking.

"Okay, okay! We'll make an exception in your case. I'll tell the Board, you'll get your jacket."

I could hardly believe it. I spoke in a trembling rush. "Oh, thank you, sir!" Suddenly I felt great. I didn't know about adrenaline[10] in those days, but I knew something was pumping through me, making me feel as tall as the sky. I wanted to yell, jump, run the mile, do something. I ran out so I could cry in the hall where there was no one to see me. At the end of the day, Mr. Schmidt winked at me and said, "I hear you're getting a scholarship jacket this year."

His face looked as happy and innocent as a baby's, but I knew better. Without answering I gave him a quick hug and ran to the bus. I cried on the walk home again, but this time because I was so happy. I couldn't wait to tell Grandpa and ran straight to the field. I joined him in the row where he was working and without saying anything I crouched down and started pulling up the weeds with my hands. Grandpa worked alongside me for a few minutes, but he didn't ask what had happened. After I had a little pile of weeds between the rows, I stood up and faced him.

"The principal said he's making an exception for me, Grandpa, and I'm getting the jacket after all. That's after I told him what you said."

Grandpa didn't say anything, he just gave me a pat on the shoulder and a smile. He pulled out the crumpled red handkerchief that he always carried in his back pocket and wiped the sweat off his forehead.

"Better go see if your grandmother needs any help with supper."

I gave him a big grin. He didn't fool me. I skipped and ran back to the house whistling some silly tune.

---

9. **vile** (vīl), *adj.* disgusting.
10. **adrenaline** (ə dren′l ən), *n.* a body chemical that speeds up the heartbeat and increases energy.

TRANSLATING GRANDFATHER'S HOUSE

ED J. VEGA

▲ This picture of a house was created by a child at the
Terezín Concentration Camp between 1942 and 1944.
It appears in the book . . . *I Never Saw Another
Butterfly. . . .*

According to my sketch,
Rows of lemon & mango
Trees frame the courtyard
Of Grandfather's stone
5 And clapboard home;
The shadow of a palomino
Gallops on the lip
Of the horizon.

The teacher says
10 The house is from
Some Zorro
Movie I've seen.

"Ask my mom," I protest.
"She was born there—
15 Right there on the second floor!"

Crossing her arms she moves on.

Memories once certain as rivets
Become confused as awakenings
In strange places and I question
20 The house, the horse, the wrens
Perched on the slate roof—
The roof Oscar Jartín
Tumbled from one hot Tuesday,
Installing a new weather vane;
25 (He broke a shin and two fingers).

Classmates finish drawings of New York City
Housing projects on Navy Street.
I draw one too, with wildgrass
Rising from sidewalk cracks like widows.
30 In big round letters I title it:

GRANDFATHER'S HOUSE

Beaming, the teacher scrawls
An A+ in the corner and tapes
It to the green blackboard.

35 To the green blackboard.

After Reading

Making Connections

1. Which narrator is more like you? On a scale of 1 to 10, rate yourself, Marta, and the narrator of the poem on each of the following: loyalty, pride, respect for authority, and self-confidence. Use graphs like the example that follows.

2. How would you feel and what would you say if a teacher reacted negatively, as in the poem, to something you were proud of?

3. If you could be the hand of fate and change events, how would you change the outcome of the poem?

4. At the end of the story, the narrator says of her grandfather, "He didn't fool me." What does she mean?

5. How would the story be different if the narrator had not overheard the conversation between the two teachers?

6. Why does the author repeat the phrase "to the green blackboard" at the end of the poem?

7. Think about the awards given at your school and how the students who receive them are chosen. Discuss fairness.

Literary Focus: Diction

You can infer or conclude a lot about authors from their **diction,** that is the words and phrases they choose to use in a story or poem. Each of these selections uses friendly, everyday language. As a result, they are easy to read and understand. Yet we know that Marta is an A+ student and, therefore, the author could have portrayed her using more difficult sentences with harder vocabulary. Her choice of simple diction tells us that Marta is a straight-forward and practical person—she is not a show-off.

Think about diction as you reread the story and poem. How would your ideas about the narrators change if the authors had chosen more difficult vocabulary?

Vocabulary Study

On your paper write the word from the list that matches each example below. One word is used twice.

valedictorian
scholarship
graffiti
coincidence
mesquite
expectation
gaunt
vile
adrenaline

1. the taste of fear and dread that Marta felt
2. the writing all over a school wall
3. a bush Marta could smell in the air
4. what Marta deserved to be
5. with reason, Marta had this regarding the jacket
6. Marta's accidental overhearing of a conversation
7. what it takes to get good grades
8. the way Marta's tall, thin principal looked
9. what made Marta feel physically energized
10. the title given to the best student to graduate

Expressing Your Ideas

Writing Choices

Dialogue Duo Look at how Marta talks to her grandfather and how Martha (as she is called at school) talks to the principal and teachers. How do these dialogues differ? Write a **comparison essay** that explains the differences in the dialogues. You may want to pay special attention to diction, or the choice of words or phrases.

Lies, Lies, Lies What if the grandfather referred to in the poem saw the phony picture of his house posted on the board? Write a **letter** from the grandfather to the poem's narrator about how he feels after seeing the picture. Include questions that the grandfather might want to ask his grandchild.

But You Don't Understand Write a **poem** about a time when someone failed to understand or believe you.

Other Options

Your Chance to Talk Imagine you are Marta. What would you say to all those gathered at the graduation ceremony—the principal, the school board, the teachers, your fellow students, and their parents? Practice and present Marta's **valedictory speech.**

House Hunting Shut your eyes and imagine your grandparents' house or apartment or another place that has been important to you as you grew up. You may focus on either the outside or an inside room. Make an **illustration** of this place. Use as many details as you can remember.

And the Winner Is . . . From the descriptions in the story, **draw** a picture of Marta wearing her scholarship jacket. Be sure to use the correct colors for the jacket.

Language Mini-Lesson

Subject-Verb Agreement: Compound Subjects

Recognize agreement problems. Compound subjects can present special agreement problems. Keep these two rules in mind when writing sentences that have compound subjects.

Rule 1: Compound subjects joined by *and* or *both . . . and* usually need a plural verb.

Both Jenny and Jackie go to the movies every Saturday.

Rule 2: If both parts of a compound subject joined by *or, either . . . or,* or *neither . . . nor* are singular, use a singular verb. If both parts are plural, use a plural verb. If one is singular and one is plural, the verb agrees with the nearer subject.

Sam or Alex is coming over this morning.

Either the senators or the lobbyists are at the White House.

Neither her friends nor her mother knows her plans.

Writing Strategy As you are writing, look to see what word or words are used to join compound subjects. Then decide which agreement rule applies to that sentence.

Activity Options

1. Tell why the verbs in the three examples given for Rule 2 are singular or plural.

2. Write five sentences with compound subjects joined by *and, both . . . and, or, either . . . or,* and *neither . . . nor.* Make sure that the subjects and verbs don't agree. Trade sentences with a partner, fix the agreement problems, and write the number of the rule you used to correct each sentence.

3. Review your last few writing products. Look for agreement problems with compound subjects. What rule should you apply to correct any problems that you might find? Give yourself a star next to the sentences you correct.

Before Reading

About Old People by Jean Little

old age sticks by E. E. Cummings

Jean Little
born 1932

When Canadian author Jean Little sits down to read, she usually chooses a book for young people. She believes children's books rejoice in life. Little celebrates life in *Hey World, Here I Am,* about two friends, Kate and Emily.

E. E. Cummings
1894–1962

Edward Estlin Cummings devoted his life to writing poetry. He played with the look of poems on a page, pioneering unusual forms. He is famous for his break with the rules of spelling, capitalization, and punctuation.

Building Background

Fear and Prejudice Recall a time when you were afraid of something you'd never tried before. It may have been a new food, a new sport, or overnight camp. Chances are that after you tried it a few times, you lost your fear and even liked it. Fear of the unknown is one cause of prejudice. We assume we don't like something just because it's strange or unfamiliar and make a judgment without enough information. What ways can you think of to prevent or overcome this kind of prejudice?

Getting into the Selections

Writer's Notebook Do older people and younger people have *anything* in common? In your notebook draw a diagram like the one below. Write down all the words you can think of for each of the categories. Write any words that could describe either category in the middle.

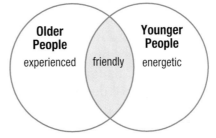

Reading Tip

Reading Poetic Selections "About Old People" is an **anecdote,** or a brief sketch in words. This anecdote is somewhat like poetry in the way lines are broken and in the way sounds and rhythms sometimes repeat.

In reading the poem by Cummings, don't be confused by strange capitalization or punctuation. As you read, look for sentences to help make sense of the poem. Reading both the anecdote and the poem aloud will help you appreciate and understand them both.

ABOUT OLD PEOPLE

JEAN LITTLE

It all started when I told Emily that I didn't like old people.
Well, I don't. They scare me—especially the really ancient[1] ones.
I never know what to say to them.
They stare as if you had dirt on your face.
They grab at you, and their hands are hard and bony.
They always want to kiss you. I hate their prickly[2] kisses.
"She's got her father's ears," they say.
As if you're made out of used parts.
Sometimes they smell musty.[3] Often they're nosy.
And you have to be polite, no matter how rude they are.
As I said, I don't like them.

When I said so to Emily, though, she was stunned![4]
You'd think I'd said I hated newborn babies or kittens.
"But you like Mrs. Thurstone, don't you?" she said at last.

I hadn't been thinking of Mrs. Thurstone.
She used to live next door to the Blairs, before they moved.
She's old all right. Eighty-six is no spring chicken.[5]
"Sure," I said, laughing.
Just thinking about Mrs. Thurstone makes me laugh.
She's so fierce and scary, and then she hands you a present.
I could see what Emily was getting at, of course.

"But she's somebody we know.
I meant I don't like old people in general."
Emily let that sink in.
I thought we'd finished with the topic.

---

1. **ancient** (ān′shənt), *adj.* very old.
2. **prickly** (prik′lē), *adj.* itchy.
3. **musty** (mus′tē), *adj.* damp or moldy.
4. **stun** (stun), *v.* bewilder or shock.
5. **spring chicken,** literally, a very young chicken; used in the phrase
   "no spring chicken" to mean a person who is no longer young.

▲ ☙ *Society* was painted by Raymond Lark. How do you think the narrator of "About Old People" would **interact** with this woman?

Then she said, all in a rush,
"You know, Kate, every old person in general
    is somebody . . .
Somebody in particular."

I blinked.
"What?" I said.
Emily took a deep breath and tried again.
"Every old person is somebody," she said.

That was when her cousin James butted in.
I haven't a clue where he sprang from or how much
    he'd heard.
All at once he was there, though, and he snorted,
"You dope, Emily, everybody is somebody.
Not just old people."

We laughed at him.
Then Emily said sternly,[6] "Don't interrupt, James.
Can't you see we're having a serious discussion?"

He took off and we went on to something else.

But, later, I got to thinking.
"Everybody is somebody," James had said.

He's only nine but he's somebody, that's for sure.
So's Emily and so's Mrs. Thurstone.
And I know I'm somebody.
And . . . old people?

---

6. **sternly** (stėrn′lē), *adv.* firmly or strictly.

old age sticks

E. E. Cummings

old age sticks
up Keep
Off
signs)&

5 youth yanks them
down(old
age
cries No

Tres)&(pas)
10 youth laughs
(sing
old age

scolds Forbid
den Stop
15 Must
n't Don't

&)youth goes
right on
gr
20 owing old

After Reading

Making Connections

1. If you had to assign "old age sticks" shapes and colors, what would they be? Why?

2. Do you agree with James in "About Old People" that "everybody is somebody"? Explain.

3. 👣 Kate indicates that she is afraid of **interactions** with old people. Describe how you think old people might feel about interacting with someone Kate's age.

4. Do you think Emily convinces Kate that old people are "somebody in particular"? Support your answer with examples from the anecdote.

5. Look through "old age sticks" and pick one unusual thing, such as parentheses, broken words, capitalization, or the "and sign." Why do you think the writer used these unconventional forms?

6. Old people are regarded differently in different cultures. Find out how the elderly are treated in China, India, or Inuit society and compare their treatment to that of the elderly in your community.

Literary Focus: Style

An author's **style,** or way of writing, is a personal stamp on what he or she writes. It includes word choice, how sentences are put together, unusual forms—everything that makes a piece of writing stand out from those written by other authors. Many of the unusual things about style in "old age sticks" are obvious. What do you find unusual about the style in "About Old People"?

Think about style as you reread the two selections. Use a chart like the one below to help organize your ideas about style.

Point of Style	"About Old People"	"old age sticks"
Complete sentences	yes	no
Punctuation	correct	different
Breaks in lines		
Breaks in words		
Word choice		
Word order in phrases		

Vocabulary Study

A. Decide if each of the following pairs are synonyms or antonyms. On your paper write *S* for synonym or *A* for antonym.

ancient
prickly
musty
stun
sternly

1. musty : fresh

2. stun : shock

3. prickly : smooth

4. ancient : aged

5. sternly : harshly

B. Choose one of the vocabulary words listed at the left and act it out in front of the class. Your classmates should guess which word you have chosen.

Expressing Your Ideas

Writing Choices

Looking Far Ahead Imagine you have just celebrated your eightieth birthday with a big party. Think about how you felt, who was there, and what they said about you. What kind of presents did you get? Write a **diary entry** describing the celebration. Be sure to use the actual date of your eightieth birthday!

Information, Please Work with a group. Choose a problem of aging, such as Alzheimer's disease, poverty, homelessness, or abuse. Research the problem and write a one-page **report** that describes the problem, tells why it occurs, and suggests what can be done about it. Select one group member to read the report to the class.

The Way We Were Interview an older person. Ask what the interviewee thought about older people when he or she was young. What misconceptions did he or she have about the elderly? What does the person think now? Write up the **interview** as it might appear in a magazine. Include a photo of the person if possible.

Other Options

Voices New and Old With a partner read "old age sticks," one taking the parts about old age and the other the lines about youth. Discuss the kind of voice each reader should have and how the lines should be read. Practice the poem and then do a **dramatic reading** of your interpretation for your classmates.

It Says It All Find a painting, a piece of sculpture, or a photograph that you feel would be good to **illustrate** the vignette or the poem. Explain to the class why you think the illustration is appropriate.

It's History Talk to a grandparent or other older person about important historical and personal events that occurred during that person's lifetime. Make a **time line** showing those events. If possible, include illustrations on your time line.

Encounters with Prejudice

Let's Be Fair

History Connection

Examples of prejudice, the belief that "my way is the one and only right way," are evident throughout history and around the world. Prejudice is often caused by fear and lack of understanding of another race, culture, religion, or social group. It can result in discrimination, and in extreme cases, slavery. In a world where prejudice exists, justice cannot.

During the Middle Ages, Jews often were blamed for deliberately contaminating public wells, and causing the Bubonic plague. That as many Jews died of the dreaded disease as did Christians made no difference to their accusers. Christians hunted and massacred Jews throughout Europe until 1351, by which time the Black Death had begun to wane. Here the victims die in fire as their executioners look on. ▽

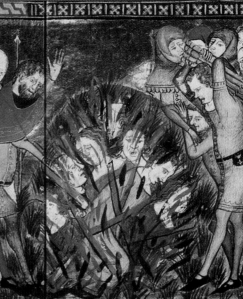

PREJUDICE ACROSS

◄ In 1844, members of the Pennsylvania state militia tried to defend themselves against anti-Catholic rioters in Philadelphia. Two Roman Catholic churches were burned and twenty-four people were killed.

A Roman slave attends to her Greek ladies. When the ancient Greek and Roman empires were strong, it was power that determined slave and master. The winner in war was the master—the loser was the slave. Fortunes could change with the next war. ►

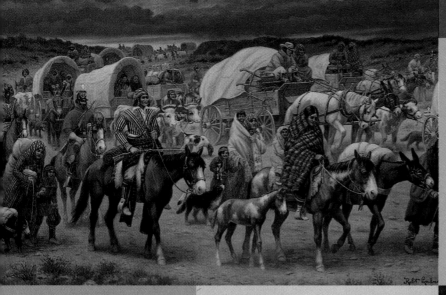

Trail of Tears by Robert Lindneux depicts the many Native Americans who were forced to leave their land, and with it their way of life, as a result of settler's lust for land. Prejudice and a lack of understanding compelled Native Americans to live on the reservations set aside by the federal government.

Long before slavery was an issue of race or religion, it was an issue of power. The winners in battle took prisoners who then became slaves to the victors. Here, African masters transport their slaves by canoe. ➤

In the name of national security, Japanese American families were forced to leave their homes and live in internment camps during World War II. Many lost their homes and businesses as well as their freedom. Here a mother and her four children are evacuated from Bainbridge Island in Washington State to a California internment camp in 1942.

THE AGES

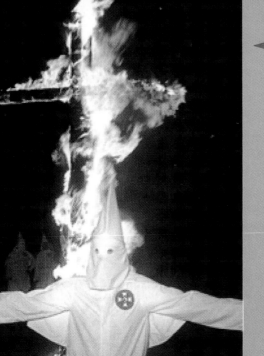

◄ Historically, members of the Ku Klux Klan have used scare tactics and violence in an attempt to eliminate what they consider to be inferior and undesirable groups from their areas. Their targets have included African Americans, Catholics, and Jews. A Klansman in traditional garb stands in front of a burning cross—a recognizable Klan symbol.

Responding

1. Prejudice results when a judgment is made about a person or a group of persons before looking carefully at the facts. Is prejudice ever justified? Explain your answer.

2. Prejudice is at least as old as recorded history. Can prejudice ever be eliminated? What can you do?

Babies are not born prejudiced. As they grow and encounter prejudice in older children and adults, they learn it. These third graders discovered that prejudice hurts. It is best to do unto others as you would like to have them do unto you.

negative

inferior

prejudice

"Teacher, Billy pushed me!"

wails the girl with blond pigtails.

"Well, Jenny, that's because Billy has blue eyes," answers her teacher, as the children quietly file into the room and sit down. "And we all know that blue-eyed people aren't as civilized as brown-eyed people. You can't expect him to act nicely."

Jenny looks smug, as Billy slides down into his seat, kicking the chair in front of him. All the blue-eyed children in the room keep their eyes down, while the ones with brown eyes look around eagerly.

The children in this class have been having one of the hardest school days of their lives. They are learning firsthand what discrimination is like.

Brown Eyes Only

by Pam Deyell Gingold

discrimination

Their class has been divided up according to the color of their eyes. Today the brown-eyed people are "superior," with many privileges like extra recess time and lining up first, getting seconds for lunch, and using the classroom's drinking fountain (a sign on it reads "Brown Eyes Only"). The "inferior" blue-eyed students have been criticized by the teacher all day long. They can't use the playground equipment, and they can't play with brown-eyed children unless invited. Before long, they are angry and depressed, doing poor schoolwork and getting into trouble.

Jane Elliott, a third-grade teacher in Riceville, Iowa, created this lesson back in 1968 following the death of Dr. Martin Luther King, Jr. Shattered by the assassination of the man she admired, and sickened by the racism that swept the country, Elliott felt compelled to find a way to stop racial prejudice from spreading to the next generation.

Although Elliott's students lived in an all-white town with no opportunities for getting to know African Americans, Elliott found that they had already picked up many negative racial stereotypes: Black people get into trouble a lot, are violent and dirty, and are not as smart as white people. Listening to what her students thought they knew about black people, Elliott determined that no children would ever again leave her classroom with such attitudes unchallenged.

"It was the hardest lesson I've ever taught," Elliott says. "All day long, I found fault with everything the blue-eyed children did and praised the brown-eyed ones. Within a couple of hours, I no longer had to look at their eyes. The 'superior' children were happy and proud, doing better schoolwork than I'd ever believed possible, all because they were expected to. The oppressed blue-eyed group was devastated. Their posture, their expressions, everything about them showed how badly they felt. They looked and acted as if they were, in fact, inferior."

The following day, the tables were turned: The blue-eyes were "superior," while the brown-eyes found out how it felt to be discriminated against. Later the class discussed what they had learned from their experiences. They agreed that discrimination makes people feel and act inferior and powerless to do anything about it.

"I felt like a dog on a leash," one boy said.

They also felt very angry at being treated unfairly. "I felt like slapping a brown-eyed person. It made me mad," wrote a blue-eyed boy.

"I felt dirty. And I did not feel as smart as I had," one girl wrote.

A classmate added, "I do not like discrimination. It makes me sad. I would not like to be angry all my life."

Elliott has repeated the same lesson each year with new students, with similar results. Each class has agreed that judging people by the color of their skin is just as illogical as judging them by the color of their eyes.

Elliott notes, "The total unfairness of this experience made my students see that society can act in irrational ways. After the lesson, they began to question everything, and once they started to think for themselves, they realized they never had to be prejudiced again."

Responding

1. Do you believe that once you start to think for yourself, you never have to be prejudiced again? Explain your answer.

2. What steps can people take to eliminate unfair prejudice in their community?

Sociology Connection

Some people live life with blinders on. They understand and accept only one way of thinking, acting, or dressing—their own. There is so much in life they will miss unless they can learn to become more tolerant.

3 Reasons to Become More Tolerant

by Lynn Duvall

Have you ever heard someone say, "Give me one good reason why I should do that"? Here are three good reasons why you should become more tolerant.

1 The more you learn, the less you fear.
Remember when you were sure there were monsters under your bed? Or how afraid you were the first time you went swimming and put your face in the water? Then you looked under the bed and put your face in the water a few more times and suddenly you weren't afraid anymore. Unlearning prejudices works the same way.

Have you ever had a notion about a person, then found out you were wrong once you got to know him or her? That's how tolerance begins. Once you learn you have nothing to fear, you become willing to try more new things, share ideas, and accept new people. As you practice tolerance and become more comfortable with differences by experiencing them firsthand through relationships, curiosity replaces fear. Your mind opens. You start respecting other people's opinions, practices, and behaviors. You gain a deeper understanding of yourself and others.

2 Tolerant people are more self-confident and comfortable in all kinds of situations.
Who wouldn't like to feel safer and more secure anytime, anywhere? Studies have shown that people who get along with different kinds of people are emotionally and physically healthier—and more successful in their careers—than those who don't.

3 Tolerance makes life more interesting.
What if you were allowed to read books by only one author? If you had to wear blue jeans, a white T-shirt, and black sneakers every day? What if you were never allowed to try anything new, not even a new soft drink or video game? What if all of your friends looked, thought, and behaved exactly alike? What if they all had to be the same age, religion, gender, and race?

Bo-ring. That's what life without diversity would be like.

Responding

What culture or religion or ethnic group would you like to learn more about? Do some research. If possible, meet and talk with someone from that group to get firsthand knowledge. Exchange ideas. Share with your class what you have learned.

Reading Mini-Lesson

Drawing Conclusions

You see 2 4 6 8 ___.

What is the next number? Most of us draw the conclusion that 10 is the next number. How can you tell? *Can* you tell for sure?

Your thinking probably went something like this: "The numbers each increased by 2, so the last number also should be two more than one before it." You are confident that your conclusion is right.

But, you're wrong! The series is 2 4 6 8 8 6 4 2. You had enough information to try to come to a conclusion, but not enough evidence to be able to test or support your conclusion.

Drawing a conclusion involves connecting knowns and unknowns. If only a few items are given, you will have to supply or invent the others; so coming to a conclusion is taking a step into the unknown. Scientists need to draw conclusions, but they like to find out if their conclusions are right. Therefore, they test their conclusions with experiments or studies and throw out the bad conclusions that the evidence doesn't support.

When you are reading, you need to be careful not to jump to conclusions that can't be supported. For example, in the article "Brown Eyes Only" on pages 314–315, Jane Elliott's students had jumped to conclusions about African Americans, even though they had no experience with any black people.

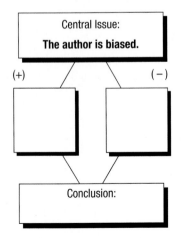

Central Issue:

The author is biased.

(+)   (−)

Conclusion:

Activity Options

1. Skim through "Brown Eyes Only" again to look for evidence to support or to disprove this conclusion: "Blue-eyed children are better and smarter than brown-eyed children." Jot down bits of evidence from the selection. After you read, state whether you think the conclusion is a good conclusion or a bad one, and give the evidence on which you base your decision.

2. A Compare-Contrast Frame like the one shown here can help you make decisions and analyze conclusions. Use a Compare-Contrast Frame to decide if this conclusion is a good one: "The article's author, Pam Deyell Gingold, is biased."

Writing Workshop

Explaining Feelings

Assignment How does Margot feel about the way the other children treat her in "All Summer in a Day"? Be Margot and write a letter to explain how you feel. See the Writer's Blueprint for details.

WRITER'S BLUEPRINT

Product   A letter

Purpose   To explore one character's feelings about unjust treatment at the hands of other characters

Audience   The characters who were unjust

Specs   As the writer of a successful letter, you should:

❏ Be Margot five years after the incident. Write a letter to the children in your class back on Venus. Think about how Margot might say things and write the letter in her voice.

❏ Begin by reminding the others who you are. Describe your present situation, including information about where you live now and what you are doing.

❏ Go on to explain why you're writing. Discuss why you think the others treated you as they did when you lived among them. Explore the children's final act of cruelty.

❏ Conclude your letter by expressing what you learned from the experience.

❏ Use concrete language in your examples and details.

❏ Follow the rules for correct grammar, usage, spelling, and mechanics. Use pronouns correctly.

The instructions that follow should help you write a successful letter.

STEP **1** PREWRITING

Chart Margot's relationship with the other children. Throughout the story, the author provides details of Margot's relationship with the other children. Make a chart to organize these details.

What Margot says and does	How the children react	What I infer about their relationship from this
Writes a poem about the sun	William doubts that Margot wrote it herself.	Maybe William is jealous because Margot knows more about the sun than he does.

In the Literary Source, Ray Bradbury shows one example of Margot's behavior.

Make a personality profile of Margot. What do the events in your chart show about Margot? What do they show about the other children? Work with a partner to brainstorm personality traits of Margot. What kind of person is she? What will she be like in the future? Make a list of Margot's personality traits. Then draw Margot as she appears in this story. Write a description to go with the drawing.

Predict what Margot will be like as a teenager. Can Margot recover from the trauma of being locked in the closet? How much of what she becomes will be determined by where she lives? Picture Margot five years in the future and cluster what she will be like, taking into consideration where she lives.

OR . . .
Go directly to "Try a quickwrite" and jot down ideas about Margot now and as a teenager.

If Margot goes elsewhere (you decide), she will be . . .

If Margot stays on Venus, she will be . . .

If Margot returns to Earth, she will be . . .

Try a quickwrite. For a few minutes, first be Margot inside the locked closet. Describe what you are thinking and feeling. Now, be Margot five years later. As Margot looking back, write a few sentences about what happened then and how you feel about it now.

Even five years later, I'm still angry and hurt. I can't believe you were so cruel. Have you changed? I doubt it.

STUDENT MODEL

Plan your narrative. Use your quickwrite and your notes to help you plan your letter. Divide your letter into four parts similar to these. Jot down details to answer each question.

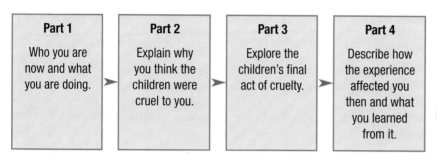

Part 1	Part 2	Part 3	Part 4
Who you are now and what you are doing.	Explain why you think the children were cruel to you.	Explore the children's final act of cruelty.	Describe how the experience affected you then and what you learned from it.

OR . . . If you would rather not follow this format, you might want to make an outline to organize the four parts of your letter.

Ask a partner: *How is my plan working?* Have you addressed the issues in each part of your plan? Use your partner's comments to help you revise your plan.

STEP

 DRAFTING

Before you write, review your quickwrite, your charts, and any other notes you have made. Then begin your draft.

As you draft, don't worry about mistakes with spelling and punctuation. Concentrate on getting your ideas on paper. In a letter like this, you'll want to say exactly what you mean. Look ahead to the Revising Strategy on using concrete language. Here are some ideas for getting started.

- Introduce yourself by describing how you felt about life on Venus.

- Begin by reminding your readers what they did to you the day the sun came out.

- Begin by explaining why you wanted to write to your readers.

Ask your partner for comments on your draft before you revise it.

✔ Have I explained who I am and why I am writing?

✔ Have I discussed how I feel about the cruel way I was treated by the other children?

✔ Have I used language that makes my meaning concrete?

Revising Strategy

> "They surged about her, caught her up and bore her, protesting and then pleading and then crying, back into a tunnel, a room, a closet, where they slammed and locked the door. They stood looking at the door and saw it tremble from her beating and throwing herself against it."
>
> from "All Summer in a Day" by Ray Bradbury

Concrete and Specific Language

As writers, we use concrete and specific language to say exactly what we mean and create an image in the reader's mind.

Concrete words name things we experience through our five senses—taste, touch, hearing, sight, and smell. For example, *sweet, bumpy, clanging, dazzling,* and *spicy* are concrete words. Describing a sunset as *beautiful* forces the reader to fill in the blanks about the colors of the sunset. If we say *the sky was streaked with red and gold,* we've made the sunset concrete.

Specific language helps us define or clarify general terms. For example, *building* is a general word. To be specific, we want to name the kind of building: *skyscraper, cottage, mansion.* Each one creates a specific picture in the reader's mind.

Notice how Ray Bradbury uses concrete and specific language to describe how the children lock Margot in the closet.

Look at how the writer of the passage below revised wording to include more concrete language.

○ If you would have been nice to me, I might have tried to bring one

of you along with me. You would ~~get to~~ *feel the warmth of* see the sun every day. You could

see *the* sun ~~and~~ *peek out from behind white fluffy* clouds.

STUDENT MODEL

Ask a partner to review your revised draft before you edit. When you edit, watch for errors in grammar, usage, spelling, and mechanics. Pay special attention to subject and object pronouns.

Editing Strategy

Subject and Object Pronouns

You know that pronouns stand for nouns. A subject pronoun is used as the subject of a sentence.

> **We** thought the field trip was tomorrow.
> Rod and **I** decided to participate in the race.

An object pronoun is used as the direct or indirect object of a sentence or the object of a preposition.

> As soon as the benches were dry, we brought **them** inside. (direct object)
> Mom sent **me** and **her** a message during school. (indirect objects)
> During the storm, we gave our umbrella to **him.** (object of preposition)

OR . . .
More rules for subject and object pronouns are listed in the Language and Grammar Handbook.

The chart organizes subject and object pronouns for you.

	Subject Pronouns	**Object Pronouns**
1st person singular	I	me
2nd person singular	you	you
3rd person singular	he, she, it	him, her, it
1st person plural	we	us
2nd person plural	you	you
3rd person plural	they	them

Notice how the writer of the draft below uses pronouns correctly.

> I don't like the way you treated me. A lot of the things you said to me made me mad. I just wanted to be friends with you.

STUDENT MODEL

5 PRESENTING

Here are two ideas for presenting your letter.

- Within your group have a "read-around." After all the letters are read, discuss what everyone thought Margot learned from being locked in the closet and how the incident probably affected her.

- Exchange letters with a partner. Read each other's letters and identify the pronouns used. Are they subject or object pronouns?

6 LOOKING BACK

Self-evaluate. What grade would you give your paper? Look back at the Writer's Blueprint and evaluate yourself on each point, from 6 (superior) down to 1 (weak).

Reflect. Think about what you learned from writing your narrative as you write answers to these questions.

✔ Have you learned anything about yourself while examining the actions and motives of both Margot and the other children? If so, what have you learned?

✔ If you could change the focus of this letter, how would you change it? Would you focus more on what Margot's life is like now, or would you focus entirely on how Margot felt about the other children while she went to school with them?

For Your Working Portfolio: Add your letter and your reflection responses to your working portfolio.

Beyond Print

Helping Margot See the Light

In "All Summer In a Day," Margot is locked in a closet because she is different from her classmates. Has Ray Bradbury described something that might happen at your school? Are students who are different treated badly? Would your class have put her in the closet?

Use the Convince-O-Meter

Hold a contest to see who gives the most effective speech to save Margot. Use a 120-point scale in which each of the criteria is worth twenty points. Rate each speaker.

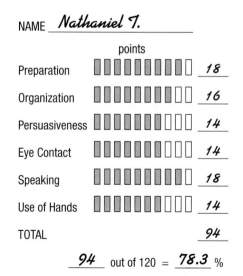

NAME _Nathaniel T._

	points	
Preparation	▮▮▮▮▮▮▮▮▮▯	_18_
Organization	▮▮▮▮▮▮▮▮▯▯	_16_
Persuasiveness	▮▮▮▮▮▮▮▯▯▯	_14_
Eye Contact	▮▮▮▮▮▮▮▯▯▯	_14_
Speaking	▮▮▮▮▮▮▮▮▮▯	_18_
Use of Hands	▮▮▮▮▮▮▮▯▯▯	_14_
TOTAL		_94_

_94_ out of 120 = _78.3_ %

Activity

Prove Ray Bradbury wrong. Help Margot see the sun by delivering an effective speech in her favor. Your classmates will play the role of Margot's classmates. You will need to do the following:

- *Preparation:* Prepare your arguments. Find reasons that will convince students. List these reasons on a piece of paper and order the reasons from the most persuasive to the least persuasive. List at least four reasons.

  - *Keep organized:* Make sure you know what you will argue and in what order. Know your arguments well enough so that you do not have to read your notes, only glance at them.

  - *Use persuasive techniques:* Be logical. Convince your classmates that the rational thing to do is to not put Margot in the closet. Appeal to their feelings and emotions.

  - *Maintain eye contact:* When you give your arguments, look your classmates in the eyes. You will be much more convincing if you speak directly to your audience.

  - *Speak clearly:* Mumbling will get you nowhere. You will only be convincing if you speak convincingly. This means you had better speak loudly, clearly, and with enough conviction to be believable.

  - *Use your hands wisely:* Gesture with your hands, but don't overdo it. Use your hands to make points. Practice using them in front of a mirror. Keep your gestures simple and natural.

Projects for Collaborative Study

Theme Connection

It's Just Not Fair! How many times have you said or heard that sentiment? Derek in the story "The Gun" may well have said these words after he was arrested for an accidental shooting. Justice is not a given. Crime and prejudice threaten all of us. What can you do if you're the victim?

■ As a class, research and discuss the remedies that are provided in your school for students who are bullied or who encounter prejudice or other forms of abuse.

■ Do victims feel that they receive justice? If not, how might the system be improved? Make a plan for constructive improvements that can be implemented in your class. Your plan might include a student court that hears complaints and decides on penalties for offenders.

Literature Connection

What Do You Make of It? The stories and poems in this and other units all have a common element—they don't tell you the whole story. You often have to put two and two together to form your own conclusions. You have to make **inferences.**

Divide into teams with four or five students in each. Pair up with another team and take turns competing to find places in the stories and poems in Unit Three where you have to infer something about the action or about a character. You may not agree about what the right inference or conclusion is, but a point should be awarded each time a team spots a place where an inference is necessary.

Life Skills Connection

Trickery. A magician uses sleight of hand and amazing illusions in her act. A soccer forward fakes a move in one direction and kicks the other way toward the goal. A poker player has a great card hand and tries not to show it on his face. How are these three situations similar? How do you feel about being tricked or tricking others?

■ Think about other forms of trickery, such as practical jokes, pranks, lying, withholding information, stealing, or cheating. Which of these have you experienced? What happened?

■ How did you feel when you were tricked? How did you feel when you used trickery?

■ As a class, debate both sides of the statement: *Deception is never justified.*

Multicultural Connection

Passive Resistance "The Revolt of the Evil Fairies" portrays the kind of highly prejudiced thinking that was common in the United States before the civil rights movement of the 1950s and 1960s. **Communication** of outrage at their treatment was achieved by African Americans through **interactions** centered on passive resistance, such as boycotts and sit-ins. As a class, debate the pros and cons of passive resistance as a remedy for discrimination. Use the following points as starters.

■ Pro: *Violence only causes more violence. Change requires time and patience.*

■ Con: *Inaction encourages oppression. Action, not words, gets results.*

Read More About Justice

Roll of Thunder, Hear My Cry (1976) by Mildred D. Taylor. An African American family living in Mississippi during the economic Depression of the 1930s encounters racial prejudice as they struggle to hold on to their land.

Summer of My German Soldier (1973) by Bette Greene. During World War II, a 12-year-old Jewish girl rebels against her abusive father and the prejudiced citizens of a small Arkansas town to help a German prisoner of war escape.

More Good Books

Sounder (1969) by William H. Armstrong. This novel, set in the South of the 1800s, portrays the hardships shared by an African American family of sharecroppers and their dog, Sounder.

I, Juan de Pareja (1965) by Elizabeth Borton de Trevino. Set in Spain in the 1600s, this biographical novel reveals the unusual bond that developed between African slave Juan de Pareja and his master, the artist Diego Velásquez.

Favorite Greek Myths (1989) by Mary Pope Osborne. In this collection, you will find colorful explanations of all kinds of natural events, from rainbows to spider webs.

The Westing Game (1978) by Ellen Raskin. In this mystery story, sixteen heirs competing for the fortune of an eccentric multimillionaire try to solve a puzzle and encounter more of a mystery than they expected.

From the Mixed-Up Files of Mrs. Basil E. Frankweiler (1967) by E. L. Konigsburg. To make her parents appreciate her more, Claudia runs away to live in a museum, where she finds a beautiful statue that leads her to Mrs. Basil E. Frankweiler.

Journeys

Travels with a Twist
Part One, pages 332–383

The Bridge to Understanding
Part Two, pages 384–449

Talking About
JOURNEYS

"I'd like to travel into my own future."

Carlos–Santa Fe, NM

Some of us are lucky enough to travel to new and interesting places. Some of us have to do our traveling by reading books or watching television. Some of us find that our greatest adventures come from traveling into our own thoughts and imaginations. Most of us enjoy a combination of all of these. We know that journeys can involve maps, passports, tours, and travel. What we must also remember is that journeys can happen while we sit in a chair and dream.

Read the comments of students like yourself. Then read the quotations from the literature you are about to read.

I took a deep breath. "I want to go forward three weeks in time."

from "LAFFF" *by Lensey Namioka, page 360*

Then came the trip west. Things were different here. She had seen ... *black families traveling west. ...*

from "Biddy Mason" by Ruth Pelz, page 366

"I'm interested in the people who moved west across the plains."

Hannah–Stevens Point, WI

On a Christmas day we were mushing our way over the Dawson trail. Talk of your cold! through the parka's fold it stabbed like a driven nail.

from "The Cremation of Sam McGee" by Robert Service, page 349

"I hope I go through a lot of my life with my family; I hope they don't die young."

Damian–Meridian, MS

I was ten years old when my mother died. Ten years old on that very day. Still she gave me a party of sorts.

from "Birthday Box" by Jane Yolen, page 410

"A journey full of action and adventure would be great!"

Amy–Baton Rouge, LA

331

Part One

Travels with a Twist

If you book a trip with your local travel agents, they're likely to put you on a plane, train, bus, or boat. But how about more adventurous kinds of travel? With a little more imagination, you can travel in outer space and even through time. So, get ready for your trip through the following selections. But buckle up tight—these travels come with a twist.

Multicultural Connection **Individuality** often involves standing up against group pressure. This may mean moving in a different direction from your own cultural background as you travel through life and find yourself in new groups. How do the characters in these selections deal with group pressure—do they express their individuality or do they yield to what others want and expect?

Literature

Rod Serling   **The Monsters Are Due on Maple Street**
                 ◆ play 334

Robert Service   **The Cremation of Sam McGee** ◆ poem 349

Lensey Namioka   **LAFFF** ◆ short story 356

Ruth Pelz   **Biddy Mason** ◆ biography 366

Rosemary and Stephen
     Vincent Benét **Western Wagons** ◆ poem 369

Hu Feng   **The Journey** ◆ poem 373

Gwendolyn Brooks   **Old Mary** ◆ poem 374

          Writing Mini-Lesson ◆ Maintaining Your Working Portfolio 377

Interdisciplinary Study Winding Roads

Three Explorers ◆ geography 378

The Adventures of Marco Polo by Simon Boughton ◆ history 381

          Reading Mini-Lesson ◆ Distinguishing Between
                    Fact and Opinion 383

Before Reading

The Monsters Are Due on Maple Street

by Rod Serling

Rod Serling
1924–1975

Serling is best known as a writer of fantasy and science fiction for the TV shows *The Twilight Zone* and *Night Gallery*. He did not set out to write fantasy, however. He began by writing plays about social problems, such as prejudice, but quickly found it was hard to get them produced. Eventually, he realized he could write about the problems that concerned him and get his plays on TV if he used science fiction or fantasy settings. "The writer's role is to be menacer of the public conscience," Serling said. He wanted his scripts for *The Twilight Zone* not only to entertain viewers, but to make them think.

Building Background

The Twilight Zone Once a week from October, 1959, to September, 1965, American television viewers left the comfort of their living rooms to enter a land between light and shadow known as *The Twilight Zone.* In this TV fantasy, viewers often met aliens or robots, but sometimes they met ordinary people as well—people whose lives took strange twists and turns. The play you are about to read first appeared on *The Twilight Zone* on March 4, 1960.

Getting into the Play

Writer's Notebook Fear, mistrust, and suspicion—while a healthy dose of these can keep you safe from harm, the characters in this play allow these emotions to get out of hand. Think about what these three words mean, what can cause the emotions, and how they can affect behavior. Then choose one word and use a chart like the following to organize your thoughts in your notebook.

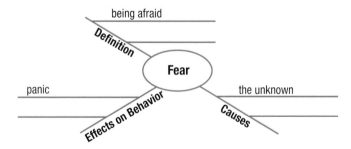

Reading Tip

Camera Instructions TV scripts are meant to be seen as well as heard, so it's important to imagine how the scenes would look. Carefully read the instructions for camera movements and lighting in the script. These instructions are printed in *italic* type. When a scene "fades in," the picture gradually appears as the darkened background lightens. When a camera "pans," it moves across a scene from top to bottom or side to side.

If you don't understand what a camera movement means, pretend that your eyes are the camera.

THE MONSTERS ARE DUE ON MAPLE STREET

ROD SERLING

CHARACTERS

NARRATOR	CHARLIE'S WIFE
FIGURE ONE	TOMMY
FIGURE TWO	SALLY, Tommy's mother
DON MARTIN	LES GOODMAN
STEVE BRAND	ETHEL GOODMAN, Les's wife
MYRA BRAND, Steve's wife	MAN ONE
PETE VAN HORN	MAN TWO
CHARLIE	WOMAN ONE

Act One

Fade in on shot of the night sky. The various heavenly bodies stand out in sharp, sparkling relief. The camera begins a slow pan across the heavens until it passes the horizon and stops on a sign which reads "Maple Street." It is daytime. Then we see the street below. It is a quiet, tree-lined, small-town American street. The houses have front porches on which people sit and swing on gliders, talking across from house to house. STEVE BRAND *is polishing his car, which is parked in front of his house. His neighbor,* DON MARTIN, *leans against the fender watching him. A Good Humor man riding a bicycle is just in the process of stopping to sell some ice cream to a couple of kids. Two women gossip on the front lawn. Another man is watering his lawn with a garden hose.*

As we see these various activities, we hear the NARRATOR'S *voice.*

NARRATOR. Maple Street, U.S.A., late summer. A tree-lined little world of front porch

▲ *Yellow Afterglow,* by Charles Burchfield, depicts a peaceful, small town scene. Do you think something sinister is approaching around the corner? Why or why not?

gliders, hopscotch, the laughter of children, and the bell of an ice cream vendor.

(*There is a pause and the camera moves over to a shot of the Good Humor man and two small boys who are standing alongside just buying ice cream.*)

NARRATOR. At the sound of the roar and the flash of the light, it will be precisely six-forty-three P.M. on Maple Street.

(*At this moment* TOMMY, *one of the two boys buying ice cream from the vendor, looks up to listen to a tremendous screeching roar from overhead. A flash of light plays on the faces of both boys and then moves down the street and disappears.*

Various people leave their porches or stop what they are doing to stare up at the sky.

STEVE BRAND, *the man who has been polishing his car, stands there* transfixed,[1] *staring upwards. He looks at* DON MARTIN, *his neighbor from across the street.*)

STEVE. What was that? A meteor?

DON. That's what it looked like. I didn't hear any crash though, did you?

STEVE. Nope. I didn't hear anything except a roar.

MYRA (*from her porch*). What was that?

STEVE (*raising his voice and looking toward the porch*). Guess it was a meteor, honey. Came awful close, didn't it?

MYRA. Too close for my money! Much too close.

(*The camera pans across the various porches to people who stand there watching and talking in low conversing tones.*)

NARRATOR. Maple Street. Six-forty-four P.M. on a late September evening. (*A pause*) Maple Street in the last calm and reflective[2] moment . . . before the monsters came!

(*The camera takes us across the porches again. A man is replacing a light bulb on a front porch. He gets down off his stool to flick the switch and finds that nothing happens.*

Another man is working on an electric power mower. He plugs in the plug, flicks the switch of the mower off and on, but nothing happens.

Through the window we see a woman pushing her finger back and forth on the dial hook of a telephone. Her voice sounds far away.)

WOMAN ONE. Operator, operator, something's wrong on the phone, operator!

(MYRA BRAND *comes out on the porch and calls to* STEVE.)

MYRA (*calling*). Steve, the power's off. I had the soup on the stove and the stove just stopped working.

WOMAN ONE. Same thing over here. I can't get anybody on the phone either. The phone seems to be dead.

(*We look down again on the street. Small, mildly disturbed voices creep up from below.*)

VOICE ONE. Electricity's off.

VOICE TWO. Phone won't work.

VOICE THREE. Can't get a thing on the radio.

VOICE FOUR. My power mower won't move, won't work at all.

VOICE FIVE. Radio's gone dead!

(PETE VAN HORN, *a tall, thin man, is seen standing in front of his house.*)

PETE. I'll cut through the back yard . . . see if the power's still on, on Floral Street. I'll be right back!

(*He walks past the side of his house and disappears into the back yard.*

The camera pans down slowly until we are looking at ten or eleven people standing around the street and overflowing to the curb and sidewalk. In the background is STEVE BRAND'S *car.*)

STEVE. Doesn't make sense. Why should the power go off all of a sudden *and* the phone line?

DON. Maybe some kind of an electrical storm or something.

CHARLIE. That don't seem likely. Sky's just as

---

1. **transfix** (tran sfiks′), *v.* make motionless with amazement.
2. **reflective** (ri flek′tiv), *adj.* thoughtful.

blue as anything. Not a cloud. No lightning. No thunder. No nothing. How could it be a storm?

WOMAN ONE. I can't get a thing on the radio. Not even the portable.

(*The people again murmur softly in wonderment.*)

CHARLIE. Well, why don't you go downtown and check with the police, though they'll probably think we're crazy or something. A little power failure and right away we get all flustered and everything—

STEVE. It isn't just the power failure, Charlie. If it was, we'd still be able to get a broadcast on the portable.

(*There is a murmur of reaction to this.* STEVE *looks from face to face and then over to his car.*)

STEVE. I'll run downtown. We'll get this all straightened out.

(*He walks over to the car, gets in, and turns the key.*

Looking through the open car door, we see the crowd watching STEVE *from the other side. He starts the engine. It turns over sluggishly and then stops dead. He tries it again, and this time he can't get it to turn over. Then very slowly he turns the key back to "off" and gets out of the car.*

The people stare at STEVE. *He stands for a moment by the car and then walks toward them.*)

STEVE. I don't understand it. It was working fine before—

DON. Out of gas?

STEVE (*shakes his head*). I just had it filled up.

WOMAN ONE. What's it mean?

CHARLIE. It's just as if . . . as if everything had stopped. (*Then he turns toward* STEVE.) We'd better *walk* downtown.

(*Another murmur of assent*[3] *to this.*)

STEVE. The two of us can go, Charlie. (*He turns to look back at the car.*) It couldn't be the meteor. A meteor couldn't do *this*.

(*He and* CHARLIE *exchange a look. Then they start to walk away from the group.*

TOMMY *comes into view. He is a serious-faced young boy in spectacles. He stands halfway between*

the group and the two men who start to walk down the sidewalk.)

TOMMY. Mr. Brand . . . you'd better not!

STEVE. Why not?

TOMMY. They don't want you to.

(STEVE *and* CHARLIE *exchange a grin and* STEVE *looks back toward the boy.*)

STEVE. *Who* doesn't want us to?

TOMMY (*jerks his head in the general direction of the distant horizon*). Them!

STEVE. Them?

CHARLIE. Who are *them*?

TOMMY (*intently*). Whoever was in that thing that came by overhead.

(STEVE *knits his brow for a moment, cocking his head questioningly. His voice is intense.*)

STEVE. What?

TOMMY. Whoever was in that thing that came over. I don't think they want us to leave here.

(STEVE *leaves* CHARLIE, *walks over to the boy, and puts his hand on the boy's shoulder. He forces his voice to remain gentle.*)

STEVE. What do you mean? What are you talking about?

TOMMY. They don't want us to leave. That's why they shut everything off.

STEVE. What makes you say that? Whatever gave you *that* idea?

WOMAN ONE (*from the crowd*). Now isn't that the craziest thing you ever heard?

TOMMY (*persistent but a little frightened*). It's always that way, in every story I ever read about a ship landing from outer space.

WOMAN ONE (*to the boy's mother,* SALLY, *who stands on the fringe of the crowd*). From outer space yet! Sally, you better get that boy of yours up to bed. He's been reading too many comic books or seeing too many movies or something!

---

3. **assent** (ə sent′), *n.* agreement.

SALLY. Tommy, come over here and stop that kind of talk.

STEVE. Go ahead, Tommy. We'll be right back. And you'll see. That wasn't any ship or anything like it. That was just a . . . a meteor or something. Likely as not— (*He turns to the group, now trying very hard to sound more optimistic than he feels.*) No doubt it did have something to do with all this power failure and the rest of it. Meteors can do some crazy things. Like sunspots.

DON (*picking up the cue*). Sure. That's the kind of thing—like sunspots. They raise Cain with radio reception all over the world. And this thing being so close—why there's no telling the sort of stuff it can do. (*He wets his lips, smiles nervously.*) Go ahead, Charlie. You and Steve go into town and see if that isn't what's causing it all.

(STEVE *and* CHARLIE *walk away from the group down the sidewalk as the people watch silently.*

TOMMY *stares at them, biting his lips, and finally calls out again.*)

TOMMY. Mr. Brand!

(*The two men stop.* TOMMY *takes a step toward them.*)

TOMMY. Mr. Brand . . . please don't leave here.

(STEVE *and* CHARLIE *stop once again and turn toward the boy. In the crowd there is a murmur of irritation and concern, as if the boy's words—even though they didn't make sense—were bringing up fears that shouldn't be brought up.*

TOMMY *is partly frightened and partly defiant.*)

TOMMY. You might not even be able to get to town. It was that way in the story. *Nobody* could leave. Nobody except—

STEVE. Except who?

TOMMY. Except the people they sent down ahead of them. They looked just like humans. And it wasn't until the ship landed that—(*The boy suddenly stops, conscious of the people staring at him and his mother and of the sudden hush of the crowd.*)

SALLY (*in a whisper, sensing the antagonism[4] of the crowd*). Tommy, please son . . . honey, don't talk that way—

MAN ONE. That kid shouldn't talk that way . . . and we shouldn't stand here listening to him. Why this is the craziest thing I ever heard of. The kid tells us a comic book plot and here we stand listening—

(STEVE *walks toward the camera, and stops beside the boy.*)

STEVE. Go ahead, Tommy. What kind of story was this? What about the people they sent out ahead?

TOMMY. That was the way they prepared things for the landing. They sent four people. A mother and a father and two kids who looked just like humans . . . but they weren't.

(*There is another silence as* STEVE *looks toward the crowd and then toward* TOMMY. *He wears a tight grin.*)

STEVE. Well, I guess what we'd better do then is to run a check on the neighborhood and see which ones of us are really human.

(*There is laughter at this, but it's a laughter that comes from a desperate attempt to lighten the atmosphere. The people look at one another in the middle of their laughter.*)

CHARLIE (*rubs his jaw nervously*). I wonder if Floral Street's got the same deal we got. (*He looks past the houses.*) Where is Pete Van Horn anyway? Didn't he get back yet?

(*Suddenly there is the sound of a car's engine starting to turn over.*

We look across the street toward the driveway of LES GOODMAN*'s house. He is at the wheel trying to start the car.*)

SALLY. Can you get started, Les?

(LES GOODMAN *gets out of the car, shaking his head.*)

LES. No dice.

---

4. antagonism (an tag′ə niz′əm), *n.* active opposition; hostility.

Eric Dinyer did not give a title to his intriguing composite photograph, which uses drawings and three-dimensional objects as part of its composition. What images can you see? ➤

(He walks toward the group. He stops suddenly as, behind him, the car engine starts up all by itself. LES *whirls around to stare at it.*

The car idles roughly, smoke coming from the exhaust, the frame shaking gently.

LES*'s eyes go wide, and he runs over to his car. The people stare at the car.)*

MAN ONE. He got the car started somehow. He got *his* car started!

(The people continue to stare, caught up by this revelation[5] and wildly frightened.)

WOMAN ONE. How come his car just up and started like that?

SALLY. All by itself. He wasn't anywheres near it. It started all by itself.

*(*DON MARTIN *approaches the group, stops a few feet away to look toward* LES*'s car and then back toward the group.)*

DON. And he never did come out to look at that thing that flew overhead. He wasn't even interested. *(He turns to the group, his face taut and serious.)* Why? Why didn't he come out with the rest of us to look?

CHARLIE. He always was an oddball. Him and his whole family. Real oddball.

DON. What do you say we ask him?

(The group start toward the house. In this brief fraction of a moment they take the first step toward a metamorphosis[6] that changes people from a group into a mob. They begin to head purposefully across the street toward the house. STEVE *stands in front*

---

5. **revelation** (rev′ə lā′shən), *n.* something made known.
6. **metamorphosis** (met′ə môr′fə sis), *n.* a noticeable or complete change of character or circumstances.

The Monsters Are Due on Maple Street—Act One   **339**

of them. For a moment their fear almost turns their walk into a wild stampede, but STEVE*'s voice, loud, incisive,*[7] *and commanding, makes them stop.*)

STEVE. Wait a minute . . . wait a minute! Let's not be a mob!

(*The people stop, pause for a moment, and then much more quietly and slowly start to walk across the street.*

Les stands alone, facing the people.)

LES. I just don't understand it. I tried to start it and it wouldn't start. You saw me. All of you saw me.

(*And now, just as suddenly as the engine started, it stops, and there is a long silence that is gradually intruded upon by the frightened murmuring of the people.*)

LES. I don't understand. I swear . . . I don't understand. What's happening?

DON. Maybe you better tell us. Nothing's working on this street. Nothing. No lights, no power, no radio. (*Then meaningfully*) Nothing except one car—*yours!*

(*The people's murmuring becomes a loud chant filling the air with accusations and demands for action. Two of the men pass* DON *and head toward* LES, *who backs away from them against his car. He is cornered.*)

LES. Wait a minute now. You keep your distance—all of you. So I've got a car that starts by itself—well, that's a freak thing— I admit it. But does that make me some kind of a criminal or something? I don't know why the car works—it just does!

(*This stops the crowd momentarily and* LES, *still backing away, goes toward his front porch. He goes up the steps and then stops, facing the mob.*)

LES. What's it all about, Steve?

STEVE (*quietly*). We're all on a monster kick, Les. Seems that the general impression holds that maybe one family isn't what we think they are. Monsters from outer space or something. Different from us. Fifth columnists from the vast beyond. (*He chuckles.*) You know anybody that might fit that description around here on Maple Street?

LES. What's this, a gag? (*He looks around the group again.*) This a practical joke or something?

(*Suddenly the car engine starts all by itself, runs for a moment, and stops. One woman begins to cry. The eyes of the crowd are cold and accusing.*)

LES. Now that's supposed to incriminate[8] me, huh? The car engine goes on and off and that really does it, doesn't it? (*He looks around the faces of the people.*) I just don't understand it . . . any more than any of you do! (*He wets his lips, looking from face to face.*) Look, you all know me. We've lived here five years. Right in this house. We're no different from any of the rest of you! We're no different at all . . . Really . . . this whole thing is just . . . just weird—

WOMAN ONE. Well, if that's the case, Les Goodman, explain why—(*She stops suddenly, clamping her mouth shut.*)

LES (*softly*). Explain what?

STEVE (*interjecting*). Look, let's forget this—

CHARLIE (*overlapping him*). Go ahead, let her talk. What about it? Explain what?

WOMAN ONE (*a little reluctantly*). Well . . . sometimes I go to bed late at night. A couple of times . . . a couple of times I'd come out here on the porch and I'd see Mr. Goodman here in the wee hours of the morning standing out in front of his house . . . looking up at the sky. (*She looks around the circle of faces.*) That's right, looking up at the sky as if . . . as if he were waiting for something. (*A pause*) As if he were looking for something.

(*There's a murmur of reaction from the crowd again as* LES *backs away.*)

LES. She's crazy. Look, I can explain that.

---

7. **incisive** (in sī′siv), *adj.* sharp or piercing.
8. **incriminate** (in krim′ə nāt), *v.* show to be guilty.

Please . . . I can really explain that . . . She's making it up anyway. (*Then he shouts.*) I tell you she's making it up!

(*He takes a step toward the crowd and they back away from him. He walks down the steps after them and they continue to back away. Suddenly he is left completely alone, and he looks like a man caught in the middle of a menacing circle as the scene slowly fades to black.*)

Act Two

SCENE 1

Fade in on Maple Street at night. On the sidewalk, little knots of people stand around talking in low voices. At the end of each conversation they look toward LES GOODMAN*'s house. From the various houses we can see candlelight but no electricity. The quiet which blankets the whole area is disturbed only by the almost whispered voices of the people standing around. In one group* CHARLIE *stands staring across at the* GOODMAN*'s house. Two men stand across the street from it in almost sentry-like*[9] *poses.*

SALLY (*in a small, hesitant voice*). It just doesn't seem right, though, keeping watch on them. Why . . . he was right when he said he was one of our neighbors. Why, I've known Ethel Goodman ever since they moved in. We've been good friends—

CHARLIE. That don't prove a thing. Any guy who'd spend his time lookin' up at the sky early in the morning—well, there's something wrong with that kind of person. There's something that ain't legitimate. Maybe under normal circumstances we could let it go by, but these aren't normal circumstances. Why, look at this street! Nothin' but candles. Why, it's like goin' back into the Dark Ages[10] or somethin'!

(STEVE *walks down the steps of his porch, down the street to the* GOODMAN*'s house, and then stops at the foot of the steps.* LES *is standing there;* ETHEL GOODMAN *behind him is very frightened.*)

LES. Just stay right where you are, Steve. We don't want any trouble, but this time if anybody sets foot on my porch—that's what they're going to get—trouble!

STEVE. Look, Les—

LES. I've already explained to you people. I don't sleep very well at night sometimes. I get up and I take a walk and I look up at the sky. I look at the stars!

ETHEL. That's exactly what he does. Why, this whole thing, it's . . . it's some kind of madness or something.

STEVE (*nods grimly*). That's exactly what it is— some kind of madness.

CHARLIE'S VOICE (*shrill, from across the street*). You best watch who you're seen with, Steve! Until we get this all straightened out, you ain't exactly above suspicion yourself.

STEVE (*whirling around toward him*). Or you, Charlie. Or any of us, it seems. From age eight on up!

WOMAN ONE. What I'd like to know is—what are we gonna do? Just stand around here all night?

CHARLIE. There's nothin' else we *can* do! (*He turns back, looking toward* STEVE *and* LES *again.*) One of 'em'll tip their hand. They *got* to.

STEVE (*raising his voice*). There's something you can do, Charlie. You can go home and keep your mouth shut. You can quit strutting around like a self-appointed hanging judge and just climb into bed and forget it.

CHARLIE. You sound real anxious to have that happen, Steve. I think we better keep our eye on you, too!

DON (*as if he were taking the bit in his teeth, takes a hesitant step to the front*). I think everything

---

9. **sentry-like** (sen′trē līk), like a soldier posted to keep watch against surprise attacks.
10. **Dark Ages,** from about A.D. 400 to about A.D. 1000, a period during which learning and culture advanced slowly in western Europe.

might as well come out now. (*He turns toward* STEVE.) Your wife's done plenty of talking, Steve, about how odd *you* are!

CHARLIE (*picking this up, his eyes widening*). Go ahead, tell us what she's said.

(STEVE *walks toward them from across the street.*)

STEVE. Go ahead, what's my wife said? Let's get it *all* out. Let's pick out every idiosyncrasy[11] of every single man, woman, and child on the street. And then we might as well set up some kind of kangaroo court.[12] How about a firing squad at dawn, Charlie, so we can get rid of all the suspects. Narrow them down. Make it easier for you.

DON. There's no need gettin' so upset, Steve. It's just that . . . well . . . Myra's talked about how there's been plenty of nights you spent hours down in your basement workin' on some kind of radio or something. Well, none of us have ever *seen* that radio—

(*By this time* STEVE *has reached the group. He stands there defiantly.*)

CHARLIE. Go ahead, Steve. What kind of "radio set" you workin' on? I never seen it. Neither has anyone else. Who do you talk to on that radio set? And who talks to you?

STEVE. I'm surprised at you, Charlie. How come you're so dense all of a sudden? (*A pause*) Who do I talk to? I talk to monsters from outer space. I talk to three-headed green men who fly over here in what look like meteors.

(MYRA BRAND *steps down from the porch, bites her lip, calls out.*)

MYRA. Steve! Steve, please. (*Then looking around, frightened, she walks toward the group.*) It's just a ham radio[13] set, that's all. I bought him a book on it myself. It's just a ham radio set. A lot of people have them. I can show it to you. It's right down in the basement.

STEVE (*whirls around toward her*). Show them nothing! If they want to look inside our house—let them get a search warrant.

CHARLIE. Look, buddy, you can't afford to—

STEVE (*interrupting him*). Charlie, don't start telling me who's dangerous and who isn't and who's safe and who's a menace. (*He turns to the group and shouts.*) And you're with him, too—all of you! You're standing here all set to crucify—all set to find a scapegoat[14]—all desperate to point some kind of a finger at a neighbor! Well now, look, friends, the only thing that's gonna happen is that we'll eat each other up alive—

(*He stops abruptly as* CHARLIE *suddenly grabs his arm.*)

CHARLIE (*in a hushed voice*). That's not the *only* thing that can happen to us.

(*Down the street, a figure has suddenly materialized in the gloom, and in the silence we hear the clickety-clack of slow, measured footsteps on concrete as the figure walks slowly toward them. One of the women lets out a stifled cry.* SALLY *grabs her boy, as do a couple of other mothers.*)

TOMMY (*shouting, frightened*). It's the monster! It's the monster!

(*Another woman lets out a wail and the people fall back in a group staring toward the darkness and the approaching figure.*

The people stand in the shadows watching. DON MARTIN *joins them, carrying a shotgun. He holds it up.*)

DON. We may need this.

STEVE. A shotgun? (*He pulls it out of* DON'*s hand.*) No! Will anybody think a thought around here? Will you people wise up? What good would a shotgun do against—

---

11. **idiosyncrasy** (id′ē ō sing′krə sē), *n.* a personal peculiarity.
12. **kangaroo court,** an unauthorized, self-appointed court in which law and justice are disregarded.
13. **ham radio,** an amateur radio station, run by a licensed operator.
14. **scapegoat** (skāp′gōt′), *n.* a person made to bear the blame for others' mistakes.

(The dark figure continues to walk toward them as the people stand there, fearful, mothers clutching children, men standing in front of their wives.)

CHARLIE *(pulling the gun from* STEVE*'s hands)*. No more talk, Steve. You're going to talk us into a grave! You'd let whatever's out there walk right over us, wouldn't yuh? Well, some of us won't!

*(*CHARLIE *swings around, raises the gun, and suddenly pulls the trigger. The sound of the shot explodes in the stillness.*

The figure suddenly lets out a small cry, stumbles forward onto his knees, and then falls forward on his face. DON, CHARLIE, *and* STEVE *race forward to him.* STEVE *is there first and turns the man over. The crowd gathers around them.)*

STEVE *(slowly looks up)*. It's Pete Van Horn.

DON *(in a hushed voice)*. Pete Van Horn! He was just gonna go over to the next block to see if the power was on—

WOMAN ONE. You killed him, Charlie. You shot him dead!

CHARLIE *(looks around at the circle of faces, his eyes frightened, his face contorted)*. But . . . but I didn't know who he was. I certainly didn't know who he was. He comes walkin' out of the darkness—how am I supposed to know who he was? *(He grabs* STEVE.*)* Steve—you know why I shot! How was I supposed to know he wasn't a monster or something? *(He grabs* DON.*)* We're all scared of the same thing. I was just tryin' to . . . tryin' to protect my home, that's all! Look, all of you, that's all I was tryin' to do. *(He looks down wildly at the body.)* I didn't know it was somebody we knew! I didn't know—

(There's a sudden hush and then an intake of breath in the group. Across the street all the lights go on in one of the houses.)

WOMAN ONE *(in a hushed voice)* Charlie . . . Charlie . . . the lights just went on in your house. Why did the lights just go on?

DON. What about it, Charlie? How come you're the only one with lights now?

LES. That's what I'd like to know.

(A pause as they all stare toward CHARLIE.*)*

LES. You were so quick to kill, Charlie, and you were so quick to tell us who we had to be careful of. Well, maybe you *had* to kill. Maybe Pete there was trying to tell us something. Maybe he'd found out something and came back to tell us who there was amongst us we should watch out for—

*(*CHARLIE *backs away from the group, his eyes wide with fright.)*

CHARLIE. No . . . no . . . it's nothing of the sort! I don't know why the lights are on. I swear I don't. Somebody's pulling a gag or something.

(He bumps against STEVE *who grabs him and whirls him around.)*

STEVE A *gag*? A gag? Charlie, there's a dead man on the sidewalk and you killed him! Does this thing look like a gag to you?

*(*CHARLIE *breaks away and screams as he runs toward his house.)*

CHARLIE. No! No! Please!

(A man breaks away from the crowd to chase CHARLIE.

As the man tackles him and lands on top of him, the other people start to run toward them. CHARLIE *gets up, breaks away from the other man's grasp, lands a couple of desperate punches that push the man aside. Then he forces his way, fighting, through the crowd and jumps up on his front porch.*

CHARLIE *is on his porch as a rock thrown from the group smashes a window beside him, the broken glass flying past him. A couple of pieces cut him. He stands there perspiring, rumpled, blood running down from a cut on the cheek. His wife breaks away from the group to throw herself into his arms. He buries his face against her. We can see the crowd converging on the porch.)*

VOICE ONE. It must have been him.

VOICE TWO. He's the one.

VOICE THREE. We got to get Charlie.

(*Another rock lands on the porch.* CHARLIE *pushes his wife behind him, facing the group.*)

CHARLIE. Look, look I swear to you . . . it isn't me . . . but I do know who it is . . . I swear to you, I do know who it is. I know who the monster is here. I know who it is that doesn't belong. I swear to you I know.

DON (*pushing his way to the front of the crowd*). All right, Charlie, let's hear it!

(CHARLIE'S *eyes dart around wildly.*)

CHARLIE. It's . . . it's . . .

MAN TWO (*screaming*). Go ahead, Charlie, tell us.

CHARLIE. It's . . . it's the kid. It's Tommy. He's the one!

(*There's a gasp from the crowd as we see* SALLY *holding the boy.* TOMMY *at first doesn't understand and then, realizing the eyes are all on him, buries his face against his mother.*)

SALLY (*backs away*). That's crazy! He's only a boy.

WOMAN ONE. But he knew! He was the only one who knew! He told us all about it. Well, how did he know? How *could* he have known?

(*Various people take this up and repeat the question.*)

VOICE ONE. How could he know?

VOICE TWO. Who told him?

VOICE THREE. Make the kid answer.

(*The crowd starts to converge around the mother, who grabs* TOMMY *and starts to run with him. The crowd starts to follow, at first walking fast, and then running after him.*

Suddenly CHARLIE'S *lights go off and the lights in other houses go on, then off.*)

MAN ONE (*shouting*). It isn't the kid . . . it's Bob Weaver's house.

WOMAN ONE. It isn't Bob Weaver's house, it's Don Martin's place.

CHARLIE. I tell you it's the kid.

DON. It's Charlie. He's the one.

(*People shout, accuse, and scream as the lights go*

on and off. Then, slowly, in the middle of this nightmarish confusion of sight and sound the camera starts to pull away until once again we have reached the opening shot looking at the Maple Street sign from high above.*)

SCENE 2

The camera continues to move away while gradually bringing into focus a field. We see the metal side of a spacecraft which sits shrouded in darkness. An open door throws out a beam of light from the illuminated interior. Two figures appear, silhouetted against the bright lights. We get only a vague feeling of form.

FIGURE ONE. Understand the procedure now? Just stop a few of their machines and radios and telephones and lawn mowers . . . throw them into darkness for a few hours, and then just sit back and watch the pattern.

FIGURE TWO. And this pattern is always the same?

FIGURE ONE. With few variations. They pick the most dangerous enemy they can find . . . and it's themselves. And all we need do is sit back . . . and watch.

FIGURE TWO. Then I take it this place . . . this Maple Street . . . is not unique.

FIGURE ONE (*shaking his head*). By no means. Their world is full of Maple Streets. And we'll go from one to the other and let them destroy themselves. One to the other . . . one to the other . . . one to the other—

SCENE 3

The camera pans up for a shot of the starry sky, and over this we hear the NARRATOR'S *voice.*

NARRATOR. The tools of conquest do not necessarily come with bombs and explosions and fallout. There are weapons that are simply thoughts, attitudes, prejudices—to be found only in the minds of men. For the record, prejudices can kill

▲ A spaceship hovers over a mountaintop in this painting by Robert McCall. Are its intentions good or evil? What do you think the artist wants us to believe?

and suspicion can destroy and a thoughtless, frightened search for a scapegoat has a fallout all its own for the children . . . and the children yet unborn. (*A pause*) And the pity of it is . . . that these things cannot be confined to . . . The Twilight Zone! (*Fade to black.*)

After Reading

Making Connections

1. If you had a chance to act in this play, which character would you like to be? Why?

2. As you read the play, did you believe Tommy's theory that an alien family lived on Maple Street? If so, who did you think it was? If not, what explanation did you have for why the characters turned on one another?

3. 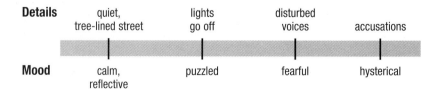 Which character seemed most able to hang on to his or her **individuality** and resist going along with the mob? Support your answer with examples from the play.

4. Look back at your notebook ideas. What changes or additions would you now make in your descriptions of the causes and effects of the emotions listed?

5. Why do you think the writer chose to use a **narrator** in this play?

6. **Science fiction** is a kind of fantasy based on science and technology. Often, it describes something that may happen in the future. Explain why you think this play is or is not science fiction.

7. Do you think the world is full of Maple Streets? Explain.

Literary Focus: Mood

The **mood,** or feeling this play creates, changes as the story unfolds. You can keep track of the changing mood by paying attention to details in the stage directions and dialogue. For example, the narrator alerts us to a change of mood early in Act One by saying Maple Street is in its "last calm and reflective moment." How would you describe the mood that develops? What details signal that mood?

By the time the "monster" approaches, the crowd is near hysteria. What details in Act Two show this? Create a story line like the one below to keep track of the changing mood and details that reveal it.

Details	quiet, tree-lined street	lights go off	disturbed voices	accusations
Mood	calm, reflective	puzzled	fearful	hysterical

Vocabulary Study

On a sheet of paper write the letter of the correct ending for each of the sentences below.

transfix
reflective
assent
antagonism
revelation
metamorphosis
incisive
incriminate
idiosyncrasy
scapegoat

1. Glimpses of the spacecraft would **transfix** the boy, making him **a.** run away quickly. **b.** stand motionless and stare. **c.** feel ill.

2. Her **incisive** comment showed **a.** she had a sharp mind. **b.** she was in touch with aliens. **c.** she was tired.

3. When they couldn't explain the power outage, the crowd picked a **scapegoat** to **a.** turn the lights back on. **b.** inform the rest of the neighborhood about it. **c.** take the blame.

4. He felt the crowd's **antagonism** when **a.** they suddenly turned on him. **b.** they laughed at his jokes about aliens. **c.** they cheered him for taking the gun.

5. We would expect a **reflective** person to **a.** get up and dance. **b.** sit calmly in thought. **c.** do what other people do.

6. The man hoped the **revelation** would **a.** solve a neighborhood mystery. **b.** turn the power back on. **c.** destroy the spacecraft.

7. The man got his neighbors' **assent** when **a.** they rejected him. **b.** they accused him. **c.** they agreed with him.

8. An **idiosyncrasy** is **a.** an engine part for a car. **b.** something unusual about an individual. **c.** a kind of mental illness.

9. After his **metamorphosis,** the quiet boy **a.** changed into a monster. **b.** spoke in a soft voice. **c.** asked for some food.

10. To **incriminate** a neighbor, the people needed **a.** no clues or evidence. **b.** a backyard barbeque. **c.** good evidence.

Expressing Your Ideas

Writing Choices

Witch Hunts The characters in this play go on a kind of witch hunt to find "aliens." Research the Salem, Massachusetts, witch hunts of 1692. Write a **comparison** of the behavior then compared to the actions in the play.

TV Time Write a **summary** of this play as it might appear in "TV Guide."

Other Options

A Nose for News Sooner or later, the news crews were bound to arrive on Maple Street. How do you think they reported the events that took place? Prepare and deliver a **TV newscast** as it might have appeared.

Quick Draw Which descriptions or short scenes from this script stand out in your mind? Choose a favorite scene to **illustrate.**

Before Reading

The Cremation of Sam McGee

by Robert Service

Robert Service
1874–1958

Service never went prospecting for Klondike gold himself, but he worked in a bank in the Yukon Territory, where he wrote down many of the stories he heard from prospectors. He thought up the plot for "The Cremation of Sam McGee" after listening to a prospector at a party he attended one night. Service was so excited by the story that he spent the entire night walking woodland trails and composing the ballad in his head. After the ballad's publication propelled him to fame, Service made a career writing poems and stories of the adventurous life in the Canadian North.

Building Background

Surviving in the Arctic In 1896 the cry of "Gold!" sent thousands of prospectors streaming into the Canadian **Yukon Territory** bordering Alaska. These adventurers soon changed that remote wilderness into the kind of rough-and-ready frontier that had characterized the California gold rush 50 years earlier. Yukon prospecting had its own problems, however. The average daily temperature in this subarctic climate was below freezing year-round, with winter temperatures regularly reaching 50 degrees below zero Fahrenheit. Despite these hardships, thousands set off in search of gold.

Getting into the Poem

Discussion "A promise is a debt unpaid," writes the narrator of this ballad. Like this narrator, many of us have made promises that are hard to keep. Can you recall a promise you made and then didn't want to keep? What did you do? Discuss it in class.

Reading Tip

Ballads "The Cremation of Sam McGee" is a **ballad**—a poem that tells a story in simple verse. The story is often a legend or a folk tale. Many ballads are sung, and even those that are not often have rhyme and rhythm that gives them a musical lilt.

To keep that rhyme and rhythm going, ballad writers may use words in unusual ways. The poet in this selection shortened the word *margin* and wrote "that night on the *marge* of Lake Lebarge" to provide rhythm and rhyme; the obvious choice, *shores,* just doesn't fit. Similarly, the poet expects the reader to pronounce *cursed* as two syllables, instead of the usual one, for the sake of rhythm in "It's the curséd cold."

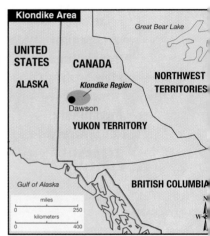

Klondike Area

Great Bear Lake

UNITED STATES

ALASKA

CANADA

Klondike Region

Dawson

YUKON TERRITORY

NORTHWEST TERRITORIES

Gulf of Alaska

BRITISH COLUMBIA

miles
0   250
kilometers
0   400

The Cremation of Sam McGee

Robert Service

There are strange things done in the midnight sun[1]
  By the men who moil for gold;
The Arctic trails have their secret tales
  That would make your blood run cold;
5 *The Northern Lights[2] have seen queer sights,*
  But the queerest they ever did see
Was that night on the marge of Lake Lebarge
  I cremated[3] Sam McGee.

Now Sam McGee was from Tennessee, where the cotton
  blooms and blows.
10 Why he left his home in the South to roam 'round the Pole,[4]
  God only knows.
He was always cold, but the land of gold seemed to hold
  him like a spell;
Though he'd often say in his homely way that "he'd sooner
  live in hell."

On a Christmas Day we were mushing our way over the
  Dawson trail.
Talk of your cold! through the parka's fold it stabbed like a
  driven nail.
15 If our eyes we'd close, then the lashes froze till sometimes
  we couldn't see;
It wasn't much fun, but the only one to whimper was Sam
  McGee.

And that very night, as we lay packed tight in our robes
  beneath the snow,

---

1. **midnight sun,** sun seen throughout the day and night in the arctic and
antarctic regions during their summers.
2. **Northern Lights,** streamers or bands of light, appearing in the sky at night, especially in polar
regions; aurora borealis.
3. **cremate** (krē′māt), *v.* burn a dead body to ashes.
4. **Pole,** North Pole.

This painting by Ted Harrison, full of "dazzling vibrations," is taken from a 1986 edition of *The Cremation of Sam McGee.* In what way does Harrison's many-hued painting capture the **individuality** of the Yukon experience?

And the dogs were fed, and the stars o'erhead were dancing
    heel and toe.
He turned to me, and "Cap," says he, "I'll cash in[5] this trip,
    I guess;
20 And if I do, I'm asking that you won't refuse my last request."

Well, he seemed so low that I couldn't say no; then he says
    with a sort of moan:
"It's the curséd cold, and it's got right hold till I'm chilled
    clean through to the bone.
Yet 'tain't being dead—it's my awful dread of the icy grave
    that pains;
So I want you to swear that, foul or fair, you'll cremate my
    last remains."
25 A pal's last need is a thing to heed,[6] so I swore I would not
    fail;
And we started on at the streak of dawn; but God! he
    looked ghastly[7] pale.
He crouched on the sleigh, and he raved all day of his home
    in Tennessee;

---

5. **cash in,** SLANG. die. [from the poker term "to cash in one's chips," meaning to end a game by exchanging poker chips for cash].
6. **heed** (hēd), *v.* pay careful attention to.
7. **ghastly** (gast′lē), *adj.* like a dead person or ghost.

And before nightfall a corpse was all that was left of Sam
    McGee.

There wasn't a breath in that land of death, and I hurried,
    horror-driven,
30 With a corpse half hid that I couldn't get rid, because of a
    promise given;
It was lashed to the sleigh, and it seemed to say: "You may
    tax your brawn and brains,
But you promised true, and it's up to you to cremate those
    last remains."

Now a promise made is a debt unpaid, and the trail has its
    own stern code.
In the days to come, though my lips were dumb, in my
    heart how I cursed that load.
35 In the long, long night, by the lone firelight, while the
    huskies,[8] round in a ring,
Howled out their woes to the homeless snows—O God! how
    I loathed the thing.

And every day that quiet clay seemed to heavy and heavier
    grow;
And on I went, though the dogs were spent and the grub
    was getting low;
The trail was bad, and I felt half mad, but I swore I would
    not give in;
40 And I'd often sing to the hateful thing, and it hearkened
    with a grin.

Till I came to the marge of Lake Lebarge, and a derelict[9]
    there lay;
It was jammed in the ice, but I saw in a trice it was called
    the "Alice May."
And I looked at it, and I thought a bit, and I looked at my
    frozen chum;
Then "Here," said I, with a sudden cry, "is my
    cre-ma-tor-eum."

45 Some planks I tore from the cabin floor, and I lit the boiler
    fire;

---

8. **husky** (hus′kē), an arctic sled dog.
9. **derelict** (der′ə likt), *n.* an abandoned ship.

Some coal I found that was lying around, and I heaped the
    fuel higher;
The flames just soared, and the furnace roared—such a
    blaze you seldom see;
And I burrowed a hole in the glowing coal, and I stuffed in
    Sam McGee.

Then I made a hike, for I didn't like to hear him sizzle so;
50 And the heavens scowled, and the huskies howled, and the
    wind began to blow.
It was icy cold, but the hot sweat rolled down my cheeks,
    and I don't know why;
And the greasy smoke in an inky cloak went streaking
    down the sky.

I do not know how long in the snow I wrestled with grisly[10]
    fear;
But the stars came out and they danced about ere again I
    ventured near;
55 I was sick with dread, but I bravely said: "I'll just take a
    peep inside.
I guess he's cooked, and it's time I looked;" . . . then the
    door I opened wide.

And there sat Sam, looking cool and calm, in the heart of
    the furnace roar;
And he wore a smile you could see a mile, and he said:
    "Please close that door.
It's fine in here, but I greatly fear you'll let in the cold and
    storm—
60 Since I left Plumtree, down in Tennessee, it's the first time
    I've been warm."

There are strange things done in the midnight sun
    By the men who moil for gold;
The Arctic trails have their secret tales
    That would make your blood run cold;
65 *The Northern Lights have seen queer sights,*
    But the queerest they ever did see
Was that night on the marge of Lake Lebarge
    I cremated Sam McGee.

---

10. **grisly** (griz′lē), *adj.* frightful; horrible.

After Reading

Making Connections

1. Would you have gone as far as the narrator did to keep a promise? Why or why not?

2. What surprised you most about the ending of this ballad?

3. Why does the poet use **repetition** of the first stanza at the end of this story?

4. Do the regular **rhyme** and **rhythm** add to or take away from your enjoyment of this poem? Explain.

5. Think back to the promises your class discussed making before reading the poem. **Compare** and **contrast** one of these promises to the promise made by the narrator. Write your comparison in outline form.

6. This poem takes a humorous look at a serious situation. Why do you suppose people turn to humor during bad times?

Literary Focus: Hyperbole

When you see **hyperbole,** or extreme exaggeration, in a poem or story, you know it is not a fact. Sam McGee claims the cold has him "chilled clean through to the bone." In fact, this is impossible. What the narrator really wants us to understand is that Sam feels very cold.

As in this ballad, hyperbole is common in legends and tall tales because exaggeration makes the heroes and their feats seem larger than life. Since such exaggeration is clearly unreal, it also tells the reader that the poem or story is entertainment rather than historical fact.

Think of some common phrases that use hyperbole, such as "My dog is as big as a horse," and share them with the class.

Vocabulary Study

On your paper write the word from the list that best completes the meaning of the sentence.

cremate
heed
ghastly
derelict
grisly

1. As we neared the shores of the remote lake, my friend's white face looked ____ in the moonlight.

2. In a brave moment, we had decided not to ____ the signs warning us to turn back, but now we were scared.

3. Ahead, we could just make out the shape of a ____ afloat near the shore.

4. Closer inspection revealed the ____ sight of charred bones and half-burnt logs on the bank.

5. Shaken, my friend whispered, "Do you think this is where someone came to ____ corpses?"

Expressing Your Ideas _____

Writing Choices

Rest His Bones What do you think the folks back in Tennessee would want to know about Sam and his life in the Yukon? Write an **obituary** to be published in his hometown paper. Be sure to include his birth and death dates and some facts about his life.

Tell Me a Story Write your own **ballad.** You may choose a story you've heard, as Robert Service did, or make up one of your own. Your ballad should use rhymed verse.

Klondike Fever Find out more about the Klondike Gold Rush, the Yukon Territory, or dog sledding. Write a four-page **research report** on the topic you've chosen.

Other Options

Read Aloud Work with a group to perform "The Cremation of Sam McGee" as a **choral reading.** Divide the ballad into parts for group reading, with solo parts for McGee and the narrator. What sounds, movement, and other special effects might you add? Perform your reading for the class.

Arctic Antics Create a **comic strip** that tells the story of Sam McGee. Your comic strip does not necessarily have to be funny. You can model it after one of the adventure strips in the Sunday newspaper.

Mood Music Ballads are traditionally sung. Some were originally written with music, but others were written as poetry and set to music later. **Compose a tune** for "The Cremation of Sam McGee" and sing the ballad for your class. If you can, provide piano or guitar accompaniment.

LAFFF

by Lensey Namioka

Lensey Namioka
born 1929

Namioka used personal experience in writing about two aspects of this story, Chinese immigrants and good math students. Born in Beijing, China, her first career was as a mathematics instructor. She began writing stories and novels for young adults after settling in Seattle, Washington, with her Japanese husband. Her writing often contains Chinese or Japanese characters. Although Namioka has always enjoyed reading science fiction, "LAFFF" is the first science-fiction story she has written.

Building Background

Science Fiction and Time Machines Would you like to walk around a Jurassic forest or experience life in the year 2500? Many science-fiction writers have played with the idea of travel into the past or future using a time machine. H. G. Wells was probably the first writer to explore this idea in English literature when he published his novel *The Time Machine* in 1895. Hundreds of these imaginary machines have shown up over the years in stories.

Getting into the Story

Writer's Notebook Imagine that you have built a time machine. This is your chance to go anywhere, past or future. Will you choose a personal event, such as your eighteenth birthday, or a historical day, such as the Boston Tea Party? In your notebook, make a time line with the year of your birth in the middle. Add places or years above the line that you would like to travel to in a time machine. Below the line give your reason for wanting to visit each place and time.

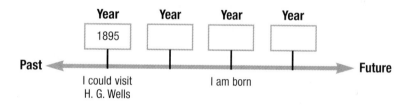

Reading Tip

Stereotypes Describe the characteristics of a nerd. Does this description pop into your mind: thin, wears glasses, and talks like an encyclopedia? That's the **stereotype** some people think of when they find out a student is interested in science, math, or computers. A stereotype is an overly simple image that represents a group of people. Writers use stereotypes as shorthand to let readers know something about a character without a lot of description. Writers also break stereotypes by giving a character who appears to be a stereotype some unique personality traits.

Masculine? Feminine? City? Suburb? Math Whiz? Literary Type? Linda Nelson takes a unique look at **individuality** in this 1995 illustration. What do you think she is trying to tell us?

Lafff

▶ **LENSEY NAMIOKA**

In movies, geniuses have frizzy white hair, right? They wear thick glasses and have names like Dr. Zweistein.

Peter Lu didn't have frizzy white hair. He had straight hair, as black as licorice. He didn't wear thick glasses, either, since his vision was normal.

Peter's family, like ours, had immigrated from China, but they had settled here first. When we moved into a house just two doors down from the Lus, they gave us some good advice on how to get along in America.

I went to the same school as Peter, and we walked to the school bus together every morning. Like many Chinese parents, mine made sure that I worked very hard in school.

In spite of all I could do, my grades were nothing compared to Peter's. He was at the top in all his classes. We walked to the school bus without talking because I was a little scared of him. Besides, he was always deep in thought.

Peter didn't have any friends. Most of the kids thought he was a nerd because they saw his head always buried in books. I didn't think he even tried to join the rest of us or cared what the others thought of him.

Then on Halloween he surprised us all. As I went down the block trick-or-treating, dressed as a zucchini in my green sweats, I heard a strange, deep voice behind me say, "How do you do."

I yelped and turned around. Peter was wearing a long, black Chinese gown with slits in the sides. On his head he had a little round cap, and down each side of his mouth drooped a thin, long mustache.

"I am Dr. Lu Manchu, the mad scientist," he announced, putting his hands in his sleeves and bowing.

He smiled when he saw me staring at his costume. I smiled back. I knew he was making fun of the way some kids believed in stereotypes about Chinese people. Still his was a scary smile, somehow.

Some of the other kids came up, and when they saw Peter, they were impressed. "Hey, neat!" said one boy.

I hadn't expected Peter to put on a costume and go trick-or-treating like a normal kid. So maybe he did want to join the others after all—at least some of the time. After that night he wasn't a nerd anymore. He was Dr. Lu Manchu. Even some of the teachers began to call him that.

When we became too old for trick-or-treating, Peter was still Dr. Lu Manchu. The rumor was that he was working on a fantastic machine in his parents' garage. But nobody had any idea what it was.

One evening, as I was coming home from a baby-sitting job, I cut across the Lus' backyard. Passing their garage, I saw through a little window that the light was on. My curiosity got the better of me, and I peeked in.

I saw a booth that looked like a shower stall. A stool stood in the middle of the stall, and hanging over the stool was something that looked like a great big shower head.

Suddenly a deep voice behind me said, "Good evening, Angela." Peter bowed and smiled his scary smile. He didn't have his costume on and he didn't have the long, droopy mustache. But he was Dr. Lu Manchu.

"What are you doing?" I squeaked.

Still in his strange, deep voice, Peter said, "What are *you* doing? After all, this is my garage."

"I was just cutting across your yard to get home. Your parents never complained before."

"I thought you were spying on me," said Peter. "I thought you wanted to know about my machine." He hissed when he said the word *machine*.

QUESTION: What more do you want to know about Peter Lu's machine? Write your questions in your notebook.

Honestly, he was beginning to frighten me. "What machine?" I demanded. "You mean this shower-stall thing?"

He drew himself up and narrowed his eyes, making them into thin slits. "This is my time machine!"

I goggled at him. "You mean . . . you mean . . . this machine can send you forward and backward in time?"

"Well, actually, I can only send things forward in time," admitted Peter, speaking in his normal voice again. "That's why I'm calling the machine LAFFF. It stands for Lu's Artifact For Fast Forward."

Of course Peter always won first prize at the annual statewide science fair. But that's a long way from making a time machine. Minus his mustache and long Chinese gown, he was just Peter Lu.

"I don't believe it!" I said. "I bet LAFFF is only good for a laugh."

"Okay, Angela. I'll show you!" hissed Peter.

He sat down on the stool and twisted a dial. I heard some *bleeps, cheeps,* and *gurgles.* Peter disappeared.

He must have done it with mirrors. I looked around the garage. I peeked under the tool bench. There was no sign of him.

"Okay, I give up," I told him. "It's a good trick, Peter. You can come out now."

Bleep, cheep, and *gurgle* went the machine, and there was Peter, sitting on the stool. He held a red rose in his hand. "What do you think of that?"

I blinked. "So you produced a flower. Maybe you had it under the stool."

"Roses bloom in June, right?" he demanded.

That was true. And this was December.

"I sent myself forward in time to June when the flowers were blooming," said Peter. "And I picked the rose from our yard. Convinced, Angela?"

It was too hard to swallow. "You said you couldn't send things back in time," I objected. "So how did you bring the rose back?"

But even as I spoke I saw that his hands were empty. The rose was gone.

"That's one of the problems with the machine," said Peter. "When I send myself forward, I can't seem to stay there for long. I snap back to my own time after only a minute. Anything I bring with me snaps back to its own time, too. So my rose has gone back to this June."

I was finally convinced, and I began to see possibilities. "Wow, just think: If I don't want to do the dishes, I can send myself forward to the time when the dishes are already done."

"That won't do you much good," said Peter. "You'd soon pop back to the time when the dishes were still dirty."

Too bad. "There must be something your machine is good for," I said. Then I had another idea. "Hey, you can bring me back a piece of fudge from the future, and I can eat it twice: once now, and again in the future."

"Yes, but the fudge wouldn't stay in your stomach," said Peter. "It would go back to the future."

"That's even better!" I said. "I can enjoy eating the fudge over and over again without getting fat!"

It was late, and I had to go home before my parents started to worry. Before I left, Peter said, "Look Angela, there's still a lot of work to do on LAFFF. Please don't tell anybody about the machine until I've got it right."

A few days later I asked him how he was doing.

"I can stay in the future time a bit longer now," he said. "Once I got it up to four minutes."

"Is that enough time to bring me back some fudge from the future?" I asked.

"We don't keep many sweets around the house," he said. "But I'll see what I can do."

A few minutes later, he came back with a spring roll for me. "My mother was frying these in the kitchen, and I snatched one while she wasn't looking."

I bit into the hot, crunchy spring roll, but before I finished chewing, it disappeared. The taste of soy sauce, green onions, and bean sprouts stayed a little longer in my mouth, though.

It was fun to play around with LAFFF, but it wasn't really useful. I didn't know what a great help it would turn out to be.

very year our school held a writing contest, and the winning story for each grade got printed in our school magazine. I wanted desperately to win. I worked awfully hard in school, but my parents still thought I could do better.

Winning the writing contest would show my parents that I was really good in something. I love writing stories, and I have lots of ideas. But when I actually write them down, my stories never turn out as good as I thought. I just can't seem to find the right words, because English isn't my first language.

I got an honorable mention last year, but it wasn't the same as winning and showing my parents my name, Angela Tang, printed in the school magazine.

The deadline for the contest was getting close, and I had a pile of stories written, but none of them looked like a winner.

Then, the day before the deadline, *boing,* a brilliant idea hit me.

I thought of Peter and his LAFFF machine.

I rushed over to the Lus' garage and, just as I had hoped, Peter was there, tinkering with his machine.

"I've got this great idea for winning the story contest," I told him breathlessly. "You see, to be certain of winning, I have to write the story that would be the winner."

"That's obvious," Peter said dryly. "In fact, you're going around in a circle."

"Wait, listen!" I said. "I want to use LAFFF and go forward to the time when the next issue of the school magazine is out. Then I can read the winning story."

After a moment Peter nodded. "I see. You plan to write down the winning story after you've read it and then send it in to the contest."

I nodded eagerly. "The story would *have* to win, because it's the winner!"

Peter began to look interested. "I've got LAFFF to the point where I can stay in the future for seven minutes now. Will that be long enough for you?"

"I'll just have to work quickly," I said.

Peter smiled. It wasn't his scary Lu Manchu

smile, but a nice smile. He was getting as excited as I was. "Okay, Angela. Let's go for it."

He led me to the stool. "What's your destination?" he asked. "I mean, *when's* your destination?"

Suddenly I was nervous. I told myself that Peter had made many time trips, and he looked perfectly healthy.

Why not? What have I got to lose—except time?

I took a deep breath. "I want to go forward three weeks in time." By then I'd have a copy of the new school magazine in my room.

"Ready, Angela?" asked Peter.

"As ready as I'll ever be," I whispered.

Bleep, cheep, and *gurgle.* Suddenly Peter disappeared.

What went wrong? Did Peter get sent by mistake, instead of me?

Then I realized what had happened. Three weeks later in time Peter might be somewhere else. No wonder I couldn't see him.

There was no time to be lost. Rushing out of Peter's garage, I ran over to our house and entered through the back door.

Mother was in the kitchen. When she saw me, she stared. "Angela! I thought you were upstairs taking a shower!"

"Sorry!" I panted. "No time to talk!"

I dashed up to my room. Then I suddenly had a strange idea. What if I met *myself* in my room? Argh! It was a spooky thought.

There was nobody in my room. Where was I? I mean, where was the I of three weeks later?

Wait. Mother had just said she thought I was taking a shower. Down the hall, I could hear the water running in the bathroom. Okay. That meant I wouldn't run into me for a while.

I went to the shelf above my desk and frantically pawed through the junk piled there. I found it! I found the latest issues of the school magazine, the one with the winning stories printed in it.

How much time had passed? Better hurry.

The shower had stopped running. This meant the other me was out of the bathroom. Have to get out of here!

Too late. Just as I started down the stairs, I heard Mother talking again. "Angela! A minute ago you were all dressed! Now you're in your robe again and your hair's all wet! I don't understand."

I shivered. It was scary, listening to Mother talking to myself downstairs. I heard my other self answering something, then the sound of her—my—steps coming up the stairs. In a panic, I dodged into the spare room and closed the door.

I heard the steps—my steps—go past and into my room.

The minute I heard the door of my room close, I rushed out and down the stairs.

Mother was standing at the foot of the stairs. When she saw me, her mouth dropped. "But . . . but . . . just a minute ago you were in your robe and your hair was all wet!"

"See you later, Mother," I panted. And I ran.

Behind me I heard Mother muttering, "I'm going mad!"

I didn't stop and try to explain. I might go mad, too.

It would be great if I could just keep the magazine with me. But, like the spring roll, it would get carried back to its own time after a few minutes. So the next best thing was to read the magazine as fast as I could.

It was hard to run and flip though the magazine at the same time. But I made it back to Peter's garage and plopped down on the stool.

At last I found the story: the story that had won the contest in our grade. I started to read.

Suddenly I heard *bleep, cheep,* and *gurgle,* and Peter loomed up in front of me. I was back in my original time again.

But I still had the magazine! Now I had to read the story before the magazine popped back to the future. It was hard to concentrate with Peter jumping up and down impatiently, so different from his usual calm, collected self.

I read a few paragraphs, and I was beginning to see how the story would shape up. But before I got any further, the magazine disappeared from my hand.

So I didn't finish reading the story. I didn't reach the end, where the name of the winning writer was printed.

That night I stayed up very late to write down what I remembered of the story. It had a neat plot, and I could see why it was the winner.

I hadn't read the entire story, so I had to make up the ending myself. But that was okay, since I knew how it should come out.

EVALUATE: Is Angela's idea for winning the contest a good one?

The winners of the writing contest would be announced at the school assembly on Friday. After we had filed into the assembly hall and sat down, the principal gave a speech. I tried not to fidget while he explained about the contest.

Suddenly I was struck by a dreadful thought. Somebody in my class had written the winning story, the one I had copied. Wouldn't that person be declared the winner, instead of me?

The principal started announcing the winners. I chewed my knuckles in an agony of suspense, as I waited to see who would be announced as the winner in my class. Slowly, the principal began with the lowest grade. Each winner walked in slow motion to the stage, while the principal slowly explained why the story was good.

At last, at last, he came to our grade. "The winner is . . ." He stopped, slowly got out his handkerchief, and slowly blew his nose. Then

The *Light Space Modulator* was created by the artist Laszlo Moholy-Nagy between the years 1923 and 1930. Do you think Peter Lu's time machine might look something like Moholy-Nagy's creation?

he cleared his throat. "The winning story is 'Around and Around,' by Angela Tang."

I sat like a stone, unable to move. Peter nudged me. "Go on, Angela! They're waiting for you."

I got up and walked up to the stage in a daze. The principal's voice seemed to be coming from far, far away as he told the audience that I had written a science fiction story about time travel.

The winners each got a notebook bound in imitation leather for writing more stories. Inside the cover of the notebook was a ballpoint pen. But the best prize was having my story in the school magazine with my name printed at the end.

Then why didn't I feel good about winning?

After assembly, the kids in our class crowded around to congratulate me. Peter formally shook my hand. "Good work, Angela," he said, and winked at me.

That didn't make me feel any better. I hadn't won the contest fairly. Instead of writing the story myself, I had copied it from the school magazine.

That meant someone in our class—one of the kids here—had actually written the story. Who was it?

My heart was knocking against my ribs as I stood there and waited for someone to complain that I had stolen his story.

Nobody did.

As we were riding the school bus home, Peter looked at me. "You don't seem very happy about winning the contest, Angela."

"No, I'm not," I mumbled. "I feel just awful."

"Tell you what," suggested Peter. "Come over to my house and we'll discuss it."

"What is there to discuss?" I asked glumly. "I won the contest because I cheated."

"Come on over, anyway. My mother bought a fresh package of humbow in Chinatown."

I couldn't turn down that invitation. Humbow, a roll stuffed with barbecued pork, is my favorite snack.

Peter's mother came into the kitchen while we were munching, and he told her about the contest.

Mrs. Lu looked pleased. "I'm very glad, Angela. You have a terrific imagination, and you deserve to win."

"I like Angela's stories," said Peter. "They're original."

It was the first compliment he had ever paid me, and I felt my face turning red.

After Mrs. Lu left us, Peter and I each had another humbow. But I was still miserable. "I wish I had never started this. I feel like such a jerk."

Peter looked at me, and I swear he was enjoying himself. "If you stole another student's story, why didn't that person complain?"

"I don't know!" I wailed.

"Think!" said Peter. "You're smart, Angela. Come on, figure it out."

Me, smart? I was so overcome to hear myself called smart by a genius like Peter that I just stared at him.

He had to repeat himself. "Figure it out, Angela!"

I tried to concentrate. Why was Peter looking so amused?

The light finally dawned. "Got it," I said slowly. "*I'm* the one who wrote the story."

"The winning story is your own, Angela, because that's the one that won."

My head began to go around and around. "But where did the original idea for the story come from?"

"What made the plot so good?" asked Peter. His voice sounded unsteady.

"Well, in my story, my character used a time machine to go forward in time . . ."

"Okay, whose idea was it to use a time machine?"

"It was mine," I said slowly. I remembered the moment when the idea had hit me with a *boing.*

"So you s-stole f-from yourself!" sputtered Peter. He started to roar with laughter. I had never seen him break down like that. At this rate, he might wind up being human.

When he could talk again, he asked me to read my story to him.

I began. "'In movies, geniuses have frizzy white hair, right? They wear thick glasses and have names like Dr. Zweistein. . . .'"

After Reading

Making Connections

1. If you had a chance to take a trip in an untried time machine, would you? Why or why not?

2. Were any of the reasons you wanted to go to specific times and places, as recorded in your Writer's Notebook, at all like Angela's reason for taking a time trip? Tell why or why not.

3. If you could change the ending of the story, what would you have happen after Angela steps into the time machine?

4. What difficulties would you face in turning this story into a play?

5. The author brings up interesting problems that might occur during time travel into the future. What might have happened to Angela if she had run into herself?

6. What problems other than those described in this story might arise if people had the ability to travel across time?

7. 🐾 Angela's and Peter's families have both emigrated from China. Their **individuality** in part stems from this background. How are their lives different from or similar to other teenagers whose families have been in the United States longer?

Literary Focus: The Importance of Time in Setting and Plot

When a **setting**—the time and place in which a story occurs—is unusual, you need to ask yourself how it affects the story. In this story the author uses time in an unusual way. The action takes place over a few weeks, but the characters also travel forward and back in time. These time changes form a central part of the **plot,** or plan, of the story.

Reread the first and last paragraphs of the story. How is the use of time unusual here? A story circle map may help you organize your thoughts. Begin with the event shown, then summarize the remaining events in order.

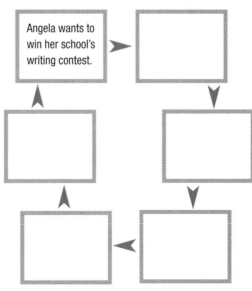

Angela wants to win her school's writing contest.

Vocabulary Study

"LAFFF" is about a boy, Peter Lu, who is a *genius* and a *scientist*. Use these two words and fill in two separate word maps like the one below, completed for the word *athlete*.

Person who has physical strength, speed, and skill

Definition

Description

They run like swift animals and move like dancers.

ATHLETE

Examples

Monica Seles   Michael Jordan   Cal Ripken, Jr.

Expressing Your Ideas

Writing Choices

Back to the Future? The time machine in this story will only send people forward in time. What if Peter's machine would only travel backward in time? Write a one-page **story** about what might happen.

Laboratory Lingo Peter could win the state science fair again if he writes up the results of his experiments with LAFFF. Imagine you are Peter. Then use the events of the story and write them up as a **laboratory experiment**, stating what you are trying to prove, how you went about it, what the results were, and what you can conclude.

How-To How do you operate a time machine? Write an **instruction manual** to go with LAFFF, including technical illustrations if needed. You may want to use an instruction manual for a television, or other household appliance, as a model.

Other Options

Imagine an Illustration Peter's time machine is described early in the story. Use that description and your imagination to make a **drawing** that shows what you think the machine might look like. Label the important operating parts.

Everyone Needs a LAFFF Make an illustrated **brochure** a salesperson might hand you if you were interested in purchasing a time machine. Your brochure should focus on the benefits that such a machine will provide to the buyer.

Yoo-hoo! It's Me! Work with a partner to perform a short **skit** that shows someone who travels into the future and meets himself or herself. One partner can take the role of the present self and the other, the future self. Perform your skit for the class.

Before Reading

Biddy Mason by Ruth Pelz
Western Wagons by Rosemary and Stephen Vincent Benét

Ruth Pelz

Her interest in history led Pelz to a career as a teacher, writer, and editor. She selected Biddy Mason's story for her book *Black Heroes of the Wild West* because Mason was a founder of Los Angeles.

Rosemary and Stephen Vincent Benét

"Western Wagons" is one of several poems written by this husband and wife. Like this poem, much of their work is about events and people in American history. Stephen Vincent Benét twice won the Pulitzer Prize for poetry—in 1929 for the epic *John Brown's Body* and in 1944, one year after his death, for *Western Star.*

Building Background

The Pioneer Spirit Just as those before them had crossed the ocean in sailing schooners, the American pioneers climbed aboard their **prairie schooners,** or covered wagons, to push on west. Their reasons for going were as varied as the people who went. Some, lured by the promise of free government land to be cleared and claimed, fled the poverty and hardships of their failed farms at home. Others saw a get-rich-quick scheme in the California gold rush. Still others just followed a dream—the hope and promise of a new land. Look for the reasons the pioneers in these selections headed west.

Getting into the Selections

Discussion The selections you will read are about people moving to the American West, a popular destination in the mid-1800s. What area or place draws people today? Participate in a discussion and class survey in which you and your classmates say where and why you would move if you could. You can choose anywhere in the world. Appoint a class member to keep track of everyone's answers on the board.

Reading Tip

Using Maps As the pioneers pushed west, they settled in different places. The first selection describes the westward journey of one who started in Mississippi, went first to Utah, then pushed on to San Bernardino and eventually to Los Angeles, California. The second selection mentions Iowa, Nebraska, Wyoming, and California as common western destinations. Before you read the selections, locate all of these places and trace the journey shown on the present-day map above.

Biddy MASON

Ruth Pelz

"Mama, I'm tired," said the little girl. "It's hot and I'm tired of walking. Why can't we stop now? Why can't we stay where we are?"

"Hush now," said Biddy, comforting her daughter. "I know you're tired. I've had enough of traveling myself, more than enough. But it isn't my choice, child. It's Mr. Robert Smith says if we're walking or staying. And Mr. Smith is a traveling kind of man. You get up in the wagon with your sister for a while."

Sometimes it seemed they would never stop traveling. First there had been the long trip to Utah. All day Biddy had walked along behind the wagons, tending the cattle. For months they walked, getting farther and farther from Mississippi. It was a hard trip, especially for the children. But what could Biddy do? She was born a slave. She was a slave today. Her master told her to walk across the plains and she did it.

They had stayed in Utah only one year. Then word came of a new settlement in Southern California. Robert Smith decided to go. Again the wagons were packed. Again they began the long days of walking.

Biddy had plenty of time for thinking along the way. What she mostly thought about was freedom. As a child she had never known a black person who wasn't a slave. Oh, she heard about them, about the ones who escaped to the North. But it was all so hard to imagine!

Then came the trip west. Things were different here. She had seen families, *black families,* traveling west with their own wagons! Just think of it! They planned to find their own land,

Centennial Progress by Montgomery Tiers depicts an unusually tranquil scene in the lives of people moving West. 🐾 Choose one of the characters and examine his or her face. What do you think this **individual's** concerns are? ➤

start their own farms, or find work in the towns. Biddy had thought about them for days.

Then there was Salt Lake City. Mormon[1] families had come there from all over the country. Some came from the South and brought slaves with them. Many families came from the northern states, though, where slavery wasn't allowed. It was different, all right. It got you thinking.

Biddy looked down at her bare feet. They were tired and sore and covered with dust. "These feet walked every mile from Mississippi," she thought. "And they remember every step. They have walked for Mr. Smith and his family. They have walked after his crops and his wagons and his cattle. But someday they are going to walk for me. Some day these feet will walk me to freedom! I'm sure of it."

A few days later, the tired travelers arrived at San Bernardino, California. It was a lovely place. It was their new home.

There were many reasons to enjoy living in California in 1852. The climate was pleasant. The land was good. The air was fresh and warm. Cities were booming. Everywhere there was a sense of promise and excitement.

The most important thing for Biddy was the promise of freedom. She had heard people talking. The new state of California did not permit slavery, they said. By law all people here were free. Biddy looked again at her dusty traveling feet. "Soon," she said to herself, "soon."

Three years passed. Life was pretty good, but Mr. Smith must have loved traveling. Even this beautiful settlement could not hold him. He decided to move again, this time to Texas. The wagons were loaded and made ready to go.

Biddy knew she had to act. As soon as the wagons left San Bernardino, she began looking for an opportunity. She found one.

Somehow she sent word to the sheriff in Los Angeles. He stopped the wagons before they left California.

"I hear you have slaves in your party," said the sheriff. "I suppose you know that's against the law. Is it true?"

Biddy came forward. In all her life this was the first time she had ever spoken to a white sheriff. Still her voice was strong. "It is true," she said. "Mr. Smith is taking us to Texas and we don't want to go."

That statement led to the most important slavery trial in Southern California. Biddy and another slave woman and their children were taken to court. Biddy spoke to the judge, and once again, her words were strong and clear: "I want to stay in California. I want to be free."

The judge sided with Biddy. He scolded Mr. Smith for breaking the law. He gave all the slaves their freedom.

Biddy gathered up her children and said, "We are moving once more, but it won't be very far. We are going to Los Angeles, and this time," she said, looking at her tired feet, "I am walking for me!"

She started her new life by taking as her full name, Biddy Mason. She went to work as a nurse and a housekeeper. Before long she saved enough to buy a house. Soon she bought other property too. Biddy Mason was a good businesswoman. She became one of the wealthiest blacks in Los Angeles.

She shared that wealth with others. She gave land to build schools and hospitals and nursing homes. She supported the education of black children and helped people in need. Biddy Mason had come a long way from that slave's cabin in Mississippi. She still remembered the walking. And she made sure she helped others along their way.

---

1. **Mormon** (môr′mən), member of the Church of Jesus Christ of Latter-Day Saints, founded in 1830 by Joseph Smith.

WESTERN WAGONS

Rosemary and Stephen Vincent Benét

They went with axe and rifle, when the trail was still to blaze,
They went with wife and children, in the prairie-schooner days,
With banjo and with frying pan—Susanna, don't you cry!
For I'm off to California to get rich out there or die!

5 We've broken land and cleared it, but we're tired of where we
      are.
They say that wild Nebraska is a better place by far.
There's gold in far Wyoming, there's black earth in Ioway,
So pack up the kids and blankets, for we're moving out today!

10 The cowards never started and the weak died on the road,
And all across the continent, the endless campfires glowed.
We'd taken land and settled—but a traveler passed by—
And we're going West tomorrow—Lordy, never ask us why!

We're going West tomorrow, where the promises can't fail.
15 O'er the hills in legions, boys, and crowd the dusty trail!
We shall starve and freeze and suffer. We shall die, and tame the
      lands.
But we're going West tomorrow, with our fortune in our hands.

After Reading

Making Connections

1. Would you want to be a pioneer blazing new trails? Why or why not?

2. What lessons can you learn from Biddy Mason?

3. 👣 If you were given the chance to design a memorial wall in Los Angeles to honor Biddy Mason, what images would you put on it to represent her special **individuality**? Why?

4. Were the reasons people in the selections went westward like the reasons given in your class discussion and survey? Explain.

5. Biddy Mason's **biography** is based on fact, but the author has added story elements to make it more enjoyable to read. Look back through the selection. What do you think is fact, and what may have been fictionalized?

6. Reread the two lines of the poem in italic type. What do the authors suggest is an important reason people went west?

7. Who are the pioneers of today? What are they doing?

Literary Focus: Third-Person Point of View

You can figure out **point of view** by asking yourself: Who is telling the story and about whom? In "Biddy Mason" you read, "Biddy knew she had to act. . . . Somehow she sent word to the sheriff in Los Angeles." You can conclude from the third-person pronoun *she* that a narrator is telling this story about someone else. It is written from a **third-person point of view**.

Third person is the most common point of view in **biography**. A narrator who knows everything—even what another person is thinking—is omniscient, or all-knowing. The narrator of this biography writes, "Biddy had plenty of time for thinking along the way. What she mostly thought about was freedom." Look back through the biography for other examples that show this is an **omniscient narrator** who in addition to telling facts about a person also describes what that person thinks and feels. Organize your findings on a chart like the one that follows.

Third-Person Point of View: Omniscient Narrator	
Facts	**Thoughts and Feelings**
Biddy got the sheriff.	She thought about freedom.

Vocabulary Study

In the poem "Western Wagons" the authors use the word *legions* in the line "O'er the hills in legions, boys, and crowd the dusty trail!"

Create a word map for *legion.* Use the form shown below. Under Synonyms and Antonyms, include any words that you think relate to the word *legion.* Under Examples, list things that you think might come in legions. Refer to a dictionary, as needed.

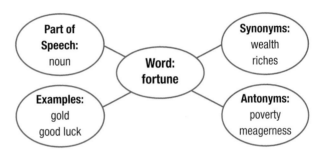

Expressing Your Ideas

Writing Choices

With Love, Biddy Imagine you are Biddy Mason. A friend expresses admiration for your courage and confesses that he himself is afraid to follow his dream. Write a **letter** of advice to encourage your friend.

Nothing Ventured Choose either the biography or the poem, and think about a lesson you learned from it or its moral. Then boil that down to a single sentence and express it in a **proverb**—a short, wise saying like "A stitch in time saves nine." Be prepared to explain how your proverb represents the selection.

Remember Biddy Imagine you have been chosen to speak at Biddy Mason's funeral. Your job is to deliver the **eulogy**, a speech praising her accomplishments and life. Write the eulogy you will give.

Other Options

Show Time With a group, discuss how you might turn the poem "Western Wagons" into a song, or otherwise perform it. Practice and present your **performance** to the class.

Timely Events Biddy Mason lived from 1820 to 1891. Make an illustrated **time line** that marks important events that occurred during her life. You may choose events that happened anywhere in the world.

Word of Mouth Compose an **oral history** of Biddy Mason's story that her little girl may have passed on later to her own children. Rely on your memory and use as few notes as possible. Present your oral history to the class.

Before Reading

The Journey by Hu Feng
Old Mary by Gwendolyn Brooks

Hu Feng
1905?–1955?

Hu Feng often felt torn between the beauties of love and art and the realities of life. To satisfy both demands, he wrote poetry and participated in the political life of China. He felt it was important in poetry to reveal individual feelings, as he does in this poem. Hu Feng disappeared during the political struggles in China in the 1950s.

Gwendolyn Brooks
born 1917

Brooks began writing poetry at the age of seven. She enjoyed studying great poets in high school and junior college and used their works as models for her own poetry. Brooks has won many prizes for her poetry, including the Pulitzer Prize, the highest honor awarded to American poets.

Building Background

Beyond the Road Not all travels involve going from one place to another. Some travelers, like American writer Henry David Thoreau, journey far without ever leaving home. "I have traveled much in Concord," Thoreau wrote in *Walden.* He wasn't, of course, talking about trips to the post office or corner store. He was talking about having an imaginative mind . . . traveling through books, conversation, and sitting alone with one's thoughts. Rich or poor, journeys of the mind are free for all of us.

Getting into the Poems

Writer's Notebook Most people hope that in old age they'll be able to look back over their lives and say "My dreams have all come true." The people in the poems "The Journey" and "Old Mary" examine their lives and find some faded dreams and disappointments.

What do you hope to accomplish or to experience during your life? Do your goals include career, family, adventure, world travel? What are your dreams? Write about them in your notebook.

Reading Tip

Poetic Structure Have you ever wondered why poets arrange the lines of a poem a certain way on the page? Sometimes the **stanzas,** or groups of lines, are about the same length; other times it looks as though the poet didn't care. No matter how a poem looks, the poet has a plan. Poetic structure is important to the meaning of the poem.

One poem in the following selections has only six lines, arranged in **couplets**. Couplets are pairs of lines. They do not have to rhyme, but in this poem they do. The other poem has four stanzas of different lengths. The first three stanzas have five lines, while the last has seven. Adding extra lines to the last stanza of a poem is a common practice. It gives the poet a chance to express an important idea. As you read these poems, ask yourself: How would these poems change if their structure changed?

THE JOURNEY

by Hu Feng

I hold on to a faded dream,
Sauntering[1] on a deserted road.
The chill sad call of the swan sweeps through the sky,
An immense cold bleakness[2] all around—
5 I know it's evening.

I carry on my back a faded dream,
Strolling along in cold blurred twilight.
A belt of pine trees lies ahead,
Huge dark shadows lie ahead—
10 I sit down, all my courage gone.

I lean on a faded dream,
Among the clusters of withered weeds.
Gazing at the misty moon,
Hearing faintly the night watchman's gong—
15 I contemplate[3] the blessed multitude[4] of lives.

I prop myself on a faded dream,
And sleep fitfully.
When I wake up
The moon is already down,
20 Darkness reigns all around—
Ah, embrace me tightly
My good friend the dark night.

Late autumn 1926
Wild Flowers and Arrows, 20–22

Travelers Among Mountains and Streams is an early eleventh-century hanging scroll by Fan Kuan. How does nature impact the lonely traveler's **individuality** in this ink on silk creation?

---

1. saunter (sôn′tər), *v.* walk along slowly and happily; stroll.
2. bleakness (blēk′nəs), *n.* a bare and cheerless condition.
3. contemplate (kon′təm plāt), *v.* think about for a long time.
4. multitude (mul′tə tüd), *n.* a great many; crowd.

Old Mary

Gwendolyn Brooks

Robert Gwathmey's *Portrait of a Farmer's Wife* was painted in 1951. Does this woman look to you like one who regrets the past? ➤

My last defense
Is the present tense.

It little hurts me now to know
I shall not go

5 Cathedral[1]-hunting in Spain
Nor cherrying in Michigan or Maine.

---

1. cathedral (kə thēʹdrəl), *n.* a large or important church.

After Reading

Making Connections

1. If the dreams that you wrote about in your Writer's Notebook don't come true, will your reaction be similar to or different from those described in the poems? Explain.

2. In the first three **stanzas** of "The Journey," the poet creates an imaginary landscape. Draw this landscape.

3. If you could meet Old Mary and the narrator of "The Journey," what would you ask them?

4. Explain the first **couplet** in "Old Mary": "My last defense/Is the present tense."

5. Look back at the first line of each **stanza** in "The Journey" and explain the narrator's changing connection to the "faded dream."

6. The last stanza of "The Journey" has the same structure as the first three, but an extra couplet is added at the end. How does the narrator feel about the "dark night" in this couplet?

Literary Focus: Symbolism

You can better understand the meaning of many poems if you look for **symbolism,** or the use of symbols. A symbol is a person, place, event, or object that has a meaning in itself but also suggests other meanings as well. For example, "The Journey" begins with a symbol in its title. The poem seems to be about an actual journey—a trip the narrator takes down "a deserted road." It also suggests another kind of journey—the trip the narrator is taking toward the end of his life and of his dream.

Look over the poem for more key words or actions in the poem that support the journey/life trip symbolism. Use a diagram like the one below to organize your thoughts.

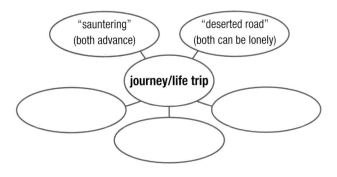

Vocabulary Study

Choose a word from the list that has the same meaning as the underlined words. Write it on your paper.

saunter
bleakness
contemplate
multitude
cathedral

1. I had no time to <u>walk slowly</u> on this journey.
2. I had come to this spot to <u>think about</u> my life and my goals.
3. Slowly, I opened the huge doors of the <u>big church</u>.
4. At first I felt afraid of its <u>depressing emptiness.</u>
5. My spirits lifted when a <u>large crowd</u> of birds in a nearby tree began to sing.

Expressing Your Ideas

Writing Choices

Biog Bits We meet both Old Mary and the narrator of "The Journey" at the end of their lives. What do you think these people were like at a younger age? What did they do in their lives? Choose either character and write an imaginary **biographical sketch.**

Car Trips and Head Trips Choose a real or symbolic journey in your life—one you've taken, or one you've contemplated taking. Then write a **poem** about that journey.

Goal Getter Look back at the goals you set for yourself in your notebook. Imagine yourself achieving one of those goals. How did you do it? How did it feel? What is your life like now? Write a **journal entry** that describes how it feels when a dream becomes real.

Other Options

Tell Me a Story Reread each stanza of "The Journey" and think about the story it tells. Then divide a piece of poster paper into four equal parts. Create a **storyboard** by drawing a picture for each of the four verses in the poem.

Finding Favorites Gwendolyn Brooks has written many poems and received many prizes for her poetry. Find and read as many of her poems as you can. Conduct a **poetry reading** in which you share your favorites with the class.

Destination: Life Make a **map** of your life's journey to this point. You might include places you have lived, important events, and turning points in the way you think. End your map with pointers to future directions you hope to take.

Writing Mini-Lesson

Maintaining Your Working Portfolio

Whether you have been keeping your working portfolio or your teacher has been keeping it, now is the time to review it.

- First, review the statement of your goals. Do you have pieces in your portfolio that show that you are working toward or have met each goal? If not, what kinds of writing do you need?

- Next, look at your writing samples. Do you have planning pieces, first drafts, revised and edited drafts, and the final copies for all your samples? Do you have some different kinds of writing—critical writing, reports, narratives, poems, etc.?

- Finally, is there anything in your portfolio that you don't think should be there? What pieces do you really like? What pieces are not examples of your best work? Make a list of items that you need to add or remove before you prepare your presentation portfolio at the end of the year.

Making a Mid-Course Correction

What about the goals themselves? Review your goals. Are they still the ones that you want to reach? Also, think about your progress in reaching the goals. Did you take on more than you can accomplish, or did you underestimate yourself? You might ask a partner for a second opinion on your goals and the written pieces you have produced.

Take some time to rewrite your goals. If you have already met your goals, then set some new ones. Be sure to include the changes you want to make in your portfolio and what you plan to accomplish for the next grading period.

Travels with a Twist

Winding Roads

Geography Connection

What do all great explorers have in common? They must relish adventure. They must yearn for travels with a twist. They must be willing to accept winding roads as their homes. They must display patience, perseverance, and inner strength.

THREE EXPLORERS

Three extraordinary men dedicated their lives to the pursuit of adventure and information about foreign lands.

Marco Polo and his uncles arrive at Hormuz, a Moslem city on the Persian Gulf. ➤

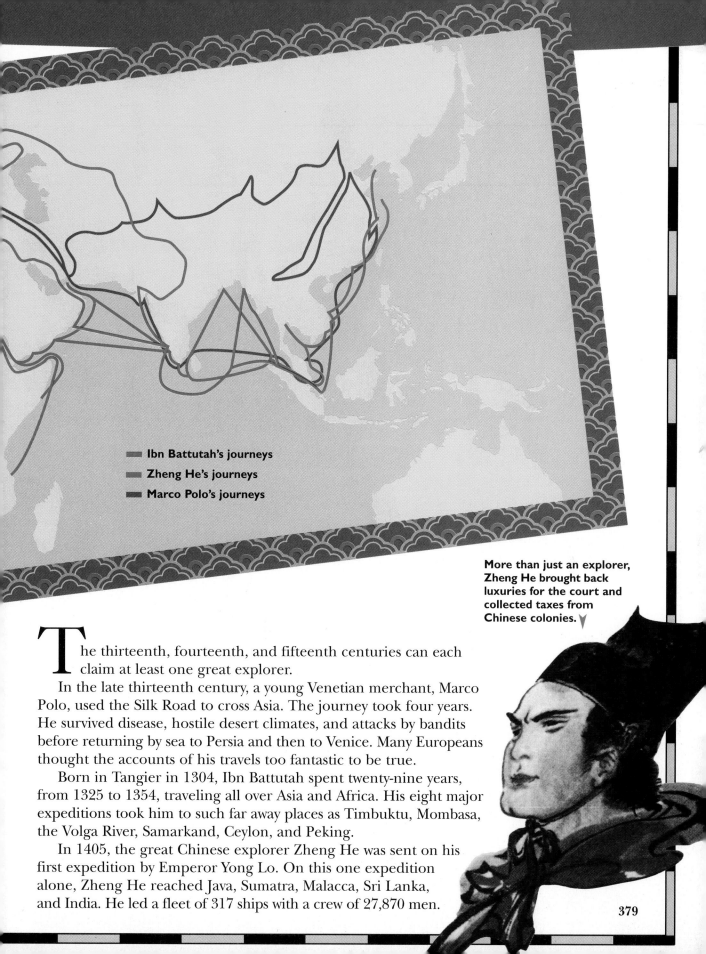

Ibn Battutah's journeys
Zheng He's journeys
Marco Polo's journeys

More than just an explorer, Zheng He brought back luxuries for the court and collected taxes from Chinese colonies. ▼

The thirteenth, fourteenth, and fifteenth centuries can each claim at least one great explorer.

In the late thirteenth century, a young Venetian merchant, Marco Polo, used the Silk Road to cross Asia. The journey took four years. He survived disease, hostile desert climates, and attacks by bandits before returning by sea to Persia and then to Venice. Many Europeans thought the accounts of his travels too fantastic to be true.

Born in Tangier in 1304, Ibn Battutah spent twenty-nine years, from 1325 to 1354, traveling all over Asia and Africa. His eight major expeditions took him to such far away places as Timbuktu, Mombasa, the Volga River, Samarkand, Ceylon, and Peking.

In 1405, the great Chinese explorer Zheng He was sent on his first expedition by Emperor Yong Lo. On this one expedition alone, Zheng He reached Java, Sumatra, Malacca, Sri Lanka, and India. He led a fleet of 317 ships with a crew of 27,870 men.

379

Long before Zheng He made his journeys of exploration in the fifteenth century, the Chinese were charting the heavens on star maps. This tenth-century map shows the Great Bear (The Big Dipper) and the group of constellations that were known to the Chinese as the Purple Enclosure. ▼

▲ This thirteenth-century Arab dhow carried a characteristically large payload and small crew.

▲ Emperor Kubla Khan hands the Polos his golden seal at the city of Khan-balik.

Responding

Research the life of an astronaut. Write a paragraph comparing this explorer of space and the three explorers presented in this section. Share your paragraph with the class.

THE ADVENTURES OF
MARCO POLO

BY SIMON BOUGHTON

LOADED CAMELS.

▲ Spices, silks, jade, and other valuable items eventually were transported to Europe by ship, but first they were carried in camel caravans over land.

When Marco Polo returned to his home in Venice after twenty years in the Far East, he had probably traveled farther than anybody before him. Not even Arab explorers, who had reached China by sea, had ventured far from the coast. Marco Polo traveled overland, from Acre on the coast of Palestine, through Persia and Turkestan, across the vast Gobi Desert and into China itself. There, at the city of Khan-balik, he became a favorite of the great Mongol Emperor Kubla Khan, who sent him on further journeys—to the south, to Burma and Indochina, to Tibet in the west, and to the city of Karakorum and northern China.

People in Europe had known of vast lands to the east for centuries, since Alexander the Great had conquered parts of India in the fourth century B.C. But there were many reasons why nobody had tried to explore them. In the first place, great distances and many natural dangers were involved. Marco Polo described some of these: wild animals, hostile warriors belonging to the nomadic tribes living in central Asia, bandits—and the landscape itself, sometimes arid, sometimes mountainous, and always unknown. Besides, for centuries nobody had had any good reason to go venturing into unfamiliar and dangerous territory. By Marco Polo's day, however, this had changed. Europe had become a community of merchants and traders, and Venice was one of its wealthiest and fastest-growing states. The East was a

◄ Marco Polo leaves Venice in search of adventure. Although Polo began his journeys by ship, he also spent many years trekking across desolate miles on land. The artist is anonymous, but paintings such as this were traditionally done by monks.

rich source of gems, spices, silks, and other precious goods, and merchants began looking for new and more profitable trade routes.

There were other problems: politics and religion. The Middle East was controlled by Muslims, and centuries of conflict between them and the Christians meant that any journey to the East by a European could be dangerous. Beyond the Muslim communities lived the Mongols, an alliance of Asian tribes deeply feared for their ferocity and military skill. By the thirteenth century, the Mongol Empire stretched from the edge of Europe to China.

Despite the dangers, in 1260 two of Marco Polo's uncles set out for China, and eventually visited the Emperor Kubla Khan. He instructed them to return, and this they did, leaving Venice in 1271, and this time taking the seventeen-year-old Marco Polo along with them. After crossing Asia, the party reached the Khan's palace at Khan-balik in 1275. For the next twenty years Marco Polo acted as a diplomat for the Khan, traveling on missions throughout the empire, and recording what he saw. In 1293, Marco Polo

and his uncles left, escorting an imperial princess to her wedding in Persia. Two years later they reached Venice.

Marco did not write anything of his adventures until he was captured during a war between Venice and the city of Genoa and imprisoned. There he met a writer named Rustichello, and together they composed Marco Polo's *Description of the World* (now known simply as the *Travels*). It became one of the best-known books of the age before the invention of printing. Marco Polo's name has survived to this day as belonging to one of history's greatest travelers.

Responding

1. One of the most treacherous parts of Marco Polo's journeys was traveling the Silk Road of Asia. Research the Silk Road. Write a paragraph describing the challenges travelers faced on this route.

2. Marco Polo began his journeys at an age when most people today are still in high school. Imagine you are Marco Polo. Write a journal entry describing the first days of your journey.

Reading Mini-Lesson

Distinguishing Between Fact and Opinion

Which of the following statements are facts?

1. Franklin Delano Roosevelt was the best President we ever had.
2. Girls are smarter than boys.
3. The worst state in the United States to live in is (you fill it in).

Did you say that none of the statements is a fact? If so, you're right! All three statements are opinions—they are personal views that may or may not be based on evidence. When trying to separate fact from opinion, be wary of words such as *always, never, everybody, nobody, best, worst, all,* and *none.* These words usually reveal a personal judgment or viewpoint.

In judging fact and opinion, *who* the reporter is makes a difference. We have several reporters in the article about Marco Polo on pages 381–382. First, in the original source, we have Marco Polo and his co-author, Rustichello. Then we have the present-day writer of the article, who also has opinions. Look at the last sentence of the first paragraph. Whose opinion is it that Marco Polo became a favorite of the Emperor? It could be any one of the three contributors.

How do you recognize a fact? One measure is universality. For example, in the metric system, 1000 milliliters is *always* 1 liter, no matter whom you ask and no matter where you are. Another measure is that facts can usually be verified or demonstrated by others. Reports by just a single observer are not accepted as fact.

Activity Options

Opinion: Marco Polo is one of history's greatest travelers.
Evidence 1:
Evidence 2:

1. The article on Marco Polo ends with the opinion that Marco Polo is "one of history's greatest travelers." Find two pieces of evidence in the selection that can be used to support this opinion. Set up your work as at the left.

2. Review the Marco Polo article carefully and find two more examples of opinions that are *not* signaled by key words such as *always, never, everybody, nobody, best, worst, all,* and *none.*

3. Work with a partner to go on a fact-and-opinion-finding mission in your local newspaper.

Part Two

The Bridge to Understanding

We know how important bridges across bodies of water are in linking people together. Other kinds of bridges also exist that make equally important connections. These bridges enlarge our understanding of the world and help us sense a oneness with others.

✿ **Multicultural Connection** Being a member of a **group** involves appreciating others and identifying with them both within and across cultural boundaries. Learning how you connect to various groups helps you better understand yourself. The stories and poems that follow are all about people who have reached beyond themselves, from one person or group to another, to build bridges to understanding.

Literature

Walter Dean Myers	**Jeremiah's Song** ◆ short story	 386
Ashley Bryan	**Storyteller** ◆ poem	 393
Beryl Markham	**Brothers Are the Same** ◆ short story	 397
Jane Yolen	**Birthday Box** ◆ short story	 410
Merrill Markoe	**The Dog Diaries** ◆ essay	 416
Shuntarō Tanikawa	**On Destiny** ◆ poem	 423
Zia Hyder	**Under This Sky** ◆ poem	 424
Laurence Yep	**We Are All One** ◆ Chinese folk tale	 429

Language Mini-Lesson ◆ Adding Punctuation for Clarity 434

Interdisciplinary Study Timeless Tales

Sundiata Keita: The Legend and the King by Patricia and
    Fredrick McKissack ◆ history 435
The Storytellers ◆ art 438

Reading Mini-Lesson ◆ Using Time Order Relationships 440

Writing Workshop Narrative Writing

Bridging the Gap 441

Beyond Print Media Literacy

A Monster of a Storyboard 447

Before Reading

Jeremiah's Song by Walter Dean Myers

Storyteller by Ashley Bryan

Walter Dean Myers
born 1937

As a child, Myers loved writing, but never thought it could be a "real job." He worked as a mail clerk and a messenger, until he decided to quit and just write. This story is about strong Southerners. It differs from much of his work because it is not set in New York City.

Ashley Bryan
born 1923

Author, poet, and illustrator, Bryan grew up in a tough neighborhood in New York City. He decided at a young age that drawing and painting were his best talents. Poetry, he feels, crosses all barriers, and is meaningful for everyone.

Building Background

Oral Tradition Storytelling is an ancient art. Long before people could write, they kept track of their histories by telling stories about them. Some groups even chose a person to memorize and tell those stories. Often, that person began in childhood to learn the group's history from an elder. As people learned to write, many tales that had passed by oral tradition from one storyteller to another were written down.

Getting into the Selections

Writer's Notebook As a character in one of these selections points out, stories about our past help us live in the present. That's one reason families often like to tell their own stories. Think about your family stories and the relatives who most enjoy telling them. In your notebook, make a list of family stories you have heard and who told them. If you don't have a storytelling family, list stories about yourself that you would like to tell your children.

Reading Tip

English Dialect Spoken language is usually less formal than written. When people talk with one another, they may use **colloquial** language, or everyday words. You might hear, "he was *fixing to* die," instead of "he was *preparing to* die." You also may hear ungrammatical language such as "you *ain't never* had *no*" instead of "you *haven't ever* had *any*." Writers use dialect in stories and poems to make characters seem more real. As you read "Jeremiah's Song," add other such expressions to a chart like the one below. Then tell what you think they mean.

English Dialect	Standard English
fixing to	preparing to
have a regular fit	become very angry
make no notice of	pay no attention to

Jeremiah's Song

WALTER DEAN MYERS

I knowed my cousin Ellie was gonna be mad when Macon Smith come around to the house. She didn't have no use for Macon even when things was going right, and when Grandpa Jeremiah was fixing to die I just knowed she wasn't gonna be liking him hanging around. Grandpa Jeremiah raised Ellie after her folks died and they used to be real close. Then she got to go on to college and when she come back the first year she was different. She didn't want to hear all them stories he used to tell her anymore. Ellie said the stories wasn't true, and that's why she didn't want to hear them.

I didn't know if they was true or not. Tell the truth I didn't think much on it either way, but I liked to hear them stories. Grandpa Jeremiah said they wasn't stories anyway, they was songs.

"They the songs of my people," he used to say.

I didn't see how they was songs, not regular songs anyway. Every little thing we did down in Curry seemed to matter to Ellie that first summer she come home from college. You couldn't do nothin' that was gonna please her. She didn't even come to church much. 'Course she come on Sunday or everybody would have had a regular fit, but she didn't come on Thursday nights and she didn't come on Saturday even though she used to sing in the gospel choir.

"I guess they teachin' her somethin' worthwhile up there at Greensboro," Grandpa Jeremiah said to Sister Todd. "I sure don't see what it is, though."

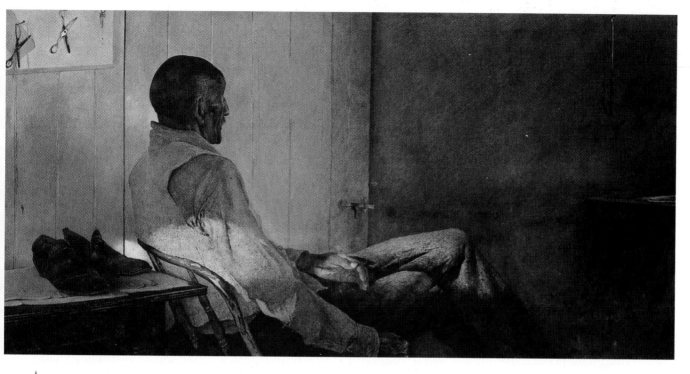

Andrew Wyeth painted *That Gentleman* in 1960 from a rather unusual perspective. Why do you think Wyeth approached his subject from this angle? Do you think it reveals something about the seated gentleman?

"You ain't never had no book learning, Jeremiah," Sister Todd shot back. She wiped at where a trickle of sweat made a little path through the white dusting powder she put on her chest to keep cool. "Them old ways you got ain't got nothing for these young folks."

"I guess you right," Grandpa Jeremiah said.

He said it but I could see he didn't like it none. He was a big man with a big head and had most all his hair even if it was white. All that summer, instead of sitting on the porch telling stories like he used to when I was real little, he would sit out there by himself while Ellie stayed in the house and watched the television or read a book. Sometimes I would think about asking him to tell me one of them stories he used to tell but

they was too scary now that I didn't have nobody to sleep with but myself. I asked Ellie to sleep with me but she wouldn't.

"You're nine years old," she said, sounding real proper. "You're old enough to sleep alone."

I *knew* that. I just wanted her to sleep with me because I liked sleeping with her. Before she went off to college she used to put cocoa butter on her arms and face and it would smell real nice. When she come back from college she put something else on, but that smelled nice too.

It was right after Ellie went back to school that Grandpa Jeremiah had him a stroke[1] and Macon started coming

---

1. **stroke,** a sudden loss of power to feel, think, or move, caused by a blood clot or bleeding in the brain.

around. I think his mama probably made him come at first, but you could see he liked it. Macon had always been around, sitting over near the stuck window at church or going on the blueberry truck when he went picking down at Mister Gregory's place. For a long time he was just another kid, even though he was older'n me, but then, all of a sudden, he growed something fierce. I used to be up to his shoulder one time and then, before I could turn around good, I was only up to his shirt pocket. He changed too. When he used to just hang around with the other boys and play ball or shoot at birds he would laugh a lot. He didn't laugh so much anymore and I figured he was just about grown. When Grandpa got sick he used to come around and help out with things around the house that was too hard for me to do. I mean, I could have done all the chores, but it would just take me longer.

When the work for the day was finished and the sows fed, Grandpa would kind of ease into one of his stories and Macon, he would sit and listen to them and be real interested. I didn't mind listening to the stories when Grandpa told them to Macon because he would be telling them in the middle of the afternoon and they would be past my mind by the time I had to go to bed.

Macon had an old guitar he used to mess with, too. He wasn't too bad on it, and sometimes Grandpa would tell him to play a tune. He could play something he called "the Delta Blues" real good, but when Sister Todd or somebody from the church come around he'd play "Precious Lord" or "Just a Closer Walk With Thee."

Grandpa Jeremiah had been feeling poorly from that stroke, and one of his legs got a little drag to it. Just about the time Ellie come from school the next summer he was real sick. He was breathing loud so you could hear it even in the next room and he would stay in bed a lot even when there was something that needed doing or fixing.

"I don't think he's going to make it much longer," Dr. Crawford said. "The only thing I can do is to give him something for the pain."

"Are you sure of your diagnosis?" Ellie asked. She was sitting around the table with Sister Todd, Deacon Turner, and his little skinny yellow wife.

Dr. Crawford looked at Ellie like he was surprised to hear her talking. "Yes, I'm sure," he said. "He had tests a few weeks ago and his condition was bad then."

"How much time he got?" Sister Todd asked.

"Maybe a week or two at best," Dr. Crawford said.

When he said that, Deacon Turner's wife started crying and goin' on and I give her a hard look but she just went on. I was the one who loved Grandpa Jeremiah the most and she didn't hardly even know him so I didn't see why she was crying.

Everybody started tiptoeing around the house after that. They would go in and ask Grandpa Jeremiah if he was comfortable and stuff like that or take him some food or a cold glass of lemonade. Sister Todd come over and stayed with us. Mostly what she did is make supper and do a lot of praying, which was good because I figured that maybe God would do something to make Grandpa Jeremiah well. When she wasn't doing that she was piecing on a fancy quilt she was making for some white people in Wilmington.

Ellie, she went around asking everybody how they felt about Dr. Crawford and then she went into town and asked about the tests and things. Sister Jenkins asked her if she thought she knowed more than Dr. Crawford, and Ellie rolled her eyes at her, but Sister Jenkins was reading out her Bible and didn't make no notice of it.

Then Macon come over.

He had been away on what he called "a little piece of a job" and hadn't heard how bad off Grandpa Jeremiah was. When he come over he talked to Ellie and she told him what was going on and then he got him a soft drink from the refrigerator and sat out on the porch and before you know it he was crying.

"He got Grandpa telling those old stories again," Ellie said.

You could look at his face and tell the difference between him sweating and the tears. The sweat was close against his skin and shiny and the tears come down fatter and more sparkly.

Macon sat on the porch, without saying a word, until the sun went down and the crickets started chirping and carrying on. Then he went in to where Grandpa Jeremiah was and stayed in there for a long time.

Sister Todd was saying that Grandpa Jeremiah needed his rest and Ellie went in to see what Macon was doing. Then she come out real mad.

"He got Grandpa telling those old stories again," Ellie said. "I told him Grandpa needed his rest and for him not to be staying all night."

He did leave soon, but bright and early the next morning Macon was back again. This time he brought his guitar with him and he went on in to Grandpa Jeremiah's room. I went in, too.

Grandpa Jeremiah's room smelled terrible. It was all closed up so no drafts could get on him and the whole room was smelled down with disinfect and medicine. Grandpa Jeremiah lay propped up on the bed and he was so gray he looked scary. His hair wasn't combed down and his head on the pillow with his white hair sticking out was enough to send me flying if Macon hadn't been there. He was

skinny, too. He looked like his skin got loose on his bones, and when he lifted his arms, it hung down like he was just wearing it instead of it being a part of him.

Macon sat slant-shouldered with his guitar across his lap. He was messin' with the guitar, not making any music, but just going over the strings as Grandpa talked.

"Old Carrie went around out back to where they kept the pigs penned up and she felt a cold wind across her face. . . ."

Grandpa Jeremiah was telling the story about how a old woman out-tricked the Devil and got her son back. I had heard the story before, and I knew it was pretty scary. "When she felt the cold breeze she didn't blink nary an eye, but looked straight ahead. . . ."

All the time Grandpa Jeremiah was talking I could see Macon fingering his guitar. I tried to imagine what it would be like if he was actually plucking the strings. I tried to fix my mind on that because I didn't like the way the story went with the old woman wrestling with the Devil.

We sat there for nearly all the afternoon until Ellie and Sister Todd come in and said that supper was ready. Me and Macon went out and ate some collard greens, ham hocks, and rice. Then Macon he went back in and listened to some more of Grandpa's stories until it was time for him to go home. I wasn't about to go in there and listen to no stories at night.

Dr. Crawford come around a few days later and said that Grandpa Jeremiah was doing a little better.

"You think the Good Lord gonna pull him through?" Sister Todd asked.

"I don't tell the Good Lord what He should or should not be doing," Dr. Crawford said, looking over at Sister Todd and at Ellie. "I just said that *my* patient seems to be doing okay for his condition."

have to get away from the kind of life that keeps us in the past."

She didn't say why we should be trying to get away from the stories and I really didn't care too much. All I knew was that when Macon was sitting in the room with Grandpa Jeremiah I wasn't nearly as scared as I used to be when it was just me and Ellie listening. I told that to Macon.

"You getting to be a big man, that's all," he said.

That was true. Me and Macon was getting to be good friends, too. I didn't even mind so much when he started being friends with Ellie later. It seemed kind of natural, almost like Macon was supposed to be there with us instead of just visiting.

Grandpa wasn't getting no better, but he wasn't getting no worse, either.

"You liking Macon now?" I asked Ellie when we got to the middle of July. She was dishing out a plate of smothered chops for him and I hadn't even heard him ask for anything to eat.

"Macon's funny," Ellie said, not answering my question. "He's in there listening to all of those old stories like he's really interested in them. It's almost as if he and Grandpa Jeremiah are talking about something more than the stories, a secret language."

I didn't think I was supposed to say anything about that to Macon, but once, when Ellie, Sister Todd, and Macon were out on the porch shelling butter beans after Grandpa got

"He been telling Macon all his stories," I said.

"Macon doesn't seem to understand that Grandpa Jeremiah needs his strength," Ellie said. "Now that he's improving, we don't want him to have a setback."

"No use in stopping him from telling his stories," Dr. Crawford said. "If it makes him feel good it's as good as any medicine I can give him."

I saw that this didn't set with Ellie, and when Dr. Crawford had left I asked her why.

"Dr. Crawford means well," she said, "but we

tired and was resting, I went into his room and told him what Ellie had said.

"She said that?" Grandpa Jeremiah's face was skinny and old looking but his eyes looked like a baby's, they was so bright.

"Right there in the kitchen is where she said it," I said. "And I don't know what it mean but I was wondering about it."

"I didn't think she had any feeling for them stories," Grandpa Jeremiah said. "If she think we talking secrets, maybe she don't."

"I think she getting a feeling for Macon," I said.

"That's okay, too," Grandpa Jeremiah said. "They both young."

"Yeah, but them stories you be telling, Grandpa, they about old people who lived a long time ago," I said.

"Well, those the folks you got to know about," Grandpa Jeremiah said. "You think on what those folks been through, and what they was feeling, and you add it up with what you been through and what you been feeling, then you got you something."

"What you got, Grandpa?"

"You got you a bridge," Grandpa said. "And a meaning. Then when things get so hard you about to break, you can sneak across that bridge and see some folks who went before you and see how they didn't break. Some got bent and some got twisted and a few fell along the way, but they didn't break."

"Am I going to break, Grandpa?"

"You? As strong as you is?" Grandpa Jeremiah pushed himself up on his elbow and give me a look. "No way you going to break, boy. You gonna be strong as they come. One day you gonna tell all them stories I told you to your young'uns and they'll be as strong as you."

"Suppose I ain't got no stories, can I make some up?"

"Sure you can, boy. You make 'em up and twist 'em around. Don't make no mind. Long as you got 'em."

"Is that what Macon is doing?" I asked. "Making up stories to play on his guitar?"

"He'll do with 'em what he see fit, I suppose," Grandpa Jeremiah said. "Can't ask more than that from a man."

Then when things get so hard...you can sneak across that bridge and see some folks who went before you.

It rained the first three days of August. It wasn't a hard rain but it rained anyway. The mailman said it was good for the crops over East but I didn't care about that so I didn't pay him no mind. What I did mind was when it rain like that the field mice come in and get in things like the flour bin and I always got the blame for leaving it open.

When the rain stopped I was pretty glad. Macon come over and sat with Grandpa and had something to eat with us. Sister Todd come over, too.

"How Grandpa doing?" Sister Todd asked. "They been asking about him in the church."

"He's doing all right," Ellie said.

"He's kind of quiet today," Macon said. "He was just talking about how the hogs needed breeding."

"He must have run out of stories to tell," Sister Todd said. "He'll be repeating on himself like my father used to do. That's the way I *hear* old folks get."

Everybody laughed at that because Sister Todd was pretty old, too. Maybe we was all happy because the sun was out after so much rain. When Sister Todd went in to take Grandpa Jeremiah a plate of potato salad with no mayonnaise like he liked it, she told him about how people was asking for him and he told her to tell them he was doing okay and to remember him in their prayers.

Sister Todd came over the next afternoon, too, with some rhubarb pie with cheese on it, which is my favorite pie. When she took a piece into Grandpa Jeremiah's room she come right out again and told Ellie to go fetch the Bible.

I cried hard even though I told myself that I wasn't going to cry...

It was a hot day when they had the funeral. Mostly everybody was there. The church was hot as anything, even though they had the window open. Some yellowjacks flew in and buzzed around Sister Todd's niece and then around Deacon Turner's wife and settled right on her hat and stayed there until we all stood and sang "Soon-a Will Be Done."

At the graveyard Macon played "Precious Lord" and I cried hard even though I told myself that I wasn't going to cry the way Ellie and Sister Todd was, but it was such a sad thing when we left and Grandpa Jeremiah was still out to the grave that I couldn't help it.

During the funeral and all, Macon kind of told everybody where to go and where to sit and which of the three cars to ride in. After it was over he come by the house and sat on the front porch and played on his guitar. Ellie was standing leaning against the rail and she was crying but it wasn't a hard crying. It was a soft crying, the kind that last inside of you for a long time.

Macon was playing a tune I hadn't heard before. I thought it might have been what he was working at when Grandpa Jeremiah was telling him those stories and I watched his fingers but I couldn't tell if it was or not. It wasn't nothing special, that tune Macon was playing, maybe halfway between them Delta blues he would do when Sister Todd wasn't around and something you would play at church. It was something different and something the same at the same time. I watched his fingers go over that guitar and figured I could learn that tune one day if I had a mind to.

Storyteller

Ashley Bryan

Emerald
Grew up in flowers
Hibiscus, poinsettia, bougainvillea
Birds pieced her stories together
5 With song

She sheltered
Under stories
Tropical rains, lightning,
War of thunder
10 Couldn't disturb her

Later she told stories
To grandchildren
Backed by Gabriel's horn[1]
Her words skirted thorns
15 Winged
Agile as birdsong
Dazzling as jazz

---

1. **Gabriel's horn** (gā′brē əlz), in the Bible,
the angel Gabriel is God's messenger;
traditionally, he blows a trumpet to
announce good news.

Ashley Bryan, who wrote the poem "Storyteller," also painted
this picture. In what ways are the poem and the painting
similar?

After Reading

Making Connections

1. If the characters in the story "Jeremiah's Song" were musical instruments, which would each be? Explain your choices.

2. Which of the characters in the story or poem do you think has the greatest understanding of what life is about? Explain.

3. How would the story change if the author had used formal language instead of **dialect**?

4. How did storytelling help both Grandpa Jeremiah in the story and Emerald in the poem?

5. What valuable lesson or **moral** could you learn from Macon?

6. After she goes to college and gets "book learning," Ellie changes. What do you think Ellie failed to learn in college, and why?

7. The narrator in the story doesn't like scary stories. Explain what kind of stories you like best, and why.

Literary Focus: Setting

You can figure out a story's **setting**—where and when it takes place—through what the writer states and suggests. The writer of "Jeremiah's Song" says the story takes place in Curry, but leaves it up to you to figure out that Curry is probably in North Carolina through the indirect clue that Ellie attends college at Greensboro. The writer never describes Curry, but the details he chooses suggest what it is like. You may assume that the narrator lives in a community in which most people are not highly educated, judging by their colloquial language. What can you infer about the time period of the story from the references to a "blueberry truck," a "flour bin," and a doctor who treats patients in their own homes?

Vocabulary Study

Copy the following form and fill it in for the word *diagnosis.*

Word: diagnosis

Source: (Write the source sentence from the story and underline the word.)

Best Guess: (the meaning you get from the surrounding context)

Dictionary Meaning: (part of speech and definition)

Sentence: (Make up a new sentence that correctly uses the word.)

Expressing Your Ideas

Writing Choices

Create a Bridge Refer to the list of family stories that you entered in your notebook. Select one of the stories to write out as a piece of **family history.** Include details and dialogue where relevant.

Your Opinion Counts Do you agree with Grandpa Jeremiah that knowing the stories of those who went before us helps us in the present? Write a **statement of opinion** in which you argue your case.

Gravestone Engraving Think about what you know about Grandpa Jeremiah, his life, and his stories. What should be put on his gravestone? Write a suitable **epitaph** for him, a short statement in his memory that sums up something important about his life or character.

Other Options

Sing it Out Grandpa Jeremiah suggests the stories he tells are like a song—the song of his people. Write a real **song** that tells one of your family stories, then perform it for the class. If you prefer, you can tape your song and play the tape for the class.

Quilting Bee Birds pieced Emerald's story together "with song" in the poem "Storyteller." Piece together your own **quilt design** representing Emerald's life that could be called "Storyteller's Song." Color your design or use pieces of colored paper or cloth.

Make a Meal Collard greens and ham hocks are just two of the traditional Southern foods mentioned in this story. Do some research on cooking in the southeastern United States. Then work with a group to create a **menu** for a restaurant that features traditional Southern foods. Name your restaurant, list the foods (giving tasty descriptions), and decorate your menu.

Before Reading

Brothers Are the Same

by Beryl Markham

Beryl Markham
1902–1986

Beryl Markham arrived in British East Africa from England as a child. While her father farmed the rich land, young Beryl hunted with the local tribal chief, played with his son, and soon learned to speak the African languages Swahili, Nandi, and Masai. She continued her unusual life as an adult, becoming first a racehorse trainer, then a commercial pilot. She was one of the first pilots to offer big game hunts by air, scouting the plains and flying hunters to their prey. In September 1936, Markham made the first solo flight across the Atlantic from east to west. She began to write later in life, putting down her memories of life in Africa.

Building Background

The Masai People On the border between Kenya and Tanzania, in the shadow of Mt. Kilimanjaro, lies the Serengeti Plain. This vast region varies from treeless grassland to thick forest and is home to millions of game animals, including lions, hyenas, gazelles, and zebras. Evidence shows that the Masai people have shared this homeland with the animals for at least 1,000 years. Originally they were warriors, but they have herded cattle on the dry grasslands of this region since about A.D. 900.

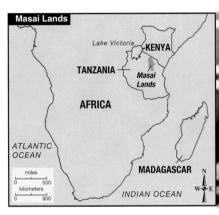

Getting into the Story

Writer's Notebook President Franklin D. Roosevelt once said, "The only thing we have to fear is fear itself." Sometimes when you're faced with a difficult task, the fear you might fail is so strong it is hard to get started. If you can get past that fear, the task itself often seems much easier. In your notebook, comment on Roosevelt's words. Have you ever had to overcome fear in order to accomplish something? How did you do it?

Reading Tip

Stop to Check Comprehension Have you ever been reading along and realized you had no idea what the last two paragraphs said? A good way to keep up your concentration is to stop occasionally and check your comprehension. Here are three ways to do that. First, you can ask yourself **questions** about what you've read and try to answer them. The printed questions in this story will help you do that. Second, if a really difficult sentence or paragraph trips you up, you can stop to **paraphrase,** or retell it in your own words. Third, stop from time to time to **summarize** sections of a story. Of course, if you find you don't understand something, you must reread it. Try using these suggestions as you read this story.

BROTHERS ARE THE SAME

BERYL MARKHAM

They are tall men, cleanly built and straight as the shafts of the spears they carry, and no one knows their tribal history, but there is some of Egypt in their eyes and the look of ancient Greece about their bodies. They are the Masai.

They are the color of worn copper and, with their graceful women, they live on the Serengeti Plain, which makes a carpet at the feet of high Kilimanjaro. In all of Africa there are today no better husbandmen[1] of cattle.

But once they were warriors and they have not forgotten that, nor have they let tradition die. They go armed, and to keep well-tempered the mettle[2] of their men, each youth among them must, when his hour comes, prove his right to manhood. He must meet in combat the only worthy enemy his people recognize—the destroyer of their cattle, the marauding master of the plains—the lion.

Thus, just before the dawning of a day in what these Masai call the Month of the Little Rains, such a youth with such a test before

him lay in a cleft of rock and watched the shadowed outlines of a deep ravine. For at least eight of his sixteen years, this youth, this young Temas, had waited for his moment. He had dreamed of it and lived it in a dozen ways—all of them glorious.

In all of the dreams he had confronted the lion with casual courage, he had presented his spear on the charging enemy with steadiness born of brave contempt—and always he had won the swift duel with half a smile on his lips. Always—in the dreams.

Now it was different. Now as he watched the place where the real lion lay, he had no smile.

He did not fear the beast. He was sure that in his bones and in his blood and in his heart he was not afraid. He was Masai, and legend said that no Masai had ever feared.

Yet in his mind Temas now trembled. Fear

---

1. **husbandman** (huz′bənd mən), farmer.
2. **mettle** (met′l), spirit; character.

of battle was a nonexistent thing—but fear of failure could be real, and was. It was real and living—and kept alive by the nearness of an enemy more formidable[3] than any lion—an enemy with the hated name Medoto.

It did not seem that he, Temas, could . . . prove equal to his comrades.

He thought of Medoto—of that Medoto who lay not far away in the deep grass watching the same ravine. Of that Medoto who, out of hate and jealousy over a mere girl, now hoped in his heart that Temas would flinch at the moment of his trial. That was it. That was the thing that kept the specter of failure dancing in his mind, until already it looked like truth.

CLARIFY: Explain what Temas fears most.

There were ten youths hidden about the ravine, and they would stage and witness the coming fight. They had tracked the lion to this, his lair,[4] and when the moment came, they would drive him, angered, upon Temas and then would judge his courage and his skill. Good or bad, that judgement would, like a brand mark, cling to him all his life.

But it was Medoto who would watch the closest for a sign, a gesture, a breath of fear in Temas. It was Medoto who would spread the word—Medoto who surely would cry "Coward!" if he could.

Temas squirmed under the heavy, unwholesome thought, then lifted his head and pierced the dim light with his eyes. To the east, the escarpment[5] stood like a wall against the rising sun. But to the north and to the west and to the south there were no horizons; the grey sky and the grey plain were part and

counterpart, and he was himself a shadow in his cleft of rock.

He was a long shadow, a lean shadow. The *shuka*[6] that he wore was now bound about his waist, giving freedom to his legs and arms. His necklace and bracelets were of shining copper, drawn fine and finely spiraled, and around each of his slender ankles there was a copper chain.

His long hair, bound by beaded threads, was a chaste[7] black column that lay between his shoulders, and his ears were pierced and hung with gleaming pendants. His nose was straight, with nostrils delicately flanged. The bones of his cheeks were high, the ridges of his jaw were hard, and his eyes were long and dark and a little brooding. He used them now to glance at his weapons, which lay beside him— a spear, a rawhide shield. These, and a short sword at his belt, were his armament.

He lowered his glance to the place he watched. The ravine was overgrown with a thicket of thorns and the light had not burst through it yet. When it did the lion within it would wake, and the moment would come.

A feeling almost of hopelessness surged through him. It did not seem that he, Temas, could in this great test prove equal to his comrades. All had passed it; all had earned the warrior's title—and none had faltered. Even Medoto—especially Medoto—had proven brave and more than ready for his cloak of manhood. Songs were sung about Medoto. In the evenings in the *manyatta*[8] when the cattle drowsed and the old men drank their honey wine, the girls would gather, and the young

---

3. **formidable** (fôr′mə də bəl), *adj.* hard to overcome; to be dreaded.
4. **lair** (ler, lar), den or resting place of a wild animal.
5. **escarpment** (e skärp′mənt), a steep slope; cliff.
6. **shuka** (shü′kə), a loose garment worn by Masai.
7. **chaste** (chāst), simple in style; undecorated.
8. **manyatta** (män yä′tə), a Masai camp.

▲ William Vincent created this colorful painting titled *Maasai, Masai Mara.* ☙ This warrior belongs to a **group** that places a high value on courage and tradition. Find examples from the story that illustrate these values.

Brothers Are the Same   **399**

men, too, and they would chant to the heroes of their hearts.

But none chanted to Temas. Not yet. Perhaps they never would—not one of them. Not even . . .

He shook his head in anger. He had not meant to think of her—of Kileghen of the soft, deep-smiling eyes and the reedbuck's grace. Even she, so rightly named after the star Venus, had only last night sung to Medoto, and he to her, laughing the while, as Temas, the yet unproven, had clung to the saving shadows, letting his fury burn. Could she not make up her mind between them? Must it always be first one and then the other?

He saw it all with the eye of his memory—all too clearly. He saw even the sneer of Medoto on the day the elder warrior, the chief of them all, had tendered Temas his spear with the wise words: "Now at last this weapon is your own, but it is only wood and steel and means nothing until it changes to honor, or to shame, within your grasp. Soon we shall know!"

And soon they should! But Medoto had laughed then. Medoto had said, "It seems a heavy spear, my comrade, for one so slight— a big weight for any but a man!" And Temas had made no answer. How could he with Kileghen leaning there against the *boma*[9] as though she heard nothing, yet denying her innocence with that quiet, ever-questing smile? At whom had she smiled? At Medoto for his needless malice[10]—or at Temas for his acceptance of it?

> **CONNECT:** If you were Kileghen, how would you have felt about the actions of these two young men?

He did not know. He knew only that he had walked away carrying the unstained spear

a little awkwardly. And that the joy of having it was quickly dead.

Now he spat on the earth where he rested. He raised a curse against Medoto—a harsh, a bitter curse. But in the midst of it he stiffened and grew tense. Suddenly he lay as still as sleep and watched only the ravine and listened, as to the tone of some familiar silence.

It was the silence of a waking lion, for morning light had breached the thicket, and within his lair the lion was roused.

Within his lair the lion sought wakefulness as suspicion came to him on the cool, unmoving air. Under the bars of sunlight that latticed his flanks and belly, his coat was short and shining. His mane was black and evenly grown. The muscles of his forelegs were not corded, but flat, and the muscles of his shoulders were laminated like sheaths of metal.

Now he smelled men. Now as the sunlight fell in streams upon his sorrel coat and warmed his flanks, his suspicion and then his anger came alive. He had no fear. Whatever lived he judged by strength—or lack of it— and men were puny. And yet the scent of them kindled fire in his brooding eyes and made him contemplate his massive paws.

He arose slowly, without sound—almost without motion—and peered outward through the wall of thorns. The earth was mute, expectant, and he did not break the spell. He only breathed.

The lion breathed and swung his tail in easy, rhythmic arcs and watched the slender figure of a human near him in a cleft of rock.

Temas had risen, too. On one knee now, he waited for the signal of the lifted spears.

Of his ten comrades he could see but two or three—a tuft of warrior's feathers; here and there a gleaming arm. Presently all would leap from the places where they hid, and the

---

9. **boma** (bō′mə), the wall around a Masai camp.
10. **malice** (mal′is), *n.* a wish to hurt or make suffer; spite.

Masai battle cry would slash through the silence. And then the lion would act.

But the silence held. The interminable[11] instant hung like a drop that would not fall, and Temas remembered many of the rules, the laws that governed combat with a lion—but not enough, for stubbornly, wastefully, foolishly, his mind nagged at fear of disgrace—fear of failure. Fear of Medoto's ringing laughter in the *manyatta*—of Kileghen's every-questing smile.

"I shall fail," he thought. "I shall fail before Medoto and, through his eyes, she will see my failure. I must fail," he said, "because now I see that I am trembling."

And he was. His hand was loose upon the long steel spear—too loose, the arm that held the rawhide shield was hot and too unsteady. If he had ever learned to weep he would have wept—had there been time.

F rom the deep grass, from the shade of anthills, from clustered rocks, warriors sprang like flames. . . .

But the instant vanished—and with it, silence. From the deep grass, from the shade of anthills, from clustered rocks, warriors sprang like flames, and as they sprang they hurled upon the waiting lion their shrill arrogant[12] challenge, their scream of battle.

Suddenly the world was small and inescapable. It was an arena whose walls were tall young men that shone like worn gold in the sun, and in this shrunken world there were Temas and the lion.

He did not know when or how he had left the rock. It was as if the battle cry had lifted him from it and placed him where he stood—a dozen paces from the thicket. He did not know when the lion had come forward to the challenge, but the lion was there.

The lion waited. The ring of warriors waited. Temas did not move.

His long Egyptian eyes swept around the circle. All was perfect—too perfect. At every point a warrior stood blocking the lion from improbable retreat—and of these Medoto was one. Medoto stood near—a little behind Temas and to the right. His shield bore proud colors of the proven warrior. He was lean and proud, and upon his level stare he weighed each movement Temas made, though these were hesitant and few.

For the lion did not seek escape, nor want it. His shifting yellow eyes burned with even fire. They held neither fear nor fury—only the hard and regal wrath of the challenged tyrant. The strength of either of his forearms was alone greater than the entire strength of any of these men; his speed in the attack was blinding speed, shattering speed. And with such knowledge, with such sureness of himself, the lion stood in the tawny grass and stared his scorn while the sun rose higher and warmed the scarcely breathing men.

The lion would charge. He would choose one of the many and charge that one. Yet the choice must not be his to make, for through the generations—centuries, perhaps—the code of the Masai decreed that the challenger must draw the lion upon him. By gesture and by voice it can be done. By movement, by courage.

Temas knew the time for this had come. He straightened where he stood and gripped his heavy spear. He held his shield before him, tight on his arm, and he advanced, step by slow step.

The gaze of the lion did not at once swing

---

11. **interminable** (in tėr′mə nə bəl), *adj.* seemingly endless.
12. **arrogant** (ar′ə gənt), *adj.* overly proud and rude, especially to those considered inferior.

to him. But every eye was on him, and the strength of one pair—Medoto's—burned in his back like an unhealed scar.

A kind of anger began to run in Temas's blood. It seemed unjust to him that in this crucial moment, at this first great trial of his courage, his enemy and harshest judge must be a witness. Surely Medoto could see the points of sweat that now rose on his forehead and about his lips as he moved upon the embattled lion. Surely Medoto could see—or sense—the hesitance of his advance—almost hear, perhaps, the pounding of his heart!

He gripped the shaft of his spear until pain stung the muscles of his hand. The lion had crouched and Temas stood suddenly within the radius of his leap. The circle of warriors had drawn closer, tighter, and there was no sound save the sound of their uneven breathing.

The lion crouched against the reddish earth, head forward. The muscles of his massive quarters were taut, his body was a drawn bow. And, as a swordsman unsheaths his blade, so he unsheathed his fangs and chose his man.

It was not Temas.

As if in contempt for this confused and untried youth who paused within his reach, the lion's eyes passed him by and fastened hard upon the stronger figure of another, upon the figure of Casaro, a warrior of many combats and countless victories.

All saw it. Temas saw it, and for an instant—for a shameless breath of time—he felt an overwhelming ease of heart, relief, deliverance, not from danger, but from trial. He swept his glance around the ring. None watched him now. All action, all thought was frozen by the duel of wills between Casaro and the beast.

Slowly the veteran Casaro sank upon one knee and raised his shield. Slowly the lion gathered the power of his body for the leap. And then it happened.

From behind Temas, flung by Medoto's hand, a stone no larger than a grain of maize shot through the air and struck the lion.

No more was needed. The bolt was loosed.

But not upon Casaro, for if from choice the regal prowler of the wilderness had first preferred an opponent worthy of *his* worth, he now, under the sting of a hurled pebble, preferred to kill that human whose hand was guilty.

SUMMARIZE: Briefly describe the lion hunt to this point.

He charged at once, and as he charged, the young Temas was, in a breath, transformed from doubting boy to man. All fear was gone—all fear of fear—and as he took the charge, a light almost of ecstasy burned in his eyes, and the spirit of his people came to him.

Over the rim of his shield he saw fury take form. Light was blotted from his eyes as the dark shape descended upon him—for the lion's last leap carried him above the shield, the spear, the youth, so that, looking upward from his crouch, Temas, for a sliver of time, was intimate[13] with death.

He did not yield. He did not think or feel or consciously react. All was simple. All now happened as in the dreams, and his mind was an observer of his acts.

He saw his own spear rise in a swift arc, his own shield leap on his bended arm, his own eyes seek the vital spot—and miss it.

But he struck. He struck hard, not wildly or too soon, but exactly at the precise, the ripened moment, and saw his point drive full into the shoulder of the beast. It was not enough. In that moment his spear was torn from his grasp, his shield vanished, claws

---

13. **intimate** (in′tə mit), *adj.* very familiar; closely acquainted.

▲ *Majestic King* was also painted by William Vincent. Does this image portray the characterisics of the lion that the author depicts in the story?

furrowed the flesh of his chest, ripping deep. The weight and the power of the charge overwhelmed him.

He was down. Dust and blood and grass and the pungent[14] lion smell were mingled, blended, and in his ears an enraged, triumphant roar overlaid the shrill, high human cry of his comrades.

His friends were about to make the kill that must be his. Yet his hands were empty, he was caught, he was being dragged. He had scarcely felt the long crescentic[15] teeth close on his thigh, it had been so swift. Time itself could not have moved so fast.

A lion can drag a fallen man, even a fighting man, into thicket or deep grass with incredible ease and with such speed as to outdistance even a hurled spear. But sometimes this urge to plunder first and destroy later is a saving thing. It saved Temas. That and his Masai sword, which now was suddenly in his hand.

Perhaps pain dulled his reason, but reason

---

14. **pungent** (pun′jənt), *adj.* sharp; powerful.
15. **crescentic** (kre sen′tik), shaped like a crescent, or first-quarter moon.

is a sluggard ally to any on the edge of death. Temas made a cylinder of his slender body, and holding the sword flat against his leg, he whirled, and whirling, felt the fangs tear loose the flesh of his thigh, freeing it, freeing him. And, as he felt it, he lunged.

It was quick. It was impossible, it was mad, but it was Masai madness, and it was done. Dust clothed the tangled bodies of the lion and the youth so that those who clamored[16] close to strike the saving blows saw nothing but this cloud and could not aim into its form-less shape. Nor had they need to. Suddenly, as if *En-Gai* himself—God and protector of these men of wilderness—had stilled the scene with a lifted hand, all movement stopped, all sound was dead.

The dust was gone like a vanquished[17] shadow, and the great rust body of the lion lay quiet on the rust-red earth. Over it, upon it, his sword still tight in his hand, the youth lay breathing, bleeding. And, beyond that, he also smiled.

He could smile because the chant of vic-tory burst now like drumbeats from his com-rades' throats—the paeans[18] of praise fell on him where he lay, the sun struck bright through shattered clouds; the dream was true. In a dozen places he was hurt, but these would heal.

And so he smiled. He raised himself, and swaying slightly like any warrior weak in sinew but strong in spirit from his wounds, he stood with pride and took his accolade.[19]

And then his smile left him. It was outdone by the broader, harder smile of another—for Medoto was tall and straight before him, and with his eyes and with his lips Medoto seemed to say: "It is well—this cheer-ing and this honor. But it will pass—and we two have a secret, have we not? We know who threw the stone that brought the lion upon you when you stood hoping in your heart that

it would charge another. You stood in fear then, you stood in cowardice. We two know this, and no one else. But there is one who might, if she were told, look not to you but to the earth in shame when you pass by. Is this not so?"

Yes, it was so, and Temas, so lately happy, shrank within himself and swayed again. He saw the young Kileghen's eyes and did not wish to see them. But for Medoto's stone, the spear of Temas would yet be virgin, clean, unproved—a thing of futile vanity.

PREDICT: What do you think will happen next between the two enemies?

He straightened. His comrades—the true warriors, of which even now he was not one—had in honor to a fierce and vanquished enemy laid the dead lion on a shield and lifted him. In triumph and with songs of praise (mistaken praise!) for Temas, they were already beginning their march toward the waiting *manyatta.*

Temas turned from his field of momentary triumph, but Medoto lingered at his side.

And now it will come, Temas thought. Now what he has said with his eyes he will say with his mouth, and I am forced to listen. He looked into Medoto's face—a calm, unmov-ing face—and thought: It is true that this, my enemy, saw the shame of my first fear. He will tell it to everyone—and to her. So, since I am lost, it is just as well to strike a blow against him. I am not so hurt that I cannot fight at least once more.

His sword still hung at his side. He grasped it now and said, "We are alone and we are ene-mies. What you are about to charge me with is

---

16. **clamor** (klam′ər), *v.* make a loud noise or uproar.
17. **vanquish** (vang′kwish), *v.* overcome; defeat.
18. **paean** (pē′ən), song of praise, joy, or triumph.
19. **accolade** (ak′ə lād), *n.* praise or recognition.

true—but, if I was a coward before the lion, I am not a coward before you, and I will not listen to sneering words!"

For a long moment, Medoto's eyes peered into the eyes of Temas. The two youths stood together on the now deserted plain and neither moved. Overhead the sun hung low and red and poured its burning light upon the drying grass, upon the thorn trees that stood in lonely clusters, upon the steepled shrines of drudging ants. There was no sound of birds, no rasping of cicada wings, no whispering of wind.

And into this dearth, into this poverty of sound, Medoto cast his laugh. His lips parted, and the low music of his throat was laughter without mirth; there was sadness in it, a note of incredulity,[20] but not more, not mockery, not challenge.

A man asks not the motives of a friend, but demands reason from his enemy.

He stared into the proud unhappy face of Temas. He plunged the shaft of his spear into the earth and slipped the shield from his arm. At last he spoke.

He said, "My comrade, we who are Masai know the saying: 'A man asks not the motives of a friend, but demands reason from his enemy.' It is a just demand. If, until now, I have seemed your enemy, it was because I feared you would be braver than I, for when I fought my lion my knees trembled and my heart was white—until that charge was made. No one knew that, and I am called Medoto, the unflinching, but I flinched. I trembled."

He stepped closer to Temas. He smiled. "It is no good to lie," he said. "I wanted you to

fail, but when I saw you hesitate I could not bear it because I remembered my own hour of fear. It was then I threw the stone—not to shame you, but to save you from shame—for I saw that your fear was not fear of death, but fear of failure—and this I understood. You are a greater warrior than I—than any—for who but the bravest would do what you have done?" Medoto paused and watched a light of wonderment kindle in Temas's eye. The hand of Temas slipped from his sword, his muscles relaxed. Yet, for a moment, he did not speak, and as he looked at Medoto, it was clear to both that the identical thought, the identical vision, had come to each of them. It was the vision that must and always will come to young men everywhere, the vision of a girl.

Now this vision stood between them, and nothing else. But it stood like a barrier, the last barrier.

And Medoto destroyed it. Deliberately, casually, he reached under the folds of his flowing *shuka* and brought from it a slender belt of leather crusted with beads. It was the work and the possession of a girl, and both knew which girl. Kileghen's handiwork was rare enough, but recognized in many places.

"This," said Medoto, "this, I was told to bring, and I was told in these words: 'If in his battle the young Temas proves himself a warrior and a man, make this belt my gift to him so that I may see him wear it when he returns. But if he proves a coward, Medoto, the belt is for you to keep.'"

Medoto looked at the bright gift in his hands. "It is yours, Temas!" He held it out. "I meant to keep it. I planned ways to cheat you of it, but I do not think a man can cheat the truth. I have seen you fight better than I have ever fought, and now this gift belongs to you.

---

20. **incredulity** (in′krə dyü′lə tē), *n.* lack of belief; doubt.

It is her wish and between us you are at last her choice." He laid the belt on the palm of Temas's open hand and reached once more for his shield and spear. "We will return now," Medoto said, "for the people are waiting. She is waiting. I will help you walk."

But Temas did not move. Through the sharp sting of his wounds, above his joy in the promise that now lay in his hands, he felt another thing, a curious, swelling pride in this new friendship. He looked into the face of Medoto and smiled, timidly, then broadly. And then he laughed and drew his sword and cut the beaded belt in half.

"No," he said. "If she has chosen, then she must choose again, for we are brothers now and brothers are the same!"

He entwined one half of the severed belt in the arm band of Medoto, and the other half he hung, as plainly, on himself.

"We begin again," he said, "for we are equal to each other, and this is a truth that she must know. She must make her choice on other things but skill in battle, since only men may judge a warrior for his worth!"

It was not far to the *manyatta* and they walked it arm in arm. They were tall together, and strong and young, and somehow full of song. Temas walked brokenly for he was hurt, and yet he sang:

Oi-Konyek of the splendid shield
Has heard the lowing of the kine . . .

And when they entered the gates of the *manyatta*, there were many of every age to welcome Temas, for his lion had been brought and his story told. They cheered and cried his name and led him past the open doors to the peaceful earthen houses to the *singara*, which is the place reserved for warriors.

Medoto did not leave him, nor he Medoto, and it was strange to some to see the enemies transformed and strong in friendship, when yesterday their only bond was hate.

It was strange to one who stood against the *boma* wall, a slender girl of fragile beauty and level, seeking eyes. She was as young as morning, as anticipant. But this anticipation quickly dimmed as she saw the token she had made, one half borne hopefully by Medoto, the other as hopefully carried by Temas!

Both sought her in the gathered crowd, both caught her glance and gave the question with their eyes. Both, in the smug, self-satisfied way of men, swaggered a little.

So the girl paused for an instant and frowned a woman's frown. But then, with musing, lidded eyes, she smiled a woman's smile—and stranger yet, the smile had more of triumph in it, and less of wonder, than it might have had.

After Reading

Making Connections

1. What do you think about the Masai test of manhood? Explain.

2. If you were Kileghen, which warrior would you choose, and why?

3. Do you think Temas and Medoto will remain friends after Kileghen chooses one or the other? Explain.

4. Rank the characters Temas, Medoto, Kileghen, and the lion in order of importance from one (as most important) to four according to how much each moved along the **plot** of the story. Explain your rankings.

5. ☝ This story involves certain **group** expectations the Masai have for their youth. Could the author have written a similar story about American youth? Explain.

6. Look back through the story at how the author describes the Masai. Tell what you learn about their **character** and appearance.

7. In the end of the story, Temas and Medoto feel a strong bond. Describe a similar bond you have with a friend or sibling.

Literary Focus: Plot

Most stories are built around a problem that must be solved. The **plot,** or story line, is divided into three parts: the events that lead to solving the problem, or **rising action;** the **climax,** or turning point; and the outcome, or **falling action.** These three parts can be shown on a diagram such as this.

In this story Temas must fight a lion, but he is not really most afraid of that. The real problem is his fear of failing. At what point in the story does that fear disappear? That is the climax. What events conclude the story? Use your answers to fill in a plot structure map organized like the one above.

Vocabulary Study

Decide if the following pairs of words are synonyms or antonyms, then write your answers on another sheet of paper.

formidable
malice
interminable
arrogant
intimate
pungent
clamor
vanquish
accolade
incredulity

1. arrogant - humble
2. pungent - mild
3. praise - accolade
4. interminable - endless
5. certainty - incredulity
6. vanquish - conquer
7. whisper - clamor
8. unfamiliar - intimate
9. formidable - terrible
10. malice - kindness

Expressing Your Ideas

Writing Choices

Family Ties Temas and Medoto are not really brothers. What do you think the title "Brothers Are the Same" means? Explain your answer in a short **essay.** Use quotes from the story to support your ideas.

Fight Your Lion Fighting a lion as a rite of passage to adulthood is not practical or desirable for young people today. There are other challenges that young Americans must meet, however. Work with a group to think of and **classify** in lists some of the tests that you face as you grow to maturity. Refer to the situation you described in your notebook.

Rites of Passage Temas was not specially selected to hunt a lion. Every young Masai man was put through the same ordeal. This rite of passage to adulthood was always conducted in the same way. Look back through the story and write a **summary** of the Masai ritual that made a boy a man.

Other Options

Tell Me a Story Temas's lion hunt will become part of the oral tradition of his people. How will storytellers of the future tell his story? Imagine you are a Masai storyteller and do a **dramatic presentation** of this story for the class.

On Display Collect illustrations and information on Masai life, including their weapons, jewelry, shelter, cattle, and so on. Work with a group to create a **bulletin board** on the Masai.

Lion Hunt Find details in the story that describe the area where Temas hunted his lion. Then use those details to create a **map** or **3-D model** of the hunting ground. You may wish to find some pictures of the Serengeti Plain to give you a better idea of how the area looks before you begin.

Before Reading

Birthday Box

by Jane Yolen

Jane Yolen
born 1939

"Stories do give us permission to have feelings; not only do they give permission to the author, but they also give it to the reader," Yolen says. She experienced the power of stories to help and heal people while writing a book after her mother's illness and death. That is one of the reasons Yolen writes stories like "Birthday Box." Another reason is that she simply enjoys telling a good story. She says, "I hope my stories amuse and entertain and move people, but in truth I'm just telling a story and what happens between the story and the listener is between the story and the listener." She began her writing career in first grade with a play about vegetables and over the years has written numerous books and stories of all kinds, many for children.

Building Background

Variations on a Theme Do you ever wonder where writers get their ideas? Johanna Hurwitz decided to explore this question in an unusual way. She proposed to put together a book in which every story had the same basic idea. She thought it would be interesting to see how many different ways authors could use the idea. So she invited writers to send her stories about a child who receives a beautifully wrapped but empty box on his or her birthday. The response she got included fantasy, fairy tales, poetry and realistic stories, including this one. No two stories were alike.

Getting into the Story

Discussion Almost any child would be disappointed to receive an empty box for a birthday gift. Have you ever received a gift you didn't understand or appreciate? Maybe it was something that was too old for you or too difficult to use or something that was "good for you" that you didn't want. Tell the class about any such gift that you can recall. How did you react when you received it? Did you ever begin to appreciate the gift? How would other class members have reacted to the same gift?

Reading Tip

Inferences Good readers use the details authors provide plus their own experience to make **inferences,** or form conclusions, about the characters and events in a story. For example, the main character in this story states, "But as Mama always reminded me whenever Dad finally remembered to send me something, it was the thought that counted, not the actual gift." From this detail, you can make the inference that the character's parents are divorced or separated and that she lives with her mother. What else can you infer?

   As you read the story, look for other opportunities the author presents for you to make inferences about characters and events.

Birthday Box

JANE YOLEN

I was ten years old when my mother died. Ten years old on that very day. Still she gave me a party of sorts. Sick as she was, Mama had seen to it, organizing it at the hospital. She made sure the doctors and nurses all brought me presents. We were good friends with them all by that time, because Mama had been in the hospital for so long.

The head nurse, V. Louise Higgins (I never did know what that *V* stood for), gave me a little box, which was sort of funny because she was the biggest of all the nurses there. I mean she was tremendous. And she was the only one who insisted on wearing all white. Mama had called her the great white shark when she was first admitted, only not to V. Louise's face. "All those needles," Mama had said. "Like teeth." But V. Louise was sweet, not sharklike at all, and she'd been so gentle with Mama.

I opened the little present first. It was a fountain pen, a real one, not a fake one like you get at Kmart.

"Now you can write beautiful stories, Katie," V. Louise said to me.

I didn't say that stories come out of your head, not out of a pen. That wouldn't have been polite, and Mama—even sick—was real big on politeness.

"Thanks, V. Louise," I said.

The Stardust Twins—which is what Mama called Patty and Tracey-lynn because they reminded her of dancers in an old-fashioned ballroom—gave me a present together. It was a diary and had a picture of a little girl in pink, reading in a garden swing. A little young for me, a little too cute. I mean, I read Stephen King and want to write like him. But as Mama always reminded me whenever Dad finally remembered to send me something, it was the thought that counted, not the actual gift.

"It's great," I told them. "I'll write in it with my new pen." And I wrote my name on the first page just to show them I meant it.

They hugged me and winked at Mama. She tried to wink back but was just too tired and shut both her eyes instead.

Lily, who is from Jamaica, had baked me some sweet bread. Mary Margaret gave me a gold cross blessed by the pope, which I put on even though Mama and I weren't church-goers. That was Dad's thing.

Then Dr. Dann, the intern who was on days, and Dr. Pucci, the oncologist (which is the fancy name for a cancer doctor), gave me a big box filled to the top with little presents, each wrapped up individually. All things they knew I'd love—paperback books and writing paper and erasers with funny animal heads and colored paper clips and a rubber stamp that printed FROM KATIE'S DESK and other stuff. They must have raided a stationery store.

There was one box, though, they held out till the end. It was about the size of a large top hat. The paper was deep blue and covered with stars; not fake stars but real stars, I mean, like a map of the night sky. The ribbon was two shades of blue with silver threads running through. There was no name on the card.

"Who's it from?" I asked.

None of the nurses answered, and the doctors both suddenly were studying the ceiling tiles with the kind of intensity[1] they usually

---

1. **intensity** (in ten′sə tē), *n.* great energy or strong feeling.

Eva Hesse, who painted this untitled image in 1964, once wrote of her art, "What counts most is involvement . . . one must be able to give lots." What other professional **groups** might make the same claim?

saved for X rays. No one spoke. In fact the only sound for the longest time was Mama's breathing machine going in and out and in and out. It was a harsh, horrible, insistent[2] sound, and usually I talked and talked to cover up the noise. But I was waiting for someone to tell me.

At last V. Louise said, "It's from your mama, Katie. She told us what she wanted. And where to get it."

I turned and looked at Mama then, and her eyes were open again. Funny, but sickness had made her even more beautiful than good health had. Her skin was like that old paper, the kind they used to write on with quill pens, and stretched out over her bones so she looked like a model. Her eyes, which had been a deep, brilliant blue, were now like the fall sky, bleached and softened. She was like a

---

2. insistent (in sis′tənt), *adj.* impossible to overlook or disregard.

faded photograph of herself. She smiled a very small smile at me. I knew it was an effort.

"It's you," she mouthed. I read her lips. I had gotten real good at that. I thought she meant it was a present for me.

"Of course it is," I said cheerfully. I had gotten good at that, too, being cheerful when I didn't feel like it. "Of course it is."

I took the paper off the box carefully, not tearing it but folding it into a tidy packet. I twisted the ribbons around my hand and then put them on the pillow by her hand. It made the stark white hospital bed look almost festive.[3]

Under the wrapping, the box was beautiful itself. It was made of a heavy cardboard and covered with a linen material that had a pattern of cloud-filled skies.

I opened the box slowly and . . .

"It's empty," I said. "Is this a joke?" I turned to ask Mama, but she was gone. I mean, her body was there, but she wasn't. It was as if she was as empty as the box.

Dr. Pucci leaned over her and listened with a stethoscope, then almost absently patted Mama's head. Then, with infinite[4] care, V. Louise closed Mama's eyes, ran her hand across Mama's cheek, and turned off the breathing machine.

"Mama!" I cried. And to the nurses and doctors, I screamed, "Do something!" And because the room had suddenly become so silent, my voice echoed back at me. "Mama, do something."

I cried steadily for, I think, a week. Then I cried at night for a couple of months. And then for about a year I cried at anniversaries, like Mama's birthday or mine, at Thanksgiving, on Mother's Day. I stopped writing. I stopped reading except for school assignments. I was pretty mean to my half brothers and totally rotten to my stepmother and Dad. I felt empty and angry, and they all left me pretty much alone.

And then one night, right after my first birthday without Mama, I woke up remembering how she had said, "It's you." Not, "It's for you," just "It's you." Now Mama had been a high school English teacher and a writer herself. She'd had poems published in little magazines. She didn't use words carelessly. In the end she could hardly use any words at all. So—I asked myself in that dark room—why had she said, "It's you"? Why were they the very last words she had ever said to me, forced out with her last breath?

I turned on the bedside light and got out of bed. The room was full of shadows, not all of them real.

ulling the desk chair over to my closet, I climbed up and felt along the top shelf, and against the back wall, there was the birthday box, just where I had thrown it the day I had moved in with my dad.

I pulled it down and opened it. It was as empty as the day I had put it away.

"It's you," I whispered to the box.

And then suddenly I knew.

Mama had meant *I* was the box, solid and sturdy, maybe even beautiful or at least interesting on the outside. But I had to fill up the box to make it all it could be. And I had to fill me up as well. She had guessed what might happen to me, had told me in a subtle[5] way. In the two words she could manage.

I stopped crying and got some paper out of the desk drawer. I got out my fountain pen. I started writing, and I haven't stopped since. The first thing I wrote was about that birthday. I put it in the box, and pretty soon that box was overflowing with stories. And poems. And memories.

And so was I.

And so was I.

---

3. **festive** (fes′tiv), *adj.* suitable for a feast or holiday; merry.

4. **infinite** (in′fə nit), *adj.* extremely great.

5. **subtle** (sut′l), *adj.* skillful or clever.

After Reading

Making Connections

1. Draw and decorate an empty box that stands as a **symbol** for you. What would you use to fill it?

2. Why do you think it takes Katie a whole year to figure out what the box means?

3. Why does Katie's mother say, "It's you?" instead of "It's for you?" Explain the difference.

4. Imagine the author were to write more stories about Katie. What do you think they might be about?

5. The author did not have the original idea for this story—she was given the topic and was asked to devise a story. How did she manage to make the topic her own?

6. Why is it important for us to keep "filling our boxes." What does this **metaphor** mean?

7. What is the greatest gift one person can give another? Explain.

Literary Focus: Symbolism

Understanding the **symbolism** in a story or poem can help you to understand the plot or theme. In this story the author uses the empty birthday box as a symbol. It is a real box that Katie can hold in her hands, but it suggests other meanings as well. Why is it important to Katie to understand what the box means? How interesting would the story be if the box were really just an empty box?

You can tell a symbol is important to a plot or theme if it is stressed or repeated. Beginning with the title, skim over the story again and notice how the author emphasizes the importance of the box.

Vocabulary Study

On your paper write the word from the list below that best completes the meaning of each sentence.

infinite
insistent
subtle
festive
intensity

1. After the party the writer arrived home in a ____ mood.
2. The atmosphere changed after she answered the ____ ringing of her phone.
3. The doctor on the other end of the line could find no ____ way to give her the bad news.
4. "Your mother has a very serious illness," he said with great ____.
5. The doctor then took ____ care to explain all the details of the lab report.

Expressing Your Ideas

Writing Choices

Boxed In In writing this story, the author accepted a challenge to create a story about a child who receives an empty box as a birthday present. Accept that challenge yourself by writing your own **story** on this topic.

Surface Impressions Imagine that the wrapping paper on an empty box that you got for your birthday repeated this picture.

Interpret the meaning that you think the giver meant to convey by using this particular wrapping. Write a **paragraph** telling what you think the meaning is.

Other Options

Come to a Party What will the invitations to Katie's twelfth birthday party look like? Create the party **invitation** she may send out. Don't forget to say who the party is for, where and when it will take place, and what the event is. Illustrate your work.

A New Life Imagine you are Katie, and have gone to live with your father, stepmother, and half brothers. Write a **skit** in which Katie and her half brothers talk about how she and they feel about her new situation. Work with a group to present your skit to the class.

Title Twist What other titles can you think of that would fit this story? Create the best **title** you can. Write it using your most imaginative handwriting, and explain your design to the class.

Before Reading

The Dog Diaries

by Merrill Markoe

Merrill Markoe
born 1949

Markoe is a former head writer for *Late Night with David Letterman*, for which she won four of television's top-ranking Emmy Awards. She also has won awards for her appearances on *Not Necessarily the News* and has written and starred in a number of television specials. In addition, her humor and highly original views of life have appeared in popular magazines. Markoe lives in California with her two dogs, Lewis and Beau.

Building Background

Dog Behavior About 12,000 years ago, people started to domesticate dogs by adopting and breeding friendly wild dogs to help guard their homes. Little by little these dogs developed into the many breeds we see today, but they never lost their pack instincts. Pet dogs today are still social animals, but their packs are now their human families. If their human pack leaders are firm with them, dogs will behave nicely. If not, dogs can get into all kinds of mischief, as you will see in the following selection.

Getting into the Selection

Writer's Notebook Pets sometimes do things that seem ridiculous to us. The author of "The Dog Diaries" wonders why dogs act as they do and sets about answering her questions in an unusual way. If you could talk to a favorite pet or a zoo animal, what questions would you ask? In your notebook, write these questions.

Reading Tip

Using Context You're reading along at a good clip when a new word suddenly rears its unfamiliar head. What do you do? Do you just skip the word or make a wild guess at its meaning? Before diving for the dictionary, experienced readers look for clues in the **context,** words or sentences around the unknown word. For example, you might not be familiar with the word *incident* when you read, "everyone else seemed to have forgotten about the fence incident by this time." You might guess from its context that *incident* probably means "something that happened." Using context can speed up your reading so that you enjoy it more.

Jot down unfamiliar words and your guesses on a chart like the one below. After reading, compare your guesses with the dictionary definitions.

Word	Guess at meaning	Dictionary definition
incident	something that happened	a happening or event; occurrence

The Dog Diaries

MERRILL MARKOE

I pick dogs that remind me of myself—scrappy, mutt-faced, with a hint of mange.[1] People look for a reflection of their own personalities or the person they dream of being in the eyes of an animal companion. That is the reason I sometimes look into the face of my dog Stan and see wistful[2] sadness and existential angst,[3] when all he is actually doing is slowly scanning the ceiling for flies.

We pet owners demand a great deal from our pets. When we give them the job, it's a career position. Pets are required to listen to us blithely,[4] even if we talk to them in infantile[5] and goofy tones of voice that we'd never dare use around another human being for fear of being forced into psychiatric observation. On top of that, we make them wear little sweaters or jackets, and not just the cool kind with the push-up sleeves, either, but weird little felt ones that say, *It's raining cats and dogs.*

We are pretty sure that we and our pets share the same reality, until one day we come home to find that our wistful, intelligent friend who reminds us of our better self has decided a good way to spend the day is to open a box of Brillo pads, unravel a few, distribute some throughout the house, and eat or wear all the rest. And we shake our heads in an inability to comprehend what went wrong here.

Is he bored or is he just out for revenge? He certainly can't be as stupid as this would indicate. In order to answer these questions

more fully, I felt I needed some kind of new perspective, a perspective that comes from really knowing both sides of the story.

Thus, I made up my mind to live with my pets as one of them: to share their hopes, their fears, their squeaking vinyl lamb chops, their drinking space at the toilet.

What follows is the revealing, sometimes shocking, sometimes terrifying, sometimes really stupid diary that resulted.

8:45 A.M. We have been lying on our sides in the kitchen for almost an hour now. We started out in the bedroom with just our heads under the bed. But then one of us heard something, and we all ran to the back door. I think our quick response was rather effective because, although I never ascertained[6] exactly what we heard to begin with, I also can't say I recall ever hearing it again.

9:00 A.M. We carefully inspected the molding in the hallway, which led us straight to the

---

1. **mange** (mānj), a skin disease of animals, caused by parasitic mites and marked by scabs and hair loss.
2. **wistful** (wist′fəl), *adj.* full of desire; longing.
3. **existential angst** (eg′zi sten′shəl ängst), an uneasiness caused by worrying about philosophical questions such as why and how one should live.
4. **blithely** (blīᴛʜ′lē), *adv.* cheerfully.
5. **infantile** (in′fən tīl), *adj.* babyish; like an infant.
6. **ascertain** (as′ər tān′), *v.* to find out for certain; make sure of.

▲ *Blue Dog on a Red Rug* was painted by George Rodrique, who has painted an entire series of blue dog portraits. How would you like to come home to this colorful fellow?

heating duct by the bedroom. Just a coincidence? None of us was really sure. So we watched it suspiciously for a while. Then we watched it for a little while longer.

Then, never letting it out of our sight, we all took a nap.

10:00 A.M. I don't really know whose idea it was to yank back the edge of the carpet and pull apart the carpet pad, but talk about a rousing good time! How strange that I could have lived in this house for all these years, and never before felt the fur of a carpet between my teeth. Or actually bit into a moist, chewy chunk of carpet padding. I will never again think of the carpet as simply a covering for the floor.

11:15 A.M. When we all wound up in the kitchen, the other two began to stare at me eagerly. Their meaning was clear. The pressure was on for me to produce snacks. They remembered the old me—the one with the prehensile thumb,[7] the one who could open refrigerators and cabinets. I saw they didn't yet realize that today I intended to live as their equal. But as they continued their staring, I soon became caught up in their obsession. That is the only explanation I have as to why I helped them topple over the garbage. At first I was nervous, watching the murky[8] fluids soak into the floor. But the heady sense of acceptance I felt when we all dove headfirst into the can more than made up for my compromised sense of right and wrong. Pack etiquette demanded that I be the last in line. By the time I really got my head in there, the really good stuff was gone. But wait! I spied a tiny piece of tinfoil hidden in a giant clump of hair, and inside, a wad of previously chewed gum, lightly coated with sugar or salt. I was settling down to my treasure when I had the sense that I was being watched. Raising my head just slightly, I looked into the noses of my companions. Their eyes were glued to that

hard rubber mass. Their drools were long and elastic, and so, succumbing[9] to peer pressure, I split up my gum wad three ways. But I am not sure that I did the right thing. As is so often the case with wanting popularity, I may have gained their short-term acceptance. But I think that in the long run, I lost their real respect. No dog of reasonable intelligence would ever divide up something that could still be chewed.

11:50 A.M. Someone spotted a fly, and all three of us decided to catch him in our teeth. I was greatly relieved when one of the others got to him first.

12:20 P.M. Someone heard something, and in a flash, we were all in the backyard, running back and forth by the fence, periodically[10] hooting. Then one of us spotted a larger-than-usual space between two of the fence boards, and using both teeth and nails, began to make the space larger. Pretty soon, all three of us were doing everything in our power to help. This was a case where the old prehensile thumb really came in handy. Grabbing hold of one of the splinters, I was able to enlarge the hole immediately. Ironically, I alone was unable to squeeze through to freedom, and so I watched with envy as the others ran in pointless circles in the lot next door. What was I going to do? All of my choices were difficult. Sure, I could go back into the house and get a hacksaw, or I could simply let myself out the back gate, but if I did that, did I not betray my companions? And would I not then be obligated to round us all up and punish us? No, I was a collaborator,[11] and I had the lip splinters

---

7. **prehensile thumb,** a thumb such as that of humans and primates that can grasp or hold.
8. **murky** (mėr′kē), *adj.* thick and dark.
9. **succumb** (sə kum′), *v.* give in.
10. **periodically** (pir′ē od′ik lē), *adv.* every now and then.
11. **collaborator** (kə lab′ə rā′tər), *n.* a person who aids or cooperates with another.

to prove it. So I went back to the hole and continued chewing. Only a few hundred dollars' worth of fence damage later, I was able to squeeze through that darn hole myself.

1:30 P.M. The extra time I took was just enough for me to lose sight of my two companions. And so, for the first time, I had to rely on my keen, new animal instincts. Like the wild creature I had become, I was able to spot their tracks immediately. They led me in a series of ever-widening circles, then across the lot at a forty-five-degree angle, then into a series of zigzags, then back to the hole again. Finally, I decided to abandon the tracking and head out to the sidewalk. Seconds later, I spotted them both across the street, where they were racing up and back in front of the neighbor's house. They seemed glad to see me, and so I eagerly joined them in their project. The three of us had only been running and hooting for less than an hour when the apparent owner of the house came to the front door. And while I admit this may not have been the best of circumstances for a first introduction, nevertheless I still feel the manner in which he threatened to turn the hose on us was both excessively violent and unnecessarily vulgar.[12]

Clearly, it was up to me to encourage our group to relocate, and I was shocked at how easily I could still take command of our unit. A simple "Let's go, boys," and everyone was willing to follow me home. (It's such a power-packed phrase. That's how I met my last boyfriend!)

3:00 P.M. By the time we had moved our running and hooting activities into our own front yard, we were all getting a little tired. So we lay down on our sides on the porch.

4:10 P.M. We all changed sides.

4:45 P.M. We all changed sides again.

5:20 P.M. We all lay on our backs. (What a nice change of pace!)

6:00 P.M. Everyone was starting to grow restless. Occasionally, one of us would get up, scratch the front door, and moan. I wrestled silently with the temptation simply to let us all in. But then I realized I didn't have any keys on me. Of course, it occurred to me that we could all go back through the new hole in the fence, but everyone else seemed to have forgotten about the entire fence incident by this time. As they say, "a word to the wise." And so, taking a hint from my friends, I began to forget about the whole thing myself.

6:30 P.M. The sound of an approaching car as it pulls into the driveway. The man who shares this house with us is coming home. He is both surprised and perplexed[13] to see us all out in the front yard running in circles. He is also quickly irritated by the fact that no one offers any explanations. And once he opens the front door, he unleashes a furious string of harsh words as he confronts the mounds of garbage someone has strewn all over the house. We have nothing but sympathy for him in his tragic misfortune. But since none of us knows anything about it, we all retire to the coat closet until the whole thing blows over. And later, as he eats his dinner, I sit quietly under the table. As I watch him, a pleasant feeling of calm overtakes me as I realize just how much I have grown as a person. Perhaps that is why the cruel things he says to me seem to have no effect. And so, when he gets up to pour himself another beverage, I raise my head up to his plate, and, with my teeth, I lift off his sandwich.

---

12. **vulgar** (vul′gər), *adj.* showing a lack of manners.
13. **perplexed** (pər plekst′), *adj.* puzzled; bewildered.

After Reading

Making Connections

1. Describe any feelings you experienced while reading about what the narrator did as a dog.

2. Imagine what the narrator looked like as she went about her day with the dogs. Choose a favorite scene from the diary and illustrate it.

3. Look back through the selection and find examples of humor. What makes this narrative funny?

4. Do you think the author really did any of the things she describes in the selection? Explain.

5. As she begins the diary, the author writes as if she were a dog. How does this **point of view** add to the humor?

6. Look back at the questions you asked in your Writer's Notebook. Imagine you are the animal and answer your questions.

7. Do you think we can understand ourselves better by understanding animal behavior? Explain.

Literary Focus: Point of View

You can tell from the narrator's use of the pronouns "I" and "we" that this selection is written from a first-person **point of view.**

Early in the selection, however, "we" means the narrator and her fellow human beings. Once the diary begins, "we" means the narrator and her two dogs. The point of view stays first person, but the subjects shift somewhat. Diaries such as this, journals, and letters are always written from a first-person point of view. Writers of fiction often like to use imaginary diaries, journals, and letters because their first-person point of view makes the reader feel closer to the action. What other reasons might the author have had for choosing a first-person point of view in this selection?

"Well, here we go again . . . Did anyone here *not* eat his or her homework on the way to school?"

Vocabulary Study

On your paper write the letter of the word that does not belong with the other words in the set.

wistful
blithely
infantile
ascertain
murky
succumb
periodically
collaborator
vulgar
perplexed

1. **a.** partner   **b.** collaborator **c.** botanist   **d.** teammate
2. **a.** succumb   **b.** overcome   **c.** accomplish   **d.** achieve
3. **a.** occasionally **b.** continuously **c.** periodically **d.** infrequently
4. **a.** cheerfully   **b.** unworriedly   **c.** seriously   **d.** blithely
5. **a.** assure   **b.** ascertain   **c.** determine   **d.** ignore
6. **a.** clear   **b.** murky   **c.** transparent   **d.** uncolored
7. **a.** confused   **b.** contracted   **c.** puzzled   **d.** perplexed
8. **a.** infantry   **b.** babyish   **c.** infantile   **d.** childish
9. **a.** polite   **b.** courteous   **c.** mannerly   **d.** vulgar
10. **a.** wistful   **b.** painful   **c.** unpleasant   **d.** disagreeable

Expressing Your Ideas

Writing Choices

Doggy Thoughts What did the dogs think when their owner got on her hands and knees and started chewing the carpet? Pick any incident you enjoyed from the story. Rewrite it as an **anecdote,** or short account, from the dogs' point of view.

Dog Diaries: The Sequel What do you think happened the day after the narrator finished her dog diaries? What did she learn from her experiences? Did she have problems relating to other people as a human being again? Write a **diary entry** from the narrator's point of view for the following day.

Turn the Tables Work with a small group to find pictures of dogs and other pets engaged in various forms of behavior, or draw your own pictures. Cooperate with your group to write **captions** from the pet's point of view. Try to make your captions as funny as possible. Display the results.

Other Options

You Wouldn't Believe Imagine you are the neighbor who caught the dogs romping on his lawn. Prepare a **dramatic monologue** in which you tell your family what you saw. Practice delivering it aloud and present it to the class.

If You Ask Me Do you have a dog, or would you like to have one? Why or why not? Write your **opinion** of dog behavior in an introductory paragraph and then support it with a **chart** in which you list what you see as the pluses and minuses of dog ownership.

Wasting Time The narrator's dogs had a pretty full day. What does your pet do all day? Make a **time line** of its activities for one 24-hour day. If you don't have a pet choose any pet that interests you—dog, gerbil, fish, cat, lizard, or whatever, and make an imaginary time line of its day.

Before Reading

On Destiny by Shuntarō Tanikawa
Under This Sky by Zia Hyder

Shuntarō Tanikawa
born 1931

Although he has written everything from children's books
and song lyrics to television
scripts, Tanikawa is mainly a
poet. He is well known in
Japan as the translator of the
"Peanuts" comic strip.

Zia Hyder
born 1936

Hyder was born in what was
then the Indian state of Bengal. In 1971 East Bengal
became Bangladesh. Its capital is Dhaka. She is presently a
professor of dramatic arts.

Building Background

The Human Condition No matter what color skin or eyes you
have, whether you're male or female, or what country you call
home, you share certain experiences with humankind. We are all
born and we all die. We get hot in the sun and wet when it rains.
Often we have very similar life experiences. In her book *This Same
Sky,* poet and editor Naomi Shihab Nye has collected the work of
poets from around the world. The two poems that follow are from
Japan and Bangladesh. Despite the differences in the original languages and cultures of the poets, many of the themes are universal. These poems speak to every human being as they explore the
human condition.

Getting into the Poems

Writer's Notebook At first glance we may not think we will like a
person who appears to be different from ourselves. Sometimes
the differences just seem too great: different ages, different taste
in clothes, even different native languages. Often, though, after we
get to know someone, we find we have much more in common
than we originally thought. Recall a time when you were surprised
to find you had common interests with a new and different
acquaintance and write about it in your notebook.

Reading Tip

Imagery Poets use **imagery,** or words that help the reader
experience how things look, sound, smell, taste, or feel.
Sometimes imagery can so stimulate the imagination that the
reader is transported to another world. At other times the imagery
brings to mind an ordinary world that is real and familiar to every
reader. In the poems that follow, the images of spring flowers, a
hand-sewn quilt, an old woman in a kitchen, and a train station
platform help the reader share the poets' experiences.

As you read the poems look for other imagery that the poets
use. Be aware of which images build the most powerful bridges
between the poet's experience and your own.

ON DESTINY

SHUNTARŌ TANIKAWA

translated by Harold Wright

Lined up on a station platform
grade school children
grade school children
grade school children
5 grade school children
talking, playing, eating.

"Aren't they cute."
"Remember?"
Lined up on a station platform
10 grown ups
grown ups
grown ups
grown ups
looking, talking, longing.

15 "Just fifty years and fifty billion kilometers."
"Remember?"
Lined up on a station platform
angels
angels
20 angels
angels
silent and watching
silent and glowing.

▲ Roxana Villa created this swirling picture that
seems to encompass the moon, the heavens,
and humanity. It has no title. What do you think
the title should be?

Under This Sky

Zia Hyder

translated by Bhabani Sengupta with Naomi Shihab Nye

There's an enormous comfort knowing
we all live under this same sky,
whether in New York or Dhaka,
we see the same sun and same moon.

5 When it is night in New York,
the sun shines in Dhaka,
but that doesn't matter.
Flowers that blossom here in spring
are unknown in meadows of distant Bengal—
10 that too doesn't matter.
There's no rainy season here—
the peasant in Bengal welcomes the new crop
with homemade sweets
while here, winter brings mountains of snow.

15 No one here knows Grandmother's hand-sewn quilt—
even that doesn't matter.
There's an enormous comfort knowing
we all live under this same sky.

The Hudson River freezes,
20 automobiles can't move.
Slowly city workers will remove the snow.
The old lady next door won't go to work—
it's too cold.
Maybe my old mother far away
25 will also enter her kitchen late.
Naked trees in Central Park and Ramna Park
quiver with dreams of new life and love.

Fog hangs on the horizon—
suddenly New York, Broadway, and Times Square
30 look dimly like Dhaka, Buriganga, and Laxmi Bazaar.

This panoramic view of the outskirts of the Dutch city of Haarlem was painted in 1670 by Ruisdael. Do you find it comforting that "we all live under this same sky"?

After Reading

Making Connections

1. What for you is the most memorable **image** from these poems? Why?

2. 👁 Which of these two poems do you think builds a better bridge between cultural **groups**? Explain.

3. Why do you think the poet Tanikawa chose the **title,** "On Destiny"?

4. Who is speaking the quoted lines in Tanikawa's poem?

5. If you had to pick one word from the poem "Under This Sky" to **summarize** its meaning, what would it be? Why?

6. Name some experiences that human beings share across continents and cultures.

Literary Focus: Repetition

A central part of poetry, **repetition,** or the repeating of sounds, words, phrases, or lines, adds to the enjoyment of a poem and helps to focus its meaning as well. Repetition is an important part of both of these poems. In "On Destiny" the repetition stands out and is easy to recognize. What words and lines are repeated in "Under This Sky"? Be sure to begin with the title in answering this question. Is there a regular pattern to this repetition, as in "On Destiny"?

Compare and contrast the ways the poets use repetition in these poems to emphasize a thought or theme. Look at the phrase "that doesn't matter" that you found repeated in "Under This Sky." How is it important to understanding the meaning of the poem?

Expressing Your Ideas

Writing Choices

Media Switch Reread the poem "On Destiny," and paraphrase it to yourself. Then write the poem as one or more **prose paragraphs,** being careful to get across the same ideas and feelings.

Stranger in Paradise In "Under This Sky," the poet tries to comfort herself in a strange place by remembering that the whole world shares the same sky. Whether you spent the night at a friend's or traveled across continents, recall a time you were homesick. Write a **journal entry** about that experience that shows what you thought or did to comfort yourself.

Alert Your Senses Keep a record of the imagery that most affects you during a day—jot down phrases that describe what you see, hear, smell, taste, and touch. Select from these familiar images as you write a piece of **prose** or a **poem** of your choice.

Other Options

See the World Two cities, New York and Dhaka (the capital of the poet's home country of Bangladesh), are compared in "Under This Sky." Choose one of these places and make a **travel poster** or **brochure** to encourage tourism. Illustrate points of interest.

Beyond Words Each of these poems creates a mood. Choose either poem and capture that mood by finding a piece of **music** or **visual images** that you feel go with the poem. Use the music or artwork as part of a presentation of the poem to the class.

Around the World Trace the outline of the map of the world below. Locate New York City and Dhaka. Keep your map and continue to use it to locate places mentioned in other selections. ▾

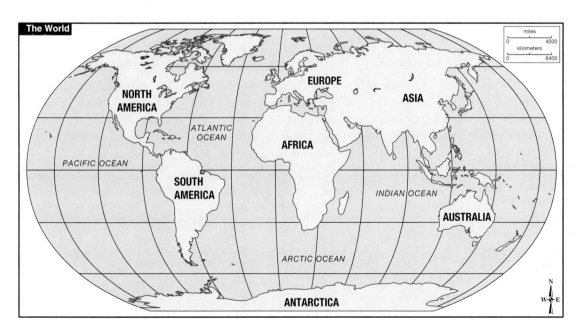

Before Reading

We Are All One

a Chinese folk tale retold by Laurence Yep

Laurence Yep
born 1948

As a third-generation Chinese American, Laurence Yep says his cultural heritage made him feel like an outsider during his childhood in San Francisco. He was not Chinese enough to speak the language of more recent immigrants, and not yet American enough to fit into his high school. That feeling sent Yep on a search for the cultural traditions of his ancestors. Later, his heritage inspired many of Yep's best-known books for young adults, such as *Dragonwings* and *The Star Fisher.* In *The Rainbow People,* from which this selection comes, Yep has tried to create a bridge between the American culture he was born into and the Chinese culture of his ancestors by collecting and retelling Chinese folk tales.

Building Background

Chinese Folk Tales Early Chinese immigrants to the United States found that telling Chinese tales kept up their spirits. These stories connected them to the lives and families they had left behind in China and helped them express their hopes and fears for their new lives. The telling and retelling of tales such as this one by the old-timers in San Francisco's Chinatown made these stories part of the Chinese American experience.

Getting into the Tale

Discussion In "We Are All One," a poor man shows respect for all forms of life by helping insects. Not everyone treats bugs in such a kind way. Do you squash them or leave them alone? Talk with your classmates about whether they feel human beings have a duty to protect lower forms of life or the right to destroy them. After everyone has expressed themselves, take an **opinion poll** and tally the results on the board.

Reading Tip

Stereotypes Just about every culture in the world seems to have folk tales. And whether the tale comes from China, Europe, or North America, the contents often include **stereotypes,** characters with easily identified, simplified traits. For example, like "Aladdin" from the Middle East and "The Brave Little Tailor" from Europe, this Chinese folk tale is about a poor man and a rich man. The chart below lists ways some folk tales are similar to one another. Try to think of other stereotypes and examples to add to the list.

Content	Similar Folk Tales
poor man/rich man	Aladdin; The Brave Little Tailor
greedy person	Rumpelstiltskin
good person rewarded	Cinderella

WE ARE ALL ONE

LAURENCE YEP

Long ago there was a rich man with a disease in his eyes. For many years, the pain was so great that he could not sleep at night. He saw every doctor he could, but none of them could help him.

"What good is all my money?" he groaned. Finally, he became so desperate that he sent criers through the city offering a reward to anyone who could cure him.

Now in that city lived an old candy peddler. He would walk around with his baskets of candy, but he was so kind-hearted that he gave away as much as he sold, so he was always poor.

When the old peddler heard the announcement, he remembered something his mother had said. She had once told him about a magical herb that was good for the eyes. So he packed up his baskets and went back to the single tiny room in which his family lived.

When he told his plan to his wife, she scolded him, "If you go off on this crazy hunt, how are we supposed to eat?"

Usually the peddler gave in to his wife, but this time he was stubborn. "There are two baskets of candy," he said. "I'll be back before they're gone."

The next morning, as soon as the soldiers opened the gates, he was the first one to leave the city. He did not stop until he was deep inside the woods. As a boy, he had often wandered there. He had liked to pretend that the shadowy forest was a green sea and he was a fish slipping through the cool waters.

As he examined the ground, he noticed ants scurrying about. On their backs were larvae like white grains of rice. A rock had fallen into a stream, so the water now spilled into the ants' nest.

"We're all one," the kind-hearted peddler said. So he waded into the shallow stream and put the rock on the bank. Then with a sharp stick, he dug a shallow ditch that sent the rest of the water back into the stream.

Without another thought about his good deed, he began to search through the forest. He looked everywhere; but as the day went on, he grew sleepy. "Ho-hum. I got up too early. I'll take just a short nap," he decided, and lay down in the shade of an old tree, where he fell right asleep.

In his dreams, the old peddler found himself standing in the middle of a great city. Tall buildings rose high overhead. He couldn't see the sky even when he tilted back his head. An escort of soldiers marched up to him with a loud clatter of their black lacquer armor. "Our queen wishes to see you," the captain said.

The frightened peddler could only obey and let the fierce soldiers lead him into a shining palace. There, a woman with a high crown sat upon a tall throne. Trembling, the old peddler fell to his knees and touched his forehead against the floor.

But the queen ordered him to stand. "Like the great Emperor Yü of long ago, you tamed the great flood. We are all one now. You have only to ask, and I or any of my people will come to your aid."

The old peddler cleared his throat. "I am looking for a certain herb. It will cure any disease of the eyes."

The queen shook her head regretfully. "I have never heard of that herb. But you will surely find it if you keep looking for it."

And then the old peddler woke. Sitting up, he saw that in his wanderings he had come back to the ants' nest. It was there he had taken his nap. His dream city had been the ants' nest itself.

"This is a good omen," he said to himself, and he began searching even harder. He was so determined to find the herb that he did not notice how time had passed. He was surprised when he saw how the light was fading. He looked all around then. There was no sight of his city—only strange hills. He realized then that he had searched so far he had gotten lost.

Night was coming fast and with it the cold. He rubbed his arms and hunted for shelter. In the twilight, he thought he could see the green tiles of a roof.

He stumbled through the growing darkness until he reached a ruined temple. Weeds grew through cracks in the stones and most of the roof itself had fallen in. Still, the ruins would provide some protection.

As he started inside, he saw a centipede with bright orange skin and red tufts of fur along its back. Yellow dots covered its sides like a dozen tiny eyes. It was also rushing into the temple as fast as it could, but there was a bird swooping down toward it.

The old peddler waved his arms and shouted, scaring the bird away. Then he put down his palm in front of the insect. "We are all one, you and I." The many feet tickled his skin as the centipede climbed onto his hand.

Inside the temple, he gathered dried leaves and found old sticks of wood and soon he had a fire going. The peddler even picked some fresh leaves for the centipede from a bush near the temple doorway. "I may have to go hungry, but you don't have to, friend."

Stretching out beside the fire, the old peddler pillowed his head on his arms. He was so tired that he soon fell asleep, but even in his sleep he dreamed he was still searching in the woods. Suddenly he thought he heard footsteps near his head. He woke instantly and looked about, but he only saw the brightly colored centipede.

"Was it you, friend?" The old peddler chuckled and, lying down, he closed his eyes again. "I must be getting nervous."

"We are one, you and I," a voice said faintly—as if from a long distance. "If you go south, you will find a pine tree with two trunks. By its roots, you will find a magic bead. A cousin of mine spat on it years ago. Dissolve that bead in wine and tell the rich man to drink it if he wants to heal his eyes."

The old peddler trembled when he heard the voice, because he realized that the centipede was magical. He wanted to run from the temple, but he couldn't even get up. It was as if he were glued to the floor.

But then the old peddler reasoned with himself: If the centipede had wanted to hurt me, it could have long ago. Instead, it seems to want to help me.

So the old peddler stayed where he was, but he did not dare open his eyes. When the first sunlight fell through the roof, he raised one eyelid cautiously. There was no sign of the centipede. He sat up and looked around, but the magical centipede was gone.

He followed the centipede's instructions when he left the temple. Traveling south, he kept a sharp eye out for the pine tree with two trunks. He walked until late in the afternoon, but all he saw were normal pine trees.

Wearily he sat down and sighed. Even if he found the pine tree, he couldn't be sure that he would find the bead. Someone else might even have discovered it a long time ago.

But something made him look a little longer. Just when he was thinking about turning back, he saw the odd tree. Somehow his tired legs managed to carry him over to the

tree, and he got down on his knees. But the ground was covered with pine needles and his old eyes were too weak. The old peddler could have wept with frustration, and then he remembered the ants.

He began to call, "Ants, ants, we are all one."

Almost immediately, thousands of ants came boiling out of nowhere. Delighted, the old man held up his fingers. "I'm looking for a bead. It might be very tiny."

Then, careful not to crush any of his little helpers, the old man sat down to wait. In no time, the ants reappeared with a tiny bead. With trembling fingers, the old man took the bead from them and examined it. It was colored orange and looked as if it had yellow eyes on the sides.

There was nothing very special about the bead, but the old peddler treated it like a fine jewel. Putting the bead into his pouch, the old peddler bowed his head. "I thank you and I thank your queen," the old man said. After the ants disappeared among the pine needles, he made his way out of the woods.

The next day, he reached the house of the rich man. However, he was so poor and ragged that the gatekeeper only laughed at him. "How could an old beggar like you help my master?"

The old peddler tried to argue. "Beggar or rich man, we are all one."

But it so happened that the rich man was passing by the gates. He went over to the old peddler. "I said anyone could see me. But it'll mean a stick across your back if you're wasting my time."

The old peddler took out the pouch. "Dissolve this bead in some wine and drink it down." Then, turning the pouch upside down, he shook the tiny bead onto his palm and handed it to the rich man.

The rich man immediately called for a cup of wine. Dropping the bead into the wine, he waited a moment and then drank it down. Instantly the pain vanished. Shortly after that, his eyes healed.

The rich man was so happy and grateful that he doubled the reward. And the kindly old peddler and his family lived comfortably for the rest of their lives.

We Are All One   **431**

After Reading

Making Connections

1. Would you have set off on the same kind of seemingly impossible search that the peddler did? Explain.

2. 👆 Folk tales like this one often erase the usual boundaries between **groups.** Do you believe, like the peddler and the ants, that "we are all one"? Explain why or why not.

3. If you wanted to make this folk tale into a children's movie, would you use cartoon animation or human actors and puppets? Explain your choice.

4. As part of his **characterization** of the peddler, the writer gives him positive human qualities. List those you found.

5. What lessons does this story teach? Explain.

6. Why do you think the writer chose to use insects in this story instead of more intelligent or appealing animals?

7. How can the story of the peddler help us better understand some of the problems we face and the decisions we must make in our own lives?

Literary Focus: Characterization

When you read a folk tale, you can make assumptions about **characterization** that you can't make when you read other forms of fiction. That's because many folk tales use familiar **stock characters.** These stereotypes keep the story simple and give the reader a quick picture of what's happening. Whether it is a peddler, a fisherman, or a housemaid, there are many similar "poor but good" folk tale heroes. The peddler's wife in this story is also a stock character—the unsympathetic wife who scolds a seemingly crazy husband.

Look back at the descriptions and actions of the main characters in the story. Which of their traits remind you of other familiar folk-tale characters? A web like the one below is a good way to identify stock characters. Name a trait, such as "Kind," then give an example of the trait.

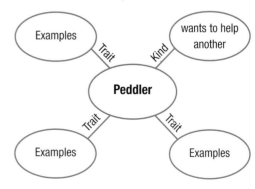

Vocabulary Study

Find out what the word *lacquer* means and how it looks. Then draw a picture of the ants changed into fierce soldiers with black lacquer armor in the peddler's dream. If you prefer, you may write a description of the soldiers, taking care to use imagery that makes them come alive.

Expressing Your Ideas

Writing Choices

Ant Speaks! Do you glance at the tabloid newspapers in the checkout line of the grocery? The headlines are often quite unbelievable. If treated as true, this story offers good material for the tabloids. Take the peddler's experiences and sum them up in **tabloid headlines.**

Familiar Story Use this story as a model to write a similar **story** set in your school or neighborhood about you and your friends. You can use any or all of the following elements from "We Are All One": the general plot outline, its themes, and typical stock characters.

Ask Away If you were a radio host, what would you like to ask guest author Laurence Yep about his folk tales or other writing or about his Chinese American background? Write out the **questions** you would ask him for an **interview** on the air. Then conduct your interview, with a partner responding as author Yep. Change roles and respond as the author to your partner's questions.

Other Options

Give and Take What did the peddler tell his wife about what happened while he was gone? Work with a partner to create a **dialogue** that might have occurred between the peddler and his wife after his return. Be sure to include her reactions to his account. Practice and deliver the dialogue to the class.

On Second Thought Before you read "We Are All One," your class conducted an **opinion poll** on the question of whether human beings have a duty to protect lower forms of life or not. Did the folk tale provoke thought that changed any opinions on this question? Poll the class again and **compare** the results.

Musically Yours Write or choose some **theme music** for each of the major characters in this story, including the insects. With a group, practice reading the story and playing the music when each character is introduced. Perform your musical folk tale for the class.

Language Mini-Lesson

Adding Punctuation for Clarity

Suppose you read the following in a sports magazine:

Sign up today to improve your soccer skills. There will be three classes—in January, February, and March, May, June, and July, and September.

Are you clear about when the three classes occur? Read it again and imagine a semicolon after *March* and after *July.* Now do you know when the classes occur? Adding the semicolons makes the meaning clear. Now read this sentence.

Soon after the classes were filled.

In this sentence words run together in a confusing way. It needs a comma to make its meaning clear. Where would you put the comma? Why?

Writing Strategy Read your writing aloud to check if you have punctuated your sentences correctly. Remember, the goal is to make yourself understood. Check to see that you have the correct punctuation when you pause or have items in a series in a sentence.

Activity Options

1. Add semicolons and/or commas to clarify the meaning of each sentence:

   • The next day Wednesday was chosen for the next meeting.

   • If only she hadn't slipped out the cat wouldn't be lost now.

2. Review the contents of your working portfolio and check for sentences that seem unclear. Can you improve them with additional punctuation? Put a star in the margin next to each sentence you clarify.

3. Be the teacher and make up sentences for your students to correct. Write five sentences that are confusing without punctuation. Exchange papers and correct each other's work.

The Bridge to Understanding

Timeless Tales

History Connection

Timeless tales all have something in common—they are bridges of understanding that touch all people and cross generations. Some human experiences, such as love and hate, joy and sorrow, triumph and despair, are universal. Stories that build on these experiences appeal to people of all times and places. The story of Sundiata is one such tale.

S undiata Keita [sùn/dē ä′tə kē tə] was a warrior-king [of Mali] who united a weak and scattered people, and, under his benevolent leadership, ushered in a glorious period of peace and prosperity. The Keita griots [grē′ōz] of Mali, who preserved the history and wisdom of their great kings, have told the story of Sundiata for centuries. A villager begins the tale:

> *Listen then, sons of Mali, children of the black people, listen to my word, for I am going to tell you of Sundiata, the father of the Bright Country, of the savanna land, the ancestor of those who draw the bow, the master of a hundred vanquished kings.*

SUNDIATA KEITA
THE LEGEND AND THE KING

by Patricia and Fredrick McKissack

Two hunters told Maghan Kon Fatta [Sundiata's father] that if he married Sogolon [Sundiata's mother], their son would be a leader without equal, and so the king did. The day Sundiata was born a storm foretold of his greatness. "The lion child, the buffalo child, is born," said the midwife. "The Almighty has made the thunder peal, the white sky has lit up, and the earth has trembled."

Sundiata's father favored Sundiata and his mother, which angered the father's first wife, Sassouma Berete. Sassouma's jealousy of Sogolon was matched only by her hatred of Sundiata. She plotted to destroy them both to make sure her son, Touman, would become king after King Fatta died.

As Sundiata grew, the situation took an odd twist. Sundiata was seven years old, yet he couldn't walk! People were shocked and surprised to see a boy his age crawling around like a baby. Sassouma used every opportunity to embarrass Sogolon and hurl insults at her son. She pushed her beautiful child up front during all ceremonies, so he could be seen and adored.

As long as the king lived, Sundiata was protected and Sassouma's scheming was kept in check, but Maghan Kon Fatta died when Sundiata was very young. Against Fatta's wishes, the royal council was coerced into making Touman the mansa [leader], and Sassouma became the power behind the throne.

Free to carry out her threats, she did her best to humiliate Sogolon and her children. Sogolon was forced to live in a storage hut out behind the palace and Sassouma encouraged children to tease and poke fun at them.

Sundiata was determined to overcome his physical handicap. With the help of a blacksmith who made braces for his legs, and the loving support of his family, Sundiata learned to walk upright. On that day his mother sang:

> Oh, day, what a beautiful day,
> Oh, day, day of joy;
> Allah Almighty, you never created a finer day.
> So my son is going to walk!

Through rigorous exercise and hard work the young prince grew tall and strong

◄ Malian antelope sculpture made of carved wood

and became a very good archer. A prince needed to be fit, but Sogolon taught her son that a good ruler also needed to be wise. She taught Sundiata to respect Mandinka [Sundiata's people] customs and traditions, their history and law.

Because of his courage and leadership, Sundiata was chosen to be mansa of Mali, which he ruled from 1230 to 1255. Mali means "the hippopotamus," which is often used in association with Sundiata, as are the lion, the symbol of the Keita clan, and the buffalo of his mother's clan.

According to the griots' story, Sundiata began his rule by first moving his seat of government to Niani, the place of his birth. Then he established a solid hold over the gold and salt trade.

> *If you want salt, if you want gold, if you want cloth, go to Niani, for the Mecca road passes by Niani. If you want fish, go to Niani, for it is there that the fishermen come to sell their catches. If you want meat, go to Niani, the country of the great hunters, and the land of the ox and the sheep. If you want to see an army, go to Niani, for it is there that the united forces of Mali are found. If you want to see a great king, go to Niani, for it is there that the son of Sogolon lives, the man with two names.*

Mandinkans called Niani the "Bright Country," which later applied to all of Mali, and Sundiata was its beloved king. He was a charismatic leader whose subjects adored him. Known for his kindness, wit, and good sense of humor, he was often asked to resolve disputes among kings. His justice was swift and cruel by today's standards. A convicted thief was sentenced to have his hand cut off. A liar lost his tongue. Repeat offenders were killed. Banishment was also a common sentence. In spite of these severe laws, songs praised Sundiata for his fairness in dealings with the privileged as well as the poor, the

strong as well as the weak. When he returned from a trip, people from the villages lined the streets for miles and cheered as he passed.

Sundiata did not believe in showing off his wealth, choosing instead to wear the garments of a *simbon* (a hunter)—a plain smock, tight trousers, and a bow slung across his back. He valued friendship and never forgot a kindness, and he expected others to follow his example.

Based on experiences learned during his exile, Sundiata set up a system of cultural exchange. His sons and daughters were sent to live in the courts of distant kings, and the princes and princesses of other rulers were invited to stay at Niani. He reasoned that children who grow up together were less likely to attack one another as adult leaders.

Sundiata died in 1255. He may have been struck by a stray arrow during a celebration in Niani or simply died of natural causes. One account says he drowned.

▲ restoration of the Mohammedan Mosque at Jenné in Mali

Responding

What universal human experiences are included in the story of Sundiata?

Art Connection

Long before written language developed, people told stories. Storytellers entertained, taught, and preserved history. As storytellers journeyed from place to place, so did their tales. As storytellers taught their skills to younger generations, tales journeyed through time.

THE STORYTELLERS

A court jester entertains his king in fifteenth-century France. During the reign of Louis XIV two centuries later, folktales and fairytales became the fashionable story genre of the French court. ▼

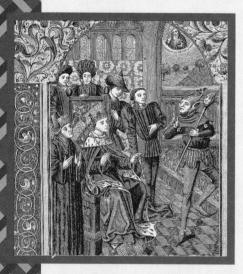

According to legend, Homer composed the two famous Greek epic poems, *The Iliad* and *The Odyssey,* around 850 B.C. Since there was no written Greek language at this time, the poems were kept alive by bards who recited them from memory. ➤

▲ Stories are forever changing. Each storyteller spins a slightly different web of words and the tale changes a bit. This young girl is sure to tell the story she is hearing in her own special style.

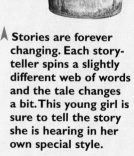

An Arabian poet recites the history of her tribe. Many nomadic peoples through the ages have relied on storytellers to preserve their history, especially the good times, the victories, and the triumphs over adversity. ▼

◄ The *Arabian Nights* begins with the story of Scheherazade, who tells the sultan a new tale every night for a thousand and one nights. By that time, the sultan is so enchanted with her storytelling that he falls in love with her. Scheherazade is then able to escape the fate of the king's previous favorites—beheading.

▲ A storyteller uses puppets to help tell his tale. He may be telling one of many Chinese fairy tales with a cast of genies, mandarins, peasants, emperors, and warriors.

◄ The Rogers Brothers perform in vaudeville, an early twentieth-century phenomenon that included a wide range of entertainment, from storytelling to singing, dancing, and slapstick comedy.

Responding

1. A stand-up comedian is a contemporary storyteller. Who is your favorite comedian? What qualities make that person a good storyteller?

2. If possible, attend a live poetry reading or listen to a storyteller in person. Report to the class on the techniques used to engage the audience.

Reading Mini-Lesson

Using Time Order Relationships

When you read, you need to keep events in order so that you can understand their progression. The history of Sundiata Keita on pages 435–437 contains many events. It also contains many words and phrases called *time markers.* Some of these are ordinary verbs. By their tenses, they point to past, present, and future events. Other time markers, such as *before, after, later, at the same time,* and *as long as,* help us to understand the relationship of events. Find three time markers in the story.

Activity Options

1. Complete the time line shown here by copying it and adding four more significant events in the story of Sundiata. You may not be able to date an event, but you should be able to put events in their proper order.

Events:

Hunters make   **Sundiata**
prediction   **dies**

Date: **1255**

2. Recall the three time markers you found in the story of Sundiata. Copy the sentences or phrases on your paper. Write the time marker in capital letters and underline the events it connects. For example: . . . to make sure <u>her son . . . would become king</u> AFTER <u>King Fatta died.</u>

3. Here are three events in the story of Sundiata. Place them in the proper time order and explain why this order is important in understanding how Sundiata became "the master of a hundred vanquished kings."
   a. Sundiata was often asked to resolve disputes among kings.
   b. Sundiata learned to respect Mandinka customs, traditions, history, and law.
   c. The seat of government moved to Niani.

Writing Workshop

Bridging the Gap

Assignment You've read about characters who build bridges between themselves and others. Imagine that two characters appear on a talk show to discuss their experiences. Write a story about what happens. See the Writer's Blueprint for details.

WRITER'S BLUEPRINT

Product   A narrative about two characters who appear on a talk show

Purpose   To describe how two characters from the literature bridge the gap with others

Audience   Your teacher, friends, and classmates

Specs   As the writer of a successful narrative, you should:

❏ Begin by describing how the talk show host opens the day's program and introduces the two characters you've chosen from the literature.

❏ Go on to relate the conversation that takes place between the characters and the talk show host. Tell how the characters describe their experiences.

❏ Include questions the talk show host and members of the studio audience pose, as well as how the characters respond to these questions.

❏ End by having the host summarize the main points of the discussion and sign off.

❏ Reveal aspects of your character's personality and attitude through the dialogue that you write.

❏ Follow the rules for correct grammar, usage, spelling, and mechanics. Make sure you've used commas correctly in your narrative.

The instructions that follow should lead you to write a successful narrative.

Chart connections from the literature. Fill in a chart like the one below about the "bridges to understanding" in the stories. List the main characters, how they are connected, and a key quote to show the connection. Use the completed chart to help you choose two characters for your story.

Story	Main Characters	Their Bridge	Quote
"Jeremiah's Song"	Narrator and Grandpa Jeremiah	Story-songs that Grandpa Jeremiah would tell	"You gonna be strong as they come. One day you gonna tell all them stories I told you to your young'uns and they'll be as strong as you."

Research talk shows. Have you noticed how TV talk shows begin? Watch the beginning of two different talk shows. Take notes on how each host opens the show and introduces the guests. Use these notes to create the opening of the talk show in your story.

Brainstorm questions for the characters. When a character is interesting or sympathetic, you may want to know more about him or her than the story tells. What would you like to find out about the two characters in your story? Jot down some questions that the host and people in the audience can ask in your story.

Try two quickwrites. Briefly read over passages in the literature in which one of your characters is thinking or talking. Then take three minutes or so to quickwrite that character's story of bridging the gap in his or her own style of speech. Remember to use the pronouns *I* and *me* to show first-person point of view. Repeat the process for your other character. Here is part of one student's quickwrite.

10 years ago—my 12th birthday—mom gave me a box. The box was beautiful, but it was empty! She said that the box was me. I said what? How? It didn't make any sense. Mom died soon after. I kept the box and filled it with stories and poems I wrote. Years later I understood.

STUDENT MODEL

Plan the story. On a large sheet of drawing paper, sketch the set of the talk show in your story. Include sketches of the host, and the two "guest" characters. Around the people in your sketch include notes about what they will say and how they will react. Your finished plan should provide an outline of how the talk show conversation will unfold.

OR . . .
Instead of sketching the talk show set, you might want to describe the set and the people in words. Fill out your descriptions with notes on what the characters will say.

Guest 1	Guest 2
"Birthday Box" narrator Notes:	Temas Notes:

Host
Sample questions:

Ask a partner: *How does my plan shape up?*

✔ Does my plan give the main points of the conversation between the characters and the talk show host?

✔ Do I make clear what the gap is and how the characters bridge it?

Use your partner's comments to help you revise your plan.

STEP 2 DRAFTING

Before you write, review your literature chart, talk show research notes, brainstorm questions, quickwrites, writing plan, and any other notes you've made. Reread the Writer's Blueprint.

As you draft, concentrate on getting your story down on paper. Here are some ideas for getting started.

• Begin with the host briefly introducing each character.

• Begin with the two characters describing their "bridges of understanding."

• Begin with a description of the technical parts of the show: lights coming up, theme music playing, and audience applauding.

As you write dialogue, try to reveal aspects of each character's personality and attitude. See the Revising Strategy for tips on this.

Ask your partner for comments on your draft before you revise it.

✔ Does the beginning clearly present the characters?

✔ Does the host end with a summary of the main points of the discussion?

✔ Does the dialogue reveal aspects of each character's personality?

Revising Strategy

LITERARY SOURCE
"'He must have run out of stories to tell,' Sister Todd said. 'He'll be repeating on himself like my father used to do. That's the way I *hear* old folks get.'
Everybody laughed at that because Sister Todd was pretty old, too."
from "Jeremiah's Song" by Walter Dean Myers

Dialogue That Reveals Personality

People reveal things about themselves with everything they say and do. A kind person's sympathy will come through. An inquisitive person will ask a lot of questions. A timid person will speak softly—and not that often.

As you revise the dialogue for your story, think about the personality and attitude of each speaker. Try to make the words tell more about that personality. For example:

Poor—"Ms. Hyder, what is a bridge to understanding?" asked the host.

Better—"Who better to explain a bridge to understanding," beamed the host, "than Zia Hyder?"

Notice that the host in the second example has a more outgoing personality. Notice how the writer of the passage below revised dialogue based on a partner's comments.

An audience member ~~went~~ *bounded* up to the microphone and ~~asked,~~ *breathlessly gushed* "How did you figure out what the box meant?" *I'm just dying to know.*

Katie ~~answered,~~ *smiled and shrugged* "I don't know. One day I was sorting through the writing I kept in the box, and it hit me all of a sudden."

STUDENT MODEL

Ask a partner to review your revised draft before you edit. When you edit, watch for errors in grammar, usage, spelling, and mechanics. Pay special attention to using commas correctly.

Editing Strategy

FOR REFERENCE . . .
More rules for using commas correctly are listed in the Language and Grammar Handbook.

Using Commas Correctly

Commas help make your writing clearer. Using them correctly enables your reader to get the meaning you intend. Here are some examples of how commas help clarify meaning.

- A comma sets off the name of a person who is being spoken to.

Wrong: "Temas is not a brave man deserving of gifts?" asked Medoto.
Right: "Temas, is not a brave man deserving of gifts?" asked Medoto.

- Commas set off phrases that are parenthetical.

Wrong: Tears on the other hand were falling freely.
Right: Tears, on the other hand, were falling freely.

- Commas set off nonrestrictive clauses. Notice how the use of commas can change the meaning of a sentence.

The doctors who knew what I wanted gave me writing materials. (Only certain doctors knew what I wanted—the ones who gave me writing materials.)

The doctors, who knew what I wanted, gave me writing materials. (All the doctors knew what I wanted.)

Notice how the writer of the draft below edited for careful comma use.

○ Glenda introduced the next guest. "Audience please give Frank

Fuller a warm Glenda Show welcome." Frank entered the stage slowly

○ and sat down. Still a little short of breath he started his story. He said

that he had gone off seeking a magical herb to cure his king's eyes. **STUDENT MODEL**

STEP **5** PRESENTING

Here are two ideas for presenting your story.

- Hold a read-around with classmates. Organize a group and read your stories to each other. Discuss each story in turn.

- Keyboard and format your story on a computer. Print it and make several copies. Distribute copies to your friends.

STEP **6** LOOKING BACK

Self-evaluate. What grade would *you* give your paper? Look back at the Writer's Blueprint and evaluate yourself on each point, from 6 (superior) down to 1 (weak).

Reflect. Think about what you learned from writing your story as you write answers to these questions.

✔ Have you had a "bridge to understanding" with someone? What was it?

✔ What did you learn from the two characters you selected about how to bridge a gap in understanding?

For Your Working Portfolio: Add your story and your reflection responses to your working portfolio.

Beyond Print

A Monster of a Storyboard

In this unit you read the television play *The Monsters Are Due on Maple Street.* You know that to film a script for TV, assorted cameras, lights, microphones, sets, and costumes are needed. Did you know that **storyboards**—a series of simple drawings that tell the camera operators how to shape the scene—are equally important?

Activity

Select a scene from the play and create a storyboard. Use as many panels as you need. Consider the following:

• What will the camera show in the scene? The look of the people and objects is important.

• How will the camera show it? For instance, will you put the camera in the middle of the mob to give your viewers a sense of chaos, or will you show a mob from a long shot, as a large group of people approaching the victim? Close-ups create a sense of intensity; long shots make viewers feel they are not part of the action.

• How will images move? You can show a sense of movement by drawing where people or things are positioned from panel to panel. Movement is very exciting for viewers. Think about whether to move the people or the camera. For instance, will you keep your camera anchored and pan a runner, or will you follow a runner with the camera? Will you shoot from the side, the front, or the rear? How will your decision affect the viewer?

• How will the scene be lit? Do you want to give a sense of sunlight as the scene opens by using full flood lamps? Will you later create an eerie effect by using flat lighting from the front? Since this play was originally filmed in black and white, you may want to do the same. This will require more creativity in lighting the scene.

• How will you use sound? Will you use music or background noise? Note any uses of sound at the bottom of your storyboard.

Projects for Collaborative Study

Theme Connection

Where on Earth . . . ? In the journeys we have taken in this unit we have traveled both to actual places and to places existing only in the mind or imagination. The real places can and should be located so that we can clearly see where we've been. To do this, we need a large map of the world. You can either draw a map or use a classroom map.

■ As a class, make a list of the all the actual places mentioned in the selections in this unit.

■ Write these place names on small, self-stick removable notes. Take turns putting these notes on the map in the right locations.

Literature Connection

Symbol Hunt Writers of poetry often use **symbolism** to express deeper meanings. In the poem "The Journey," you discovered that the journey symbolized the narrator's trip through life. Other selections, including some prose, also may contain symbolism that you might not have spotted as you read them. To sharpen your symbol-spotting skills, let's go on a Symbol Hunt!

■ Divide into equal teams of four or six members. Assign pairs of team members different parts of this book or others that you may have in your classroom or library.

■ The pairs look for symbols for their team and write down each one that they find. Include the book and selection title, the page number, the symbol, and what it stands for. Teams compete to find the most symbols. Discuss the symbols you find.

Life Skills Connection

Fear Buster Some people say that forty percent of what we worry about never happens and another thirty percent is past and can't be changed! Yet we often find ourselves wondering, "What if I don't make the team" or "What if I don't go to the dance?" Let's explore a way to handle our fears.

■ As a class, select and write a common worry, such as "What if I flunk the test?" Then write how likely this outcome is: "50/50," "not too likely," or so on.

■ What would you do if your negative case did happen? What positive things might occur? Brainstorm possible responses to both questions, such as "study more" or "get more help."

■ Select your favorite response. This is your Fear Buster for that worry. Repeat this method with your own concerns and end by saying, "I'll handle it!"

Multicultural Connection

Me and Them We all have a unique **individuality,** but much of our behavior is conditioned by the **group** culture around us. To test that statement, try this.

■ Work with a group of classmates. Have each person write the name of a foreign country that he or she finds interesting. Mix up the names and draw one.

■ With your group, brainstorm a list of all the things that would change if you suddenly were dropped from the sky into that culture. Include language, food, customs, schooling, clothing, recreation, transportation, employment, religion, housing, government, etc.

Read More About Journeys

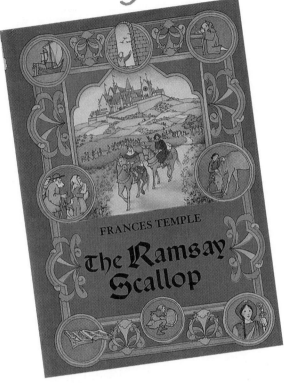

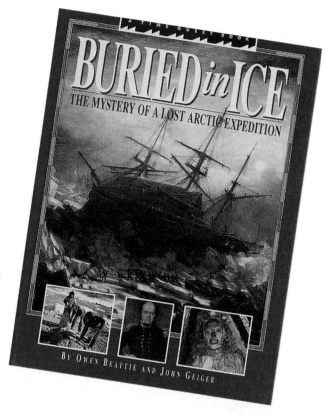

The Ramsay Scallop (1994) by Frances Temple. Set in the 1300s in Europe, this story of a fourteen-year-old orphan girl unwillingly betrothed to an also reluctant returning crusader becomes a journey of service, self-realization, and finally love.

Buried in Ice: The Mystery of a Lost Arctic Expedition (1992) by Owen Beattie and John Geiger. Anthropologists Beattie and Geiger solve the 147-year-old mystery of what happened to Sir John Franklin's expedition from England to search for the fabled Northwest Passage.

More Good Books

Julie of the Wolves (1972) by Jean Craighead George. A thirteen-year-old Eskimo girl lives with wolves to escape conflict between the old Eskimo ways and the new ways introduced by whites.

Homesick (1982) by Jean Fritz. Although labeled fiction, this book is largely an autobiographical account of Fritz's life in China from 1925, when she was ten, to 1927.

A Wizard of Earthsea (1968) by Ursula K. Le Guin. In this fantasy, set in the island world of Earthsea, a wizard-in-training named Ged explores magic and spells and confronts the true nature of evil.

When the Nightingale Sings (1992) by Joyce Carol Thomas. Like Cinderella, Marigold must escape from a mean adopted mother and her bickering twin daughters to find her destiny at a convention of gospel singers.

The Giver (1993) by Lois Lowry. Twelve-year-old Jonas, living in an ideal society with no color, pain, or past, is chosen to be the Receiver of Memory, a task that leads him to flee the Community.

Change

Turning Points
Part One, pages 454–499

New Directions
Part Two, pages 500–559

Talking About
CHANGE

There is no escaping it, change is always with us. Some changes we revel in—growing, learning, setting off in new directions. Other changes cause us to wonder why this is happening and when things will get back to normal. Sometimes we wish things would just stay the same and never change at all. At other times we look forward to the change that is on the way.

Notice that the students' comments on these pages are similar to the thoughts expressed in the literature you will be reading.

"**A serious sudden illness changes everything.**"

Kyle—Cleveland, OH

She was hardly there, just bones and eyes, and a few pale wisps of hair bleached by malnutrition.

from "Niña" by Margarita Mondrus Engle, page 490

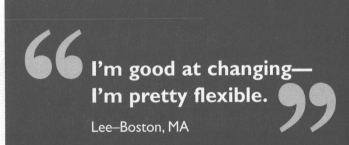

I'm good at changing— I'm pretty flexible.

Lee—Boston, MA

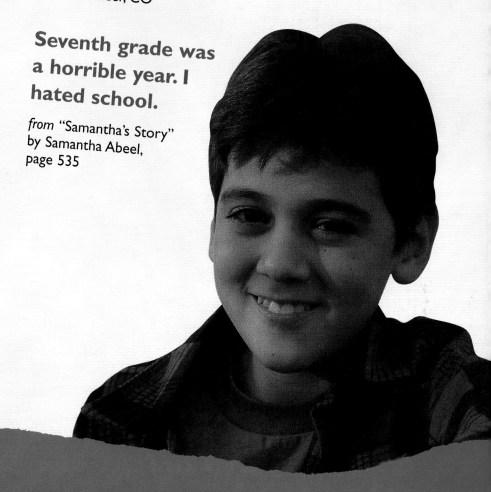

"Everyone says, 'deal with change and make the best of it;' but how?"

Jason—Boulder, CO

"Nobody can make me change; I want to stay the same."

Latoya—Mobile, AL

Seventh grade was a horrible year. I hated school.

from "Samantha's Story" by Samantha Abeel, page 535

To his surprise, he discovered the young women liked him very much, just the way he was.

from "Rabbit Dances with the People" retold by Gayle Ross, page 543

. . . I could for the first time pick up a book and read and now begin to understand what the book was saying. Anyone who has read a great deal can imagine the new world that opened.

from "The Autobiography of Malcolm X" by Malcolm X and Alex Haley, p 482

Part One

Turning Points

Every time you blink, you change. Literally. Change is so constant in your life, you barely notice . . . unless it's a turning point. That's a change you remember because something—your point of view or maybe your whole life—is different from then on. Anything can serve as a turning point— an accident, a trip, or just a wicked case of the measles. Just remember, a turning point doesn't stop to ask if you're ready. The upcoming stories show some amazing changes people make, ready or not.

Multicultural Connection **Perspective** is the point of view from which one person views another person or event. Your cultural background may influence your perspective, but unique personal experiences can add new dimension to your view of life and equip you well for the changes that lie ahead. From what perspective do the people in these stories view change?

Literature

MacKinlay Kantor	**A Man Who Had No Eyes** ◆ short story	.456
Bailey White	**Turkeys** ◆ autobiography	.462
James Herriot	**Alfred: The Sweet-Shop Cat**	
	◆ narrative nonfiction	.468
Malcolm X with Alex Haley	**The Autobiography of Malcolm X**	
	◆ autobiography	.480
Mae Jackson	**i remember** ◆ poem	.483
	Writing Mini-Lesson ◆ Research Technique:	
	Finding Information	.486
Margarita Mondrus Engle	**Niña** ◆ short story	.488

Interdisciplinary Study Science on the March

What's in the Blood That Can Make You Sick? ◆ life science	494
Breakthroughs in Medicine ◆ science	.496
Reading Mini-Lesson ◆ Recalling Details	499

Before Reading

A Man Who Had No Eyes

by MacKinlay Kantor

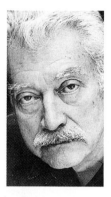

MacKinlay Kantor
1904–1977

At the age of 17, Kantor was a reporter for his hometown newspaper in Webster City, Iowa. While working for the paper, he entered a short-story contest and won first prize. That's when Kantor made up his mind to be a writer, a dream that warmed him when he couldn't afford a winter coat. When World War II broke out in 1939, Kantor was an established writer. He went to England and sent home stories about the heroism of American and British airmen. Later, he won the Pulitzer Prize for *Andersonville,* a book about the hated Confederate prison of the American Civil War. Many readers, however, were first hooked on Kantor's short stories with his trademark "snapper"—a perfect ending you don't expect.

Building Background

Pennies for Good Thoughts "A Man Who Had No Eyes" was published in 1931, a time when the world was down on its luck due to the crushing **Great Depression.** For a nickel or a dime, people could forget their troubles by reading one of the gripping stories in a "slick"—a magazine with a glossy, bright cover. These slicks also helped writers through hard times, paying them a penny a word for a good story. MacKinlay Kantor was one of the serious authors who first became known to readers by writing stories that dealt with the dreams that gave hungry people hope.

Getting into the Story

Writer's Notebook You may have guessed that "A Man Who Had No Eyes" has something to do with being sightless. Have you ever wondered what your life would be like if you couldn't see? With a partner, take turns being guided around the room blindfolded. Afterward, in your notebook, write your thoughts about the experience. Try to imagine how you would adapt to blindness. As you read, try to draw on your impressions.

Reading Tip

Dashes and Dots No, we will not be discussing Morse code here. The dashes and dots referred to are used by the author. Dashes (like this —) and "dots," called *ellipses* (like this . . .), are used as writing techniques. Dashes indicate a pause. Ellipses indicate that words have been left out or are being thought instead of spoken. Dashes and ellipses are really a part of everyday conversation. One speaker may cut off another, a speaker's sentence may trail off, or a train of thought may wander. In this story, dashes and ellipses make the characters' conversation natural and realistic.

A Man Who

▲ *Extra Paper (State Street Scene)* is a watercolor by A. J. Motley painted in 1946. 👁 Notice the **perspective** and the way the artist has filled the space. What does this scene tell you about the artist's view of Chicago in the 1940's?

Had No Eyes

MACKINLAY KANTOR

A beggar was coming down the avenue just as Mr. Parsons emerged from his hotel.

He was a blind beggar, carrying the traditional battered cane, and thumping his way before him with the cautious, half-furtive[1] effort of the sightless. He was a shaggy, thick-necked fellow; his coat was greasy about the lapels and pockets, and his hand splayed[2] over the cane's crook with a futile[3] sort of clinging. He wore a black pouch slung over his shoulder. Apparently he had something to sell.

The air was rich with spring; sun was warm and yellowed on the asphalt. Mr. Parsons, standing there in front of his hotel and noting the clack-clack approach of the sightless man, felt a sudden and foolish sort of pity for all blind creatures.

And, thought Mr. Parsons, he was very glad to be alive. A few years ago he had been little more than a skilled laborer; now he was successful, respected, admired. . . . Insurance. . . . And he had done it alone, unaided, struggling beneath handicaps. . . . And he was still young. The blue air of spring, fresh from its memories of windy pools and lush shrubbery, could thrill him with eagerness.

He took a step forward just as the tapping blind man passed him by. Quickly the shabby fellow turned.

"Listen, guv'nor.[4] Just a minute of your time."

Mr. Parsons said, "It's late. I have an appointment. Do you want me to give you something?"

"I ain't no beggar, guv'nor. You bet I ain't.

I got a handy little article here"—he fumbled until he could press a small object into Mr. Parsons' hand—"that I sell. One buck. Best cigarette lighter made."

Mr. Parsons stood there, somewhat annoyed and embarrassed. He was a handsome figure with his immaculate gray suit and gray hat and malacca stick.[5] Of course the man with the cigarette lighters could not see him. . . . "But I don't smoke," he said.

"Listen. I bet you know plenty people who smoke. Nice little present," wheedled[6] the man. "And, mister, you wouldn't mind helping a poor guy out?" He clung to Mr. Parsons' sleeve.

Mr. Parsons sighed and felt in his vest pocket. He brought out two half dollars and pressed them into the man's hand. "Certainly. I'll help you out. As you say, I can give it to someone. Maybe the elevator boy would—" He hesitated, not wishing to be boorish[7] and inquisitive,[8] even with a blind peddler. "Have you lost your sight entirely?"

---

1. **furtive** (fėr′tiv), *adj.* quickly done in a sly or secret manner.
2. **splay** (splā), *v.* spread out; extend.
3. **futile** (fyü′tl), *adj.* useless; not successful.
4. **guv'nor**, a shortened form of governor, used to address someone of superior rank.
5. **malacca stick**, a walking stick made of a kind of wood that comes from the city of Malacca in Malaysia.
6. **wheedle** (hwē′dl), *v.* use soft speech and flattering words to persuade.
7. **boorish** (bùr′ish), *adj.* having bad manners; rude.
8. **inquisitive** (in kwiz′ə tiv), *adj.* too curious; nosy.

The shabby man pocketed the two half dollars. "Fourteen years, guv'nor." Then he added with an insane sort of pride: "Westbury, sir. I was one of 'em."

"Westbury," repeated Mr. Parsons. "Ah, yes. The chemical explosion. . . . The papers haven't mentioned it for years. But at the time it was supposed to be one of the greatest disasters in—"

"They've all forgot about it." The fellow shifted his feet wearily. "I tell you, guv'nor, a man who was in it don't forget about it. Last thing I ever saw was C shop going up in one grand smudge, and gas pouring in all the busted windows."

Mr. Parsons coughed. But the blind peddler was caught up with the train of his one dramatic reminiscence.[9] And, also, he was thinking that there might be more half dollars in Mr. Parsons' pocket.

"Just think about it, guv'nor. There was a hundred and eight people killed, about two hundred injured, and over fifty of them lost their eyes. Blind as bats—" He groped forward until his dirty hand rested against Mr. Parsons' coat. "I tell you, sir, there wasn't nothing worse than that in the war. If I had lost my eyes in the war, okay. I would have been well took care of. But I was just a workman, working for what was in it. And I got it. You're darn right I got it, while the capitalists[10] were making their dough! They was insured, don't worry about that. They—"

"Insured," repeated his listener. "Yes. That's what I sell—"

"You want to know how I lost my eyes?" cried the man. "Well here it is!" His words fell with the bitter and studied drama of a story often told, and told for money. "I was there in C shop, last of all the folks rushing out. Out in the air there was a chance, even with buildings exploding right and left. A lot of guys made it safe out the door and got away. And just when I was about there, crawling along

between those big vats, a guy behind me grabs my leg. He says, 'Let me past, you—!' Maybe he was nuts. I dunno. I try to forgive him in my heart, guv'nor. But he was bigger than me. He hauls me back and climbs right over me! Tramples me into the dirt. And he gets out, and I lie there with all that poison gas pouring down on all sides of me, and flame and stuff. . . ." He swallowed—a studied sob—and stood dumbly expectant. He could imagine the next words: *Tough luck, my man. Now, I want to*—"That's the story, guv'nor."

The spring wind shrilled past them, damp and quivering.

"Not quite," said Mr. Parsons.

The blind peddler shivered crazily. "Not quite? What do you mean, you—"

"The story is true," Mr. Parsons said, "except that it was the other way around."

"Other way around?" He croaked unamiably.[11] "Say, guv'nor—"

"I was in C shop," said Mr. Parsons. "It was the other way around. You were the fellow who hauled back on me and climbed over me. You were bigger than I was, Markwardt."

The blind man stood for a long time, swallowing hoarsely. He gulped: "Parsons. I thought you—" And then he screamed fiendishly:[12] "Yes. Maybe so. Maybe so. But I'm blind! I'm blind, and you've been standing here letting me spout to you, and laughing at me every minute! I'm blind."

People in the street turned to stare at him.

"You got away, but I'm blind! Do you hear? I'm—"

"Well," said Mr. Parsons, "don't make such a row about it, Markwardt. . . . So am I."

---

9. **reminiscence** (rem′ə nis′ns), *n.* a remembering or recalling of past events.

10. **capitalist** (kap′ə tə list), *n.* person who favors private ownership of business; often, a rich person.

11. **unamiably** (un ā′mē ə blē), *adv.* in an unpleasant or disagreeable manner.

12. **fiendishly** (fēn′dish lē), *adv.* in a cruel or wicked manner.

After Reading

Making Connections

1. What do you suppose Parsons and Markwardt might be thinking as they walk away from each other?

2. Look back at what you wrote in your notebook. What moments in the story brought your experience back to mind?

3. If you turned this story into a **fable**—a story with a lesson—what animals would you use to represent the two characters? Why?

4. What clues does the author give at the beginning of the story that Parsons is blind?

5. 👆 Parsons's **perspective** on being blind is very different from Markwardt's. Create a web that shows the various ways each exhibits his perspective. Here's one way to begin your web:

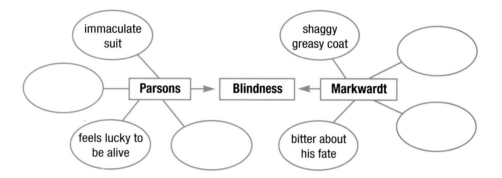

6. How was the explosion a turning point in each character's life?

7. What do you think makes the biggest difference in how a person deals with a life-changing event such as going blind?

Literary Focus: Irony

Now you can understand the popularity of MacKinlay Kantor's famous "snapper." The final revelation that Parsons too is blind is called **irony**—a situation that is the opposite of what it appears.

On a chart, list some ironic situations you've found in other stories. Compare your examples to this story.

Other Stories	The Irony	Similarity to This Story
Cinderella	The most unfortunate girl in the kingdom wins the prince.	Like Markwardt, her family learns the truth about a person they mistreated.

Vocabulary Study

Read the rhyming riddles below. Then look at the vocabulary list and answer the question "WHAT WORD AM I?"

furtive
splay
futile
wheedle
boorish
inquisitive
reminiscence
capitalist
unamiably
fiendishly

1. I can buy a lot with all my money,
   But my wealth can't make misfortune funny.

2. I beg and flatter to get spare change.
   I want things my way—is that so strange?

3. I'm the wicked way that thrives on bad.
   Listen for my cackle when you're feeling sad.

4. I get called *useless*. I take such abuse!
   I could try a bit harder, but what's the use?

5. I'm the disagreeable way to get through life.
   I treat friends like enemies and stir up strife.

6. I'm what you remember from your past.
   If you try to change me, I'll laugh last.

7. Pull myself together? That's easy to say!
   Try being spread out like me some day.

8. Do you want to be sly? I'll show you how.
   I'm sneaky and quick. Watch me! Where am I now?

9. Don't follow me when you want to be nice.
   I'm the *rude* part of *crude*. I turn feelings to ice.

10. They say I'm nosy and overly curious.
    I'm so full of questions, I make people furious.

Expressing Your Ideas

Writing Choices

Brief Encounter In an **essay,** compare the lives of Parsons and Markwardt between the time of the explosion and their chance meeting.

New Vision Advancements in science have helped the blind live productive lives. Create the copy for a **brochure** about a recent invention for the visually impaired.

Once Upon a Time Write a **fable** in which you use animal characters to relate the moral of this story.

Other Options

It Happened Like This Imagine Parsons as an old man reminiscing about his life. Retell his **story** as he might tell it to a grandchild.

Roving Reporters Form a group to enact on-the-street **interviews** of Parsons and Markwardt. Go back to the story to get ideas for questions to ask the characters.

Easy Living, Inc. Draw a **floor plan** for a home that would accommodate the special needs of a blind person.

Turkeys

by Bailey White

Bailey White
born 1950

Bailey White became famous doing the very thing she hates doing most—talking on the radio. Speaking to the public is so scary to White, that her voice gets crackly. Still, her audience loves hearing her stories. White thinks of herself as a writer, not a storyteller, but says teaching first grade is her "honorable job." The love of writing, however, is a family trait. Bailey White's father, Robb White, was a scriptwriter for the *Perry Mason* TV series and Hollywood thrillers. Her strong-willed and witty mother, Rose, provides much of her daughter's writing material, putting in an appearance in "Turkeys." Rose is also the straightforward writing critic who noted that Bailey "is a much better writer than her father ever was."

Building Background

Let's Talk Turkey Certain habitats attract certain kinds of birds, which in turn attract a certain kind of scientist—an *ornithologist.* Ornithologists study birds of all kinds. Ornithology includes all aspects of bird life—physical characteristics, behavior, and habitat. Guess the kind of bird the ornithologists study in this selection.

The Wild Turkey

Getting into the Autobiography

Writer's Notebook Have you ever missed someone you've never met—like an ichthyornis? This bird has been extinct for millions of years, but birds are disappearing from the Earth even now. Many others are endangered, but may still be saved. In your notebook, write your thoughts about disappearing wildlife.

Reading Tip

Field Notes The author writes about birds that are familiar to people in Georgia, where she grew up. Are any familiar to you?

Bird	Characteristics
red cockaded woodpecker	Named for the red cockades, or tufts of feathers, on the male's crest. Threatened due to its limited habitat.
ivory billed woodpecker	Largest North American woodpecker. Once found in Southern forests, last seen in 1971.
chuck-will's-widow	Night-flying bird that nests on the ground. It catches insects in flight and has a rhythmic call.
Carolina parakeet	North American parrot, extinct since 1918. Shot as a pest in fields and orchards.
wild turkey	Large bird with a loud gobble, it makes a nest on the ground for 8 to 15 eggs.

BAILEY WHITE

Something about my mother attracts ornithologists. It all started years ago when a couple of them discovered she had a rare species of woodpecker coming to her bird feeder. They came in the house and sat around the window, exclaiming and taking pictures with big fancy cameras. But long after the red cockaded woodpeckers had gone to roost in their sticky little holes in the red hearts of our big old pine trees, and the chuck-will's-widows had started to sing their night chorus, the ornithologists were still there. There always seemed to be three or four of them wandering around our place, discussing the body fat of hummingbirds, telling cruel jokes about people who couldn't tell a pileated woodpecker from an ivory bill, and staying for supper.

In those days, during the 1950s, the big concern of ornithologists in our area was the wild turkey. They were rare, and the pure-strain wild turkeys had begun to interbreed with farmers' domestic stock. The species was being degraded.[1] It was extinction by dilution,[2] and to the ornithologists it was just as tragic as the more dramatic demise[3] of the passenger pigeon or the Carolina parakeet.

One ornithologist had devised a formula to compute the ratio of domestic to pure-strain wild turkey in an individual bird by comparing the angle of flight at takeoff and the rate of acceleration. And in those sad days, the turkeys were flying low and slow.

It was during that time, the spring when I was six years old, that I caught the measles. I had a high fever, and my mother was worried about me. She kept the house quiet and dark and crept around silently, trying different methods of cooling me down.

Even the ornithologists stayed away—but

---

1. **degrade** (di grād′), *v.* lower the quality of; make less pure.
2. **dilution** (də lü′shən), *n.* the act of making something weaker or less pure by the addition of something else.
3. **demise** (di mīz′), *n.* death.

▲ *In Bed* was painted in 1891 by Edouard Vuillard. Why do you suppose Vuillard chose these particular colors for his painting?

not out of fear of the measles or respect for a household with sickness. The fact was, they had discovered a wild turkey nest. According to the formula, the hen was pure-strain wild—not a taint of the sluggish domestic bird in her blood—and the ornithologists were camping in the woods, protecting her nest from predators and taking pictures.

One night our phone rang. It was one of the ornithologists. "Does your little girl still have measles?" he asked.

"Yes," said my mother. "She's very sick. Her temperature is 102."

"I'll be right over," said the ornithologist.

In five minutes a whole carload of them arrived. They marched solemnly into the house, carrying a cardboard box. "A hundred two, did you say? Where is she?" they asked my mother.

They crept into my room and set the box down on the bed. I was barely conscious, and when I opened my eyes, their worried faces hovering over me seemed to float out of the darkness like giant, glowing eggs. They snatched the covers off me and felt me all over. They consulted in whispers.

"A hundred two—can't miss if we tuck them up close and she lies still."

I closed my eyes then, and after a while the ornithologists drifted away, their pale faces bobbing up and down on the black wave of fever.

The next morning I was better. For the first time in days I could think. The memory of the ornithologists with their whispered voices and their bony, cool hands was like a dream from another life. But when I pulled down the covers, there staring up at me with googly eyes and wide mouths, were sixteen fuzzy baby turkeys and the cracked chips and caps of sixteen brown speckled eggs.

I was a sensible child. I gently stretched myself out. The eggshells crackled, and the turkey babies fluttered and cheeped and snuggled against me. I laid my aching head back on the pillow and closed my eyes. "The ornithologists," I whispered. "The ornithologists have been here."

It seems the turkey hen had been so disturbed by the elaborate[4] protective measures that had been undertaken in her behalf that she had abandoned her nest on the night the eggs were due to hatch. It was a cold night. The ornithologists, not having an incubator to hand, used their heads and came up with the next best thing.

The baby turkeys and I gained our strength together. When I was finally able to get out of bed and feebly creep around the house, the turkeys peeped and cheeped around my ankles, scrambling to keep up with me and tripping over their own big spraddle-toed feet. When I went outside for the first time, the turkeys tumbled after me down the steps and scratched around in the yard while I sat in the sun.

Finally, in late summer, the day came when they were ready to fly for the first time as adult birds. The ornithologists gathered. I ran down the hill, and the turkeys ran too. Then, one by one, they took off. They flew high and fast. The ornithologists made V's with their thumbs and forefingers, measuring angles. They consulted their stopwatches and paced off distances. They scribbled in their tiny notebooks. Finally they looked at each other. They sighed. They smiled. They jumped up and down and hugged each other. "One hundred percent pure wild turkey!" they said.

Nearly forty years have passed since then. In many ways the world is a worse place now. But there's a vaccine for measles. And the woods where I live are full of pure wild turkeys. I like to think they are all descendants of those sixteen birds I saved from the vigilance[5] of the ornithologists.

They scribbled in their tiny notebooks. Finally they looked at each other. They sighed. They smiled.

---

4. **elaborate** (i lab′ər it), *adj.* very careful and detailed.
5. **vigilance** (vij′ə ləns), *n.* watchfulness.

After Reading

Making Connections

1. Have you ever had an experience that was stranger than fiction? How did people react when you told them what happened?

2. Who do you think cares most about birds in this selection? Explain.

3. Does the author intend her account to be serious or amusing? Find examples to support your answer.

4. Frequently writers are advised to "write about what you know." How does following that rule make this autobiography unique?

5. What in this selection has to do with change?

6. The narrator likes to recall her small part in helping to save wild turkeys. Reflect on what you wrote in your notebook before reading. How might you help an endangered species survive?

Literary Focus: Tone

You can tell that narrator of this selection really wanted to

(A) become an ornithologist.

(B) see ornithologists return every summer.

(C) show that wild birds need ornithologists.

(D) do none of the above.

If you answered "D," you caught the narrator's **tone**—her attitude toward someone or something in the selection.

One way to determine tone is by noticing the author's choice of words and details. Consider how the narrator describes the ornithologists' appearance and behavior. What do her descriptions suggest about her attitude? You can organize your findings on a chart like the one below.

Ornithologists	Attitude Revealed
Appearance	
faces like giant eggs	They are so wrapped up in eggs they look like them. Their faces are as bland and featureless as an egg.
Behavior	
tell cruel jokes	

Vocabulary Study

A. Number a sheet of paper from one to five. After each number, add dashes and squares as shown below. Fill in the dashes and squares with the letters of the words defined on the right.

degrade
dilution
demise
elaborate
vigilance

WORDS   DEFINITIONS

1. □ __ __ __ __ □ □ __   something made weaker

2. __ __ __ □ __ __ __ □ __   watchfulness

3. __ __ __ □ __ □ __ □ __   careful and detailed

4. __ __ □ __ □ __   death

5. __ □ __ __ __ □ __   make less pure

B. Rearrange the letters in the squares to answer this riddle: What kind of fowl do ornithologists ignore?

__ __ __ __ __ __ __ __ __   __ __ __ __

Expressing Your Ideas

Writing Choices

Rabbit Attack!
Imagine you woke up one morning to find this furry fellow at the foot of your bed! How would you react? Do you think its presence would change your life? Write a **short story** about the experience.

Back to Nature Spend an hour observing something in nature, such as a bird, an insect, a plant, or the weather. Take **field notes** on what you see, hear, and smell.

Bird Watcher's Notebook Imagine you are an ornithologist. Log several **journal entries** about the life cycle of turkey eggs.

Other Options

Here Today . . . The Carolina parakeet became extinct in your great-grandparents' generation. **Research** and **report on** an endangered bird you hope your great-grandchildren will get to see—alive. Make drawings for your presentation.

Little Chicks' Turkeys Bird stories really "fly" with children. Turn "Turkeys" into a picture book for a young child you know. You might try out your work by reading it to a kindergarten class.

Cheeps 'n' Peeps Listen to the birds in your community or to a recording to learn various bird calls. Imitate and teach some bird calls to classmates. Then hold a bird-calling contest to see who the birds are most likely to answer.

Before Reading

Alfred: The Sweet-Shop Cat

by James Herriot

James Herriot
1916–1995

James Wight was best known by his pen name, James Herriot. Herriot was both the author and the country veterinarian in the books and films based on his life. *All Creatures Great and Small* and *All Things Bright and Beautiful* are two you may know. As a boy, Herriot explored the Scottish highlands with his dog. By the age of thirteen he knew he would be a veterinarian, and he let nothing get in his way—not even pitiful grades in science. He soon discovered his dream job was "dirty, uncomfortable, sometimes dangerous . . . and terribly hard work." He loved it. At age fifty, Herriot taught himself how to write while practicing veterinary medicine full time. His greatest pleasure was hearing his words spoken by fine actors.

Building Background

Alfred's World What do American veterinarians do in spring while British veterinarians are *lambing?* They do the same! Tending female sheep who are giving birth to their young (called *lambing* by the British) happens in rural areas everywhere. British words and ways are just part of the fun of the story you are about to read, which takes place in a *sweet shop*, or English candy store. For more about what goes on there, bite into this selection.

Getting into the Selection

Writer's Notebook You are going to read about a special friendship between a man and his cat . . . or perhaps it's a cat and his man. In any case, you've probably met people who are such good friends with their pets that they seem to look alike. Write about it in your notebook.

Reading Tip

Briticisms The chart below will help you understand this story's **Briticisms,** words used and spelled in a typically British way.

	British	**American**
Spelling	vapour, flavour, colour	vapor, flavor, color
	favourite, honour	favorite, honor
	Geoff	Jeff
	liquorice	licorice
	recognise, realise	recognize, realize
	anaesthetic	anesthetic
Words	bonny	pretty
	aye	yes
	nay	no
Dialect	'ave, 'ad, 'im	have, had, him
	summat	something
	o'	of
	t'	the
	nowt	nothing

Alfred the Sweet-Shop Cat

James Herriot

My throat was killing me. Three successive nocturnal lambings on the windswept hillsides in my shirt-sleeves had left me with the beginnings of a cold and I felt in urgent need of a packet of Geoff Hatfield's cough drops. An unscientific treatment, perhaps, but I had a childish faith in those powerful little candies which exploded in the mouth, sending a blast of medicated vapour surging through the bronchial tubes.

The shop was down a side alley, almost hidden away, and it was so tiny—not much more than a cubby hole—that there was hardly room for the sign, GEOFFREY HATFIELD, CONFECTIONER,[1] above the window. But it was full. It was always full, and, this being market day, it was packed out.

---

1. **confectioner,** a person who sell candies and cakes.

Geoffrey Hatfield's shop in a little side alley in North Yorkshire, England, as perceived by Lesley Holmes. 🐾 What does this **perspective** tell you about the village? ➤

The little bell went "ching" as I opened the door and squeezed into the crush of local ladies and farmers' wives. I'd have to wait for a while but I didn't mind, because watching Mr. Hatfield in action was one of the rewarding things in my life.

I had come at a good time, too, because the proprietor[2] was in the middle of one of his selection struggles. He had his back to me, the silver-haired, leonine[3] head nodding slightly on the broad shoulders as he surveyed the rows of tall glass sweet jars against the wall. His hands, clasped behind him, tensed and relaxed repeatedly as he fought his inner battle, then he took a few strides along the row, gazing intently at each jar in turn. It struck me that Lord Nelson pacing the quarterdeck of the *Victory*,[4] wondering how best to engage the enemy, could not have displayed a more portentous[5] concentration.

The tension in the little shop rose palpably[6] as he reached up a hand, then withdrew it with a shake of the head, but a sigh went up from the assembled ladies as, with a final grave nod and a squaring of the shoulders, he extended both arms, seized a jar and swung round to face the company. His large Roman Senator face was crinkled into a benign smile.

"Now, Mrs. Moffat," he boomed at a stout matron and, holding out the glass vessel with both hands, inclined it slightly with all the grace and deference of a Cartier jeweller displaying a diamond necklace, "I wonder if I can interest you in this."

Mrs. Moffat, clutching her shopping basket, peered closely at the paper-wrapped confections in the jar. "Well, ah don't know. . . ."

"If I remember rightly, madam, you indicated that you were seeking something in the nature of a Russian caramel, and I can thoroughly recommend these little sweetmeats.[7] Not quite a Russian, but nevertheless a very nice, smooth-eating toffee." His expression became serious, expectant.

The fruity tones rolling round his description made me want to grab the sweets and devour them on the spot, and they seemed to have the same effect on the lady. "Right, Mr. Hatfield," she said eagerly, "I'll 'ave half a pound."

The shopkeeper gave a slight bow. "Thank you so much, madam, I'm sure you will not regret your choice." His features relaxed into a gracious smile and, as he lovingly trickled the toffees onto his scales before bagging them with a professional twirl, I felt a renewed desire to get at the things.

Mr. Hatfield, leaning forward with both hands on the counter, kept his gaze on his customer until he had bowed her out of the shop with a courteous, "Good day to you, madam," then he turned to face the congregation. "Ah, Mrs. Dawson, how very nice to see you. And what is your pleasure this morning?"

The lady, obviously delighted, beamed at him. "I'd like some of them fudge chocolates I 'ad last week, Mr. Hatfield. They were lovely. Have you still got some?"

"Indeed I have, madam, and I am delighted that you approve of my recommendation. Such a deliciously creamy flavour. Also, it so happens that I have just received a consignment in a special presentation box for Easter." He lifted one from the shelf and balanced it on the palm of his hand. "Really pretty and attractive, don't you think?"

Mrs. Dawson nodded rapidly. "Oh, aye, that's real bonny. I'll take a box and there's

---

2. **proprietor** (prə prī′ə tər), *n.* shop owner.
3. **leonine** (lē′ə nīn), like a lion.
4. **Lord Nelson . . . of the *Victory*.** In the Battle of Trafalger, 1805, Vice Admiral Nelson commanded the ship *Victory*, leading England to victory over France.
5. **portentous** (pôr ten′təs), threatening.
6. **palpably** (pal′pə blē), *adv.* plainly; obviously.
7. **sweetmeats,** candied fruits and sugar-coated nuts.

summat else I want. A right big bag of nice boiled sweets[8] for the family to suck at. Mixed colours, you know. What 'ave you got?"

Mr. Hatfield steepled his fingers, gazed at her fixedly and took a long, contemplative[9] breath. He held this pose for several seconds, then he swung round, clasped his hands behind him, and recommenced his inspection of the jars.

There was no doubt he was a cat of enormous presence.

That was my favourite bit and, as always, I was enjoying it. It was a familiar scene. The tiny, crowded shop, the proprietor wrestling with his assignment and Alfred sitting at the far end of the counter.

Alfred was Geoff's cat and he was always there, seated upright and majestic on the polished boards near the curtained doorway which led to the Hatfield sitting room. As usual, he seemed to be taking a keen interest in the proceedings, his gaze moving from his master's face to the customer's, and though it may have been my imagination I felt that his expression registered a grave involvement in the negotiations and a deep satisfaction at the outcome. He never left his place or encroached[10] on the rest of the counter, but occasionally one or other of the ladies would stroke his cheek and he would respond with a booming purr and a gracious movement of the head towards them.

It was typical that he never yielded to any unseemly display of emotion. That would have been undignified, and dignity was an unchanging part of him. Even as a kitten he had never indulged in immoderate playfulness. I had neutered him three years earlier—for which he appeared to bear me no ill will—and he had grown into a massive, benevolent[11] tabby.[12] I looked at him now, sitting in his place. Vast, imperturbable, at peace with his world. There was no doubt he was a cat of enormous presence.

And it had always struck me forcibly that he was exactly like his master in that respect. They were two of a kind and it was no surprise that they were such devoted friends.

When it came to my turn I was able to reach Alfred and I tickled him under his chin. He liked that and raised his head high while the purring rumbled up from the furry rib cage until it resounded throughout the shop.

Even collecting my cough drops had its touch of ceremony. The big man behind the counter sniffed gravely at the packet and then clapped his hand a few times against his chest. "You can smell the goodness, Mr. Herriot, the beneficial vapours. These will have you right in no time." He bowed and smiled and I could swear that Alfred smiled with him.

I squeezed my way out through the ladies and as I walked down the alley I marvelled for the umpteenth time at the phenomenon of Geoffrey Hatfield. There were several other sweet shops in Darrowby, big double-fronted places with their wares attractively displayed in the windows, but none of them did anything like the trade of the poky establishment I had just left. There was no doubt that it was all due to Geoff's unique selling technique

---

8. **boiled sweets,** hard candies in many flavors and colors.
9. **contemplative** (kon′təm plā′tiv), *adj.* deeply thoughtful.
10. **encroach** (en krōch′), *v.* to go beyond proper limits.
11. **benevolent** (bə nev′ə lənt), *adj.* kindly; charitable.
12. **tabby,** a gray or brownish-yellow cat with dark stripes.

Alfred: The Sweet-Shop Cat **471**

▲ Lesley Holmes painted this watercolor interpretation of Alfred in 1994. Does this cat strike you as "majestic"?

and it was certainly not an act on his part, it was born of a completely sincere devotion to his calling, a delight in what he was doing.

His manner and "posh" diction gave rise to a certain amount of ribald[13] comment from men who had left the local school with him at the age of fourteen, and in the pubs he was often referred to as "the bishop," but it was good-natured stuff because he was a well-liked man. And, of course, the ladies adored him and flocked to bask in his attentions.

About a month later I was in the shop again to get some of Rosie's favourite liquorice all-sorts and the picture was the same—Geoffrey smiling and booming, Alfred in his place, following every move, the pair of them radiating dignity and well-being. As I collected my sweets, the proprietor whispered in my ear.

"I'll be closing for lunch at twelve noon, Mr. Herriot. Would you be so kind as to call in and examine Alfred?"

"Yes, of course." I looked along the counter at the big cat. "Is he ill?"

"Oh, no, no . . . but I just feel there's something not right."

Later I knocked at the closed door and Geoffrey let me into the shop, empty for once, then through the curtained doorway into his sitting room. Mrs. Hatfield was at a table, drinking tea. She was a much earthier character than her husband. "Now then, Mr. Herriot, you've come to see t'little cat."

"He isn't so little," I said, laughing. And indeed, Alfred looked more massive than ever seated by the fire, looking calmly into the flames. When he saw me he got up, stalked unhurriedly over the carpet and arched his back against my legs. I felt strangely honoured.

"He's really beautiful, isn't he?" I murmured. I hadn't had a close look at him for some time and the friendly face with the dark stripes running down to the intelligent eyes appealed to me as never before. "Yes," I said, stroking the fur which shone luxuriantly in the flickering firelight, "you're a big beautiful fellow."

I turned to Mr. Hatfield. "He looks fine to me. What is it that's worrying you?"

"Oh, maybe it's nothing at all. His appearance certainly has not altered in the slightest, but for over a week now I've noticed that he is not quite so keen on his food, not quite so lively. He's not really ill . . . he's just different."

"I see. Well, let's have a look at him." I went over the cat carefully. Temperature was normal, mucous membranes a healthy pink. I got out my stethoscope and listened to heart and lungs—nothing abnormal to hear. Feeling around the abdomen produced no clue.

"Well, Mr. Hatfield," I said, "there doesn't seem to be anything obviously wrong with him. He's maybe a bit run down, but he doesn't look it. Anyway, I'll give him a vitamin injection. That should buck him up. Let me know in a few days if he's no better.

"Thank you indeed, sir. I am most grateful. You have set my mind at rest." The big man reached out a hand to his pet. The confident resonance[14] of his voice was belied by the expression of concern on his face. Seeing them together made me sense anew the similarity of man and cat—human and animal, yes, but alike in their impressiveness.

I heard nothing about Alfred for a week and assumed that he had returned to normal, but then his master telephoned. "He's just the same, Mr. Herriot. In fact, if anything, he has deteriorated slightly. I would be obliged if you would look at him again."

It was just as before. Nothing definite to see even on close examination. I put him on to a course of mixed minerals and vitamin tablets. There was no point in launching into

---

13. **ribald** (rib′əld), mocking and offensive.
14. **resonance** (rez′n əns), *n.* a full, echoing quality.

treatment with our new antibiotics—there was no elevation of temperature, no indication of any infectious[15] agent.

I passed the alley every day—it was only about a hundred yards from Skeldale House—and I fell into the habit of stopping and looking in through the little window of the shop. Each day, the familiar scene presented itself; Geoff bowing and smiling to his customers and Alfred sitting in his place at the end of the counter. Everything seemed right, and yet . . . there *was* something different about the cat.

I called in one evening and examined him again. "He's losing weight," I said.

Geoffrey nodded. "Yes, I do think so. He is still eating fairly well, but not as much as before."

"Give him another few days on the tablets," I said, "and if he's no better I'll have to get him round to the surgery and go into this thing a bit more deeply."

I had a nasty feeling there would be no improvement and there wasn't, so one evening I took a cat cage round to the shop. Alfred was so huge that there was a problem fitting him into the container, but he didn't resist as I bundled him gently inside.

At the surgery I took a blood sample from him and X-rayed him. The plate was perfectly clear and when the report came back from the laboratory it showed no abnormality.

In a way, it was reassuring, but that did not help because the steady decline continued. The next few weeks were something like a nightmare. My anxious peering through the shop window became a daily ordeal. The big cat was still in his place, but he was getting thinner and thinner until he was almost unrecognisable. I rang the changes with every drug and treatment I could think of, but nothing did any good. I had Siegfried examine him, but he thought as I did. The progressive emaciation was the sort of thing you would expect from an internal tumour, but further

X-rays still showed nothing. Alfred must have been thoroughly fed up of all the pushing around, the tests, the kneading of his abdomen, but at no time did he show any annoyance. He accepted the whole thing placidly as was his wont.[16]

There was another factor which made the situation much worse. Geoff himself was wilting under the strain. His comfortable coating of flesh was dropping steadily away from him, the normally florid cheeks were pale and sunken and, worse still, his dramatic selling style appeared to be deserting him. One day I left my viewpoint at the window and pushed my way into the press of ladies in the shop. It was a harrowing scene. Geoff, bowed and shrunken, was taking the orders without even a smile, pouring the sweets listlessly[17] into their bags and mumbling a word or two. Gone was the booming voice and the happy chatter of the customers, and a strange silence hung over the company. It was just like any other sweet shop.

Saddest sight of all was Alfred, still sitting bravely upright in his place. He was unbelievably gaunt, his fur had lost its bloom and he stared straight ahead, dead-eyed, as though nothing interested him any more. He was like a feline scarecrow.

I couldn't stand it any longer. That evening I went round to see Geoff Hatfield.

"I saw your cat today," I said, "and he's going rapidly downhill. Are there any new symptoms?"

The big man nodded dully. "Yes, as a matter of fact. I was going to ring you. He's been vomiting a bit."

I dug my nails into my palms. "There it is again. Everything points to something

---

15. **infectious** (in fek′shəs), *adj.* spreading by germs or virus.
16. **as was his wont,** according to his usual way.
17. **listlessly** (list′lis lē), *adv.* without interest; seeming too tired to care.

abnormal inside him and yet I can't find a thing." I bent down and stroked Alfred. "I hate to see him like this. Look at his fur. It used to be so glossy."

"That's right," replied Geoff, "he's neglecting himself. He never washes himself now. It's as though he can't be bothered. And before, he was always at it—lick, lick, lick for hours on end."

"We've got to do something or this cat is going to die."

I stared at him. His words had sparked something in my mind. "Lick, lick, lick." I paused in thought. "Yes . . . when I think about it, no cat I ever knew washed himself as much as Alfred. . . ." The spark suddenly became a flame and I jerked upright in my chair.

"Mr. Hatfield," I said, "I want to do an exploratory operation!"

"What do you mean?"

"I think he's got a hair-ball inside him and I want to operate to see if I'm right."

"Open him up, you mean?"

"That's right."

He put a hand over his eyes and his chin sank onto his chest. He stayed like that for a long time, then he looked at me with haunted eyes. "Oh, I don't know. I've never thought of anything like that."

"We've got to do something or this cat is going to die."

He bent and stroked Alfred's head again and again, then without looking up he spoke in a husky voice. "All right, when?"

"Tomorrow morning."

Next day, in the operating room, as Siegfried and I bent over the sleeping cat, my mind was racing. We had been doing much more small-animal surgery lately, but I had always known what to expect. This time I felt as though I was venturing into the unknown.

I made an incision and in the stomach I found a large, matted hair-ball, the cause of all the trouble. Something which wouldn't show up on an X-ray plate.

Siegfried grinned. "Well, now we know!"

"Yes," I said as the great waves of relief swept over me. "Now we know."

I found more, smaller hair-balls, all of which had to be removed and then the incision stitched. I didn't like this. It meant a bigger trauma and shock to my patient, but finally all was done and only a neat row of skin sutures[18] was visible.

When I returned Alfred to his home, his master could hardly bear to look at him. At length he took a timid glance at the cat, still sleeping under the anaesthetic. "Will he live?" he whispered.

"He has a good chance," I replied. "He has had some major surgery and it might take him some time to get over it, but he's young and strong. He should be all right."

I could see Geoff wasn't convinced, and that was how it was over the next few days. I kept visiting the little room behind the shop to give the cat penicillin injections and it was obvious that Geoff had made up his mind that Alfred was going to die.

Mrs. Hatfield was more optimistic, but she was worried about her husband.

"Eee, he's given up hope," she said. "And it's all because Alfred just lies in his bed all day. I've tried to tell 'im that it'll be a bit o' time before the cat starts runnin' around, but he won't listen."

She looked at me with anxious eyes. "And, you know, it's gettin' him down, Mr. Herriot. He's a different man. Sometimes I wonder if he'll ever be the same again."

---

18. **sutures,** stitches made to sew up a wound.

I went over and peeped past the curtain into the shop. Geoff was there, doing his job like an automaton. Haggard, unsmiling, silently handing out the sweets. When he did speak it was in a listless monotone and I realised with a sense of shock that his voice had lost all its old timbre. Mrs. Hatfield was right. He was a different man. And, I thought, if he stayed different, what would happen to his clientele? So far they had remained faithful, but I had a feeling they would soon start to drift away.

It was a week before the picture began to change for the better. I entered the sitting room, but Alfred wasn't there.

Mrs. Hatfield jumped up from her chair. "He's a lot better, Mr. Herriot," she said eagerly. "Eating well and seemed to want to go into t'shop. He's in there with Geoff now."

Again I took a surreptitious[19] look past the curtain. Alfred was back in his place, skinny but sitting upright. But his master didn't look any better.

I turned back into the room. "Well, I won't need to come any more, Mrs. Hatfield. Your cat is well on the way to recovery. He should soon be as good as new." I was quite confident about this, but I wasn't so sure about Geoff.

At this point, the rush of spring lambing and post-lambing troubles overwhelmed me as it did every year, and I had little time to think about my other cases. It must have been three weeks before I visited the sweet shop to buy some chocolates for Helen. The place was packed and as I pushed my way inside all my fears came rushing back and I looked anxiously at man and cat.

Alfred, massive and dignified again, sat like a king at the far end of the counter. Geoff was leaning on the counter with both hands, gazing closely into a lady's face. "As I understand you, Mrs. Hird, you are looking for something in the nature of a softer sweetmeat." The rich voice reverberated[20] round the little shop. "Could you perhaps mean a Turkish Delight?"

"Nay, Mr. Hatfield, it wasn't that. . . ."

His head fell on his chest and he studied the polished boards of the counter with fierce concentration. Then he looked up and pushed his face nearer to the lady's. "A pastille,[21] possibly . . . ?"

"Nay . . . nay."

"A truffle? A soft caramel? A peppermint cream?"

"No, nowt like that."

He straightened up. This was a tough one. He folded his arms across his chest and as he stared into space and took the long inhalation I remembered so well I could see that he was a big man again, his shoulders spreading wide, his face ruddy and well fleshed.

Nothing having evolved from his cogitations,[22] his jaw jutted and he turned his face upwards, seeking further inspiration from the ceiling. Alfred, I noticed, looked upwards, too.

There was a tense silence as Geoff held this pose, then a smile crept slowly over his noble features. He raised a finger. "Madam," he said, "I do fancy I have it. Whitish, you said . . . sometimes pink . . . rather squashy. May I suggest to you . . . marshmallow?"

Mrs. Hird thumped the counter. "Aye, that's it, Mr. Hatfield. I just couldn't think of t'name."

"Ha-ha, I thought so," boomed the proprietor, his organ tones rolling to the roof. He laughed, the ladies laughed, and I was positive that Alfred laughed, too.

All was well again. Everybody in the shop was happy—Geoff, Alfred, the ladies and, not least, James Herriot.

---

19. **surreptitious** (sėr/əp tish/əs), *adj.* secret; stealthy.
20. **reverberate** (ri vėr/bə rāt/), *v.* echo back.
21. **pastille,** a medicated candy or cough drop.
22. **cogitation,** deep thought; careful consideration.

After Reading

Making Connections

1. Can you relate to Mr. Hatfield's devotion to his cat? Explain.

2. Look back at your Writer's Notebook. How do Mr. Hatfield and Alfred compare with the pair you wrote about?

3. James Herriot is known for his lifelike descriptions of people and animals. Discuss two descriptive phrases that brought Alfred's personality to life for you.

4. What changes in Alfred and Mr. Hatfield led up to the turning point in the story? Use a plot line like the one below.

turning point _____

next change in Alfred and Hatfield _____

_____

next change in Alfred and Hatfield _____

_____

a change in Hatfield _____

a change in Alfred _____

as story opens Mr. Hatfield runs his shop like Lord Nelson on the
_____ quarterdeck. Alfred is majestic. _____

5. 🐾 The veterinarian and the sweet-shop owner each have a different **perspective** regarding Alfred. Compare and contrast their views of this majestic cat.

6. Based on this story and your own experience, list three benefits and three responsibilities of having a pet.

Literary Focus: Dialect

You've learned something about British dialect by reading this selection. By using such true-to-life language, an author can suggest a great deal about the characters, such as native origin, years of education, social status, and so on.

You can tune your ear for dialect, by playing **"Who Said?"** Here's how: On slips of paper, write short phrases spoken by the various characters in the story. Mix the slips in a container. Form two teams. A member of one team draws a slip and says, "Who said (and reads the slip)?" The other team gets one guess.

Vocabulary Study

Match each vocabulary word at the left with its descriptive rhyme.

proprietor
palpably
contemplative
encroach
benevolent
resonance
infectious
listlessly
surreptitious
reverberate

1. This word describes what's behind the scene—
   A secret glance, a quiet hiss . . . you know what I mean.

2. Here's a word for a cat deep in thought,
   Plotting its strategies for mice to be caught.

3. A wise cat who wants to avoid disaster
   Will find a home with this kind of master.

4. *Not* doing this is knowing your place,
   Keeping your distance, and leaving no trace.

5. When you meow at the moon in full, booming tones,
   Your voice has this quality, which jiggles your bones.

6. This is the way sounds echo through halls:
   They repeat themselves and bounce off walls.

7. No interest in life? Too tired to purr?
   The symptoms of this word call for a cure.

8. This word tells how feelings fill a room
   Till you can almost "see" joy, worry, or gloom.

9. I'd like to be this person in a candy store,
   I'd own all the candy and a whole lot more.

10. This is a word that makes the rounds,
    Spreading germs to people, cats, and hounds.

Expressing Your Ideas

Writing Choices

Here, Kitty, Kitty Some people say a cat makes the perfect companion. Others prefer a dog or a fish. Write a **thumbnail sketch** of the perfect animal for you.

Service with a Smile James Herriot observed that Hatfield showed "a completely sincere devotion to his calling, a delight in what he was doing." Write a **character sketch** about someone you know who fits this description.

Other Options

Kindness to Animals Taking good care of an animal is the best way to keep it healthy. Give a **demonstration** to the class on how to care for a pet of your choosing.

Body Language Communication between pets and owners is very common. Most people become experts on their pet's body language. Produce a **cartoon strip** that shows what your pet means by its movements and postures.

Before Reading

from The Autobiography of Malcolm X

by Malcolm X with Alex Haley

Malcolm X
1925–1965

The writing of *The Autobiography of Malcolm X* was a joint effort. Alex Haley urged Malcolm X to tell his story, and Malcolm agreed after deciding he could be an example of change through faith. Malcolm wanted to express himself in the most effective way, and so he teamed up with Haley, a professional writer.

Alex Haley
1921–1992

Haley's experience with Malcolm X inspired him to write his own story, *Roots: The Saga of an American Family*, which won the Pulitzer Prize.

Building Background

A Man for Change At age twenty—when college graduates look toward a future with promise—Malcolm Little entered Charlestown State Prison in Massachusetts for burglary. It was a predictable outcome for a junior-high dropout who was "majoring" in crime.

Six years later, in 1952, Malcolm was free—and changed. He converted to the Black Muslim religion and took the name Malcolm X, symbolizing his break with the past. He became a Black Muslim, urging African Americans to use "whatever force necessary" to gain their rights. Then, on a journey to Mecca, the home of the Islamic religion, Malcolm X changed again. He began to urge all races to fight for justice—*together* and in peace. On February 21, 1965, bullets silenced Malcolm X as he gave a speech.

Getting into the Autobiography

Writer's Notebook Egric zblog ik jittle? Xqi flonkity blib! Remember when words looked like that—*before* you learned to read? In your notebook, describe your feelings about learning to read.

Reading Tip

Chronology This selection begins with some background information. Then it goes further back to a life-changing event that unfolded over time. By using clues to **chronology,** or the sequence of events, you can keep pace with Malcolm X every step of the way. Here are some words and phrases that give you clues to the chronology.

CALENDAR OF EVENTS				
Monday	**Tuesday**	**Wednesday**	**Thursday**	**Friday**
It had really begun back in . . .	Finally, . . .	Then, . . .	. . . next morning	. . . for the first time
		. . . eventually . . .	. . . up to then . . .	

from The Autobiography of

MALCOLM X

MALCOLM X WITH ALEX HALEY

It was because of my letters that I happened to stumble upon starting to acquire some kind of homemade education.

I became increasingly frustrated at not being able to express what I wanted to convey[1] in letters that I wrote, especially those to Mr. Elijah Muhammad.[2] In the street, I had been the most articulate[3] hustler out there—I had commanded attention when I said something. But now, trying to write simple English, I not only wasn't articulate, I wasn't even functional.[4] How would I sound writing in slang, the way I would *say* it, something such as, "Look, daddy, let me pull your coat about a cat, Elijah Muhammad—"[5]

Many who today hear me somewhere in person, or on television, or those who read something I've said, will think I went to school far beyond the eighth grade. This impression is due entirely to my prison studies.

It had really begun back in the Charlestown Prison, when Bimbi[6] first made me feel envy of his stock of knowledge. Bimbi had always taken charge of any conversation he was in, and I had tried to emulate[7] him. But every book I picked up had few sentences which didn't contain anywhere from one to nearly all of the words that might as well have

1. **convey** (kən vā′), *v.* communicate; make known.
2. **Mr. Elijah Muhammad,** the African-American leader of the Black Muslim religion in the United States.
3. **articulate** (är tik′yə lit), *adj.* being able to put thoughts into words easily.
4. **functional** (fungk′shə nəl), *adj.* capable of reading and writing well enough to meet everyday needs.
5. **"Look, daddy . . . Elijah Muhammad—,"** street slang meaning "Look, pal. I'd like to tell you about a man called Elijah Muhammad."
6. **Bimbi,** a fellow prisoner at Charlestown Prison.
7. **emulate** (em′yə lāt), *v.* imitate an admired person.

▲ *The Library* was created in 1960 by Jacob Lawrence. Imagine the sounds in this scene.
  Try to describe them.

been in Chinese. When I just skipped those words, of course, I really ended up with little idea of what the book said. So I had come to the Norfolk Prison Colony still going through only book-reading motions. Pretty soon, I would have quit even these motions, unless I had received the motivation that I did.

I saw that the best thing I could do was get hold of a dictionary—to study, to learn some words. I was lucky enough to reason also that I should try to improve my penmanship. It was sad. I couldn't even write in a straight line. It was both ideas together that moved me to request a dictionary along with some tablets

and pencils from the Norfolk Prison Colony school.

I spent two days just riffling[8] uncertainly through the dictionary's pages. I'd never realized so many words existed! I didn't know *which* words I needed to learn. Finally, just to start some kind of action, I began copying.

In my slow, painstaking,[9] ragged handwriting, I copied into my tablet everything printed on that first page, down to the punctuation marks.

---

8. **riffle** (rif′əl), *v.* leaf through pages.
9. **painstaking** (pānz′tā′king), *adj.* very careful.

I believe it took me a day. Then, aloud, I read back to myself everything I'd written on the tablet. Over and over, aloud, to myself, I read my own handwriting.

I woke up the next morning, thinking about those words—immensely proud to realize that not only had I written so much at one time, but I'd written words that I never knew were in the world. Moreover, with a little effort, I also could remember what many of these words meant. I reviewed the words whose meanings I didn't remember. Funny thing, from the dictionary first page right now, that "aardvark" springs to my mind. The dictionary had a picture of it, a long-tailed, long-eared, burrowing African mammal, which lives off termites caught by sticking out its tongue as an anteater does for ants.

I was so fascinated that I went on—I copied the dictionary's next page. And the same experience came when I studied that. With every succeeding page, I also learned of people and places and events from history. Actually, the dictionary is like a miniature encyclopedia. Finally, the dictionary's A section had filled a whole tablet—and I went on into the B's. That was the way I started copying what eventually became the entire dictionary. It went a lot faster after so much practice helped me to pick up handwriting speed. Between what I wrote in my tablet, and writing letters, during the rest of my time in prison I would guess I wrote a million words.

I suppose it was inevitable[10] that as my word-base broadened, I could for the first time pick up a book and read and now begin to understand what the book was saying. Anyone who has read a great deal can imagine the new world that opened. Let me tell you something: from then until I left that prison, in every free moment I had, if I was not reading in the library, I was reading on my bunk. You couldn't have gotten me out of books with a wedge. Between Mr. Muhammad's teachings, my correspondence, my visitors—usually Ella and Reginald[11]—and my reading of books, months passed without my even thinking about being imprisoned. In fact, up to then, I never had been so truly free in my life.

CLARIFY: Why does Malcolm X feel more truly free inside prison than he did in the street?

The Norfolk Prison Colony's library was in the school building. A variety of classes was taught there by instructors who came from such places as Harvard and Boston universities. The weekly debates between inmate teams were also held in the school building. You would be astonished to know how worked up convict debaters and audiences would get over subjects like "Should Babies Be Fed Milk?"

Available on the prison library's shelves were books on just about every general subject. Much of the big private collection that Parkhurst had willed to the prison was still in crates and boxes in the back of the library—thousands of old books. Some of them looked ancient: covers faded, old-time parchment-looking binding. Parkhurst,[12] I've mentioned, seemed to have been principally interested in history and religion. He had the money and the special interest to have a lot of books that you wouldn't have in general circulation. Any college library would have been lucky to get that collection.

As you can imagine, especially in a prison where there was heavy emphasis on rehabilitation,[13] an inmate was smiled upon if

---

10. **inevitable** (in ev′ə tə bəl), not to be avoided; certain to happen.
11. **Ella and Reginald,** Malcolm X's sister and brother.
12. **Parkhurst,** a rich man who wanted to help prisoners get an education.
13. **rehabilitation** (rē′hə bil′ə tā′shən), n. restoring one to good health or positive behavior.

he demonstrated an unusually intense interest in books. There was a sizable number of well-read inmates, especially the popular debaters. Some were said by many to be practically walking encyclopedias. They were almost celebrities. No university would ask any student to devour[14] literature as I did when this new world opened to me, of being able to read and *understand*.

I read more in my room than in the library itself. An inmate who was known to read a lot could check out more than the permitted maximum number of books. I preferred reading in the total isolation of my own room.

When I had progressed to really serious reading, every night at about ten P.M. I would be outraged with the "lights out." It always seemed to catch me right in the middle of something engrossing.[15]

Fortunately, right outside my door was a corridor light that cast a glow into my room.

The glow was enough to read by, once my eyes adjusted to it. So when "lights out" came, I would sit on the floor where I could continue reading in that glow.

At one-hour intervals the night guards paced past every room. Each time I heard the approaching footsteps, I jumped into bed and feigned[16] sleep. And as soon as the guard passed, I got back out of bed onto the floor area of that light-glow, where I would read for another fifty-eight minutes—until the guard approached again. That went on until three or four every morning. Three or four hours of sleep a night was enough for me. Often in the years in the streets I had slept less than that.

---

14. **devour** (di vour′), *v.* take in with the eyes or ears in a hungry way.
15. **engrossing** (en grō′sing), *adj.* taking up one's complete attention.
16. **feign** (fān), *v.* make believe; pretend.

Another Voice

i remember . . .

Mae Jackson

i remember . . .

january,

1968

its snow,

5 the desire that i had to build

a black snowman

and place him upon

Malcolm's grave.

8/15/68

After Reading

Making Connections

1. Look back to what you wrote about learning to read in your Writer's Notebook. Were your experiences different than those of Malcolm X? Do you see any similarities? Explain.

2. If you had a large book collection to leave behind as Parkhurst did, whom would you leave it to, and why?

3. Mae Jackson's poem "i remember" expresses a strong emotional reaction to Malcolm X's death. What qualities do you see in him that might have evoked such a reaction?

4. Malcolm X said his motivation to read began with his envy of Bimbi's knowledge and ability to talk. How did his motivation to read change over time?

5. Chart Malcolm X's process of learning to read and write, from being *frustrated* to feeling *truly free*. Record your data on a **cause-and-effect chart,** expanding or shortening it as you see fit.

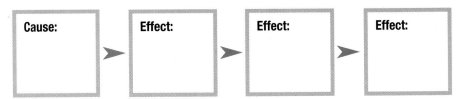

6. For most of us, going to a library is an ordinary event. Why do you think going to the prison library was such a significant experience for Malcolm X?

7. This dramatic autobiography tells how literacy changed the life of an extraordinary man. What difference can literacy make in the lives of ordinary people?

Literary Focus: Symbolism

A word is a word and also a **symbol**—something that represents an idea or holds special meaning. The word *book,* for example, is a group of letters arranged in a way you can recognize and pronounce. An *unabridged* or uncut dictionary, lists over twenty meanings for *book* as a noun—plus almost a dozen more as a verb. From Malcolm X's point of view, however, *book* has still another meaning not found in a dictionary—*freedom.*

How does a book symbolize freedom in this selection? How is ignorance like a prison? With classmates, brainstorm other things a book may symbolize.

Vocabulary Study

Match each underlined phrase below with the appropriate vocabulary word at left.

convey
articulate
functional
emulate
riffle
painstaking
rehabilitation
devour
engrossing
feign

1. A convict can undergo <u>change for the better</u> through education.
2. Some find reading to be <u>taking all their attention.</u>
3. Education can help prisoners become <u>able to work</u> in society.
4. When we are impressed with others, we may <u>try to be like</u> them.
5. The scholar was <u>very careful</u> when taking notes for his exam.
6. He would <u>take in hungrily</u> all that he read.
7. The prisoner who earns a degree may <u>pretend</u> not to care, but must be very proud.
8. A <u>well-spoken</u> request has a better chance of being understood.
9. The warden began <u>to leaf through</u> a report on the prisoner.
10. Prisoners may <u>communicate</u> their feelings through art.

Expressing Your Ideas

Writing Choices

All the Difference Learning to read changed Malcolm X's life. Write an **autobiographical essay** about an experience that has had a major impact on your life.

As Told By . . . Work with a partner. Interview each other about an activity each of you enjoy as much as Malcolm X enjoyed reading. Then **ghostwrite** each other's story as Alex Haley helped Malcolm X write his autobiography.

Prison Without Bars What changed Malcolm Little the small-time crook into Malcolm X the civil rights leader? In an **essay,** discuss how one makes such a transition. Use examples from the selection to illustrate your ideas.

Other Options

Lights On for Reading Form a **special-interest group** to read more of *The Autobiography of Malcolm X.* You could divide the book into parts. Each member then reads and reports on one section.

Performance Reading One effective way to share a writer's work is to read some of it aloud to others. Give a **dramatic reading** in class of one of Malcolm X's writings as he himself would have liked to hear it spoken— *with feeling*.

Warning: This Book May Be Hazardous to Ignorance! Design a **bookplate** to paste on the inside cover of every book you own. Include an original saying in the design.

Writing Mini-Lesson

Research Technique: Finding Information

Kinds of Sources There are two kinds of sources for research.

- **Primary sources** are firsthand accounts of an event. Primary sources include letters, speeches, and diaries; eyewitness reports; literary works; follow-up reports to observations or experiments; your own interviews, letters, journal entries, or observations.

- **Secondary sources** are reports of information from other sources. Your history book is a secondary source. Encyclopedia entries, history books, and biographies are also secondary sources.

Locating Sources

Check the following for primary and secondary materials:

- **Your school or public library database or card catalog.** Some libraries have special collections of primary source materials.

- **Museums and historical societies.**

- **Public and private organizations involved in your research topic.**

- **People in your community.** People who remember a person or event are valuable sources of information.

Activity Options

1. Classify the following items about World War II as a primary or secondary source: letters from a soldier, a newspaper article about D-Day, a biography of President Roosevelt, an autobiography of a concentration camp survivor, a diary from 1943, a chapter from your history book, recruitment posters.

2. Learn how to use library materials such as reference materials, the *Reader's Guide to Periodical Literature*, the card catalog, and other databases.

3. As you research a topic, make notes about where you looked for your sources and what you found in your search. Compare your methods and results with your classmates.

Before Reading

Niña

by Margarita Mondrus Engle

Margarita Mondrus Engle

Building Background

Land in Change The tropical island of Cuba was formed long ago by volcanic eruption. The original Cubans were South American Indians who spoke Arawakan. Today, Cubans trace their roots to Europe and Africa and speak mainly Spanish.

After a fiery revolution in the 1960s, Cuba came under communist rule, aided by the Soviet Union. With the Soviet collapse, Cuba is again at the crossroads of change.

Getting into the Story

Discussion In this story, a trip to Cuba is a turning point in a young girl's life. The different customs of the people she visits changes her view of the world. Talk about a time when you encountered customs different from yours. How did you react? As you read, think about the way the narrator handles the customs she encounters.

Reading Tip

Words from Cuba It's always good to know some of the language of a country you are visiting. Use this chart for reference on your "trip" to Cuba in this story.

Terms in the Story	Meanings and Descriptions
Abuelita (ä´bwä lē´tä)	Grandma (-*ita* is added as an endearment)
anon fruit	a tropical pulpy tart fruit with fleshy spines
bohio (bō ē´ō)	hut
Estados Unidos (es ta´dōs ü nē´ dōs)	United States
mamonsillo fruit (ma mon´sē yo)	papaya
tarantula	a large, hairy spider with a painful sting
Yanquis	Yankees, Cubans' word for Americans

Niña

Margarita Mondrus Engle

My mother was afraid it might be our last chance to visit her family in Cuba. The revolution was almost two years old, and already there was talk of an impending[1] crisis.

At the airport in Miami she gave us three instructions.

"Never tell anyone you are tomboys."

"Why?"

"They wouldn't understand. Also, don't tell the other children about your allowance. You have more money in the bank than their fathers make in a year."

"So?"

"So, they would feel bad."

"Oh."

"And the most important, don't bring animals into your grandmother's house."

"But mom . . ."

"No animals. They don't like having animals in the house. Do you understand?"

At the airport in Havana we released the caterpillars we had hidden in our luggage.

"Just in case there are no butterflies here," my sister and I reassured each other.

We had no idea what to expect, but the island did not disappoint us. Abuelita's house was on the outer fringe of Havana, and there were animals everywhere. We put the lizards in beds, and tarantulas and scorpions in the living room. The fisherman who lived across the street gave us a ripe swordfish snout to play with. When it really started to stink my mother threw it on the roof, where it rotted quickly in the sun.

The fisherman's daughter asked me if I had money for ice cream. "Yes," I said with pride, "I have eighty dollars in the bank, which I saved all my myself."

"Dollars? Really?" I could see she didn't believe a word of it. I squirmed inside, remembering my mother's admonition.[2]

"Well, I have something better," the girl offered. "Crabs. When my father gets home you can have one to cook for dinner."

She was right, of course. The crabs were better than my money. Her father came home with a truckload of them, bright orange crabs as big as cats. We put ours on a leash, and led it up and down the street until it died.

My sister liked dogs better than crabs. She begged my mother for a can of dogfood for my great-grandmother's mangy[3] hound. We had to go all the way downtown, to Woolworth's, just to find dogfood in cans. It

---

◄ *The Sick Child* was painted by Edvard Munch. Judging by the mother's posture, how grave would you judge the child's illness to be?

1. **impending** (im pen′ding), *adj.* likely to happen soon; threatening.
2. **admonition** (ad′mə nish′ən), *n.* warning.
3. **mangy** (mān′jē), *adj.* shabby and dirty.

cost more than a month's supply of real food, corn meal, black beans and rice.

Just to make sure there were no sins left uncommitted, I went across the street and told the fisherman's daughter I was a tomboy.

"Oh no," she said horrified. "You're not a tomboy, don't worry. You will be fine." She fluffed her petticoat and curled a lock of hair with her fingers.

My collection of revolutionary bullets were growing. They were everywhere, in Abuelita's front yard, and in the weeds where we searched for tarantulas, which we caught with wads of gum attached to strings. There were bullets in the open field beyond the city, and in the passion vines[4] which clung to the walls of houses.

On one of my solitary expeditions I wandered far beyond those walls, beyond the open fields and into a mud floored hut with a thatched roof and many inhabitants. The family greeted me as if I had some right to invade their home. The children came outside to introduce me to their mule, their chickens, and the sensitive Mimosa plant which closed its leaves at the touch of a child's finger.

One of the children was called Niña, meaning "girl." I assumed her parents had simply run out of names by the time they got round to her. In Niña's case her name was more unusual than her appearance. She was hardly there, just bones and eyes, and a few pale wisps of hair bleached by malnutrition.[5]

"Doesn't she get enough to eat?" I asked my mother when I reached home.

"They say she has a hole in her stomach."

One day I was standing in the sun of the front porch, watching a black storm cloud sweep across the sky, bringing towards me its thunder and lightning, which fell only in one small corner of the sky. A motionless circle of vultures hung from the cloud, listless, with black wings barely trembling in the wind.

"Come in," my mother warned. "Don't forget your uncle who was killed by lightning, right in his own kitchen."

I ignored her. If it could happen in the kitchen, then why bother to go inside? I was just as safe outside.

Niña crept up to the porch, smiling her death's head smile, like the skull and cross-bones on a bottle of medicine.

"Here," she said, offering me half of the anon fruit she was eating. I took it. Together we ate and stared and smiled at each other, not knowing what to say. We both knew my half of the seedy, juicy fruit was going into my body, making flesh and fat, while hers was going right out of the gaping invisible hole in her stomach.

Something like a shiver passed through my shoulder.

"Someone stepped on your grave," Niña giggled.

"What do you mean?"

"They say when you shiver like that it's because someone stepped on the spot where your grave will be."

I stared at Niña's huge eyes, wondering who could have been cruel enough to inform her that she would ever have a grave.

When we trooped down the street to the bingo games at my great-grandmother's house, Niña tagged along. An endless array of uncles and cousins filed in and out, a few boasting revolutionary beards and uniforms, but most outfitted in their farmers' Sunday best, their hands brown and calloused.[6]

Niña was quiet. She poured burnt-milk candy through the hole in her stomach, and watched. The size of her eyes made her watching feel like staring, but no one seemed to notice. Children like Niña surprised no one.

---

4. **passion vine,** a vine with a large, showy flower.
5. **malnutrition** (mal′nü trish′ən), *n.* poor health due to lack of good food.
6. **calloused** (kal′əst), *adj.* hardened.

On the anniversary of the revolution the streets filled with truckloads of bearded men on their way to the mountains to celebrate. A man with a loudspeaker walked along our street announcing the treachery of the Yanquis. I was listening inside my grandmother's house. Suddenly his voice changed.

"Let me clarify," he was saying, "that it is not the common people of the United States who we oppose, but the government which has . . ." I stopped listening. Niña was at the open door, smiling her bony smile.

"I told him," she said very quietly, "that you are from Estados Unidos. I didn't want him to hurt your feelings."

At the beach, my sister and I went swimming inside shark fences. We imagined the gliding fins beyond the fence. Afterwards, our mother extracted[7] the spines of bristly sea urchins from the soles of our feet.

We visited huge caverns gleaming with stalactites.[8] How wonderfully the Cuban Indians must have lived, I thought, with no home but a cave, nothing to eat but fruit and shellfish, nothing to do but swim and sing. "We were born a thousand years too late," I told my sister.

With a square old-fashioned camera, I took pictures of pigs, dogs, turkeys, horses and mules. Not once did it occur to me to put a friend or relative into one of my photos. I was from Los Angeles. There were more than enough people in the world, and far too few creatures. When my uncle cut sugar cane, it was the stiff, sweet cane itself which caught my eye, and the gnats clinging to his eyes. His strong arms and wizened[9] face were just part of the landscape. When my cousins picked mamonsillo fruit, it was the tree I looked at, and not the boys showing off by climbing it. I thrived on the wet smell of green land after a rain, and the treasures I found crawling in red mud or dangling from the leaves of weeds and vines. I trapped lizards, netted butterflies, and once, with the help of my sister, I snared a vulture with an elaborate hand-rigged snare. Our relatives were horrified. What could one do with a vulture? It was just the way I felt about everything which mattered to them. If the goal of the revolution was to uproot happy people from their thatched havens,[10] and deposit them in concrete high-rise apartment buildings, who needed it? Thatched huts, after all, were natural, wild, primitive. They were as good as camping. When my mother explained that the people living in the bohios were tired of it, I grew sulky. Only an adult would be foolish enough to believe that any normal human being could prefer comfort to wilderness, roses to weeds, radios to the chants of night-singing frogs.

I knew the hole in Niña's stomach was growing. She was disappearing, vanishing before my eyes. Her parents seemed resigned[11] to her departure. People spoke of her as if she had never really been there. Niña was not solid. She didn't really exist.

On the day of her death, it occurred to me to ask my mother, "Why didn't they just take her to a doctor?"

"They had no money."

I went out to the front porch, abandoning the tarantula I had been about to feed. As I gazed across the open fields toward Niña's bohio, the reality of her death permeated[12] the humid summer air. In my mind, I sifted through a stack of foals and ducks, caterpillars and vultures. Somewhere in that stack, I realized, there should have been an image of Niña.

---

7. extract (ek strakt′), v. pull out.
8. **stalactite,** a formation of lime, shaped like an icicle, hanging from the roof of a cave.
9. wizened (wiz′nd), adj. withered, old.
10. haven (hā′vən), n. place of safety and shelter.
11. resigned (ri zīnd′), adj. accepting what happens without complaint.
12. permeate (pèr′mē āt), v. to spread through all of something.

After Reading

Making Connections

1. The narrator learned something new in Cuba at every turn. What is something she learned that had an effect on you?

2. How do you think knowing Niña changed the narrator's life?

3. ✿ Before reading, you wrote about your experience with customs different from yours. What **perspective** might the people in this story have on some American customs?

4. What are some early clues to the narrator's expectations of what Cuba would be like? How did her expectations differ from her experience?

5. ✿ The revolution in Cuba caused conflict among Cubans and between Cuba and the United States. What does the narrator say that shows her **perspective** on the revolution?

6. Imagine that Abuelita is visiting your community for the first time. Describe the things you would like to show her.

Literary Focus: Foreshadowing

At what point in the story did you expect Niña's death? What details up until then led you to that conclusion?

An author can use **foreshadowing**—hints and clues about what will happen—to prepare readers for an important event. While the narrator of "Niña" describes many happy occasions typical of a vacation, many details in the story prepare you for death to be part of the experience.

List several examples of foreshadowing. You can use a chart like the one below to note your findings. Share your findings with the class.

Description of Niña	Other Hints of Death	Well-Known Symbols
She was hardly there	hole in her stomach	black storm cloud

Vocabulary Study

Choose the correct vocabulary word to complete the sentences.

impending
admonition
mangy
malnutrition
calloused
extract
wizened
haven
resigned
permeate

1. An **impending** turning point in the revolution suggests the turning point was **a.** planned. **b.** delayed. **c.** about to happen.

2. Remembering her mother's **admonition** not to talk suggests her talking is **a.** inappropriate. **b.** in a foreign language. **c.** untrue.

3. The children buy food for the **mangy** hound, which suggests the hound is **a.** well cared for. **b.** neglected. **c.** fat.

4. Niña eventually dies from **malnutrition,** which suggests that Niña was **a.** starving. **b.** overeating. **c.** too picky.

5. The farmer's hands were **calloused,** which suggests that farming is **a.** easy work. **b.** low-paid. **c.** hard labor.

6. If Mother must **extract** urchin spines from the girl's feet, this suggests the spines are **a.** red. **b.** sharp. **c.** blunt.

7. Uncle's **wizened** face in the cane field suggests that cane is cut **a.** under a hot sun. **b.** in the rain. **c.** at night.

8. The revolution took each person from a thatched **haven,** suggesting that the people's homes were **a.** unlocked. **b.** safe. **c.** uncomfortable.

9. Niña's family was **resigned** to her death, which suggests they were **a.** uncaring. **b.** without hope. **c.** very shocked.

10. Niña's absence was said to **permeate** the air, suggesting her absence was **a.** felt everywhere. **b.** iced. **c.** like a dream.

Expressing Your Ideas

Writing Choices

Virtual History The narrator regreted being born too late to live as the Cuban Indians did. Imagine spending a day in any place at any time you wish. **Describe** your day.

Bon Voyage! With a small group, research the customs and points of interest of another country. Write a **travel guide** for visitors.

Dear Abuelita You are the narrator back at home in the U.S. Write a letter to your grandmother in Cuba.

Other Options

See the USA! Put together a **tour package** for a Cuban student touring the USA. Include pictures of must-see places, maps, tickets, and a tape of useful English phrases.

Cuba's Revolution In a small group, research the Cuban revolution. Make an **illustrated time line** to record key events.

Niña Remembered Create a **memorial** that captures Niña's spirit. Possibilities are a piece of art, a song, poem, or dance.

Life Science Connection
Science is on the march. The more we learn about ourselves and the world in which we live, the more we can improve the quality of life for everyone. How healthy are you? Your blood often holds the secret to that question.

What's in the Blood That Can Make You Sick?

It was just a stomachache. Joey said he had had it for a few days. The doctor wasn't sure what was causing it. He told his nurse to take some blood from Joey's arm so that he could do a blood test.

"A blood test! Why?" asked Joey. "All I have is a stomachache."

"The blood test will tell me if there is an infection," the doctor said. "It will also tell me a lot of other things."

Red, White, and...

In the blood there are both red and white blood cells. And there are *platelets*, another type of blood cell. Together, they make up about half our blood; the other half is a liquid called *plasma*.

With a blood test, doctors look for changes in the blood. Any changes in the different cells tell them that something is wrong.

For example, the red blood cells carry oxygen to all parts of the body. They also contain *hemoglobin*, a red, iron-rich substance. The oxygen helps us to stay alive. If the blood test shows that you don't have enough red blood cells, it means your body is not getting all the oxygen it needs to work well.

Anemia—A Lack of Red Cells

A shortage of red blood cells means you have *anemia*. Anemias are the most common blood disorders. A person with anemia becomes pale and breathless, loses energy, and tires quickly. An anemic person may feel weak, dizzy, and drowsy.

A common cause of anemia in growing children is a diet poor in iron. Other causes include infection and the use of certain drugs.

Another form of anemia, called *sickle cell anemia*, also can be found by blood examination. In this disease, the red blood cells

Blood Types in the U.S.

Type O: positive–37.4% or 1 in 3; negative–6.6% or 1 in 15

Type A: positive–35.7% or 1 in 3; negative–6.3% or 1 in 16

Type B: positive–8.5% or 1 in 12; negative–1.5% or 1 in 67

Type AB: positive–3.4% or 1 in 29; negative–.6% or 1 in 140

become stiff and shaped like crescents. Because of their shape, they cause a lot of pain as they circulate in the bloodstream. Most sickle cell anemia is found in persons of African American descent.

Out-of-Control White Cells

Some blood disorders are a type of cancer. One of these is *leukemia*. It results from a change in the white blood cells, which normally help protect the body against infection from bacteria and viruses.

Leukemia is the most common form of cancer in young children. The disease causes abnormal, harmful white blood cells to multiply wildly. These bad cells crowd out the healthy blood cells. They spill over into the bloodstream and make it a great deal more difficult for the immune system to fight off infection.

Leukemia is a disease that affects the entire body; it is not contagious. Treatment has improved greatly in recent years by the use of new drugs and procedures such as bone marrow transplants. Many people with this disease now recover.

Damaged Blood Vessels

What about the platelets in the blood? Their job is to repair damaged blood vessels. When you get an injury that causes you to bleed, the platelets get together to plug up the place where the bleeding occurs. They help the blood to clot and the bleeding to stop.

But some people's blood does not clot normally. They are missing a protein in the blood that is important for clotting to occur.

"Pull out, Betty! Pull out!. . .You've hit an artery!"

These people, almost always male, don't stop bleeding after an injury. Without treatment, they can bleed to death. They have a disease called *hemophilia*, which is inherited.

The treatment for young people with hemophilia is better today than ever before. Patients are taught to inject themselves with a protein solution that replaces the missing substance in their blood.

Blood Tests—Important Tools

Anemias, leukemia, and hemophilia are not the only problems that are found by blood tests. A blood test tells the doctor whether there is too much *cholesterol*, a fat, in the blood. If there is a high level of cholesterol, there may be a risk for heart disease.

A blood test can measure the amount of sugar (also called glucose) in your bloodstream. If there is high blood sugar, it means the body is not using the glucose properly. This tells the doctor to look for *diabetes*.

Blood transfusions are sometimes a necessary part of the treatment of a person who has a blood disorder. Blood is vital for life. Each year, millions of lives are saved because people give their blood to help those with blood disorders.

Responding

With each turning point in science and medicine, the quality of human life has improved and the average life span has increased. Some people argue that scientists should no longer work to lengthen life span because quality of life decreases with age. Do you agree? Explain.

Science Connection

Change is inevitable. However, the changes in science and medicine go far beyond most. They are nothing short of remarkable. Take a look at some of the the turning points in medicine that have so improved the quality of life in the past few centuries.

English physician and anatomist William Harvey demonstrates his theory of blood circulation. Harvey developed his theory in 1628. His work became the basis for modern research on the circulatory system. ▼

The first public demonstration of the use of anesthesia was given at Massachusetts General Hospital in 1846. The development of anesthesia allowed doctors to safely perform complex surgeries, giving patients with a variety of illnesses a new chance at life.

In 1796, British physician Edward Jenner introduced vaccination with cowpox virus to prevent smallpox. By the late 1970s, the vaccine had wiped out the disfiguring and often fatal disease. Here, a doctor vaccinates patients in his parlor with virus taken directly from an infected cow.

Scientist Louis Pasteur was the first to prove that many diseases are caused by germs that multiply in the body. Pasteur developed vaccinations to fight the germs and eliminate the diseases they caused. He first used his rabies vaccination on a human patient in 1885 when a young boy was bitten by a rabid dog. Here Pasteur vaccinates a patient.

Breakthroughs in Medicine

German physicist Wilhelm Conrad Roentgen discovered X rays in 1895. His discovery revolutionized diagnostic and surgical procedures in medicine. The X ray of the hand above was taken in 1896 in Hamburg, Germany, using Roentgen's technique. The digitized X ray on the right was taken in 1992.

Sir Alexander Fleming, who discovered penicillin in 1928, works in his laboratory in St. Mary's Hospital, London. The development of penicillin opened a new chapter in medicine, and in 1940 it came into general use in the fight against infection. World War II was the stage for the first field trial of the new miracle drug.

Dr. Jonas Salk administers a polio vaccine to a student in Pittsburgh in 1955. Salk developed the vaccine that virtually eliminated this crippling and contagious viral disease.

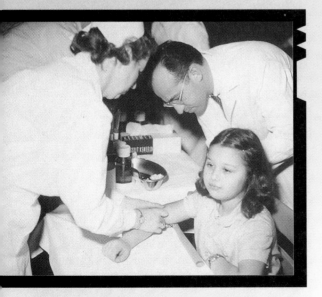

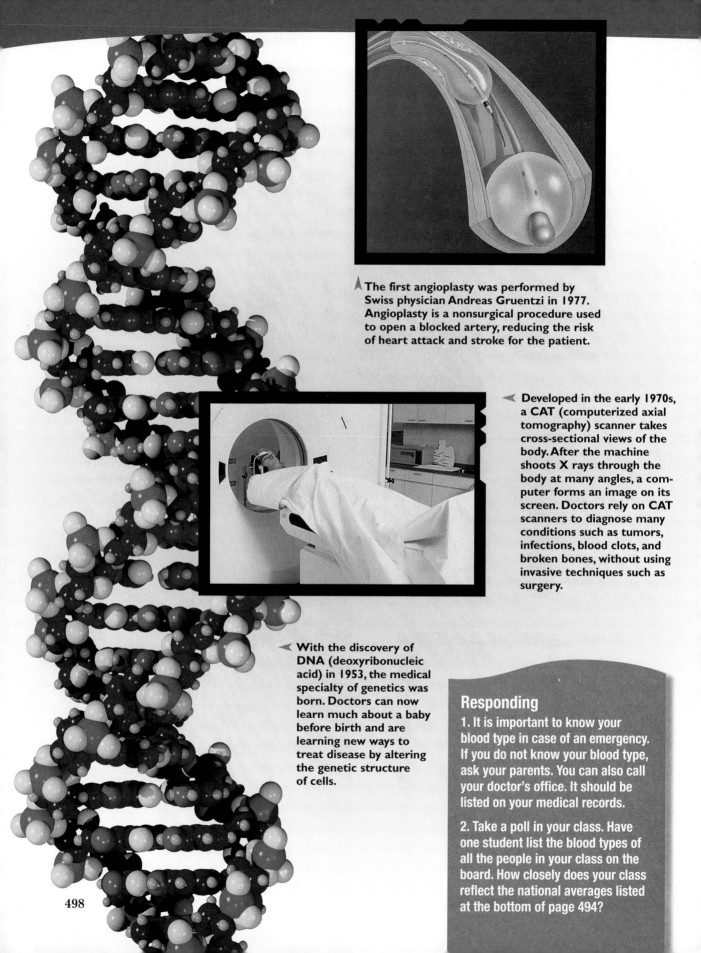

The first angioplasty was performed by Swiss physician Andreas Gruentzi in 1977. Angioplasty is a nonsurgical procedure used to open a blocked artery, reducing the risk of heart attack and stroke for the patient.

Developed in the early 1970s, a CAT (computerized axial tomography) scanner takes cross-sectional views of the body. After the machine shoots X rays through the body at many angles, a computer forms an image on its screen. Doctors rely on CAT scanners to diagnose many conditions such as tumors, infections, blood clots, and broken bones, without using invasive techniques such as surgery.

With the discovery of DNA (deoxyribonucleic acid) in 1953, the medical specialty of genetics was born. Doctors can now learn much about a baby before birth and are learning new ways to treat disease by altering the genetic structure of cells.

Responding

1. It is important to know your blood type in case of an emergency. If you do not know your blood type, ask your parents. You can also call your doctor's office. It should be listed on your medical records.

2. Take a poll in your class. Have one student list the blood types of all the people in your class on the board. How closely does your class reflect the national averages listed at the bottom of page 494?

Reading Mini-Lesson

Recalling Details

Did you ever forget the last part of a telephone number as you were dialing? What happened to your memory? Did you forget to turn it on?

Memory is tricky. It's not something you "turn on" after you read. If you want your memory to work well, you have to turn it on *before* you start reading. This is like making a shopping list before you go to the store. You're more likely to return with everything you need.

Using a K-W-L chart like the one below will help you warm up your memory. In the "K" (Know) column you brainstorm what you know about the subject. In the "W" (Want) column you list questions you want to have answered when you read. After you read, you fill in the "L" (Learned) column with what you learned as you read.

For example, to get started with the article on blood on pages 494–495, you would scan the article for subject matter clues. You'll find clues in the title and headings, and by rapidly skimming the text. Here are some entries you might make in the K and W columns of the K-W-L chart before you read the first part of the article. Entries you might make after reading are shown in the L column.

K-W-L Chart		
Topic: What's in the Blood That Can Make You Sick?		
What We Know	**What We Want to Know**	**What We Learned**
Blood has red and white cells.	What else is in the blood?	platelets, plasma, oxygen, hemoglobin
	What makes one sick?	lack of oxygen-carrying red blood cells

Activity Options

1. Copy the K-W-L chart above and fill in the K and W sections for the remaining parts of the article. Then after reading (or, in this case, rereading) the article, fill in the L column.

2. Find another informational article in a book or magazine and use a K-W-L chart to turn on and warm up your memory.

Part Two

New Directions

Have you ever planned a day at the beach and found it raining when you awoke? You probably have plans for your life too—school, a career, travel and adventure, a family. But what happens if any of those plans get rained on? In the selections that follow, you will meet characters who have experienced firsthand the saying "Into each life some rain must fall." Instead of just standing there getting wet, they have risked going in new directions.

Multicultural Connection **Interactions** involve dealing with dynamic changes that occur as groups of people interact with one another. Your cultural background influences the way you react to others. How do the characters in these selections interact with members of other groups?

Literature

M. E. Kerr	**The Author** ◆ short story	.502
Buson	**The Reader** ◆ poem	.507
	Language Mini-Lesson ◆ Consistent Verb Tense	.510
Maya Angelou	**New Directions** ◆ biography	.512
Borden Deal	**Antaeus** ◆ short story	.518
Robert F. Kennedy	**On the Death of Martin Luther King, Jr.** ◆ speech	.530
Samantha Abeel	**Samantha's Story** ◆ autobiography	.535
	Self Portrait ◆ poem	.538
Gayle Ross	**Rabbit Dances with the People** ◆ Cherokee legend	.542

Interdisciplinary Study From Pen to Printout

Words on the Page ◆ history 546

A Short History of Punctuation by Polly M. Robertus ◆ language 548

    Reading Mini-Lesson ◆ Comparing and Contrasting 550

Writing Workshop Narrative Writing

Taking New Directions 551

Beyond Print Technology Skills

Wake Things Up with Multimedia 557

Before Reading

The Author

by M. E. Kerr

M. E. Kerr
born 1927

M. E. Kerr is one of a series of pen names used by Marijane Meaker during her long writing career. As far back as she can remember, Meaker wanted to become a writer. Her father read constantly and encouraged her to read too. Her mother, who enjoyed gossip, was a good model for the use of facts to invent fiction. During her teens Meaker escaped everyday life by creating stories. A rebellious student, she had many difficulties in high school and college. Later Meaker couldn't hold down a job because she was too busy writing and trying to sell her stories. Her first big sale at age 23 began a highly successful career as a writer of mysteries, thrillers, and novels for adult and young adult readers.

Building Background

Author Biographies Have you ever wanted to learn more about a writer whose stories interest you? There are lots of ways to find out about authors. Many books carry a picture and short biography on the book jacket or last page. Several special reference books are devoted to author biographies.

You might want to write to an author. If the address is not available in a reference book, you can address the author in care of the publisher at the address on the copyright page.

Getting into the Selection

Discussion In "The Author," the narrator decides that he likes stories that are "close to home." What kinds of literature do you and your classmates most like to read? Take a poll of your classmates to see what most of them choose to read. **Classify** and record their responses under categories such as fiction, nonfiction, poetry, plays, and so on. Which is most popular, and why?

Reading Tip

Reading Fiction and Poetry Reading a **short story** is somewhat like watching a movie. Reading a poem might be likened to looking at a snapshot. It takes a while to read a short story, and when you read the last word, it seems complete. Poems usually are a much quicker read. Like a snapshot, you see the whole thing at once, but it invites you back to take a more careful, thoughtful look.

The following selection is followed by a short poem by the Japanese poet Buson. It is similar to a Japanese haiku, in that it is about nature. Don't read the poem as quickly as you would the first lines of the story. Good readers match the way they read to the material they are reading. Read the poem slowly and allow each word and phrase to suggest new images that change the picture developing in your mind. Later, you can reread it in a different mood, perhaps with different outcomes.

The Author

M. E. Kerr

Before the author comes to school, we all have to write him, saying we are glad he is coming and we like his books.

That is Ms. Terripelli's idea. She is our English teacher and she was the one who first got the idea to have real, live authors visit Leighton Middle School.

She wants the author to feel welcome.

You are my favorite author, I write.

I have never read anything he's written.

Please send me an autographed picture, I write. I am sure this will raise my English grade, something I need desperately, since it is not one of my best subjects.

The truth is: I have best friends and best clothes and best times, but not best subjects.

I am going to be an author, too, someday, I write, surprised to see the words pop up on the screen. But I am writing on the computer in the school library and there is something wonderful about the way any old thought can become little green letters in seconds, which you can erase with one touch of your finger.

I don't push WordEraser, however.

I like writing that I am going to be an author.

The person I am writing to is Peter Sand.

My name happens to be Peter too.

Peter Sangetti.

I might shorten my name to Peter Sang, when I become an author, I write. *Then maybe people will buy my books by mistake, thinking they are getting yours. (Ha! Ha!)*

Well, I write, *before this turns into a book and you sell it for money, I will sign off, but I will be looking for you when you show up at our school.*

I sign it *Sincerely,* although that's not exactly true.

The night before the author visit, my dad comes over to see me. My stepfather and my mother have gone off to see my stepbrother, Tom, in Leighton High School's version of *The Sound of Music.*

To myself, and sometimes to my mother, I call him Tom Terrific. Naturally, he has the lead in the musical. He is Captain Von Trapp.

▲ Fairfield Porter painted *John Ashbery and James Schuyler Writing "A Nest of Ninnies"* in 1967. 🐾 **Interactions** which draw from the cultural backgrounds of two authors can produce rich literature. What does the painter show you about how these two authors work with one another?

If they ever make the Bible into a play, he will be God.

I like him all right, but I am tired of playing second fiddle to him always. He is older, smarter, and better looking, and his last name is Prince. Really.

I can't compete with him.

It's funny, because the first words out of my dad's mouth that night are, "I can't compete with that."

He is admiring the new CD audio system my stepfather had ordered from the Sharper Image catalog. It is an Aiwa with built-in BBE sound.[1]

"It's really for Tom Terrific," I say, but it is in the living room, not Tom's bedroom, and Dad knows my CD collection is my pride and joy.

I suppose just as I try to compete with Tom Terrific, my dad tries to compete with Thomas Prince, Sr. . . . Both of us are losing the game, it seems. My dad is even out of work just now, although it is our secret . . . not to be shared with my mom or stepfather.

The plant where he worked was closed. He'd have to move out of the state to find the same kind of job he had there, and he doesn't want to leave me.

"I'm not worried about you," I lie. And then I hurry to change the subject, and tell him about the author's visit, next day.

He smiles and shakes his head. "Funny. I once wanted to be a writer."

"I never knew that."

"Sure. One time I got this idea for a story about our cat. She was always sitting in the window of our apartment building, looking out. She could never get out, but she'd sit there, and I'd think it'd be her dream come true if she could see a little of the world! Know what I mean, Pete?"

"Sure I do." I also know my dad always wished he could travel. He is the only person I've ever known who actually reads *National Geographic*.[2]

He laughs. "So I invented a story about the day she got out. Here was her big chance to run around the block!"

"What happened?"

"A paper bag fell from one of the apartments above ours. It landed right on Petunia's head. She ran around the block, all right, but she didn't see a thing."

Both of us roar at the idea, but deep down I don't think it is that hilarious,[3] considering it is my dad who dreamed it up.

What's he think—that he'll never see the world? Never have his dreams come true?

"Hey, what's the matter?" he says. "You look down in the dumps suddenly."

"Not me," I say.

"Aw, that was a dumb story," he says. "Stupid!"

"It was fine," I say.

"No, it wasn't," he says. "I come over here and say things to spoil your evening. You'd rather hear your music."

"No, I wouldn't," I say, but he is getting up to go.

We are losing touch not living in the same house anymore.

Whenever I go over to his apartment, he spends a lot of time apologizing for it. It is too small. It isn't very cheerful. It needs a woman's touch. I want to tell him that if he'd just stop pointing out all the things wrong with it, I'd like it fine . . . but it is turning out that we aren't great talkers anymore. I don't say everything on my mind anymore.

He shoots me a mock[4] punch at the door and tells me that next week he'll get some tickets to a hockey game. Okay with me? I say he doesn't have to, thinking of the money, and he

---

1. **BBE sound,** the manufacturer's name for stereo sound with extended bass.
2. ***National Geographic,*** magazine with articles and photographs about places and peoples throughout the world.
3. hilarious (hə ler′ē əs), *adj.* very funny.
4. mock (mok), *adj.* pretend; not real.

Peter's father tells an amusing story he invented about his cat Petunia's dream come true. Do you think the cat in this picture by Nicolas Tarkhoff has a similar scheme in mind? ➤

says I know it's not like going to the World Series or anything. I'd gone to the World Series the year before with my stepfather.

"Let up," I mumble.

"What?" he says.

"Nothing."

He says, "I heard you, Pete. You're right. You're right."

Next day, waiting for me out front is Ms. Terripelli.

"He asked for you, Pete! You're going to be Mr. Sand's guide for the day."

"Why me?" I ask.

"Because you want to be a writer?" She looks at me and I look at her.

"Oh, that," I say.

"You never told the class that," she says.

"It's too personal."

"Do you write in secret, Pete?"

"I have a lot of ideas," I say.

"Good for you!" says Ms. Terripelli, and she hands me a photograph of Peter Sand. It is autographed. It also has written on it, "Maybe someday I'll be asking for yours, so don't change your name. Make me wish it was mine, instead."

"What does all that mean?" Ms. Terripelli asks me.

"Just author stuff," I say.

I put the picture in my locker and go to the faculty lounge to meet him.

He is short and plump, with a mustache. He looks like a little colonel of some sort, because he has this booming voice and a way about him that makes you feel he knows his stuff.

"I never write fantasy," he says. "I write close to home. When you read my books, you're reading about something that happened to me! . . . Some authors write both fantasy and reality!"

At the end of his talks he answers all these questions about his books and he autographs paperback copies.

The Author   505

I hang out with him the whole time.

We don't get to say much to each other until lunch.

The school doesn't dare serve him what we get in the cafeteria, so they send out for heros, and set up a little party for him in the lounge.

The principal shows up, and some librarians from the Leighton Town Library.

When we do get a few minutes to talk he asks me what I am writing.

I say, "We had this cat, Petunia, who was always looking out the window . . ."

He is looking right into my eyes as though he is fascinated, and I finish the story.

"Wow!" he says. "Wow!"

"It's sort of sad," I say.

"It has heart and it has humor, Pete," he says. "The best stories always do."

His last session is in the school library, and members of the town are invited.

About fifty people show up.

He talks about his books for a while, and then he starts talking about me.

He tells the story about Petunia. He calls it wistful and amusing, and he says anyone who can think up a story like that knows a lot about the world already.

I get a lot of pats on the back afterward, and Ms. Terripelli says, "Well, you've had quite a day for yourself, Pete."

By this time I am having trouble looking her in the eye.

Things are a little out of hand, but what the heck—he is on his way to the airport and back to Maine, where he lives. What did it hurt that I told a few fibs?

Next day, the *Leighton Lamplighter* has the whole story. I hadn't even known there was a reporter present. There is the same photograph Peter Sand has given to me, and there is my name in the article about the author visit.

My name. Dad's story of Petunia, with no mention of Dad.

"Neat story!" says Tom Terrific.

My stepfather says if I show him a short story all finished and ready to send out somewhere, he'll think about getting me a word processor.

"I don't write for gain,"[5] I say.

Mom giggles. "You're a wiseguy, Pete."

"Among other things," I say.

Like a liar, I am thinking. Like a liar and a cheat.

When Dad calls, I am waiting for the tirade.[6]

He has a bad temper. He is the type who leaves nothing unsaid when he blows. I expect him to blow blue: he does when he loses his temper. He comes up with slang that would knock the socks off the Marine Corps.

"Hey, Pete," he says, "you really liked my story, didn't you?"

"Too much, I guess. That's why you didn't get any credit."

"What's mine is yours, kid. I've always told you that."

"I went off the deep end, I guess, telling him I want to be a writer."

"An apple never falls far from the tree, Pete. That was my ambition when I was your age."

"Yeah, you told me. . . . But *me*. What do I know?"

"You have a good imagination, son. And you convinced Peter Sand what you were saying was true."

"I'm a good liar, I guess."

"Or a good storyteller. . . . Which one?"

Why does he have to say which one?

Why does he have to act so pleased to have given me something?

The story of Petunia isn't really a gift. I realize that now. It was more like a loan.

I can tell the story, just as my dad told it to

---

5. gain (gān), *n.* getting something; profit.
6. tirade (tī′rād), *n.* a long, scolding speech.

me, but when I try to turn myself from a liar into a storyteller, it doesn't work on paper.

I fool around with it for a while. I try.

The thing is: fantasy is not for me.

I finally find out what is when I come up with a first sentence which begins:

Before the author comes to school, we all have to write him, saying we are glad he is coming and we like his books.

You see, I am an author who writes close to home.

Another Voice

The Reader

Buson

This butterfly
Which on a poppy clings
Opens, shuts
Its book of tiny paper wings.

This color-splashed impression of a butterfly was painted by Diana Ong in 1990. In what ways does Ong's interpretation of a butterfly differ from Buson's?

After Reading

Making Connections

1. Imagine you could have lunch with one of your favorite authors. Describe what it would be like.

2. 👁 Do you think your **interaction** with the poem is different than or similar to that of a Japanese reader? Explain.

3. Is Pete a born storyteller, or just a liar? Explain.

4. Be Miss Terripelli and give Pete grades on a report card for creativity, honesty, and sensitivity.

5. How does the story "The Author" fit the theme "New Directions"?

Literary Focus: Genre

You can often tell by the way something looks on the page what **genre,** or kind of material, you are about to read. One of these selections has short, broken lines, which tells you it is **poetry.** A **play** would begin with a cast of characters and have dialogue following the characters' names.

Separating **fiction** from **nonfiction** often can't be done just by looking at it. How far did you have to read before you knew that "The Author" was fiction, and not nonfiction? What clues did you use to figure it out?

Look back at the selections you just read and ask yourself why the author chose the **genre** in each case. Would the poem have made a good piece of fiction or the story a good poem? Why or why not?

Vocabulary Study

Use context clues to find the correct word from the list for each numbered blank. One of the words will be used twice.

hilarious
mock
gain
tirade

Why did Eddie Smith, who never won anything, decide to enter the World's Biggest Liar contest? Maybe it was because of his mother's __(1)__ the last time he lied about where he'd been. "You're a real liar!" she had yelled. He might have entered for the __(2)__, because there was a prize, a gold-painted crown with a __(3)__ diamond pasted in the middle. Whatever his reasons for entering, we laughed heartily at Eddie's __(4)__ story. Unfortunately, the judges awarded the crown to another liar. Eddie was furious and went into a __(5)__ you could hear a block away.

Expressing Your Ideas

Writing Choices

Invite an Author If you could meet any author, who would you pick? Write a **letter** to your favorite author inviting him or her to visit your English class. Be sure to use the correct form for a friendly letter.

The Plot Thickens Could you come up with a story like Pete's dad did? Think of a plot for a short story you would like to write and make an **outline** of it. Your story may be fantasy, like the one about Petunia, or it can be taken from real life. Check to see that your outline includes setting, characters, a conflict, rising action, climax, and falling action.

Scooped Reporters like truth, and if they found out the real story behind Peter Sangetti and the author they would surely publish it. Imagine you are a reporter for the *Leighton Lamplighter* and write a **news article** that gives Peter's true story.

Other Options

Never Judge. . . Design a **book jacket** for "The Author" or another story or novel you have read. Include an illustration, the title, a short review on the inside flap, and a biography of the author on the back flap.

Talk of the Town Work with a group to create a **radio** or **TV play** in which a talk show host interviews the characters from "The Author" to get at the truth of what happened. Rehearse and present your play to the class.

Dance Duo Work with a partner. Choose some music that you think represents the poem you read. Create a **dance** to the music. You might name your dance "The Reader." Rehearse a performance of the poem and dance and present it to the class.

Language Mini-Lesson

Consistent Verb Tense

As you write, pay close attention to verb tense. Shift tense only when you mean to show a change in the time of the action. Compare the first paragraph, where verb tense shifts unintentionally, to the second paragraph which has consistent verb tense.

INCONSISTENT
Jeff took a deep bow, while the crowd cheers and applauds. After several curtain calls, he thanks the audience for the last time and went backstage to greet his family.

CONSISTENT
Jeff took a deep bow, while the crowd cheered and applauded. After several curtain calls, he thanked the audience for the last time and went backstage to greet his family.

Writing Strategy Look through your writing and note any shifts in verb tense. If you have trouble finding them, try reading your work aloud and listening for shifts. Then, for each shift, think about whether there is a good reason for the tense to change. If there isn't a good reason, make verb tenses consistent.

Activity Options

1. Work with a partner to choose a passage from literature and rewrite it in a different tense. For example, if it is written in the past tense, rewrite it in the present tense. Double-check to make sure you maintain consistent verb tense in your rewrite.

2. Write a paragraph about a conversation you've had and include direct quotations. Underline sections where the verb tense shifts. If the shift is unnecessary, correct it. If the shift is needed, explain why.

3. Go over the assignments in your working portfolio to check for inconsistent verb tense. Work with a partner to correct any problems that you find.

New Directions

by Maya Angelou

Maya Angelou
born 1928

Singer, actress, director, poet, and author Maya Angelou has never been afraid to try new directions in her life. Born Marguerita Johnson, young Maya's home life was split between times with her grandmother Annie Henderson, a general store owner in Stamps, Arkansas, and with her glamorous mother Vivian Baxter in St. Louis and in San Francisco. Angelou tried many jobs before beginning an artistic career. She also joined Martin Luther King, Jr., in the civil rights movement and then worked in Africa for several years. Angelou's best-known works are autobiographical. In 1992 she was chosen to deliver a poem at President Clinton's inauguration.

Building Background

Entrepreneurs We call people who have a vision and go after it, *entrepreneurs*. "New Directions" is about a woman who became an entrepreneur. The word *entrepreneur* is often associated with people like Andrew Carnegie, who was a 12-year-old immigrant when he began work in a factory for $1.20 a week. Fifty years later, Carnegie was one of the richest men in the United States. His wealth was exceptional, but many Americans see a need for a product or service and start successful businesses.

Getting into the Selection

Writer's Notebook "New Directions" is based on the life of the author's grandmother, a woman who has a vision and takes steps to change her life when it is going wrong. What do you do when things in your life are going wrong? Recall a time when you were facing a problem. In your notebook explain how you responded to it.

Reading Tip

Storyteller's Art The author's attitude about a subject is called **tone.** We can recognize the tone by the words the author chooses, the sentence structure, the imagery, and the treatment of characters. Perhaps the easiest way to recognize tone is by reading aloud, since tone in writing is similar to tone of voice in speaking.

The following selection is the story of a simple woman told in a slow-paced, dignified way that creates a tone of respect. As you read, look for examples of how the author sets this tone. Use a web like the one below to record your observations.

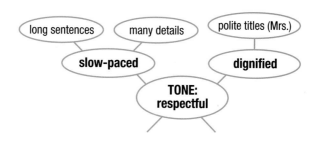

long sentences — many details — polite titles (Mrs.)

slow-paced — **dignified**

TONE: respectful

New Directions

Maya Angelou

In 1903 the late Mrs. Annie Johnson of Arkansas found herself with two toddling sons, very little money, a slight ability to read and add simple numbers. To this picture add a disastrous marriage and the burdensome fact that Mrs. Johnson was a Negro.

When she told her husband, Mr. William Johnson, of her dissatisfaction with their marriage, he conceded that he too found it to be less than he expected, and had been secretly hoping to leave and study religion. He added that he thought God was calling him not only to preach but to do so in Enid, Oklahoma. He did not tell her that he knew a minister in Enid with whom he could study and who had a friendly, unmarried daughter. They parted amicably, Annie keeping the one-room house and William taking most of the cash to carry himself to Oklahoma.

Annie, over six feet tall, big-boned, decided that she would not go to work as a domestic and leave her "precious babes" to anyone else's care. There was no possibility of being hired at the town's cotton gin[1] or lumber mill, but maybe there was a way to make the two factories work for her. In her words, "I looked up the road I was going and back the way I come, and since I wasn't satisfied, I decided to step off the road and cut me a new path." She told herself that she wasn't a fancy cook but that she could "mix groceries well enough to scare hungry away and from starving a man."

---

1. **cotton gin** (jin), machine for separating the fibers of cotton from the seeds; in this case, a factory with such machines.

▲ *Maudell Sleet's Magic Garden,* a collage on board, was created by Romare
Bearden in 1978. 🐾 Does this woman's **interaction** with her garden seem to
give her satisfaction?

She made her plans meticulously[2] and in secret. One early evening to see if she was ready, she placed stones in two five-gallon pails and carried them three miles to the cotton gin. She rested a little, and then discarding[3] some rocks, she walked in the darkness to the saw mill five miles farther along the dirt road. On her way back to her little house and her babies, she dumped the remaining rocks along the path.

That same night she worked into the early hours boiling chicken and frying ham. She made dough and filled the rolled-out pastry with meat. At last she went to sleep.

The next morning she left her house carrying the meat pies, lard, an iron brazier,[4] and coals for a fire. Just before lunch she appeared in an empty lot behind the cotton gin. As the dinner noon bell rang, she dropped the savors[5] into boiling fat and aroma rose and floated over to the workers who spilled out of the gin, covered with white lint, looking like specters.[6]

Most workers had brought their lunches of pinto beans and biscuits or crackers, onions and cans of sardines, but they were tempted by the hot meat pies which Annie ladled out of the fat. She wrapped them in newspapers, which soaked up the grease, and offered them for sale at a nickel each. Although business was slow, those first days Annie was determined. She balanced her appearances between the two hours of activity.

So, on Monday if she offered hot fresh pies at the cotton gin and sold the remaining cooled-down pies at the lumber mill for three cents, then on Tuesday she went first to the lumber mill presenting fresh, just-cooked pies as the lumbermen covered in sawdust emerged[7] from the mill.

For the next few years, on balmy spring days, blistering summer noons, and cold, wet, and wintry middays, Annie never disappointed her customers, who could count on seeing the tall, brown-skin woman bent over her brazier, carefully turning the meat pies. When she felt certain that the workers had become dependent on her, she built a stall between the two hives of industry and let the men run to her for their lunchtime provisions.[8]

She had indeed stepped from the road which seemed to have been chosen for her and cut herself a brand-new path. In years that stall became a store where customers could buy cheese, meal, syrup, cookies, candy, writing tablets, pickles, canned goods, fresh fruit, soft drinks, coal, oil, and leather soles for worn-out shoes.

Each of us has the right and the responsibility to assess the roads which lie ahead, and those over which we have traveled, and if the future road looms[9] ominous[10] or unpromising, and the roads back uninviting, then we need to gather our resolve and, carrying only the necessary baggage, step off that road into another direction. If the new choice is also unpalatable,[11] without embarrassment, we must be ready to change that as well.

---

2. **meticulously** (mə tik′yə ləs lē), *adv.* in such a way as to be extremely careful about details.
3. **discard** (dis kärd′), *v.* get rid of; throw aside.
4. **brazier** (brā′ zhər), a large metal pan that holds burning coals. Food may be heated on a brazier.
5. **savor** (sā′vər), flavoring; seasoning.
6. **specter** (spek′tər), *n.* a ghost or phantom, often of terrifying appearance.
7. **emerge** (i mėrj′), *v.* come out.
8. **provisions** (prə vizh′ənz), *n. pl.* supply of food and drinks.
9. **loom** (lüm), *v.* appear, often in a threatening way.
10. **ominous** (om′ə nəs), *adj.* unfavorable; threatening.
11. **unpalatable** (un pal′ə tə bəl), *adj.* unpleasant; distasteful.

After Reading

Making Connections

1. Describe how you felt at the end of this selection.

2. What kind of boss do you think Annie Johnson would be? Explain.

3. 👣 **Interactions** in life are not always positive. A saying goes "If life hands you a lemon, make lemonade." How does this saying relate to the story?

4. Look back through the selection. What qualities does Annie Johnson have that enabled her to succeed?

5. Why do you think Maya Angelou chose to write this biography?

6. Briefly summarize the story's **message.**

7. How would the use of more regional dialect and more direct quotations from Annie Johnson change the **tone** of this story?

8. Tell the story of another entrepreneur you know, personally or through reading. What qualities does that person share with Annie Johnson and with you?

Literary Focus: Diction

Diction means choice of words. Excellent diction, or using just the right words, sets good writers apart from mediocre or poor writers. English is a very rich language which has many words with similar meanings. Knowing and selecting just the right word tests an author's skill. For example, in "New Directions," Maya Angelou wrote that Mrs. Annie Johnson had "a disastrous marriage." Think of all the other words Angelou might have used in place of *disastrous.* What word would you have used? Would you have picked a simple word like *bad, poor,* or *rotten?* Or would you have gone for a big, $50-word like *calamitous* or *catastrophic?* Do you agree that *disastrous* was the best choice?

Although most authors know lots of big words with which they could impress their readers, they usually choose to use the most simple and natural-seeming language that can express exactly what they want to tell the reader. Skim the selection again, looking for other words the author uses that strike you as good choices. No writer is perfect—do you find some words that you would like to change?

Vocabulary Study

On your paper write the letter of the word pair that best expresses a relationship like that expressed in the first pair.

meticulously
discard
specter
emerge
provisions
loom
ominous
unpalatable

1. **meticulously : carefully :: a.** silently : quietly **b.** stupidly : cleverly **c.** politely : rudely **d.** joyfully : tearfully

2. **specter : scare :: a.** horse : mule **b.** cat : furry **c.** clown : laugh **d.** baby : young

3. **enter : emerge :: a.** move : dance **b.** inhale : exhale **c.** start : begin **d.** gallop : trot

4. **discard : garbage :: a.** sing : bird **b.** float : canoe **c.** toss : ball **d.** rise : dough

5. **supplies : provisions :: a.** food : drink **b.** trees : forest **c.** stoves : sinks **d.** cups : mugs

6. **tasty : unpalatable :: a.** pretty : ugly **b.** red : scarlet **c.** spotless : clean **d.** small : young

7. **spook : specter :: a.** shoe : foot **b.** dancer : ballerina **c.** tire : car **d.** rabbit : fox

8. **ominous : shark :: a.** sweet : lemon **b.** gigantic : mouse **c.** crescent : moon **d.** funny : clown

9. **exit : emerge :: a.** say : predict **b.** emergency : ambulance **c.** climb : opening **d.** entrance : enter

10. **loom : disappear :: a.** fade : vanish **b.** saunter : walk **c.** open : shut **d.** horrify : scare

Expressing Your Ideas _____

Writing Choices

For Hire Imagine you are looking for a job and hear that Annie Johnson needs a clerk in her store. Fill out a **job application** that gives your personal information, qualifications, and reasons for wanting the job.

Half a Cup of Love If Annie Johnson could write out her recipe for happiness, it would include a lot of hard work and determination. What do you think happiness is made of? Write out your own **recipe** for happiness.

Other Options

Only a Nickel Design an **advertising flyer** that can be handed out to attract customers for Annie Johnson's meat pies.

Annie's Award Imagine that the success of Annie Johnson's store has earned her the Businesswoman of the Year award. Design an appropriate **award** to be presented to her. The award might be a certificate, a plaque, or a trophy.

Before Reading

Antaeus

by Borden Deal

Borden Deal
1922–1985

Deal was born in Mississippi and drew on settings and characters from the South for most of his writing. His stories are full of working people and realistic scenes from their lives. He believed that what people today think and feel isn't very different from what is expressed in ancient myths. His characters often resemble the heroes of myths. The idea for this story came to Deal in a dream. It took ten years to get it published, but once in print, "Antaeus" became his most popular short story.

Building Background

The Antaeus Myth In Greek mythology, the bloodthirsty monster Antaeus (an tē′əs) was the offspring of Mother Earth and the Serpent of Chaos. Although Antaeus was unbeatable in battle with human beings, his mother feared he might lose if he fought a god. Mother Earth put a healing spell on her son. Each time Antaeus was hurt, he had only to fall to the ground and the power of Earth would heal him at once. Antaeus was unbeatable until Hercules came to challenge him. At first the challenge looked hopeless for Hercules, but the clever hero discovered Antaeus's secret, lifted him from the ground, and killed him.

Getting into the Story

Writer's Notebook Whether it was a few bean sprouts in a wet paper towel, acres of corn, or weeds in a vacant lot, you have probably watched many plants grow. What were your feelings when you saw the first tiny green sprouts or leaves? Recall a time when you planted and nurtured a seed, or noticed wildflowers come out in spring. In your notebook, write about your feelings.

Reading Tip

Dialect Speakers of English who have grown up in each region of the United States have slightly different words and expressions for the same thing. Those differences are part of the **regional dialect** of an area. In this story, a character from Alabama uses many words typical of Southern speech. The chart below lists words and meanings of some of the Southern dialect you will find in the selection. Are any of these terms used where you live?

Dialect	Meaning	Dialect	Meaning
you-all	you	a-laying	lying
offen	off, from	fixing to	about to
ever'	every	wan't	weren't
ourn	ours	toted	carried

ANT

B O R D E N   D E A L

This was during the wartime, when lots of people were coming North for jobs in factories and war industries, when people moved around a lot more than they do now and sometimes kids were thrown into new groups and new lives that were completely different from anything they had ever known before. I remember this one kid, T. J. his name was, from somewhere down South, whose family moved into our building during that time. They'd come North with everything they owned piled into the back seat of an old-model sedan that you wouldn't expect could make the trip, with T. J. and his three younger sisters riding shakily on top of the load of junk.

Our building was just like all the others there, with families crowded into a few rooms, and I guess there were twenty-five or thirty kids about my age in that one building. Of course, there were a few of us who formed

In this painting by Gina Carra, city rooftops are brought to life with colors reflected from the setting sun. In the story, T. J. also sees life when he looks at a barren rooftop. How does his vision differ from the artist's? ➤

a gang and ran together all the time after school, and I was the one who brought T. J. in and started the whole thing.

The building right next door to us was a factory where they made walking dolls. It was a low building with a flat, tarred roof that had a parapet[1] all around it about head high and we'd found out a long time before that no one, not even the watchman, paid any attention to the roof because it was higher than any of the other buildings around. So my gang used the roof as a headquarters. We could get up there by crossing over to the fire escape from our own roof on a plank and then going on up. It was a secret place for us, where nobody else could go without our permission.

HE TALKED DIFFERENT FROM ANY OF US AND YOU NOTICED IT RIGHT AWAY. BUT I LIKED HIM ANYWAY, SO I TOLD HIM TO COME ON UP.

I remember the day I first took T. J. up there to meet the gang. He was a stocky, robust[2] kid with a shock of white hair, nothing sissy about him except his voice—he talked in this slow, gentle voice like you never heard before. He talked different from any of us and you noticed it right away. But I liked him anyway, so I told him to come on up.

We climbed up over the parapet and dropped down on the roof. The rest of the gang were already there.

"Hi," I said. I jerked my thumb at T. J. "He just moved into the building yesterday."

He just stood there, not scared or anything, just looking, like the first time you see somebody you're not sure you're going to like.

"Hi," Blackie said. "Where are you from?"

"Marion County," T. J. said.

We laughed. "Marion County?" I said. "Where's that?"

He looked at me for a moment like I was a stranger, too. "It's in Alabama," he said, like I ought to know where it was.

"What's your name?" Charley said.

"T. J.," he said, looking back at him. He had pale blue eyes that looked washed-out but he looked directly at Charley, waiting for his reaction. He'll be all right, I thought. No sissy in him . . . except that voice. Who ever talked like that?

"T. J.," Blackie said. "That's just initials. What's your real name? Nobody in the world has just initials."

"I do," he said. "And they're T. J. That's all the name I got."

His voice was resolute[3] with the knowledge of his rightness and for a moment no one had anything to say. T. J. looked around at the rooftop and down at the black tar under his feet. "Down yonder where I come from," he said, "we played out in woods. Don't you-all have no woods around here?"

"Naw," Blackie said. "There's the park a few blocks over, but it's full of kids and cops and old women. You can't do a thing."

T. J. kept looking at the tar under his feet. "You mean you ain't got no fields to raise nothing in? . . . No watermelons or nothing?"

"Naw," I said scornfully. "What do you want to grow something for? The folks can buy everything they need at the store."

He looked at me again with that strange, unknowing look. "In Marion County," he said, "I had my own acre of cotton and my own acre of corn. It was mine to plant and make ever' year."

He sounded like it was something to be

---

1. **parapet** (par′ə pet), *n.* a low wall at the edge of a roof.
2. **robust** (rō bust′), *adj.* strong and healthy.
3. **resolute** (rez′ə lüt), *adj.* determined; firm.

proud of, and in some obscure[4] way it made the rest of us angry. "Who'd want to have their own acre of cotton and corn?" Blackie said. "That's just work. What can you do with an acre of cotton and corn?"

T. J. looked at him. "Well, you get part of the bale offen your acre," he said seriously. "And I fed my acre of corn to my calf."

EVALUATE: What kind of a boy is T. J.?

We didn't really know what he was talking about, so we were more puzzled than angry; otherwise, I guess, we'd have chased him off the roof and wouldn't have let him be part of our gang. But he was strange and different and we were all attracted by his stolid[5] sense of rightness and belonging, maybe by the strange softness of his voice contrasting our own tones of speech into harshness.

He moved his foot against the black tar. "We could make our own field right here," he said softly, thoughtfully. "Come spring we could raise us what we want to . . . watermelons and garden truck and no telling what all."

"You'd have to be a good farmer to make these tar roofs grow any watermelons," I said. We all laughed.

But T. J. looked serious. "We could haul us some dirt up here," he said. "And spread it out even and water it and before you know it we'd have us a crop in here." He looked at us intently. "Wouldn't that be fun?"

"They wouldn't let us," Blackie said quickly.

"I thought you said this was you-all's roof," T. J. said to me. "That you-all could do anything you wanted to up here."

"They've never bothered us," I said. I felt the idea beginning to catch fire in me. It was a big idea and it took a while for it to sink in but the more I thought about it the better I liked it. "Say," I said to the gang. "He might have something there. Just make us a regular

roof garden, with flowers and grass and trees and everything. And all ours, too," I said. "We wouldn't let anybody up here except the ones we wanted to."

"It'd take a while to grow trees," T. J. said quickly, but we weren't paying any attention to him. They were all talking about it suddenly, all excited with the idea after I'd put it in a way they could catch hold of it. Only rich people had roof gardens, we knew, and the idea of our own private domain[6] excited them.

"We could bring it up in sacks and boxes," Blackie said. "We'd have to do it while the folks weren't paying any attention to us, for we'd have to come up to the roof of our building and then cross over with it."

"Where could we get the dirt?" somebody said worriedly.

"Out of those vacant lots over close to school," Blackie said. "Nobody'd notice if we scraped it up."

I slapped T. J. on the shoulder. "Man, you had a wonderful idea," I said, and everybody grinned at him, remembering that he had started it. "Our own private roof garden."

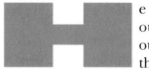e grinned back. "It'll be ourn," he said. "All ourn." Then he looked thoughtful again. "Maybe I can lay my hands on some cotton seed, too. You think we could raise us some cotton?"

We'd started big projects before at one time or another, like any gang of kids, but they'd always petered out[7] for lack of organization and direction. But this one didn't . . . somehow or other T. J. kept it going all through the winter months. He kept talking about the

---

4. **obscure** (əb skyùr′), *adj.* hard to understand.
5. **stolid** (stol′id), not easily excited; showing no emotion.
6. **domain** (dō mān′), *n.* land owned by one person, or in this case, by one group.
7. **peter out,** gradually come to an end; fail.

watermelons and the cotton we'd raise, come spring, and when even that wouldn't work he'd switch around to my idea of flowers and grass and trees, though he was always honest enough to add that it'd take a while to get any trees started. He always had it on his mind and he'd mention it in school, getting them lined up to carry dirt that afternoon, saying in a casual way that he reckoned a few more weeks ought to see the job through.

Our little area of private earth grew slowly. T. J. was smart enough to start in one corner of the building, heaping up the carried earth two to three feet thick, so that we had an immediate result to look at, to contemplate with awe. Some of the evenings T. J. alone was carrying earth up to the building, the rest of the gang distracted by other enterprises or interests, but T. J. kept plugging along on his own and eventually we'd all come back to him again and then our own little acre would grow more rapidly.

He was careful about the kind of dirt he'd let us carry up there and more than once he dumped a sandy load over the parapet into the areaway below because it wasn't good enough. He found out the kinds of earth in all the vacant lots for blocks around. He'd pick it up and feel it and smell it, frozen though it was sometimes, and then he'd say it was good growing soil or it wasn't worth anything and we'd have to go on somewhere else.

Thinking about it now, I don't see how he kept us at it. It was hard work, lugging paper sacks and boxes of dirt all the way up the stairs of our own building, keeping out of the way of the grownups so they wouldn't catch on to what we were doing. They probably wouldn't have cared, for they didn't pay much attention to us, but we wanted to keep it secret anyway. Then we had to go through the trap door to our roof, teeter over a plank to the fire escape, then climb two or three stories to the parapet and drop down onto the roof. All that for a small pile of earth that sometimes didn't seem worth the effort. But T. J. kept the vision bright within us, his words shrewd and calculated toward the fulfillment of his dream; and he worked harder than any of us. He seemed driven toward a goal that we couldn't see, a particular point in time that would be definitely marked by signs and wonders that only he could see.

The laborious[8] earth just lay there during the cold months, inert[9] and lifeless, the clods lumpy and cold under our feet when we walked over it. But one day it rained and afterward there was a softness in the air and the earth was alive and giving again with moisture and warmth. That evening T. J. smelled the air, his nostrils dilating with the odor of the earth under his feet.

"It's spring," he said, and there was a gladness rising in his voice that filled us all with the same feeling. "It's mighty late for it, but it's spring. I'd just about decided it wasn't never gonna get here at all."

PREDICT: Will T. J. and the gang succeed in their plans?

We were all sniffing at the air, too, trying to smell it the way that T. J. did, and I can still remember the sweet odor of the earth under our feet. It was the first time in my life that spring and spring earth had meant anything to me. I looked at T. J. then, knowing in a faint way the hunger within him through the toilsome winter months, knowing the dream that lay behind his plan. He was a new Antaeus, preparing his own bed of strength.

8. **laborious** (lə bôr′ē əs), *adj.* requiring much hard work.
9. **inert** (in ėrt′), *adj.* having no power to move or act; inactive.

"Planting time," he said. "We'll have to find us some seed."

"What do we do?" Blackie said. "How do we do it?"

"First we'll have to break up the clods," T. J. said. "That won't be hard to do. Then we plant the seed and after a while they come up. Then you got you a crop." He frowned. "But you ain't got it raised yet. You got to tend it and hoe it and take care of it and all the time it's growing and growing, while you're awake and while you're asleep. Then you lay it by[10] when it's growed and let it ripen and then you got you a crop."

WE COULDN'T KEEP FROM LOOKING AT IT, UNABLE TO BELIEVE THAT WE HAD CREATED THIS DELICATE GROWTH.

"There's those wholesale seed houses over on Sixth," I said. "We could probably swipe some grass seed over there."

T. J. looked at the earth. "You-all seem mighty set on raising some grass," he said. "I ain't never put no effort into that. I spent all my life trying not to raise grass."

"But it's pretty," Blackie said. "We could play on it and take sunbaths on it. Like having our own lawn. Lots of people got lawns."

"Well," T. J. said. He looked at the rest of us, hesitant for the first time. He kept on looking at us for a moment. "I did have it in mind to raise some corn and vegetables. But we'll plant grass."

He was smart. He knew where to give in. And I don't suppose it made any difference to him, really. He just wanted to grow something, even if it was grass.

"Of course," he said, "I do think we ought to plant a row of watermelons. They'd be mighty nice to eat while we was a-laying on that grass."

We all laughed. "All right," I said. "We'll plant us a row of watermelons."

Things went very quickly then. Perhaps half the roof was covered with the earth, the half that wasn't broken by ventilators,[11] and we swiped pocketfuls of grass seed from the open bins in the wholesale seed house, mingling among the buyers on Saturdays and during the school lunch hour. T. J. showed us how to prepare the earth, breaking up the clods and smoothing it and sowing the grass seed. It looked rich and black now with moisture, receiving of the seed, and it seemed that the grass sprang up overnight, pale green in the early spring.

We couldn't keep from looking at it, unable to believe that we had created this delicate growth. We looked at T. J. with understanding now, knowing the fulfillment of the plan he had carried alone within his mind. We had worked without full understanding of the task but he had known all the time.

We found that we couldn't walk or play on the delicate blades, as we had expected to, but we didn't mind. It was enough just to look at it, to realize that it was the work of our own hands, and each evening the whole gang was there, trying to measure the growth that had been achieved that day.

One time a foot was placed on the plot of ground . . . one time only, Blackie stepping onto it with sudden bravado. Then he looked at the crushed blades and there was shame in his face. He did not do it again. This was his grass, too, and not to be desecrated.[12] No one said anything, for it was not necessary.

---

10. **lay it by,** save; put away for future use.
11. **ventilator** (ven′tl ā′tər), any opening or device for providing fresh air to an enclosed space.
12. **desecrate** (des′ə krāt), v. treat or use without respect.

CONNECT: How have the boys changed since the beginning of the story?

T. J. had reserved a small section for watermelons and he was still trying to find some seed for it. The wholesale house didn't have any watermelon seed and we didn't know where we could lay our hands on them. T. J. shaped the earth into mounds, ready to receive them, three mounds lying in a straight line along the edge of the grass plot.

We had just about decided that we'd have to buy the seed if we were to get them. It was a violation of our principles, but we were anxious to get the watermelons started. Somewhere or other, T. J. got his hands on a seed catalogue and brought it one evening to our roof garden.

"We can order them now," he said, showing us the catalogue. "Look!"

We all crowded around, looking at the fat, green watermelons pictured in full color on the pages. Some of them were split open, showing the red, tempting meat, making our mouths water.

"Now we got to scrape up some seed money," T. J. said, looking at us. "I got a quarter. How much you-all got?"

We made up a couple of dollars between us and T. J. nodded his head. "That'll be more than enough. Now we got to decide what kind to get. I think them Kleckley Sweets. What do you-all think?"

He was going into esoteric[13] matters beyond our reach. We hadn't even known there were different kinds of melons. So we just nodded our heads and agreed that Yes, we thought the Kleckley Sweets too.

"I'll order them tonight," T. J. said. "We ought to have them in a few days."

"What are you boys doing up here?" an adult voice said behind us.

It startled us, for no one had ever come up here before, in all the time we had been using

▲ Painted in 1964, Robert Vickrey's *The Corner Seat* shows a young boy sitting quietly, perhaps daydreaming. If this were T. J., what might he be dreaming of?

the roof of the factory. We jerked around and saw three men standing near the trap door at the other end of the roof. They weren't policemen, or night watchmen, but three men in plump business suits, looking at us. They walked toward us.

"What are you boys doing up here?" the one in the middle said again.

We stood still, guilt heavy among us, levied by the tone of voice, and looked at the three strangers.

The men stared at the grass flourishing behind us. "What's this?" the man said. "How did this get up here?"

"Sure is growing good, ain't it?" T. J. said conversationally. "We planted it."

13. **esoteric** (es/ə ter′ik), *adj.* understood only by a select few.

The men kept looking at the grass as if they didn't believe it. It was a thick carpet over the earth now, a patch of deep greenness startling in the sterile[14] industrial surroundings.

THE REST OF US WERE SILENT, FRIGHTENED BY THE AUTHORITY OF HIS VOICE.

"Yes sir," T. J. said proudly. "We toted that earth up here and planted that grass." He fluttered the seed catalogue. "And we're just fixing to plant us some watermelon."

The man looked at him then, his eyes strange and faraway. "What do you mean, putting this on the roof of my building?" he said. "Do you want to go to jail?"

T. J. looked shaken. The rest of us were silent, frightened by the authority of his voice. We had grown up aware of adult authority, of policemen and night watchmen and teachers, and this man sounded like all the others. But it was a new thing to T. J.

"Well, you wan't using the roof," T. J. said. He paused a moment and added shrewdly, "So we just thought to pretty it up a little bit."

"And sag it so I'd have to rebuild it," the man said sharply. He started turning away, saying to another man beside him. "See that all that junk is shoveled off by tomorrow."

"Yes sir," the man said.

T. J. started forward. "You can't do that," he said. "We toted it up here and it's our earth. We planted it and raised it and toted it up here."

The man stared at him coldly. "But it's my building," he said. "It's to be shoveled off tomorrow."

"It's our earth," T. J. said desperately. "You ain't got no right!"

The men walked on without listening and descended clumsily through the trap door. T. J. stood looking after them, his body tense with anger, until they had disappeared. They wouldn't even argue with him, wouldn't let him defend his earth-rights.

He turned to us. "We won't let 'em do it," he said fiercely. "We'll stay up here all day tomorrow and the day after that and we won't let 'em do it."

We just looked at him. We knew that there was no stopping it. He saw it in our faces and his face wavered for a moment before he gripped it into determination.

"They ain't got no right," he said. "It's our earth. It's our land. Can't nobody touch a man's own land."

We kept on looking at him, listening to the words but knowing that it was no use. The adult world had descended on us even in our richest dream and we knew there was no calculating the adult world, no fighting it, no winning against it.

We started moving slowly toward the parapet and the fire escape, avoiding a last look at the green beauty of the earth that T. J. had planted for us . . . had planted deeply in our minds as well as in our experience. We filed slowly over the edge and down the steps to the plank, T. J. coming last, and all of us could feel the weight of his grief behind us.

SUMMARIZE: Retell what happened when the adults arrived on the roof.

"Wait a minute," he said suddenly, his voice harsh with the effort of calling. We stopped and turned, held by the tone of his voice, and looked up at him standing above us on the fire escape.

"We can't stop them?" he said, looking down at us, his face strange in the dusky light. "There ain't no way to stop 'em?"

"No," Blackie said with finality. "They own the building."

---

14. **sterile** (ster'əl), *adj.* unable to produce life; barren.

Antaeus   **525**

We stood still for a moment, looking up at T. J., caught into inaction by the decision working in his face. He stared back at us and his face was pale and mean in the poor light, with a bald nakedness in his skin like sick people have sometimes.

"They ain't gonna touch my earth," he said fiercely. "They ain't gonna lay a hand on it! Come on."

He turned around and started up the fire escape again, almost running against the effort of climbing. We followed more slowly, not knowing what he intended. By the time we reached him, he had seized a board and thrust it into the soil, scooping it up and flinging it over the parapet into the areaway below. He straightened and looked at us.

"They can't touch it," he said. "I won't let 'em lay a dirty hand on it!"

We saw it then. He stooped to his labor again and we followed, the gusts of his anger moving in frenzied labor among us as we scattered along the edge of earth, scooping it and throwing it over the parapet, destroying with anger the growth we had nurtured with such tender care. The soil carried so laboriously upward to the light and the sun cascaded swiftly into the dark areaway, the green blades of grass crumpled and twisted in the falling.

It took less time than you would think . . . the task of destruction is infinitely easier than that of creation. We stopped at the end, leaving only a scattering of loose soil,

and when it was finally over, a stillness stood among the group and over the factory building. We looked down at the bare sterility of black tar, felt the harsh texture of it under the soles of our shoes, and the anger had gone out of us, leaving only a sore aching in our minds like overstretched muscles.

T. J. stood for a moment, his breathing slowing from anger and effort, caught into the same contemplation of destruction as all of us. He stooped slowly, finally, and picked up a lonely blade of grass left trampled under our feet and put it between his teeth, tasting it, sucking the greenness out of it into his mouth. Then he started walking toward the fire escape, moving before any of us were ready to move, and disappeared over the edge.

We followed him but he was already halfway down to the ground, going on past the board where we crossed over, climbing down into the areaway. We saw the last section swing down with his weight and then he stood on the concrete below us, looking at the small pile of anonymous earth scattered by our throwing. Then he walked across the place where we could see him and disappeared toward the street without glancing back, without looking up to see us watching him.

They did not find him for two weeks. Then the Nashville police caught him just outside the Nashville freight yards. He was walking along the railroad track; still heading south, still heading home.

As for us, who had no remembered home to call us . . . none of us ever again climbed the escape-way to the roof.

After Reading

Making Connections

1. Would you have joined the gang in their efforts to create a garden? Why or why not?

2. Who was in the right, the businessman or the boys?

3. What did creating the rooftop garden **symbolize** for T. J.? Refer to the story to support your answer.

4. What **conclusions** can we draw about the personalities of T. J. and the narrator from what they say and do in the story? Use a character web like the one below to describe each of them.

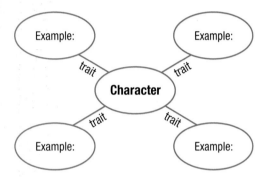

5. Why did the author choose to call the story "Antaeus" instead of something like "T. J. and the Gang," or "The Garden"?

6. How would the story change if the author had T. J. tell his own story?

7. What options might the boys have had for creating a garden if they lived in your community?

Literary Focus: Formal and Informal Language

When T. J., the gang, and even the adults in this story talk, they use the **informal language** of ordinary speech. They sometimes make grammatical errors and may not speak in whole sentences, as when Blackie says, "We could play on it and take sunbaths on it. Like having our own lawn. Lots of people got lawns." In contrast, the narrator uses **formal language** to tell the story. The vocabulary is precise and there is no slang. He also uses complicated sentence structure.

Look back over the story. Compare the way the author writes dialogue for the gang and the formal language the author uses when the narrator tells the story. Why do you think the author chose to use both formal and informal language in this story?

Vocabulary Study

On your paper write the letter of the correct ending.

parapet
robust
resolute
obscure
domain
laborious
inert
desecrate
esoteric
sterile

1. Looking over his **domain,** the owner **a.** checked his bank balance. **b.** toured his property. **c.** enjoyed TV.

2. To **desecrate** a garden, it takes **a.** a determined gardener. **b.** a large scarecrow. **c.** two hungry deer.

3. T. J. looked **robust** because he was: **a.** from the South. **b.** strong and healthy. **c.** sunburned from working in the garden.

4. The **obscure** directions on the seed package **a.** made planting easy. **b.** were very helpful. **c.** were difficult to understand.

5. To remove the **inert** material, the gardener **a.** took out the stones. **b.** pulled weeds. **c.** harvested the vegetables.

6. The most **laborious** task in making a garden is **a.** sprinkling it. **b.** planting seeds. **c.** hauling dirt.

7. A **resolute** gardener will **a.** get the job done. **b.** put off tasks. **c.** look for advice.

8. A rooftop is a **sterile** place if it **a.** gets all-day sunlight. **b.** collects rainwater. **c.** has no life on it.

9. To a gardener an **esoteric** subject might be **a.** effects of rainfall. **b.** kinds of soil. **c.** computer programs.

10. If you stood on a **parapet,** you might worry about **a.** giving a speech. **b.** missing your flight. **c.** falling off.

Expressing Your Ideas

Writing Choices

Profile of a Gardener Look back through the story and observe what T. J. says and does, and what others say about him. Then write a **profile** of T. J. in which you describe not only the way he looks, but the way he thinks and feels.

Dear Sir If the boys had tried, they might have gotten permission to plant their garden. Write a **persuasive** letter to the building owner that explains why the garden would be a good idea.

Other Options

Those Alabama Blues Think about the things that made T. J. sad or angry. Then write the words for a blues song he might have sung and set the words to music you compose or to a blues tune you know. Perform it for the class.

Dream On T. J.'s dream garden didn't work out as he'd planned. Draw **diagrams** of the garden T. J. wanted to plant and of the real garden the boys eventually did plant.

Before Reading

On the Death of Martin Luther King, Jr.

by Robert F. Kennedy

Robert F. Kennedy
1925–1968

"Bobby" Kennedy, as he was usually known, was the seventh of nine children born to Joseph P. and Rose Fitzgerald Kennedy. As a youngster, Kennedy traveled abroad with his father, received letters from President Franklin D. Roosevelt, and met the Pope. As a small boy, Kennedy enjoyed proving himself by taking risks. When his older brother John was elected President, he appointed Bobby his Attorney General. Kennedy used this position to help further the cause of civil rights. After his brother's assassination, he was elected Senator from New York. Many people believe Robert Kennedy would have won the Democratic presidential nomination in 1968 if he had not been assassinated.

Building Background

Senator Robert F. Kennedy On April 4, 1968, Sen. Robert F. Kennedy was in Indiana campaigning for the Democratic nomination for President when he learned that Dr. Martin Luther King, Jr., had been shot. Kennedy's brother, President John F. Kennedy, also had been shot and killed by an assassin in 1963. That evening at a rally with a mostly black crowd, Robert Kennedy announced King's death in the heartfelt speech that you will read. Kennedy went on to win the Indiana primary. On June 4, after he won the California primary, a man approached him as if to shake hands. A shot rang out, and Robert Kennedy crumpled to the floor. Two days later he, too, died.

Getting into the Speech

Discussion With the growing civil rights movement and protests against the Vietnam War, the late 1960s were a time of unrest in the United States. Think about what you've read and heard from others about that time in history. In a class discussion, tell what you know about the late 1960s. Then work together to make a time line of events from the assassination of John F. Kennedy to 1970.

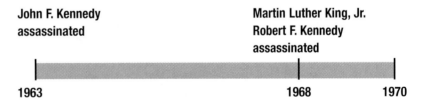

John F. Kennedy assassinated		Martin Luther King, Jr. Robert F. Kennedy assassinated	
1963		1968	1970

Reading Tip

Reading a Speech Reading a speech is almost a contradiction, because speeches are meant to be spoken. The sentence structure of speeches may be less formal than written language. Some of the best speeches may not be written down until after they're given. The speaker uses notes as guidelines.

As you read the following speech, imagine how the speaker delivered it. Then read it aloud with expression.

On the Death of
MARTIN LUTHER KING, JR.

Robert F. Kennedy

I have bad news for you, for all of our fellow citizens, and people who love peace all over the world, and that is that Martin Luther King was shot and killed tonight.

Martin Luther King dedicated[1] his life to love and to justice for his fellow human beings, and he died because of that effort.

In this difficult day, in this difficult time for the United States, it is perhaps well to ask what kind of a nation we are and what direction we want to move in. For those of you who are black—considering the evidence there evidently[2] is that there were white people who were responsible—you can be filled with bitterness, with hatred, and a desire for revenge. We can move in that direction as a country, in great polarization[3]—black people amongst black, white people amongst white, filled with hatred toward one another.

Or we can make an effort, as Martin Luther King did, to understand and to comprehend, and to replace that violence, that stain of bloodshed that has spread across our land, with an effort to understand with compassion[4] and love.

For those of you who are black and are tempted to be filled with hatred and distrust at the injustice of such an act, against all white people, I can only say that I feel in my own heart the same kind of feeling. I had a member of my family killed, but he was killed by a white man. But we have to make an effort in the United States, we have to make an effort to understand, to go beyond these rather difficult times.

My favorite poet was Aeschylus.[5] He wrote: "In our sleep, pain which cannot forget falls drop by drop upon the heart until, in our own despair, against our will, comes wisdom through the awful grace of God."

What we need in the United States is not division; what we need in the United States is not hatred; what we need in the United States is not

---

1. **dedicate** (ded′ə kāt), *v.* give up wholly to some purpose; devote.
2. **evidently** (ev′ə dənt lē), *adv.* plainly; clearly.
3. **polarization** (pō′lər ə zā′shən), *n.* breaking up or separating into two opposing sides.
4. **compassion** (kəm pash′ən), *n.* sympathy or pity.
5. **Aeschylus** (es′kə ləs), Greek poet and playwright who lived from 525–456 B.C.

Martin Luther King, Jr. (left front) and Robert F. Kennedy stand side by side in a meeting with then Vice-President Lyndon B. Johnson (right front). Johnson became President after the assassination of Robert Kennedy's brother, President John F. Kennedy, in 1963.

violence or lawlessness, but love and wisdom, and compassion toward one another, and a feeling of justice towards those who still suffer within our country, whether they be white or they be black.

So I shall ask you tonight to return home, to say a prayer for the family of Martin Luther King, that's true, but more importantly to say a prayer for our own country, which all of us love— a prayer for understanding and that compassion of which I spoke.

We can do well in this country. We will have difficult times. We've had difficult times in the past. We will have difficult times in the future. It is not the end of violence; it is not the end of lawlessness; it is not the end of disorder.

But the vast majority of white people and the vast majority of black people in this country want to live together, want to improve the quality of our life, and want justice for all human beings who abide[6] in our land.

Let us dedicate ourselves to what the Greeks wrote so many years ago: to tame the savageness of man and to make gentle the life of this world.

Let us dedicate ourselves to that, and say a prayer for our country and for our people.

_____

6. **abide** (ə bīd′), v. live; reside.

After Reading

Making Connections

1. How did you feel after reading Robert Kennedy's speech?

2. Do you agree with Kennedy that "the vast majority of white people and the vast majority of black people in this country want to live together . . . and want justice for all human beings"? Explain.

3. 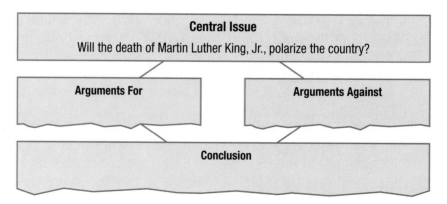 What kinds of racial **interactions** did Kennedy hope to prevent and to promote by making this speech?

4. What does the quote from Aeschylus mean?

5. Do you agree with Aeschylus, or not? Use events from your own life, the lives of friends, or stories you know to support your choice.

6. What issue do you think most divides our country today? What do you think could help resolve the division?

Literary Focus: Speeches

A speech given at the signing of a peace treaty after a war would be very different from a speech at a memorial service for children who died in a fire. How a speech is written and delivered depends on its topic and purpose, the occasion, and the audience. The crowd that listened to Robert Kennedy's speech undoubtedly heard the news of the death of Dr. Martin Luther King, Jr., with great sorrow and anger. The purpose of the speech was to **persuade** the crowd not to react to the terrible event with hatred and violence.

Look back over the speech and think about how it accomplishes that purpose. Using a chart like the one below may help you organize your ideas.

Central Issue
Will the death of Martin Luther King, Jr., polarize the country?

Arguments For

Arguments Against

Conclusion

Vocabulary Study

On your paper write the word from the list at the left that is most clearly related to the sentence.

dedicate
evidently
polarization
compassion
abide

1. Kennedy asked the crowd to remember that all citizens should obey the law of the land.

2. After the Indiana primary, Kennedy continued to devote all his time and energy to winning the Democratic presidential nomination.

3. Kennedy showed his sympathy to Coretta King by calling her and offering the use of an airplane.

4. After the police investigated, the facts seemed to show that an unhappy Palestinian immigrant, apparently acting alone, shot Robert Kennedy.

5. Racial equality and the Vietnam War were two issues that divided people in the United States in the late 1960s.

Expressing Your Ideas

Writing Choices

My Fellow Americans Had Kennedy not been scheduled to speak the night Martin Luther King, Jr., was shot, he might have chosen another way to get his message across. Rewrite this speech as a **letter** to the American people Kennedy might have sent to a major newspaper to publish.

Soapbox Write your own **speech** on any issue that is important to you. Try in your speech, as Kennedy did, to persuade your audience to agree with you.

Lessons from Life Choose either Martin Luther King, Jr., or Robert F. Kennedy and research that person's life. Use your knowledge of the person to write a **homily.** A homily is a serious talk, like a sermon, that gives advice or a warning.

Other Options

Meeting of Minds What do you think Robert Kennedy and Martin Luther King talked about when they met? Work with a partner to imagine this meeting. Reenact the **scene** you have imagined for the class.

Calling All Artists Design a suitable **memorial** for either Robert Kennedy, Martin Luther King, Jr., or both men together. Your memorial can be a **mural,** a **statue,** a **building,** or any other form you wish. Choose an appropriate location for your memorial as part of the project.

On the Air Imagine you were one of the many reporters who crowded around Kennedy after his speech. Work with a partner to re-create the **TV interview** you held with him that night.

Before Reading

Samantha's Story and Self Portrait

by Samantha Abeel

Samantha Abeel
born 1977

Samantha Abeel's keen interest in creative writing suggested the poetry project that resulted in her first book, "Reach for the Moon." Abeel was still a high school student in Traverse City, Michigan, when the book was published. Besides writing, her active interests include music and art. She also enjoys outdoor activities and learning about history. Abeel continues to cope with the daily challenges of having a learning disability.

Building Background

Reach for the Moon When Samantha Abeel discovered that she had a learning disability, she and her family felt a rush of relief. Finally, they understood why Samantha could win prizes in creative writing but could barely tell time. Her problem was in learning numbers. Samantha got the extra help she needed in math. She also decided to prove to herself and others what she could do well, so she set out on a creative writing project. Gazing at watercolors by her friend, Charles Murphy, Samantha wrote poems. Eventually that project became a book.

Getting into the Selections

Writer's Notebook Like Samantha, we all have different talents and learning styles. Imagine that your assignment is to learn about a Civil War battle. Would you rather read about it, listen to a tape, watch a video, take notes, or draw a diagram? In your notebook, create a graph like the one below. On the scale (with five the best), show how you learn by filling in the squares.

	1	2	3	4	5
Reading	▓				
Listening		▓			
Seeing				▓	
Writing			▓		
Doing					▓

Reading Tip

Poetic Devices When writers want to reveal their feelings, they often use the kind of **expressive language** found in poetry. In the essay and poem that follow, the writer uses poetic language to tell how it feels to have a learning disability. She begins the essay with the **image** of a tree bathed in moonlight, and goes on to use a **metaphor** about her "ocean of troubles." Look for other examples.

SAMANTHA'S STORY

Samantha Abeel

A tree that stands in the moonlight reflects the light, yet also casts a shadow. People are the same. They have gifts that let them shine, yet they also have disabilities, shadows that obscure the light. When I started this project in the seventh grade, I had trouble telling time, counting money, remembering even the simplest of addition and subtraction problems. Yet no matter how hard it was to stay afloat in this ocean of troubles, there was something inside of me, something that became my life preserver—and that was writing.

Seventh grade was a horrible year. I hated school. Every night I would come home and kiss the floor and revel that I had made it through one more day without totally messing up, or if I had, at least I was still alive. Then I would remember that I had to go back the next day and brave through all the same trials. With that thought, the tears and panic attacks[1] grew. Yet one hour of my day was a refuge.[2] Here, there weren't any concepts with numbers, measurements, algebra, or failure. It was my seventh-grade writing class. I had begun to experiment with creative writing in

---

1. **panic attack,** a sense of intense fear and discomfort for no apparent reason.
2. refuge (ref′üj), *n.* shelter from danger or trouble.

sixth grade, but in seventh grade I discovered how much writing was a part of me and I was a part of it.

To build on this, my mother asked Mrs. Williams, who was my English teacher, if she would work with me by giving me writing assignments and critiquing[3] them as a way of focusing on what was right with me and not on what was wrong. Charles Murphy, a family friend, lent us slides and pictures of his beautiful watercolors. I began to write using his images as inspiration. I discovered that by crawling inside and becoming what I wrote, it made my writing and ideas more powerful.

In eighth grade I was finally recognized as learning disabled. I was taken from my seventh grade algebra class, where I was totally lost and placed in a special education resource classroom. Special education changed my life. It was the best thing that ever happened to me. I could raise my hand in that class, even when being taught the most elementary concepts, and say, "I don't get it." It was the most wonderful feeling in the world. Eighth grade was my best year at the junior high. It is an illusion that students in special education have no abilities. Special education just means that you learn differently. I am so thankful for specially trained teachers who have been able to help me and many other kids like me.

If you struggle with a disability, the first thing you need to do is find something that you are good at, whether it's singing or skate boarding, an interest in science or acting, even just being good with people. Then do something with that. If you are good with people, then volunteer at a nursing home or at a day care center; if you love skate boarding, work toward a competition. If it's singing, join a school choir. Even if you can't read music (like me) or read a script, you can always find ways of coping and compensating.

Never let your disability stop you from doing what you are good at or want to do. I have trouble spelling and I'm horrible at grammar, but I was lucky enough to have teachers who graded me on the content of what I had to say instead of how bad my spelling and punctuation were. I was able to use a computer to compensate.

Remember that if you have trouble in school, it might not be because you don't fit the school, it might be because the school doesn't fit you. Be an advocate[4] for yourself. Keep trying. You may not fit in now, but whether you're seven or seventy, one day you will find a place where you excel.[5]

At the beginning of ninth grade we realized that what had started out as an art/poetry project had grown into something more. Because getting the right teachers and having the right educational placement made such a difference in my life, we realized it was a message we wanted to share. LD does not mean "lazy and dumb." It just means you have another way of looking at the world. I hope through my writing to remind people that if you're standing in the shadow of the tree, you may need to walk to the other side to see the light it reflects. They are both part of the same tree; both need to be recognized and understood. This is my reflection of the light.

---

3. **critique** (kri tēk′), *v.* review or criticize.
4. **advocate** (ad′və kit), *n.* a person who speaks or writes in favor of a cause.
5. **excel** (ek sel′), *v.* be outstanding; be better.

Self Portrait

Samantha Abeel

To show you who I am
I crawled inside a tree, became its roots, bark and leaves,
listened to its whispers in the wind.
When fall came and painted the leaves red and gold
5 I wanted to shake them across your lawn
to transform the grass into a quilt, a gift spread at your feet,
but their numbers eluded me,
so I turned a piece of paper into my soul
to send to you so that you might see
10 how easily it can be crumpled and flattened out again.
I wanted you to see my resilience,[1]
but I wasn't sure how to arrange the numbers in your address,
so I danced with the Indians in the forest
and collected the feathers that fell from the eagle's wings,
15 each one a wish for my future,
but I lost track of their numbers, gathered too many,
and was unable to carry them home
so I reaped the wind with my hair,
relived its journey through my senses, and
20 felt its whispered loneliness, like lakes in winter,
but it was too far and you could not follow me.

Now I've written out their shadows
like the wind collects its secrets
to whisper into receptive ears, and I
25 will leave them at your doorstep,
a reminder of what others cannot see,
a reminder of what I can and cannot be.

---

1. **resilience** (ri zil′ē əns), *n.* power of recovering rapidly.

In this 1994 picture of a tree, photographer Jerry N. Uelsmann combines images to produce a startling and mysterious effect. What phrase or line from Abeel's poem would be a good caption for his work of art? ➤

After Reading

Making Connections

1. If you were to buy Samantha a birthday gift, what would you get her? Explain your choice.

2. To the right is Samantha's desk. What do you think she keeps there?

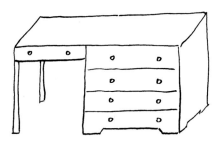

3. Samantha calls writing a "life preserver" that keeps her "afloat in this ocean of troubles." Do you have a life preserver? Explain.

4. Reread the first three sentences of the story. Do you agree with Samantha that all people have both gifts and disabilities? Why or why not?

5. Poets often repeat sounds within a line of poetry. Find examples of such **repetition** in Samantha's poem "Self Portrait."

6. Do you think Samantha would say that having a learning disability has its positive side? Find evidence in the story to support your view.

7. Samantha gives advice to people who are struggling with a disability. Do you think her advice applies to others too? Explain.

8. Find out what services your school offers to students with learning disabilities. What is the first thing students should do if they need help?

Literary Focus: Alliteration

When you read Samantha's poem aloud, you can hear **alliteration,** or the repetition of sounds, especially consonant sounds. These sounds may be repeated at the beginnings of words (as the *f* in "feathers that fell") or within and at the ends of words (as the *s* in "whispered loneliness"). Writers use alliteration to set a mood, to add an appealing musical quality to their writing, or to point out important words.

Alliteration can add a poetic touch to prose writing too. Reread the first few lines of "Samantha's Story," and notice the number of words that begin with *sh.* Then notice the other words with the *s* sound in various positions. What quality or mood does this alliteration give to Samantha's prose?

Vocabulary Study

refuge
critique
advocate
excel
resilience

See the sample word web below for the word *disability*. Create a similar web for each word on the list. Place the word in the center and fill in the web with words, such as synonyms, antonyms, and others, that you relate to its meaning.

Expressing Your Ideas

Writing Choices

Seventh Heaven? Samantha wrote movingly of her experiences in seventh grade. Do you share any of them? Write a **description** of your life as a seventh grader. Make sure you include both high points and low points, as Samantha did.

Perfect Poets Pen Poems Write a **poem** that contains **alliteration,** or repeated sounds. Remember that the repeated sounds can come anywhere in a word. Your poem should make sense as well as having interesting sounds.

Mass Appeal One purpose Samantha had in publishing her project was to send a message of hope and encouragement to others with disabilities. Write a similar **inspirational message** on a theme of your choice.

Other Options

Say a Song of Sounds Find a poem, or a piece of prose, that has obvious **alliteration.** Practice reading it aloud and then present it to the class as your classmates listen for and identify the repeated sounds.

Gifts Galore Just like the sunny side of the tree in "Samantha's Story," each student in your class has gifts that let that person shine. Work in groups to **survey** your members about their interests and strengths. Discuss the results, and then introduce one another to the class based on your survey.

Information, Please! Think of some questions you would like to ask Samantha about her book, and imagine her answers. With a partner conduct an **interview** in which one is the interviewer and the other is Samantha. Reverse roles so that each partner gets to ask and answer questions.

Before Reading

Rabbit Dances with the People

a Cherokee legend retold by Gayle Ross

Gayle Ross
born 1951

Following in her grand-mother's footsteps, Cherokee storyteller Gayle Ross has told the tales and legends of the Cherokee people to audiences across the United States and Canada. She is a descendant of the well-known Cherokee chief, John Ross, who led the struggle to defend the rights of his people in the 1830s. Gayle Ross collected the Rabbit stories both to honor her ancestors and to commu-nicate these traditional tales to children of this generation. The stories of Rabbit, trickster and hero, form a central part of the Cherokee storytelling tradition.

Building Background

Trickster Tales Everyone loves a good practical joke—as long as it's played on someone else. That may be one reason for the popularity of trickster tales. In a trickster tale, one character outwits another in a devious, or tricky, way. Tricksters come from many parts of the world. A French trickster, Reynard the Fox, dupes fishermen into giving him a ride in the back of their truck, where he steals all their eels. Anansi is an African trickster who appears as either a spider or a man. His pranks even carry him to Central America, where he tries to trick a business partner out of half a farm. Whether fox, spider, or rabbit, as in this Cherokee trickster tale, it's better to read about a trickster than to meet one.

Getting into the Story

Writer's Notebook Not all trickster tales end happily for the character who plays the trick. Sometimes the trick backfires, and the trickster learns a lesson. Have you ever tried to play a practical joke that didn't turn out as you'd planned? In your notebook, write about a time you tried to trick someone. What happened?

Reading Tip

Legends and Lessons Like many legends and folk tales, the Cherokee trickster tale that follows passes along a lesson. This lesson, which is the main point of the tale, neatly wraps up the story. As you read this story, keep in mind that it is leading toward a lesson at the end. A chart like the one below may help you keep track of the details that reveal the lesson in this story.

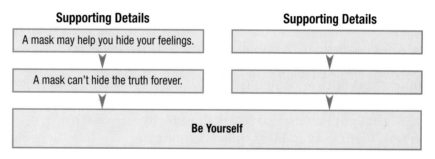

Supporting Details	Supporting Details
A mask may help you hide your feelings.	
A mask can't hide the truth forever.	
Be Yourself	

Rabbit Dances with the People

retold by Gayle Ross

A long time ago, there was a young man who was ashamed of his face. He had quite a nice face, but for some reason he felt he was ugly. He was a very good artist, though, and he hit on the idea of carving a mask for himself. This mask was very handsome, and the boy felt very good when he had it on. He wore the mask to all the dances, and the people thought it was his natural face.

Now, there were seven young women who were enchanted with the face on the mask. They watched for the young man at all the dances. They would talk to the boy between rounds of songs, and each thought of him as a special friend.

One night Rabbit was hiding in the bushes and watching the people dance. He had come hoping to learn some new songs. He watched the young man with all the pretty girls following him, and, as usual, Rabbit was jealous. He thought, "I would like to be that young fellow!"

After the dance, Rabbit followed the young man to his house, hoping to learn some of his attracting medicine. Imagine his surprise when he saw the boy take off his face! "Ho," thought Rabbit, "that mask must be his secret!" Right away, Rabbit began scheming to get his hands on the boy's mask. He watched very carefully to see where the boy hid it.

Some time later, Rabbit heard about a big dance the people were planning, and he made up his mind to go. In the middle of the night, when everything was dark, Rabbit crept into the young man's house and stole away with the mask.

The next night, Rabbit dressed in his finest dance clothes, put on the mask, and headed out to where the people were dancing. At first he was having a fine time. Rabbit was a good dancer, and the seven young women gave him a warm welcome. But after a time the girls said, "We're tired of dancing. Come sit and talk with us." So Rabbit followed the young women to a place where they could sit and talk.

"It is a fine night for a dance," Rabbit began, but he broke off when he saw the girls staring at him in amazement.

"My friend," said one young woman, "what has happened to your voice? It is so high and squeaky!"

"Oh," said Rabbit, thinking quickly, "I choked on a bone caught in my throat yesterday. Perhaps that is what makes my voice so scratchy!"

But the girls were suspicious. "And why

▲ Native American artist Joe H. Herrera painted this watercolor of the *Cochiti Green Corn Dance* in 1947. In Native American cultural tradition, art is visual prayer, a community rather than an individual expression. Although a successful mainstream artist, **interactions** between his two cultures created pressures that caused Herrera to stop painting in 1958. What cultural conflicts do you imagine he might have faced?

have you stayed away from us for so long?" asked another.

"Well," said Rabbit, "that is just because I have been away on some very important business!"

"Then who was that dancing with us just last night?" cried the girls. They began to giggle and pinch Rabbit until he was black and blue all over! Suddenly the mask slipped sideways and the girls saw Rabbit's face. "Oh, this is just Rabbit, up to his tricks!" cried the girls. And they chased him away from the dance ground.

When Rabbit was safely away from the angry young women, he threw the mask down and headed home. "I do not think I will ever dance with those people again," thought Rabbit. "They have a lot to learn about good manners!"

Meanwhile, the young man was very worried when he discovered that his mask was missing. He searched and searched until he found it on the ground where Rabbit had dropped it. Happily, he put the mask on and hurried to the dance ground. He was very surprised when he saw the way the young women treated him, though. They would not even talk to him! Whenever he came near, they called him names and ran away!

At last, the young man thought to put away the mask and go to the dance wearing his own face. To his surprise, he discovered the young women liked him very much, just the way he was.

After Reading

Making Connections

1. If you had the **choice,** would you want to change your appearance? How might you change it?

2. How would you feel about a person who arrived wearing a mask at a dance you were attending?

3. What does the mask do for the young man in this tale?

4. Why do you think the trickster in this tale is a rabbit rather than some other animal?

5. One purpose of folk tales is to teach people lessons. What **lesson** is taught in this story?

6. While wearing the mask, Rabbit and the young man are rejected by the girls, but their reactions to rejection are quite different. **Compare** and **contrast** how Rabbit and the young man react to the girls' treatment.

7. Do you think people today can learn anything from an old folk tale such as this? Explain.

Literary Focus: Symbolism

A symbol is something that stands for something else. For example, a dove is a symbol for peace. If you need help in uncovering the **symbolism** in a story, pick out the most important items and ask yourself what they suggest. The most important object in this story is the mask. Masks are used to cover, hide, or change things. How do you feel about those uses? Your answer will help you identify what the mask symbolizes.

A diagram like the one below can help you uncover the levels of meaning a symbol may have. Write down all the ideas that come to you. Don't initially reject any ideas as wrong. Remember that two readers may see the meaning of a symbol in different ways and both may be right, as long as their views make sense in the story.

mask = **1st level** hides covers changes = **2nd level** pretending deceiving misleading = trying to be what one isn't *(meaning)*

Vocabulary Study

Adjectives that describe people, such as *scheming, suspicious, worried,* and *angry,* are important in this story. Find in the story and list on separate slips of paper as many of these adjectives as you can. Place the slips face down in a pile. Use these adjectives to play a game of Vocabulary Charades. Work in two teams. Have the first team draw an adjective and act it out silently. The second team must guess the adjective. Then have that team draw an adjective, and so on. Award one point for each correct guess.

Expressing Your Ideas

Writing Choices

Lots o' Limericks Limericks are five-line poems that always follow this sing-song rhyme pattern:

A silly young man from New York
Thought he'd eat applesauce with a fork.
But each time he tried
The mixture would slide
'Til he had to admit it won't work.

Take the situation in the story "Rabbit Dances with the People" and turn it into a **limerick.** You will probably want to begin "There was a young man . . ."

What's Up, Doc? From Peter Rabbit to Bugs Bunny, rabbit characters pop up in a number of legends, stories, and cartoons. You may even know one or more real rabbits. In an **essay,** compare the rabbit from this story to other rabbits you have read about or known.

Tricky, Trickier, Trickiest Using what you have learned from reading "Rabbit Dances with the People" write your own **trickster tale.** You will need to choose an animal to be the trickster and create a plot that teaches a lesson that is obvious at the end of the story.

Other Options

Story Time Use your school or community library to research other American Indian folk tales. Choose your favorite tale and learn it so that you can tell it to the class in an **oral presentation.** Use body actions and changes of voice during dialogues as you tell the story.

Mask Maker What kind of mask would be magical enough to fool seven girls at a dance? Use papier-mâché (made by mixing paper pulp with glue), cardboard, wood, or other materials, to create the **mask** you think the young man might have worn to the dance.

Playtime Work with a group to turn this tale into a **skit.** Assign parts, work out dialogue, rehearse it, and present your production for a younger class. You may want to use a mask made in the activity above as a prop.

New Directions

From Pen to Printout

History Connection

Some changes occur slowly. All books and manuscripts were written by hand for centuries before the invention of the printing press. Other changes seem to take place over-night. In 1984 very few American homes had a computer. Ten years later, Americans bought more home computers than television sets. At whatever speed, many new directions have been explored on the road from pen to printout.

◀ Johann Gutenberg is credited with the invention of movable type in the fifteenth century. His gothic type was modeled after the lettering used by scribes of his time. Far more elaborate than our alphabet and punctuation, Gutenberg's type included 290 characters.

▲ This page from the Codex Mendoza, an ancient Aztec manuscript, shows the symbolism of clothing. The first two rows illustrate how a priest earns the right to wear increasingly elaborate costumes with each captive he takes. The third row shows the dress of officials, and military commanders in the last row wear feathered tassels.

◀ Dated A.D. 868, the Chinese *Diamond Sutra* is believed to be the oldest complete printed book in existence. Pages were printed using a series of woodblocks. The printed sheets then were glued together, forming a sixteen-foot scroll. This sutra, one of Buddha's sermons, was written in Sanskrit.

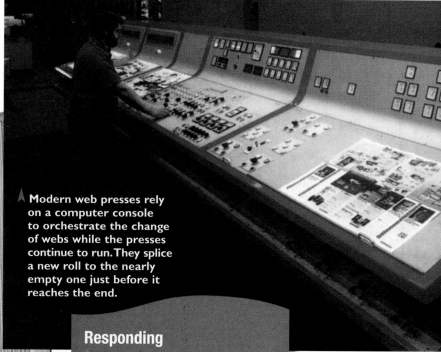

Gutenberg developed the printing press and in 1448 set up his own business in Germany. With new business partners, he soon printed a Turkish Calendar and his famous forty-two line Bible, so called because most of its pages have forty-two lines. Gutenberg's printing career came to an end when he lost his business in 1455. ➤

The British Walter Press was the first to use large rolls of paper, called webs, around 1869. The web press needed to be completely shut down to change the huge rolls. ➤

Below is Gutenberg's Bible of forty-two lines per column. At the time of its printing, many European men and women shared a great desire to read this great work. ▼

Modern web presses rely on a computer console to orchestrate the change of webs while the presses continue to run. They splice a new roll to the nearly empty one just before it reaches the end.

Responding

Some scientists and experts in technology believe that the next step in the evolution of the written word is a "paperless society." They say that the computer of the future will completely eliminate the need for pen and paper. Do you think this will ever happen? Explain your answer.

A Short History of Punctuation

by Polly M. Robertus

EARLYGREEKSHADHARDLYANYPUNCTUATION
FONOITCERIDEHTDEGNAHCNEVEDNA*
THEIRWRITINGATTHEENDOFEACHLINELATER
TAHTGNITIRWFOYAWAOTDEGNAHCYEHT
FAVOREDRIGHTHANDEDPEOPLEANDSHOWED
WHEREANEWPARAGRAPHBEGANBYUNDERLINING
THEFIRSTLINEOFIT<u>LATERTHEGREEKPLAYWRIGHT</u>
ARISTOPHANES • INVENTEDMARKSTOSHOW • WHERE
THEREADERSHOULDTAKEABREATH:
THE • ROMANS • MADE • WRITING • MUCH • EASIER •
TO • READ • BY • PUTTING • DOTS • BETWEEN • WORDS •
AND • BY • MOVING • THE • FIRST • LETTER • OF • A •
PARAGRAPH • INTO • THE • LEFT • MARGIN: THEY •
ADAPTED • SOME • OF • THE • GREEK • MARKS • SUCH • AS •
THE • COLON • MARK • TO • INDICATE • PHRASE • ENDINGS:
INTHEEARLYMIDDLEAGESTHISSYSTEMOFPUNCTUATION
BROKEDOWNBECAUSEVERYFEWPEOPLECOULDREAD
ANDWRITE   BUTWRITERSKEPTASPACEATTHEENDOF
ASENTENCEANDCONTINUEDTOMARKPARAGRAPHS
EVENTUALLY WORDS WERE SEPARATED AGAIN AND
NEW SENTENCES BEGAN WITH A LARGER LETTER

*Hint: Try reading from right to left.

The educational reforms of Charlemagne led to the invention of lowercase letters which could be written and read much faster / Phrases and sentence endings were indicated either by ∴ or by a slash /

As time went on writers looked for more ways to clarify meaning / In medieval music notation they found a way to indicate how a voice should rise or fall at the end of a sentence or phrase. Can you hear your voice rise at the end of a question? Our question mark came directly from medieval music notation. When a long sentence broke in the middle > they put a new mark that became our semicolon and colon. The hy= phen appeared as two lines instead of one.

Around A.D. 1500 the indented paragraph appeared, as did the comma and period as we know them. Printers of the Renaissance invented new marks like the exclamation point and quotation marks. By that time, people were commonly reading silently, and punctuation came to depend more on grammatical groups than breath groups.

(Parentheses and dashes appeared with the advent of printing.)

By the end of the seventeenth century, our punctuation system was in place for the most part, though sometimes details varied. Just think, though: After only a few lessons in school—and with lots of practice reading and writing—you can boast that you've mastered a system that took Westerners many centuries to develop!

Responding

1. Based on this reading, what do you think is the main purpose of punctuation?

2. Do your own experiment to test the importance of punctuation. Choose a paragraph from any story in this book—the more suspenseful the better. Write the paragraph without using any punctuation. Ask another student to read it. Then ask the same person to read the original paragraph from the book. What difference did punctuation make in the reading?

Reading Mini-Lesson

Comparing and Contrasting

What do you do when you compare and contrast? You look at the similarities and differences between two or more things, often with the purpose of judging which is better or best. We do this all the time when trying to decide between brands of cereal or sneakers or when channel-hopping to find the best TV show to view.

Comparing and contrasting also are important when reading or learning about something new. Skill in spotting differences and similarities helps you better understand what you read and relates new information to what you already know.

Differences or contrasts help us see the importance of change. Advertisers use "before-and-after" pictures to show dramatic changes that will happen after you buy and use their products. "A Short History of Punctuation" on pages 548–549 gives us similar before-and-after contrasts. In this selection, samples of early Greek writing make us appreciate how convenient present-day rules of writing, that we take for granted, are.

A chart is a good way to compare and contrast. It allows the kind of side-by-side comparison that really makes clear the similarities and differences. The chart at the left contrasts similarities and differences between early Greek and Roman writing.

Feature of Writing	Early Greek	Roman
Letter form:	all capitals	all capitals
Direction of writing:	both directions	left to right
Space markers:	none	dots between words

Activity Options

1. Make a chart, similar to the one above, that compares and contrasts (a) the way the early Greeks wrote, (b) the way people in Charlemagne's time wrote, and (c) the way we write today. Include these features: letter forms (capital/lower case), space markers, direction of writing, and punctuation marks.

2. If you could make improvements on our present-day system of writing and punctuation, what would they be? Invent your own system and show on a chart how it compares with that in use today.

Writing Workshop

Taking New Directions

Assignment The characters you read about took their lives in new directions. When have you cut a new path for yourself? Write about an incident in which you turned your life in a new direction. See the Writer's Blueprint for details.

WRITER'S BLUEPRINT

Product   An autobiographical essay
Purpose   To describe a time when you turned your life in a new direction
Audience   A close friend or family member
Specs   As the writer of a successful essay, you should:

❏ Start with an opener that draws your audience into the situation.

❏ Continue by describing the events before and during the incident.

❏ Include details about setting, time frame, people involved, and action to help your readers visualize the incident. Use dialogue where appropriate.

❏ Conclude by explaining how the incident caused an important change in your life.

❏ Vary your sentences to keep readers engaged.

❏ Follow the rules for grammar, usage, spelling, and mechanics. Be sure your pronoun reference is clear throughout your essay.

The instructions that follow will help you write a successful autobiographical essay.

STEP **1** PREWRITING

Chart new directions from the literature. Each selection deals with someone who has taken his or her life in a new direction. Create a chart for the literature like the one below. It may remind you of an incident in which your life turned in a new direction.

Character	Situation at Beginning of Story	New Direction Taken
Peter	not a good student; losing touch with his father	grows closer to his father; becomes interested in putting words down on paper

In the Literary Source, what new direction does author M. E. Kerr show that Peter's life has taken?

Brainstorm new directions from your own life. Does anything from the literature remind you of your own life? Think back to times when you think your life took a new direction. These may have been because of a conscious effort on your part or because of events you didn't control. Make a list of those times. Select one that you think is most interesting and you'd like to share with others.

OR . . .

Instead of doing a quick-write, you might draw the incident that changed your life. Be sure to include the result in your drawing.

Use your senses to explore the incident. Close your eyes and visualize the incident. What sensory impressions do you have? Examine details about setting, people, and action through your five senses. List these details in a chart. Write the senses down the side and *setting, people,* and *action* across the top.

Quickwrite about your incident for a few minutes. Be sure to use the first person pronouns *I* and *me* when you write to show that you are telling the story. Here is part of one student's quickwrite.

August 10, 1992. Moving day. We'll be in the same city, but it's a new neighborhood and new school. New house, new room. This is going to be a tough change for me. I wasn't happy about moving. I'm also a little bit nervous about all this new stuff!

STUDENT MODEL

Ask yourself: *Do I have all the information I need?* Look at your quickwrite. If you have left anything out, you might:

- Review the results of the incident and work back to the events that preceded them.

- Talk to people who knew about the incident at the time it took place.

Plan your narrative. Using your list of details and your quickwrite, divide your incident into a series of events on a storyboard. Draw the events before, during, and after your incident. Beneath each, write details about that part of the incident. Arrange your events in chronological order. Summarize with a sentence that explains how the incident created an important change in your life.

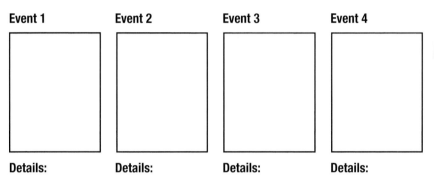

OR . . . If you would rather not do a storyboard, put your events in chronological order on a time line.

Event 1	Event 2	Event 3	Event 4

Details: Details: Details: Details:

This incident created an important change in my life because . . .

DRAFTING

Before you write, review the Writer's Blueprint. You should also review your Prewriting steps.

As you draft, don't worry about mistakes with spelling and punctuation. Concentrate on getting your ideas on paper. To keep your writing interesting, try to vary your sentence structure. For tips on this, look ahead to the Revising Strategy on varied sentence structure. Here are some ideas for getting started.

• Begin by explaining how your incident changed your life and then describe the incident.

• Explain why the incident is so important to you.

• Begin with the first event you put on your storyboard or time line.

Remember, you want your opener to grab your audience and make them want to continue reading.

Ask a partner for comments on your draft before you revise it.

✔ Have I followed the specs in the Writer's Blueprint?

✔ Does my opening draw my reader into the situation?

✔ Have I used enough sensory details to help my reader visualize the situation?

✔ Do I vary the structure of my sentences?

Revising Strategy

Varied Sentence Structure

Writers vary the structure of their sentences to make their writing more interesting. Look at the Literary Source. How has M. E. Kerr created variety in these sentences?

With time you'll find that sentence variety comes naturally as you put your ideas on paper, but you'll need to practice. Here are some suggestions that will help you achieve variety.

- Vary sentence length, using short, declarative sentences and longer compound or complex sentences.

- Vary sentence beginnings with phrases and clauses.

- When possible, combine sentences with similar ideas.

- Vary the types of sentences you use. Sometimes a declarative sentence is more effective if it's written as a question.

LITERARY SOURCE

"The night before the author visit, my dad comes over to see me. My step-father and my mother have gone off to see my step-brother, Tom, in Leighton High School's version of *The Sound of Music.*

To myself, and sometimes to my mother, I call him Tom Terrific."

from "The Author" by M. E. Kerr

Notice how the writer of the passage below revised sentence structure based on a comment from a partner.

School started in September. Fifth grade. *During the school year,* I made many friends, ~~during the school year.~~ My friends and I have had many great times together. We go to the movies, have sleepovers, and play sports. I still see my old friends. The move hasn't been as tough as I thought it would be.

STUDENT MODEL

Ask a partner to review your revised draft before you edit. When you edit, watch for errors in grammar, usage, spelling, and mechanics. Pay special attention to pronoun reference.

Editing Strategy

FOR REFERENCE... More rules for pronoun reference are provided in the Language and Grammar Handbook.

Clear Pronoun Reference

When you use pronouns in writing, make sure that your reference to an antecedent is clear.

- Avoid using pronouns so that they seem to refer to more than one noun.

Confusing: Ms. Walton used Grace's essay as an example because she pointed out the differences between the two characters.
Clear: Because Grace's essay pointed out the differences between the two characters, Ms. Walton used it as an example.

- Make sure that the antecedent is stated and not implied.

Confusing: To study for the test, he reviewed his notes and did further research. This helped him get a good grade.
Clear: To study for the test, he reviewed his notes and did further research. These preparations helped him do well.

- Avoid placing a pronoun too far away from its antecedent.

Confusing: The kids got caught in the rain who walked home from school.
Clear: The kids who walked home from school got caught in the rain.

Notice how the writer of the draft below paid attention to pronoun reference.

The night before the move, my brother and I slept over at my grandmother's. She made us popcorn, and we watched movies. I think she wanted us to relax.

STUDENT MODEL

5 PRESENTING

Here are two ideas for presenting your narrative.

- Turn your incident into a script for a TV talk show concerning a topic such as "People who have turned their lives around." Work with a group to present several essays as an entire production and present it to the class.

- Present your essay aloud to the class as if it were an inspirational, motivational program, such as a self-improvement program similar to an infomercial on cable television.

6 LOOKING BACK

Self-evaluate. What grade would you give your paper? Look back at the Writer's Blueprint and evaluate yourself on each point, from 6 (superior) down to 1 (weak).

Reflect. Think about what you learned from writing your narrative as you write answers to these questions.

✔ Has this particular incident continued to influence your life? How?

✔ If you could change the manner in which you wrote this essay, what would it be? Would you expand the brainstorming session, add steps to the Prewriting stage, or spend more time planning how to construct your essay?

For Your Working Portfolio: Add your narrative and your reflection responses to your working portfolio.

Beyond Print

Hints for Using Multimedia

- Use pictures and music that don't distract the audience.
- Use large text in projections so everyone will be able to read it.
- Don't try to put all your information on the screen.
- Use headings in an outline form and present the details orally.
- Don't create posters or computer screens that are "busy" and unclear.
- Use colors that will stand out from across the room.
- Project your voice clearly so everyone can hear you.
- Create clear transitions from one section to another with the media. Fade in music that relates to the next section as you are finishing the current section.
- Run through your presentation several times before you present it.

Wake Things Up with Multimedia

Any time you use more than one way of communicating with an audience, you are using multimedia. When used in various combinations, speeches, posters, slides, video, computers, recordings, or even skits are powerful tools for presenting your information.

Multimedia presentations come in two formats: passive and interactive. *Passive multimedia* is used successfully in oral presentations in which a chart or graph is added to make it easier to explain complex ideas. Simply watching a movie is passive, but it includes both video and sound. *Interactive multimedia* involves the viewer. A computer presentation that asks the user to enter information into a computer is interactive.

Good writing skills form the basis of all successful multimedia presentations. Projected text should be clear and large, since viewers may be seated far away and will have only a few seconds to read. Correct spelling is also important.

You should begin planning by making an outline and writing a clear thesis. Then, in the presentation, try to create a strong beginning, middle, and end that will make your point clear to the audience, just as you would in an essay.

Activity

Using at least one type of media, prepare an oral presentation based on "A Short History of Punctuation." Start by simply adding a graphic to the speech by creating a poster, transparency, slide, or computer image. Or try incorporating music into the speech. Later, try adding other types of media to the presentation.

Projects for Collaborative Study

Theme Connection

A Change of Pace Every time we open a magazine we see images sending signals as to how we should look or act. Look like this model and have friends galore! Drive this car and impress your neighbors! Are you buying any of it? It's often hard not to.

■ As a class, gather images from newspapers and magazines of all kinds of people—fashion models, political and sports figures, people in science, business, literature, etc. Display them on a bulletin board. What strikes you about them? Compare and contrast your impressions.

■ Next go the local library and find advertisements and news stories featuring men and women from the 1920s through the 1980s. Display these on a table below the bulletin board. Compare and contrast today's images to those of the past. Discuss what you can gather about change from all this.

Literature Connection

Plot It Out When someone asks you what a movie or book is about, they are asking about the **plot**—what goes on in the story. When discussing a plot, be sure to do so in broad outline—don't give too much away. Tell a bit about how the story begins, how it develops, and where it leads. Don't give away the ending (unless you are asked to).

Divide into teams with two or three students in each. Take turns very broadly describing the plot of one of the selections you have read. The first to correctly name the selection wins a point. The first team to acquire ten points is the winner.

Life Skills Connection

A Change of Habit One of the more difficult things to change is a habit. A habit is something you do without much conscious thought. Some habits are useful. Some get in the way. Others are destructive. What are some of your beneficial habits? How are they useful? What are some of your less beneficial habits? How do they limit you?

A way to break a habit is to substitute your usual behavior with a new approach. At first, you will be very conscious of your changed behavior. When you reach the point that you automatically substitute the new approach, you will be on the road to a new and better habit.

■ Substitute a new behavior for a habit that's not useful to you. What might be its benefits?

■ For two weeks make a conscious effort to practice this new behavior and break your old habit. Keep a journal of your progress.

Multicultural Connection

The View from Here Perspective is a term used in art, literature, and even life. In art it refers to the artist's physical relationship to the object being represented. In literature it is the author's view of the subject being written about. In life, it is how we view our world— how we **interact** with what goes on. Look back over Unit Five and find a selection or image that has a perspective that you find interesting. Then answer these questions:

■ How would you interact in this setting?

■ What would your perspective be here?

Read More About Change

The Clay Marble (1993) by Minfong Ho. Twelve-year-old Dara and her family are Cambodian refugees on the Thailand border. The tragic death of her friend Jantu brings Dara to an appreciation of creativity, family, and home.

Keeping Secrets (1995) by Mary E. Lyons. The diaries of famous nineteenth-century women such as Louisa May Alcott, Ida B. Wells, and Kate Chopin reveal their secret yearnings and frustrations. This book makes very clear the diary's ability to help people find their innermost selves.

More Good Books

Dawn Land (1993) by Joseph Bruchac. This novel, set in the Ice Age some 10,000 years ago, follows Young Hunter, who sets off on a mythical journey. Along the way, he learns to use the Long Thrower, a weapon of peace, and discovers that strangers are not necessarily enemies.

The Land I Lost (1982) by Quang Nhuong Huynh. The author writes simply and vividly about the homeland he lost—a hamlet in the Vietnamese highlands.

The Dandelion Garden (1995) by Budge Wilson. In her latest collection of stories, Wilson tells about ten different characters ranging in age from seven to 76. Their experiences are universal.

All Creatures Great and Small (1972) by James Herriot. The first in the popular series of autobiographical stories about a veterinarian in Yorkshire, England, this book describes the young vet's first year on the job with spirit and warmth.

A Light in the Forest (1953) by Conrad Richter. Raised by the Delaware, a boy must return to his forgotten birth family. He is unhappy in this new environment and returns to his Indian friends. He must choose between the opposing expectations of these two cultures.

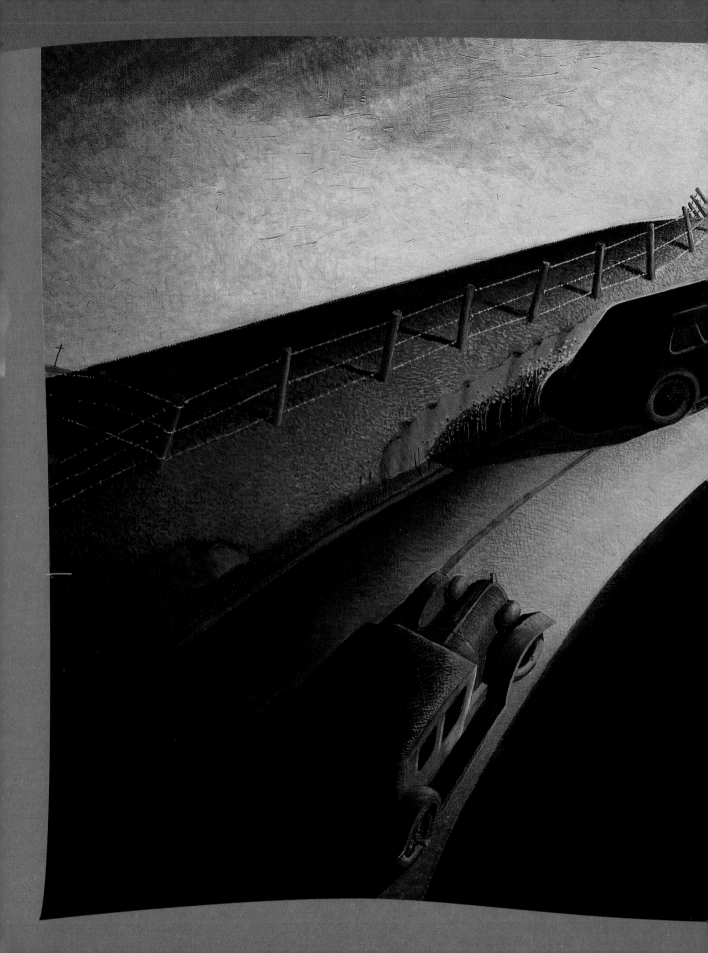

Conflict and Resolution

You're Invading My Space!
Part One, pages 564–615

Standing Your Ground
Part Two, pages 616–679

Talking About
CONFLICT AND
RESOLUTION

Disappointment, confusion, and anger are emotions that we all feel at one time or another. They are feelings that may lead to conflict—but before they do, there are steps we can take to resolve them. Talking about how we feel is very important. Trying to see all sides of the issue is important also. Stop—calm down—count to twenty before you say or do something that may lead to conflict. Concentrate on ways to reach a resolution. You'll feel much better if you do.

Read the thoughts of students from across the nation. Compare their ideas to those of the literature you are about to read.

The question is: Did he willingly and illegally take the life of a fellow creature?

from Survival *by Alfred Brenner, page 629*

Aquarium (detail), by Carol Hoy, 1993.

"Some resolutions have a bad effect as well as a good one."

Benita—Portland, OR

"When I try to explain something I did to my friends, they won't listen"

Sunjay–Charleston, NC

"This guy hassles that guy. This group gangs up on that group. This country overruns that country. It's everywhere!"

Nat–Sedona, AZ

A redcoat troop came marching—
Marching—marching—
King George's men came marching,
up to the old inn door.

from "The Highwayman" by Alfred Noyes, page 642

I would like for her to disappear. I just know that on Monday my friends, and my enemies, in the barrio will have a lot of senile-grandmother jokes to tell in front of me.

from "Abuela Invents the Zero" by Judith Ortiz Cofer, page 590

563

Part One

You're Invading My Space!

Most of us feel the need for what we call "breathing room"—some space to call our own. The boundaries we set may be as simple as a wall around a garden or as complicated as the unspoken feelings we want others to notice and respect. No matter how the lines are drawn, crossing uninvited into others' territory is the surest way to cause conflict.

 **Multicultural Connection** **Perspective** involves trying to look beyond our own experiences and cultural background. Cultural forces may lead you to come into conflict with those of other groups. Resolving these kinds of group conflicts can often be accomplished by learning to see the other group's perspectives. Which of the characters in these stories gain new perspectives when someone or something invades their space?

Literature

Toni Cade Bambara	**The War of the Wall** ♦ short story	566
Edwin Markham	**Outwitted** ♦ poem	573
Roald Dahl	**The Green Mamba** ♦ autobiography	577
Robert Frost	**A Minor Bird** ♦ poem	583
Judith Ortiz Cofer	**Abuela Invents the Zero** ♦ short story	587
Rudyard Kipling	**Rikki-tikki-tavi** ♦ short story	594
	Language Mini-Lesson ♦ Checking Your Spelling	609

Interdisciplinary Study Guest or Pest?

Animal and Plant Invaders ♦ earth science	610
Mongoose on the Loose ♦ science	613
Reading Mini-Lesson ♦ Finding Cause-and-Effect Relationships	615

Before Reading

The War of the Wall

by Toni Cade Bambara

Toni Cade Bambara
1939–1995

Toni Cade Bambara knew people. She was a teacher, a social worker, a film maker, and a keen observer of human beings since her childhood in New York City. Bambara listened closely to *what* people had to say and *how* they said it, which shows in the realistic way her characters talk. She also asked herself questions. She said about this story, "I wondered how people in the neighborhood would react if a stranger started painting on a wall, their wall." That's how "The War of the Wall" began. This story also pursues the fascinating thought, "If only walls could talk. . . ." Toni Cade Bambara died in Philadelphia at the age of 56.

Building Background

Wall to Wall Think about the title of this story. We usually think of walls as barriers built to enclose or divide areas. Some walls protect those inside or serve to separate people. Other walls, as in this story, are opportunities for self-expression that can bring people together.

Getting into the Story

Writer's Notebook "The War of the Wall" has to do with first impressions. In your notebook write about a first impression you had of someone or something that turned out to be quite different from what you first thought. You may want to use these questions for starters: What was your first impression and why? How did your view change and why? As you read, compare your experience with that of the narrator.

Reading Tip

Colorful Expressions Although English is spoken throughout the United States, people in various regions of the country may use expressions you have never heard. The chart below gives the meaning of some expressions that are used in the following story. Cover the right column with your hand and see how many of them you already know.

Expressions	Meanings
flat out	directly or openly; without hesitation
leaning hipshot	leaning with one hip stuck out
paid us no mind	did not notice us
fix her wagon	scold her; put her in her place
hunching each other	shoving or pushing
laying down a heavy rap	saying something important

The War of the Wall

Toni Cade Bambara

Me and Lou had no time for courtesies. We were late for school. So we just flat out told the painter lady to quit messing with the wall. It was our wall, and she had no right coming into our neighborhood painting on it. Stirring in the paint bucket and not even looking at us, she mumbled something about Mr. Eubanks, the barber, giving her permission. That had nothing to do with it as far as we were concerned. We've been pitching pennies against that wall since we were little kids. Old folks have been dragging their chairs out to sit in the shade of the wall for years. Big kids have been playing handball against the wall since so-called integration[1] when the crazies 'cross town poured cement in our pool so we couldn't use it. I'd sprained my neck one time boosting my cousin Lou up to chisel Jimmy Lyons's name

into the wall when we found out he was never coming home from the war in Vietnam to take us fishing.

"If you lean close," Lou said, leaning hip-shot against her beat-up car, "you'll get a whiff of bubble gum and kids' sweat. And that'll tell you something—that this wall belongs to the kids of Taliaferro Street." I thought Lou sounded very convincing. But the painter lady paid us no mind. She just snapped the brim of her straw hat down and hauled her bucket up the ladder.

"You're not even from around here," I hollered up after her. The license plates on her old piece of car said "New York." Lou

---

1. integration (in′tə grā′shən), *n.* including people of all races on an equal basis in schools, parks, neighborhoods, and so on.

dragged me away because I was about to grab hold of that ladder and shake it. And then we'd really be late for school.

When we came from school, the wall was slick with white. The painter lady was running string across the wall and taping it here and there. Me and Lou leaned against the gum ball machine outside the pool hall and watched. She had strings up and down and back and forth. Then she began chalking them with a hunk of blue chalk.

The Morris twins crossed the street, hanging back at the curb next to the beat-up car. The twin with the red ribbons was hugging a jug of cloudy lemonade. The one with yellow ribbons was holding a plate of dinner away from her dress. The painter lady began snapping the strings. The blue chalk dust measured off halves and quarters up and down and sideways too. Lou was about to say how hip it all was, but I dropped my book satchel on his toes to remind him we were at war.

Some good aromas were drifting our way from the plate leaking pot likker[2] onto the Morris girl's white socks. I could tell from where I stood that under the tinfoil was baked ham, collard greens, and candied yams. And knowing Mrs. Morris, who sometimes bakes for my mama's restaurant, a slab of buttered cornbread was probably up under there too, sopping up some of the pot likker. Me and Lou rolled our eyes, wishing somebody would send us some dinner. But the painter lady didn't even turn around. She was pulling the strings down and prying bits of tape loose.

Side Pocket came strolling out of the pool hall to see what Lou and me were studying so hard. He gave the painter lady the once-over, checking out her paint-spattered jeans, her chalky T-shirt, her floppy-brimmed straw hat. He hitched up his pants and glided over toward the painter lady, who kept right on with what she was doing.

Self Portrait, painted in 1927 by Mexican artist Rufino Tamayo, is a kind of opaque watercolor over black chalk. Which character in the story do you think might have posed for this portrait? What about the painting made you select that person?

"Watcha got there, Sweetheart?" he asked the twin with the plate.

"Suppah," she said, all soft and country-like.

"For her," the one with the jug added, jerking her chin toward the painter lady's back.

Still she didn't turn around. She was rearing back on her heels, her hands jammed into her back pockets, her face squinched up like the masterpiece she had in mind was taking shape on the wall by magic. We could have been gophers crawled up into a rotten hollow for all she cared. She didn't even say hello to

2. **pot likker,** the broth in which meat or vegetables have been cooked.

anybody. Lou was muttering something about how great her concentration was. I butt him with my hip, and his elbow slid off the gum machine.

"Good evening," Side Pocket said in his best ain't-I-fine voice. But the painter lady was moving from the milk crate to the stepstool to the ladder, moving up and down fast, scribbling all over the wall like a crazy person. We looked at Side Pocket. He looked at the twins. The twins looked at us. The painter lady was giving a show. It was like those old-timey music movies where the dancer taps on the table top and then starts jumping all over the furniture, kicking chairs over and not skipping a beat. She didn't even look where she was stepping. And for a minute there, hanging on the ladder to reach a far spot, she looked like she was going to tip right over.

"Ahh," Side Pocket cleared his throat and moved fast to catch the ladder. "These young ladies here have brought you some supper."

"Ma'am?" The twins stepped forward. Finally the painter turned around, her eyes "full of sky," as my grandmama would say. Then she stepped down like she was in a trance. She wiped her hands on her jeans as the Morris twins offered up the plate and the jug. She rolled back the tinfoil, then wagged her head as though something terrible was on the plate.

"Thank your mother very much," she said, sounding like her mouth was full of sky too. "I've brought my own dinner along." And then, without even excusing herself, she went back up the ladder, drawing on the wall in a wild way. Side Pocket whistled one of those oh-brother breathy whistles and went back into the pool hall. The Morris twins shifted their weight from one foot to the other, then

crossed the street and went home. Lou had to drag me away, I was so mad. We couldn't wait to get to the firehouse to tell my daddy all about this rude woman who'd stolen our wall.

All the way back to the block to help my mama out at the restaurant, me and Lou kept asking my daddy for ways to run the painter lady out of town. But my daddy was busy talking about the trip to the country and telling Lou he could come too because Grandmama can always use an extra pair of hands on the farm.

> **Finally the painter turned around, her eyes "full of sky," as my grandmama would say.**

Later that night, while me and Lou were in the back doing our chores, we found out that the painter lady was a liar. She came into the restaurant and leaned against the glass of the steam table, talking about how starved she was. I was scrubbing pots and Lou was chopping onions, but we could hear her through the service window. She was asking Mama was that a ham hock in the greens, and was that a neck bone in the pole beans, and were there any vegetables cooked without meat, especially pork.

"I don't care who your spiritual leader is," Mama said in that way of hers. "If you eat in the community, sistuh, you gonna eat pig by-and-by, one way or t'other."

CLARIFY: Why are the painter lady and Mama in conflict?

Me and Lou were cracking up in the kitchen, and several customers at the counter were clearing their throats waiting for Mama to really fix her wagon for not speaking to the elders when she came in. The painter lady took a stool at the counter and went right on with her questions. Was there cheese in the baked macaroni, she wanted to know? Were there eggs in the salad? Was it honey or sugar in the iced tea? Mama was fixing Pop Johnson's plate. And every time the painter lady asked a fool question, Mama would dump another spoonful of rice on the pile. She was tapping her foot and heating up in a dangerous way. But Pop Johnson was happy as he could be. Me and Lou peeked through the service window, wondering what planet the painter lady came from. Who ever heard of baked macaroni without cheese, or potato salad without eggs?

"Do you have any bread made with unbleached flour?" the painter lady asked Mama. There was a long pause, as though everybody in the restaurant was holding their breath, wondering if Mama would dump the next spoonful on the painter lady's head. She didn't. But when she set Pop Johnson's plate down, it came down with a bang.

When Mama finally took her order, the starving lady all of a sudden couldn't make up her mind whether she wanted a vegetable plate or fish and a salad. She finally settled on the broiled trout and a tossed salad. But just when Mama reached for a plate to serve her, the painter lady leaned over the counter with her finger all up in the air.

"Excuse me," she said. "One more thing." Mama was holding the plate like a Frisbee, tapping that foot, one hand on her hip. "Can I get raw beets in that tossed salad?"

"You will get," Mama said, leaning her face close to the painter lady's, "whatever Lou back there tossed. Now sit down." And the painter lady sat back down on her stool and shut right up.

All the way to the country, me and Lou tried to get Mama to open fire on the painter lady. But Mama said that seeing as how she was from the North, you couldn't expect her to have any manners. Then Mama said she was sorry she'd been so impatient with the woman because she seemed like a decent person and was simply trying to stick to a very strict diet. Me and Lou didn't want to hear that. Who did that lady think she was, coming into our neighborhood and taking over our wall?

"Wellllll," Mama drawled,[3] pulling into the filling station so Daddy could take the wheel, "it's hard on an artist, ya know. They can't always get people to look at their work. So she's just doing her work in the open, that's all."

Me and Lou definitely did not want to hear that. Why couldn't she set up an easel downtown or draw on the sidewalk in her own neighborhood? Mama told us to quit fussing so much; she was tired and wanted to rest. She climbed into the back seat and dropped down into the warm hollow Daddy had made in the pillow.

All weekend long, me and Lou tried to scheme[4] up ways to recapture our wall. Daddy and Mama said they were sick of hearing about it. Grandmama turned up the TV to drown us out. On the late news was a story about the New York subways. When a train came roaring into the station all covered from top to bottom, windows too, with writings and drawings done with spray paint, me and Lou slapped five. Mama said it was too bad kids in New York had nothing better to do than spray paint all over the trains. Daddy said that in the cities, even grown-ups wrote all over the trains and buildings too. Daddy called it "graffiti." Grandmama called it a shame.

---

3. **drawl** (drôl), *v.* talk in a slow way, drawing out certain sounds.

4. **scheme** (skēm), *v.* plot or plan in a secret way.

The Wall of Respect in Chicago, photographed by Tom Medcalf, was painted in 1967 by nine artists belonging to the Visual Art Workshop of the Organization of Black American Culture. This mural inspired thousands of other such murals worldwide. Look for ways in which this wall is similar to the one described in the story. ➤

PREDICT: What do you think the narrator and Lou may do to recapture the wall?

We couldn't wait to get out of school on Monday. We couldn't find any black spray paint anywhere. But in a junky hardware store downtown we found a can of white epoxy paint, the kind you touch up old refrigerators with when they get splotchy and peely. We spent our whole allowance on it. And because it was too late to use our bus passes, we had to walk all the way home lugging our book satchels and gym shoes, and the bag with the epoxy.

When we reached the corner of Taliaferro and Fifth, it looked like a block party or something. Half the neighborhood was gathered on the sidewalk in front of the wall. I looked at Lou, he looked at me. We both looked at the bag with the epoxy and wondered how we were going to work our scheme. The painter lady's car was nowhere in sight. But there were too many people standing around to do anything. Side Pocket and his buddies were leaning on their cue sticks, hunching each other. Daddy was there with a lineman[5] he catches a ride with on Mondays. Mrs. Morris had her arms flung around the shoulders of the twins on either side of her. Mama was talking with some of her customers, many of them with napkins still at the throat. Mr. Eubanks came out of the barber shop, followed by a man in a striped poncho, half his face shaved, the other half full of foam.

"She really did it, didn't she?" Mr. Eubanks huffed out his chest. Lots of folks answered right quick that she surely did when they saw the straight razor in his hand.

Mama beckoned us over. And then we saw it. The wall. Reds, greens, figures outlined in black. Swirls of purple and orange. Storms of blues and yellows. It was something. I recognized some of the faces right off. There was

---

5. **lineman,** a person who sets up and repairs telephone or electric power lines.

Martin Luther King, Jr. And there was a man with glasses on and his mouth open like he was laying down a heavy rap. Daddy came up alongside and reminded us that he was Minister Malcolm X. The serious woman with a rifle I knew was Harriet Tubman because my grandmama has pictures of her all over the house. And I knew Mrs. Fannie Lou Hamer 'cause a signed photograph of her hangs in the restaurant next to the calendar.

Then I let my eyes follow what looked like a vine. It trailed past a man with a horn, a woman with a big white flower in her hair, a handsome dude in a tuxedo seated at a piano, and a man with a goatee holding a book. When I looked more closely, I realized that what had looked like flowers were really faces. One face with yellow petals looked just like Frieda Morris. One with red petals looked just like Hattie Morris. I could hardly believe my eyes.

"Notice," Side Pocket said, stepping close to the wall with his cue stick like a classroom pointer. "These are the flags of <u>liberation</u>,"[6] he said in a voice I'd never heard him use before. We all stepped closer while he pointed and spoke. "Red, black, and green," he said, his pointer falling on the leaflike flags of the vine. "Our liberation flag. And here Ghana, there Tanzania. Guinea-Bissau, Angola, Mozambique."[7] Side Pocket sounded very tall, as though he'd been waiting all his life to give this lesson.

Mama tapped us on the shoulder and pointed to a high section of the wall. There was a fierce-looking man with his arms crossed against his chest guarding a bunch of children. His muscles bulged, and he looked a lot like my daddy. One kid was looking at a row of books. Lou hunched me 'cause the kid looked like me. The one that looked like Lou was spinning a globe on the tip of his finger like a basketball. There were other kids there with microscopes and compasses. And the more I looked, the more it looked like the fierce man was not so much guarding the kids as defending their right to do what they were doing.

Then Lou gasped and dropped the paint bag and ran forward, running his hands over a rainbow. He had to tiptoe and stretch to do it, it was so high. I couldn't breathe either. The painter lady had found the chisel marks and had painted Jimmy Lyons's name in a rainbow.

"Read the <u>inscription</u>,[8] honey," Mrs. Morris said, urging little Frieda forward. She didn't have to urge much. Frieda marched right up, bent down, and in a loud voice that made everybody quit oohing and ahhing and listen, she read,

> *To the People of Taliaferro Street*
> *I Dedicate This Wall of Respect*
> *Painted in Memory of My Cousin*
> *Jimmy Lyons*

---

6. liberation (lib′ə rā′shən), *n.* setting or being set free.
7. **Ghana** (gä′nə), **Tanzania** (tan′zə nē′ə), **Guinea-Bissau** (gin′ē bi sou′), **Angola** (ang gō′lə), **Mozambique** (mō′zam bēk′), countries in Africa.
8. inscription (in skrip′shən), *n.* words written or engraved on stone, metal, paper, and so on.

Outwitted

Edwin Markham

He drew a circle that shut me out—

Heretic, rebel, a thing to flout.

But Love and I had the wit to win:

We drew a circle that took him in!

After Reading

Making Connections

1. Copy the scale below onto your paper. Put a *B* on the line to show whose side you were on at the beginning of the story and an *E* to show where you stood at the end. Explain your answers.

Narrator   Painter
and Lou_____Lady

2. Do you think the narrator was justified in being upset with the painter lady? Why or why not?

3. What are some other ways that the narrator and Lou might have solved their problem with the painter lady?

4. Choose a character in the story you would most like to be. Find examples of things the character says and does that show why you would like to be this character.

5. 👐 What differences in **perspective** caused the **conflict** between the neighborhood and the painter lady? What resolved the conflict?

6. How would people react if the painter lady came into your neighborhood to paint a public wall?

Literary Focus: Dialogue

You can draw conclusions about the characters from their **dialogue**—the words they say to one another. Early in the story the narrator "hollers" at the painter lady, "You're not even from around here." From this line of dialogue, you can conclude that the narrator is angry at the painter lady for invading the neighborhood.

Look back at the story for examples of what the characters say to each other. Ask yourself: What does this dialogue tell me about how the character feels and thinks?

A chart can help you better understand the characters in the story. List the character, the dialogue that shows something important about that character, and what that dialogue helps you conclude about the character. Here is an example to get you started.

Character	Character's Dialogue	My Conclusions
narrator	"You're not even from around here."	angry, feels the neighborhood has been invaded

Vocabulary Study

On your paper write a synonym chosen from the vocabulary list for each underlined word or phrase.

integration
drawl
scheme
liberation
inscription

1. The civil rights movement of the 1960s was about the <u>mixing</u> of all races in our communities.

2. Many "Walls of Respect" were painted in the 1960s to portray <u>freedom</u>.

3. Sometimes artists had to plan or even <u>plot</u> to get approval to paint walls.

4. An <u>engraving</u> was sometimes added to a Wall of Respect to honor a civil rights leader.

5. Side Pocket did not <u>speak slowly</u> as he talked about the Wall of Respect.

Expressing Your Ideas

Writing Choices

A Space Case Think about why people in the narrator's neighborhood felt threatened when the painter lady went to work on their wall. Write a brief **description** of how this story relates to the theme "You're Invading My Space!"

Dear Painter Lady Unfortunately, the painter lady didn't get to see the effect her mural had on the narrator. Imagine that you are the narrator and write a **personal note** to the painter lady to let her know how you feel about her completed work of art.

Pushed to the Wall In a small group, divide the story into scenes. Have each person rewrite a different **scene** from the point of view of the painter lady. Everyone should read aloud his or her new version of the scene to the group. If possible, the new version of the story can then be read aloud to the entire class.

Other Options

Counter Revolution Work in a small group. Look back at the restaurant scene in the story and prepare a **skit** to perform for the class. Look for clues in the dialogue and descriptive passages as to how your character looks, acts, and talks. Really *be* that character.

Painter Kids Who and what have made your community proud? With classmates, plan a **wall of respect** for your community. Obtain permission to paint a wall and consult teachers and other experts on local history and mural planning and painting.

Smart Play In the 1960s several countries in Africa gained their independence, new ones came into being, and others changed their names. Invent a **game** that requires players to know—or learn as they play—the names of the African countries *plus* at least one important fact about each one.

Before Reading

The Green Mamba by Roald Dahl

A Minor Bird by Robert Frost

Roald Dahl
1916–1990

British author Roald Dahl began by writing adventure stories for magazines and telling bedtime stories to his children, whom he considered excellent writing teachers. "Children," he said, "are highly critical. And they lose interest so quickly. You have to keep things ticking along."

Robert Frost
1874–1963

Robert Frost—one of the most important American poets of this century—did not gain recognition as a U.S. poet until he moved to England. His poetry reveals his deep love of nature.

Building Background

Drawing the Line We civilized humans have a trait in common with wild animals—we're territorial. We stake out our territory as animals stake out theirs. Sometimes we gladly share our place in nature, especially if the intruder is a beautiful butterfly and not a stinging hornet. We call certain animals, who show up where they aren't welcome, pests. In large numbers, pests can become big problems. The following story and poem deal with when, where, and how we draw the line between our space and theirs.

Getting into the Selections

Writer's Notebook Some people hang up feeders to attract birds but panic when they see a harmless kind of snake in their yard. You, too, may feel drawn to certain kinds of animal life and repelled by others—but what in general is your attitude toward wildlife? In your notebook draw a scale like the one below and put an X on the spot that best shows how you usually feel when a wild creature walks, hops, creeps, crawls, slithers, or flies into your space.

Like_____Undecided_____Dislike

Reading Tip

Descriptive Writing When you go to a play, do you head for a front-row seat where you can see, hear, and almost feel the action? Good writers take you to a front row in your imagination with vivid descriptions that bring characters and events to life. As you read the "The Green Mamba" and "A Minor Bird," look for details that help you visualize scenes as though you were there.

THE GREEN MAMBA

ROALD DAHL

Oh, those snakes! How I hated them! They were the only fearful thing about Tanganyika,[1] and a newcomer very quickly learnt to identify most of them and to know which were deadly and which were simply poisonous. The killers, apart from the black mambas, were the green mambas, the cobras, and the tiny little puff adders that looked very much like small sticks lying motionless in the middle of a dusty path, and so easy to step on.

One Sunday evening I was invited to go and have a sundowner[2] at the house of an Englishman called Fuller who worked in the Customs office in Dar es Salaam.[3] He lived with his wife and two small children in a plain white wooden house that stood alone some way back from the road in a rough grassy piece of ground with coconut trees scattered about. I was walking across the grass towards the house and was about twenty yards away when I saw a large green snake go gliding straight up the veranda[4] steps of Fuller's house and in through the open front door. The brilliant yellowy-green skin and its great size made me certain it was a green mamba, a creature almost as deadly as the black mamba, and for a few seconds I was so startled and dumbfounded[5] and horrified that I froze to the spot. Then I pulled myself together and ran round to the back of the house shouting, "Mr. Fuller! Mr. Fuller!"

---

1. **Tanganyika** (tang′gə nyē′kə), former country in East Africa, now part of Tanzania.
2. **sundowner,** a drink at the end of the day.
3. **Dar es Salaam** (där es sə läm), a seaport in Tanzania, once the capital of Tanganyika.
4. veranda (və ran′də), *n.* a large porch along one or more sides of a house.
5. **dumbfounded** (dum′foun′dəd), *adj.* amazed.

Mrs. Fuller popped her head out of an upstairs window. "What on earth's the matter?" she said.

"You've got a large green mamba in your front room!" I shouted. "I saw it go up the veranda steps and right in through the door!"

"Fred!" Mrs. Fuller shouted, turning round. "Fred! Come here!"

Freddy Fuller's round red face appeared at the window beside his wife. "What's up?" he asked.

"There's a green mamba in your living room!" I shouted.

Without hesitation and without wasting time with more questions, he said to me, "Stay there. I'm going to lower the children down to you one at a time." He was completely cool and unruffled. He didn't even raise his voice.

A small girl was lowered down to me by her wrists, and I was able to catch her easily by the legs. Then came a small boy. Then Freddy Fuller lowered his wife, and I caught her by the waist and put her on the ground. Then came Fuller himself. He hung by his hands from the windowsill and when he let go he landed neatly on his two feet.

We stood in a little group on the grass at the back of the house, and I told Fuller exactly what I had seen.

The mother was holding the two children by the hand, one on each side of her. They didn't seem to be particularly alarmed.

"What happens now?" I asked.

"Go down the road, all of you," Fuller said. "I'm off to fetch the snake-man." He trotted away and got into his small ancient black car and drove off. Mrs. Fuller and the two small children and I went down to the road and sat in the shade of a large mango tree.

"Who is this snake-man?" I asked Mrs. Fuller.

"He is an old Englishman who has been out here for years," Mrs. Fuller said. "He actually *likes* snakes. He understands them and never kills them. He catches them and sells them to zoos and laboratories all over the world. Every native for miles around knows about him and whenever one of them sees a snake, he marks its hiding place and runs, often for great distances, to tell the snake-man. Then the snake-man comes along and captures it. The snake-man's strict rule is that he will never buy a captured snake from the natives."

"Why not?" I asked.

"To discourage them from trying to catch snakes themselves," Mrs. Fuller said. "In his early days he used to buy caught snakes, but so many natives got bitten trying to catch them, and so many died, that he decided to put a stop to it. Now any native who brings in a caught snake, no matter how rare, gets turned away."

"That's good," I said.

"What is the snake-man's name?" I asked.

"Donald Macfarlane," she said. "I believe he's Scottish."

"Is the snake in the house, Mummy?" the small girl asked.

"Yes, darling. But the snake-man is going to get it out."

"He'll bite Jack," the girl said.

"Oh!" Mrs. Fuller cried, jumping to her feet. "I forgot about Jack!" She began calling out, "Jack! Come here, Jack! Jack! . . . Jack! . . . Jack!"

The children jumped up as well, and all of them started calling to the dog. But no dog came out of the open front door.

"He's bitten Jack!" the small girl cried out. "He must have bitten him!" She began to cry and so did her brother, who was a year or so younger than she was. Mrs. Fuller looked grim.

"Jack's probably hiding upstairs," she said. "You know how clever he is."

Mrs. Fuller and I seated ourselves again on the grass, but the children remained standing. In between their tears they went on calling to the dog.

The art on this cloth flag made by African warriors of the Fante people of Ghana depicts the proverb "Without the head, the snake is nothing but rope." 🐾 What other cultures do you think might share this **perspective** on snakes? Which might not?

"Would you like me to take you down to the Maddens' house?" their mother asked.

"No!" they cried. "No, no, no! We want Jack!"

"Here's Daddy!" Mrs. Fuller cried, pointing at the tiny black car coming up the road in a swirl of dust. I noticed a long wooden pole sticking out through one of the car windows.

The children ran to meet the car. "Jack's inside the house and he's been bitten by the snake!" they wailed. "We know he's been bitten! He doesn't come when we call him!"

Mr. Fuller and the snake-man got out of the car. The snake-man was small and very old, probably over seventy. He wore leather boots made of thick cowhide, and he had long gauntlet[6]-type gloves on his hands made of the same stuff. The gloves reached above his elbows. In his right hand he carried an extraordinary implement,[7] an eight-foot-long wooden pole with a forked end. The two prongs of the fork were made, so it seemed, of black rubber, about an inch thick and quite

---

6. gauntlet (gônt′lit), *n.* a sturdy, heavy glove, with a flaring cuff that covers part of the arm.
7. implement (im′plə mənt), *n.* tool or piece of equipment.

The Green Mamba   579

flexible, and it was clear that if the fork was pressed against the ground the two prongs would bend outwards, allowing the neck of the fork to go down as close to the ground as necessary. In his left hand he carried an ordinary brown sack.

Donald Macfarlane, the snake-man, may have been old and small but he was an impressive-looking character. His eyes were pale blue, deep-set in a face round and dark and wrinkled as a walnut. Above the blue eyes, the eyebrows were thick and startlingly white, but the hair on his head was almost black. In spite of the thick leather boots, he moved like a leopard, with soft slow catlike strides, and he came straight up to me and said, "Who are you?"

"He's with the oil company," Fuller said. "He hasn't been here long."

"You want to watch?" the snake-man said to me.

"Watch?" I said, wavering. "Watch? How do you mean watch? I mean where from? Not in the house?"

"You can stand out on the veranda and look through the window," the snake-man said.

"Come on," Fuller said. "We'll both watch."

"Now don't do anything silly," Mrs. Fuller said.

The two children stood there forlorn and miserable, with tears all over their cheeks.

The snake-man and Fuller and I walked over the grass towards the house, and as we approached the veranda steps the snake-man whispered, "Tread softly on the wooden boards or he'll pick up the vibration. Wait until I've gone in, then walk up quietly and stand by the window."

The snake-man went up the steps first and he made absolutely no sound at all with his feet. He moved soft and catlike onto the veranda and straight through the front door, and then he quickly but very quietly closed the door behind him.

I felt better with the door closed. What I mean is I felt better for myself. I certainly didn't feel better for the snake-man. I figured he was committing suicide. I followed Fuller onto the veranda and we both crept over to the window. The window was open, but it had a fine mesh mosquito netting all over it. That made me feel better still. We peered through the netting.

The living room was simple and ordinary, coconut matting[8] on the floor, a red sofa, a coffee table, and a couple of armchairs. The dog was sprawled on the matting under the coffee table, a large Airedale with curly brown and black hair. He was stone dead.

The snake-man was standing absolutely still just inside the door of the living room. The brown sack was now slung over his left shoulder, and he was grasping the long pole with both hands, holding it out in front of him, parallel to the ground. I couldn't see the snake. I didn't think the snake-man had seen it yet either.

A minute went by . . . two minutes . . . three . . . four . . . five. Nobody moved. There was death in that room. The air was heavy with death and the snake-man stood as motionless as a pillar of stone, with the long rod held out in front of him.

And still he waited. Another minute . . . and another . . . and another.

And now I saw the snake-man beginning to bend his knees. Very slowly he bent his knees until he was almost squatting on the floor, and from that position he tried to peer under the sofa and the armchairs.

And still it didn't look as though he was seeing anything.

Slowly he straightened his legs again, and then his head began to swivel around the room. Over to the right, in the far corner, a staircase led up to the floor above. The snake-man looked at the stairs, and I knew very well what

---

8. **coconut matting,** floor covering made from fiber of the coconut palm.

was going through his head. Quite abruptly, he took one step forward and stopped.

Nothing happened.

A moment later I caught sight of the snake. It was lying full-length along the skirting of the right-hand wall, but hidden from the snake-man's view by the back of the sofa. It lay there like a long, beautiful, deadly shaft[9] of green glass, quite motionless, perhaps asleep. It was facing away from us who were at the window, with its small triangular head resting on the matting near the foot of the stairs.

I nudged Fuller and whispered, "It's over there against the wall." I pointed and Fuller saw the snake. At once, he started waving both hands, palms outward, back and forth across the window, hoping to get the snake-man's attention. The snake-man didn't see him. Very softly, Fuller said, "Pssst!" and the snake-man looked up sharply. Fuller pointed. The snake-man understood and gave a nod.

Now the snake-man began working his way very, very slowly to the back wall of the room so as to get a view of the snake behind the sofa. He never walked on his toes as you or I would have done. His feet remained flat on the ground all the time. The cowhide boots were like moccasins, with neither soles nor heels. Gradually, he worked his way over to the back wall, and from there he was able to see at least the head and two or three feet of the snake itself.

But the snake also saw him. With a movement so fast it was invisible, the snake's head came up about two feet off the floor, and the front of the body arched backwards, ready to strike. Almost simultaneously, it bunched its whole body into a series of curves, ready to flash forward.

The snake-man was just a bit too far away from the snake to reach it with the end of his pole. He waited, staring at the snake, and the snake stared back at him with two small malevolent[10] black eyes.

The Fante warriors of Ghana also make flags that identify them with strong or powerful animals, in this case a large, fierce dog. Large dogs, however, are not always immune to danger. What fate does the dog Jack in the story suffer?

Then the snake-man started speaking to the snake. "Come along, my pretty," he whispered in a soft wheedling[11] voice. "There's a good boy. Nobody's going to hurt you. Nobody's going to harm you, my pretty little thing. Just lie still and relax . . ." He took a step forward towards the snake, holding the pole out in front of him.

What the snake did next was so fast that the whole movement couldn't have taken more than a hundredth of a second, like the flick of a camera shutter. There was a green flash as the snake darted forward at least ten feet and struck at the snake-man's leg.

---

9. **shaft** (shaft), *n*. long, narrow part of a spear or an arrow.
10. **malevolent** (mə lev′ə lənt), *adj*. showing ill will; spiteful.
11. **wheedling** (hwē′dling), *adj*. soft and persuasive; coaxing.

The Green Mamba **581**

Nobody could have got out of the way of that one. I heard the snake's head strike against the thick cowhide boot with a sharp little *crack*, and then at once the head was back in that same deadly backward-curving position, ready to strike again.

"There's a good boy," the snake-man said softly. "There's a clever boy. There's a lovely fellow. You mustn't get excited. Keep calm and everything's going to be all right." As he was speaking, he was slowly lowering the end of the pole until the forked prongs were about twelve inches above the middle of the snake's body. "There's a lovely fellow," he whispered. "There's a good kind little chap. Keep still now, my beauty. Keep still, my pretty. Keep quite still. Daddy's not going to hurt you."

I could see a thin dark trickle of venom[12] running down the snake-man's right boot where the snake had struck.

The snake, head raised and arcing backwards, was as tense as a tight-wound spring and ready to strike again. "Keep still, my lovely," the snake-man whispered. "Don't move now. Keep still. No one's going to hurt you."

Then *wham*, the rubber prongs came down right across the snake's body, about midway along its length, and pinned it to the floor. All I could see was a green blur as the snake thrashed around furiously in an effort to free itself. But the snake-man kept up the pressure on the prongs and the snake was trapped.

What happens next? I wondered. There was no way he could catch hold of that madly twisting flailing[13] length of green muscle with his hands, and even if he could have done so, the head would surely have flashed around and bitten him in the face.

Holding the very end of the eight-foot pole, the snake-man began to work his way round the room until he was at the tail end of the snake. Then, in spite of the flailing and the thrashing, he started pushing the prongs forward along the snake's body towards the head. Very very slowly he did it, pushing the rubber prongs forward over the snake's flailing body, keeping the snake pinned down all the time and pushing, pushing, pushing the long wooden rod forward millimeter by millimeter. It was a fascinating and frightening thing to watch, the little man with white eyebrows and black hair carefully manipulating[14] his long implement and sliding the fork ever so slowly along the length of the twisting snake towards the head. The snake's body was thumping against the coconut matting with such a noise that if you had been upstairs you might have thought two big men were wrestling on the floor.

Then at last the prongs were right behind the head itself, pinning it down, and at that point the snake-man reached forward with one gloved hand and grasped the snake very firmly by the neck. He threw away the pole. He took the sack off his shoulder with his free hand. He lifted the great, still twisting length of the deadly green snake and pushed the head into the sack. Then he let go the head and bundled the rest of the creature in and closed the sack. The sack started jumping about as though there were fifty angry rats inside it, but the snake-man was now totally relaxed, and he held the sack casually in one hand as if it contained no more than a few pounds of potatoes. He stooped and picked up his pole from the floor, then he turned and looked towards the window where we were peering in.

"Pity about the dog," he said. "You'd better get it out of the way before the children see it."

---

12. **venom** (ven′əm), *n.* the poison produced by some snakes, spiders, scorpions, lizards, and so on.
13. **flailing** (flā′ling), *adj.* beating; thrashing.
14. **manipulate** (mə nip′yə lāt), *v.* to handle skillfully.

A Minor Bird

Robert Frost

I have wished a bird would fly away,
And not sing by my house all day;

Have clapped my hands at him from the door
When it seemed as if I could bear no more.

5 The fault must partly have been in me,
The bird was not to blame for his key.

And of course there must be something wrong
In wanting to silence any song.

In his *Queen Anne's Lace and American Goldfinch,* painted in 1982, artist Robert Bateman celebrates the natural world that the narrator in the poem wants to shut out. What might account for such differences in **perspective?**

After Reading

Making Connections

1. On the like/dislike scale you made in your notebook before reading, put an *M* for Macfarlane and an *S* for the speaker in the poem to show where they each stand in relation to nature. Explain your placements.

2. The snake-man and the speaker in the poem show different relationships with nature. Which one is more like yours?

3. If you could meet the snake-man, what would you like to ask him?

4. How do the autobiography and the poem relate to the theme "You're Invading My Space!"?

5. Mrs. Fuller's **dialogue,** or the words she speaks, tells us Macfarlane "*likes* snakes." How else does the author reveal Macfarlane's feelings about snakes?

6. How does the author use timing to heighten the suspense as Macfarlane stalks the snake?

7. What is a high-risk profession you have observed? In what ways is it similar to Macfarlane's snake catching?

Literary Focus: Imagery

Now that you have read "The Green Mamba," can you imagine what it would be like to meet this snake on the loose? If so, you are reacting to the use of **imagery**—details that activate your senses so you *see, hear,* and *feel* what you read. Vivid mental images can turn what you read into virtual reality, the kind of you-are-there experience that certain computer headsets try to give us. The difference is, *your mind* supplies the images.

Look at chart below. It classifies three images from the story under *Sight, Sound,* and *Feeling*. Make a similar chart. Add other images you find in the story and poem to the chart.

	Sight	Sound	Feeling
"The Green Mamba"	a green blur	thumping against coconut matting	air heavy with death
"A Minor Bird"			

Vocabulary Study

Choose the most appropriate word from the list to complete each sentence.

veranda
dumbfounded
gauntlet
implement
shaft
malevolent
wheedling
venom
flailing
manipulate

1. Mambas, which are found only in Africa, attack when they sense danger not because they have a ____ nature.

2. The black mamba has the most deadly ____ of any snake in Africa.

3. You won't see an animal in a twisting, ____ struggle to escape after a mamba bite, as it quickly paralyzes its prey.

4. A black mamba lying straight in the grass could be mistaken for the ____ of a spear.

5. Meeting a mamba in the wild may leave you ____ , but you won't be any more startled than the mamba.

6. Despite the legendary speed of mambas, it's safer to run away than to use an ____ to move one out of your path.

7. Mambas would rather avoid humankind than listen to ____ words no matter how flattering.

8. A green mamba prefers to spend its time in a tree, not in your house or on your ____.

9. Skillful "milkers" purposely ____ poisonous snakes into striking in order to harvest poison for snakebite medicine.

10. If you decide to milk snakes for a living, protect your hands and arms with ____ gloves.

Expressing Your Ideas

Writing Choices

Snake Strikes Out! That's one possible headline for a magazine or newspaper feature on the snake-man. Write a **human-interest story** about his work. Make up a striking headline readers can't ignore.

Keeping Your Cool Macfarlane's success with the green mamba had a lot to do with his staying calm. Write a **descriptive essay** about an encounter that required you to stay calm. Use vivid imagery to bring the event to life for readers.

Other Options

Bag Unruly Reptiles Let people know how they can give uninvited snakes the sack. Produce a **TV commercial** to advertise the snake-man's services.

Form a Tableau That means don't move . . . for fun, not out of fear. In a group, position your bodies to form a **tableau** that depicts a scene from the story or poem. See if your audience can identify the scene and each person's part in it.

Before Reading

Abuela Invents the Zero

by Judith Ortiz Cofer

Judith Ortiz Cofer
born 1952

Cofer grew up in two worlds—Paterson, New Jersey, and the Island, meaning Puerto Rico, where she was born. She felt at home in the cool, quiet apartment home where she lived with her parents in the United States. Yet she also looked forward to returning to the warmth of her tropical home and her large family of cousins, aunts, uncles, and grandparents in Puerto Rico. Her grandmother in Puerto Rico was a powerful presence in Cofer's life. She recalls afternoons spent at her grandmother's house, where the women of the family gathered for coffee. They would share the day's news and tell stories full of history, information, and lessons for the young girls to hear. As an author, now living in Georgia, Cofer continues her family tradition of being a storyteller and historian.

Building Background

Long Distance Between Close Neighbors As a result of the American victory in the Spanish-American War, the United States gained control over Puerto Rico in 1898. Puerto Ricans became self-governing U.S. citizens in 1917. People can come and go freely between the island and the States, but Puerto Ricans cannot vote in U.S. elections and some issues of citizenship are still unresolved.

Puerto Ricans are Spanish-speaking people of mixed European, American Indian, and African ancestry and tradition. Some come to the United States mainland hoping for better opportunities. Too often these U.S. citizens run into prejudice, as if they were invaders rather than fellow Americans. Some go back to Puerto Rico. Those who stay and adopt the mainland culture can seem like aliens to the friends and family they leave behind in Puerto Rico. This story shows what can happen when the two cultures clash in one family.

Getting into the Story

Writer's Notebook Sometimes being different is "cool" and sometimes it's just plain puzzling. Have you ever been embarrassed in public by someone who attracted attention because he or she looked unusual or behaved differently? In your notebook, write about what happened.

Reading Tip

Easing into Spanish The author of "Abuela Invents the Zero" is bilingual, meaning that she moves easily between her two languages, Spanish and English. As a writer, she weaves in Spanish expressions and explains their special meanings so skillfully that readers who don't know Spanish understand every word.

In the first sentence, for example, you will learn the meanings of three Spanish words: *un, cero,* and *nada.* If you don't know the meaning of *Abuela* in the title, don't worry. The English translation appears in sentence three.

Abuela Invents the Zero

JUDITH ORTIZ COFER

"You made me feel like a zero, like a nothing," she says in Spanish, *un cero, nada.* She is trembling, an angry little old woman lost in a heavy winter coat that belongs to my mother. And I end up being sent to my room, like I was a child, to think about my grandmother's idea of math.

It all began with Abuela coming up from the Island for a visit—her first time in the United States. My mother and father paid her way here so that she wouldn't die without seeing snow, though if you asked me, and nobody has, the dirty slush in this city is not worth the price of a ticket. But I guess she deserves some kind of award for having had ten kids and survived to tell about it. My mother is the youngest of the bunch. Right up to the time when we're supposed to pick up the old lady at the airport, my mother is telling me stories about how hard times were for la familia on la isla,[1] and how *la abuela* worked night and day to support them after their father died of a heart attack. I'd die of a heart attack too if I had a troop like that to support. Anyway, I had seen her only three or four times in my entire life, whenever we would go for somebody's funeral. I was born here and I have lived in this building all my life. But when Mami says, "Connie, please be nice to Abuela. She doesn't have too many years left. Do you promise me, Constancia?"— when she uses my full name, I know she means business. So I say, "Sure." Why wouldn't I be nice? I'm not a monster, after all.

So we go to Kennedy to get la abuela and she is the last to come out of the airplane, on the arm of the cabin attendant, all wrapped

---

1. **la familia on la isla,** the family on the Island, or Puerto Rico.

up in a black shawl. He hands her over to my parents like she was a package sent airmail. It is January, two feet of snow on the ground, and she's wearing a shawl over a thin black dress. That's just the start.

Once home, she refuses to let my mother buy her a coat because it's a waste of money for the two weeks she'll be in *el Polo Norte*, as she calls New Jersey, the North Pole. So since she's only four feet eleven inches tall, she walks around in my mother's big black coat looking ridiculous. I try to walk far behind them in public so that no one will think we're together. I plan to stay very busy the whole time she's with us so that I won't be asked to take her anywhere, but my plan is ruined when my mother comes down with the flu and Abuela absolutely *has* to attend Sunday mass[2] or her soul will be eternally[3] damned. She's more Catholic than the Pope. My father decides that he should stay home with my mother and that I should escort[4] la abuela to church. He tells me this on Saturday night as I'm getting ready to go out to the mall with my friends.

"No way," I say.

I go for the car keys on the kitchen table: he usually leaves them there for me on Friday and Saturday nights. He beats me to them.

"No way," he says, pocketing them and grinning at me.

Needless to say, we come to a compromise[5] very quickly. I do have a responsibility to Sandra and Anita, who don't drive yet. There is a Harley-Davidson fashion show[6] at Brookline Square that we *cannot* miss.

"The mass in Spanish is at ten sharp tomorrow morning, entiendes?" My father is dangling the car keys in front of my nose and pulling them back when I try to reach for them. He's really enjoying himself.

"I understand. Ten o'clock. I'm out of here." I pry his fingers off the key ring. He knows that I'm late, so he makes it just a little

difficult. Then he laughs. I run out of our apartment before he changes his mind. I have no idea what I'm getting myself into.

Sunday morning I have to walk two blocks on dirty snow to retrieve[7] the car. I warm it up for Abuela as instructed by my parents, and drive it to the front of our building. My father walks her by the hand in baby steps on the slippery snow. The sight of her little head with a bun on top of it sticking out of that huge coat makes me want to run back into my room and get under the covers. I just hope that nobody I know sees us together. I'm dreaming, of course. The mass is packed with people from our block. It's a holy day of obligation[8] and everyone I ever met is there.

I have to help her climb the steps, and she stops to take a deep breath after each one, then I lead her down the aisle so that everybody can see me with my bizarre[9] grandmother. If I were a good Catholic, I'm sure I'd get some purgatory time taken off for my sacrifice. She is walking as slow as Captain Cousteau[10] exploring the bottom of the sea, looking around, taking her sweet time. Finally she chooses a pew, but she wants to sit in the *other* end. It's like she had a spot picked out for some unknown reason, and although it's the most inconvenient seat in the house,

---

2. **mass,** the main Roman Catholic Church worship service.
3. eternally (i tėr′nl ē), *adv.* always and forever.
4. escort (ə skôrt′), *v.* go with someone as a show of courtesy or honor.
5. compromise (kom′prə mīz), *n.* settlement of a dispute by agreement that each side will give up something.
6. **Harley-Davidson fashion show,** show featuring the kind of clothing often worn by riders of Harley-Davidson and other motorcycles.
7. retrieve (ri trēv′), *v.* find and bring back.
8. **holy day of obligation,** one of various holy days that Catholics honor by going to mass.
9. bizarre (bə zär′), *adj.* strikingly odd looking.
10. **Captain Cousteau** (kü stō′), Jacques-Yves (zhäk′ēv′) Cousteau, a French sea captain and author, famous as an undersea explorer.

▲ In *Aquarium,* painted in 1993, the artist Carol Hoy appears to be depicting feelings and tensions like those experienced by Connie in the story. What mood does the position of the figure communicate? What meaning might the aquarium have?

that's where she has to sit. So we squeeze by all the people already sitting there, saying, "Excuse me, please, *con permiso*, pardon me," getting annoyed looks the whole way. By the time we settle in, I'm drenched in sweat. I keep my head down like I'm praying so as not to see or be seen. She is praying loud, in Spanish, and singing hymns at the top of her creaky voice.

I ignore her when she gets up with a hundred other people to go take communion.[11] I'm actually praying hard now—that this will all be over soon. But the next time I look up, I see a black coat dragging around and around the church, stopping here and there so a little gray head can peek out like a periscope on a submarine. There are giggles in the church, and even the priest has frozen in the middle of a blessing, his hands above his head like he is about to lead the congregation[12] in a set of jumping jacks.

I realize to my horror that my grandmother is lost. She can't find her way back to the pew. I am so embarrassed that even though the woman next to me is shooting daggers at me with her eyes, I just can't move to go get her. I put my hands over my face like I'm praying, but it's really to hide my burning cheeks. I would like for her to disappear. I just know that on Monday my friends, and my enemies, in the barrio[13] will have a lot of senile-grandmother jokes to tell in front of me. I am frozen to my seat. So the same woman who wants me dead on the spot does it for me. She makes a big deal out of getting up and hurrying to get Abuela.

The rest of the mass is a blur. All I know is that my grandmother kneels the whole time with her hands over *her* face. She doesn't speak to me on the way home, and she doesn't let me help her walk, even though she almost falls a couple of times.

When we get to the apartment, my parents are at the kitchen table, where my mother is trying to eat some soup. They can see right away that something is wrong. Then Abuela points her finger at me like a judge passing a sentence on a criminal. She says in Spanish, "You made me feel like a zero, like a nothing." Then she goes to her room.

I try to explain what happened. "I don't understand why she's so upset. She just got lost and wandered around for a while," I tell them. But it sounds lame, even to my own ears. My mother gives me a look that makes me cringe and goes in to Abuela's room to get her version of the story. She comes out with tears in her eyes.

"Your grandmother says to tell you that of all the hurtful things you can do to a person, the worst is to make them feel as if they are worth nothing."

I can feel myself shrinking right there in front of her. But I can't bring myself to tell my mother that I think I understand how I made Abuela feel. I might be sent into the old lady's room to apologize, and it's not easy to admit you've been a jerk—at least, not right away with everybody watching. So I just sit there not saying anything.

My mother looks at me for a long time, like she feels sorry for me. Then she says, "You should know, Constancia, that if it wasn't for this old woman whose existence[14] you don't seem to value, you and I would not be here."

That's when *I'm* sent to *my* room to consider a number I hadn't thought much about—until today.

---

11. **communion** (kə myü′nyən), the sharing of bread and wine in memory of the death of Jesus Christ.
12. **congregation** (kong′grə gā′shən), *n.* people gathered for a religious service.
13. **barrio** (bär′ē ō), *n.* a neighborhood, often urban, where mainly Spanish-speaking people live.
14. **existence** (eg zis′təns), *n.* being; life.

After Reading

Making Connections

1. Rate the way Connie treated her grandmother on a scale of zero (terribly) to ten (wonderfully). Explain your rating.

2. How does the embarrassing situation you wrote about before reading compare with Connie's experience in church with Abuela? How would you rate your actions on the zero-to-ten scale?

3. Reflect on the scene in church where Connie is embarrassed. How do you think she would handle the situation in the future?

4. Both Abuela and Connie felt like zeroes. What did each one need to feel she mattered?

5. What came to your mind when you first read the story **title?** What did the title mean to you after reading the story?

6. Do you feel that the **conflict** between Connie and Abuela was resolved in this story? Why or why not?

7. ☺ Has this story given you any new **perspective** or insight into how to treat elders? What lesson can you learn from the story?

Literary Focus: Idioms

Connie's reply to her father's request that she take Abuela to church is "No way." Which of these interpretations explains what she means?

(a) The roads to the church are blocked.

(b) The car won't start.

(c) Not me!

    C is the only answer that would occur to someone who understands current American English **idioms**—expressions with meanings that cannot be understood from the ordinary meanings of the words in it. Every language has idioms that make no sense to non-native speakers. To make matters more confusing, every generation invents new ones, like the idioms in this story.

    Make a chart like the one below and find and list other idioms in the story. Write what you think each one means.

Idioms in the Story	Meanings of the Idioms
No way	Not me . . . I won't do it.

Abuela Invents the Zero   **591**

Vocabulary Study

On a sheet of paper, write the letter of the word pair that best shows a relationship similar to that expressed in the original pair.

eternally
escort
compromise
retrieve
bizarre
congregation
barrio
existence

1. BARRIO : DISTRICT :: **a.** city : nation **b.** fire : smoke
   c. rain : drought **d.** community : neighborhood

2. BIZARRE : ORDINARY :: **a.** weird : odd **b.** strange : common
   c. unique : different **d.** typical : usual

3. COMPROMISE : AGREEMENT :: **a.** love : hate **b.** despair : hope
   c. argument : conflict **d.** button : shirt

4. CONGREGATION : CHURCH :: **a.** audience : theater
   b. mob : individual **c.** flock : herd **d.** school : hospital

5. ESCORT : ACCOMPANY :: **a.** play : work **b.** assist : help
   c. lead : follow **d.** obey : defy

6. BIZARRE : UNUSUAL :: **a.** disappointed : glad
   b. strange : common **c.** unique : different **d.** wet : dry

7. EXISTENCE : BEING :: **a.** living : dying **b.** water : dripping
   c. birth : death **d.** death : dying

8. RETRIEVE : STICK :: **a.** swim : pool **b.** fetch : ball
   c. skate : wheels **d.** talk : telephone

9. CONGREGATION : WORSHIP :: **a.** audience : applaud
   b. assembly : auditorium **c.** gang : crowd **d.** person : group

10. ETERNALLY : FOREVER :: **a.** immediately : later **b.** then : now
    c. always : ever **d.** soon : never

Expressing Your Ideas _____

Writing Choices

Turnaround Is Fair Play Imagine what might happen if Connie visited Abuela. Write a **one-act play** in which the tables are turned, and Connie is the odd one out.

Dear Abuela . . . What do you think Connie wanted to say to Abuela when she realized how she made her grandmother feel? Write a **letter** to Abuela as if you were Connie after realizing you had been "a jerk."

Other Options

Say What? Suppose someone took every idiom you used literally—such as "Chill out," "Let's kick it," or "Snap out of it." With a partner, make up a **comedy routine** in which idioms cause communication mix-ups.

These Kids Today! How do older people see you? With a partner, **interview** several older people to find how they feel about your generation. Take notes or use a tape recorder. Present your findings to the class.

Before Reading

Rikki-tikki-tavi

by Rudyard Kipling

Rudyard Kipling
1865–1936

Rudyard Kipling was an Englishman who was born in Bombay, India. He spent a not-so-happy boyhood back in England, but he kept his sense of humor, which showed up early in poems he wrote. At sixteen, he put together his own book of witty verse and gave copies to his friends. The next year he went to work in a bustling newspaper office in India where he learned to write at a furious pace, earning him the title "Phrase-Maker." Whenever he had a free moment, he worked on his colorful stories and poems about life in India. Kipling lived at the center of conflict, being an Englishman in India during its growing rebellion against British rule. His defense of England's control drew harsh criticism, but his storytelling genius made Kipling the first British citizen to win a Nobel prize in literature.

Building Background

A Living Legend A traditional theme in legends of India is about a mongoose who saves a sleeping child from a deadly cobra while the parents are away. The parents return to find the mongoose covered with the snake's blood. Assuming it has killed their child, they kill the mongoose and then discover their tragic mistake. Weeping in shame, they call the mongoose their *other son* or *brother*. A real-life mongoose would settle for being called *friend*. It's an animal who loves company and likes to play.

Getting into the Story

Discussion Nature equips wildlife for survival, but sometimes an animal needs help. Have you, or has someone you know, ever tried to rescue a wild animal in trouble? If so, what was the problem and how was it discovered? What rescue attempt was made? What was the outcome? In a small group, share your experiences with giving nature a hand.

Reading Tip

Pronunciation The animal characters in "Rikki-tikki-tavi" live in India and have Indian names. This chart tells you who's who and how to pronounce their names when you meet them in the story.

Name	Pronunciation	Description
Rikki-tikki-tavi	(rik′ē tik′ē tav′ē)	a daring mongoose
Darzee	(där zē′)	a chatty tailorbird
Chuchundra	(chü chun′drə)	a timid muskrat
Nag	(näg)	a big black cobra
Nagaina	(nä gān′ə)	Nag's wicked wife
Karait	(kä rit′)	a sly little snake
Chua	(chü′ə)	a knowing rat

RIKKI-TIKKI-TAVI

Rudyard Kipling

This is the story of the great war that Rikki-tikki-tavi fought single-handed, through the bathrooms of the big bungalow[1] in Segowlee cantonment.[2] Darzee the Tailorbird helped him, and Chuchundra the Muskrat, who never comes out into the middle of the floor, but always creeps round by the wall, gave him advice, but Rikki-tikki did the real fighting.

He was a mongoose, rather like a little cat in his fur and his tail, but quite like a weasel in his head and his habits. His eyes and the end of his restless nose were pink. He could scratch himself anywhere he pleased with any leg, front or back, that he chose to use. He could fluff up his tail till it looked like a bottle brush, and his war cry as he scuttled through the long grass was: *Rikk-tikk-tikki-tikki-tchk!*

One day, a high summer flood washed him out of the burrow where he lived with his father and mother, and carried him, kicking and clucking, down a roadside ditch. He found a little wisp of grass floating there, and clung to it till he lost his senses. When he revived,[3] he was lying in the hot sun on the middle of a garden path, very draggled indeed, and a small boy was saying, "Here's a dead mongoose. Let's have a funeral."

"No," said his mother, "let's take him in and dry him. Perhaps he isn't really dead."

They took him into the house, and a big man picked him up between his finger and thumb and said he was not dead but half choked. So they wrapped him in cotton wool, and warmed him over a little fire, and he opened his eyes and sneezed.

"Now," said the big man (he was an Englishman who had just moved into the bungalow), "don't frighten him, and we'll see what he'll do."

It is the hardest thing in the world to frighten a mongoose, because he is eaten up from nose to tail with curiosity. The motto of

---

1. **bungalow** (bung′gə lō), *n.* a one-story house with low, sweeping lines.
2. **Segowlee cantonment** (sə gou′lē kan ton′mənt), area in Segowlee, India, where British soldiers were stationed.
3. **revive** (ri vīv′), *v.* come back to life or consciousness.

all the mongoose family is "Run and find out," and Rikki-tikki was a true mongoose. He looked at the cotton wool, decided that it was not good to eat, ran all around the table, sat up and put his fur in order, scratched himself, and jumped on the small boy's shoulder.

"Don't be frightened, Teddy," said his father. "That's his way of making friends."

"Ouch! He's tickling under my chin," said Teddy.

Rikki-tikki looked down between the boy's collar and neck, snuffed at his ear, and climbed down to the floor, where he sat rubbing his nose.

"Good gracious," said Teddy's mother, "and that's a wild creature! I suppose he's so tame because we've been kind to him."

"All mongooses are like that," said her husband. "If Teddy doesn't pick him up by the tail, or try to put him in a cage, he'll run in and out of the house all day long. Let's give him something to eat."

CLARIFY: Why is Rikki-tikki unafraid of humans?

They gave him a little piece of raw meat. Rikki-tikki liked it immensely, and when it was finished he went out into the veranda and sat in the sunshine and fluffed up his fur to make it dry to the roots. Then he felt better.

"There are more things to find out about in this house," he said to himself, "than all my family could find out in all their lives. I shall certainly stay and find out."

He spent all that day roaming over the house. He nearly drowned himself in the bathtubs, put his nose into the ink on a writing table, and burned it on the end of the big man's cigar, for he climbed up in the big man's lap to see how writing was done. At nightfall he ran into Teddy's nursery to watch how kerosene lamps were lighted, and when Teddy went to bed Rikki-tikki climbed up too.

But he was a restless companion, because he had to get up and attend to every noise all through the night, and find out what made it. Teddy's mother and father came in, the last thing, to look at their boy, and Rikki-tikki was awake on the pillow.

"I don't like that," said Teddy's mother. "He may bite the child."

"He'll do no such thing," said the father. "Teddy is safer with that little beast than if he had a bloodhound to watch him. If a snake came into the nursery now—"

But Teddy's mother wouldn't think of anything so awful.

Early in the morning Rikki-tikki came to early breakfast in the veranda riding on Teddy's shoulder, and they gave him banana and some boiled egg. He sat on all their laps one after the other, because every well-brought-up mongoose always hopes to be a house mongoose some day and have rooms to run about in; and Rikki-tikki's mother (she used to live in the general's house at Segowlee) had carefully told Rikki what to do if ever he came across white men.

Then Rikki-tikki went out into the garden to see what was to be seen. It was a large garden, only half cultivated,[4] with bushes, as big as summerhouses, of Marshal Niel roses, lime and orange trees, clumps of bamboos, and thickets of high grass. Rikki-tikki licked his lips. "This is a splendid hunting ground," he said, and his tail grew bottle-brushy at the thought of it, and he scuttled up and down the garden, snuffing here and there till he heard very sorrowful voices in a thornbush. It was Darzee the Tailorbird and his wife. They had made a beautiful nest by pulling two big leaves together and stitching them up the edges with fibers, and had filled the hollow

---

4. **cultivate** (kul′tə vāt), *adj.* tame or develop.

◄ This young boy was drawn by Charles Gibson around the turn of the century. What qualities do you think he might share with Teddy?

with cotton and downy fluff. The nest swayed to and fro, as they sat on the rim and cried.

"What is the matter?" asked Rikki-tikki.

"We are very miserable," said Darzee. "One of our babies fell out of the nest yesterday and Nag ate him."

"H'm," said Rikki-tikki, "that is very sad—but I am a stranger here. Who is Nag?"

Darzee and his wife only cowered[5] down in the nest without answering, for from the thick grass at the foot of the bush there came a low hiss—a horrid cold sound that made Rikki-tikki jump back two clear feet. Then inch by inch out of the grass rose up the head and spread hood of Nag, the big black cobra, and he was five feet long from tongue to tail. When he had lifted one-third of himself clear of the ground, he stayed balancing to and fro exactly as a dandelion tuft balances in the wind, and he looked at Rikki-tikki with the wicked snake's eyes that never change their expression, whatever the snake may be thinking of.

"Who is Nag?" said he. "*I* am Nag. The great God Brahm[6] put his mark upon all our people, when the first cobra spread his hood to keep the sun off Brahm as he slept. Look, and be afraid!"

He spread out his hood more than ever, and Rikki-tikki saw the spectacle mark on the back of it that looks exactly like the eye part of a hook-and-eye fastening. He was afraid for the minute, but it is impossible for a mongoose to stay frightened for any length of time, and though Rikki-tikki had never met a live cobra before, his mother had fed him on dead ones, and he knew that all a grown mongoose's business in life was to fight and eat snakes. Nag knew that too and, at the bottom of his cold heart, he was afraid.

"Well," said Rikki-tikki, and his tail began to fluff up again, "marks or no marks, do you think it is right for you to eat fledglings out of a nest?"

Nag was thinking to himself, and watching the least little movement in the grass behind Rikki-tikki. He knew that mongooses in the garden meant death sooner or later for him and his family, but he wanted to get Rikki-tikki

---

5. **cower** (kou′ər), *v.* crouch or draw back in fear.
6. **the great God Brahm,** also spelled Brahma, the Hindu god of creation.

off his guard. So he dropped his head a little, and put it on one side.

"Let us talk," he said. "You eat eggs. Why should not I eat birds?"

"Behind you! Look behind you!" sang Darzee.

"Be careful. I am Death!" It was Karait, the dusty brown snakeling. . . .

Rikki-tikki knew better than to waste time in staring. He jumped up in the air as high as he could go, and just under him whizzed by the head of Nagaina, Nag's wicked wife. She had crept up behind him as he was talking, to make an end of him. He heard her savage hiss as the stroke missed. He came down almost across her back, and if he had been an old mongoose he would have known that then was the time to break her back with one bite; but he was afraid of the terrible lashing return stroke of the cobra. He bit, indeed, but did not bite long enough, and he jumped clear of the whisking tail, leaving Nagaina torn and angry.

"Wicked, wicked Darzee!" said Nag, lashing up as high as he could reach toward the nest in the thornbush. But Darzee had built it out of reach of snakes, and it only swayed to and fro.

CLARIFY: What has caused conflict between Rikki-tikki and Nag and Nagaina?

Rikki-tikki felt his eyes growing red and hot (when a mongoose's eyes grow red, he is angry), and he sat back on his tail and hind legs like a little kangaroo, and looked all round him, and chattered with rage. But Nag and Nagaina had disappeared into the grass. When a snake misses its stroke, it never says anything or gives any sign of what it means to do next. Rikki-tikki did not care to follow them, for he did not feel sure that he could manage two snakes at once. So he trotted off to the gravel path near the house, and sat down to think. It was a serious matter for him.

If you read the old books of natural history, you will find they say that when the mongoose fights the snake and happens to get bitten, he runs off and eats some herb that cures him. That is not true. The victory is only a matter of quickness of eye and quickness of foot—snake's blow against mongoose's jump—and as no eye can follow the motion of a snake's head when it strikes, this makes things much more wonderful than any magic herb. Rikki-tikki knew he was a young mongoose, and it made him all the more pleased to think that he had managed to escape a blow from behind.

It gave him confidence in himself, and when Teddy came running down the path, Rikki-tikki was ready to be petted. But just as Teddy was stooping, something wriggled a little in the dust, and a tiny voice said: "Be careful. I am Death!" It was Karait, the dusty brown snakeling that lies for choice on the dusty earth; and his bite is as dangerous as the cobra's. But he is so small that nobody thinks of him, and so he does the more harm to people.

Rikki-tikki's eyes grew red again, and he danced up to Karait with the peculiar rocking, swaying motion that he had inherited from his family. It looks very funny, but it is so perfectly balanced a gait that you can fly off from it at any angle you please, and in dealing with snakes this is an advantage.

If Rikki-tikki had only known, he was doing a much more dangerous thing than fighting Nag, for Karait is so small, and can turn so quickly, that unless Rikki bit him close to the back of the head, he would get the return stroke in his eye or his lip. But Rikki did not know. His eyes were all red, and he rocked back and forth, looking for a good place to hold. Karait struck out. Rikki jumped sideways and tried to run in, but the wicked little dusty gray head lashed within a fraction of his shoulder, and he had to jump over the body, and the head followed his heels close.

Teddy shouted to the house: "Oh, look here! Our mongoose is killing a snake." And Rikki-tikki heard a scream from Teddy's mother. His father ran out with a stick, but by the time he came up, Karait had lunged out once too far, and Rikki-tikki had sprung, jumped on the snake's back, dropped his head far back between his forelegs, bitten as high up the back as he could get hold, and rolled away.

That bite paralyzed Karait, and Rikki-tikki was just going to eat him up from the tail, after the custom of his family at dinner, when he remembered that a full meal makes a slow mongoose, and if he wanted all his strength and quickness ready, he must keep himself thin. He went away for a dust bath under the castor-oil bushes, while Teddy's father beat the dead Karait.

"What is the use of that?" thought Rikki-tikki. "I have settled it all."

And then Teddy's mother picked him up from the dust and hugged him, crying that he had saved Teddy from death, and Teddy's father said that he was a providence,[7] and Teddy looked on with big scared eyes. Rikki-tikki was rather amused at all the fuss, which, of course, he did not understand. Teddy's mother might just as well have petted Teddy for playing in the dust. Rikki was thoroughly enjoying himself.

That night at dinner, walking to and fro among the wineglasses on the table, he might have stuffed himself three times over with nice things. But he remembered Nag and Nagaina, and though it was very pleasant to be patted and petted by Teddy's mother, and to sit on Teddy's shoulder, his eyes would get red from time to time, and he would go off into his long war cry of *"Rikk-tikk-tikki-tikki-tchk!"*

Teddy carried him off to bed and insisted on Rikki-tikki sleeping under his chin. Rikki-tikki was too well bred to bite or scratch, but as soon as Teddy was asleep he went off for his nightly walk round the house, and in the dark he ran up against Chuchundra the Muskrat creeping around by the wall. Chuchundra is a brokenhearted little beast. He whimpers and cheeps all the night, trying to make up his mind to run into the middle of the room. But he never gets there.

"Don't kill me," said Chuchundra, almost weeping. "Rikki-tikki, don't kill me!"

"Do you think a snake-killer kills muskrats?" said Rikki-tikki scornfully.

"Those who kill snakes get killed by snakes," said Chuchundra, more sorrowfully than ever. "And how am I to be sure that Nag won't mistake me for you some dark night?"

"There's not the least danger," said Rikki-tikki. "But Nag is in the garden, and I know you don't go there."

"My cousin Chua the Rat told me—" said Chuchundra, and then he stopped.

"Told you what?"

"H'sh! Nag is everywhere, Rikki-tikki. You should have talked to Chua in the garden."

"I didn't—so you must tell me. Quick, Chuchundra, or I'll bite you!"

Chuchundra sat down and cried till the tears rolled off his whiskers. "I am a very poor man," he sobbed. "I never had spirit enough to run out into the middle of the room. H'sh! I mustn't tell you anything. Can't you *hear,* Rikki-tikki?"

Rikki-tikki listened. The house was as still as still, but he thought he could just catch the faintest *scratch-scratch* in the world—a noise as faint as that of a wasp walking on the window-

---

7. providence (prov′ə dəns), *n.* God's care and help.

A This watercolor of the Calcutta residence of Percy Brown was painted in the early twentieth century. Look carefully at the details of the room. What do they tell you about the people who lived here?

pane—the dry scratch of a snake's scales on brickwork.

"That's Nag or Nagaina," he said to himself, "and he is crawling into the bathroom sluice. You're right, Chuchundra; I should have talked to Chua."

He stole off to Teddy's bathroom, but there was nothing there, and then to Teddy's mother's bathroom. At the bottom of the smooth plaster wall there was a brick pulled out to make a sluice[8] for the bath water, and as Rikki-tikki stole in by the masonry curb where the bath is put, he heard Nag and Nagaina whispering together outside in the moonlight.

"When the house is emptied of people," said Nagaina to her husband, "*he* will have to go away, and then the garden will be our own again. Go in quietly, and remember that the big man who killed Karait is the first one to bite. Then come out and tell me, and we will hunt for Rikki-tikki together."

"But are you sure that there is anything to be gained by killing the people?" said Nag.

"Everything. When there were no people in the bungalow, did we have any mongoose in the garden? So long as the bungalow is empty, we are king and queen of the garden;

---

8. **sluice,** a canal with a gate that controls the flow of water.

and remember that as soon as our eggs in the melon bed hatch (as they may tomorrow), our children will need room and quiet."

"I had not thought of that," said Nag. "I will go, but there is no need that we should hunt for Rikki-tikki afterwards. I will kill the big man and his wife, and the child if I can, and come away quietly. Then the bungalow will be empty, and Rikki-tikki will go."

Angry as he was, Rikki-tikki was very frightened as he saw the size of the big cobra.

Rikki-tikki tingled all over with rage and hatred at this, and then Nag's head came through the sluice, and his five feet of cold body followed it. Angry as he was, Rikki-tikki was very frightened as he saw the size of the big cobra. Nag coiled himself up, raised his head, and looked into the bathroom in the dark, and Rikki could see his eyes glitter.

"Now, if I kill him here, Nagaina will know; and if I fight him on the open floor, the odds are in his favor. What am I to do?" said Rikki-tikki-tavi.

PREDICT: What do you think Rikki-tikki will do?

Nag waved to and fro, and then Rikki-tikki heard him drinking from the biggest water jar that was used to fill the bath. "That is good," said the snake. "Now, when Karait was killed, the big man had a stick. He may have that stick still, but when he comes in to bathe in the morning he will not have a stick. I shall wait here till he comes. Nagaina—do you hear me?—I shall wait here in the cool till daytime."

There was no answer from outside, so Rikki-tikki knew Nagaina had gone away. Nag coiled himself down, coil by coil, round the bulge at the bottom of the water jar, and Rikki-tikki stayed still as death. After an hour he began to move, muscle by muscle, toward the jar. Nag was asleep, and Rikki-tikki looked at his big back, wondering which would be the best place for a good hold. "If I don't break his back at the first jump," said Rikki, "he can still fight. And if he fights—O Rikki!" He looked at the thickness of the neck below the hood, but that was too much for him; and a bite near the tail would only make Nag savage.

"It must be the head," he said at last; "the head above the hood. And, when I am once there, I must not let go."

Then he jumped. The head was lying a little clear of the water jar, under the curve of it; and, as his teeth met, Rikki braced his back against the bulge of the red earthenware to hold down his head. This gave him just one second's purchase,[9] and he made the most of it. Then he was battered to and fro as a rat is shaken by a dog—to and fro on the floor, up and down, and around in great circles, but his eyes were red and he held on as the body cart-whipped over the floor, upsetting the tin dipper and the soap dish and the flesh brush, and banged against the tin side of the bath.

As he held he closed his jaws tighter and tighter, for he made sure he would be banged to death, and, for the honor of his family, he preferred to be found with his teeth locked. He was dizzy, aching, and felt shaken to pieces when something went off like a thunderclap just behind him. A hot wind knocked him senseless and red fire singed[10] his fur. The big man had been wakened by the noise, and had fired both barrels of a shotgun into Nag just behind the hood.

---

9. **purchase** (pėr′chəs), *n.* a firm hold.
10. **singe** (sinj), *v.* burn a little.

Rikki-tikki held on with his eyes shut, for now he was quite sure he was dead. But the head did not move, and the big man picked him up and said, "It's the mongoose again, Alice. The little chap has saved *our* lives now."

Then Teddy's mother came in with a very white face, and saw what was left of Nag, and Rikki-tikki dragged himself to Teddy's bedroom and spent half the rest of the night shaking himself tenderly to find out whether he really was broken into forty pieces, as he fancied.[11]

When morning came he was very stiff, but well pleased with his doings. "Now I have Nagaina to settle with, and she will be worse than five Nags, and there's no knowing when the eggs she spoke of will hatch. Goodness! I must go and see Darzee," he said.

Without waiting for breakfast, Rikki-tikki ran to the thornbush where Darzee was singing a song of triumph at the top of his voice. The news of Nag's death was all over the garden, for the sweeper had thrown the body on the rubbish heap.

"Oh, you stupid tuft of feathers!" said Rikki-tikki angrily. "Is this the time to sing?"

"Nag is dead—is dead—is dead!" sang Darzee. "The valiant[12] Rikki-tikki caught him by the head and held fast. The big man brought the bang stick, and Nag fell in two pieces! He will never eat my babies again."

"All that's true enough. But where's Nagaina?" said Rikki-tikki, looking carefully round him.

"Nagaina came to the bathroom sluice and called for Nag," Darzee went on, "and Nag came out on the end of a stick—the sweeper picked him up on the end of a stick and threw him upon the rubbish heap. Let us sing about the great, the red-eyed Rikki-tikki!" And Darzee filled his throat and sang.

"If I could get up to your nest, I'd roll your babies out!" said Rikki-tikki. "You don't know

when to do the right thing at the right time. You're safe enough in your nest there, but it's war for me down here. Stop singing a minute, Darzee."

"For the great, the beautiful Rikki-tikki's sake I will stop," said Darzee. "What is it, O Killer of the terrible Nag?"

"Where is Nagaina, for the third time?"

"On the rubbish heap by the stables, mourning for Nag. Great is Rikki-tikki with the white teeth."

"Bother my white teeth! Have you ever heard where she keeps her eggs?"

"In the melon bed, on the end nearest the wall, where the sun strikes nearly all day. She hid them there weeks ago."

"And you never thought it worthwhile to tell me? The end nearest the wall, you said?"

"Rikki-tikki, you are not going to eat her eggs?"

"Not eat exactly, no. Darzee, if you have a grain of sense you will fly off to the stables and pretend that your wing is broken, and let Nagaina chase you away to this bush. I must get to the melon bed, and if I went there now she'd see me."

Darzee was a feather-brained little fellow who could never hold more than one idea at a time in his head. And just because he knew that Nagaina's children were born in eggs like his own, he didn't think at first that it was fair to kill them. But his wife was a sensible bird, and she knew that cobra's eggs meant young cobras later on. So she flew off from the nest, and left Darzee to keep the babies warm, and continue his song about the death of Nag. Darzee was very like a man in some ways.

---

11. **fancy** (fan′sē), *v.* picture to oneself; imagine.
12. **valiant** (val′yənt), *adj.* showing courage; brave.

She fluttered in front of Nagaina by the rubbish heap and cried out, "Oh, my wing is broken! The boy in the house threw a stone at me and broke it." Then she fluttered more desperately than ever.

Nagaina lifted up her head and hissed. "You warned Rikki-tikki when I would have killed him. Indeed and truly, you've chosen a bad place to be lame in." And she moved toward Darzee's wife, slipping along over the dust.

"The boy broke it with a stone!" shrieked Darzee's wife.

"Well! It may be some consolation[13] to you when you're dead to know that I shall settle accounts with the boy. My husband lies on the rubbish heap this morning, but before night the boy in the house will lie very still. What is the use of running away? I am sure to catch you. Little fool, look at me!"

Darzee's wife knew better than to do *that*, for a bird who looks at a snake's eyes gets so frightened that she cannot move. Darzee's wife fluttered on, piping sorrowfully, and never leaving the ground, and Nagaina quickened her pace.

Rikki-tikki heard them going up the path from the stables, and he raced for the end of the melon patch near the wall. There, in the warm litter above the melons, very cunningly hidden, he found twenty-five eggs, about the size of a bantam's eggs, but with whitish skins instead of shells.

"I was not a day too soon," he said, for he could see the baby cobras curled up inside the skin, and he knew that the minute they were hatched they could each kill a man or a mongoose. He bit off the tops of the eggs as fast as he could, taking care to crush the young cobras, and turned over the litter from time to time to see whether he had missed any. At last there were only three eggs left, and Rikki-tikki began to chuckle to himself, when he heard Darzee's wife screaming:

"Rikki-tikki, I led Nagaina toward the house, and she has gone into the veranda, and—oh, come quickly—she means killing!"

Rikki-tikki smashed two eggs, and tumbled backward down the melon bed with the third egg in his mouth, and scuttled to the veranda as hard as he could put foot to ground. Teddy and his mother and father were there at early breakfast, but Rikki-tikki saw that they were not eating anything. They sat stone-still, and their faces were white. Nagaina was coiled up on the matting by Teddy's chair, within easy striking distance of Teddy's bare leg, and she was swaying to and fro, singing a song of triumph.

"Son of the big man that killed Nag," she hissed, "stay still. I am not ready yet. Wait a little. Keep very still, all you three! If you move I strike, and if you do not move I strike. Oh, foolish people who killed my Nag!"

Teddy's eyes were fixed on his father, and all his father could do was to whisper, "Sit still, Teddy. You mustn't move. Teddy, keep still."

Then Rikki-tikki came up and cried, "Turn round, Nagaina. Turn and fight!"

"All in good time," said she, without moving her eyes. "I will settle my account with *you* presently. Look at your friends, Rikki-tikki. They are still and white. They are afraid. They dare not move, and if you come a step nearer I strike."

"Look at your eggs," said Rikki-tikki, "in the melon bed near the wall. Go and look, Nagaina!"

The big snake turned half around, and saw the egg on the veranda. "Ah-h! Give it to me," she said.

Rikki-tikki put his paws one on each side of the egg, and his eyes were blood-red. "What price for a snake's egg? For a young cobra? For a young king cobra? For the last—the very last of the brood? The ants are eating all the others down by the melon bed."

---

13. **consolation** (kon′sə lā′shən), *n.* comfort.

Nagaina spun clear round, forgetting everything for the sake of the one egg. Rikki-tikki saw Teddy's father shoot out a big hand, catch Teddy by the shoulder, and drag him across the little table with the teacups, safe and out of reach of Nagaina.

"Tricked! Tricked! Tricked! *Rikk-tck-tck!*" chuckled Rikki-tikki. "The boy is safe, and it was I—I—I that caught Nag by the hood last night in the bathroom." Then he began to jump up and down, all four feet together, his head close to the floor. "He threw me to and fro, but he could not shake me off. He was dead before the big man blew him in two. I did it! *Rikki-tikki-tck-tck!* Come then, Nagaina. Come and fight with me. You shall not be a widow long."

Again and again and again she struck, . . .

Nagaina saw that she had lost her chance of killing Teddy, and the egg lay between Rikki-tikki's paws. "Give me the egg, Rikki-tikki. Give me the last of my eggs, and I will go away and never come back," she said, lowering her hood.

"Yes, you will go away, and you will never come back. For you will go to the rubbish heap with Nag. Fight, widow! The big man has gone for his gun. Fight!"

Rikki-tikki was bounding all round Nagaina, keeping just out of reach of her stroke, his little eyes like hot coals. Nagaina gathered herself together and flung out at him. Rikki-tikki jumped up and backward. Again and again and again she struck, and each time her head came with a whack on the matting of the veranda and she gathered herself together like a watch spring. Then Rikki-tikki danced in a circle to get behind her, and Nagaina spun round to keep her head to his head, so that the rustle of her tail on the matting sounded like dry leaves blown along by the wind.

He had forgotten the egg. It still lay on the veranda, and Nagaina came nearer and nearer to it, till at last, while Rikki-tikki was drawing breath, she caught it in her mouth, turned to the veranda steps, and flew like an arrow down the path, with Rikki-tikki behind her. When the cobra runs for her life, she goes like a whiplash flicked across a horse's neck. Rikki-tikki knew that he must catch her, or all the trouble would begin again.

She headed straight for the long grass by the thornbush, and as he was running Rikki-tikki heard Darzee still singing his foolish little song of triumph. But Darzee's wife was wiser. She flew off her nest as Nagaina came along, and flapped her wings about Nagaina's head. If Darzee had helped her they might have turned her, but Nagaina only lowered her hood and went on. Still, the instant's delay brought Rikki-tikki up to her, and as she plunged into the rathole where she and Nag used to live, his little white teeth were clenched on her tail, and he went down with her—and very few mongooses, however wise and old they may be, care to follow a cobra into its hole.

It was dark in the hole; and Rikki-tikki never knew when it might open out and give Nagaina room to turn and strike at him. He held on savagely, and stuck out his feet to act as brakes on the dark slope of the hot, moist earth.

PREDICT: What do you think the outcome of the underground battle will be?

Then the grass by the mouth of the hole stopped waving, and Darzee said, "It is all over with Rikki-tikki! We must sing his death song. Valiant Rikki-tikki is dead! For Nagaina will surely kill him underground."

So he sang a very mournful song that he made up on the spur of the minute, and just as he got to the most touching part, the grass quivered again, and Rikki-tikki, covered with dirt, dragged himself out of the hole leg by leg, licking his whiskers. Darzee stopped with a little shout. Rikki-tikki shook some of the dust out of his fur and sneezed. "It is all over," he said. "The widow will never come out again." And the red ants that live between the grass stems heard him, and began to troop down one after another to see if he had spoken the truth.

Rikki-tikki curled himself up in the grass and slept where he was—slept and slept till it was late in the afternoon, for he had done a hard day's work.

"Now," he said, when he awoke, "I will go back to the house. Tell the Coppersmith, Darzee, and he will tell the garden that Nagaina is dead."

The Coppersmith is a bird who makes a noise exactly like the beating of a little hammer on a copper pot. The reason he is always making it is because he is the town crier to every Indian garden, and tells all the news to everybody who cares to listen. As Rikki-tikki went up the path, he heard his "attention" notes like a tiny dinner gong, and then the steady "*Ding-dong-tock!* Nag is dead—*dong!* Nagaina is dead! *Ding-dong-tock!*" That set all the birds in the garden singing, and the frogs croaking, for Nag and Nagaina used to eat frogs as well as little birds.

When Rikki got to the house, Teddy and Teddy's mother (she looked very white still, for she had been fainting) and Teddy's father came out and almost cried over him; and that night he ate all that was given him till he could eat no more, and went to bed on Teddy's shoulder, where Teddy's mother saw him when she came to look late at night.

"He saved our lives and Teddy's life," she said to her husband. "Just think, he saved all our lives."

Rikki-tikki woke up with a jump, for the mongooses are light sleepers.

"Oh, it's you," said he. "What are you bothering for? All the cobras are dead. And if they weren't, I'm here."

Rikki-tikki had a right to be proud of himself. But he did not grow too proud, and he kept that garden as a mongoose should keep it, with tooth and jump and spring and bite, till never a cobra dared show its head inside the walls.

After Reading

Making Connections

1. What do you see as the single most important moment in the story?

2. Do you think Nag and Nagaina deserve any sympathy? Why or why not?

3. After Rikki-tikki was rescued from a summer flood, he showed his gratitude in a dramatic, storybook way. How did the real-life animals you discussed before reading respond to being rescued?

4. Throughout the story, Kipling uses **anthropomorphism,** that is, he gives all the animals human traits. 🐾 They see life from a human **perspective.** Find examples of how Nag and Darzee view life as humans do.

5. Is the **conflict** in this story just about ownership of space or territory, or are other issues also involved? Explain.

6. This story is similar in some ways to **folk tales** and **legends,** which usually teach lessons. What lesson, if any, does this story teach?

7. If the **setting,** or location of this story, were moved to your region, what in the story would change? Who might the hero and the villain be?

Literary Focus: Onomatopoeia

In one of Darzee's victory songs, he calls a shotgun a "bang stick." Why is that a fitting name? If you say it's because a shotgun firing sounds like *BANG* you are explaining **onomatopoeia**—words that sound like what they mean. What difference would it make if Darzee's name for a shotgun were "loud stick"? Go back to the story and find and list other examples of words or names that sound like what they stand for.

Vocabulary Study

A. On your paper copy the boxes and blanks as shown below. Use the clues on the right to find the correct word from the vocabulary list and fill in the letters in the boxes and blanks.

bungalow
revive
cultivate
cower
providence
purchase
singe
fancy
valiant
consolation

WORDS	CLUES
1. _ _ _ _ _ □	may be done with air
2. _ _ _ □ _	done with fire
3. _ _ _ □ _	picture in your head
4. _ _ □ _ _ _ _	a firm grip
5. _ _ _ _ □ _ _	a word for a brave hero
6. _ □ _ _ _ _ _	a low, wide house
7. _ □ _ _ _	what the fearful do
8. _ □ _ _ _ _ _ _	tend and care for
9. _ _ □ _ _ _ _ _ _	divine help
10. _ _ _ □ _ _ _ _ _ _	comforting words

B. Rearrange the letters from the boxes to find the mystery word that describes Rikki-tikki.

Expressing Your Ideas

Writing Choices

Song for a *Living* Legend A problem with Darzee's "death song" for Rikki-tikki is that the mongoose lived. Write **lyrics** for a "life song" that tells Rikki-tikki's story. Try to incorporate onomatopoetic words—words that sound like what they are.

RADD (Reptiles Against Deadly Discrimination) Snakes are often hunted and killed just for sport. As a supporter of RADD, write a **science article** about an endangered snake.

Other Options

X Marks the Spot Make a **tourist map** for the bungalow and garden where Rikki-tikki lived with his friends and foes. Use different symbols to show who lived where and to mark sites of important events.

Story Hour Create posterboard **cutouts** of the characters in the story. Use the figures to present a dramatic retelling of the story to a kindergarten or primary class.

What a Team! Even a brave hero like Rikki-tikki relies on some help from his friends. Make awards for Rikki-tikki and the other animals who helped him.

Language Mini-Lesson

Checking Your Spelling

Recognize spelling problems. Sometimes the worst kinds of spelling mistakes we make are the most obvious. These are words that we know, but they are so familiar to us that we don't "see" them when we proofread. Which words are misspelled in the sentences below?

- Your invited to a party for my freind Jack on Saturday.

- I no you won't go too the party without a gift.

- After the party, their was trash everywere.

Writing Strategy Make yourself aware of words that are easily misspelled. Here are some tips.

- Know the spellings and definitions for words that sound alike.

- Watch out for silent letters. They can fool you. Look up a word in a dictionary if you're unsure of its spelling.

- Proofread for meaning when you write. A word that looks right may actually be wrong.

Computer Terms

If you're using a computer, remember that the spell check software can check spelling but not meaning. If you use the wrong word in a sentence and spell it correctly, the spell checker won't catch it. Be sure to proofread carefully.

Activity Options

1. Misspellings are everywhere. Sometimes they're intentional, such as when "quick" is spelled "kwik." Begin a list of misspellings that you see every day, intentional or not. Write down the incorrect and correct spellings. Compare your lists with other students. You might want to have a contest to see who can find the most misspellings.

2. Write five sentences that include the following words, but spell them incorrectly: *everybody, they're, their, there, something, buy,* and *our.* Exchange papers with a partner and correct each other's sentences.

3. Keep a "Careless Errors" list of words you sometimes misspell. Add words from your other subjects too. Compare your list with others to see how many words you have in common.

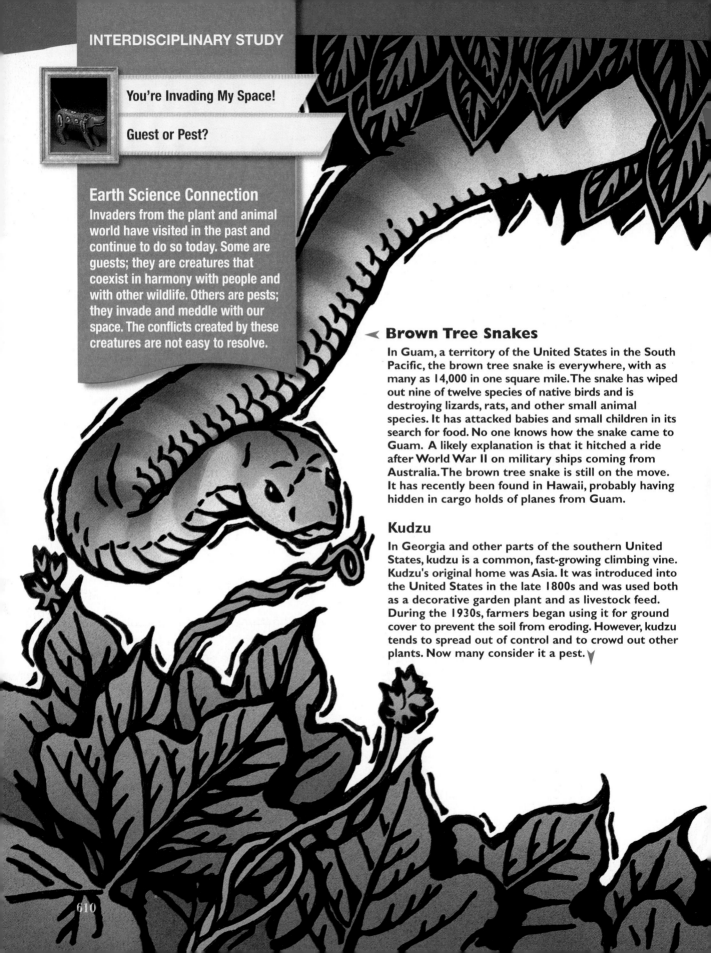

You're Invading My Space!

Guest or Pest?

Earth Science Connection

Invaders from the plant and animal world have visited in the past and continue to do so today. Some are guests; they are creatures that coexist in harmony with people and with other wildlife. Others are pests; they invade and meddle with our space. The conflicts created by these creatures are not easy to resolve.

◄ Brown Tree Snakes

In Guam, a territory of the United States in the South Pacific, the brown tree snake is everywhere, with as many as 14,000 in one square mile. The snake has wiped out nine of twelve species of native birds and is destroying lizards, rats, and other small animal species. It has attacked babies and small children in its search for food. No one knows how the snake came to Guam. A likely explanation is that it hitched a ride after World War II on military ships coming from Australia. The brown tree snake is still on the move. It has recently been found in Hawaii, probably having hidden in cargo holds of planes from Guam.

Kudzu

In Georgia and other parts of the southern United States, kudzu is a common, fast-growing climbing vine. Kudzu's original home was Asia. It was introduced into the United States in the late 1800s and was used both as a decorative garden plant and as livestock feed. During the 1930s, farmers began using it for ground cover to prevent the soil from eroding. However, kudzu tends to spread out of control and to crowd out other plants. Now many consider it a pest. ▼

Animal and Plant Invaders

◄ Wild Pigs

The pig, not native to the Americas, probably came when Christopher Columbus landed in Cuba on one of his voyages. Spanish explorers who followed Columbus in the 1500s—Hernando Cortés and Hernando DeSoto—brought these pigs to help feed their men. Today there may be a million or more across the United States. They have caused great damage, eating bark and roots, toppling underbrush and trees, and disrupting the delicate forest ecosystem.

Killer Bees

Swarms of "killer bees" have been found in Texas. These aggressive bees developed in Brazil some forty years ago when imported African honey bees escaped and mated with local bees. The resulting hybrid bees soon spread throughout much of South America and traveled northward into Central America, Mexico, and eventually Texas. "Killer bees" attack fiercely in large numbers when their hive is disturbed, and have been known to kill animals and people. ►

Nutria

In the wet marshlands of southern Louisiana, the nutria, a ten-pound water rat, is causing a major environmental problem. Nutria are destroying marsh plants that are the breeding ground for shrimp and other shellfish. The plants also help prevent soil erosion on the vast network of canals and drainage ditches that keep the low-lying suburbs of New Orleans from flooding. Nutria were brought into Louisiana from South America by E. A. McIlhenny, the creator of Tabasco sauce. He intended to raise the nutria for their fur. During a hurricane in 1937, the nutria escaped from their cages. With an endless supply of food, they have since grown and multiplied in the wild.

Water Hyacinths

A beautiful but troublesome plant in the southern United States is the water hyacinth. It originally grew in tropical regions in South America, where insects and diseases kept its growth in check. However, in Florida and other states where it was introduced, the plant has no natural enemies. Water hyacinths grow quickly, creating a thick, matted cover on the water. Sunlight and oxygen are blocked, and plant and animal life underneath the surface dies out. ➤

Med Flies

Californians have been concerned in recent years with the Med fly, the common name for the Mediterranean fruit fly. Med flies lay their eggs on fruit. When they hatch, the maggots tunnel through the fruit, making it unfit to eat. Travelers are asked not to bring fruit into the state because it might be infected with this destructive pest.

Responding

1. Based on the descriptions you have read, how would you define "plant and animal invaders"?

2. Are there any animal or plant invaders in your region? What is being done to control them?

Science Connection

Balance in nature is delicate. Tampering with the natural order can cause many problems. In the case of the mongoose, the introduction of a guest with no natural enemies into the ecosystem to eliminate a pest backfired. Instead of one kind of pest, there are now two.

Mongoose on the Loose

by Larry Luxner

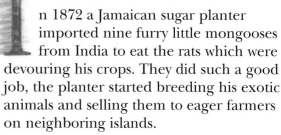

In 1872 a Jamaican sugar planter imported nine furry little mongooses from India to eat the rats which were devouring his crops. They did such a good job, the planter started breeding his exotic animals and selling them to eager farmers on neighboring islands.

With no natural predators—like wolves, coyotes, or poisonous snakes—the mongoose population exploded, and within a few years, they were killing not just rats but pigs, lambs, chickens, puppies, and kittens. Dr. G. Roy Horst, a U.S. expert on mongooses, says that today mongooses live on seventeen Caribbean islands as well as Hawaii and Fiji, where they have attacked small animals, threatened endangered species, and have even spread minor rabies epidemics.

In Puerto Rico there are from 800,000 to one million of them. That is about one mongoose for every four humans. In St. Croix, there are 100,000 mongooses, about twice as many as the human population. "It's impossible to eliminate the mongoose population, short of nuclear war," says Horst. "You can't poison them, because cats, dogs, and chickens get poisoned, too. I'm not a prophet crying in the wilderness, but the potential for real trouble is there," says Horst.

According to Horst, great efforts have been made to rid the islands of mongooses, which have killed off a number of species including the Amevia lizard on St. Croix, presumed extinct for several decades. On Hawaii, the combination of mongooses and sports hunting has reduced the Hawaiian goose, or nene, to less than two dozen individuals.

The fifty-nine-year-old biology professor, who teaches at Potsdam College in upstate New York, recently finished his third season at the 500-acre Cabo Rojo National Wildlife Refuge in southwestern Puerto Rico, using microchips to study the life cycle and reproductive habits of the Caribbean mongoose.

▲ A mongoose gets tagged.

(He is also doing similar work at the Sandy Point Fish and Wildlife Refuge on St. Croix in the U.S. Virgin Islands.) "I want to know what happens when you take a small animal and put him in an area with no competition. This is a model that doesn't exist anywhere else in the world."

Horst's five-year, $60,000 study is being sponsored by Earthwatch Incorporated, a non-profit group that has funded some 1,300 research projects in eighty-seven countries. Volunteers pay $1,500 each (not including airfare) to come to Puerto Rico for ten days and help Horst set out mongoose traps, study

This is a model that doesn't exist anywhere else in the world.

the animals, and keep records. Often he and his volunteers spend a sweaty day walking about ten miles while setting out mongoose traps in the wilderness. Later, they perform surgery on their unwilling subjects to implant the electronic devices that will allow them to track the animal's habits.

Horst has tagged more than 400 mongooses with PITs (permanently implanted transponders), a new microchip technology, which he says has changed his work dramatically. "You couldn't do this with ear tags. It was very hard to permanently mark these animals until this technology came along," he said.

Horst has caught thousands of mongooses and has reached some interesting conclusions. Among them: mongooses have a life expectancy of six to ten years, much longer than the previously accepted figure of three years. Horst says his research will provide local and federal health officials with extremely valuable information if they ever decide to launch a campaign against rabies in Puerto Rico or the U.S. Virgin Islands.

Responding

1. What lesson can be learned from this story of the mongoose?

2. Once the mongoose population began to grow, it proved very difficult to control. What measures might be taken to limit the mongoose population?

Reading Mini-Lesson

Finding Cause-and-Effect Relationships

Finding the pattern a writer has used to organize information can help you understand and remember what you read. Cause and effect is one pattern often found in writing. An event happens, and then another event happens as a result. Sometimes there is a chain reaction of effects, with one effect causing another effect.

"Mongoose on the Loose" on pages 613–614 begins with the information that in 1872 a Jamaican sugar planter's crops were threatened by rats. That's the first event. What does the planter do as a result? What happens then? Drawing a diagram can help you understand cause-and-effect relationships. For example:

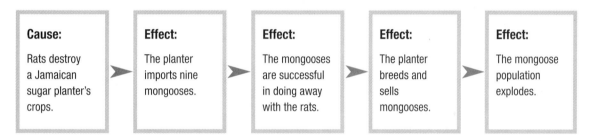

Cause:	**Effect:**	**Effect:**	**Effect:**	**Effect:**
Rats destroy a Jamaican sugar planter's crops.	The planter imports nine mongooses.	The mongooses are successful in doing away with the rats.	The planter breeds and sells mongooses.	The mongoose population explodes.

Activity Options

1. Think about all the effects of the mongoose population explosion. One involves endangered species, but there are other effects too. Continue the chart begun above. You may want to include Dr. G. Roy Horst's study and its expected results.

2. Work with a group of classmates. Find and talk about cause-and-effect relationships in "Animal and Plant Invaders." Create a poster or bulletin board display to show some of the cause-and-effect relationships in the picture essay on pages 610–612.

3. Find a newspaper or magazine article that is organized by cause-and-effect relationships. Bring the article to class and work with a partner to draw a diagram that traces the causes and effects.

Part Two

Standing Your Ground

Stick up for yourself! Hang in there! Just say no! Hold firm! These are just a few of the ways we say, "Stand your ground." Often, we don't know our own strength until something really gets in our way. Someone or something may threaten to take what is ours, or try to force us to do the wrong thing, or stop us from doing the right thing, or keep us from a goal. That's when we find out just what we're made of . . . and so does everyone else.

🐾 **Multicultural Connection** **Choice** involves balancing cultural traditions with the conflicts inherent in a changing world. Sometimes those conflicts arise when people cross into new cultural situations. What does it take to stand one's ground when faced with conflict? Does it take courage or stubbornness? Mind or muscle? Quiet determination or a loud roar? Look for the choices the characters in the selections make in addressing conflicts.

Literature

Alfred Brenner   **Survival** ◆ play 618
Alfred Noyes   **The Highwayman** ◆ poem 640
Langston Hughes   **Mother to Son** ◆ poem 647
Alice Walker   **Women** ◆ poem 648
Juan A. A. Sedillo   **Gentleman of Rio en Medio** ◆ short story 652
Ricardo E. Alegría   **The Rabbit and the Tiger** ◆ Puerto Rican
                     folk tale 658
          Writing Mini-Lesson ◆ Preparing Your Presentation Portfolio 665

Interdisciplinary Study Women Making Waves

Pursuing Equality ◆ sociology 666
Fabric of Life by Donna Johnson ◆ anthropology 668
          Reading Mini-lesson ◆ Summarizing 670

Writing Workshop Persuasive Writing

Expressing an Opinion 671

Beyond Print Critical Thinking

Yes, We Have No Bananas 677

Before Reading

Survival

by Alfred Brenner

Alfred Brenner
born 1916

Alfred Brenner's interest in drama was sparked while he was still in high school. As a teenager, he was already at work writing plays of his own. After completing college, he had many of his plays produced on television. *Survival* aired on television in 1957 and was voted one of the best dramas of the year. The following year, Brenner was honored with an Emmy for his shorter television plays. He continued as a playwright for film and live theater.

Building Background

Lifeboat Roulette Imagine being on a sinking ship carrying 2,225 people with lifeboats for only 1,178. That was the situation on the luxurious *Titanic* when it rammed into an iceberg and sank, taking over 1,500 lives. Only after that famous tragedy in 1912, did the rule "lifeboats for everyone" come into existence. In 1841, however, the time in which the play *Survival* is set, having lifeboats for all on board was considered an "unnecessary luxury." And in those days, crossing the ocean was a dangerous undertaking. Storms, fog, and sea ice made any voyage a risky venture. A voyage from Ireland to the United States could take nearly 40 days.

Getting into the Play

Writer's Notebook *Survival* is based on a difficult choice one man had to make. Have you ever had to make a very difficult decision, such as putting a pet to sleep? What options did you have to consider? Who helped you make your decision? In your notebook, write about a time you had to make and stand by a tough decision.

Reading Tip

Terms Used at Sea This drama, based on fact, contains words commonly heard on ships of the era. Some may be new to you. Use the chart below to "navigate" through some oceangoing terms.

hatchway	a hole in the deck of a ship leading to lower decks
hold	the inside of a ship, where cargo is carried
jollyboat	a small boat carried on a ship
league	about 5 kilometers, or 3 miles
lee'ard	leeward—the side away from the wind
longboat	the largest boat carried by a sailing ship
maritime	having to do with the sea or sailing
mast	the long center pole that supports a ship's sails
mizzenmast	a mast nearest the rear of a ship with more than one mast
seafaring	traveling or working on the sea

SURVIVAL

ALFRED BRENNER

CAST

DAVID HOLMES	FRANK ASKIN
LANDLADY	MARY O'BRIEN
TWO POLICEMEN	THOMAS ABLE
PAT ASKIN	LORNA QUINN
ARMSTRONG	STENOGRAPHER
CLERK	CAPTAIN AMOS TILTON
JUDGE	MRS. RESTON
DALLAS	FOREMAN OF THE JURY

TIME *1842*

PLACE *A rooming house and courtroom in Philadelphia, with some suggested scenes at sea*

PLAYING TIME *About fifty minutes*

Act One

(Fade in.)

(A street in Philadelphia near the water front, 1842. A single street lamp drops a vague puddle of light on the cobbles. All we can see are the fronts of several buildings, some barrels, a coil of rope. DAVID HOLMES, *a thick, heavy-set seaman with hard, worried eyes, about thirty, carrying a seabag over his shoulder, is walking slowly along past buildings.)*

NARRATOR *(over).* This story is based on a real case. It was tried in the U.S. Circuit Court[1] in the City of Philadelphia, on the 13th of April, 1842. It bears the title U.S. versus Holmes.

*(*HOLMES *halts abruptly at the door of a house over which hangs a sign:*

THE JOLLY REST
Rooms For Seamen
And Their Guests

He knocks on door. We hear footsteps within, a rusty lock turns; then door opens a crack and we see a landlady in nightdress, holding a candle, looking out suspiciously.)

LANDLADY *(looking him up and down).* Rent's two dollars a week . . . in advance . . .

---

1. **circuit court,** the court of general jurisdiction in a state.

◄ *Portrait of Joseph Roulin* was painted by Vincent Van Gogh in 1888. Do you think this hardy old fellow would know his way around a sailing ship?

(HOLMES *glances at her swiftly, stiff, tense.*)

Wait'll I tell Mrs. Brannigan I got a *hero* boardin' with me . . .

HOLMES (*leaping toward her, grabbing her throat, hissing*). You don't tell nobody who you got! Nobody!

(*He slowly drops his hands. They stare at each other. An awkward silence. Suddenly she turns on her heels, leaves. He stands there, staring after her, exhausted. Abruptly he shakes it off, bends down beside his seabag, opens it, takes out several sheets of paper, pen, ink, goes to desk, sits down and begins to write. He writes slowly, painfully. There is no sound except the scratching of the pen. Camera pans away from him, moves slowly around room.*)

(*Dissolve to:* HOLMES *slumped across desk, asleep. A partly addressed envelope is lying beside him. A shaft of sunlight lights up his face. It is morning. There is a knock on the door. His eyes open. He starts up, suddenly awake, springs to his feet.*)

HOLMES. Who is it?

(*Door opens, two* POLICEMEN, *followed by* LANDLADY *enter.*)

FIRST POLICEMAN. David Holmes, we have a warrant[2] for your arrest . . . (*Grabs* HOLMES' *arm.*)

HOLMES (*pulls away stiffly*). Take your hands off me!

(HOLMES *reaches for his money bag, takes out several coins, drops them into her hand. She counts them quickly, glances up at him again.*)

This way . . .

(*He enters a hallway, follows her a few steps to a door. She opens it, goes into a small dingy room containing a bed, small table and chair. He steps in after her.*)

You just come off ship? (*He nods.*) What's yer name?

HOLMES (*throwing bag down, feeling bed*). Holmes . . .

LANDLADY (*examining him carefully*). Say, you ain't the one who brought in that longboat, saved all them women?

_____

2. **warrant** (wôr′ənt), *n.* written order giving authority.

(He walks toward door almost proudly, exits. POLICEMEN *follow him out quickly.* LANDLADY *glances around room, notices something on the table. The letter* HOLMES *wrote is still there. She picks up envelope, looks at it.)*

(Cut to: closeup of envelope. We read the name "Pat Askin" on it.)

(Dissolve to: PAT ASKIN, *an attractive girl in her twenties, standing somewhat nervously among a small knot of men and women outside a pair of paneled doors on which is printed:*

U.S. CIRCUIT COURT FOR THE THIRD EASTERN DISTRICT OF PENNSYLVANIA

A buzz of excited conversation rises from the men and women. Suddenly PAT *sees someone. Her whole body stiffens. The others, following her eyes, turn, stare at* HOLMES, *who has just arrived. Beside him is his attorney,* ARMSTRONG, *a well-dressed man in his forties holding a brief case under his arm.* HOLMES *catches sight of* PAT, *halts, stiffens. But* ARMSTRONG *quickly grabs his arm, pulls him through paneled doors, into courtroom.)*

(Cut to: HOLMES *and* ARMSTRONG *inside courtroom coming down the aisle. Suddenly* HOLMES *stops, his eyes fixed on something just ahead, an old weather-beaten longboat. We are able to read the name, William Brown, printed on the side of a boat near the bow.)*

ARMSTRONG *(glancing at* HOLMES*).* Exhibit A for the prosecution.

(He leads HOLMES *to defense table. They sit down.)*
I tried to get a postponement . . .

HOLMES *(becoming angry).* Who said I wanted a postponement?

ARMSTRONG. If I did everything you wanted, Holmes, there'd be a noose around your neck right now.

HOLMES. I'm gonna plead guilty.

ARMSTRONG. No!

HOLMES *(defiantly).* I did everything they said I did! I'm not gonna deny it. Armstrong, you didn't have to come all the way down

here from Boston to defend me . . . Why did you?

ARMSTRONG. I'm not sure. Maybe it's because I've never seen Philadelphia before.

(Pat Askin is coming down the aisle.)
Holmes, why don't you stop fighting me?

HOLMES *(snapping).* I told you the facts—

ARMSTRONG. I understand the facts! What I need to understand is *you!*

(But HOLMES *is not listening. He is staring out toward spectators.* ARMSTRONG, *following his eyes, sees* PAT. *She takes a seat among six or seven girls in first row.)*
What about Pat Askin?

HOLMES *(turning on him angrily).* Listen, Armstrong! Why don't you let them sentence me and be done with it?

(The rapping of the gavel interrupts him.)

CLERK *(calling out).* Oyez! Oyez! The United States Circuit Court for the Third Eastern District of Pennsylvania is now in session. The United States versus Holmes. Will everyone rise.

(Everyone rises. JUDGE *enters, sits on bench. All are seated.)*

JUDGE. Is the accused ready for trial?

*(*ARMSTRONG *motions for* HOLMES *to rise.)*

HOLMES *(on his feet).* Yes, sir . . .

CLERK *(reading aloud from paper in his hands).* "In that David Holmes, ordinary seaman, on or about April 20, 1841, did commit manslaughter[3] by unlawfully and feloniously[4] making an assault upon and casting Frank Askin, a passenger, from a longboat belonging to the merchant ship, the *William Brown,* into the Atlantic Ocean, by means of which Askin was suffocated and drowned . . ." David Holmes, you have

---

3. **manslaughter** (man′slô′tər), *n.* the killing of a human being but without deliberate intent.
4. **feloniously** (fə lō′nē əs lē), having to do with a serious crime or felony.

heard the charge against you: how say you, guilty or not guilty ?

HOLMES (*A pause. He looks around hesitantly*). I . . . Not guilty . . .

PAT (*crying out*). He's lying! I saw him! He . . .

(*PAT leaps to her feet. She breaks, sobbing. Several other girls move to her side quickly, hold and comfort her. Sounds of excited conversation . . . confusion in the courtroom.*)

JUDGE (*pounding the gavel*). Order! Order in the Court!

(*Noise gradually ceases. He turns to prosecutor.[5]*)

Mr. Dallas, the United States District Attorney,[6] will present the case for the people.

DALLAS (*rises, steps toward jury*). Gentlemen of the Jury, four months ago an American merchant ship, the *William Brown*, set sail from Liverpool, England . . . (*His voice fades.*)

(*Dissolve to:* DALLAS *from a different angle, still addressing jury. His jacket is open now, and he is loosening his collar and mopping his brow. He had been talking for a while and is beginning to wind up his address . . .*)

Although the members of the crew and the mate have all disappeared and have still not been reached, fortunately there are a number of witnesses present who were on that longboat, who saw these horrible deeds with their own eyes . . .

(*He turns toward women sitting in first row, who are watching, listening intently.*)

Why did Holmes do such a thing? I suggest, gentlemen, you will find the reason . . . the motive, if you will—in the character of the man himself . . .

(*We see* HOLMES *sitting in his chair, his right hand clenched on the table. He is motionless, expressionless.* ARMSTRONG *keeps glancing at him.*)

A man who in a moment of panic exploded, and sent not only Frank Askin, but eleven of his fellow passengers to their death!

(DALLAS *turns, walks slowly back to his seat.* JUDGE *looks questioningly at* ARMSTRONG. ARMSTRONG *says something to* HOLMES *who does not react. Finally he rises.*)

ARMSTRONG. Your Honor, the defense will not address the jury at this time. (*He is seated.*)

JUDGE (*looks at him questioningly, then to* DALLAS). Prosecution will proceed . . .

CLERK. Miss Pat Askin will take the stand . . .

(PAT *crosses up aisle to stand.* HOLMES *watches her carefully.*)

Raise your right hand— Do you solemnly swear that the testimony[7] you are about to give will be the truth . . . the whole truth and nothing but the truth, so help you God?

PAT. I do.

CLERK. State your name.

PAT. Patricia Askin.

DALLAS (*approaches*). You are the sister of Frank Askin who was thrown off a longboat and drowned in the Atlantic Ocean on April 20 of this year?

PAT. Yes.

DALLAS. Were you on that same longboat at that time?

PAT. I was.

DALLAS (*points to boat*). Is that the longboat?

PAT. Yes . . .

DALLAS. Miss Askin, did you see the defendant, David Holmes, forcibly throw your brother, Frank, out of *this* longboat and thus cause him to drown?

PAT. Yes . . . I did.

(*Murmuring, voices from courtroom.* JUDGE *bangs gavel.*)

---

5. **prosecutor** (pros′ə kyü′tər), *n.* the lawyer who takes the government's side of a case against an accused person.

6. **district attorney,** the lawyer who handles cases for the government of a certain district of a state.

7. **testimony** (tes′tə mō′nē), *n.* a statement used for evidence or proof.

JUDGE. Did I hear an objection,[8] Mr. Armstrong?

ARMSTRONG (*from far away*). What . . . ? No, Your Honor.

JUDGE (*to* DALLAS). Proceed.

DALLAS (*to* PAT). You and Frank were not the only passengers aboard the ship, the *William Brown*, were you, Miss Askin?

PAT. No . . . there were about thirty others with us.

DALLAS. Where were you coming from?

PAT. Ireland.

DALLAS. Why did you decide to come to America?

PAT. Well . . . it was the famine[9] . . . my father died . . . Frank and I decided to sell our little plot and seek a better life in this country.

DALLAS. Miss Askin, please tell the Court what happened on the night of April 19th.

PAT. An iceberg hit the ship.

DALLAS. Would you describe the circumstances.

PAT. Well, I was asleep when it happened. When I opened my eyes, everyone was in their nightclothes screaming . . . someone was yelling: "On deck! Into the boats!" We piled up the hatchway with the seas crashing down. Some climbed into the little jollyboat. But most of us got into the longboat . . . Soon after the two boats were lowered into the sea, the ship went down. . . .

DALLAS. Miss Askin, I am now going to ask you to step down from the stand and get into the longboat, taking the exact position you were in that night.

(DALLAS *begins to help her out of stand.*)

JUDGE. One moment—would the prosecutor please explain his purpose?

DALLAS. If it please the Court. It is necessary to show Miss Askin's position in the boat in order to show that she could see what was going on.

JUDGE. You may proceed.

(DALLAS *leads* PAT *to longboat, helps her inside.*)

DALLAS. Is this where you were sitting?

PAT. Yes.

DALLAS. What were you doing?

PAT. Bailing . . .

DALLAS (*over*). Bailing? There was water in the boat?

PAT. Oh, a great deal.

(*Super: film, sound of sea, winds up.*)

PAT (*continues*). Besides, we had sprung a leak . . . My clothes were soaked and I was exhausted. My brother was sitting in front of me. Then I saw Holmes. Beside him were two seamen. He had a terrible look as he faced my brother.

(*We are in close, can almost see what* PAT *is describing.*)

Frank asked him what was happening. For a moment there was no reply—then Holmes took my brother by the shoulders and said, "It's your turn, Frank. You've got to go."

(*There is a look of horror on* FRANK's *face.*)

Then they threw my brother over the side. (*She screams.*) Leave him be! Leave him be!

(*We are in for a closeup of her face.*)

(*Sound of storm down and out. We hear nothing but* PAT's *sobbing. Lights come up on* DALLAS *in courtroom.*)

DALLAS. On that night, your brother as well as other male passengers were thrown over—Miss Askin, were any of the *crew* thrown overboard?

PAT. No.

DALLAS. No further questions. (*Begins to help her down.*)

ARMSTRONG (*rising*). You may remain where

---

8. **objection,** a reason or argument against something

9. **famine,** a time of starving. In 1845, disease ruined Ireland's potato crops, causing the Irish Potato Famine. A million people died, and over a million fled Ireland.

you are, Miss Askin. You just stated that none of the crew members were thrown overboard. Could you tell me why?

PAT. Well . . . they . . . Holmes said they were needed to row.

ARMSTRONG. No more questions.

(*He turns away. Court attendant helps* PAT *down.*)

JUDGE. Is that the extent of your cross-examination of this important witness, Mr. Armstrong?

ARMSTRONG. Miss Askin will be called as a witness for the defense, Your Honor.

JUDGE. For the *defense?*

ARMSTRONG. Yes, Your Honor.

(JUDGE *stares at him, shrugs, turns toward clerk.*)

CLERK. Miss Mary O'Brien.

(MARY *comes forward, glances angrily at* HOLMES. *He is gazing across at* PAT. ARMSTRONG *notices the look on his face.*)

(*Dissolve to:* DALLAS *at stand.*)

DALLAS. Miss O'Brien, was Holmes in command of the longboat immediately after the ship went down?

MARY (*in stand*). No, sir, John Widdows was— the first mate.

DALLAS. Oh?

MARY. Holmes took over later.

DALLAS. Took over? Forcibly? Did he fight with the mate?

MARY. Not right away. But he started to argue with him.

DALLAS. What about, Miss O'Brien?

MARY. The direction we was to take . . . The mate told Holmes to head west for land. Holmes refused. He said our only chance was to head south where we might pick up a ship . . . Well, sir, that's what we did—we went south.

DALLAS. Then Holmes actually took command.

MARY. All night long I heard his voice shoutin', cussin', threatenin' . . . I tell you, I'm not a shrinkin' violet[10] of a woman, but

I was scared of him . . . He's crazy!

DALLAS. Crazy?

MARY. Yes, sir.

DALLAS. Thank you, Miss O'Brien . . . Your witness.

ARMSTRONG (*rising*). How would you describe a man who was crazy, Miss O'Brien?

MARY. Well . . . Out of his mind . . . You know.

ARMSTRONG. Would you say that a man who is crazy doesn't know what he's doing?

MARY. Yes, sir! That's it!

ARMSTRONG. You mean Holmes didn't know what he was doing on that longboat?

MARY. I didn't say that . . .

ARMSTRONG. Well . . . You said he was crazy.

MARY. Well . . . He wasn't exactly *crazy* . . . He . . .

ARMSTRONG. No more questions.

(*He goes back to table. Camera stays on him and* HOLMES)

CLERK (*over, calling*). Thomas Able.

(*Dissolve to: Witness stand.* THOMAS ABLE, *a little withered seaman, sitting there looking at* DALLAS, *who has just begun to question him.*)

DALLAS. Mr. Able, how long were you and Holmes members of the crew of the *William Brown?*

ABLE. Five years.

DALLAS. At the time of the sinking, where did you go?

ABLE. In the jollyboat.

DALLAS. When you heard what had happened aboard the longboat, were you surprised?

ABLE. No, sir. I wouldn't be surprised at anything Holmes did. He's capable of anything. He's like gunpowder, ready to explode at any time . . .

DALLAS. Had he ever done anything like that before?

---

10. **shrinking violet,** a shy, timid person.

ABLE. No, not exactly . . . but, well, he was proud . . .

DALLAS. Proud?

ABLE. Well, he always had to be the first one up on the crow's nest . . . even during the worst weather. I see him hanging on to the top of the mizzenmast once with the ship practically layin' over on her side in the sea . . . and the mast all icy. An' when he came down later, his hands all bloody, he didn't say one word . . . even when some of the men slapped his shoulder and told him he did a nice job. He was crazy!

DALLAS *(smiles).* Did you like him as a shipmate?

ABLE. Nobody likes him.

DALLAS. Why not?

ABLE. Well, he was different . . . Kept apart . . . Never swapped a yarn . . . Never took a drink . . . I don't trust a man who don't take a drink . . . Not a seafarin' man . . .

DALLAS. Thank you, Mr. Able.

(He returns to table. ARMSTRONG *approaches stand.)*

ARMSTRONG. Tell me, Mr. Able, is Holmes a good seaman? In your opinion?

ABLE. Aye.

ARMSTRONG. A brave man?

ABLE. Aye, I guess he's got courage, but it's stupid . . .

ARMSTRONG. *(sharply).* Would you just answer my questions, please! Now, Mr. Able, in all the years that you knew the defendant, did he every willfully harm anyone?

ABLE. Well . . . no.

ARMSTRONG. No further questions.

(He turns away.)

DALLAS. That's all, Mr. Able.

*(*ABLE *steps down.)*

CLERK *(calling).* Miss Lorna Quinn.

*(*LORNA *rises from among row of women. As she does, we see* ARMSTRONG *at defense table making a few notes.* HOLMES *glances at him.)*

ARMSTRONG. That Tom Able reminds me of a

man I once shipped with . . .

HOLMES. What did *you* ever wanna go to sea for? It was a stupid thing to do.

(Dissolve to: LORNA QUINN *on stand being questioned by* DALLAS. *She is nervous.)*

DALLAS. . . . Do you actually mean, Miss Quinn, that on the night of April 20th, the night following the sinking of the *William Brown,* you heard the defendant order the crew to throw the male passengers overboard?

LORNA. I even saw it happen. I saw Holmes and two of the crew go up to Riley and they told him to stand up . . . and when Riley stood up, they gave him a shove and he went right overboard.

DALLAS. How close were you to Riley when this happened?

LORNA. Well, no further than you are from me right now.

DALLAS. Then what happened?

LORNA. Well, they threw over Duffy next, then Charlie Conlin . . . Charlie offered Holmes five sovereigns if he'd spare his life, but Holmes wouldn't even listen to him . . . and, well, this went on until every one of the men passengers except Ed McKenzie and Patrick Whelan were thrown over. Holmes spared those two because their wives were aboard.

DALLAS. Are you able to tell the Court—from your observation—how many men were thrown overboard during that terrible night?

LORNA. Well, there was Riley, Duffy, Charlie Conlin, Frank Askin . . . There were twelve.

DALLAS *(turning away swiftly).* Your witness.

ARMSTRONG *(rises, approaches* LORNA*).* Miss Quinn, did you personally feel safer—when you saw that the boat had been lighted by those men?

DALLAS. Objection!

▲ *The Rainbow* was painted by the Russian artist Ivan Aivazovsky in the late nineteenth century. Imagine being in that small storm-tossed boat. How would you feel?

JUDGE. You are placing the witness in a very difficult situation, Mr. Armstrong . . .

ARMSTRONG. If it please the Court, the defendant was faced with exactly the same difficult situation.

JUDGE (*after a pause*). Objection overruled.[11]

ARMSTRONG. Miss Quinn, I asked you if you felt safer—more secure—when you saw that the boat had been lightened by those men. Remember, you're under oath.

LORNA (*almost in tears*). I . . . I . . . don't know . . .

ARMSTRONG. That's all, Miss Quinn.

(*He returns to defense table. She steps down.*

DALLAS *comes forward.*)

CLERK. Miss Ann Flaherty.

ARMSTRONG (*rising*). If the Court please, I understand the United States Prosecutor intends to call at least ten survivors as witnesses . . .

DALLAS. That's correct . . .

ARMSTRONG. The defense agrees that the testimony of these witnesses will confirm the testimony already heard.

---

11. **overrule** (ō′vər rül′), *v.* rule or decide against an argument or objection.

JUDGE. Mr. Armstrong, you are yielding a rather important point . . .

ARMSTRONG. Your Honor, the defense does not deny that Holmes was responsible for casting Frank Askin and other male passengers overboard . . .

JUDGE. Oh! *(He studies* ARMSTRONG. *A silence.)* Mr. Armstrong, the Court understands you came all the way down from Boston to conduct this defense . . .

ARMSTRONG. That's correct, Your Honor . . .

JUDGE. You attended college in Boston?

ARMSTRONG. Harvard College, Your Honor.

JUDGE. Do you have any personal interest in this case, Mr. Armstrong?

ARMSTRONG. Your Honor, the effect of maritime law is felt in Boston as well as in Philadelphia; on land as well as on sea. I believe that this trial has meaning for all who travel on the sea—seamen and passengers. That is my personal interest.

JUDGE. The prosecution will proceed.

*(*ARMSTRONG *is seated.)*

CLERK. Captain Amos Tilton.

*(*CAPTAIN TILTON, *lean, hard, tanned, in sea uniform, approaches.)*

(Cut to: ARMSTRONG *and* HOLMES. HOLMES *is tensely watching* PAT. *Then to* PAT.*)*

(Dissolve to: Witness stand. DALLAS *is questioning the* CAPTAIN.*)*

DALLAS. Captain Tilton, how long were you in command of the *William Brown?*

CAPTAIN. Eight years.

DALLAS. During her last voyage, how many had she on board?

CAPTAIN. A crew of 13 and 39 passengers, Scotch and Irish immigrants, as well as a heavy cargo.

DALLAS. What happened when she was hit by the iceberg?

CAPTAIN. Well, there was panic among the passengers, sir, but the crew with one exception handled themselves well. . . . The second mate, seven of the crew, two passengers, and myself got into the small jollyboat, while the first mate, four seamen, and thirty-seven passengers got into the longboat. We in the jollyboat were picked up six days later.

DALLAS. How many male passengers were in the longboat?

CAPTAIN. Sixteen, sir.

DALLAS. Captain, you just stated that you in the jollyboat were picked up six days later.

CAPTAIN. Yes sir.

DALLAS. During those six days conditions were extremely difficult. There was the same storm, the same rough sea as that which the longboat met . . . and yet you brought your boat into safety with all aboard?

CAPTAIN. Yes, sir.

DALLAS. Now, Captain—had *you* instead of Holmes been in command of the longboat—would you have given the same order—in other words, would you have sacrificed the lives of any of the passengers, just to save your own life?

ARMSTRONG. Objection!

JUDGE *(quickly).* Overruled! The Court considers the captain an expert witness.

DALLAS. Well, Captain? Would you have committed manslaughter?

CAPTAIN. I . . . No, sir.

(Uproar in crowd.)

(Cut to: HOLMES *and* ARMSTRONG *for reaction. Both are deeply shaken. Uproar swells—)*

(Quick fade out.)

After Reading

Making Connections

1. Thus far in the play, what is your opinion of David Holmes?

2. What does the testimony of the various witnesses tell us about the character of Holmes? You can note your ideas on a chart like the one below.

Clues to Holmes's Character		
Witness	**Testimony**	**Trait Revealed**
Pat Askin	Holmes did not throw crew overboard because they were needed to row.	practical
Lorna Quinn		
Captain Tilton		

3. How would this play be different if it were produced for live theater instead of for TV?

4. Look back at your Writer's Notebook. How does the decision you faced compare with the choices Holmes made in the longboat?

Vocabulary Study

Choose the word from the list that answers the question "What Am I?"

warrant
manslaughter
prosecutor
testimony
overrule

1. You didn't mean to kill, or so you pled.
   But because of this, somebody is dead.

2. Police who forget me when searching for clues,
   Don't follow the law, and their case they may lose.

3. Success for me is proving guilt.
   When I win, defense lawyers wilt.

4. When you hear a judge say this word,
   It means, "Sorry, but your protest won't be heard."

5. Whenever a witness takes the stand,
   This is given, after raising the right hand.

Act Two

(Fade in: The courtroom. No time lapse. CAPTAIN TILTON *is in the witness stand. Uproar continues.* JUDGE *is rapping for order.)*

DALLAS. Your witness.

ARMSTRONG *(approaches stand).* Captain, in your testimony you stated that the crew with one exception[1] handled themselves well. Please explain the exception.

CAPTAIN. John Widdows, first mate . . .

ARMSTRONG *(surprised).* The first mate?

CAPTAIN. I would have taken him out of the longboat, but it was impossible due to the storm—the panic and all.

ARMSTRONG. Why?

CAPTAIN. He was a coward.

ARMSTRONG. And so Holmes took over. *(CAPTAIN looks down at his hands.)* Captain Tilton, how many people could the longboat normally hold?

CAPTAIN. She was built to hold twenty, sir.

ARMSTRONG. And how many were aboard?

CAPTAIN. Forty-two.

ARMSTRONG. Captain Tilton, what was the condition of the longboat?

CAPTAIN. I felt she was in grave[2] danger, sir . . .

ARMSTRONG. Captain, based upon your experience, how did you judge your chances of survival?

CAPTAIN. At the time? Not one chance in a hundred.

ARMSTRONG. Did the crew agree?

CAPTAIN. Yes, sir.

ARMSTRONG. When the jollyboat and the longboat were lowered into the water, where did you send Holmes?

CAPTAIN. To the jollyboat.

ARMSTRONG *(surprised).* The jollyboat? How did he get into the longboat? Did you order him to go?

CAPTAIN. No, sir. He offered.

ARMSTRONG. Do you mean he offered to go into the longboat, knowing that he was possibly going to his death?

CAPTAIN. Yes.

ARMSTRONG. Do you know why Holmes offered to go?

CAPTAIN. No, sir.

ARMSTRONG. Did you have a chance to watch the defendant at the time the *William Brown* was hit by the iceberg?

CAPTAIN. Yes, sir.

ARMSTRONG. How did he act?

CAPTAIN. His efforts to save the passengers were outstanding, sir. Without him I'm sure more lives would have been lost.

ARMSTRONG. Captain, is it possible that Holmes offered to go into the longboat because he thought he could save the boat?

DALLAS *(jumping up).* Objection! This is a guess, suggestion . . . It is not evidence . . .

JUDGE. Sustained.[3]

ARMSTRONG. All right . . . Captain, the longboat did survive . . . in spite of all the odds against her, and she was finally picked up. How do you account for this? Would you say it was due to Holmes' seamanship?

CAPTAIN. Well, Holmes is a fine seaman. It was very likely due to—

ARMSTRONG *(quickly).* Due to the fact that the boat was lightened?

DALLAS *(shouting).* Objection!

ARMSTRONG. I am only asking for the captain's expert opinion, Your Honor. It is important to this case to show why this longboat stayed afloat.

JUDGE. It is a reasonable question. Objection overruled.

---

1. **exception** (ek sep′shən), *n.* person or thing that is left out.
2. **grave** (grāv), *adj.* dangerous, threatening to life.
3. **sustain** (sə stān′), *v.* allow or approve. Here, the judge is approving the prosecution's objection.

ARMSTRONG. Captain, in your opinion, was the lightening of the longboat by about a ton important to its survival?

CAPTAIN. I cannot answer a question. . .

JUDGE. This is a court of law, not the deck of a ship. Answer the question!

CAPTAIN (*unwillingly*). Yes, it was possible . . .

ARMSTRONG. Thank you, Captain.

(*He turns away.* CAPTAIN *starts to leave stand.*)

DALLAS (*rising*). One moment, Captain . . . (CAPTAIN *remains in stand.*) Could the longboat have survived *without* Holmes? If he had *not* lightened the boat by throwing twelve human beings to their doom? Was there any chance at all, Captain?

CAPTAIN. There are always miracles, sir . . .

DALLAS. Will you answer my question, please! Yes, or no?

CAPTAIN. It was possible, sir . . .

DALLAS (*turning away*). No further questions.

(CAPTAIN *rises, steps out of stand.*)

JUDGE. Captain Tilton, you may leave the stand.

(CAPTAIN *hurries away.*)

DALLAS. Prosecution rests.

JUDGE. Is defense ready to present its care?

ARMSTRONG (*rising*). Yes, Your Honor.

JUDGE. Proceed.

(ARMSTRONG *nods to clerk.*)

CLERK (*calling out*). Mrs. Margaret Reston. Please take the stand.

(MRS. RESTON *rises, comes forward.*)

(*Cut to:* HOLMES *watching her.*)

(*Dissolve to: Witness stand.*)

ARMSTRONG. You have a daughter, Mrs. Reston?

MRS. RESTON. Aye . . . Isabel . . . She's nine years old.

ARMSTRONG. Mrs. Reston, will you please tell the Court what happened to your daughter on the night the *William Brown* was struck by the iceberg . . .

MRS. RESTON. Well, she was left behind on the sinking ship.

ARMSTRONG. What did you do when you discovered this?

MRS. RESTON. Well, I was like out of my mind . . . I cried out for help . . . And, praise God, one of the seamen, he climbed back on to the ship just as she was turning over and rescued my daughter. Oh, I'll never forget it. That seaman didn't even know me, yet he risked his life.

ARMSTRONG. Who was that seaman, Mrs. Reston?

MRS. RESTON. David Holmes.

ARMSTRONG. Thank you, Mrs. Reston. Your witness.

DALLAS. Mrs. Reston, I'm sure there was a great deal of bravery shown. The question is: Did he willingly and illegally take the life of a fellow creature? I therefore ask you: While you were in the longboat, did you see him cause any of the passengers to be thrown into the sea?

MRS. RESTON. I . . . I . . .

DALLAS (*angrily*). Well, Mrs. Reston?

MRS. RESTON. I . . . I . . . Please . . . Please don't ask me . . .

(*She sobs.* ARMSTRONG *is on his feet.*)

ARMSTRONG. Objection. Is it necessary to bully the witness, Your Honor?

DALLAS. Your Honor, I would like to reserve the right to reexamine this witness later when she is more capable of answering questions.

JUDGE. Permission granted.

DALLAS. No further questions.

(*He turns away.* MRS. RESTON *comes down from stand.*)

CLERK (*calling out*). Miss Patricia Askin.

(PAT *rises nervously, comes forward, takes stand.*)

ARMSTRONG. Miss Askin, when did you first meet the defendant?

PAT. On the *William Brown.* During the first week of the voyage.

ARMSTRONG. Can you describe the circumstances?

PAT. My brother introduced us.

ARMSTRONG. Oh, he knew Holmes then?

PAT. Well, he met him aboard ship, too.

ARMSTRONG. Did he and Holmes see a lot of each other during the voyage?

PAT. Well, yes . . .

ARMSTRONG. Your brother tilled the soil in Ireland, didn't he?

PAT. Yes. Farming was his whole life. His dream was to get some land in America.

ARMSTRONG. Looking back on it now, doesn't it seem unusual to you that your brother and Holmes should have struck up such a speedy friendship . . . considering the fact that Holmes is supposed to be such a difficult man to know, that he doesn't mix easily . . . and that *his* first love is the sea?

PAT. David Holmes' first love is *not* the sea.

ARMSTRONG. Oh, no, what is it then?

PAT. Farming.

ARMSTRONG. He told you that?

PAT. Yes . . . All he wanted was to own a farm.

ARMSTRONG. No one else on board ship was aware of Holmes' attitude toward farming. You must have been quite friendly for him to trust in you like that.

DALLAS. Objection! I can see no purpose in this line of questioning, Your Honor . . .

ARMSTRONG. If it please the Court, I am trying to show why Holmes offered to go into the longboat at the risk of his life. I believe he had good reason. To understand it, however, it is necessary to understand his relationship with Pat and Frank Askin.

JUDGE. Objection overruled.

ARMSTRONG. How friendly with the defendant were you, Miss Askin?

PAT. Well, we used to talk a lot . . . that's all . . .

ARMSTRONG (*quickly*). You liked Holmes, didn't you?

PAT. I was blind . . .

ARMSTRONG (*sharply*). Were you in love with him?

PAT (*bursting out*). I didn't say that!

ARMSTRONG. Were you?

PAT. Well . . . I . . . don't know . . .

ARMSTRONG. Was he in love with you?

PAT. I don't know! Ask him!

ARMSTRONG. He thought a great deal of your brother, didn't he?

PAT. I . . . don't know . . .

ARMSTRONG. Didn't his actions show it?

PAT. I don't know!

ARMSTRONG. Miss Askin, during the ocean crossing, did you or your brother make any plans for the future in which the defendant was included?

PAT (*her voice low, broken*). I made plans, hundreds of them . . . What good are they now?

ARMSTRONG. Miss Askin, on the morning of April 21st, the morning after that terrible night in which your brother and the others were thrown overboard . . . Did you think there was any chance of rescue?

PAT. No, I didn't care . . .

ARMSTRONG. Would you say that David Holmes—by his own efforts and at the risk of his own life—was responsible for saving that longboat?

DALLAS (*jumping up*). Objection!

JUDGE. Sustained!

ARMSTRONG (*turns away*). No further questions . . .

(JUDGE *looks at* DALLAS. DALLAS *shakes his head.*)

JUDGE. You may step down, Miss Askin.
(*She does.*)

ARMSTRONG (*rises*). I call the accused.

(HOLMES *stands.*)

This *Portrait of a Young Woman* was painted by Pierre-Auguste Renoir, probably in the 1880s. How would you describe her? ➤

JUDGE. Does the accused request that he be permitted to testify?

HOLMES *(after a pause).* I do.

JUDGE. You have the right to do so. You also have the right not to take the stand. If you don't testify, that fact won't be held against you. If you do, you may undergo a severe cross-examination.

HOLMES. I understand, Your Honor. (HOLMES *goes to stand.*)

CLERK. Raise your right hand. *(He does.)* Do you solemnly swear that the evidence you are about to give shall be the truth, the whole truth, and nothing but the truth, so help you God?

HOLMES. I do.*(He is seated.)*

ARMSTRONG. David Holmes, how long have you been a seaman?

HOLMES. Since I was fourteen.

ARMSTRONG. Do you like the sea?

HOLMES. I hate it!

ARMSTRONG. Yet you have been a seaman all your life. Why?

HOLMES. I had no other occupation . . . no money to buy a farm . . .

ARMSTRONG. Is that your ambition in life? To own a farm?

HOLMES. Yes.

ARMSTRONG. Have you ever worked on a farm?

HOLMES. My father's farm.

ARMSTRONG. Where was this?

HOLMES. New York State. Near Albany.

ARMSTRONG. Did you like the life, the work?

HOLMES. For me it's the only life.

ARMSTRONG. Why did you leave?

(A long silence. HOLMES *doesn't answer.)*
Did you hear my question?

HOLMES *(to* JUDGE*).* Can I leave the stand?

JUDGE. Why?

HOLMES. I'm not gonna answer these questions!
(Reaction from jury.)

ARMSTRONG. May it please the Court, I beg for an opportunity to speak to my client. A brief delay. Two minutes.

JUDGE *(raps gavel).* There will be a two-minute pause in the proceedings.

ARMSTRONG *(to* HOLMES *in a low tone, angry).* If you leave the stand now, I walk out.

HOLMES. Go ahead!

ARMSTRONG. Holmes, what are you afraid of? A little rough questioning? Or maybe you threw Frank Askin overboard because you were frightened!

HOLMES. No!

ARMSTRONG. Well, prove it then! If not to me, to Pat. Answer the questions I ask you before the whole world.

(*He walks away from stand.*)

JUDGE (*raps gavel*). Mr. Holmes, do you intend to submit to questioning, or do you wish to step down?

(*There is a pause.* HOLMES *looks across at* ARMSTRONG.)

You will not have another chance to change your mind.

HOLMES. I'll answer.

ARMSTRONG. Your father had a farm. Why did he leave it?

HOLMES. They took it away from my father.

ARMSTRONG. Why did they take it away?

HOLMES (*resisting*). I dunno! (*Then, after a silence, as* ARMSTRONG *watches him, with great effort*) He owed money on it . . . He never told anybody . . . He was too proud . . . When a man came to take it away, my father shot him dead. I saw it . . . Then more men came and took my father, and they got a rope . . . (*His voice chokes, remembering.*) I couldn't stand it . . . I ran away . . .

ARMSTRONG. Where did you go?

HOLMES. New York City.

ARMSTRONG. What did you do there?

HOLMES. I hung around the water front, slept in doorways . . . One night some men came. They beat me unconscious. When I came to I was in the hold of a ship.

ARMSTRONG. How old were you?

HOLMES. Fourteen.

ARMSTRONG. What happened on the ship? Did you become part of the crew?

HOLMES. The mate sent me up the mast the first day out. I couldn't stay there. I got

dizzy . . . I fell. Musta been laying on the deck for hours. But them seamen—they just laughed. We were at sea eighteen months and they kept laughing at me. I couldn't do anything right. I hated them. (HOLMES *is wound up, talking with difficulty.* ARMSTRONG *steps back, listens politely.*) I made up my mind then I'd show them. It took me a year, two, three . . . I don't know how long. I hated the sea, but I fought it . . . I fought *them* . . . I swore an oath to myself that I'd get my father's farm back. Someday I'd return. That's all I lived for . . . I saved my money . . .

ARMSTRONG. What money?

HOLMES. My pay . . .

ARMSTRONG. What is your pay?

HOLMES. Eleven dollars a month.

ARMSTRONG. You mean you thought you could save enough out of *that* to buy back your father's farm?

HOLMES (*triumphantly*). I did! The money is in a bank in New York City right now . . .

ARMSTRONG. How long did it take you to save that much money?

HOLMES. Thirteen years.

ARMSTRONG. Thirteen years? Is that why you never went ashore with your shipmates?

HOLMES. I couldn't afford to.

ARMSTRONG. Well, if you had all this money, why didn't you leave the sea?

HOLMES. After this trip I was gonna quit.

ARMSTRONG. David Holmes, during the last voyage of the *William Brown* you met Frank Askin. Explain the circumstances.

HOLMES. Well . . . I heard some of the passengers one night . . . I was on the lee'ard watch. Frank Askin was talking about farming . . . He seemed to know what he was talking about, and he spoke like it really meant something to him. So I sought him out and asked him questions.

ARMSTRONG. You became friends?

HOLMES. Yes.

ARMSTRONG. In the course of your friendship with him, did you often speak with his sister, Pat?

HOLMES. Yes.

ARMSTRONG. What was your relationship with her?

HOLMES. We got along.

ARMSTRONG. Is that all?

HOLMES. We got along!

ARMSTRONG. Did you ask her to marry you?

HOLMES. No!

ARMSTRONG. Did you *think* of asking her? (*As* HOLMES *hesitates*) Did you?

HOLMES. I thought of a lot of things!

ARMSTRONG (*reaches inside his jacket, takes out a letter, shows it to* JUDGE). Your Honor, this has been recorded as Exhibit B for the defense. (*Turns to* HOLMES) Have you ever seen this letter before? David Holmes, did you write this letter? Is this your signature? (*Shows it to him*) It was given to me by Mrs. Althea Temple, landlady of the boarding house you stayed in on your first night ashore. It is addressed to Miss Pat Askin. Did you write this letter? (HOLMES *nods— unable to speak.*) Please read it to the court. (*He hands it to him.*)

HOLMES (*choked*). I didn't know what I was doing when I wrote it . . . I . . .

ARMSTRONG. I understand that. Please read it.

HOLMES (*mumbling, hunched over, after a long pause, reading*). "Dear Pat. I am going to ship out on the first vessel. I have some money. I want you to have it. Don't think of it as mine. Think of it as Frank's, that he left it for you . . . Pat, I want you to know that I loved Frank, too. I know you hate me, but there was nothing else I could have done . . . I don't know if he told you . . ."

(HOLMES *breaks.* ARMSTRONG *takes letter, continues reading.*)

ARMSTRONG. "I don't know if he told you, but we planned to farm together, as partners. I had hoped you would be with us. I am going to ship out on the first vessel. David Holmes . . ."

(*Silence.* HOLMES *is sitting there, his head bowed.* ARMSTRONG *looks at him gently.*)

Thank you, David. Now can you tell the Court why you offered to go into the longboat?

HOLMES (*his voice low*). To save it. Everything I had was on that boat. (*Then crying out in pain*) I *had* to save it! *And I did!* I did what I could! God, what else could I do? But I had to do it. I *had* to. *I loved them.*

(*Fade out*)

Act Three

(*Fade in: The courtroom.* HOLMES *still on stand.* DALLAS, *having just completed his re-examination, returns to table.* JUDGE *looks across at* ARMSTRONG *questioningly.*)

DALLAS. No further questions.

ARMSTRONG. No re-examination. Your Honor, the defense rests.

JUDGE. You may leave the stand, Mr. Holmes.

(HOLMES *steps down. There is a pause as* JUDGE *checks his notes, looks up.*)

Gentlemen, are you ready for summation?

(*The* FOREMAN OF THE JURY *rises.*)

FOREMAN. Just a minute! Your Honor!

(*Commotion in the courtroom.*)

JUDGE (*pounding gavel*). What is the cause of this outburst?

FOREMAN. There's been a mistake in some of the testimony.

JUDGE (*stern*). Mistake?

FOREMAN. Your Honor, maybe if you could have a part of Captain Tilton's and Lorna Quinn's testimony that tells about the number of men thrown overboard. . .

JUDGE (*staring at* FOREMAN, *after a long pause, to* STENO[4]). You may do as he asks.

STENO (*flipping through notes, reads*). "Question by Mr. Dallas to Miss Quinn: From your observation, are you able to tell the Court how many men were thrown overboard during that terrible night? Answer: Well . . . there was Riley, Duffy, Charlie Conlin, Frank Askin. There were twelve."

FOREMAN (*quickly*). Now could you read the part where Captain Tilton tells how many men passengers were on the longboat.

STENO (*flipping through notes, reads*). "Question by Mr. Dallas: How many male passengers were in the longboat? Answer by Captain Tilton: Sixteen, sir."

FOREMAN. There you are, sir! Since there were sixteen men passengers originally in the longboat, and twelve were thrown overboard, *four* must have survived. But according to Miss Quinn's testimony, only *two* men passengers survived. She said they were not thrown overboard because their wives were present. Well, Your Honor, that leaves two men not accounted for. I'd like to know what happened to them!

DALLAS (*rises*). If the Court please, both the defense and the prosecution are aware that two of the male passengers are not accounted for . . . the fact is, no one seems to know what happened to them . . . and it has no bearing on this case.

JUDGE. Gentlemen, the question you must decide involves only one point: is the defendant, David Holmes, guilty of the manslaughter of Frank Askin? Only Frank Askin. None other.

FOREMAN. But Your Honor! How can we come to a decision unless the evidence regarding those two men . . .

JUDGE. You're out of order, sir.

VOICE. Your Honor! Your Honor!

(*Everyone turns. We see* MRS. RESTON *extremely upset, coming forward. Suddenly she halts, frightened*

at the JUDGE's *stern look.*)

Excuse me, sir . . . I . . . Perhaps I can explain . . . I mean, about those two men . . .

JUDGE (*severely*). Do you know what happened to them?

MRS. RESTON. Yes. Yes.

(*Reaction from the court.*)

ARMSTRONG (*rising*). Please the Court! I request that this witness be allowed to take the stand! I have no idea what she will say, but her evidence might have a bearing on this case . . .

JUDGE. Any objection, Mr. Dallas?

DALLAS. No objection.

JUDGE. Mrs. Reston, you may take the stand . . .

ARMSTRONG (*comes forward*). Now, Mrs. Reston, your testimony will bear directly upon the question which is disturbing the jury . . . It will include nothing else.

MRS. RESTON. Yes . . . (*glancing across at* HOLMES *with difficulty*). I didn't say before; I didn't want to hurt anybody—I—but it is eating away inside me, and I must get it out or I will never be able to look anyone in the face again. It is something I saw . . .

ARMSTRONG. What did you see?

MRS. RESTON. It was just before dawn (*Hit film*) after that awful night. I mean the night the men were cast over. The storm had quieted at that moment, and we were trying to rest when I noticed a movement beneath the canvas on the bottom of the boat . . . two of the men passengers were hidden. Their feet were sticking out. I realized that they had hidden during the night to escape being thrown over. Just then I saw that two of the seamen had also noticed them. They didn't know that I was

---

4. **steno,** stenographer, person who takes notes. Courtroom stenographers use a special machine to take down all that is said in court.

watching. They bent down and struck and struck, and then they threw the two unconscious[5] bodies overboard. *(film out)* They didn't have to do it. There was no need for it any more. Yet they threw those men over anyway. I sat there too frightened to say anything. *(She is sobbing.)*

ARMSTRONG. Thank you, Mrs. Reston.

(He crosses to defense table, sits beside HOLMES.)

HOLMES *(shocked deeply).* I didn't know . . . I didn't know . . .

JUDGE. Mr. Dallas?

DALLAS *(rises).* No questions, Mrs. Reston. *(She leaves stand.)* Your Honor, I waive my right to final summation and would like to address the jury now.

JUDGE. Mr. Armstrong?

ARMSTRONG. Agreed.

DALLAS. Please the Court, Gentlemen of the Jury. The act just described by Mrs. Reston is murder—vicious, stupid, unreasonable killing for its own sake. Why did those seamen cast two human beings into the sea, when any need for such an act was clearly at an end? Because they had been ordered to kill and because once they started to kill, all sense of right and wrong broke down. They couldn't stop. Who was responsible for it? The prisoner, David Holmes, for it was he alone who made the decision to take the lives of his fellow men! Did David Holmes have the right to give such an order? Did he have the right to place himself above his fellow men and select those who should die and those who should live? Does any man have that right? Gentlemen, this case does not deal only with the guilt or innocence of one man. In a sense we are all on that longboat, and at stake is a question of greatest importance. It is this: that *all* men's lives are sacred, of equal value . . . that in a crisis where some men have to die in order to save the rest, the decisions as to who will go cannot be left to one man but must be decided upon equally by all. Gentlemen, David Holmes not only committed manslaughter but he broke the law upon which our democracy rests! Therefore you have no choice . . . but to find the defendant GUILTY!

(Uproar of crowd. JUDGE pounds gavel, courtroom becomes quiet. He looks toward ARMSTRONG. ARMSTRONG rises slowly now, approaches JUDGE and jury.)

ARMSTRONG. Your Honor, Gentlemen of the Jury. As you sit here in the courtroom judging David Holmes . . . I ask you to look for one moment into your own hearts. What would *you* have done on the night of April 20th? A hundred leagues from land . . . A boat filled with water . . . Women screaming, knowing that at any moment all may die . . . What would you have done? Talked about the law and democratic rights? Taken a vote? As an experienced seaman, Holmes knew there was only one way to save the boat . . . a terrible way . . . lighten it. And that is what he did. Considering the women and children first, he gave the order to cast over the male passengers . . . among them a man he loved and admired . . . a man in whom all his hopes for the future were placed—indeed, the very person he had come to save. Can you imagine the dreams which will torment him for the rest of his life? *(quietly, but with rising strength).* Holmes acted out of duty, because it was his duty to save the boat, and out of love, because he believed human lives to be sacred . . . And so he saved most of the passengers. *(He turns suddenly to face the witnesses.)* Look at them. Would they be here today if it were not for Holmes? *(turns swiftly to jury)* How can you declare him guilty?

---

5. **unconscious** (un kon′shəs), *adj.* not able to feel or think, unaware.

(Fade out.)

(Fade in slowly: HOLMES *is standing before* JUDGE*.)*

CLERK. Gentlemen of the Jury, have you agreed upon a verdict?

FOREMAN. We have.

CLERK. And how do you find, gentlemen?

FOREMAN. We find the defendant . . . *guilty.* *(We hear a gasp, a cry from spectators.)* But we recommend mercy.

(We hear murmuring in courtroom.)

JUDGE *(pounds gavel).* Order. *(Murmuring dies out.)* David Holmes, you have broken the law upon which our civilization rests. You have taken into your hands a right which lies only in the people at large and in God himself. Although there are many circumstances which are of a sort to make you admired by this court and indeed by all humanity—the law demands punishment.

In accordance[6] with the jury's recommendation of mercy, I hereby sentence you, David Holmes, to six months in prison. Court dismissed!

(Noise in court. HOLMES *stands there swaying.)*

*(*ARMSTRONG *comes up to him, places his arm about his shoulder, leads him slowly down aisle toward doors in rear. As they reach doors, Pat approaches.)*

PAT *(choked, trembling).* David . . . I understand . . . *(They look at each other.)* Don't go back to sea . . . *(pause).* Buy the farm . . .

HOLMES *(speechless).* Yes . . .

*(*ARMSTRONG *takes him off.* PAT *continues to watch until the two men have disappeared down the corridor. Her eyes are wet.)*

(Slow fade.)

---

6. **accordance** (ə kôrd′ns), *n.* agreement.

After Reading

Acts Two and Three

Making Connections

1. What new things do we learn about David Holmes in these two acts that make him seem more three-dimensional?

2. Do you think Mrs. Reston's testimony about the two men who had been unaccounted for helped David Holmes's case? Why or why not?

3. If you were a member of the jury, would you have found Holmes guilty? Why or why not?

4. Do you think his six-month sentence was appropriate? Explain.

5. After the trial, Pat tells Holmes she understands and encourages him to buy the farm. Do you think that means she forgives him for her brother's death? Why or why not?

6. Do you think a person ever has the right to decide whether another human being lives or dies? Explain.

Literary Focus: Theme

Like any literary work, *Survival* has a **theme**—a central idea based on an observation of human behavior or experience. While the *subject* of a work is the topic on which an author has chosen to write, the *theme* makes a statement or expresses an opinion about that topic. For example, the topic of the play *Survival* is the main character's decision to sacrifice certain lives to save others; the theme is the deeply contested question of whether any human being has the right to make such a decision.

What does this play's theme say to you? See if you can state your answer in one sentence which includes any three of the words below.

survival *sacrifice* CONFLICT weak FIRM STRONG

Vocabulary Study

Choose the word from the list that answers the question "What Am I?"

exception
grave
sustain
unconscious
accordance

1. I'm here to back up whatever you say.
   I'm the word you need in a courtroom fray.

2. Play by the rules and stick with me.
   We'll do what's right and we'll all agree.

3. I'm different, unique, the one and only.
   While others mass together I stand lonely.

4. I'm a serious and sometimes deadly word.
   Danger is near when my name is heard.

5. I'm a word caught in nothingness—
   Just a blank trapped in thoughtlessness.

Expressing Your Ideas

Writing Choices

April 15, 1841 . . . A ship captain's job includes keeping a **daily log** during a voyage. Write several entries as if you were Captain Tilton recording events up to and including the iceberg accident.

A New Start Imagine Holmes on the day he is released from prison. Write a **description** of what happens. What does he do? Where does he go? How does he feel?

Dear Friend/Enemy What do you think Holmes wanted to say to Pat Askin at the end of the trial? With a partner, write **letters** that he and she send one another while he is serving his sentence.

Other Options

Casting Parts With a group, imagine being the producers of a new TV production of *Survival.* **Cast** the parts of Holmes, Pat Askin, Armstrong, Judge, and Dallas. Display your choices on a chart and explain your reasons.

His Eyes, Fixed . . . Did you picture the characters in your mind? Be a courtroom artist and **sketch** some of the important characters as you imagine they looked when testifying.

Hero or Killer? Mrs. Brannigan calls Holmes a hero. Dallas says he's a vicious murderer. With a partner, take the parts of Brannigan and Dallas and **debate** whether Holmes is a hero or a dangerous killer.

Before Reading

The Highwayman

by Alfred Noyes

Alfred Noyes
1880–1958

Growing up in England near a fir-tree forest he called the "bewitching woods," Noyes explored nature and read poetry, alone but not lonely. At the age of nine, he was inspired by the colors of a tiger moth to write his first poem. Several years later, nature caught his attention again. This time the "wind was a torrent of darkness," which became the first line of "The Highwayman." Of all the volumes of poetry and scholarly works Noyes produced in over fifty years as a writer and professor, he is remembered best for this ballad, the poem he wrote in two blustery days at the age of twenty-four.

Building Background

Travel Expenses "The Highwayman" is a **narrative** poem, meaning it tells a story. This poem mixes a tale of adventure and romance with factual history. The events are set in England about 250 years ago, during the reign of King George II. It was a time when lonely travelers in distant regions risked meeting the kind of company they did *not* want—highwaymen. A highwayman was a robber on horseback who thrived on adventure and "lightening the load" of the rich by taking their gold. Wherever the highwaymen went, the king's lawmen, known as redcoats, were sure to follow. What could happen if they met? Read on to find out.

Getting into the Poem

Writer's Notebook Alfred Noyes said his ideas for the events in the "The Highwayman" could be traced back to the colorful "two-penny" adventure stories he read as a boy. What kind of adventure captures your imagination? In your notebook, jot down your thoughts on what you consider material for a romantic adventure.

Reading Tip

Poetic Language This poem is a **romantic ballad,** it tells a story that is set in a distant time and place. The poet chose words for their meaning, sound, rhythm, and power to capture the spirit of the time. Are some of these words familiar to you?

bonny	pretty to see
breeches	short pants fastened below the knee
cobbles	rounded stones used for pavement
galleon	a large, tall ship used long ago
musket	a gun used before rifles were invented
ostler	one who cares for horses at an inn
plaiting	braiding
rapier	a long, light sword
stable-wicket	a small stable gate or window

The HIGHWAYMAN

by Alfred Noyes

Part One:

The wind was a torrent[1] of darkness among the gusty trees;
The moon was a ghostly galleon tossed upon cloudy seas;
The road was a ribbon of moonlight over the purple moor;
And the highwayman came riding—
5   Riding—riding—
The highwayman came riding, up to the old inn door.

He'd a French cocked hat on his forehead, a bunch of lace at his chin,
A coat of claret[2] velvet, and breeches of brown doeskin;
They fitted with never a wrinkle; his boots were up to the thigh!
10 And he rode with a jeweled twinkle,
     His pistol butts a-twinkle,
His rapier hilt a-twinkle, under the jeweled sky.

Over the cobbles he clattered and clashed in the dark inn yard;
And he tapped with his whip on the shutters, but all was locked and barred;
15 He whistled a tune to the window, and who should be waiting there
But the landlord's black-eyed daughter,
     Bess, the landlord's daughter,
Plaiting a dark red love knot into her long black hair.

And dark in the dark old inn yard a stable-wicket creaked
20 Where Tim the ostler listened; his face was white and peaked;
His eyes were hollows of madness, his hair like moldy hay,
But he loved the landlord's daughter,
     The landlord's red-lipped daughter;
Dumb as a dog he listened, and he heard the robber say—

---

1. **torrent** (tôr′ənt), *n.* a violent rushing stream.
2. **claret** (klar′ət), *adj.* dark purplish-red.

▲ An unknown eighteenth-century artist painted this scene of a highway robber and his victims. 🗣 What might lead someone to a **choice** that involves robbing others at the point of a pistol?

25 "One kiss, my bonny sweetheart; I'm after a prize tonight;
But I shall be back with yellow gold before the morning light;
Yet, if they press me sharply, and harry me through the day,
Then look for me by moonlight,
        Watch for me by moonlight,
30 I'll come to thee by moonlight, though hell should bar the way."

He rose upright in the stirrups; he scarce could reach her hand,
But she loosened her hair i' the casement![3] His face burned like a brand
As the black cascade[4] of perfume came tumbling over his breast;
And he kissed its waves in the moonlight
35   (Oh sweet black waves in the moonlight!);
Then he tugged at his rein in the moonlight, and galloped away to the West.

_____

3. **casement** (kās′mənt), *n.* a window that opens on hinges.
4. **cascade** (kas kād′), *n.* something that flows like a waterfall.

Part Two:

He did not come in the dawning[5]; he did not come at noon;
And out o' the tawny[6] sunset, before the rise o' the moon,
When the road <u>was a</u> gypsy's ribbon, looping the purple <u>moor</u>,[7]
40 A redcoat troop came marching—
     Marching—marching—
King George's men came marching, up to the old inn door.

They said no word to the landlord; they drank his ale instead;
But they gagged his daughter and bound her to the foot of her narrow bed;
45 Two of them knelt at her casement, with muskets at their side!
There was death at every window,
     And hell at one dark window,
For Bess could see, through her casement, the road that *he* would ride.

They had tied her up to attention, with many a <u>sniggering</u>[8] jest;
50 They had bound a musket beside her, with the <u>barrel</u> beneath her breast!
"Now keep good watch!" and they kissed her.
She heard the dead man say:
Look for me by moonlight,
     Watch for me by moonlight,
55 *I'll come to thee by moonlight, though hell should bar the way!*

She twisted her hands behind her, but all the knots held good!
She writhed her hands till her fingers were wet with sweat or blood!
They stretched and strained in the darkness, and the hours crawled by like years,
Till, now, on the stroke of midnight,
60   Cold on the stroke of midnight,
The tip of one finger touched it! The trigger at least was hers!

The tip of one finger touched it; she strove no more for the rest!
Up she stood, to attention, with the barrel beneath her breast.
She would not risk their hearing; she would not strive again;
65 For the road lay bare in the moonlight,
     Blank and bare in the moonlight,
And the blood of her veins in the moonlight throbbed to her love's <u>refrain</u>.[9]

Tlot-tlot; tlot-tlot! Had they heard it? The horse-hoofs ringing clear;
Tlot-tlot, tlot-tlot, in the distance! Were they deaf that they did not hear?

---

5. **in the dawning,** at sunrise.
6. tawny (tô′nē), *adj.* brownish-yellow.
7. moor (mu̇r), *n.* open land covered with small purple flowers.
8. snigger (snig′ər), *n.* mocking, disrespectful laughter.
9. refrain (ri frān′), *n.* repeated phrase of a verse.

70 Down the ribbon of moonlight, over the brow of the hill,
The highwayman came riding—
        Riding—riding—
The redcoats looked to their priming![10] She stood up, straight and still!

Tlot-tlot, in the frosty silence! *Tlot-tlot,* in the echoing night!
75 Nearer he came and nearer! Her face was like a light!
Her eyes grew wide for a moment; she drew one last deep breath;
Then her finger moved in the moonlight,
        Her musket shattered the moonlight,
Shattered her breast in the moonlight and warned him—with her death.

80 He turned; he spurred to the westward; he did not know who stood
Bowed, with her head o'er the musket, drenched with her own red blood!
Not till the dawn he heard it; and slowly blanched[11] to hear
How Bess, the landlord's daughter,
        The landlord's black-eyed daughter,
85 Had watched for her love in the moonlight, and died in the darkness there.

Back he spurred like a madman, shrieking a curse to the sky,
With the white road smoking behind him, and his rapier brandished[12] high!
Blood-red were his spurs i' the golden noon; wine-red was his velvet coat,
When they shot him down on the highway,
90   Down like a dog on the highway,
And he lay in his blood on the highway, with the bunch of lace at his throat.

And still of a winter's night, they say, when the wind is in the trees,
When the moon is a ghostly galleon tossed upon cloudy seas,
When the road is a ribbon of moonlight over the purple moor,
95 *A highwayman comes riding—*
        Riding—riding—
A highwayman comes riding, up to the old inn door.

Over the cobbles he clatters and clangs in the dark inn yard;
And he taps with his whip on the shutters, but all is locked and barred;
100 *He whistles a tune to the window, and who should be waiting there*
But the landlord's black-eyed daughter,
        Bess, the landlord's daughter,
Plaiting a dark red love knot into her long black hair.

---

10. **priming** (prī′ming), powder or other material used to set fire to an explosive.
11. blanch (blanch), *v.* become pale, turn white.
12. brandish (bran′dish), *v.* wave or shake in a threatening way.

After Reading

Making Connections

1. Were you surprised by the events in this poem? Explain.

2. Reflect on what you wrote in your notebook before reading. Is this poem your idea of a romantic adventure? Why or why not?

3. Who would you say this poem is really about—the highwayman or Bess? Explain.

4. How does this ballad illustrate the theme "Standing Your Ground"?

5. Find some examples of **repetition** in this poem. What effect do they have? You can organize your notes on a chart like this:

Repetitions	Effects
riding, riding, riding	hurry, determination

6. 🐾 Bess's predicament is unlikely in real life, but it does show how intense emotional stress can affect the **choice** a person makes. What advice would you give to someone making a critical decision in life?

Literary Focus: Sound Devices

Imagine the chase scene in an adventure movie without sound. No music. No squealing brakes. No pounding hoofs. No life! Just as the drama in a film is heightened with music and sound, poetry brings a scene to life with **sound devices**—words and techniques that play on your imagination's own "stereo system." This ballad is a classic example of the "high-amp" effects a writer can use. Look for examples of these sound devices in "The Highwayman."

Rhyme:	two or more words that sound alike (*gold, bold, told*)
Rhythm:	the beat, or repeated pattern of accented sounds (*clip-**clop**, clip-**clop***)
Onomatopoeia:	words that sound like what they mean (*click, hiss, thud*)
Alliteration:	repetition of consonant sounds at the beginning or inside of words (*plodding along muddy roads with heavy heart*)

Which of these sound effects dramatize the scene of Bess's fatal warning in lines 74–79?

Vocabulary Study

Each of the following words is paired with a synonym or an antonym. On a piece of paper, write *S* for synonym or *A* for antonym.

torrent
claret
casement
cascade
tawny
moor
snigger
refrain
blanch
brandish

1. brandish - threaten
2. casement - window
3. cascade - droplet
4. claret - red
5. moor - mall
6. refrain - repetition
7. snigger - sulk
8. blanch - blush
9. torrent - trickle
10. tawny - golden

Expressing Your Ideas

Writing Choices

R.I.P. Bess and her highwayman, like Romeo and Juliet, died for the sake of love. Write **epitaphs** that might be inscribed on headstones for this doomed, devoted pair.

In Other Words There's always more than one way to say something—your way, for example. **Paraphrase** lines 25 through 30 of "The Highwayman." Use different words to express the lines.

To the Rescue! "The pen is mightier than the sword." You can save Bess and her highwayman with your pen. Just **rewrite** a few stanzas in the style of Alfred Noyes to help the troubled pair escape alive.

Other Options

Clattering Cobblestones! The dramatic emotion of this poem has inspired humorous versions that made even the poet laugh. With a group, perform "The Highwayman" as a **melodrama**—a play that exaggerates emotions for comic effect.

All Together The most exciting way to read "The Highwayman" is aloud. With a small group, perform a **choral reading** of the poem. Use materials on hand and your imagination to create sound effects.

Yee Hah! Work with a partner to turn "The Highwayman" into a **country-western song** to perform for the class. You can set your lyrics to a familiar tune or make up your own.

Before Reading

Mother to Son by Langston Hughes
Women by Alice Walker

Langston Hughes
1902–1967

Hughes learned about standing his ground from the women who raised him. He spent much of his boyhood in Kansas with his grandmother, the first black woman to attend Oberlin College in Ohio. In eighth grade, Hughes wrote a sixteen-stanza graduation poem—the first he ever wrote.

Alice Walker
born 1944

Alice Walker's mother worked from sunup to sundown to raise her eight children. Reading was a vital part of Walker's life. When Walker was twenty-two she met Hughes. His kindness inspired her to write a children's book about him.

Building Background

Job Wanted People usually look for a job to make money. There is one job, however, that many people want more than anything in the world, which *costs* money. Working conditions include 24-hour workdays, 7-day workweeks, no time off, and invisible benefits (occasional moments of extreme joy and the highest possible satisfaction for good work). The job also involves a substantial risk—outcome not guaranteed. Have you guessed what the job is? Raising a child!

Getting into the Poems

Discussion As you no doubt realize, being a good parent takes a lot more than money. In a small group, discuss what you consider the most important thing a parent can give a child. Have a volunteer write some of the ideas you and your classmates come up with on the board.

Reading Tip

A Common Theme These poems are about mothers who have very little money but give their children what money can't buy. As you read, compare how the women portrayed in these poems achieve their purpose as parents.

Mother to Son

Langston Hughes

Well, son, I'll tell you:
Life for me ain't been no crystal stair.
It's had tacks in it,
And splinters,
5 And boards torn up,
And places with no carpet on the floor—
Bare.
But all the time
I'se been a-climbin' on,
10 And reachin' landin's,
And turnin' corners,
And sometimes goin' in the dark
Where there ain't been no light.
So boy, don't you turn back.
15 Don't you set down on the steps
'Cause you finds it's kinder hard.
Don't you fall now—
For I'se still goin', honey,
I'se still climbin',
20 And life for me ain't been no crystal stair.

"Industries attempted to board their labor in quarters that were oftentimes very unhealthy. Labor camps were numerous." Panel #46 from the Migration Series, 1940-41. Text and title revised by the artist, 1993

▲ Jacob Lawrence painted this scene as part of "The Migration Series," works of art that depict the African American experience. Do you think these stairs speak of hope or despair?

▲ *Women of the Setting Sun* was painted by Xavier Jones. Compare the postures of these women to the woman on page 631.

Women

Alice Walker

They were women then
My mama's generation
Husky of voice—Stout of
Step
5 With fists as well as
Hands
How they battered down
Doors
And ironed
10 Starched white
Shirts
How they led
Armies
Headragged Generals
15 Across mined
Fields
Booby-trapped
Ditches
To discover books
20 Desks
A place for us
How they knew what we
Must know
Without knowing a page
25 Of it
Themselves.

After Reading

Making Connections

1. Which poem has a stronger message for you? Explain.

2. Look back at your discussion notes. Compare your thoughts on what good parents give their children with what the women in these poems gave their children.

3. Point out some images in each poem and their effects. Make a comparison of the **imagery** used in the two poems. You can note your examples and ideas on a chart like this:

Poem	Images	Effects
"Mother to Son"		
"Women"		
Comparison		

4. There is a saying, "When the going gets tough, the tough get going." How might the women described in these poems respond to that saying? Find examples in the poems to support your answer.

5. The women in the poems stood their ground in different ways. Which do you see as more effective or realistic?

6. The women in the poems set examples for their children. What kinds of things do you think parents should do to set good examples?

Literary Focus: Word Choice

What's in a Word? Here's what a poet might say: A word is made up of sound + rhythm + feeling + **connotation**, a word's own special meanings. For example, dictionary definitions of the word *stout* include *fat, large, strongly built, firm, strong, brave, bold,* and *stubborn.*

Connotation includes the attitudes that surround a word in a certain time, place, and situation. For instance, the word *stout* is sometimes used as a dainty way of saying *overweight*. What do you think *stout* means in the poem "Women"? What do the sound and rhythm of *stout* add to its meaning? Try walking across the room in the way Alice Walker means by the phrase "stout of step." How does it feel?

Vocabulary Study

Word roots *generate* or "sprout" more words. The word *generation,* for example, comes from the Latin root *genus,* meaning any group of similar things. Create a word web around *generation,* adding four related words with their meanings. Here's how your web may look when you begin:

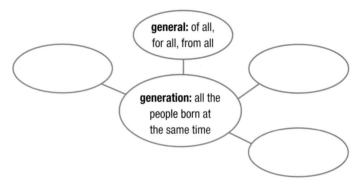

general: of all, for all, from all

generation: all the people born at the same time

Expressing Your Ideas ——

Writing Choices

Looking Back Imagine you are an adult looking back on your life. Write a **poem** for your child in which you pass on an important observation you have made about life.

Signed, Wimpy Imagine you write the advice column for a teen magazine. Make up a **letter** from a reader whose problem has to do with not standing his or her ground. Then answer the letter with your advice.

Holding the Line Write an **essay** about what you have learned about standing your ground. Include examples to support your ideas. Some questions to consider: When is standing your ground important? Why is it important? How do you do it?

Other Options

Close-ups The images in these poems are pictures for the mind's eye. Take some **photographs** that represent images in the poems. You can arrange them with captions from the poems, such as "Boards Torn Up" and "Starched White Shirts."

A Confrontation Look at the fifteenth-century tile at the left. Imagine you are the peasant, about to turn and see the soldier on horseback. With a partner, create and perform the **dialogue** that might occur.

Before Reading

Gentleman of Rio en Medio

by Juan A. A. Sedillo

Juan A. A. Sedillo
1902–1982

Born in Mexico, Juan A. A. Sedillo was descended from the earliest Spanish settlers of the southwestern United States and Mexico. He lived in both countries and worked as a lawyer and judge in the city of Santa Fe. He shared his experiences by writing newspaper columns and stories. "Gentleman of Rio en Medio" is based on an incident from his legal career.

Building Background

A New Idea on Old Ground The idea of *owning* land is new in America. It arrived just a little over 500 years ago with the European explorers. They brought their tradition of claiming land, including what was *on* it and *in* it. To the people whose ancestors had been living on this continent for thousands of years, owning land was a strange idea. Stranger still was the idea of owning nature. They viewed everything that grows on earth—including themselves—as part of nature, which no one can own.

Today, we consider it a basic right to own a piece of land and all that lies within its borders. Yet there are descendants of older American cultures who feel the "right" to own nature makes no more sense than owning a rainbow.

Getting into the Story

Writer's Notebook Does the place you call home sometimes feel like it's part of you? Can you imagine it belonging to someone else? If you had to leave it, how would you feel? In your notebook, begin writing with one of these sentences:

- If I were to leave my home, I would feel. . . .
- When I left the place that was my home, I felt. . . .

Reading Tip

Details of Characterization In a short story, a writer must use every opportunity to show what a character is like. Revealing clues can be a simple gesture, a way of walking or standing, or certain articles of clothing. Every detail is like the stroke of an artist's brush, painting a picture for you to complete in your mind. As you read, notice the details that create the character of Don Anselmo, the gentleman of Rio en Medio.

GENTLEMAN OF RIO EN MEDIO

Juan A. A. Sedillo

It took months of negotiation[1] to come to an understanding with the old man. He was in no hurry. What he had the most of was time. He lived up in Rio en Medio, where his people had been for hundreds of years. He tilled[2] the same land they had tilled. His house was small and wretched,[3] but quaint.[4] The little creek ran through his land. His orchard was gnarled[5] and beautiful.

The day of the sale he came into the office. His coat was old, green and faded. I thought of Senator Catron, who had been such a power with these people up there in the mountains. Perhaps it was one of his old Prince Alberts.[6] He also wore gloves. They were old and torn and his finger tips showed through them. He carried a cane, but it was only the skeleton of a worn out umbrella. Behind him walked one of his innumerable[7] kin—a dark young man with eyes like a gazelle.

The old man bowed to all of us in the room. Then he removed his hat and gloves, slowly and carefully. Chaplin[8] once did that in a picture, in a bank—he was the janitor. Then he handed his things to the boy, who stood obediently behind the old man's chair.

There was a great deal of conversation, about rain and about his family. He was very proud of his large family. Finally we got down to business. Yes, he would sell, as he had agreed, for twelve hundred dollars, in cash. We would buy, and the money was ready. "Don[9] Anselmo," I said to him in Spanish, "We have made a discovery. You remember that we sent that surveyor,[10] that engineer, up there to survey your land so as to make the deed. Well, he finds that you own more than eight acres. He tells us that your land extends across the river and that you own almost twice as much as you thought." He didn't know that.

---

1. **negotiation** (ni gō′shē ā′shən), *n.* talking over terms.
2. **till** (til), *v.* to plow or cultivate land
3. **wretched** (rech′id), *adj.* miserable or very unsatisfactory.
4. **quaint** (kwānt), *adj.* odd in a pleasing way.
5. **gnarled** (närld), *adj.* twisted and knotted.
6. **Prince Alberts,** a long, double-breasted coat (perhaps a hand-me-down from Senator Catron).
7. **innumerable** (i nü′mər ə bəl), *adj.* very many; too many to count.
8. **Chaplin,** the silent-film actor Charlie Chaplin.
9. **Don,** Spanish word for Mr.
10. **surveyor** (sər vā′ər), *n.* a person who examines land.

R. Douglas Wiggins painted *Morning Star Over Cerro Gordo.* How would you describe the houses and trees in this painting?

"And now, Don Anselmo," I added, "These Americans are *buena gente,* they are good people, and they are willing to pay you for the additional land as well, at the same rate per acre, so that instead of twelve hundred dollars you will get almost twice as much, and the money is here for you."

The old man hung his head for a moment in thought. Then he stood up and stared at me. "Friend," he said, "I do not like to have you speak to me in that manner." I kept still and let him have his say. "I know these Americans are good people, and that is why I have agreed to sell to them. But I do not care to be insulted. I have agreed to sell my house and land for twelve hundred dollars and that is the price."

I argued with him but it was useless. Finally he signed the deed and took the money but refused to take more than the amount agreed upon. Then he shook hands all around, put on his ragged gloves, took his stick and walked out with the boy behind him.

A month later my friends had moved into Rio en Medio. They had replastered the old adobe house, pruned the trees, patched the fence, and moved in for the summer. One day they came back to the office to complain. The children of the village were overrunning their property. They came every day and played under the trees, built little play fences around them, and took blossoms. When they were spoken to they only laughed and talked back good-naturedly in Spanish.

"I SOLD THEM MY PROPERTY BECAUSE I KNEW THEY WERE GOOD PEOPLE, BUT I DID NOT SELL THEM THE TREES. . . ."

I sent a messenger up to the mountains for Don Anselmo. It took a week to arrange another meeting. When he arrived he repeated his previous preliminary[11] performance. He wore the same faded cutaway, carried the same stick and was accompanied by the boy again. He shook hands all around, sat down with the boy behind his chair, and talked about the weather. Finally I broached[12] the subject. "Don Anselmo, about the ranch you sold to these people. They are good people and want to be your friends and neighbors always. When you sold to them you signed a document, a deed, and in that deed you agreed to several things. One thing was that they were to have the complete possession of the property. Now, Don Anselmo, it seems that every day the children of the village overrun the orchard and spend most of their time there. We would like to know if you, as the most respected man in the village, could not stop them from doing so in order that these people may enjoy their new home more in peace."

Don Anselmo stood up. "We have all learned to love these Americans," he said, "Because they are good people and good neighbors. I sold them my property because I knew they were good people, but I did not sell them the trees in the orchard."

This was bad. "Don Anselmo," I pleaded, "When one signs a deed and sells real property one sells also everything that grows on the land, and those trees, every one of them, are on the land and inside the boundaries of what you sold."

"Yes, I admit that," he said. "You know," he added, "I am the oldest man in the village. Almost everyone there is my relative and all the children of Rio en Medio are my sobrinos and nietos,[13] my descendants.[14] Every time a child has been born in Rio en Medio since I took possession of the house from my mother I have planted a tree for that child. The trees in that orchard are not mine, Señor,[15] they belong to the children of the village. Every person in Rio en Medio born since the railroad came to Santa Fé owns a tree in that orchard. I did not sell the trees because I could not. They are not mine."

There was nothing we could do. Legally we owned the trees but the old man had been so generous, refusing what amounted to a fortune for him. It took most of the following winter to buy the trees, individually, from the descendants of Don Anselmo in the valley of Rio en Medio.

---

11. preliminary (pri lim′ə ner′ē), *adj.* leading up to the main business.
12. broach (brōch), *v.* begin to speak about.
13. sobrinos (sō brē′ nōs) and nietos (nyā′tōs), sobrinos are nephews and nieces; nietos are children and grandchildren.
14. descendant (di sen′dənt), *n.* person born to a certain family—children, grandchildren, nieces, nephews, and so on.
15. Señor (sā nyôr′), Spanish word for sir or gentleman.

After Reading

Making Connections

1. If you were one of Don Anselmo's descendants, would you sell your tree to the new owners? Why or why not?

2. If you could visit with Don Anselmo, what would you like to talk about?

3. What **character traits** of Don Anselmo would you like to have?

4. How is the title "Gentleman of Rio en Medio" suitable for this story?

5. What word would you choose to describe the way Don Anselmo stood his ground? What part of the story illustrates your word?

6. How do you think Don Anselmo's background affects the **choices** he makes regarding his property?

7. Do you think people transacting a land deal today would ever agree to Don Anselmo's terms? Why or why not?

Literary Focus: Characterization

Picture in your mind a hero who battles forces that threaten to destroy his people's culture. What image comes to mind? Is it a frail old man who uses a worn-out umbrella for a cane? That's one of the ways the author **characterizes,** or portrays, Don Anselmo. How do the details of Don Anselmo's character make him a hero who stands his ground?

Go back to the story for clues to Don Anselmo's character. A chart like this can help you organize and summarize your findings:

The Makings of a Hero		
Appearance	**Actions**	**Speech**
old, uses a worn-out umbrella for a cane		
Summary		

Vocabulary Study

On your paper write the letter of the correct ending.

negotiation
till
wretched
quaint
gnarled
innumerable
surveyor
preliminary
broach
descendant

1. When you **broach** a subject, you intend to **a.** discuss something. **b.** avoid conversation. **c.** stop discussion.

2. Your **descendant** is most likely to **a.** pass on physical traits to you. **b.** marry your grandchild. **c.** inherit your possessions.

3. A **gnarled** tree stands **a.** straight and tall. **b.** crooked and bent. **c.** near a waterfall.

4. If you had **innumerable** plans, your mind would be **a.** busy. **b.** blank. **c.** inactive.

5. A **negotiation** will most likely lead to **a.** a misunderstanding. **b.** a standoff. **c.** an agreement.

6. During **preliminary** meetings you would **a.** complete your assignment. **b.** organize your notes. **c.** make closing comments.

7. When visiting a **quaint** village you might say, **a.** "How charming!" **b.** "This place is scary!" **c.** "What will science do next?"

8. Ask the advice of a **surveyor** before you **a.** build a fence. **b.** go to sea in a small boat. **c.** buy expensive gems.

9. When it's time to **till** your land, the most useful item is **a.** a deep well. **b.** a silo to hold grain. **c.** a tractor.

10. You could expect to feel **wretched** if you **a.** stood your ground and won. **b.** gave in to the opposition. **c.** made a fair deal.

Expressing Your Ideas

Writing Choices

Family Trees With a small group, imagine you are the new owners of Don Anselmo's land. Compose a **form letter** to the tree owners asking to purchase their trees. Each of you then answers the letter as one of the owners, explaining why you will or won't sell your tree.

Leaving Home How do you think Don Anselmo felt about selling his home? Write a **journal entry** he might have made, describing his feelings about leaving. Draw on the ideas you recorded in your notebook.

Other Options

Celebrate! With several classmates, imagine you are villagers in Rio en Medio. Plan a **victory party** for Don Anselmo. Each of you should honor him with a suitable gift and a short speech about him.

Images of Don Anselmo's Life Create a **collage** representing Don Anselmo's life, home, and victory. Things you may want to represent include his homestead and orchard, his descendants, the village, his character, and his new home.

Before Reading

The Rabbit and the Tiger

a Puerto Rican folk tale adapted by Ricardo E. Alegría

Ricardo E. Alegría
born 1921

With training in history, archaeology, and anthropology, Ricardo Alegría truly understands the mixed heritage of Puerto Rico. He has published books on Native Americans of Puerto Rico, the Spanish conquest and colonization of Puerto Rico, and the archaeology of the West Indies. He has collected Puerto Rican folk tales and adapted them for children. About these folk tales he wrote, "they have been handed from father to son over four centuries. Some of these traditional stories originated in the Orient and were carried to Spain by the Arabs. . . . Others were brought from West Africa by the Negro slaves. After countless retellings they have been adapted to the geography and cultural environment of Puerto Rico."

Building Background

Tricksters at Large Puerto Rican culture includes a rich blend of Native American, Spanish, and West African elements. For example, the trickster, a character who plays practical jokes on others, is common in Native American and West African folk tales. The tiger, a main character in "The Rabbit and the Tiger," is not native to Puerto Rico, but to Africa. Many elements of plot in some Puerto Rican folk tales are very similar to elements in the Ananzi tales from West Africa, in which a clever spider tricks a leopard and other animals.

Getting into the Story

Discussion One of the animals in "The Rabbit and the Tiger" is a trickster. Predict which animal mentioned in the title you think it might be. Discuss the kinds of tricks this animal might play on the other and why. Write your predictions on the board.

Reading Tip

Causes and Effects Tricks are an important part of "The Rabbit and the Tiger." Each trick has a series of different causes and/or effects. Make a diagram like one of the ones below. As you read, think about the causes and effects of each of the different tricks. After reading, go back and read one trick again to identify causes and effects. Create a new diagram to show how the trick works.

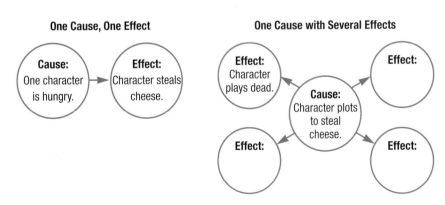

One Cause, One Effect

Cause: One character is hungry. → **Effect:** Character steals cheese.

One Cause with Several Effects

Cause: Character plots to steal cheese.

Effect: Character plays dead.

Effect:

Effect:

Effect:

The Rabbit

(El Conejo y el Tigre)

Once upon a time there were two great friends— a rabbit and a tiger. The rabbit, who was much quicker than the tiger, was forever playing tricks upon his friend; and the tiger was forever chasing the rabbit to eat him. So, they were great friends.

One day, when the rabbit had nothing to eat, he remembered that this was the day when his friend the tiger took the cheese he had made to the market. The rabbit was very hungry and decided he would eat the tiger's cheese. He went to the road he knew the tiger would take and stretched out upon it as though he were dead. The tiger came along and saw him.

"A dead rabbit. I'll pick it up to eat on my way back," he said, and went on to the market. As soon as he had gone, the rabbit jumped up and hurried by way of a shortcut he knew to a place farther along the road. There he lay down again and pretended to be dead. When the tiger came to the spot and saw the rabbit lying there, he said, "Another dead rabbit! With this and the first one I saw, I'll have a fine meal!" Although his appetite increased with the thought of the rabbit dish he would make, the tiger decided to go on to the market with his cheese. As soon as he had passed, the rabbit jumped off a ledge and landed below, just in the turning of the road that the tiger would have to pass. Again he stretched out and pretended to be dead. The tiger came along dreaming of

and the Tiger

adapted by Ricardo E. Alegría

the fine rabbit stew he was going to enjoy, and when he saw the rabbit on the road—it was too much!

"I'm going to eat these rabbits now!" he exclaimed. He threw down his cheeses and hurried back to collect the other two he had seen.

As soon as he left, the rabbit jumped up, collected the cheeses, and ran off with them to hide from the tiger and eat in peace.

The tiger searched and searched, but he did not find a single dead rabbit; but he did begin to suspect his friend of playing tricks. He lost no time in hurrying back to rescue his cheeses. But he found neither rabbit nor cheeses. He was furious and set out to find the rabbit so that he could kill and eat him!

After looking a long time, the tiger saw the rabbit on the side of a hill. The rabbit had eaten all the cheeses and was resting.

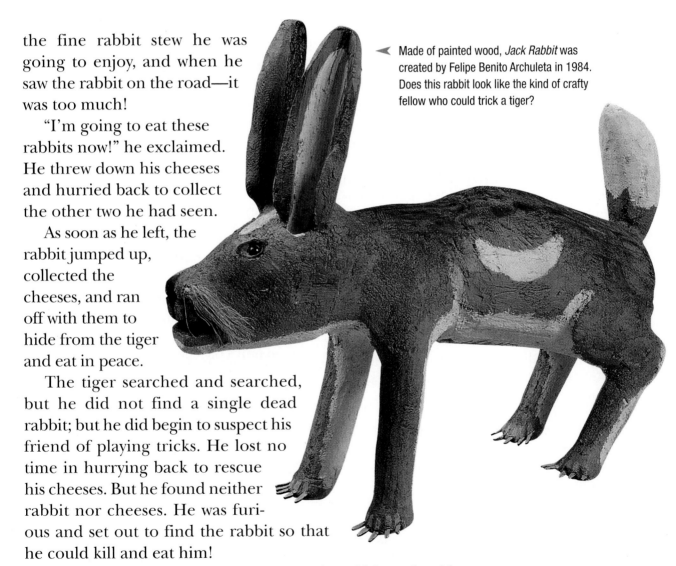

◄ Made of painted wood, *Jack Rabbit* was created by Felipe Benito Archuleta in 1984. Does this rabbit look like the kind of crafty fellow who could trick a tiger?

The Rabbit and the Tiger   **659**

When he saw the tiger coming, he knew there was no escape. He got up and braced himself against a great rock, as though he were holding it on the hill.

The tiger came, ready to eat him, but when he saw that the rabbit did not run away but stood fast against the rock, he asked, "My friend, what is the matter? Why are you huddled against that rock?"

The rabbit, who was expecting this question, answered, "Aye, my friend, help me hold this rock! It is rolling down, and if it falls all the way, the world will end!"

The tiger grew very frightened at these words and braced himself against the rock. The rabbit told him to hold fast while he went for help. He said that he would return with other animals, and he ran off, laughing at the tiger. The tiger stayed there many hours until his strength gave out and he let go. To his surprise, nothing happened; the stone didn't move. When he realized that he had been fooled again by his friend the rabbit, he was furious and set off to find him.

He knew how quick the rabbit was and decided to see if he could catch his sly friend with one of his own tricks. He hid in the rabbit's house, hoping to catch him and eat him when he came home.

But the rabbit was suspicious[1] and ready for him. As he drew near his house, he called out, "My house, my house, how are things in my house?"

The tiger heard him but kept still.

Then the rabbit said, in a louder voice, "My goodness! Something is the matter with my house; someone must be in it, or it would answer me," and he called again.

"My house, my house, how are things in my house?"

The tiger, who was stupid enough to believe all that he heard, tried to disguise his voice and answered, "Come in, rabbit, come in. No one is here."

The rabbit recognized the tiger's voice, laughed, and said, "Houses don't talk, stupid!" Then he ran as fast as he could and hid in the woods. The tiger saw that he had been stupid in telling the rabbit he wasn't there, and, angrier than ever, he swore he'd get even with his friend.

One day when the rabbit was fishing in the river, the tiger came along and said, "You won't escape me this time."

The rabbit smiled and answered, "Ah, my friend, you have come at a bad time. I was about to pull a big cheese out of the river, and now you're going to eat me."

The tiger, who was a glutton,[2] no sooner heard the word "cheese" than his mouth began to water, and he asked the rabbit where it was. The rabbit pointed to a great bundle lying on the river bed. The tiger said he would get it and eat it with the rabbit stew he was going to have. The rabbit said that that was a

---

1. **suspicious** (sə spish′əs), *adj.* suspecting something; imagining something might occur.
2. **glutton** (glut′n), *n.* a greedy eater; someone who eats too much.

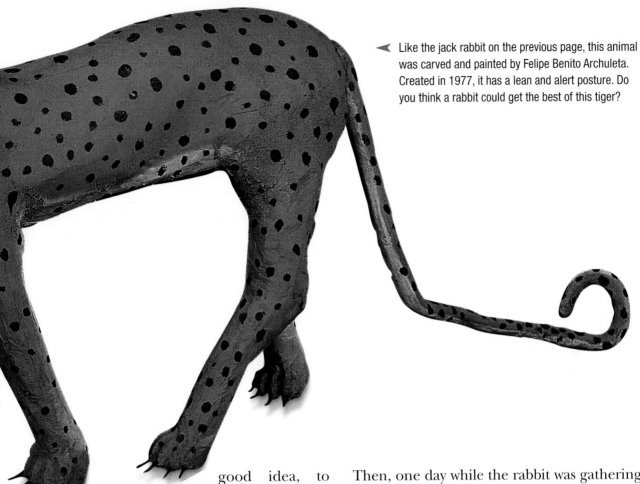

Like the jack rabbit on the previous page, this animal was carved and painted by Felipe Benito Archuleta. Created in 1977, it has a lean and alert posture. Do you think a rabbit could get the best of this tiger?

good idea, to jump in and get the cheese, but in order to reach the bottom of the river, he'd better tie himself to a big stone. So the tiger, thinking only of the cheese he was going to get, tied a big stone to his tail and jumped into the river. When he reached the bottom, he found that the rabbit had fooled him again.

What he had seen and believed to be cheese was nothing but the reflection of the moon on the water. The rabbit stood on the river bank laughing uproariously[3] at the stupidity of his friend who by now was on the point of drowning. He barely managed to pull himself out of the river, and by then the rabbit was nowhere to be seen.

Some time passed, and the tiger continued to be annoyed with the rabbit. He looked everywhere for him, to kill him and eat him.

Then, one day while the rabbit was gathering vines with which to make ropes, the tiger came along and said, "Now, nothing can save you, my friend. I'm going to eat you this time!"

The rabbit saw that he was lost; the tiger was too near; there was no escape, so he said, "Ah, my friend, what a shame you chose today for eating me. You see, there is a great storm approaching, and I am gathering vines to tie myself down so that the wind won't blow me away."

The tiger knew what a hurricane[4] could do and became frightened. He cried to the rabbit, "Give me those vines! Tie me tightly to the tree so that I won't be blown away!"

---

3. **uproariously** (up rôr′ē əs lē), *adv.* loudly and with great humor.
4. **hurricane** (hėr′ə kān), *n.* storm with violent wind and, usually very heavy rain. The wind in a hurricane blows with a speed above 75 (121 kilometers) miles per hour.

The rabbit used all the vines and tied the tiger to the tree, and when he was sure he could not get loose, he said to him, "My friend, here comes the hurricane!" and, picking up a switch, he began beating the tiger, who shouted and swore that he was being killed. He also knew he was being made a fool of! The rabbit went off and left the tiger abandoned there for several days until he managed to get free himself. He reached home half dead.

The rabbit boasted to everyone about what he had done, and he made a bet that he could ride the tiger through the streets of the town as though he were a horse.

First he sent a letter to the tiger saying that he was sick and most sorry and apologetic[5] for all the tricks he had played and that he wanted the tiger to come and eat him. When the tiger received the letter, he thought that at last his problems were ended, and he went to his friend's house. When the rabbit saw him coming, he got in bed and pretended to be sick. "Aye, my friend!" He sighed as the tiger leaned over him. "I'm so sick! Please eat me so that I can repay you for all the grief I have caused."

The tiger said that was all very well, but he could not eat a sick rabbit because he might be poisoned or the disease might be contagious.[6]

Then the rabbit, who knew this was how the tiger would feel, said, "My friend, carry me to your house, and you can eat me when I am better." The tiger said this was a good idea and would the rabbit please get up and come home with him. The rabbit made an effort to

rise, then fell back and sighed. "Aye, my friend, I can't walk. You'll have to carry me on your back." The tiger said that was fine and to get on his back. So the rabbit climbed up, but he fell off again, saying, "Aye, my friend, if I ride on your back, I'll need a saddle." The tiger said that was all right, so the rabbit put a saddle on his back and climbed up, but he fell off again, saying, "Aye my friend, I can't hold on without reins and a bit."[7] The tiger answered that he didn't like the idea, but to hurry up and get it over with. The rabbit, chuckling to himself, fastened on the harness and adjusted the bit in the tiger's mouth. Then he climbed up, and as soon as he saw that all was just right, he gave a jerk on the reins that sent the tiger running through the town where everyone could see the rabbit mounted on the tiger.

The tiger was so angry that he ran as though he were crazy and wouldn't stop. So the rabbit jumped off his back and hid among the rocks. Later he returned to town and collected the bets he had won by riding the tiger.

The tiger still looks for the rabbit to kill and eat him. But he hasn't found him to this day.

And red, white, and blue,
THE END—
This is true!

---

5. **apologetic** (ə pol′ə jet′ ik), *adj.* making an excuse.
6. **contagious** (kən tā′jəs), spreading by contact.
7. **reins and a bit**, a set of long narrow straps (reins) used to guide an animal; these straps are attached to a thin, metal bar (bit) which is held in the animal's mouth.

After Reading

Making Connections

1. Look back at the predictions you made about who the trickster would be in this story and what kinds of tricks would be played. How did your predictions compare with what actually occurred in the story?

2. In your opinion, does the tiger deserve what happens to him? Explain your answer.

3. The author describes the rabbit and tiger as friends. Do you think he shows that they are friends in this story? Give examples to defend your answer.

4. Look over the cause-and-effect diagrams you made after reading this story. What does each trick have in common? Use this information to explain why the tiger was fooled so easily.

5. Trickster tales appear in folk literature from all parts of the world. Why do you think the trickster is such a universally popular character?

6. 🐾 Think about the perspective of people who play tricks on others as compared to those being tricked. Why do you think some people are usually the trickster while others are often the victim?

Literary Focus: Humor

Humor in life and in literature is often a combination of the expected and the unexpected. You may expect a tiger to be strong and an easy winner in a contest with a rabbit. So, you laugh when he fails. You don't expect the rabbit to always get out of tight situations with the tiger. So, you laugh when the rabbit tricks the tiger with an almost impossible scheme.

Think about the humor of the different tricks in "The Rabbit and the Tiger." Which trick do you think is the funniest? What part of the trick did you expect to happen? Which part of the trick was unexpected? Draw a cartoon or a series of cartoons that highlights the humor of your favorite trick in this story.

Vocabulary Study

The rabbit has written a trickster's guide on how to fool the tiger. For each of the tips below, write the letter of the word that best completes the sentence.

suspicious
glutton
uproariously
hurricane
apologetic

1. DO tempt the tiger with good food. He'll fall for it every time. He's a ____.
   a. charger   **b.** glutton   **c.** hurricane

2. DON'T worry about being rude to the tiger. You can trick him all you like and never feel ____.
   a. contagious   **b.** apologetic   **c.** suspicious

3. DO use the tiger's fear of storms to play tricks on him. You can get him to do what you suggest, if you explain it's a way to keep himself safe from a ____.
   a. zoo   **b.** glutton   **c.** hurricane

4. DON'T be afraid to tease the tiger and laugh at him ____.
   a. suspicious   **b.** horribly   **c.** uproariously

5. DO be aware of the tiger's whereabouts at all times. He cannot surprise you if you are always ____.
   a. suspicious   **b.** ferocious   **c.** apologetic

Expressing Your Ideas _____

Writing Choices

All Is Vanity Make up a **vanity license plate** for each animal that tells something about his character. You can use up to eight letters, numerals, or spaces per plate. Trade vanity license plates with a classmate and try to figure what each other's plates mean.

Signed Dear Abby Rabbit and Tiger are both unhappy. Take the part of either animal and write a letter to an **advice column** asking for suggestions on how to repair the friendship. Then, exchange papers with a classmate who has also chosen this activity and write a reply the columnist might give.

Other Options

Use Your Hands Make hand puppets, stick puppets, or marionettes of the rabbit and the tiger and put on a **puppet show** to tell a story about the animals. Write a script for a narrator and the two characters. Make or gather props to enhance the performance. Put on your puppet show for younger children in your school or another school.

See You in Court! Tiger has decided to sue Rabbit for physical harassment. Stage a mock **trial** with a judge, lawyers for both parties, witnesses, and a jury.

Writing Mini-Lesson

Preparing Your Presentation Portfolio

Now is the time to change your **working portfolio** into your **presentation portfolio.** This is the collection of written work that will be presented to others to show how you have met your goals for the year.

Reviewing and Selecting Samples

- Start by checking with your teacher to find out the requirements for the presentation portfolio.

- Next, decide which pieces you will include in your presentation portfolio. Divide your work into three stacks: **definitely use, definitely not use,** and **unsure.** (Go back through the third stack again.) Use your goal statements as a guide to review each piece of work. You might also consider your reflections, your self-evaluations, and comments from others.

Arranging Your Portfolio

There are several ways to arrange your portfolio.

- Chronological—Arrange your samples from the beginning of the year to the end. This order helps show what you have learned.

- By category—Group the same kinds of writing together, such as narratives, poems, plays, and so forth. This arrangement shows how you've changed as a writer.

- By theme—Sort your pieces by mood or topic. This arrangement highlights the major themes in your writing.

Completing the Package

- Write an introduction that first explains the entire portfolio and then each piece. This will help the reader see your work the way you want them to see it.

- Finalize the cover.

- Skim over the portfolio to make sure no pages are missing, and that they're ordered the way you'd like.

Standing Your Ground

Women Making Waves

Sociology Connection

Throughout history, women have pursued equality. Many have undertaken this occasionally treacherous journey by quietly standing their ground and slowly making progress. Other women have publicly and loudly pursued equality, never afraid to make waves. Both types are represented here.

QUEEN HATSHEPSUT

Queen Hatshepsut was one of only five women pharaohs in three thousand years of ancient Egyptian civilization. The queen, who reigned from 1486 to 1468 B.C., strengthened her title by claiming to have the approval of Egypt's god, Amon-Ra. She also wore traditional male royal clothing—a kilt, headdress, and false beard.

SAPPHO

This image from a Herculaneum fresco is believed to be Sappho around 100 B.C. Although there were other women poets in ancient Greece, Sappho was considered to be one of the best of all poets of her time.

TRIEU AU

In A.D. 248, a peasant woman, Trieu Au, dressed in golden armor and rode an elephant to lead her Vietnamese army into battle against Chinese invaders. When her army was eventually defeated, Trieu Au committed suicide rather than surrender.

NIGERIAN QUEEN

This sculpture depicts a Nigerian queen of the twelfth or thirteenth century. She may have been one of at least two women who ruled the forest state of Benin, located in what is now southern Nigeria. Women of the Benin state had their own councils and religious ceremonies. The government was just, and the people enjoyed a comfortable way of life.

PURSUING EQUALITY

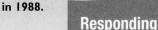

DAW AUNG SAN SUU KYI

Daw Aung San Suu Kyi was awarded the 1991 Nobel Peace Prize for her nonviolent resistance to the dictatorship in Myanmar, a country in Southeast Asia known as Burma until 1989. Her struggle for equality and human rights resulted in her arrest in 1989. She was released in July of 1995, but the Burmese military government blocked her from leading the political party she helped found. Here she speaks to a crowd in Burma in 1988.

HILLARY CLINTON

Hillary Clinton, first lady of the United States, speaks at the United Nations World Conference on Women held in September 1995 in Beijing, China. The conference focused on women's concerns worldwide, now and in the future.

QUEEN ELIZABETH

In the sixteenth century, an age of strong antifeminism, Europe's greatest monarch was a woman who brilliantly ruled England for forty-five years. Wearing armor, Queen Elizabeth addressed her troops as they waited for the expected invasion of the Spanish Armada. "I know I have the body of a weak and feeble woman, but I have the heart and stomach of a king, and of a king of England, too."

SARAH WINNEMUCCA

Sarah Winnemucca was the chief of her Piute tribe in the late nineteenth century. After her people were forced to leave their land, Sarah Winnemucca traveled to Washington to make an appeal to President Hayes. Although she was not allowed to speak to the President, she lectured throughout the East and publicized government injustices toward Native Americans.

Responding

1. What qualities do many of the women pictured on these pages share?

2. Take a look at yourself. Is there a cause you believe in strongly enough to work for? Would you more likely be the quiet support behind the leader, or would you be the leader?

Anthropology Connection

In the conflict between the traditional Kuna Indian way of life and encroaching modern society, the women of the tribe have found a resolution. They are standing their ground by preserving their native craft of mola-making. They are also accepting the inevitable arrival of modern society and prospering by selling their work to outsiders.

A A Kuna woman shows her work to a tourist.

FABRIC OF LIFE

by Donna Johnson

A nimals talk to the Kuna Indians of northeastern Panama, and sometimes they even do it in the Kuna's own language. Accustomed to hearing Kuna voices in the forest, wild parrots have been known to mimic their human neighbors from tree branches.

In turn, some Kunas imitate the parrots—not orally but visually—by depicting them on fabric art called molas. Kuna women spend many hours creating these panels to decorate blouses or to use as wall hangings.

Mola-making has been a custom among the Kuna for more than a century. Now, as the Kuna struggle to preserve their way of life from encroaching development, their art has become a record of the nature around them and an important commodity for the tourist trade.

Tourism is a new source of income for the 30,000 Kuna Indians that inhabit Panama's San Blas Islands and the adjacent strip of mainland called Kuna Yala. As central America's last unassimilated indigenous tribe, the Kuna have stepped into modern times with both their culture and their political autonomy intact. They have even managed to preserve a portion of their forested land—60,000 hectares (148,000 acres)—in the form of a national park.

Despite these accomplishments, Kunas still feel threatened. Each year in Panama nearly 80,000 hectares (200,000 acres) of rain forest are felled illegally. "For twenty years, the Kuna park has been invaded by colonists, cattle ranchers, and hunters who indiscriminately cut trees," says Guillermo. Archibold, Kuna Indian and technical director of the preserve.

This contemporary shirt illustrates the mola maker's ability to assimilate the modern world while keeping tradition alive. ➤

Bright colors, reflecting the sunlit colors of the tropics, are used in molas. ▼

Molas sometimes depict historical events. This one portrays a conquistador. ➤

The Kuna lands at risk represent one of the richest biological regions in Central America and a unique source of inspiration for mola-makers. The rain forest harbors toucans, coatimundis, rare golden frogs, giant anteaters, and many species of migratory songbirds. On the coast, rainbow-hued tropical fish, hermit crabs, and long-legged shorebirds make their home. All find their way onto molas.

Kuna women begin the mola-making process by cutting animal shapes from commercial cloth. Working between chores, the artisans sew the shapes onto panels in techniques known as appliqué and reverse appliqué. Details, such as the teeth on a shark, are embroidered later with painstaking care.

Each creation takes weeks to complete, but the thimblework pays off. By selling molas to tourists, some women make more money than their husbands.

And no wonder molas sell. Taking one home is like taking home a vision of Panama. Each scene is a unique interpretation of the country's wildlife—especially some very talkative parrots.

Responding
The Kuna women have found a way to coexist with modern society. Do you think their efforts will be enough to ensure the survival of the tribe and its traditions? Explain your answer.

Interdisciplinary Study   **669**

Reading Mini-Lesson

Summarizing

If you were to build a small-scale model of a sports car, you would want your model to have the same shape and proportions as the actual car. People looking at your model should get a good idea of what the real thing looks like.

When "building" a good summary of a selection, you also want to provide a clear view of the original. Here are some tips for uncovering the essentials.

- Get the topic—what the selection is *about*—firmly in mind.

- Use headings as subtopic guides. If there are no headings, write your own. Pay special attention to first sentences of paragraphs.

- Think visually. You might make a topics web, like the one started below, to provide an overview of the main topic and subtopics for the article "Fabric of Life," on pages 668–669. A summary of this article should include all of the information on the completed web.

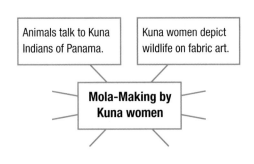

Sometimes selections contain built-in summaries in introductions, conclusions, and key paragraphs. Look for these as you read. As you write a summary, look for opportunities to tighten it up by combining several ideas into one sentence.

Activity Options

1. Image that you are an editor who has the task of writing a brief heading for each of the main parts of the "Fabric of Life" article. Count the paragraphs and put a paragraph number by each of your headings to indicate where it should go.

2. Work with a partner. Copy the topic web started above and complete it by writing in the remaining subtopics about the Kuna women and their mola-making.

3. Write a brief summary of the article. If you completed the topic web, you may want to use it as a basis for your summary.

Writing Workshop

Expressing an Opinion

Assignment In the selections you've read, characters must make choices and stand their ground. Consider David Holmes's case in *Survival.* Imagine you're on the jury. Express your opinion about Holmes's innocence or guilt. See the Writer's Blueprint for details.

WRITER'S BLUEPRINT

Product	Written opinion of a jury member
Purpose	To evaluate the facts in the case of David Holmes and make a reasoned judgment based on those facts
Audience	Other members of the jury
Specs	As the writer of a successful paper, you should:

❏ Begin by stating your purpose for writing and whether you think David Holmes is innocent or guilty.

❏ Go on to discuss how the evidence supports your opinion.

❏ Next, discuss other factors which helped you to form your opinion. These might include the unusual circumstances surrounding the incident and what you know of Holmes's character as presented by witnesses.

❏ Conclude by restating your opinion and encouraging other jury members to agree with you.

❏ Use an interesting beginning that will hook your readers.

❏ Follow the rules for grammar, usage, spelling, and mechanics. Watch that you don't confuse adjectives and adverbs.

The instructions that follow should help you write a successful paper.

Chart key quotes from the literature. Members of a jury often take notes to remember important statements. As a jury member in David Holmes's manslaughter case, you should first list key statements from witnesses. Find quotes from the play *Survival* that provide evidence about Holmes's guilt or innocence. Organize the information in a chart like this.

Character/witness	Evidence/quote	Is evidence fact or opinion?	Supports guilt or innocence?
Patricia Askin	"—Then Holmes took my brother by the shoulders and said, 'It's your turn, Frank. You've got to go.' Then they threw my brother over the side."	Fact	Guilt

Research the law on homicide. *Homicide* is the killing of one person by another. In order to rule on Holmes's case, you must understand the law on homicide. Is homicide always illegal? Is it sometimes justified? Look up the terms *homicide, manslaughter,* and *murder* in an encyclopedia. Be sure you understand how they differ.

OR . . .
Research the laws in your own state concerning these crimes. What are the punishments for them? If you can, talk with a judge, law professor, criminal lawyer, or the state's attorney's office for more information.

Chart reasons for guilt and innocence. To prepare an opinion, it often helps to jot down the strongest arguments for both sides. Prepare a chart like the one below. On the left, list five reasons for declaring Holmes guilty. On the right, list five reasons for declaring him innocent. Then review both sides of your chart and complete this statement: I think Holmes is (<u>guilty or innocent</u>) because _____.

Reasons for declaring guilty	Reasons for declaring innocent
Captain's expert opinion: longboat might have survived even with the extra weight.	Captain admitted it would have taken a miracle for the longboat to survive with the extra weight.

Try a quickwrite. For five minutes or so, describe the unusual circumstances in the case. Why did Holmes act as he did? What makes it difficult to determine whether he is guilty or innocent?

Plan the opinion. Chart your opinion essay about the Holmes case. Include all the specs listed in the Writer's Blueprint on page 671. Your chart might look like the one below.

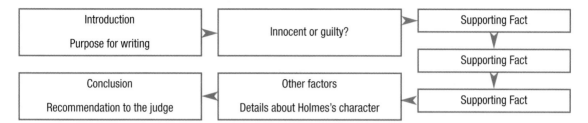

Introduction Purpose for writing	→	Innocent or guilty?	→	Supporting Fact
				↓
				Supporting Fact
				↓
Conclusion Recommendation to the judge	←	Other factors Details about Holmes's character	←	Supporting Fact

Plan your opening paragraph. This is an important essay you're writing, and you'll want to grab your readers' interest at the beginning. Think of a way to "hook" your readers in your opening paragraph. Look ahead to the Revising Strategy for ideas on how to write a hook. Try it out before you begin your draft.

STEP 2 DRAFTING

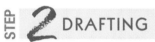

Before you write, review your literature chart, research notes, and any other notes you've made. Reread the Writer's Blueprint too.

As you draft, don't worry about mistakes with spelling and punctuation. Concentrate on getting your ideas on paper. Here are some ideas for getting started.

- Begin with a key quote from the play.

- Begin with a quick rundown of the facts in the case.

- Begin with a question that sets forth your dilemma as a member of the jury.

STEP 3 REVISING

Ask your partner for comments on your draft before you revise it.

✔ Have I followed the specs in the Writer's Blueprint?

✔ Have I stated my opinion on the case clearly?

✔ Do the facts and examples I've chosen from the play support my opinion?

✔ Is my recommendation to the other jury members convincing?

✔ Does my beginning hook the reader?

Revising Strategy

LITERARY SOURCE
"It took months of negotiation to come to an understanding with the old man. He was in no hurry. What he had the most of was time. He lived up in Rio en Medio, where his people had been for hundreds of years. He tilled the same land they had tilled. His house was small and wretched, but quaint."
from "Gentleman of Rio en Medio" by Juan A. A. Sedillo

Interesting Beginnings

The beginning of an essay sets the tone for the whole piece. A good beginning "hooks" the reader by grabbing her or his attention. Be creative with your beginning sentences. Here are some tips for better beginnings.

- Experiment! Try a quote, a question, or a shocking piece of information.

- State your opinion as quickly as possible.

- Choose the point in your opinion that interests you most and get that into your beginning sentence.

- Don't worry about explaining everything at once. If you successfully "tease" the reader with a few key facts, he or she will read on for a fuller explanation.

Take a look at the Literary Source. How does Juan A. A. Sedillo tease the reader in the opening paragraph of "Gentleman of Rio en Medio"? What does he make you want to find out?

Notice how the writer of the draft below hooked the reader with an interesting beginning.

"He's like gunpowder, ready to explode at any time . . . ." This is how Thomas Able described David Holmes in his testimony of that awful night in April when Holmes forced twelve innocent men overboard. How can we acquit someone who sent these men to watery graves, forcing others in the lifeboat to listen to their dying screams?

STUDENT MODEL

4 EDITING

Ask a partner to review your revised draft before you edit. When you edit, watch for errors in grammar, usage, spelling, and mechanics. Pay attention to distinguishing between adjectives and adverbs.

Editing Strategy

Distinguishing Between Adjectives and Adverbs

In editing your opinion, check to see that you use adjectives and adverbs correctly. Both can modify other words and both can end in -ly. For example, *friendly* is an adjective. *Not, never,* and *always* are adverbs. Look at the sentences below.

Adjective—The plan was *perfect* for that situation.
Adverb—The plan worked *perfectly.*
Adverb—The plan was *perfectly* obvious.

Confused about whether to use an adjective or an adverb? Be sure you know what kind of word you want to modify. Adjectives modify nouns and pronouns and tell *what kind, which one,* or *how many.* Adverbs modify verbs, adjectives, or other adverbs. They tell *how, when, where,* or *to what extent.* What words do the adjectives and adverbs in the examples above modify?

Notice how the writer of the draft below used adjectives and adverbs correctly.

> **FOR REFERENCE . . .**
> More information about distinguishing between adjectives and adverbs is listed in the Language and Grammar Handbook.

○   My first example is Mrs. Reston and her story about David

     Holmes on that terrible night. She said that her nine-year-old daughter

○   was left alone and frightened on the sinking ship. David Holmes, who

     didn't know mother or daughter, bravely jumped back on the ship and

○   rescued Mrs. Reston's daughter.

STUDENT MODEL

5 PRESENTING

Here are two ideas for presenting your opinion.

- Participate in a jury of your peers. Get together with twelve class-mates and take turns reading your opinions. Can you reach a consensus?

- Allow a friend or family member to read *Survival* and then your opinion. Discuss how a modern jury might rule on the case.

6 LOOKING BACK

Self-evaluate. What grade would *you* give your paper? Look back at the Writer's Blueprint and evaluate yourself on each point, from 6 (superior) down to 1 (weak).

Reflect. Think about what you learned from writing your opinion as you write answers to these questions.

✔ Would you like to serve as a jury member? How could writing this paper help you be a successful jury member?

✔ What part of the planning process was most helpful in writing your opinion? Can you think of another planning step that would have helped?

For Your Working Portfolio: Add your opinion and your reflection responses to your working portfolio.

Beyond Print

A Few Advertising Techniques

Bandwagon encourages people to do something because everyone else does.

Testimonial uses a role model or a celebrity to sell a product.

Transfer makes a connection between a product and a positive value.

What's that green stuff in my Banana BoBana???

Yes, We Have No Bananas

The CEO leans back in her hand-rubbed Naugahyde leather, executive swivel-with-ease chair and stares at the vice-president who brought her the news.

"How many boxes of the stuff did we make?" she asks.
The vice-president replies, "Exactly 552,721."

Ever since being named CEO of the Sunset Cereal Corporation, she has had nothing but success, much of it due to her ideas for breakfast cereals that appeal to children. Chocolate Marshmallow Munchie sold in the millions. But now something strange has happened to Banana BoBana. The cereal is packaged in the same plant as a freeze-dried vegetable line. Broccoli ended up in 552,721 boxes of Banana BoBana.

"This will bankrupt us!" the CEO screams.

The vice-president tries to paint a happier picture. The nutrition people are very pleased. This is the healthiest cereal any company has yet produced. It is whispered around the company, however, that the taste resembles "grass a la banana peel."

Activity

It is your job to develop an ad campaign to sell this cereal to young people. In groups of two to four, write a two-minute commercial for Banana BoBana using mocked-up cereal boxes, slogans, and whatever else you feel will be successful. Try to use one of the advertising techniques mentioned at the left above. Oh, and there is one major rule of this ad campaign. . . .

YOU CANNOT LIE ABOUT THE CEREAL!

You might want to consider using some of these strategies:

Use a celebrity.	Employ happy kids.	Emphasize nutrition.
Write a snappy jingle.	Change the name.	Give away prizes.

Projects for Collaborative Study

Theme Connection

Fight or Flight? The conflicts in this unit were settled in many different ways. Some resulted in physical battles. Others were resolved peacefully. Physical confrontation is appropriate and even necessary on hunting grounds and battlefields, but what about playgrounds and football fields? How far should physical contact—pushing, shoving, and hitting—go in everyday life?

■ As a class, discuss incidents you have witnessed in which someone went too far in a conflict. *How* and *why* did it happen? *Who* or *what* stopped it? *What* were the consequences for those involved?

■ Brainstorm ways in which fighting can be avoided. Are there times when people <u>should</u> be allowed to fight? When? How?

Literature Connection

Theme The play *Survival* concerns one man's hopeless situation and the terrible decision he must make. The conflict he faces and its ultimate resolution comprise the **theme** of the play—the overriding reason behind the events, or what the author is trying to tell us. Often a story or play will have more than one theme. If you look back through this book, you will see that all of the selections are arranged according to theme.

Divide into equal teams of six members. Look at the table of contents on pages vii through xvii. Each of you chooses a different theme and a selection under that theme. Discuss why each selection fits its theme. Under which other themes could you list each selection?

Life Skills Connection

Me Versus You? Conflict often involves a struggle or a clash between opposing forces. Conflict occurs often in nature. The result may be a storm, an earthquake, or a fox eating a chicken for dinner.

Conflict is a natural occurrence in our everyday life, too—a struggle with a homework assignment or a clash with a classmate over an unkind remark. What creates conflict in your life?

■ Discuss this statement as a class:

Conflict is healthy and can produce beneficial results. True or False?

☙ Multicultural Connection

Conflict Resolution In any conflict that threatens us, we have a **choice**—we can try to avoid it, delay it, face it head on, or even welcome it. What we do depends on the situation at hand. Approaching it with a clear **perspective** helps. If we delay the conflict, will it be easier to deal with later or more difficult? If we face it head on, will trouble result?

■ Work in a small group. Name a time when you think it would be better to face a conflict than to avoid it. Name a time when you think it would be better to avoid a conflict than to face it.

■ Do you think that conflict resolution is something that people can learn? Why or why not? What would you have to learn to do it? Discuss this as a class.

Read More About Conflict and Resolution

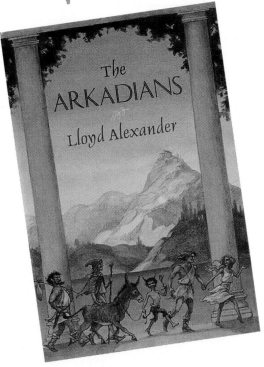

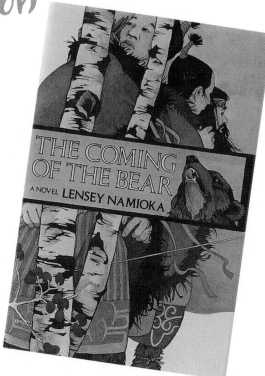

The Arkadians (1995) by Lloyd Alexander. Lucian discovers that soothsayers are stealing money from the King of Bromios and must flee or be killed. He encounters a poet who has been turned into a donkey, a girl with strange powers, and other wonderful characters.

The Coming of the Bear (1992) by Lensey Namioka. It is about 1600, and two unemployed samurai escape Japan and some enemies by boat. They are thrown off course by a storm and end up with a group of round-eyed people, the Ainu. The plot centers on a conflict between the Ainu and a Japanese settlement.

More Good Books

The Rebounder (1994) by Thomas J. Dygard. Six-feet, six-inch Chris refuses Coach Fulton's offers to join the basketball team. Chris had injured an opponent during a game and has quit playing. Fulton is a sensitive individual whose support helps Chris resolve his inner conflict and return to the sport he loves.

Her Stories (1995) by Virginia Hamilton. The nineteen stories in this book focus on magical lore, ghost stories, and creative fairy tales about African American women. These are strong, competent women who use their wits to thwart their enemies. The book is illustrated by Leo and Diane Dillon.

Where the Lilies Bloom (1969) by Vera and Bill Cleaver. Mary is a motherless fourteen-year-old who must single-handedly bury her father, earn money, and keep the landlord away from her sister, Devola.

Catherine, Called Birdy (1994) by Karen Cushman. Birdy, daughter of a thirteenth-century knight, confides her troubles and humorous schemes to her diary. She aches for independence and is determined to find her own way.

Boy: Tales of Childhood (1984) by Roald Dahl. Dahl writes about growing up in Wales during the 1920s and 1930s. Many of the episodes recount harrowing experiences in the English boarding school he attended.

Glossaries, Handbooks, and Indexes

Understanding Fiction 682

Understanding Nonfiction 684

Understanding Poetry 686

Understanding Drama 688

Glossary of Literary Terms 690

Glossary of Vocabulary Words 694

Language and Grammar Handbook 703

Index of Skills and Strategies 724

Index of Fine Art and Artists 732

Index of Authors and Titles 734

Text Acknowledgments 736

Illustration Acknowledgments 737

Understanding Fiction

Fiction is writing that comes from an author's imagination. Its purpose is to illustrate some truth about life or to entertain. A **novel** is a long work of fiction dealing with characters, actions, and scenes that copy those of real life in a complex plot. A **short story** is shorter than a novel. It often describes just one event, and the characters are usually fewer in number and not as fully developed as those in a novel. Short stories can usually be read in one sitting.

Fiction shapes our own imaginations because it provides glimpses into the past, ideas about life in the future, and understanding of the world as it is today. Fiction has several important elements.

Characters

The **characters**—the people or animals—are one of the most important elements in fiction. Authors make their characters seem real by describing such things as what they look like (Anna was tall and wore jeans), the way they speak or act (Tony spoke calmly but his hands shook), and sometimes even what they are thinking (Norman wondered why his parents disagreed).

Plot

The **plot**—what happens to the characters—is a second important element in fiction, and it is carefully worked out by the author so that one event flows logically after another. In most fiction, the plot is built around a **conflict,** a problem or struggle of some sort. The conflict may be between characters, between a character and some object or event, or between a character and that character's inner self. The conflict builds to an emotional moment called a **climax,** or turning point, when the main character takes an action to end the conflict, or when the way events are working out causes some important change.

Usually the turning point comes close to the end of the story and sometimes it is at the very end. The conclusion of a story, where the complications of the plot are worked out, is called the **resolution.** The events before the climax are often referred to as the *rising action,* while the events after the climax are called the *falling action.*

Setting

The **setting**—when and where the action takes place—is a third important element in fiction. Sometimes the setting is crucial to what happens, and then it is described in detail by the author. If the particular city or town and the exact season or year are important to the action, an author usually states them directly (New York City on a cold December Monday in 1996). Often authors do not need to be so definite. If all that happens occurs in one room and involves a character with an inner conflict, then the setting may not be described in detail because it is irrelevant to the story.

Theme

Another important thing to look for in fiction is **theme,** or underlying meaning. The theme may be directly stated by the author or only implied. Theme is not the same as subject, or topic, in that it involves a statement or an opinion about the topic. Not every work of fiction has a theme, and various readers may discover different themes in the same selection.

Mood/Tone

The author's choice of words and details to describe setting, characters, and events contributes to two additional elements of fiction—mood and tone. **Mood** refers to the atmosphere or feeling created in the reader by the author. **Tone** is the author's attitude toward the subject or toward the reader.

Strategies for Reading Fiction

When reading fiction, it is helpful to consider the following things:

- **Think about the characters.** What happens to each one? Who is your favorite character and why?

- **Think about the events.** What is the central problem or conflict? What is the moment of greatest suspense? Is the order of events important? Do you like the ending?

- **Think about when and where the action takes place.** Often the **setting** will be explained in the first few paragraphs. What are some of the other things that create a sense of time and place?

As you read, think about what the author suggests as well as what he or she actually states. When the information about the characters, events, and setting is only suggested, rather than stated, you must make **inferences.** An inference is a reasonable conclusion based on clues provided by the author. Looking for clues and making inferences will help you become a better reader.

If a story is not too long, read it through without stopping. What is it about? To become involved, **visualize** the characters and the place. After reading, it is often necessary to go back and reread sections. Try it. Be sure you know who the main characters are and what they are like. Be sure you understand where the action takes place and what the main problem is and how it is solved.

You'll also want to consider the **narrator,** or who is telling the story. Is the narrator a charac-ter participating in the events, or someone outside the story who is simply observing what happens? The two most common **points of view** are first person (a character in the story) and third person (an outsider). Ask yourself: From whose point of view am I seeing the characters, events, and setting?

As you read, stop occasionally and think about what you are reading.

Question yourself about the characters and events. "Why is this character such a bully? Is she jealous or just plain mean?"

Predict what may happen next. "Will the girl come out of the coma?"

Clarify what is happening by trying to explain things to yourself. "The carpet design helps me understand the game the boy has made up to amuse himself."

Summarize what has happened so far, an especially important step when you are reading a long story or difficult novel.

Evaluate by making judgments about the quality of the author's work. You can also evaluate such elements as a character's actions. "This story seems true to life because I think it's possible for a dog to save a person's life."

Connect the story with your own experiences—do you think the character is doing the right thing? Do you identify with the way the character feels? "I felt exactly the same way—scared and lonely—when I moved last year."

Understanding Nonfiction

Nonfiction is about real people, real places, and things that actually happened. It includes many kinds of writing but can be divided into two general groups—**informational nonfiction,** such as newspaper articles, and **narrative nonfiction,** such as biography, which has many of the same literary elements as fiction. Although narrative nonfiction may tell a story, the story should be true and based on facts.

Below are descriptions of some of the most common types of nonfiction.

Autobiography

An **autobiography** is an account of all or part of a person's life written by that person. Feelings and observations about life's experiences are often important in an autobiography. Because the author is the narrator, an autobiography is almost always told from the first-person point of view.

Shorter forms of autobiography include **diaries, memoirs,** and **journals.** Today some autobiographies of people noted for contributions in special fields, such as a politics or sports, are written with the help of a professional writer. Examples of autobiography included in this book are "Samantha's Story" by Samantha Abeel and the selection from *The Autobiography of Malcolm X* by Malcolm X with Alex Haley.

Biography

A **biography** is an account of a real person's life written by another person. Biographers try to learn about a noteworthy person and then help readers get to know that person. A biography can take us back in time or around the world to learn about fascinating people and their remarkable lives.

Doing research is part of a biographer's job, and books, letters, and journals all can be a source of details for a biography. If possible, a biographer interviews the subject of the biography, or people who have known the person. To help readers visualize time periods, places, and people, a biography may have a setting and characterization, just as fiction does. Although the goal of a biographer is to provide a truthful account, sometimes inferred details are drawn from the facts available. "Nate 'Tiny' Archibald" by Bill Littlefield is an example of biography.

Essay

An **essay** is a discussion about a specific topic and it often expresses an opinion on the topic. Some essays are primarily expository, or informative. They explain something or give more information about a subject. Essays may be classified as formal or informal. A formal essay has a serious tone and is generally intended to persuade the reader. An informal essay, more concerned with entertaining than persuading, has a personal, friendly tone. Sometimes an informal essay is humorous. "Father's Day" by Michael Dorris and "A Sea Worry" by Maxine Hong Kingston are examples of essays included in this book.

Speech

A **speech** is written to be given as a public talk, usually for a particular occasion such as a graduation, a memorial service, or a political rally. It may be formal or informal, and the topic will depend upon the intended audience. In this book, you will find the speech by Robert Kennedy titled "On the Death of Martin Luther King, Jr."

Strategies for Reading Nonfiction

When reading nonfiction, it is helpful to consider the following strategies:

• Before you actually begin reading nonfiction, **warm up by previewing.** Consider the title and read the first paragraph. Also look at any illustrations. What clues to the subject do you find? Knowing what to expect should help you better understand what you read.

• **Think about the facts and opinions presented**. Since accuracy is important in nonfiction, you'll want to distinguish between statements of fact and statements of opinion. Remember that a statement of fact can be proved while a statement of opinion expresses personal feelings, beliefs, or evaluations. Any statement about a future event is an opinion since it cannot be proved that it will happen.

• **Consider the author's purpose**. Why do you think this author wrote this particular work of nonfiction? Is it simply to inform you by providing facts? Is it to convince you of an idea? Or is the purpose to entertain?

• **Consider your own purpose for reading.** It can allow you to read with **flexibility.** For example, if you are reading a difficult article about a recent discovery in space in preparation for reporting on it in science class, you will want to slow down and pay careful attention to the details. On the other hand, if you are looking for the name of the scientist who made the discovery, you might skim the article by glancing quickly at the material to find the specific information you want.

• **Use the time-order relationships** in the material. Paying attention to when things happen is particularly important when you read a history textbook, a biography, or an autobiography. Dates and clue words, such as *in 1900,* will help you find the order of events.

• **Think about cause-and-effect relationships.** Noticing how events are linked in a pattern, one event happening as the result of another, will help you follow narrative nonfiction. Using cause-and-effect relationships is also very useful in reading the directions for a science experiment or a history text.

• **Looking for the main idea, topic, and details** in nonfiction can be a help in remembering as well as understanding what you read. Recall that the topic is the subject of the selection and the main idea is the "big" idea about that topic. Details are included to support the main idea.

Understanding Poetry

Poetry is a type of literature that creates an emotional response through the imaginative use of words. It helps you experience what you might not otherwise notice. It can surprise or delight you, and it often will suggest some new ideas for thought. Poetry dates back to the beginning of human communities when poetic forms were used in tribal ceremonies. Later, stories were told in verse and passed along from one generation to the next.

Traditional poems are written in **stanzas,** or groups of lines that are set off visually from the other lines in a poem. Many traditional poems are **narrative poems,** poems that tell stories. They have the same literary elements you find in fiction, such as plot, characters, and setting. The **repetition** of sounds is another characteristic of traditional poems.

A modern poem characteristically is written in the language of everyday speech, and it may be about a variety of subjects, from rattlesnakes to homework. Often a modern poem creates a single **image** that appeals to your senses. Many modern poems are written in **free verse,** meaning they are free from any fixed or repeated patterns.

Below are descriptions of several important elements in poetry.

Rhythm

The pattern of sounds that are stressed and not stressed in a poem provides the **rhythm.** As you read the following stanza from Robert Service's "The Cremation of Sam McGee," what syllables do you emphasize, or pronounce louder?

1　There are strange things done in the
　　　midnight sun
2　　By the men who moil for gold;
3　The Arctic trails have their secret tales
4　　That would make your blood run cold;

5　The Northern Lights have seen queer
　　　sights,
6　　But the queerest they ever did see
7　Was that night on the marge of Lake
　　　Lebarge
8　　I cremated Sam McGee.

The pattern of stressed syllables gives you a feeling for the beat of the stanza. Notice that the rhythm is not quite regular. In the first line, these syllables are stressed: *strange, done, mid-,* and *sun.* There are two unaccented syllables before *strange* (*There, are*) and between *done* and *mid-,* (*in, the*) but only one between *strange* and *done* (*things*). Rhythm makes poetry enjoyable to read.

Rhyme

The repetition of a sound in two or more words is called **rhyme.** In poetry, the last words of lines often rhyme. In the stanza from "The Cremation of Sam McGee," there is end rhyme in lines 2 and 4 (*gold, cold*) and lines 6 and 8 (*see, McGee*). Also notice the rhyme within lines (*done, sun* in line 1; *marge, Lebarge* in line 7).

Figurative Language

Figurative language goes beyond the ordinary meanings of words in order to achieve a new effect or to express an idea in a fresh way. Two of the most common figures of speech are **simile** and **metaphor.** Notice the comparisons of essentially unlike things in the following stanza from "The Highwayman" by Alfred Noyes.

1　The wind was a torrent of darkness among
　　　the gusty trees;
2　The moon was a ghostly galleon tossed
　　　upon cloudy seas;
3　The road was a ribbon of moonlight over
　　　the purple moor;
4　And the highwayman came riding—
5　　Riding—riding—

6 The highwayman came riding, up to the
    old inn door.

   The moon is compared to a galleon, or large
ship, and the road to a ribbon of moonlight.
Close your eyes. Can you use these figures of
speech to picture the moon and the road in a
new way?

Imagery

When writers help us experience things
through our senses of sight, hearing, smell,
taste, and touch, they are using images, or
imagery. Notice how the words in these lines
from "The Highwayman" help you hear the
sounds of clattering and tapping and see the
dark yard of the inn.

Over the cobbles he clattered and clashed
    in the dark inn yard;
And he tapped with his whip on the
    shutters, but all was locked and barred

Alliteration

Sound devices are an important part of poetry.
The repetition of consonant sounds at the beginnings of words or within words is called **alliteration,** as shown in these lines from "The
Cremation of Sam McGee." Notice the repeat of
the sound of *l* in *long, lone, firelight,* and *while* and
the repeat of the sound of *r* in *round* and *ring.*

   In the long, long night, by the lone
       firelight, while the huskies, round in
       a ring, . . .

Strategies for Reading Poetry

When we read poems, it's important to listen to
the words. Often they say more than they
directly tells us. Keep in mind the following tips
as you read poetry.

• **Use the title** to get a clue to the topic of the
poem.

• **Do not pause or stop at the end of a line** unless
there is a mark of punctuation indicating that
you should do so.

• **Look for the meaning.** One way to do this is to
pay attention to the punctuation. Although
lines may flow from one to the next, ideas are
often expressed as statements or questions.

• **Try to see in your mind the pictures** created by
the words.

• In a poem that tells a story, **look for the action
and visualize the characters** who determine
the action.

• In reading poetry that focuses on an image
or an emotion, **listen for the voice of the
poem.** Notice how the word choices of the
poet help you visualize an object or experience an emotion.

• **Give careful attention to each word in a poem.**
Because poets use words precisely and sparingly,
each word is significant.

• With any poem, it helps to **try reading aloud.**
By listening to the poem's sounds you will get
insight into the meaning. Hear the beat of the
rhythm, the pattern of rhyme, and the repetition of sounds.

• **Keep in mind that the speaker of a poem is not
necessarily the poet** but rather the voice the
poet has chosen to communicate the experience.

Understanding Drama

A **drama** is a literary work that is written for presentation to an audience. It tells a story through the speech and actions of the characters. It may be written in verse or in prose. Generally, plays are fictional, but occasionally they are based on true events and real people. Even a play that tells the story of something that actually happened will probably not re-create the exact words that were spoken. This happens because no one may remember just what was said at a particular moment.

As is true for fiction, the **characters** in a drama are developed in several ways. You can learn about them from what the playwright tells you, from what the characters say about themselves, from what others say the characters, and from what the characters do. Most plays have the same elements of **plot** that you find in fiction. There will be a problem, a conflict, and a resolution.

Below are descriptions of the common forms that drama takes and several important terms to know about drama.

Stage Plays

In the nineteenth and early twentieth centuries, the **stage** was seen as a room with one wall removed. The audience viewed all that happened through this invisible "fourth" wall. Before the performance and during intermissions, a curtain replaced the invisible wall. Recently the traditional stage has become less confined, and some theaters have been built with the stage in the center and seating on all sides. Stage plays are acted in front of live audiences.

Television Plays

A **television play** is performed on a stage for broadcast to television viewers. You will see this form of drama most frequently on public or educational television networks.

Movies

Usually filmed at different locations and over a period of time, **movies** can include more action than is possible in a stage or television play. Movies are produced for both large public theaters and for first-time viewing on television.

Radio Plays

The two most significant features of **radio plays** are dialogue between characters and sound effects that add to the drama. Although radio plays are not common today, they were very popular before the days of television.

Cast of Characters

If you go to the performance of a play, you will likely get a program that lists all of the **characters** who have parts in the production. The script for a play you read will have a similar cast of characters at the beginning, before the scene is described or the action starts. Sometimes this list not only names the characters in the play but also describes or identifies them for you, as in the following example from a play version of Sir Arthur Conan Doyle's *The Dying Detective*.

CHARACTERS
MRS. HUDSON
DR. WATSON
SHERLOCK HOLMES
CULVERTON SMITH "A great yellow face, coarse-grained and greasy, with heavy double chin, and two sullen, menacing grey eyes which glared at me from under tufted and sandy brows . . ."
INSPECTOR MORTON Middle-aged, tough, dressed in plain clothes.

Script

A play, whether it is performed live on stage or filmed by a camera, starts with a **script** made up of the stage directions and dialogue. In a play of more than one scene, the script shows how the play is divided into parts.

Stage Directions

Stage directions are the playwright's instructions to the performers. The setting may be described in detail in stage directions at the beginning of a play. You will notice that stage directions are usually printed in a different type, as in the following example from *The Dying Detective*.

> **SCENE ONE**
>
> SHERLOCK HOLMES's *bedroom at 221B Baker Street. The essential features are: a bed with a large wooden head, placed crosswise on the stage, . . .*

Stage directions also provide information for the actors on how to interpret lines and how to move. Reading them will help you visualize the **characters' actions**. Stage directions may be set apart in parentheses as well as different type.

> **WATSON** (*grimly*). I'm going, Holmes.
>
> (*He hurries out.*) HOLMES *remains propped up for a moment. staring after* WATSON, *then sinks back into a sleeping posture as the stage blacks out.*)

Dialogue

Since the story in the play is revealed through the words of the characters as they perform on stage, **dialogue** makes up most of the text of a play. It is the chief means of moving the plot along in a play and is made up of the lines, or speeches, of the various characters. The dialogue that follows is from *The Dying Detective:*

> **WATSON.** Oh! You . . . After all these years, Holmes, you haven't . . . confidence in me?
>
> **HOLMES.** In your friendship, Watson—yes. But facts are facts. As a medical man you're a mere general practitioner, of limited experience and mediocre qualifications.
>
> **WATSON.** Well . . . ! Well, really!
>
> **HOLMES.** It is painful to say such things, but you leave me no choice.

Strategies for Reading Drama

Reading a play is different from viewing it because you must picture the scene, imagine the characters, and interpret the actions.

- **Use the stage directions to visualize.** The information the playwright provides in the stage directions will help you picture the **setting** and the movements of the **characters.**

- **Read the stage directions carefully.** Stage directions help you imagine the scene and the action. You may be tempted to skip over the directions and focus on the dialogue, but if you do this you will miss some things you would see or hear if you were viewing the play or movie.

- **Try reading the characters' lines aloud.** Work with a partner or small group of classmates. Choose a scene and assign individuals to the different parts. Read the dialogue as you imagine the character would say the words. Consider your tone of voice as well as the signals the playwright has included in the punctuation.

- **Be alert to special terms.** A play written for filming will usually include some specific directions for the person doing the camera work. For example, *pan* means "to move horizontally or vertically to take in the larger scene."

Glossary of Literary Terms

Words in SMALL CAPITAL LETTERS refer you to other entries in the Glossary of Literary Terms.

alliteration, the REPETITION of consonant sounds at the beginnings of words or within words. Alliteration is used to create melody, establish MOOD, and call attention to important words in a poem or sentence. An example of alliteration can be found in this line from the poem "Under This Sky" by Zia Hyder (page 424): "We see the same sun and same moon."

anecdote, a short account of an interesting event in someone's life. Jean Little's "About Old People" is a good example of an anecdote.

biography, any account of a real person's life. An autobiography is the story of part or all of a person's life written by the person who lived it. "Nat 'Tiny' Archibald" by Bill Littlefield (page 134) is a good example of a biography.

characterization, the methods an author uses to acquaint a reader with the characters in a work. An author may develop a character through describing the character's physical appearance, as Cynthia Rylant does in her descriptions of Doris in "A Crush" (page 6). A character's speech, actions, and inner thoughts are also very revealing. The author may develop a character by showing how other characters react to him or her, as Borden Deal does in showing how the gang interacts with T. J. in "Antaeus" (page 518).

connotation, the emotional associations surrounding a word, as opposed to its literal meaning. In his autobiography, Malcolm X describes how the word *book* came to have a connotation of *freedom* to him (page 480).

denotation, the strict, literal meaning of a word; the definition in a dictionary.

dialogue, the conversation between one or more people in a literary work. Dialogue can serve to develop CHARACTERIZATION, as in "Jeremiah's Song" by Walter Dean Myers (page 386). It can also create the MOOD and advance the PLOT, as it does in Rod Serling's play *The Monsters Are Due on Maple Street* (page 334).

drama, see PLAY.

end rhyme, the rhyming of words at the ends of lines of poetry. Notice the end rhyme in the two lines of poetry below.

> I'm Nobody! Who are you?
> Are you nobody, too?
> —Emily Dickinson, "I'm Nobody" (page 188)

essay, a brief composition that presents a personal point of view. "A Sea Worry" by Maxine Hong Kingston (page 60) is an essay.

fable, a brief TALE, in which the characters are often animals, told to point out a moral truth.

fantasy/science fiction. Both fantasy and science fiction are works set wholly or partly in an unreal world. Often, at least one character is unlike a human being. Frequently, the plot concerns events that cannot be scientifically explained. "The Smallest Dragonboy" by Anne McCaffrey (page 170) is a good example of both.

fiction, a story, novel, or play about imagined people and events. Examples are "Charles" by Shirley Jackson (page 249) and "Key Item" by Isaac Asimov (page 81).

figurative language, language expanded beyond its ordinary literal meaning. It uses comparisons to achieve new effects, to provide fresh insights, or to express a relationship between things that are essentially different. HYPERBOLE, METAPHOR, and SIMILE are all common types of figurative language.

flashback, an interruption in the action of a story, play, or piece of nonfiction to show an episode that happened at an earlier time. A flashback is used to provide background information necessary to understanding the characters or plot. By using a flashback, an author can have some freedom to rearrange the events of a story in an order that has the strongest effect. Paul Annixter uses flashback in "Last Cover" (page 116) to describe how the wild fox came into the family's life.

foreshadowing, a hint given to the reader of what is to come in the story. In "Niña" by Margarita Mondrus Engle (page 488) hints are given by the author that Niña will die.

free verse, a type of poetry that is "free" from a fixed pattern of RHYTHM or RHYME. Poems using free verse in this book include "Birdfoot's Grampa" (page 75) and "Kidnap Poem" (page 258).

genre, a form or type of literary work. The novel, short story, poem, and play are all genres.

hero/heroine, the main character in a literary work.

hyperbole, an exaggerated statement, sometimes involving FIGURATIVE LANGUAGE. The conclusion of "The Cremation of Sam McGee" by Robert Service (page 349) is a prime example of hyperbole.

imagery, concrete words or details that appeal to the senses of sight, sound, touch, smell, taste, and to internal feelings. "Where You Are" by Jack Anderson (page 203) is rich in imagery.

inference, reasonable conclusion drawn by a reader or viewer from hints or implications that are provided by the author or artist. For example, early in the story "All Summer in a Day" (page 279), Ray Bradbury infers that Margot's classmates are cruel to her because they are jealous.

irony, a contrast between what appears to be and what really is. *Verbal irony* occurs when one says or writes the opposite of the intended meaning, as when Steve in Rod Serling's *The Monsters Are Due on Maple Street* (page 334), says to Charlie:

> Who do I talk to? I talk
> to monsters from outer space.

Irony of situation exists when an event is contrary to what is expected or appropriate, as when Merrill Markoe actually lives a dog's life in "The Dog Diaries" (page 416). *Dramatic irony* occurs when the reader or spectator knows more about the true state of affairs than a character does. For example, in "A Letter to God" by Gregorio López y Fuentes (page 127), the reader knows what Lencho doesn't—where the money he has received actually came from.

legend, a story by an unknown author, handed down through the years. "Sir Gawain and the Loathly Lady" (page 151) is an English legend and "Rabbit Dances with the People" (page 542) is a Cherokee legend.

limerick, a five-line humorous poem. The first, second, and fifth lines rhyme and the third and fourth lines rhyme. Limericks are often about the manners and peculiarities of people.

> There was a young lady from Lynn
> Who was so exceedingly thin
> That when she essayed
> To drink lemonade
> She slid down the straw and fell in.

metaphor, a figure of speech that involves an implied comparison between two basically unlike things. One example of metaphor occurs in Emily Dickinson's poem, "I'm Nobody" (page 188) where being "somebody" is compared to being a frog.

mood, the atmosphere or feeling within a work of art. The choice of setting, objects, details, images, and words all contribute to create a specific mood. The mood throughout most of the story "The Gun" by Carol Ellis (page 242) is one of foreboding.

moral, the lesson or teaching in a tale, fable, poem, or story. The moral of the legend "Rabbit Dances with the People" (page 542) is to be yourself.

myth, a traditional story connected with the religion or beliefs of a people, usually attempting to account for something in nature. Both the Greek myth "Prometheus" (page 264) and the African myth "How the Lame Boy Brought Fire from Heaven" (page 262) deal with the origins of fire.

narrative, a story or account of an event or a series of happenings. It may be true or fictional. "The Day the Sun Came Out" by Dorothy M. Johnson (page 108) is a narrative story. "The Highwayman" by Alfred Noyes (page 640) is a narrative poem.

narrator, the teller of a story. The teller may be a character in the story, as in "The Author" by M. E. Kerr (page 502), or someone outside the story, as in "After Twenty Years" by O. Henry (page 18).

nonfiction, literature about real people and events rather than imaginary ones. For example, nonfiction can be a BIOGRAPHY, an ESSAY, or an article. "Biddy Mason" (page 366) and "Father's Day" (page 54) are examples of nonfiction.

novel, a long work of FICTION dealing with characters, situations, and settings that copy those of real life. A *novella* is a short novel. *The*

Adventures of Tom Sawyer by Mark Twain is an example of a novel.

onomatopoeia, words used to imitate the sound of a thing. *Hiss, smack, buzz,* and *hum* are examples of words whose sounds suggest their sense. Below is an example from this book.

> He could fluff up his tail till it looked like a bottle brush, and his war cry as he scuttled through the long grass was: *Rikk-tikk-tikki-tikki-tchk!*
> —Rudyard Kipling, "Rikki-tikki-tavi" (page 594).

personification, a figure of speech or FIGURATIVE LANGUAGE in which human characteristics are given to nonhuman things. In "old age sticks" by E. E. Cummings (page 309), youth is personified as a rule-breaker and old age is personified as a stick-in-the-mud.

play, a composition in prose or verse written to be acted on a stage or before motion-picture or television cameras, or in front of a microphone. *The Dying Detective* (page 228), *The Monsters Are Due on Maple Street* (page 334), and *Survival* (page 618) are all plays.

plot, a series of happenings in a literary work. Plot consists of these elements: a conflict, a pattern of events, a climax, and a conclusion. In a carefully constructed plot, each event is important: the incidents are arranged in a cause-effect relationship, with each incident becoming a necessary link leading to the climax and conclusion of the work. "A Man Who Had No Eyes" by MacKinlay Kantor (page 456) has a fully developed plot.

poetry, composition in verse. The words in poetry are arranged in lines that have rhythm and, sometimes, rhyme. There are many examples of poetry in this book.

point of view, the relationship between the NARRATOR of a story and the characters and action in it. The author's choice of narrator determines the amount of information a reader will be given. The three major points of view that authors commonly use are: first person, third person limited, and third person omniscient. "The Revolt of the Evil Fairies" by Ted Poston (page 288) is told in the first person point of view. "Brothers Are the Same" by Beryl Markham (page 397) is told from a third person limited point of view—the narrator is confined to a single character's (Temas's)

perspective. "Rabbit Dances with the People" (page 542) is told from a third person omniscient point of view—the narrator sees into the minds of all the characters.

repetition, word or phrase used over and over again for emphasis, especially in poetry but also sometimes in folk tales. Repetition is used often in "The Highwayman" by Alfred Noyes (page 640).

> The road was a ribbon of moonlight over the
> purple moor;
> And the highwayman came riding—
> Riding—riding—

resolution, the tying up of the PLOT; the conclusion, where the complications in a plot are resolved.

rhyme, the REPETITION of syllable sounds. End words that share a particular sound are called END RHYMES. In "Almost Perfect" by Shel Silverstein (page 130), the two last lines in each stanza rhyme.

rhyme scheme, the pattern of END RHYMES in a poem. You can chart a rhyme scheme with letters of the alphabet by using the same letter for end words that rhyme, as in the poem below. Notice the underlined *internal rhymes* also.

> And that very <u>night</u>, as we lay packed
> <u>tight</u> in our robes beneath the snow,   A
> And the dogs were <u>fed</u>, and the stars
> o'er<u>head</u> were dancing heel to toe.   A
> He turned to <u>me</u>, and "Cap," says <u>he</u>,
> "I'll cash in this trip, I guess;   B
> And if I <u>do</u>, I'm asking that <u>you</u> won't
> refuse my last request."   B
> —Robert Service, "The Cremation of Sam McGee" (page 349)

rhythm, the arrangement of stressed and unstressed sounds in writing and speech. The rhythm in the poem below is indicated by the capital letters of the stressed words or syllables.

> "One KISS, my bonny SWEETheart: I'm after a
> PRIZE tonight:
> But I shall be BACK with yellow GOLD before the
> MORNing light;
> Yet, if they PRESS me SHARPly, and HARRy me
> through the DAY,
> Then LOOK for me by MOONlight,
> WATCH for me by MOONlight,
> I'll COME to thee by MOONlight, though HELL
> should bar the WAY."
> —Alfred Noyes, "The Highwayman" (page 640).

science fiction, see FANTASY/SCIENCE FICTION.

setting, the time, place, and general environment in which the events of a NARRATIVE occur. Details of the setting may be either stated or suggested. In some stories the setting is vital to the narrative—it may have an effect on the events of the PLOT, reveal character, or create a certain MOOD. In other stories the setting is relatively unimportant. The setting is important in "All Summer in a Day" (page 279) and "Brothers Are the Same" (page 397).

short story, a story shorter than a NOVEL. Although it generally describes just one event, it must have a beginning, a middle, and an end. The characters are usually fewer in number and not as fully developed as those in a novel. Toni Cade Bambara's "The War of the Wall" (page 566) is a short story.

simile, a comparison in which the word *like* or *as* is used to point out a similarity between two basically unlike things. Ed J. Vega uses a simile to compare memories to rivets in his poem "Translating Grandfather's House" (page 301).

speaker, the same as a NARRATOR. Often the narrator of a poem is called the speaker.

speech, a public talk that is given to inform, persuade, or entertain. Robert F. Kennedy's speech "On the Death of Martin Luther King, Jr." (page 530) was given to help his listeners come to terms with a shocking tragedy and to offer hope for America's future.

stanza, a group of lines set off visually from the other lines in a poem. "A Minor Bird" by Robert Frost (page 583) has four stanzas.

stereotype, character in fiction that fits a standardized mental picture of what members of a certain group are like, or a plot in which the action follows a predictable pattern. David

Holmes in the play *Survival* by Alfred Brenner (page 618) appears through most of the drama to represent the stereotype of a callous, hard-bitten sailor.

suspense, the method or methods an author uses to maintain a reader's interest. In *The Dying Detective* (page 228), Arthur Conan Doyle creates suspense by almost convincing the reader that the invincible Sherlock Holmes has succumbed to an evil plot to kill him.

symbol, person, place, or object that has meaning in itself but suggests other meanings as well. The jacket in the Marta Salinas story "The Scholarship Jacket" (page 296) is a symbol not only of academic achievement but of strength and dignity also.

tale, a spoken or written account of some happening. It is usually less complicated than a short story. "We Are All One" (page 429) is a Chinese folk tale. "The Rabbit and the Tiger" (page 658) is a Puerto Rican folk tale.

theme, the main idea or underlying meaning of a literary work. A theme may be directly stated, but more often it is merely implied. In Judith Ortiz Cofer's "Abuela Invents the Zero"(page 587), the topic or subject of the story is a teenager's reaction to her visiting grandmother's unfamiliar ways, but the theme is the importance of showing respect and compassion for others.

tone, an author's attitude toward the subject of a literary work or toward the reader. Tone is conveyed through the author's particular choice of words and details in describing setting, portraying characters, and presenting events. Bailey White's tone in "Turkeys" (page 462) is playful and a bit sarcastic. James Herriot's tone in "Alfred: The Sweet-Shop Cat" (page 468) is one of understanding and concern.

Glossary of Vocabulary Words

a hat	o hot	ü rule	(a in about
ā age	ō open	ch child	e in taken
ä far	ô order, all	ng long	ə { i in pencil
e let	oi oil	sh she	o in lemon
ē equal	ou out	th thin	(u in circus
ė term	u cup	ᵀʜ then	
i it	u̇ put	zh measure	
ī ice			

A

abide (ə bīd′), *v.* live; reside.

abstraction (ab strak′shən), *n.* not representing an actual object or thing; idea.

absurdity (ab sėr′də tē), *n.* something unreasonable or ridiculous.

accolade (ak′ə lād), *n.* praise or recognition.

accordance (ə kôrd′ns), *n.* agreement.

admonition (ad′mə nish′ən), *n.* warning.

adrenaline (ə dren′l ən), *n.* a body chemical that speeds up the heartbeat and increases energy.

advocate (ad′və kit), *n.* a person who speaks or writes in favor of a cause.

affix (ə fiks′), *v.* stick on; fasten; attach.

agitated (aj′ə tāt′id), *adj.* upset, disturbed.

alibi (al′ ə bī), *n.* a claim that a person was somewhere else when a crime occurred.

alleviate (ə lē′vē āt), *v.* relieve; lessen.

alliterate (ə lit′ə rāt), *v.* write something using words that start with the same letter or sound.

amiable (ā′mē ə bəl), *adj.* pleasant; agreeable.

amiss (ə mis′), *adj.* wrong.

anecdote (an′ik dōt), *n.* a short, often humorous, retelling of events.

anguish (ang′gwish), *n.* severe physical or mental pain; great suffering.

anonymous (ə non′ə məs), *adj.* nameless; unknown.

antagonism (an tag′ə niz′əm), *n.* active opposition; hostility.

apologetic (ə pol′ə jet′ik), *adj.* making an excuse.

apparatus (ap′ə rat′əs), *n.* equipment or machinery needed for a specific use.

aptitude (ap′tə tüd), *n.* talent, natural ability.

arrogant (ar′ə gənt), *adj.* overly proud and rude, especially to those considered inferior.

articulate (är tik′yə lit), *adj.* being able to put thoughts into words easily.

ascertain (as′ər tān′), *v.* to find out for certain; make sure of.

assent (ə sent′), *n.* agreement.

B

bankbook (bangk′bu̇k′), *n.* a book in which a record of a person's account at a bank is kept.

barrio (bär′ē ō), *n.* part of a city where mainly Spanish-speaking people live.

beau (bō), *n.* a young man courting a young woman.

benevolent (bə nev′ə lənt), *adj.* kindly; charitable.

bizarre (bə zär′), *adj.* strikingly odd looking.

blanch (blanch), *v.* become pale, turn white.

bleakness (blēk′nəs), *n.* a bare and cheerless condition.

blithely (blīᴛн′lē), *adv.* cheerfully.

bluff (bluf), *v.* fool by pretending confidence.

boorish (bür′ish), *adj.* having bad manners; rude.

brandish (bran′dish), *v.* wave or shake in a threatening way.

broach (brōch), *v.* begin to speak about.

bungalow (bung′gə lō), *n.* a one-story house with low, sweeping lines

C

cajole (kə jōl′), *v.* coax; persuade.

caliber (kal′ə bər), *n.* inside diameter of the barrel of a gun.

calloused (kal′əst), *adj.* hardened.

canny (kan′ē), *adj.* shrewd or cautious in dealing with others.

capitalist (kap′ə tə list), *n.* person who favors private ownership of business; often, a rich person.

captivate (kap′tə vāt), *v.* charm; fascinate.

careen (kə rēn′), *v.* rush headlong with a swaying motion.

cascade (kas kād′), *n.* something that flows like a waterfall.

casement (kās′mənt), *n.* a window that opens on hinges.

cathedral (kə thē′drəl), *n.* a large or important church.

cherish (cher′ish), *v.* hold dear; treat with affection.

chivalry (shiv′əl rē), *n.* knightly qualities, such as bravery, honor, courtesy, and respect for women.

clamor (klam′ər), *v.* make a loud noise or uproar.

claret (klar′ət), *adj.* dark purplish-red.

clinch (klinch), *v.* fix firmly; settle decisively.

coalesce (kō′ə les′), *v.* unite, grow together.

coincidence (kō in′sə dəns), *n.* two things that occur by chance at the same time.

collaborator (kə lab′ə rā′tər), *n.* a person who aids or cooperates with another.

commentary (kom′ən ter′ē), *n.* series of comments or remarks.

compassion (kəm pash′ən), *n.* sympathy or pity.

complement (*n.* kom′plə mənt; *v.* kom′plə ment), *n.* the number required to complete or fill something. —*v.* to complete or make perfect.

compound (kom pound′), *v.* combine similar parts to form a whole.

compromise (kom′prə mīz), *n.* settlement of a dispute by agreement that each side will give up something.

confound (kon found′), *v.* confuse; mix up.

confrontation (kon′frən tā′shən), *n.* face-to-face standoff or opposition.

congregation (kong′grə gā′shən), *n.* people gathered for a religious service.

consequence (kon′sə kwens), *n.* importance.

consolation (kon′sə lā′shən), *n.* comfort.

consternation (kon′stər nā′shən), *n.* great dismay.

consume (kən süm′), *v.* use up; spend.

contemplate (kon′təm plāt), *v.* think about for a long time.

contemplative (kon′təm plā′tiv), *adj.* deeply thoughtful.

contemptuous (kən temp′chü əs), *adj.* scornful or mocking.

contender (kən tend′ər), *n.* one who takes part in a major contest; competitor.

conversational (kon′vər sā′shə nəl), *adj.* talking in a friendly, easy way.

convey (kən vā′), *v.* communicate; make known.

conviction (kən vik′shən), *n.* firmness of belief.

countenance (koun′tə nəns), *n.* facial expression.

courteous (kėr′tē əs), *adj.* thoughtful of others; polite; full of courtly manners.

cower (kou′ər), *v.* crouch or draw back in fear.

cremate (krē′māt), *v.* burn a dead body to ashes.

critique (kri tēk′), *v.* review or criticize.

cultivate (kul′tə vāt), *v.* tame or develop.

cynically (sin′ik lē), *adv.* showing doubt about the goodness or sincerity of others.

D

declaim (di klām′), *v.* recite in public.

dedicate (ded′ə kāt), *v.* give up wholly to some purpose; devote.

defy (di fī′), *v.* resist or stand against authority.

degrade (di grād′), *v.* lower the quality of; make less pure.

delirious (di lir′ē əs), *adj.* out of one's senses for a time.

demise (di mīz′), *n.* death.

deprive (di prīv′), *v.* take away by force.

derelict (der′ə likt), *n.* an abandoned ship.

descendant (di sen′dənt), *n.* person born to a certain family or group.

desecrate (des′ə krāt), *v.* treat or use without respect.

devour (di vour′), *v.* take in with the eyes or ears in a hungry way.

dignified (dig′nə fīd), *adj.* having self-respect or pride.

dilution (də lü′shən), *n.* the act of making something weaker or less pure by the addition of something else.

disability (dis′ə bil′ə tē), *n.* lack of ability or power to do or act.

discard (dis kärd′), *v.* get rid of; throw aside.

discreetly (dis krēt′lē), *adv.* in a way that shows good judgment; cautiously.

disillusion (dis′i lü′zhən), *v.* set free from false ideas; disenchant.

distinctive (dis tingk′tiv), *adj.* distinguishing from others; special.

distract (dis trakt′), *v.* to draw away the attention.

domain (dō mān′), *n.* land owned by one person or by one group.

dumbfounded (dum′foun′dəd), *adj.* amazed.

E

economize (i kon′ə mīz), *v.* cut down expenses.

egotism (ē′gə tiz′əm), *n.* habit of thinking too highly of oneself; conceit.

elaborate (i lab′ər it), *adj.* very careful and detailed.

elaborately (i lab′ər it lē), *adv.* very carefully.

elective (i lek′tiv), *n.* subject or course of study that may be taken, but is not required.

emerge (i mėrj′), *v.* come out.

emulate (em′yə lāt), *v.* imitate an admired person.

encroach (en krōch′), *v.* to go beyond proper limits.

endow (en dou′), *v.* to give at birth some special ability or talent.

endure (en dur′), *v.* put up with; withstand.

enduring (en dur′ing), *adj.* lasting.

engrossing (en grō′sing), *adj.* taking up one's complete attention.

ensure (en shur′), *v.* make sure or certain.

escort (ə skôrt′), *v.* go with someone as a show of courtesy or honor.

esoteric (es′ə ter′ik), *adj.* understood only by a select few.

eternally (i tėr′nl ē), *adv.* always and forever.

evidently (ev′ə dənt lē), *adv.* plainly; clearly.

excel (ek sel′), *v.* be outstanding; be better.

exception (ek sep′shən), *n.* person or thing that is left out.

exceptionally (ek sep′shən əl lē), *adv.* unusually.

excess (ek′ses), *adj.* too much or too many; extra.

existence (eg zis′təns), *n.* being; life.

expectation (ek′spek tā′shən), *n.* anticipation; something expected.

explicit (ek splis′it), *adj.* outspoken, frank; not reserved.

extract (ek strakt′), *v.* pull out.

F

fancy (fan′sē), *v.* picture to oneself; imagine.

feign (fān), *v.* make believe; pretend.

ferment (fėr′ment), *n.* excitement or unrest.

ferocity (fə ros′ə tē), *n.* savage cruelty; fierceness.

fervent (fėr′vənt), *adj.* showing great warmth of feeling; very eager and serious.

festive (fes′tiv), *adj.* suitable for a feast or holiday; merry.

fiend (fēnd), *n.* an evil spirit, devil or demon.

fiendishly (fēn′dish lē), *adv.* in a cruel or wicked manner.

flailing (flā′ling), *adj.* beating; thrashing.

flex (fleks), *v.* bend.

formidable (fôr′mə də bəl), *adj.* hard to overcome; to be dreaded.

frail (frāl), *adj.* slender and not very strong; weak.

functional (fungk′shə nəl), *adj.* capable of reading and writing well enough to meet everyday needs.

furtive (fėr′tiv), *adj.* quickly done in a sly or secret manner.

futile (fyü′tl), *adj.* useless; not successful.

G

gain (gān), *n.* getting something; profit.

gaunt (gônt), *adj.* thin and bony, with hollow eyes.

gauntlet (gônt′lit), *n.* a sturdy, heavy glove, with a flaring cuff that covers part of the arm.

ghastly (gast′lē), *adj.* like a dead person or ghost.

glumly (glum′lē), *adv.* with bad humor; dismally.

glutton (glut′n), *n.* a greedy eater; someone who eats too much.

gnarled (närld), *adj.* twisted and knotted.

graffiti (grə fē′tē), *n.* drawings or writings scratched or scribbled, usually on a wall.

grisly (griz′lē), *adj.* frightful; horrible.

grudging (gruj′ing), *adj.* given unwillingly.

H

habitual (hə bich′ü əl), *adj.* done by habit; usual; customary.

haggard (hag′ərd), *adj.* looking worn from pain or worry.

harass (har′əs), *v.* trouble by repeated attacks; disturb or torment.

harried (har′ēd), *adj.* worried.

haven (hā′vən), *n.* place of safety and shelter.

heed (hēd), *v.* pay careful attention to.

hilarious (həler′ē əs), *adj.* very funny.

hurricane (hėr′ə kān), *n.* storm with violent wind and, usually very heavy rain.

I

idiosyncrasy (id′ē ō sing′krə sē), *n.* a personal peculiarity.

imminent (im′ə nənt), *adj.* about to happen soon.

immunization (im′yə nī zā′shən), *n.* protection from disease.

impale (im pāl′), *v.* pierce with something pointed; fasten.

impending (im pen′ding), *adj.* likely to happen soon; threatening.

implement (im′plə mənt), *n.* tool or piece of equipment.

implore (im plôr′), *v.* beg earnestly for.

improbable (im prob′ə bəl), *adj.* unlikely.

impromptu (im promp′tü), *adj.* without preparation; offhand.

incisive (in sī′siv), *adj.* sharp or piercing.

inconsolable (in′kən sō′lə bəl), *adj.* broken-hearted.

incredulity (in′krə dyü′lə tē), *n.* lack of belief; doubt.

incredulous (in krej′ə ləs), *adj.* not ready to believe; doubting.

incredulously (in krej′ə ləs lē), *adv.* doubting; not able to believe.

incriminate (in krim′ə nāt), *v.* show to be guilty.

incubation (ing′kyə bā′shən), *n.* stage of a disease from the time of infection until the first symptoms appear.

incurable (in kyŭr′ə bəl), *adj.* not capable of being cured or healed.

indifferent (in dif′ər ənt), *adj.* uncaring; showing no interest.

inert (in ėrt′), *adj.* having no power to move or act; inactive.

inevitable (in ev′ə tə bəl), *adj.* not to be avoided; certain to happen.

infantile (in′fən tīl), *adj.* babyish; like an infant.

infectious (in fek′shəs), *adj.* spreading by germs or virus.

infinite (in′fə nit), *adj.* extremely great.

infinitely (in′fə nit lē), *adv.* extremely; vastly.

innumerable (i nü′mər ə bəl), *adj.* very many; too many to count.

inquisitive (in kwiz′ə tiv), *adj.* too curious; nosy.

insatiable (in sā′shə bəl), *adj.* not able to be satisfied.

inscription (in skrip′shən), *n.* words written or engraved on stone, metal, paper, and so on.

insistent (in sis′tənt), *adj.* impossible to overlook or disregard.

insolently (in′sə lənt lē), *adv.* rudely; disrespectfully.

integration (in′tə grā′shən), *n.* including people of all races on an equal basis in schools, parks, neighborhoods, and so on.

intensity (in ten′sə tē), *n.* great energy or strong feeling.

interminable (in tėr′mə nə bəl), *adj.* seemingly endless.

internment (in tėrn′mənt), *n.* a confining; a restricting within a place, usually during wartime.

intimate (in′tə mit), *adj.* very familiar; closely acquainted.

intimately (in′tə mit lē), *adv.* closely; very well.

intricate (in′trə kit), *adj.* with many twists or turns; entangled or complicated.

invariably (in ver′ē ə blē), *adv.* without change or exception.

iridescent (ir′ə des′nt), *adj.* colorful; showing colors that change.

irksome (ėrk′səm), *adj.* annoying; tiresome.

irony (ī′rə nē), *n.* an unexpected twist.

irreverent (i rev′ər ənt), *adj.* disrespectful.

L

laborious (lə bôr′ē əs), *adj.* requiring much hard work.

liberation (lib′ə rā′shən), *n.* setting or being set free.

license (lī′sns), *n.* a card or paper that shows permission by law.

linger (ling′gər), *v.* stay, as if unwilling to leave.

listlessly (list′lis lē), *adv.* without interest; seeming too tired to care.

loathsome (lōн′səm), *adj.* making one feel sick; disgusting.

loom (lüm), *v.* appear, often in a threatening way.

M

magistrate (maj′ə strāt), *n.* a government official who has power to apply and enforce the law.

malevolent (mə lev′ə lənt), *adj.* showing ill will; spiteful.

malice (mal′is), *n.* a wish to hurt or make suffer; spite.

malnutrition (mal′nü trish′ən), *n.* poor health due to lack of good food.

mangy (mān′jē), *adj.* shabby and dirty.

manipulate (mə nip′yə lāt), *v.* to handle skillfully.

manslaughter (man′slô′tər), *n.* the killing of a human being but without deliberate intent.

martyr (mär′tər), *n.* person who dies for a belief or cause.

marvel (mär′vəl), *v.* be filled with wonder; be astonished.

mayhem (mā′hem), *n.* senseless damage.

medic (med′ik), *n.* a person in the armed forces who gives first-aid to soldiers.

mesquite (me skēt′), *n.* a common tree or shrub of the pea family found in the southwestern United States and Mexico.

metamorphosis (met′ə môr′fə sis), *n.* a noticeable or complete change of character or circumstances.

methodical (mə thod′ə kəl), *adj.* done in an orderly manner.

meticulously (mə tik′yə ləs lē), *adv.* in such a way as to be extremely careful about details.

minimum (min′ə məm), *adj.* lowest amount allowed.

mock (mok), *adj.* pretend; not real

moldy (mōl′dē), *adj.* old and decaying; musty.

moor (mùr), *n.* open land covered with small purple flowers.

mortified (môr′tə fīd), *adj.* ashamed; humiliated.

multitude (mul′tə tüd), *n.* a great many; crowd.

murky (mėr′kē), *adj.* thick and dark.

N

negotiation (ni gō′shē ā′shən), *n.* talking over terms.

neurotic (nù rot′ik), *adj.* suffering from an emotional disorder, such as depression.

nuisance (nü′sns), *n.* something that annoys or troubles.

nymph (nimf), *n.* maiden goddess of nature in Greek and Roman myths, who lived in seas, woods, or mountains.

O

oblivious (ə bliv′ē əs), *adj.* paying no attention; unaware.

obscure (əb skyùr′), *adj.* hard to understand. —*v.* hide from view; dim.

ominous (om′ə nəs), *adj.* unfavorable; threatening.

overrule (ō′vər rül′), *v.* rule or decide against an argument or objection.

P

pacific (pə sif′ik), *adj.* peaceful; calm; quiet.

painstaking (pānz′tā′king), *adj.* very careful.

palpably (pal′pə blē), *adv.* plainly; obviously.

parapet (par′ə pet), *n.* a low wall at the edge of a roof.

passive (pas′iv), *adj.* not active; being inactive.

penetrate (pen′ə trāt), *v.* enter into or pass through.

periodically (pir′ē od′ik lē), *adv.* every now and then.

permeate (pėr′mē āt), *v.* to spread through all of something.

perplexed (pər plekst′), *adj.* puzzled; bewildered.

pertain (pər tān′), *v.* have to do with; be related.

pillar (pil′ər), *n.* slender column used as support or ornament for a building.

plague (plāg), *n.* widespread trouble or calamity.

plantain (plan′tən), *n.* a plant with large leaves, similar to a banana plant.

plight (plīt), *n.* a bad or hopeless situation.

plodder (plod′ər), *n.* person who works hard, but slowly.

polarization (pō′lər ə zā′shən), *n.* breaking up or separating into two opposing sides.

portly (pôrt′lē), *adj.* having a large body; overweight.

precisely (pri sīs′lē), *adv.* exactly, definitely.

predestined (prē des′tənd), *adj.* having one's fate determined beforehand.

preliminary (pri lim′ə ner′ē), *adj.* leading up to the main business.

prodigy (prod′ə jē), *n.* a marvel or wonder.

prolific (prə lif′ik), *adj.* producing many offspring.

proprietor (prə prī′ə tər), *n.* shop owner.

prosecutor (pros′ə kyü′tər), *n.* the lawyer who takes the government's side of a case against an accused person.

providence (prov′ə dəns), *n.* God's care and help.

provisions (prə vizh′ən), *n.* pl. supply of food and drinks.

pulverize (pul′və rīz), *v.* break into pieces; grind into dust.

pungent (pun′jənt), *adj.* sharp; powerful.

purchase (pėr′chəs), *n.* a firm hold.

Q

quaint (kwānt), *adj.* odd in a pleasing way.

quirkier (kwėr′kē ər), *adj.* more peculiar; offbeat.

quiver (kwiv′ər), *v.* shake with a slight but rapid motion; shiver; tremble.

R

rationalize (rash′ə nə līz), *v.* to find an explanation or excuse for.

raucous (rô′kəs), *adj.* harsh-sounding; hoarse.

recline (ri klīn′), *v.* lean back; lie down.

reflective (ri flek′tiv), *adj.* thoughtful.

reformation (ref′ər mā′shən), *n.* a change for the better.

refrain (ri frān′), *n.* repeated phrase of a verse.

refuge (ref′üj), *n.* shelter from danger or trouble.

rehabilitation (rē′hə bil′ə tā′shən), *n.* restoring one to good health or positive behavior.

relent (ri lent′), *v.* become less harsh; be more merciful.

remembrance (ri mem′brəns), *n.* memory.

reminiscence (rem′ə nis′ns), *n.* a remembering or recalling of past events.

repercussion (rē′pər kush′ən), *n.* sound flung back; echo.

reprehensible (rep′ri hen′sə bəl), *adj.* deserving blame; hateful.

reprove (ri prüv′), *v.* scold; find fault with.

reservation (rez′ər vā′shən), *n.* land set aside by the government for a special purpose: *an Indian reservation.*

resigned (ri zīnd′), *adj.* accepting what happens without complaint.

resilience (ri zil′ē əns), *n.* power of recovering rapidly.

resilient (ri zil′ē ənt), *adj.* springing back.

resolute (rez′ə lüt), *adj.* determined; firm.

resolution (rez′ə lü′shən), *n.* something decided on.

resonance (rez′n əns), *n.* a full, echoing quality.

retrieve (ri trēv′), *v.* find and bring back.

revelation (rev′ə lā ′shən), *n.* something made known.

reverberate (ri vėr′bə rāt′), *v.* echo back.

revive (ri vīv′), *v.* come back to life or consciousness.

riffle (rif′əl), *v.* leaf through pages.

rifle (rīf′əl), *v.* search and rob; steal.

robust (rō bust′), *adj.* strong and healthy.

S

sarcasm (sar′kaz′əm), *n.* mocking humor; ridicule.

saunter (sôn′tər), *v.* walk along slowly and happily; stroll.

savor (sā′vər), *n.* flavoring; seasoning. — *v.* enjoy very much.

scapegoat (skāp′gōt′), *n.* a person made to bear the blame for others' mistakes.

scheme (skēm), *v.* to plot or plan in a secret way.

scholarship (skol′ər ship), *n.* showing knowledge gained through study.

scorn (skôrn), *v.* look down upon; despise.

scowl (skoul), *v.* look angry or sullen by lowering the eyebrows; frown.

sedately (si dāt′lē), *adv.* calmly; seriously.

self-conscious (self′kon′shəs), *adj.* embarrassed; shy.

sentiment (sen′tə mənt), *n.* feeling, especially refined or tender feeling.

shaft (shaft), *n.* long, narrow part of a spear or an arrow.

sheepishly (shē′pish lē), *adv.* in an awkwardly bashful or embarrassed manner.

simultaneously (sī′məl tā′nē əs lē), *adv.* happening at the same time.

singe (sinj), *v.* burn a little.

skittish (skit′ish), *adj.* apt to jump, start, or run.

skulk (skulk), *v.* hide in a cowardly way.

slacken (slak′ən), *v.* become slower or less active.

slain (slān), *v.* killed.

snigger (snig′ər), *n.* mocking, disrespectful laughter.

solemnly (sol′əm lē), *adv.* gloomily; seriously.

solitary (sol′ə ter′ē), *adj.* away from people; lonely.

somber (som′bər), *adj.* gloomy, dark, dismal.

sovereignty (sov′rən tē), *n.* complete control over one's own life.

specter (spek′tər), *n.* a ghost or phantom, often of terrifying appearance.

speculation (spek′yə lā′shən), *n.* a guessing; conjecture.

splay (splā), *v.* spread out; extend.

spurn (spėrn), *v.* refuse with anger and disgust.

stalwart (stôl′wərt), *adj.* strongly built; sturdy.

stanchest (stônch′əst), *adj.* most loyal (also spelled **staunchest**).

sterile (ster′əl), *adj.* unable to produce life; barren.

stolid (stol′id), *adj.* without excitement; unemotional.

submerge (səb mėrj′), *v.* cover with water.

subtle (sut′l), *adj.* skillful or clever.

succumb (sə kum′), *v.* give in.

sullenly (sul′ən lē), *adv.* silently, due to bad feeling, such as anger.

surge (sėrj), *v.* move like waves; rise up excitedly.

surreptitious (sėr′əp tish′əs), *adj.* secret; stealthy.

surveyor (sər vā′ər), *n.* a person who examines land.

suspicious (sə spish′əs), *adj.* suspecting something; imagining something might occur.

sustain (sə stān′), *v.* allow or approve. *The judge sustained the prosecution's objection.*

sustenance (sus′tə nəns), *n.* support; aid.

swarthy (swôr′ᴛʜē), *adj.* having a dark skin.

T

tantalize (tan′tl īz), *v.* tease or torment with something desired.

tawny (tô′nē), *adj.* brownish-yellow.

testimony (tes′tə mō′nē), *n.* a statement used for evidence or proof.

therapy (ther′ə pē), *n.* treatment of a disease or mental disorder.

till (til), *v.* to plow or cultivate land.

timidly (tim′id lē), *adv.* shyly; fearfully.

tirade (tī′rād), *n.* a long, scolding speech.

tolerate (tol′ə rāt′), *v.* permit; put up with.

torrent (tôr′ənt), *n.* a violent rushing stream.

transfix (tran sfiks′), *v.* make motionless with amazement.

translucent (tran slü′snt), *adj.* letting light through without being completely clear.

trudge (truj), *v.* walk wearily or with effort.

tumultuously (tü mul′chü əs lē), *adv.* in a disorderly way.

U

unamiably (un āˊmē ə blē), *adv.* in an unpleasant or disagreeable manner.

unconscious (un konˊshəs), not able to feel or think, unaware.

unpalatable (un palˊə tə bəl), *adj.* unpleasant; distasteful.

unsettling (un setˊling), *adj.* disturbing.

uproariously (up rôrˊē əs lī), *adv.* loudly and with great humor.

usher (ushˊər), *v.* guide; escort.

V

valedictorian (valˊə dik tôrˊē ən), *n.* student with the best grades who gives the farewell speech at graduation.

valiant (valˊyənt), *adj.* showing courage; brave.

vanquish (vangˊkwish), *v.* conquer; defeat.

vengeance, (venˊjəns), *n.* punishment in return for a wrong; revenge.

venom (venˊəm), *n.* the poison produced by some snakes spiders, scorpions, lizards, and so on.

veranda (və ranˊdə), *n.* a large porch along one or more sides of a house.

vigilance (vijˊə ləns), *n.* watchfulness.

vindictive (vin dikˊtiv), *adj.* wanting revenge; spiteful.

vulgar (vulˊgər), *adj.* showing a lack of manners.

W

wane (wān), *v.* decline in strength or intensity; lessen.

warrant (wôrˊənt), *n.* written order giving authority.

wheedle (hwēˊdl), *v.* use soft speech and flattering words to persuade.

wheedling (hwēˊdling), *adj.* soft and persuasive; coaxing.

wistful (wistˊfəl), *adj.* full of desire; longing.

wizened (wizˊnd), *adj.* withered, old.

wretched (rechˊid), *adj.* miserable or very unsatisfactory.

writhe (rīᴛʜ), *v.* twist and turn in pain or discomfort.

Language and Grammar Handbook

This **Handbook** is alphabetically arranged with each entry explaining a certain term or concept. For example, if you can't remember when to use *accept* and *except,* look up the entry **accept, except.** You'll find an explanation of the meaning of each word and a sentence using each word. (Many of the sentences used are from selections in this book.)

A

a, an The choice between *a* and *an* depends on the beginning sound, not the beginning letter, of the following word. *A* is used before a consonant sound, and *an* is used before a vowel sound.

◆ He bent and stroked Alfred's head again and again, then without looking up he spoke in *a* husky voice.
   from "Alfred: The Sweet-Shop Cat" by James Herriot

◆ Old man Silver doesn't blink *an* eye.
   from "The Scribe" by Kristen Hunter

accept, except The similarity in sound causes these words to be confused. *Accept* means "to take or receive; consent to receive; say yes to." It is always a verb. *Except* is most commonly used as a preposition meaning "but."

◆ "The first time you *accept* a fee, I'll close you up and run you off this corner."
   from "The Scribe" by Kristen Hunter

◆ "The story is true," Mr. Parsons said, "*except* that it was the other way around."
   from "A Man Who Had No Eyes" by MacKinlay Kantor

adjective Adjectives are modifiers that describe nouns and pronouns and make their meaning more exact. Adjectives tell *what kind, which one, or how many.*

What kind:	pink coat	beautiful sunset	cloudy sky
Which one:	this video	that ticket	those rollerblades
How many:	six planets	several computers	many messages

See *also* **articles** and **comparative forms of adjectives and adverbs.**

adverb Adverbs modify verbs, adjectives, or other adverbs, They tell *how, when,* or *where* about verbs.

How:	peacefully	quietly	quickly
When:	tomorrow	soon	yesterday
Where:	here	far	inside

See *also* **comparative forms of adjectives and adverbs.**

advice, advise The similarity in sound between these words causes confusion. *Advice* is a noun meaning "an opinion or recommendation as to what should be done"; *advise* is a verb meaning "to give advice to; to inform or recommend."

◆ This worked fine because the carpenters and plumbers and painters in town trusted Dolores and took her *advice* to heart.
　　from "A Crush" by Cynthia Rylant

◆ "That is well *advised*, Gawain," said the King.
　　from "Sir Gawain and the Loathly Lady" by Betsy Hearne

affect, effect *Affect* is a verb. It is most frequently used to mean "to influence." *Effect* is mainly used as a noun meaning "result or consequence."

"How will this news *affect* your family?" he asked.

◆ Singular coincidence, eh? Or are you going to start making accusations once again—about cause and *effect*.
　　from *The Dying Detective* by Arthur Conan Doyle (dramatized by Michael and Mollie Hardwick)

agreement

1. Subject-verb agreement. When the subject and verb of a sentence are both singular or both plural, they agree in number. This is called subject-verb agreement. Usually, singular verbs in the present tense end in *–s.* Plural verbs do not have the *–s* ending.

Jill paints. (singular subject; singular verb)

Jill and Andre paint. (plural subject; plural verb)

Pronouns generally follow the same rule. However I and you always take plural verbs.

	Singular	Plural
1st person	**I paint**	we paint
2nd person	**you paint**	you paint
3rd person	he/she/it paints	they paint

Changes also occur with the verb *to be* in both the present and past tense:

Present Tense		Past Tense	
I am	we are	I was	we were
you are	you are	you were	you were
he/she/it is	they are	he/she/it was	they were

a. Most compound subjects joined by *and* or *both. . . and* are plural and are followed by plural verbs.

◆ My *stepfather* and my *mother* have gone off to see my stepbrother, Tom. . . .
　　from "The Author" by M. E. Kerr

b. A compound subject joined by *or, either. . . or,* or *neither. . . nor* is followed by a verb that agrees in number with the closer subject.

◆ Neither did mountain *goats* nor any *beasts* of the forest ever *drink* from it.
from "Echo and Narcissus" by Anne Terry White

Problems arise when it isn't obvious what the subject is. The following rules should help you with some of the most troublesome situations:

c. Phrases or clauses coming between the subject and the verb do not affect the subject-verb agreement.

◆ The *building* right next door to us *was* a factory where they made walking dolls.
from "Antaeus" by Bordon Deal

d. Singular verbs are used with the singular indefinite pronouns *each, every, either, neither, anyone, anybody, one, everyone, everybody, someone, somebody, nobody, no one.*

◆ *One* of the children *was* called Niña, meaning "girl."
from "Niña" by Margarita Mondrus Engle

e. Plural indefinite pronouns take plural verbs. They are *both, few, many,* and *several.*

◆ A *few had* surfboards, which are against the rules at a body-surfing beach. . . .
from "A Sea Worry" by Maxine Hong Kingston

f. The indefinite pronouns *all, any, most, none,* and *some* can be either singular or plural depending on their meaning in a sentence.

Singular	Plural
None of us was really sure.	None of the invitations were mailed.
Some of the music was good.	Some of the dancers were exhausted.

g. Unusual word order does not affect agreement; the verb generally agrees with the subject, whether the subject follows or precedes it.

◆ Down by the bathing pool *was one* of the long crooknecked poles used to retrieve clothes from the hot washing troughs.
from "The Smallest Dragonboy" by Anne McCaffrey

◆ Gone *was* the booming *voice* and the happy *chatter* of the customers. . . .
from "Alfred: The Sweet-Shop Cat" by James Herriot

In informal English you may often hear sentences like "There's a book and some paper for you on my desk." *There's* is a contraction for there is. Technically, since the subject is *a book and some paper,* the verb should be plural and the sentence should begin "There are . . . ." Since this may sound strange, you may want to revise the sentence to something like "A book and some paper are on my desk." Be especially careful of sentences beginning with *There;* be sure the verb agrees with the subject.

NOTE: When writing dialogue, an author may intentionally use *there's* incorrectly for effect.

◆ There *were bullets* in the open field beyond the city, and in the passion vines which clung to the walls of the houses.
from "Niña" by Margarita Mondrus Engle

◆ There *wasn't* really a *Stan* of Stan's Hardware.
from "A Crush" by Cynthia Rylant

2. Pronoun-antecedent agreement.
a. An *antecedent* is a word, clause, or phrase to which a pronoun refers. The pronoun agrees with its antecedent in person, number, and gender.

◆ My *stepfather* says if I show *him* a short story all finished and ready to send out somewhere, *he'll* think about getting me a word processor.
from "The Author" by M. E. Kerr

b. Singular pronouns are generally used to refer to the indefinite pronouns *one, anyone, each, either, neither, everybody, everyone, somebody, someone, nobody,* and *no one.*

◆ *Each* had a wide smile on *his* face as Delores put her nose to the flowers.
from "A Crush" by Cynthia Rylant

Now look at the following sentence:

Everyone lined up early to buy her ticket.

This sentence poses problems. First, it is clearly plural in meaning but "everyone" and "her" are singular pronouns; second, "everyone" may not refer to women only. To avoid the latter problem, you could write "Everyone lined up early to buy his or her ticket." However, this solution gets clumsy and wordy. Sometimes it is best to revise:

The students lined up early to buy their tickets.

This sentence is now clear and non-sexist.

all right *All right* is generally used as an adjective and should always be spelled as two words.

◆ "It's *all right,* officer," he said reassuringly.
from "After Twenty Years" by O. Henry

among, between *Among* implies more than two persons, places, or things. *Between* usually refers to two, followed either by a plural or by two expressions joined by *and*—not by *or*.

◆ "Now move *among* the eggs," the wingsecond said.
from "The Smallest Dragonboy" by Anne McCaffrey

◆ It is her wish and *between* us you are at last her choice.
from "Brothers Are the Same" by Beryl Markham

See also **between you and me.**

anxious, eager Usually *anxious* means "worried" or "fear of being disappointed"; *eager* suggests being excited about something one wants to do or have.

◆ Why, my cabmen both enquired *anxiously* after you; and so did Inspector Morton. . . .
from *The Dying Detective* by Arthur Conan Doyle (dramatized by Michael and Mollie Hardwick)

◆ The last words came out in an *eager* rush.
from "The Scholarship Jacket" by Marta Salinas

apostrophe An apostrophe is used in possessive words and in contractions. It is also used to form the plurals of letters and numbers.

Ted's CD player	Delores's tattoo
won't hasn't	She got all A's and B's.

appositive An appositive is a noun or phrase that follows a noun and identifies or explains it. It is usually set off by commas.

◆ My father, *a career army officer,* was twenty-seven when he was killed. . . .
from "Father's Day" by Michael Dorris

◆ Tonight, Keevan's father, *K'last,* was at the main dragonrider table.
from "The Smallest Dragonboy" by Anne McCaffrey

articles *A, an,* and *the* are special adjectives called articles. *The* refers to something specific: *the* glove (that one over there). *A* and *an* refer to any item in its class: *a* glove (any glove).

awkward writing A general term (abbreviated *awk*) sometimes used in theme correcting to indicate such faults as inappropriate word choice, unnecessary repetition, clumsy phrasing, confusing word order, or any other weakness or expression that makes reading difficult.

Many writers have found that reading their first drafts aloud, helps them detect clumsy or unclear phrasing. Once identified, awkward construction can almost always be improved by rethinking and rewording.

B

bad, badly Be careful in using the modifiers *bad* and *badly*. *Bad* is an adjective. Use it to modify a noun or a pronoun. Use the adverb *badly* to modify a verb.

◆ "Well, Charles was *bad* again today."
from "Charles" by Shirley Jackson

◆ "He had tests a few weeks ago and his condition was *bad* then."
from "Jeremiah's Song" by Walter Dean Myers

The people of Maple Street were *badly* frightened by the strange events that occurred.

between you and me After prepositions such as *between,* use the objective form of the personal pronouns: *between you and* **me,** *between you and* **her,** *between you and* **him,** *between you and* **us,** *between you and* **them.**

Just *between you and me,* I know where the fox is hidden.

borrow, lend *To borrow* means to get something from someone else. To lend means to give something to someone else.

Abuela *borrowed* a black coat that was much too long for her.

Someone *lent* Malcolm X a dictionary.

bring, take To *bring* means to "carry something toward." To *take* means to "carry something away.

◆ "Do you not know, Prometheus, that every gift *brings* a penalty?"
from "Prometheus" by Bernard Evslin

◆ . . . Laurie slid off his chair, *took* a cookie, and left. . . .
from "Charles" by Shirley Jackson

capitalization

1. Capitalize all proper nouns and adjectives.

Proper Nouns	Proper Adjectives
Japan	Japanese
Africa	African
Victoria	Victorian

2. Capitalize peoples' names and titles

Herbert H. Hoover	Grandma Moses
Justice Sandra Day O'Connor	Judge Albert Ruhl
Mrs. Francis Jackson	Dr. Sara Mitchell
President of the United States	Senator Robert Dole
the Pope	the Secretary of State
Aunt Rebecca	Grandpa

3. Capitalize the names of races, languages, religions, and religious figures and writings. Also capitalize any adjectives made from these names.

Irish ballad	French
Spanish	African folk tale
the Bible	Biblical prophet
Allah	the Koran
the Lord God	the Torah

NOTE: If an article or possessive pronoun comes before a family title, the title is *not* capitalized: Everyone calls *my dad* T.J. *A sister* can be a real pest sometimes.

NOTE: Do not capitalize *god* when it refers to those found in ancient myths and legends.

Capitalize geographical names (except for articles and prepositions).

NOTE: Do not capitalize directions of the compass or adjectives that indicate direction: The storm is coming from the *east*. The tribe originated in the *southwest*.

Antarctica	North America
the Indian Ocean	Niagara Falls
the Gulf of Oman	Lake Erie
Mt. Shasta	Death Valley
the Alamo	Yosemite National Park
Route 66	the Everglades
the South	a Northeastern accent

5. Capitalize the names of structures, organizations, and bodies in the universe.

the Lincoln Memorial	the United Nations Building
Republican Party	Kennedy Middle School
the Red Cross	Second Harvest
Venus	the Solar System

Earth (when used with other planet names but *not* when preceded with *the*)

On a clear night Venus and Mars can be seen from *Earth*.

The *earth* has a core of molten lava.

6. Capitalize the names of historical events, times, and documents.

the Constitution	the Battle of Normandy
the Medieval Age	the Monroe Doctrine

7. Capitalize the names of months, days, holidays, and time abbreviations.

NOTE: *Do not* capitalize the names of the seasons: *spring, summer, fall, winter.*

February	Monday	A.M.
Valentine's Day	Presidents' Day	P.M.

8. Capitalize the first words in sentences, lines of poetry, and direct quotations.

NOTE: Some modern poetry does not begin each line with a capital letter.

◆ After Sarah was chosen for Sleeping Beauty, I went out for the Prince Charming role with all my heart.
  from "The Revolt of the Evil Fairies" by Ted Poston

◆ Macavity, Macavity, there's no one like Macavity,
  There never was a cat of such deceitfulness and suavity.
  from "Macavity: The Mystery Cat" by T. S. Eliot

◆ She said in a low voice, "I don't know how it will be if it's poison. Just do the best you can with the girls."
  from "The Day the Sun Came Out" by Dorothy M. Johnson

9. Capitalize certain parts of letters, outlines, and the first, last, and all other important words in titles,

Dear Sir or Madam: Dear Aunt Gail, Sincerely yours, Very truly yours,

I. Computers
  A. Size
    1. Desktop
    2. Laptop
    3. Notebook
  B. Brand

Book Title: *The Adventures of Tom Sawyer*
Newspaper: *The New York Times*
Play: *The Diary of Anne Frank*
Television Series: *Star Trek: The Next Generation*
Short Story: "The Gift of the Magi"
Song: "This Land Is Your Land"
Work of Art: *Mona Lisa*
Magazine: *Sassy*

clause A clause is a group of words that has a subject and a verb. A clause is *independent* when it can stand alone and make sense. A *dependent* clause has a subject and a verb, but it cannot stand alone. The reader is left wondering about the meaning.

Independent clause: Sherlock Holmes pretended to be ill.

Dependent clause: Although Sherlock Holmes pretended to be ill.

coherence If your writing has coherence (or is coherent), it means that the ideas move in a smooth, straight, uninterrupted flow from beginning to end. Coherence is achieved primarily through presenting the details in an orderly sequence that the reader can easily follow and will find sensible.

colon (:) The colon is used after the greeting of a business letter and between the hour and minutes when you write time in numbers.

    Dear Ms. Anderson: 9:25 P.M.

A colon is also used after phrases that introduce a list or a quotation.

◆ There they ate eggs and bacon and French toast among those whose work demanded rising before the *sun:* bus drivers, policemen, nurses, mill workers.
    from "A Crush" by Cynthia Rylant

◆ On the days she went sleeveless, one could see it on the taut brown skin of her upper *arm:* "Howl at the Moon."
    from "A Crush" by Cynthia Rylant

NOTES: (1) Some professional writers leave out the comma before the *and.* In general, however, student writers should include this comma unless told otherwise by their teachers. (2) If the items in the series are all separated by a word like *and,* no comma is necessary.

comma Commas are used to show a pause or separation between words and word groups in sentences, to avoid confusion in sentences, to separate items in addresses and dates, in dialogue, and in figures and friendly letters.

1. Use commas between items in a series. Words, phrases, and clauses in a series are separated by commas.

◆ It can analyze futures in *weather, politics, and economics.*
from "Key Item" by Issac Asimov

◆ *They ran among the trees, they slipped and fell, they pushed each other, they played hide-and-seek and tag. . . .*
from "All Summer in a Day" by Ray Bradbury

◆ The man who was in love with Delores and who brought her zinnias and cornflowers and nasturtiums and marigolds and asters and four o'clocks in clear mason jars did not know any of this.
from "A Crush" by Cynthia Rylant

2. Use a comma after certain introductory words and groups of words such as clauses and prepositional phrases of five words or more.

◆ *"Look,* Joann's father is not only on the Board, he owns the only store in town. . . .
from "The Scholarship Jacket" by Marta Salinas

◆ *When Etim'Ne heard that he had angered Obassi Osaw,* he set out himself for the latter's town. . . .
from "How the Lame Boy Brought Fire from Heaven"

◆ *With a basketball in his hands,* he could pretend not to hear the youngsters who were calling to him to come over and share the wine they were drinking. . . .
from "Nate 'Tiny' Archibald" by Bill Littlefield

3. Use a comma to set off nouns in direct address. The name or title by which persons (or animals) are addressed is called a noun of direct address. It is set off by commas.

◆ He ran into his friend, *Michael Torres,* by the water fountain that never turned off.
from "Seventh Grade" by Gary Soto

◆ You'll be the one in the dock, *Holmes. Inspector,* he asked me to come here.
from *The Dying Detective* by Arthur Conan Doyle (dramatized by Michael and Mollie Hardwick)

4. Use commas to set off interrupting words and appositives. Any phrase or clause that interrupts the general flow of a sentence is often set off by commas.

◆ Finally, *in late summer,* the day came when they were ready to fly for the first time as adult birds.
from "Turkeys" by Bailey White

Language and Grammar Handbook   **711**

◆ "I am Dr. Lu Manchu, *the mad scientist*," he announced, putting his hands in his sleeves and bowing.
    from "LAFFF" by Lensey Namioka

5. Use a comma before the conjunction in a compound sentence.

A comma is generally used before the coordinating conjunction *(and, but, for, or, nor, yet, so)* that joins the parts (independent clauses) of a compound sentence.

◆ Nag coiled himself down, coil by coil, round the bulge at the bottom of the water jar, *and* Rikki-tikki stayed still as death.
    from "Rikki-tikki-tavi" by Rudyard Kipling

NOTE: If the compound parts are very short, no comma is needed.

◆ I was eighteen and Jimmy was twenty.
    from "After Twenty Years" by O. Henry

6. Use a comma after a dependent clause that begins a sentence. Do not use a comma before a dependent clause that follows the independent clause.

◆ *As Teresa walked down the hall,* Victor walked the other way, looking back. . . .
    from "Seventh Grade" by Gary Soto

◆ He hadn't told them before *because he didn't want to admit any more about the gun than he had to.*
    from "The Gun" by Carol Ellis

7. Use commas to separate items in a date. If a date is within a sentence, put a comma after the year.

Eric dated the letter July 4, 1999, and put it in the time capsule.

8. Use a comma to separate items in an address. The number and street are considered one item. The state and Zip Code are also considered one item. Use a comma after the Zip Code if it is within a sentence.

Nick Katakis   Maria Gonzalez
724 W. Madison   8246 Camino Real
Green Bay, WI 54301   San Antonio, TX 78200

9. Use a comma to separate numerals greater than three digits.

84,600   156,825   267,552,832
$21,000   1,000,000

10. Use a comma after the greeting in a friendly letter and after the closing in all letters.

Dear Sarah,   Yours truly,   Very sincerely yours,

11. Use commas in punctuating dialogue. *See* dialogue.

comma splice *See* **run-on sentence.**

comparative forms of adjectives and adverbs Most adjectives and adverbs have three forms to show comparison. The **positive** form does not make a comparison, the **comparative** form compares two things, and the **superlative** form compares three or more of anything.

Most adjectives and adverbs form the comparative and superlative in regular ways.

1. Most one- and two-syllable modifiers add *-er* and *-est* to make the comparative and superlative forms.

Positive	Comparative	Superlative
big	bigger	biggest
cool	cooler	coolest
soon	sooner	soonest
crispy	crispier	crispiest
pretty	prettier	prettiest
gentle	gentler	gentlest

2. Longer modifiers use *more* and *most* to make comparisons.

Positive	Comparative	Superlative
careful	more careful	most careful
easily	more easily	most easily
sensible	more sensible	most sensible

3. Some adjectives and adverbs do not follow the usual rules. Their comparative and superlative forms are made differently.

Positive	Comparative	Superlative
good	better	best
bad	worse	worst
much	more	most
little	less	least
well	better	best
badly	worse	worst
much	more	most

conjunction A conjunction is a word that links one part of a sentence to another. It can join words, phrases, or entire sentences.

D

dash (—) The dash is used to show a sudden change in thought or to set off words that interrupt the main thought of a sentence.

◆ I passed the alley every day—it was only about a hundred yards from Skeldale House—and I fell into the habit of stopping and looking in through the little window of the shop.
  from "Alfred: The Sweet-Shop Cat" by James Herriot

◆ Tiny had handed Philadelphia a three-games-to-one advantage—a lead that a team that good was almost impossibly unlikely to lose.
  from "Nate 'Tiny' Archibald" by Bill Littlefield

Language and Grammar Handbook   **713**

desert, dessert Remember that *dessert* always refers to a treat, often at the end of a meal, (think of the extra *–s* as standing for *sweet*), and *desert* is used in all other contexts.

◆ Biddy Mason would have gladly walked through a *desert* if it meant she was walking to freedom.

◆ Angela hoped that the LAFFF machine would let her eat all the *desserts* she wanted without getting fat.

dialogue Dialogue is often used to enliven many types of writing. Notice the paragraphing and punctuation of the following passage:

◆ In English they reviewed the parts of speech. Mr. Lucas, a portly man, waddled down the aisle, asking, "What is a noun?"

"A person, place, or thing," said the class in unison.

"Yes, now somebody give me an example of a person—you, Victor Rodriguez."

"Teresa," Victor said automatically. Some of the girls giggled. They knew he had a crush on Teresa. He felt himself blushing again.

from "Seventh Grade" by Gary Soto

E

ellipsis (. . .) An ellipsis is used to indicate that words (or sentences or paragraphs) have been omitted. An ellipsis consists of three dots, but if the omitted portion would have completed the sentence, a fourth dot is added for the period.

◆ I was just taking my lamp to go to my bed on Wednesday night when I heard a faint knocking at the street door. I. . . found Mr. Holmes there.

from *The Dying Detective* by Arthur Conan Doyle (dramatized by Michael and Mollie Hardwick)

◆ The pounding in my ears drowned out the rest of the words, only a word here and there filtered through. ". . . Martha is Mexican. . . resign. . . won't do it. . . ."

from "The Scholarship Jacket" by Marta Salinas

exclamation point (!) An exclamation mark is used at the end of an exclamatory sentence—one that shows excitement or strong emotion. Exclamation points can also be used with strong interjections.

◆ "I'm blind, and you've been standing here letting me spout to you, and laughing at me every minute!"

from "A Man Who Had No Eyes" by MacKinlay Kantor

◆ "What faith! I wish I had the faith of the man who wrote this letter."

from "A Letter to God" by Gregorio López y Fuentes

F

fragment *See* **sentence fragment.**

G

good, well *Good* is used as an adjective to modify a noun or pronoun. Do not use it to modify a verb. Use the adverb *well* to modify a verb.

NOTE: When you are referring to health, both *good* and *well* can be used. They mean different things. If the meaning is "not ill," use *well:* If the meaning is "pleasant" or "in good spirits," use *good.*

◆ "I'm a *good* liar, I guess." "Or a *good* storyteller. . . . Which one?"
from "The Author" by M. E. Kerr

◆ I think I may say it worked very *well*—with your assistance, of course.
from *The Dying Detective* by Arthur Conan Doyle (dramatized by Michael and Mollie Hardwick)

◆ . . . I figured that maybe God would do something to make Grandpa Jeremiah *well.*
from "Jeremiah's Song" by Walter Dean Myers

◆ "If it makes him feel *good* it's as good as any medicine I can give him."
from "Jeremiah's Song" by Walter Dean Myers

H

hopefully This is often used to mean "it is hoped" or "I hope," as in the following sentence:

Hopefully, you'll make the team.

However, in formal writing, avoid this usage.

◆ I *hope* they don't have the same problems that I, and probably all the tomboys in the world, have had.
from "Never Fitting In" by Nereida Román

however Words like *however, moreover, nevertheless, consequently,* etc. (known as conjunctive adverbs) require special punctuation. If the word comes within a clause, it is generally set off by commas.

Rikki was surprised, *however,* at the fierceness of the cobra.

If the conjunctive adverb separates two independent clauses, a semicolon is used preceding the word and a comma is used after the word.

The boy stole fire and brought it to Earth; *consequently,* he was punished by Obassi Osaw.

I

interjection An interjection is a word or phrase used to express strong emotion.

◆ "*Yah!*" Beterli made a show of standing on his toe-tips. "You can't even see over an egg. . . . Oh, I forget, you can run fast can't you?"
from "The Smallest Dragonboy" by Anne McCaffrey

NOTE: In handwritten or non-computer writing, underlining takes the place of italics. See Capitalization, rule 10. for examples of italicized titles.

italics Italics are used to indicate titles of whole works such as books, magazines, newspapers, plays, films, and so on. They are also used to indicate foreign words and phrases and to add special emphasis to a word or phrase.

◆ The teacher beamed and said, *"Très bien. Parlez-vous français?"*
from "Seventh Grade" by Gary Soto

◆ You take advantage of that, and even if you don't ever play a day as a pro, you'll have *something*.
from "Nate 'Tiny' Archibald" by Bill Littlefield

its, it's *Its* is the possessive form of the personal pronoun *it; it's* is the contraction meaning "it is."

◆ Handle it gingerly, though. It may play *its* part at his trial. (possessive)
from *The Dying Detective* by Arthur Conan Doyle (dramatized by Michael and Mollie Hardwick)

◆ *It's* pitiful. *It's* disgusting. Makes me so mad I want to yell. (contraction of *it is*)
from "The Scribe" by Kristen Hunter

L

lay, lie This verb pair presents problems because, in addition to the similarity between the words, the past tense of *lie* is *lay.* The verb *to lay* means "to put or place something somewhere."

Present	Past	Past participle	Present Participle
lay	laid	(has) laid	(is) laying

◆ "Maybe I can *lay* my hands on some cotton seed, too."
from "Antaeus" by Bordon Deal

◆ I *laid* my aching head back on the pillow and closed my eyes.
from "Turkeys" by Bailey White

The principal parts of the verb *to lie,* which means "to rest in a flat position" are:

Present	Past	Past Participle	Present Participle
lie	lay	(has) lain	(is) lying

Notice the way the verbs are used in the following sentences:

◆ Won't take food or drink. Just *lies* there, sleeping. . .
from *The Dying Detective* by Arthur Conan Doyle (dramatized by Michael and Mollie Hardwick)

◆ He used them now to glance at his weapons, which *lay* beside him. . . .
from "Brothers Are the Same" by Beryl Markham

NOTE: When the meaning you intend is "not to tell the truth," *lie* (*lied, has lied*) is the verb to use.

◆ Great Heavens! Now, Holmes, you just *lie* quiet, and. . .
from *The Dying Detective* by Arthur Conan Doyle (dramatized by Michael and Mollie Hardwick)

learn, teach To *learn* means "to gain knowledge." To *teach* means "to give knowledge."

Present	Past	Past Participle	Present Participle
learn	learned	had learned	is learning
teach	taught	had taught	is teaching

◆ I saw that the best thing I could do was. . .to study, to *learn* some words.
   from "The Autobiography of Malcolm X" by Malcolm X with Alex Haley

◆ When the time came, she prevailed upon the elderly man next door to *teach* me how to shave.
   from "Father's Day" by Michael Dorris

lose, loose *Lose* (to lose one's way, to lose one's life, to lose a watch) is a verb; *loose* (to come loose, loose-fitting) is an adjective.

◆ "Why not? What have I got to *lose* except time?"
   from "LAFFF" by Lensey Namioka

◆ His hand was *loose* upon the long steel spear—too *loose*. . . .
   from "Brothers Are the Same" by Beryl Markham

M

myself (and himself, herself, etc.) Be careful not to use *myself* and the other reflexive and intensive pronouns when you simply need to use the personal pronoun *I* or its objective form *me*.

Incorrect: Andy and myself are lab partners.
 Correct: Andy and I are lab partners.

Incorrect: Patti gave John and myself the tickets.
 Correct: Patti gave John and me the tickets.

Reflexive pronouns reflect the action of the verb back to the subject. An intensive pronoun adds intensity to the noun or pronoun just named.

◆ I pick dogs that remind me of *myself,* scrappy, mutt-faced, with a hint of mange. (The reflexive pronoun *myself* refers back to me.)
   from "The Dog Diaries" by Merrill Markoe

Love is such a mystery, and when it strikes the heart of one as mysterious as Ernie *himself,* it can hardly be spoken of. (The intensive pronoun *himself* refers back to *Ernie.*)
   from "A Crush" by Cynthia Rylant

N

noun A noun is a word that names a person, place, thing, or idea. Most nouns are made plural by just adding *-s or -es* to the singular. When you are unsure about a plural form, check a dictionary.

P

parallel construction Items in a sentence that are of equal importance should be expressed in parallel (or similar) forms. These can take the form of noun phrases, verb phrases, and among others, prepositional phrases.

◆ *Dad toiled* at the office, *Mom baked* in the kitchen, and *brother and sister* always *had* neighborhood *friends sleeping over.*
from "Father's Day" by Michael Dorris

◆ Then she'd *wash that grease* out of Dolores's hair, *give her a* good blunt *cut, dress her* in a decent silk-blend blouse with a nice Liz Claiborne skirt from the Sports line, and, finally, *tone down* that swarthy, longshoreman look of Dolores's with a concealing beige foundation, some frosted peach lipstick, and a good gray liner for the eyes.
from "A Crush" by Cynthia Rylant

parentheses ( ) Parentheses are used to enclose words that interrupt the thought of a sentence or to enclose references to page numbers, chapters, or dates.

◆ The head nurse, V. Louise Higgins *(I never did know what that V stood for),* gave me a little box, which was sort of funny because she was the biggest of all the nurses there.
from "Birthday Box" by Jane Yolen

Edgar Allan Poe (1809-1849) led a troubled life.

possessive case The possessive case is formed in various ways. For singular nouns and indefinite pronouns, add an apostrophe and –s. *See also* **apostrophe.**

my *sister's* purse   no *one's* fault   *everybody's* assignment

◆ Alfred was *Goeff's cat* and he was always there, seated upright and majestic. . . .
from "Alfred: The Sweet-Shop Cat" by James Herriot

For plural nouns ending in an –s, add only an apostrophe.

the *doctors' office*   the *babies' pool*   the *teachers' rooms*

Anyone who damages the *books' covers* will have to pay a large fine.

However, if the plural is irregular and does not end in –s, add an apostrophe and then an –s.

men's razors   *children's parkas*   *women's gloves*

NOTE: Apostrophes are **not** *used with personal pronouns to show possession.*

◆ We both knew my half of the seedy, juicy fruit was going into my body, making flesh and fat, while *hers* was going right out of the gaping invisible hole in her stomach.
from "Ninā" by Margarita Mondrus Engle

preposition Prepositions are words that show the relationship between a noun or pronoun and some other word in a sentence.

Common prepositions include:

about	at	down	near	to
above	before	during	of	toward
across	behind	except	off	under
after	below	for	on	underneath
against	beneath	from	onto	until
along	beside	in	out	up
among	between	inside	over	upon
around	but	into	since	with
as	by	like	through	without

prepositional phrase Prepositional phrases are groups of words that begin with a preposition and end with a noun or pronoun. These phrases act as modifiers and create more vivid pictures for the reader. Notice the four prepositional phrases in the following sentence:

◆ When I went outside *for the first time,* the turkeys tumbled *after me down the steps* and scratched around *in the yard* while I sat *in the sun.*
from "Turkeys" by Bailey White

pronoun Subject pronouns are used as subjects of sentences. Object pronouns can be used as direct objects, indirect objects, or objects or prepositions.

When a pronoun is used as the subject of a sentence, the pronoun is in the nominative case and is called a *subject pronoun.*

Subject Pronouns

Singular:	I	you	he, she, it
Plural:	we	you	they

I went to the mall.   *She* and *I* went to the mall.

When a pronoun is used as an object, the pronoun is in the objective case and is called an *object pronoun.*

Object Pronouns

Singular:	me	you	him, her, it
Plural:	us	you	them

When the cookies were cool, Jeff ate *them.*

The waiter brought *him* and *me* the dessert very quickly.

HINT: When you are uncertain about whether to use a subject pronoun or an object pronoun in a sentence like the one above, take out the first pronoun to test the sentence. (You wouldn't say "The waiter brought I the dessert very quickly,")

Q

quotation marks Quotation marks enclose a speaker's exact words. They are also used to enclose some titles. When you use someone's exact words in your writing, use the following rules:

1. Enclose all quoted words within quotation marks.

◆ "You've got a large green mamba in your front room!" I shouted.
from "The Green Mamba" by Roald Dahl

2. The first word of a direct quotation begins with a capital letter. When a quotation is broken into two parts, use two sets of quotation marks. Use one capital letter if the quote is one sentence. Use two capital letters if it is two sentences.

◆ "I mean," Alabama moaned, "What tribe was it?"
   from "A Haircut" by I. S. Nakata

◆ "It sounds pretty interesting," said the policeman. "Rather a long time between meetings, though, it seems to me. Haven't you heard from your friend since you left?"
   from "After Twenty Years" by O. Henry

3. Use a comma between the words that introduce the speaker and the words that are quoted. Place the end punctuation or the comma that ends the quotation inside the quotation marks. Begin a new paragraph each time the speaker changes.

◆ "OK. . . OK," Derek said. "I had a gun."
   "Right. Where'd you get it?"
   "I found it. In a lot." Derek shook his head, remembering the fear and excitement he'd felt when he saw it.
   from "The Gun" by Carol Ellis

4. Put question marks and exclamation points inside the quotation marks if they are a part of the quotation. Put question marks and exclamation points outside the quotation marks if they are not part of the quotation.

◆ "What on earth's the matter?" she said.
   from "The Green Mamba" by Roald Dahl

Did Evan say, "I've finished reading 'The Green Mamba'"?

◆ He paused and added the key item. He said *"Please!"*
   from "Key Item" by Issac Asimov

See also **dialogue.**

5. Enclose titles of short works such as stories, songs, poems, and book chapters in quotation marks. *See* **capitalization,** rule number 9.

R

raise, rise   Use *raise* to mean "lift"; use *rise* to mean "get up."

Present	Past	Past Participle	Present Participle
rise	rose	had risen	is rising
raise	raised	had raised	is raising

◆ He says it's his "job" and *rises* each morning at 5:30 to catch the bus to Sandy Beach.
   from "A Sea Worry" by Maxine Hong Kingston

◆ . . . she dropped the savors into boiling fat and the aroma *rose* and floated over to the workers. . . .
   from "New Directions" by Maya Angelou

◆ I am sure this will *raise* my English grade, something I need desperately.
from "The Author" by M. E. Kerr

◆ He *raised* his eyes slowly and looked around. No Teresa.
from "Seventh Grade" by Gary Soto

NOTE: Notice the use of capital and lower-case letters in each correct example. You only need a capital letter when you break the run-on into two complete sentences.

run-on sentence This occurs when there is only a comma (known as a comma splice) or no punctuation between two independent clauses. Separate the clauses into two complete sentences, join them with a semicolon, or join them with a comma and a coordinating conjunction (*and, but, or, nor, yet, so, for*).

Run-on: The student received her schedule, then she went home.
Correct: The student received her schedule. Then she went home.
Correct: The student received her schedule; then she went home.
Correct: The student received her schedule, and then she went home.

semicolon (;) Use this punctuation mark to separate the two parts of a compound sentence when they are not joined by a comma and a conjunction.

◆ Mama told us to quit fussing so *much; she* was tired and wanted to rest.
from "The War of the Wall" by Toni Cade Bambara

sentence fragment A fragment, like a run-on sentence, should be avoided because it signals an error in the understanding of a sentence. A fragment often occurs when one sentence is finished, but another thought occurs to the writer and that thought is written as a complete thought. A fragment may be missing a subject, a verb, or both.

Fragment: I loved the book. Especially when Huck is trying to free Jim.
Correct: I loved the book, especially when Huck is trying to free Jim.

NOTE: As with run-ons, fragments are sometimes used by writers for effect or emphasis.

◆ "Cherokee?"
"No, not Cherokee."
"Not Sioux, are you?"
"Never been in North or South Dakota," I said.
from "A Haircut" by I. S. Nakata

sit, set *Sit* means to sit down; *set* means to put something somewhere.

Present	Past	Past Participle	Present Participle
sit	sat	had sat	is sitting
set	set	had set	is setting

◆ Even the white folks overflowed the two rows reserved for them, and a few were forced to *sit* in the intervening one.
from "The Revolt of the Evil Fairies" by Ted Poston

◆ He *sat* down on the stool and twisted a dial.
from "LAFFF" by Lensey Namioka

◆ You have *set* my mind at rest.
from "Alfred: The Sweet-Shop Cat" by James Herriot

T

than, then *Than* is used to point out comparisons; *then* is used as an indicator of time. Notice the use of *than* and *then* in the following examples:

◆ It took less time *than* you would think. . .the task of destruction is infinitely easier than that of creation.
   from "Antaeus" by Bordon Deal

◆ *Then* I remembered my P.E. shorts were still in a bag under my desk. . . .
   from "The Scholarship Jacket" by Marta Salinas

HINT: Remember that *there* has the word *here* in it; these two words are related in that they can both be indicators of place.

their, there, they're *Their* is a possessive, *there* is an introductory word or adverb of place, and *they're* is the contraction for *they are.*

◆ *Their* first time in Big Boy, Ernie was too nervous to eat. (possessive)
   from "A Crush" by Cynthia Rylant

◆ "I was *there* in C shop, last of all the folks rushing out. (adverb)
   from "A Man Who Had No Eyes" by MacKinlay Kantor

◆ "It means you've earned it by having the highest grades for eight years and that's why *they're* giving it to you." (contraction of *they are*)
   from "The Scholarship Jacket" by Marta Salinas

threw, through *Threw* is the past tense of *throw; through* is a preposition meaning "between the parts of":

◆ When it really started to stink my mother *threw* it on the roof where it rotted quickly in the sun.
   from "Niña" by Margarita Mondrus Engle

◆ I spent two days just riffling uncertainly *through* the dictionary's pages.
   from "The Autobiography of Malcolm X" by Malcolm X with Alex Haley

to, too, two *To* is a preposition that means "toward, in that direction" or is used in the infinitive form of the verb (e.g., to follow); *too* means "also" or "more than enough"; *two* means "more than one."

◆ "Ah Mrs. Dawson, how very nice *to* see you.
   from "Alfred: The Sweet-Shop Cat" by James Herriot

◆ I had come at a good time, *too,* because the proprietor was in the middle of one of his selection struggles.
   from "Alfred: The Sweet-Shop Cat" by James Herriot

◆ "There was a hundred and eight people killed, about *two* hundred injured, and over fifty of them lost their eyes."
   from "The Man Who Had No Eyes" by MacKinlay Kantor

V

verb *A verb* is a word that tells about an action or a state of being. The form or *tense* of the verb tells whether the action occurred in the past, the present, or the future.

verb shifts in tense Use the same tense to show two or more actions that occur at the same time.

> Incorrect: Rolanda *woke* (past) the boys and fixes (present) them breakfast.
> Correct: Rolanda *woke* (past) the boys and fixed (past) them breakfast.

W

weather, whether *Weather* refers to the condition of the atmosphere. *Whether* refers to a possibility.

> ◆ In such *weather* he could catch a cold. Is that not possible?
>   from "The Clever Magistrate" by Linda Fang

> ◆ If you struggle wth a disability, the first thing you need to do is find something that you are good at, *whether* it's singing or skateboarding. . . .
>   from "Samantha's Story" by Samantha Abeel

who, whom *Who* is used as a subject. *Whom* is used as a direct object or the object of a preposition.

> ◆ *Who* ever heard of baked macaroni without cheese or potato salad without eggs?
>   from "The War of the Wall" by Toni Cade Bambara

> ◆ A maiden *whom* he had spurned asked the goddess of vengeance to take her part.
>   from "Echo and Narcissus" by Anne Terry White

who's whose *Whose* is a possessive; *who's* is a contraction meaning "who is."

> ◆ "Charlie, don't start telling me *who's* dangerous and who isn't. . . (contraction of *who is*)
>   from *The Monsters Are Due on Maple Street* by Rod Serling

> ◆ And Prince Charming was one character *whose* lines Miss LaPrade never varied much. (possessive)
>   from "The Revolt of the Evil Fairies" by Ted Poston

would of This incorrect expression is often used mistakenly because it sounds like *would've,* the contraction for *would have.* In formal writing, write out *would have,* and you won't be confused.

> I *would have* gone to bed earlier if I had known what today would be like!

Y

your, you're *Your* is the possessive form of the personal pronoun *you; you're* is a contraction meaning "you are."

> ◆ "Listen guv'nor. Just a minute of *your* time." (possessive)
>   from "A Man Who Had No Eyes" by MacKinlay Kantor

> ◆ *You're* standing here all set to crucify—all set to find a scapegoat. . . . (contraction of *you are*)
>   from *The Monsters Are Due on Maple Street* by Rod Serling

Index of Skills and Strategies

Literary Genres, Terms, and Techniques

Alliteration, 259, 539, 540, 644, 690

Anecdote, 305, 421, 690

Anthropomorphism, 607

Archaic English, 150,159

Autobiography, 293, 684, 690

Ballad, 24, 348
  romantic, 639

Biography, 370, 690

Briticisms, 467, 477

Characterization, 14, 57,100, 239, 246, 432, 651, 655, 690

Characters, 15, 131, 148, 407, 432, 574
  main, 199, 432
  stock, 239

Character traits, 71, 159, 182, 655

Climax, 182, 407

Colloquial language, 385, 565

Conclusions, 267, 459, 527, 649

Conflict, 591, 607, 682

Connotation, 649, 690

Couplets, 372, 375

Devices
  poetic, 534
  sound, 644

Dialect, 385, 394, 477, 517
  regional, 517

Dialogue, 148, 246, 443, 444, 527, 574, 584, 689, 690

Diction, 159, 302, 303, 515

Drama, 617, 688, 690

End ryhme, 690

English, archaic, 150, 159

Epitaph, 395

Essay, 684, 690

Fables, 459, 460, 690

Falling action, 407

Fiction, 501, 508, 682, 690

Figurative language, 37, 686, 690
  metaphor, 37, 131, 285, 413, 534, 691
  simile, 64, 285, 693

First-person point of view, 293, 420, 692

Flashback, 124, 690

Foil, 239

Folk tales, 144, 261, 428, 541, 607, 657

Foreshadowing, 492, 690

Formal language, 394, 527

Free verse, 690

Genre, 508, 691

Haiku, 166

Hero/Heroine, 691

Humor, 293, 420, 663

Hyperbole, 353, 691

Idioms, 591

Imagery, 78, 267, 422, 426, 534, 584, 649, 687, 691

Inference, 253, 326, 409, 691
  See also Word choice, context clues in Vocabulary and Study Skills Index

Informal language, 527

Interior monologue, 246

Intonation, 269

Irony, 71, 131, 220, 459, 691

Jargon
  basketball, 133
  code of chivalry, 150
  navigation, 617
  surfing, 59
  war terms, 53

Language
  formal, 394, 527
  informal, 527

Legends, 435-37, 541, 607, 69

Limerick, 69

Main characters, 199, 432

Main idea, 51, 199

Message, 515
  See also Main Idea

Metaphor, 37, 131, 285, 413, 534, 691

Monologue, interior, 246

Mood, 113, 346, 427, 539, 682, 691

Moral, 394, 691

Moral tales, 541, 544

Motivation, 199

Myth, 39, 43, 261, 691

Narrative, 691

Narrator, 346, 465, 691
  omniscient, 370

Nonfiction, 508, 691

Novel, 691

Onomatopoeia, 607, 644, 692

Personification, 43, 259, 692

Play, 617, 688, 692

Plot, 23, 85, 148, 159, 182, 239, 253, 285, 363, 407, 504, 692

Poetic devices, 37, 259, 426, 534, 539, 607, 644

Poetry, 33, 255, 501, 508, 692
  haiku, 166
  imagery in, 201, 422, 691
  narrative, 639, 691
  repetition used in, 78, 692
  structure of, 372
  symbolism of, 448

Point of view, 31, 44, 57, 64, 71, 79, 124, 182, 293, 370, 420, 692

Repetition, 78, 131, 148, 259, 353, 426, 539, 644, 692

Resolution, 682, 692

Rhyme, 255, 259, 348, 353, 644, 686, 692

Rhyme scheme, 692

Rhythm, 33, 255, 348, 353, 639, 644, 686, 692

Rising action, 407

Science-fiction, 169, 333, 346, 355, 693

Setting, 5, 14, 15, 85, 204, 239, 246, 363, 394, 607, 682, 693

Short story, 501, 693

Simile, 64, 285, 693

Sound devices, 644

Speaker, 693

Speech, 530, 684, 693

Stage directions, 227, 689

Stanza, 372, 375, 693

Stereotype, 355, 428, 693

Stock characters, 239, 432

Style, 310

Suspense, 23, 584, 693

Symbolism, 37, 113, 199, 375, 413, 448, 484, 527, 544, 693

Tale, 693
Theme, 199, 267, 637, 682, 693
Third-person point of view, 31, 370, 693
Title, 204, 591
Tone, 142, 189, 465, 511, 515, 682, 693
    persuasive, 269
Word choice, 269

Writing Forms, Modes, and Processes

Audience, 93, 213, 269, 319, 441, 557, 671
Autobiographical essays, tips for writing, 551-556
Conclusions, 319, 671
Concrete language, 319, 321, 322
Creative writing
    additional chapter, 254
    additional stanza, 260
    alternate ending, 24
    ballads, 24, 205, 354
    biographical sketch, 376
    brochure copy, 460
    captions, 421
    character sketch, 58, 72
    daily log, 638
    definitions, 240
    dialogue, 23, 24, 149, 286
    diary entries, 149, 183, 311, 421
    epitaphs, 395, 645
    eulogy, 371
    fable, 460
    family history, 395
    form letters, 656
    ghostwriting, 485
    haiku poem, 166, 205
    headlines, 24, 240, 433, 585
    human interest story, 585
    imagery prose, 427
    imaginary day, 493
    instructional manual, 364
    interior monologue, 286
    using irony, 132
    job application, 516
    laboratory experiment, 364
    letters, 79, 143, 200, 303, 371, 493, 509, 592, 638, 650, 664

limerick, 87, 545
as Marco Polo, 382
missing-person profile, 72
myth, 44, 268
new law, 149
newspaper ad, 260
newspaper articles, 24, 240, 509
obituary, 354
personal note, 575
petition, 125
play, 268, 592
poem, 38, 65, 79, 132, 303, 354, 376, 427, 540, 650
proverb, 72, 114, 371
questionnaire, 190, 247
recipe, 516
report card, 253
resume, 143
scene, 200, 575
science-fiction story, 183
science article, 608
scripts, 200, 294
short stories, 132, 260, 466
short story outline, 509
skit, 87, 414
song lyrics, 205, 608, 645
speech, 183, 533
stories, 364, 414, 433
tabloid headlines, 433
talk-show characters, 441-46
title, 414
trickster tale, 545
vanity license plate, 664
Descriptive writing, 205, 254, 320, 376, 557
    description of an occurrence, 585, 638
    imaginary day, 493
    journal, 656
    predictions, 254
    profile of a character, 528
    soldiers, 433
    theme relationship, 575
    words, 58
Dialogue
    writing 441-446
Drafting, 95, 215, 321, 443, 559-60, 673
Editing, 97, 217, 323, 445, 555, 675

strategies for 97, 217, 323, 445, 555, 675
Expository/informative writing
    analysis, 86, 205
    comparison and contrast, 15, 32, 38, 247, 268, 303, 347, 380, 460, 545
    critical review, 93-98, 294
    essays, 15, 213-218, 268, 408, 460, 485
    explanation, 414
    field notes, 466
    how-to manual, 160
    inspirational message, 540
    instructional manual, 86, 364
    instructions, 15
    lab experiment, 364
    law, 149
    leaflet, 200
    letters, 319-24
    reports, 114, 125, 247, 268
    research reports, 72, 294, 311, 354
    summarizing a play, 347
    summarizing a ritual, 408
    summarizing a story, 72, 149, 293
    summarizing main points, 93
    time line, 371
    tips for writing, 213-218, 319-324
    travel guide, 493
"Hooking" an audience, 673, 674
Letters, tips for successful writing, 319
Main ideas, 213, 215, 216
Narrative writing
    autobiographical essay, 44, 551-556
    chronological organization in, 553
    description, 43
    interview, 311
    interview questions, 433
    paraphrasing, 645
    tips for, 441-446, 551-556
Note taking, 92, 190
Outlining, 92, 161
Paragraphs, focused, 216
Parallel structure, for clarity, 93
Peer review/editing, 97, 215, 217,

321, 323, 443, 444, 673

Personal expression
  autobiographical description, 540
  autobiographical essay, 485
  autobiographical sketch, 190
  autobiography, 44
  character sketch, 478
  essay, 114
  homily, 533
  letters, 79
  memoir, 254
  notebook entry, 5, 17, 53, 59, 80, 107, 126, 133, 150, 169, 185, 201, 227, 248, 261, 267, 278, 295, 305, 333, 355, 372, 376, 385, 396, 415, 422, 427, 455, 461, 467, 469, 479, 511, 517, 534, 541, 565, 576, 586, 617, 639, 651, 656
  personal description, 585
  personal essays, 114, 650
  personal narratives, 125, 160
  poem, 38
  poster, 24, 32, 200, 294, 427
  press release, 86
  proverb, 72, 371
  question, 190
  statement of opinion, 395
  thank-you note, 15
  thumbnail sketch, 478

Persuasive/argumentative writing
  evidence in, 671
  letters, 528
  opinion, 671-76
  paragraph, 65, 269
  tips for writing, 671-676
  tone in, 269

Portfolio presentation, preparing, 665

Portfolio, working
  arranging, 665
  getting started, 16
  introduction for, 665
  maintaining, 377
  reviewing goals for, 377
  reviewing writing in, 665
  setting up, 16
  what to include, 16

Portfolio
  working, 98, 218, 324, 446, 556, 676

Presenting, 38, 98, 218, 324, 446, 556, 676

Prewriting, 94-95, 213-15, 319-21, 442-43, 551-553, 672-73
  quickwrite, 94, 214, 320, 442, 552, 672

Quickwrite, 94-95, 214, 320, 442, 552, 672

Reflecting, 98, 218, 324, 446, 556, 676

Revising, 96, 215-16, 322, 444, 554, 673-74
  parallel structure in, 96
  strategies for, 96, 216, 322, 444, 554, 674
  writing, 444

Rewriting
  anecdote, 421
  archaic English, 159
  as a letter, 533
  as a prose paragraph, 427
  scene, 575
  stanza, 645

Specific language, 322

Summaries, 293, 441, 670
  a play, 347
  a ritual, 408
  a story, 72
  main points, 93

Supporting an opinion, 421, 671

Supporting details, 213, 215, 216, 557

Writer's notebook, 358, 504

Writing process,
  concrete language, 322
  clear pronoun reference, 555
  details, arranging, 161
  dialogue that reveals personality, 444
  distinguishing between adjectives and adverbs, 675
  misspellings, 609
  punctuation, 434, 445
  purpose in, 93, 213, 269, 319, 441, 557, 671
  research techniques for, 497
  self-evaluating, 98, 218, 324, 446, 556, 676
  subject and object pronouns, 323
  varied sentence structure, 554

verb tense, 514

Reading/Thinking Strategies

Author's purpose, 23, 57, 78, 85, 107, 113, 131, 287, 310, 426, 527, 584

Cause and effect, 346, 615, 657, 685

Chronological organization, 161
  interesting beginnings, 674

Chronology, 479

Clarifying, xxiii, 31, 37, 71, 115, 159, 267, 285, 398, 413, 482, 598, 607, 637, 649, 683

Classifying, 408, 497

Colloquial English, 565

Comparison/contrast, 14, 51, 71, 124, 126, 148, 150, 189, 199, 212, 240, 248, 267, 310, 363, 415, 426, 504, 544, 550, 565, 584, 591, 627, 644, 646, 649, 663

Comprehension, techniques for, 396

Connecting, xxiii, 37, 38, 43, 64, 142, 150, 177, 199, 208, 284, 285, 293, 310, 315, 375, 400, 407, 413, 437, 683

Context clues. See entry in Vocabulary and Study Skills index

Description, 57

Details, recalling, 499

Drawing conclusions, 14, 37, 113, 182, 189, 199, 204, 239, 241, 246, 267, 271, 285, 315, 318, 346, 370, 394, 407, 420, 426, 432, 459, 465, 484, 515, 527, 532, 539, 544, 574, 591, 612, 614, 627, 637, 644, 655, 663

Evaluating, xxiii, 14, 23, 31, 37, 43, 57, 64, 71, 78, 85, 113, 124, 131, 142, 144, 148, 159, 166, 182, 189, 199, 204, 209, 239, 241, 246, 285, 293, 310, 313, 315, 325, 353, 361, 363, 370, 394, 407, 413, 420, 432, 459, 465, 484, 492, 515, 521, 532, 539, 544, 549, 574, 584, 591, 607, 637, 649, 683

Evidence to support
conclusion, 318, 539

Facts
distinguishing from opinions, 383, 685
recognizing, 383
supporting, 383

Foreign words, 25, 487
Spanish, 487, 586

Graphic aids, in reading, 212

Illiteracy, 191
See also Literacy

Main idea, 276, 685

Mental outlines, 276

Opinions, distinguishing from facts, 383, 685

Order of importance
organization, 161

Organization, modes of, 161

Paraphrasing, as technique for comprehension, 396

Personal response, 14, 23, 31, 37, 43, 64, 66, 71, 73, 85, 113, 115, 124, 131, 142, 144, 148, 159, 163, 166, 199, 204, 211, 239, 246, 248, 253, 310, 313, 325, 346, 353, 355, 363, 370, 376, 394, 407, 413, 420, 432, 439, 459, 465, 484, 492, 495, 498, 508, 515, 527, 532, 539, 544, 574, 584, 627, 607, 637, 644, 649, 651, 663, 667

Poetry, strategies for reading, 33, 73

Predicting, xxiii, 8, 14, 31, 39, 51, 57, 64, 71, 85, 110, 124, 131, 159, 180, 208, 282, 285, 295, 320, 363, 404, 413, 527, 533, 574, 591, 601, 605, 614, 627, 657, 663, 683

Previewing, 25, 33, 39, 53, 59, 66, 73, 80, 107, 115, 126, 133, 144, 150, 169, 185, 191, 201, 227, 241, 248, 255, 277, 278, 287, 295, 305, 333, 348, 355, 365, 372, 385, 396, 409, 415, 422, 428, 454, 455, 464, 469, 479, 487, 501, 511, 517, 529, 534, 541, 565, 576, 586, 593, 617, 639, 646, 651, 657, 685

Problem-solving strategies, for reading, 80

Questioning, xxiii, 9, 23, 71, 209, 358, 375, 396, 683

Reading
note taking as aid to, 92
and remembering, 276
special-interest group for, 485

Recalling details, 499

Sequence of events, 479

Sequencing, 440

Setting a purpose for reading, 5, 17, 25, 33, 39, 53, 57, 66, 80, 107, 115, 126, 133, 144, 168, 185, 191, 201, 226, 241, 248, 255, 277, 278, 287, 295, 305, 332, 365, 372, 409, 415, 422, 454, 499, 500, 501, 511, 529, 534, 541, 564, 565, 576, 593, 616, 639, 646, 651, 657

Similarities/differences, 38, 80, 93, 126, 159, 163, 199, 204, 246, 293, 370, 375, 508, 550

Skimming, 51, 124, 318, 413, 515, 657

Special organization, 161

Summarizing, xxiii, 37, 144, 149, 172, 175, 253, 273, 396, 402, 426, 432, 637, 667, 670, 683

Supporting details, 14, 43, 276, 409, 465, 576, 649, 663, 685

Time/order relationships, 440, 685

Time markers, 440

Using prior knowledge, 25, 33, 39, 53, 59, 73, 107, 115, 126, 131, 133, 142, 144, 150, 168, 169, 185, 210, 227, 241, 248, 253, 255, 278, 287, 295, 305, 326, 333, 348, 353, 365, 372, 385, 396, 407, 409, 422, 428, 469, 479, 487, 501, 511, 517, 529, 532, 539, 541, 557-62, 576, 584, 586, 593, 612, 616, 617, 639, 646, 651

Visualizing, 5, 167, 278, 285, 576, 670

Words
faulty and funny, 66
foreign, 25, 487, 586

Vocabulary and Study Skills

Analogies, 72, 286, 592

Antonyms, 24, 86, 125, 254, 311, 408, 540

Boxes, for categorizing, 66

Card catalogue, 497

Charts
archaic English, 150
bird characteristics, 461
Briticisms, 469
calendar of events, 479
casting decisions, 638
cause/effect, 484
character's dialogue, 574
character clues, 627
characters, 261
character traits, 71, 185, 655
classifying viewpoints, 78
comparison/contrast, 126, 550
context clues, 53, 608
details, 161, 214, 320
dialects, 385, 517
dialogue, 148
dog ownership, 421
expressions, 565
favorite poems, 255
folk tales, 428
foreign words, 25, 487
friendships, 33
guilty/innocent, 672
idea organizing, 73, 532
idioms, 591
images, 584, 649
imaginary reunion, 17
interior monologue, 246
irony, 459
K-W-L, 499
literacy, 191
literature connections, 442
literature key quotes, 672
motives and methods, 267
narrator's tone, 465
navigation jargon, 617
new directions, 558
news articles, 51
opinions, 94, 673
place, people, terms, 169, 261
plot, 23

predictions, 295
problem/solution, 80
pronouns, 323
pronunciation, 593
relationships, 319-20
repetitions, 78, 644
report card, 253
sequence, 38
settings, 204
simile/metaphor, 285
sound devices, 644
Spanish word meanings, 487
stage directions, 227
style, 310
supporting details, 541
surfing jargon, 59
third-person point of view, 370
traits for success, 239
word meanings, 395, 415
writing style, 310
Cluster, predictions, 320

Diagrams
cause/effect, 615
climax, 182
garden, 528
personification, 43
plot, 407
staircase of details, 214
symbols, 544
Venn, 43, 64, 124, 182, 259, 305

Frames
comparison/contrast, 318
reasoning, 14

Graphs, 190, 212, 534

Historical societies, as a research source, 486

Individuals, as a research source, 486

Inferred meanings. See Word choice, context clues

Information, sources for, 486

Jargon
basketball, 133
surfing, 59

Lists
adjectives, 545
characterizations, 432
classification, 408
class rules, 254
clues, 253

decisions, 220
dos and don'ts, 32
fire attributes, 261
headings, 51
images, 91
new directions, 558
onomatopoeia, 607
places, 448
prejudice, 293

Maps
Africa, 396
Cuba, 487
westward movement, 365
world, 427
Yukon Territory, 348

Museums, as a research source, 486

Outlining. See Writing Forms, Modes, and Processes Index

Primary sources, 486

Public libraries, as a research source, 486

Reader's Guide to Periodical Literature, 486

Research
astronaut's life, 380
careers, 190
chromosome structure, 275
civil rights movement, 294
Cuban revolution, 493
endangered bird, 466
ethnic heritage tales, 437
firsthand knowledge, 316
genetic fingerprinting, 273
homicide law, 672
Japanese internment, 72
learning disability services, 539
pets, 125
pillories, 247
remedies, 326
savings accounts, 200
science topic, 268
Southern cooking, 395
surfer, 65
talk shows, 442
techniques for, 486
topics for, 220
travelers' challenges, 382
Yukon, 354

Root words, 39, 650

Scales
attributes, 302
beginning/end, 574
effective speech, 325
likes/dislikes, 576
values, 241
zero to ten, 591
Secondary sources, 486
Sources, for information, 486
Story circle, 363
Story line, 346
Synonyms, 15, 24, 58, 86, 114, 125, 160, 311, 408, 540, 575

Time lines, 311, 355, 421, 440
assassinations, 529
clues, 115
Cuban revolution, 493

Venn diagrams, 43, 124, 182, 259, 305

Vocabulary, older out-of-use words, 17

Vocabulary template, definitions, 190

Word choice
context clues, 17, 25, 32, 44, 53, 65, 132, 143, 149, 200, 204, 240, 260, 268, 294, 303, 347, 354, 376, 414, 421, 459, 460, 466, 478, 485, 493, 509, 516, 528, 533, 585, 608, 627, 638, 656, 664
Word maps, 86, 333, 364, 371
Words, faulty and funny, 66
Word webs
cause/effect, 657
causes, 293
characters, 527
character traits, 159, 432
connotations, 333
descriptive, 185, 189
love definition, 51
mood, 113
perspective on blindness, 459
poetry images, 255
root words, 650
setting, 5, 95
symbolism, 375
tone, 142, 511
topics, 670
word meanings, 540

Grammar, Usage, Mechanics, and Spelling

a and *and*, 703
accept and *except*, 703
Adjective
    distinguishing from adverb, 675
    as modifier, 703
Adverb, distinguishing from adjective, 675
advice or *advise*, 704
affect or *effect*, 704
Agreement problems, recognizing, 304
    subject-verb agreement, 304, 704
    pronoun-antecedent agreement, 706
all right, 706
among or *between*, 706
anxious or *eager*, 707
apostrophe, 707
appositive, 707
articles, 707
awkward writing, 707
bad or *badly*, 707
between you and me, 708
borrow or *lend*, 708
bring or *take*, 708
Capitalization, 78, 708-710
Clause, 710
Coherence, 710
Colon, 710
Comma
    rules for using, 217, 445, 711-712
Comma splices, 93, 97, 712
Comparative forms of adjectives/adverbs, 713
Complex sentences, 184
Compound sentences, 184
Compound subjects, verb subject agreement problems with, 304
Conjunction, 713
Dash, 713
desert or *dessert*, 714
Dialogue, 690, 714
Ellipsis, 455, 714
Exclamation point, 714

Fragment, 714
good or *well*, 715
Homophone, 87
hopefully, 715
however, 715
Interjection, 715
Italics, 715
its or *it's*, 716
lay or *lie*, 716
learn or *teach*, 717
lose or *loose*, 717
Misspellings, 613
myself (and *himself*, *herself*, etc.), 717
Noun, 717
Object Pronouns, 323, 719
Parallel construction, 717
Parentheses, 718
Possessive case, 718
Preposition, 718
Pronoun, 719
    object, 323, 719
    subject, 323, 719
Pronunciation, 593
Punctuation
    for clarity, 434
    purpose of, 78, 549
Quotation marks, 719-720
raise or *rise*, 720
Run-on sentences, 97, 721
Semicolon, 721
sit or *set*, 721
Sentence
    avoiding run-on, 97
    complex, 184
    compound, 184
    fragment, 721
    strategies for combining, 184
    varying structure of, 560
Spelling problems, recognizing, 609
Subject-verb agreement, with compound subjects, 304
Subject and object pronouns, 323
than or *then*, 722
their, *there*, or *they're*, 722
threw or *through*, 722

to, *too*, or *two*, 722
Verb, 722
Verb tense, consistent, 510, 723
weather or *whether*, 723
who or *whom*, 723
who's or *whose*, 723
would of, 723
your or *you're*, 723

Speaking, Listening, and Viewing

Advertising techniques, 677
Bandwagon appeal, as an advertising technique, 677
Beyond print, 99
Choral reading, 132, 354, 645
Collaborative learning
    bird-calling contest, 466
    brainstorming, 32, 64, 71, 87, 114, 191, 213-14, 220, 241, 255, 320, 442, 448, 484, 558
    comedy routine, 592
    debates, 86, 143, 247, 294, 326, 638
    games, 99, 545
    group discussions, 39, 100, 160, 220, 287, 294, 311, 326, 348, 365, 395, 408, 434, 509, 638
    interviewing, 149, 311, 540, 592
    mock trials, 260, 664
    partners, 24, 32, 33, 51, 73, 87, 96, 98, 114, 149, 161, 182, 183, 184, 205, 240, 254, 267, 276, 302, 311, 320, 324, 364, 383, 433, 455, 485, 514, 533, 540, 592, 613, 615, 638, 650, 670
    small groups, 15, 25, 38, 51, 65, 144, 161, 167, 183, 190, 199, 200, 205, 218, 241, 247, 255, 260, 268, 324, 408, 414, 493, 575, 593, 615, 645, 656, 676
    taking a poll, 220, 428, 433, 501
    town meeting, 125
Conversation, improvised, 205
Critical thinking,
    advertising, 219, 558, 677
Demonstration, 478

Dramatic presentation, 311, 408, 608
interviews, 65, 460

Interactive multimedia, 577

Interviewing, 65, 149, 311, 460, 533, 540, 592

Listening
effective, 99
strategies for, 99

Media literacy, 477
TV court dramas, 269

Multimedia, hints for using, 557

Oral history, 371

Oral presentation, 38, 65, 79, 114, 268, 557
fire safety, 268
passive multimedia used in, 557
a play, 240, 268, 509
tips for making a, 219

Oral reading, 200, 211, 218, 240, 305, 446

Oral report, 143, 160, 200, 466

Pantomime, 38, 205

Passive multimedia, 557

Performing
comedy routine, 592
melodrama, 645
skits, 58, 254, 364, 414, 575
song, 38, 354, 371, 645
puppet show, 664
western, 371

Play-by-play description, 205

Speaking
description, 58, 492
a dialogue, 433, 650
a dramatic monologue, 421
a dramatic reading, 485, 608
effective, 325
a poetry reading, 376
TV commercial, 160, 585
a TV newscast, 347

Speeches, 529, 684, 693
persuasive, 183, 325, 532,
preparing a, 325
valedictory, 303

Storytelling, 79, 385, 438-39, 460

Survey, conducting, 125, 365, 540

Tableau, presenting a, 160, 585

Technology skills, 447

computer skills, 87, 98, 446
interactive multimedia used in, 557

Testimonial, as an advertising technique, 677

Town Meeting, enacting a, 125

Transfer, an advertising technique, 677

Viewing, 219, 427
dance, 509
puppet show, 664
TV talk shows, 442

Interdisciplinary Connections

Advertising campaign, developing, 677

Advertising flyer, 516

Anthropology, courtship and marriage, 47-49

Anthropology connection, 668

Art connection, 438-439

Awards, 516, 608

Baby book, 254

Ballad, 24

Board games, 268, 575

Book jacket, 79, 509

Bookplate, 485

Brochures, 220, 364, 427

Bulletin boards, 89, 408, 615

Cartoon strips, 478, 663

Collages, 15, 16, 656

Comic books, 44, 160, 354

Community service, 210
tutoring, 210-11

Computer games, 86

Covers
book, 79
portfolio, 665

Cutouts, 608

Dance, 509

Decoration, 413

Designs
costumes, 149, 294
scenery, 294

Dioramas, 183, 240

DNA, 272-75, 498

Doing Battle, 162-66
knights, 162

Samurai, 163-65

Drawings, 16, 32, 58, 59, 72, 79, 85, 125, 132, 190, 200, 240, 260, 303, 364, 375, 413, 433, 455

Earth science connection, 610

Explorers, 378-82
Ibn Battutah, 379
Marco Polo 378-79, 381-82
Zheng He, 379-80

Floor plan, 460

From Pen to Printout, 546-49
history of printing, 546-47
history of punctuation, 548-49

Garden designs, 528

Gathering Evidence, 270-75
DNA, 272-75
fingerprints, 271
genetic fingerprinting, 272-75
historically, 270
lie detector, 271

Geography connection, 378

Getting Into Focus, 88-91
interpreting visual evidence, 90-91
vision, 88-89

Graphic aids, 557

Guest or Pest, 610
brown tree snakes, 610
killer bees, 611
kudzu, 610
med flies, 612
mongoose, 613-14
nutria, 612
water hyacinths, 612
wild pigs, 611

Hand puppets, 664

Help Is on the Way, 206-11

History connection, 162, 164, 206, 270, 311, 312, 381, 435, 546

Illustrations, 114, 142, 286, 303, 311, 347, 364, 371, 414

Language connection, 548

Let's Be Fair, 312-17

Life science connection, 88, 272, 274, 494

Literacy, worldwide, 209-11

Love Connection, The, 45-50

Maps, 167, 286, 376, 408, 608

Mask, 545
Mathematics, marriage statistics of, 50
Mathematics connection, 209
Memorials, 493, 533
Menu, 395
Models, 86
   3-D, 408
   chromosome, 275
Mural, 183
Music, 44, 65, 354, 433, 509, 528, 645

Paintings, 311
   comparison of, 91
   as inspiration, 79
   wall of respect, 575
Pamphlet, 32
Pantomime, 38, 205
Party invitation, 414
Photographs, 16, 58, 650
Picture books, 44, 466
Pictures, 58, 79
Posters, 24, 32, 200, 260, 294, 427, 557, 615
Psychology, What is love?, 45
Psychology connection, 90

Quilt design, 395

Scale drawing, 240
Science connection, 496, 613
Science on the March, 494-98
   anemia, 494-95
   anesthesia, 496
   DNA, 498
   vaccines, 496
   X-rays, 497
Scribes, in history, 206-208
Sculpture, 311
Silhouettes, 189
Sketches
   characters, 638
   costumes, 149
Sociology connection, 314, 316, 666
Songs, 38, 205, 354, 371, 395, 645
Storyboards, 376, 447
T-shirt design, 114, 183
Tableau, 160, 585
Tattoo, 15
Timeless Tales, 435-39

Tour package, 493
Vanity license plate, 72
Winding Roads, 378-82
   explorers, 378-82
   Marco Polo, 378-79, 381-82
Women Making Waves, 666-69
   equality of, 667
   historically, 666
   Kuna Indians, 668-69
Works of art, 38

Media and Technology

Advertisement
   creating an ad, 114, 160, 219
   propaganda, 677
Advertising Techniques
   bandwagon, 677
   testimonial, 677
   transfer, 677

Computer
   spell check, 609
   formatting, 446
   game, 86, 557

Television
   advertment, 160, 247, 585
   camera terms, 333, 447
   lighting, 447
   newscast, 348
   sound, 447
   storyboard, 447

Media literacy
   critical thinking, 677
   interacting with, 557
   shaping a scene, 447
Movies, 219
Multimedia, 557
   interactive, 557
   passive, 557

Multicultural Awareness and Appreciation

Change, 106, 113, 117, 124, 141, 142, 159, 220, 452-53
Choice, 544, 616, 637, 644, 655, 678
   consequences of, 162
Communication, 4, 7, 14, 26, 31, 36, 37, 100, 226, 253, 267, 326, 478

Groups, 52, 71, 411
   cultures of, 422, 426, 448
   expectations of, 399, 407
   identifying with, 57, 69
   as parent replacement, 57
   understanding between, 384, 432
Individuality, 168, 179, 189, 204, 220, 332, 346, 350, 356, 363, 366, 370, 373, 448
Interactions, 277, 285, 289, 293, 307, 310, 326, 500, 503, 508, 515, 532

Perspective, 454, 459, 492, 564, 574, 591, 607, 663, 678

Life Skills

Challenges, 104-105
Change, 106, 113, 124, 142, 159, 220, 452-53
Choices, 220
Conflicts, 562-63, 574, 591, 607
Deception, 326
Decisions, 220
Habits, 564
Prejudice, 224-25, 287, 305, 312-17, 313
   classroom exercise, 314-15
   historically, 312-13
   internment of Japanese, 313
   Ku Klux Klan, 313
   slavery, 313
   tolerance and , 316-17
Relationships, 2-3, 99
Stress, reducing, 220
Values and beliefs, 224-25, 330-31
Visualizing, 214, 558
Worries and fears, 305, 448

Index of Fine Art and Artists

African art (anonymous), bronze statue from Benin, 262; Somali courtship, 47; sculpture from Mali , 436; Fante people of Ghana, snake flag, 579, dog flag, 581; Nigerian queen, 666

Aivazovsky, Ivan, *The Rainbow,* 625

Alexander, Gregory, *from The Jungle Book,* 595

Ancient art (anonymous), Herculaneum fresco of Sappho, 666

Arabic art (anonymous), fourth-century scribes, 207

Archuleta, Felipe Benito, *Jack Rabbit,* 659, *Tiger,* 660-661

Arcimboldo, Giuseppe, *The Vegetable Gardener,* 90

Aztec art (anonymous), wedding celebration, 48; *Codex Mendosa,* 546

Bateman, Robert, *Queen Anne's Lace and American Goldfinch,* 583

Bearden, Romare, *The Block,* 192, 193; *Maudell Sleet's Magic Garden,* 513

Benally, Elsie, *Women's Basketall Team,* 187

Browning, Colleen, *Computer Cosmology,* 83; *Sly's Eye,* 245

Bryan, Ashley, *from Sing to the Sun: Poems and Pictures (Storyteller),* 393

Burchfield, Charles, *Fantasy of Heat,* 283; *Yellow Afterglow,* 335

Calcutta Residence of Percy Brown, *Untitled* (anonymous), 600

Carapaccio, Vittore, *St. Jerome in His Study,* 207

Carra, Gina, *Untitled* (rooftop scene), 518-519

Cavatio, Vince, *Untitled* (surfer in a pipeline), 60

Children's art (anonymous), from Terezin Concentration Camp, 301

Chinese art (anonymous), hired mourner doll, 145; Buddhist scribe, 206

Cossiers, Jan, *Prometheus Carrying Fire,* 265

Cottingham, Robert, *Barber Shop,* 69

Cross, Henri Edmond, *Landscape with Stars,* 76

Derain, André, *Portrait of Vlaminck,* 21

Dinyer, Eric, *Untitled* (face in a porthole), 339

Dürer, Albrecht, *The Young Hare,* 466

Eakins, Thomas, *study for Negro Boy Dancing,* 390

Egyptian art (anonymous), fresco of scribes in field, 206; Queen Hatshepsut, 666

Emslie, Alfred Edward, *Dinner at Haddo House,* xxiv

Gauguin, Paul, *The Three Huts,* 79

Gibson, Charles, *Untitled* (young boy), 597

Greek art (anonymous), sixth-century terracotta scribe, 206

Green, Jonathan, *Mt. Pleasant Dance Hall,* 1

Grotesque Old Woman (anonymous), painted in 1520, 154

Gwathmey, Robert, *Portrait of a Farmer's Wife,* 374

Haring, Keith, *Untitled lithograph* (heavy heart), 26

Harrison, Ted, *from The Cremation of Sam McGee,* 350

Hayes, Connie, *Untitled* (two boys), 117

Herrera, Joe H., *Cochiti Green Corn Dance,* 543

Hesse, Eva, *Untitled* (boxes), 411

Highwayman, *Untitled* (anonymous), 641

Holmes, Lesley, *from Cat Stories* (Hatfield's shop), 468 (cat), 472

Homer, Winslow, *Mink Pond,* 188; *Breezing Up,* 102-103

Hopper, Edward, *Brooklyn, 1932,* 205

Hoy, Carol, *Aquarium,* 589

Jin, Shang, See **Shang Jin**

Jones, Xavier, *Women of the Setting Sun,* 648

Kestrel, Steve, *Dream of the Frog,* 75

Kuan, Fan, *Travelers Among Mountains and Streams,* 373

Kuna Indian art (anonymous) molas, 668-669

Künstler, Mort, *Morning Mist,* 112

Lacy, Jean, *Welcome to My Ghetto Land,* 77

Langenstein, Michael, *American Liberty,* 222

Lark, Raymond, *Society,* 307

Lawrence, Jacob, *Vaudeville,* 289; *Grand Performance,* 291; *The Library,* 481, *"The Migration Series" image,* 647

Lichtenstein, Roy, *The Ring,* 47

Liljefors, Bruno, *Untitled* (fox), 120

Lindneux, Robert, *Trail of Tears,* 313

Lotto, Lorenzo, *Bridal Couple: Messer Marsilio and His Wife,* 48

Lundeen, George, *Woman Holding a Basket,* 108

Magana, Mardonio, *Campesino con Yunta de Bueyes (Farmer with Yoked Oxen),* 129

Magritte, Rene, *Le Faux Miroir,* 203

Marks, Cora Goldberg, *Untitled* (Jewish wedding), 49

Matisse, Henri, *The Young Sailor II,* 7
McCall, Robert, *Untitled* (spaceship), 345
Medieval art (anonymous), from the Capodilista Codex, 152; *The Battle of Najera* and Brigandine armor, 162; Christine de Pisan writing, 208
Meyers, Jeffry W., *Untitled* (school coatroom), 251
Moholy-Nagy, Laszlo, *Light Space Modulator,* 361
Motley, A. J., *Extra Paper (State Street Scene),* 456
Munch, Edvard, *The Sick Child,* 488
Mural art, *The Wall of Respect* (Visual Art Workshop collaborative), 570-571

Navoi, *Untitled* (Arabic tile), 650
Nelson, Linda, *Untitled* (male/female image), 356

Ong, Diana, *Faces III,* 414; Butterfly, 507

Paget, Walter, *Untitled* (Sherlock at the door), 235
Porter, Fairfield, *John Ashbery and James Schuyler Writing "A Nest of Ninnies,"* 503
Portrait of a Provincial Treasure, Lu Ming (anonymous), 147
Poulides, Peter, *Untitled* (gun), 243
Provensen, Alice and Martin, *Echo and Narcissus,* 40-41

Ranson, Paul, *Edge of the Forest,* 450-451
Renoir, Pierre-Auguste, *Portrait of a Young Woman,* 631
Ricks, Don, *Good Friends—Zinnias & Asters,* 10
Rivera, Diego, *Portrait of a Woman,* 296
Rivera, Pablo, *Untitled* (track meet), 202
Rodrique, George, *Blue Dog on a Red Rug,* 417
Rosenthal, Marc, *Untitled* (cat), 257
Rossetti, Dante Gabriel, *Il Ramoscello,* 157
Ruisdael, *Untitled* (Dutch scene), 425

Samurai art (anonymous), Samurai armor and Heiji Insurrection of 1159, 163; ivory statue of Kusunoki Masashige, 165
Shang Jin, *A Girl of Yi Nationality,* cover (detail), ii
Sloan, John, *The City from Greenwich Village,* 18-19

Szathmary, Kara, *In Pursuit of Paradise,* 328-329

Tagel, Peggy, *Untitled* (dancing couple), 258
Tamayo, Rufino, *Self Portrait,* 567
Tarkhoff, Nicolas, *The Black Cat on the Window Sill,* 505
Tiers, Montgomery, *Centennial Progress,* 366-367
Torak, Thomas, *After the Game,* 55
Trees and Flowers by a Stream (anonymous), screen, 431

Uelsmann, Jerrey N. *Untitled* (tree and leaf), 536; *Untitled* (tree and woman), 538
Utamaro, Kitagawa, *The Courtesan Ajeraki and Her Gallant,* 47

Van Gogh, Vincent, *Still Life: Basket with Six Oranges,* 35; *Portrait of Joseph Roulin,* 619
van der Zee, James, *Untitled* (bridal couple), 48
Velez, Walter *Untitled* (young person in toga), 174
Vickrey, Robert, *Seated Negress,* 196; *The Magic Carpet,* 280; *The Corner Seat,* 524
Vietnamese art (anonymous), Trieu Au, 666
Villa, Roxana, *Untitled* (swirling heavens), 423
Vincent, William, *Maasai, Masai Mara,* 399; *Majestic King,* 403
Visual Art Workshop, *The Wall of Respect,* 570-571
Vuillard, Edouard *In Bed,* 463

Wallop, E. H, *Untitled* (basketball players), 134-135
Watteau, Antoine, *Love Song,* 47
Whelan, Michael, *Weyrworld,* 170; *Destiny's Road,* 179
Wiggins, R. Douglas, *Morning Star Over Cerro Gordo,* 653
Wilson, Alexander, *Turkey,* 461
Wilson, Ellis, *Haitian Funeral Procession,* 36
Wilson, Maurice, *The Battle Between Nag and Rikki-tikki-tavi,* 603
Wood, Grant, *Death on Ridge Road,* 560-561
Wyeth, Andrew, *That Gentleman,* 387
Wyeth, Henriette, *Young Peter,* 252

Index of Authors and Titles

Abeel, Samantha, 534
About Old People, 306
Abuela Invents the Zero, 587
Adventures of Marco Polo, The, 381
After Twenty Years, 18
Alegría, Ricardo E., 657
Alfred: The Sweet-Shop Cat, 468
All Summer in a Day, 279
Almost Perfect, 130
Anderson, Jack, 201
Angelou, Maya, 511
Annixter, Paul, 115
Antaeus, 518
Asimov, Isaac, 80
Author, The, 502
Autobiography of Malcolm X, The, 480

Bambara, Toni Cade, 565
Baraka, Amiri, 198
Benét, Rosemary and Stephen, 365
Berry, James, 34
Biddy Mason, 366
Birdfoot's Grampa, 75
Birthday Box, 410
Boughton, Simon, 381
Bradbury, Ray, 278
Brenner, Alfred, 617
Brooks, Gwendolyn, 372
Brothers Are the Same, 397
Brown Eyes Only, 314
Bruchac, Joseph, 74
Bryan, Ashley, 385
Buson, 507

Charles, 249
Clever Magistrate, The, 145
Clifton, Lucille, 74
Cofer, Judith Ortiz, 586
Conan Doyle, Arthur, 227
Cremation of Sam McGee, The, 349
Crush, A, 6
Cummings, E. E., 305

Dahl, Roald, 576
Day the Sun Came Out, The, 108

Deal, Borden, 517
Dickinson, Emily, 185
Dinner Party, The, xxiv
Dog Diaries, The, 416
Dorris, Michael, 53
Duvall, Lynn, 316
Dying Detective, The, 228

Echo and Narcissus, 40
Eliot, T. S., 255
Ellis, Carol, 241
Engle, Margarita Mondrus, 487
Evans, Mari, 34
Evslin, Bernard, 261

Fabric of Life, 668
Fang, Linda, 144
Father's Day, 54
Feng, Hu, 372
Frost, Robert, 576

Gardner, Mona, xxiv
Genetic Fingerprinting: The Murder with No Body, 272
Gentleman of Rio en Medio, 652
Gingold, Pam Deyell, 314
Giovanni, Nikki, 255
Green Mamba, The, 577
Greensleeves, 158
Gun, The, 242

Haircut, A, 67
Haley, Alex, 479
Hardwick, Michael and Mollie, 227
Hearne, Betsy, 150
Henry, O., 17
Herriot, James, 467
Highwayman, The, 640
How the Lame Boy Brought Fire from Heaven, 262
Hughes, Langston, 646
Hunter, Kristin, 191
Hyder, Zia, 422

i remember, 483
I'm Nobody, 188
In the Inner City, 77
Interpreting Visual Evidence, 90

Jackson, Mae, 483
Jackson, Shirley, 248
Jeremiah's Song, 386
Johnson, Donna, 668
Johnson, Dorothy, 107
Journey, The, 373

Kantor, MacKinlay, 455
Kennedy, Robert F., 529
Kerr, M. E., 501
Key Item, 81
Kidnap Poem, 258
Kingston, Maxine Hong, 59
Kipling, Rudyard, 593
Kusunoki Masashige: The Loyal Samurai, 164

LAFFF, 356
Larsen, Anita, 272
Last Cover, 116
Letter to God, A, 127
Little, Jean, 34, 305
Littlefield, Bill, 133
López y Fuentes, Gregorio, 126
Luxner, Larry, 613

Macavity: The Mystery Cat, 256
Malanga, Gerard, 34
Man Who Had No Eyes, A, 456
Markham, Beryl, 396
Markham, Edwin, 573
Markoe, Merrill, 415
McCaffrey, Anne, 169
McKissack, Patricia and Fredrick, 435
Meltzer, Milton, 210
Minor Bird, A, 583
Mongoose on the Loose, 613
Monsters Are Due on Maple Street, The, 334
Moore, Ann Woodbury, 164
Morrison, Lillian, 201
Mother to Son, 647
My Hard Repair Job, 36
Myers, Walter Dean, 385

Nakata, I. S., 66
Namioka, Lensey, 355
Nate "Tiny" Archibald, 134

Never Fitting In, 186
New Directions, 512
Niña, 488
Noyes, Alfred, 639

Old Mary, 374
old age sticks, 309
On Destiny, 423
*On the Death of Martin Luther
    King, Jr.,* 530
Oranges, 35
Outwitted, 573

Pelz, Ruth, 365
Poston, Ted, 287
Prometheus, 264
Pure Poetry, 35

Rabbit and the Tiger, The, 658
Rabbit Dances with the People,
    542
Reader, The, 507
Rebel,The, 36
Revolt of the Evil Fairies, The, 288
Rikki-tikki-tavi, 594
Robertus, Polly M., 548
Rolzinski, Catherine A., 210
Román, Nereida, 185
Ross, Gayle, 541
Rylant, Cynthia, 5

Salinas, Marta, 295
Samantha's Story, 535
Scholarship Jacket, The, 296
Scribe, The, 192
Sea Worry, A, 60
Sedillo, Juan A. A., 651
Self Portrait, 538
Serling, Rod, 333
Service, Robert, 348
Seventh Grade, 26
Short History of Punctuation, A,
    548
Silverstein, Shel, 126
Sir Gawain and the Loathly Lady,
    151
Smallest Dragonboy, The, 170
SOS, 198
Soto, Gary, 25
Storyteller, 393
Students Helping Students, 210
*Sundiata Keita, the Legend and the
    King,* 435
Survival, 618

Tanikawa, Shuntarō, 422
Thomson, Dr. David, 90
*Three Reasons to Become More
    Tolerant,* 316

Translating Grandfather's House,
    301
Turkeys, 462

Under This Sky, 424

Vega, Ed J., 295

Walker, Alice, 646
War of the Wall, The, 566
We Are All One, 429
Western Wagons, 369
*When I Heard the Learn'd
    Astronomer,* 76
Where You Are, 203
White, Anne Terry, 39
White, Bailey, 641
Whitman, Walt, 74
Who Cares? Millions Do, 210
Women's 400 Meters, The, 202
Women, 648
Worth, Valerie, 13

X, Malcolm, 479

Yep, Laurence, 428
Yolen, Jane, 409

Zinnias, 13

170 "The Smallest Dragonboy" by Anne McCaffrey. Copyright © 1974 by Anne McCaffrey. Reprinted by permission of the author and the author's agent, Virginia Kidd. **186** "Never Fitting In" by Nereida Román is reprinted with permission from the publisher of *Hispanic, Female and Young: An Anthology,* edited by Phyllis Tashlik (Houston: Arte Público Press–University of Houston, 1994). **188** "I'm Nobody" from *Poems of Emily Dickinson,* Second Series, edited by T. W. Higginson and Mabel Loomis Todd. (Boston: Roberts Brothers), 1891. **192** "The Scribe" by Kristin Hunter. Copyright © 1972 by Kristin Hunter. Reprinted by permission of the author. **198** "SOS" by Amiri Baraka from *Selected Poetry of Amiri Baraka/LeRoi Jones.* Copyright © 1979 by Amiri Baraka. Reprinted by permission of Sterling Lord Literistic, Inc. **202** "The Women's 400 Meters" from *The Sidewalk Racer and Other Poems of Sports and Motion* by Lillian Morrison, page 16. Copyright © 1968, 1977 by Lillian Morrison. Reprinted by permission of Marian Reiner for the author. **203** "Where You Are" from *The Invention of New Jersey* by Jack Anderson, page 67. Copyright © 1969 by the University of Pittsburgh Press. Reprinted by permission of the University of Pittsburgh Press. **210** Milton Meltzer, *Who Cares? Millions Do . . .* New York, N.Y., Walker Publishing Company, Inc., 1994, page 98. Catherine A. Rolzinski, *The Adventure of Adolescence: Middle School Students and Community Service.* Youth Service America, pages 11, 12, 14 and 15-17. **228** "The Dying Detective" from *The Game's Afoot* by Michael and Mollie Hardwick. Copyright © 1969 by Michael and Mollie Hardwick. Reprinted by permission of John Murray (Publishers) Ltd. **242** "The Gun" by Carol Ellis. Copyright © 1995 by Carol Ellis. Reprinted by permission of the author. **249** "Charles" from *The Lottery* by Shirley Jackson. Copyright 1948, 1949 by Shirley Jackson. Copyright renewed © 1976, 1977 by Laurence Hyman, Barry Hyman, Mrs. Sarah Webster, and Mrs. Joanne Schnurer. Reprinted by permission of Farrar, Straus & Giroux, Inc. **256** "Macavity: The Mystery Cat" from *Old Possum's Book of Practical Cats* by T.S. Eliot, 1939. **258** "Kidnap Poem" from *The Women and the Men* by Nikki Giovanni. Copyright © 1970, 1974, 1975 by Nikki Giovanni. Reprinted by permission of William Morrow and Company, Inc. **262** "How the Lame Boy Brought Fire from Heaven" from *The Shadow in the Bush* by P.A. Talbot, (1912). **264** "Prometheus" from *Heroes, Gods, and Monsters of the Greek Myths* retold by Bernard Evslin. Copyright © 1966 by Scholastic, Inc. Reprinted by permission of Scholastic Inc. **272** Adapted from "'Genetic Fingerprinting': The Murder with No Body" from *True Crimes and How They Were Solved* by Anita Larsen, pages 14–17. Copyright © 1993 by Scholastic Inc. Reprinted by permission of Scholastic Inc. **279** "All Summer in a Day" by Ray Bradbury. Originally published in *Fantasy & Science Fiction Magazine.* Copyright 1954, renewed © 1982 by Ray Bradbury. Reprinted by permission of Don Congdon Associates, Inc. **288** "The Revolt of the Evil Fairies" by Ted Poston. Reprinted by permission of the Estate of Ted Poston, Ersa H. Poston and Ruth Banks. **296** "The Scholarship Jacket" by Marta Salinas from *Nosotras: Latina Literature Today,* edited by María del Carmen Boza, Beverly Silva, and Carmen Valle. Copyright © 1986 by Bilingual Press/Editorial Bilingüe (Arizona State University, Tempe, AZ). Reprinted by permission of Bilingual Press/Editorial Bilingüe. **301** "Translating Grandfather's House" by Ed J. Vega from *Cool Salsa* by Lori M. Carlson, pages 6–7. Collection copyright © 1994 by Lori M. Carlson. Reprinted by permission of Henry Holt and Company, Inc. **306** "About Old People" from *Hey World, Here I Am!* by Jean Little, pages 60 and 62–63. **309** "old age sticks" by E. E. Cummings from *Complete Poems: 1904–1962,* Edited by George J. Firmage. Copyright © 1958, 1986, 1991 by the Trustees for the E. E. Cummings Trust. Reprinted by permission of Liveright Publishing Corporation. **314** From "Brown-eyes Only" by Pam Deyell Gingold from *Faces Magazine,* Volume IX, Number VI, February 1993 issue: *Prejudice/Tolerance,* pages 14–17. Copyright © 1993 by Cobblestone Publishing, Inc., 7 School St., Peterborough, N.H. 03458. Reprinted by permission of the publisher. **316** "Three Reasons to Become More Tolerant" from *Respecting Our Differences: A Guide to Getting Along in a Changing World* by Lynn Duvall, Edited by Pamela Espeland, pages 5–6. Copyright © 1994 by Lynn Duvall. Reprinted by permission of Free Spirit Publishing Inc., Minneapolis, MN; (800) 735-7323. All rights reserved. **334** "The Monsters Are Due on Maple Street" by Rod Serling. Copyright © 1960 by Rod Serling; © 1988 by Carolyn Serling, Jodi Serling and Anne Serling. Reprinted by permission of The Rod Serling Trust. All rights reserved. **349** "The Cremation of Sam McGee" by Robert Service. Reprinted by permission of the Estate of Robert Service and Krasilovsky Copyright Agency, Inc. **356** "LAFFF" by Lensey Namioka from *Within Reach,* edited by Donald R. Gallo, pages 33–48. Copyright © 1993 by Lensey Namioka. Reprinted by permission of Ruth Cohen, Inc., Literary Agent for Lensey Namioka. All rights are reserved by Lensey Namioka. **366** "Biddy Mason" from *Black Heroes of the Wild West* by Ruth Pelz, pages 31–35. Copyright © 1990 by Open Hand Publishing Inc. Reprinted by permission of Open Hand Publishing Inc. **369** "Western Wagons" from *A Book of Americans* by Rosemary and Stephen Vincent Benét, page 36. Copyright 1933 by Rosemary and Stephen Vincent Benét. Copyright renewed © 1964 by Thomas C. Benét, Stephanie B. Mahin, and Rachel Lewis Benét. All Rights Reserved. Reprinted by permission of Brandt & Brandt Literary Agents, Inc. **373** "The Journey" by Hu Feng from *Twentieth Century Chinese Poetry: An Anthology,* Translated and Edited by Kai-yu Hsu, page 375. **374** "Old Mary" by Gwendolyn Brooks from her book *Blacks,* published by Third World Press, 1991. Copyright © 1991 by Gwendolyn Brooks. Reprinted by permission of the author. **381** Adapted from "Travels in the East" from *Great Lives* by Simon Boughton, pages 206–207. Copyright © 1988 by Grisewood and Dempsey Ltd. Reprinted by permission of Doubleday, a division of Bantam Doubleday Dell Publishing Group, Inc. **386** "Jeremiah's Song" by Walter Dean Myers from *Visions: Nineteen Short Stories by Outstanding Writers for Young Adults,* Edited by Donald R. Gallo, pages 194–202. **393** "Storyteller" and illustration from *Sing to the Sun* by Ashley Bryan. Copyright © 1992 by Ashley Bryan. Reprinted by permission of HarperCollins Publishers, Inc. **397** "Brothers Are the Same" by Beryl Markham from *The Splendid Outcast: Beryl Markham's*

African Stories, Compiled and Introduced by Mary S. Lovell, pages 51-66. Copyright © 1987 by the Beryl Markham Estate. Reprinted by permission of the Estate of Beryl Markham and Laurence Pollinger Limited.
410 "Birthday Box" by Jane Yolen. First appeared in *Birthday Surprises: Ten Great Stories to Unwrap,* Published by Morrow Junior Books, pages 27–33. Copyright © 1995 by Jane Yolen. Reprinted by permission of Curtis Brown Ltd. **416** "The Dog Diaries" from *What the Dogs Have Taught Me: And Other Amazing Things I've Learned* by Merrill Markoe, pages 37–43. Copyright © 1992 by Merrill Markoe. Reprinted by permission of Viking Penguin, a division of Penguin Books USA Inc. **423** "On Destiny" by Shuntarō Tanikawa, translated by Harold Wright from *Selected Poems of Shuntarō Tanikawa.* Copyright © 1983 by Shuntarō Tanikawa and Harold Wright. Reprinted by permission of Harold Wright. **424** "Under This Sky" from *Dur Theke Dekka* by Zia Hyder. Copyright © 1973 by Zia Hyder. Reprinted by permission of the author. **429** "We Are All One" from *The Rainbow People* by Laurence Yep, pages 73–78. Text copyright © 1989 by Laurence Yep. Reprinted by permission of HarperCollins Publishers, Inc. **435** Adapted from *The Royal Kingdoms of Ghana, Mali, and Songhay: Life in Medieval Africa* by Patricia and Fredrick McKissack, pages 47–48, 49, and 52–54. Copyright © 1994 by Patricia and Fredrick McKissack. Reprinted by permission of Henry Holt and Company, Inc. **456** "A Man Who Had No Eyes" by MacKinlay Kantor. Copyright 1931 by MacKinlay Kantor. Reprinted by permission of the MacKinlay Kantor Estate and Donald Maass Literary Agency, 157 W. 57th St., Suite 1003, New York, N.Y. 10019. **462** "Turkeys" from *Mama Makes Up Her Mind: And Other Dangers of Southern Living* by Bailey White, pages 12–16. **468** "Alfred the Sweet-Shop Cat" from *James Herriot's Cat* Stories by James Herriot, pages 1–9, and 12–19. Copyright © 1994 by James Herriot. Reprinted by permission of St. Martin's Press, Inc. and Harold Ober, Associates, Inc. **480** From *The Autobiography of Malcolm X* by Malcolm X with Alex Haley. Copyright © 1964 by Alex Haley and Malcolm X. Copyright © 1965 by Alex Haley and Betty Shabazz. Reprinted by permission of Randon House, Inc. **483** "i remember . . ." from *Can I Poet with You* by Mae Jackson. Reprinted by permission of the author. **488** "Niña" by Margarita Mondrus Engle is reprinted with permission from the publisher of *The Américas Review* (Houston: Arte Público Press–University of Houston, 1987). **494** Adapted abridgment of "What's in the Blood That Can Make You Sick?" from *Current Health 1,* Volumn 18, No. 4, October 1994, pages 28–29. **502** "The Author" by M.E. Kerr from *Funny You Should Ask,* Edited by David Gale, pages 190–198. **512** "New Directions" from *Wouldn't Take Nothing for My Journey Now* by Maya Angelou, pages 21–24. Copyright © 1993 by Maya Angelou. Reprinted by permission of Random House, Inc. **518** "Antaeus" by Borden Deal. Reprinted by permission of Ashley Deal Moss. **535** and **538** "Samantha's Story" and "Self Portrait" from *Reach for the Moon,* stories and poems by Samantha Abeel. Copyright © 1994 by Samantha Abeel. Reprinted by permission of Pfeifer-Hamilton Publishers, 210 W. Michigan, Duluth, MN 55802, 800-247-6789. **542** "Rabbit Dances with the People" from *How Rabbit Tricked Otter: And Other Cherokee Trickster Stories,* told by Gayle Ross, pages 25–28. **548** "A Short History of Punctuation" by

Polly M. Robertus from *Cricket,* June 1991, Volume 18, Number 10, pages 20–21. Copyright © 1991 by Polly M. Robertus. Reprinted by permission of the author. **566** "The War of the Wall" by Toni Cade Bambara. Copyright © 1981 by Toni Cade Bambara. Reprinted by permission of the Estate of Toni Cade Bambara. **573** "Outwitted" by Edwin Markham from *The Best Loved Poems of the American People,* selected by Hazel Felleman, page 67. **577** Adaptation of "The Green Mamba" from *Going Solo* by Roald Dahl, pages 50–58. Copyright © 1986 by Roald Dahl. Reprinted by permission of Farrar, Straus & Giroux, Inc. and Murray Pollinger Literary Agent. **583** "A Minor Bird" by Robert Frost from *The Poetry of Robert Frost,* edited by Edward Connery Lathem. Copyright © 1956 by Robert Frost. Copyright 1928, © 1969 by Henry Holt and Company, Inc. Reprinted by permission of Henry Holt and Company, Inc. **587** "Abuela Invents the Zero" from *An Island Like You* by Judith Ortiz Cofer, pages 107–111. Copyright © 1995 by Judith Ortiz Cofer. Reprinted by permission of the Publisher, Orchard Books, New York. **613** "Mongoose on the Loose" by Larry Luxner from *Américas Magazine,* July/August, 1993, page 3. **618** "Survival" by Alfred Brenner. Reprinted by permission of the author. **647** "Mother to Son" copyright 1929 by Alfred A. Knopf, Inc. and renewed 1954 by Langston Hughes. Reprinted from *Selected Poems of Langston Hughes,* by permission of Alfred A. Knopf, Inc. **648** "Women" from *Revolutionary Petunias & Other Poems,* copyright © 1970 by Alice Walker, reprinted by permission of Harcourt Brace & Company. **652** "Gentleman of Rio en Medio" by Juan A. A. Sedillo from *The New Mexico Quarterly,* August 1939. Reprinted by permission of the author. **658** "The Rabbit and the Tiger" ("El Conejo y el Tigre") from *The Three Wishes: A Collection of Puerto Rican Folktales,* Selected and adapted by Ricardo E. Alegría, Translated by Elizabeth Culbert, pages 44–47 and 49–51. Copyright © 1969 by Ricardo E. Alegría. Reprinted by permission of Ricardo E. Alegría. **668** Adapted from "Fabric of Life" by Donna Johnson from *International Wildlife,* Volume 24, Number 4, July-August 1994, page 12. Copyright © 1994 by National Wildlife Federation. Reprinted by permission of National Wildlife Federation.

Illustrations

Unless otherwise acknowledged, all photographs are the property of Scott, Foresman and Company. Page abbreviations are as follows: (t)top, (c)center, (b)bottom, (l)left, (r)right, (ins)inset.

cover (detail), ii Shang Jin, *"Girl of Yi Nationality,"* 1993. Courtesy of Quast Galleries, Taos, NM **vii** Jonathan Green, *"Mt. Pleasant Dance Hall,"* 1991. Oil on masonite, 16 x 20 inches. Courtesy of Jonathan Green, Naples, Florida **ix** *"Breezing Up," (A Fair Wind)* 1876 Oil on canvas 35⅝ x 49¾ Homer, Winslow, National Gallery of Art, Washington, DC, Gift of the W. L. and May T. Mellon Foundation **xi** "American Liberty, New York,"1984 © Michael Langenstein, computer graphics created on a Dicomed D38, Collection of the Artist **xiii** *"In Pursuit of Paradise"* © Kara Szathmary **xv** Paul Ranson, Christie's, London/Superstock **xvii** *"Death on the Ridge Road,"* Grant Wood, 1935, Williams College Museum of Art, Gift of Cole Porter **xxiv** National Portrait Gallery, London/Superstock

0–1 Jonathan Green, "*Mt. Pleasant Dance Hall,*" 1991. Oil on masonite, 16 x 20 inches. Courtesy of Jonathan Green, Naples, Florida **1, 4, 16, 45, 51(icon)** Diana Ong, "*Crowd #2,*" Private Collection/Superstock **5** Courtesy of the author **7** Henry Matisse, "*The Young Sailor II,*" 1906. Oil on canvas. 40 x 32¾ inches. The Jacques and Natasha Gelman Collection. Photograph by Malcolm Varon/Courtesy Metropolitan Museum of Art **10** Don Ricks, "*Good Friends—Zinnias & Astors,*" Courtesy Vanier & Roberts, Ltd. Fine Art **17** Corbis-Bettmann Archive **18–19** John Sloan, "*The City from Greenwich Village.*" 1922. Oil on canvas, 26" x 33¾ inches. Gift of Helen Farr Sloan. ©1995 Board of Trustees, The National Gallery of Art, Washington **21** Musee des Beaux-Arts, Chartres, France/Giraudon/Art Resource **25** Carolyn Soto **26** Keith Haring, "*Untitled,*" 1985, Lithograph. © The Estate of Keith Haring, 1995 **34(tc)** Courtesy of Gerard Malanga, Photo by Virginia Vincent **34(bc)** Courtesy, Harcourt, Brace, Jovanovich **34(b)** Courtesy, William, Morrow and Company **36** Ellis Wilson, "*Haitian Funeral Procession,*" ca.1950s, 30½" x 29¼", Aaron Douglas Collection, The Amistad Research Center at Tulane University, New Orleans, LA **45** Stewart Cohen/Index Stock Photography, Inc. **46** Cass O'Keefe **47(cl)** National Gallery, Washington, DC/Superstock, Inc. **47(l)** Abdim Dr. No, "Courtship"/Superstock **47(cr)** Kitagawa Utamaro, "*The Courtesan Ajeraki and Her Gallant*"/Bridgeman Art Library, London/Superstock **47(r)** Roy Lichenstein, "*The Ring,*" 1962. Private Collection, Italy. © Roy Lichtenstein **48(l)** Lorenzo Lotto, "*Bridal Couple: Messer Marsillio and his Wife,*"/Museo del Prado, Madrid/Scala/Art Resource **48(c)** From "*The World of Weddings:* an Illustrated Celebration" by Brian Michael Murphy. Copyright © 1978 Brian M. Murphy. Photo: Cottie Burland. **48(r)** Photograph by James Van Der Zee, courtesy of Donna Van Der Zee. **49(tl)** Joe Viesti/Viesti Associates, Inc. **49(bl)** From "*The Bride*" by Barbara Tober. Published by Harry N. Abrams, Inc. Illustrations copyright ©1984 Conde Nast Publications, Inc. Illustration by Cara Goldberg Marks. **49(c)** Eliott Elisofon/Life Magazine, © Time Warner, Inc. **49(r)** Bill Aron/Tony Stone Images **50** Comstock Inc. **53** Courtesy Milkweed Press **55** Thomas Torak, "*After The Game.*" Oil on canvas, 20 x 30 inches. G.C.Lucas Gallery, Indianapolis, IN **59** © Franco Salmoiraghi **60** Vince Cavatio 1995/Allsport **62** Photo by Joli, From "*The Next Wave* " by Nick Carroll. Copyright Weldon Russell Pty Ltd. 1991. Published by Abbeville Press. **69** Robert Cottingham, "*Barber Shop,*" 1988. Oil on canvas, 32 x 32". Private Collection. Courtesy Louis K. Meisel Gallery, New York. Photo: Aaron J. Miller **74(t)** Photo by Carol Bruchac **74(b)** Pennsylvania Academy of Fine Arts **75** "*Dream of the Frog*" 12½"h x 5½"w x 5"d Steve Kestrel **76** Henri Edmond Cross, "*Landscape with Stars.*" Watercolor on paper. Metropolitan Museum of Art, Robert Lehman Collection, 1975.1.592 **77** Jean Lacy, "*Welcome to My Ghetto Land,*" 1986. Paint, gesso, gold leaf on wood panel, 6 x 3 inches. Dallas Museum of Art, Metropolitan Life Foundation Purchase Grant. **80** Courtesy Isaac Asimov **83** Colleen Browning, "*Computer Cosmology,*" 1980. Oil on canvas, 42 x 40½ inches. Private Collection. Photograph courtesy of Kennedy Galleries Inc., New York City **85** Courtesy of Sperry Corporation **89(all)** Pseudo Isochromatic Plates engraved and printed by the Beck Engraving Co., Inc. copyright 1940. **90(t)** ED141951 8205 "*The Vegetable Gardener*" by Arcimboldo, Giuseppe (1527–93), Museo Civico Ala Ponzone, Cremona/The Bridgeman Art Library, London **91(t)** © N.E.Thing Enterprises, Inc. Reprinted with permission of "Andrews & McMeel." All rights reserved. **91(b)** Illustration by Ivan Ripley, *Visual Magic* **102–103** "*Breezing Up,*" (A Fair Wind) 1876 Oil on canvas 35⅝ x 49¾, Homer, Winslow, National Gallery of Art, Washington, DC, Gift of the W. L. and May T. Mellon Foundation **103, 106, 161, 162, 167, 168, 184(icon)** Superstock, **104** E. H. Wallop/Stock Market **105** David Young-Wolff/PhotoEdit **107** Courtesy University of Montana Alumni Association, Missoula **108** George Lundeen **112** Mort Kunstler **117** Connie Hayes/Stock Illustration Source, Inc. **120** Bruno Liljefors, "*Foxes,*" 1886. Oil on canvas, 28⅔ x 36½ inches. Courtesy of The Gothenburg Art Gallery (Goteborgs Konstmuseum), Sweden. Photograph by Ebbe Carlsson. **126(b)** AP/Wide World **129** Mardonio Magana, "*Campesino con Yunta de Bueyes,*" c. 1928. Wood CNCA/INBA, Museo Nacional de Art, Mexico City **133** Courtesy the Author **134–135** E.H.Wallop/Stock Market **139** Jerry Wachter/Focus on Sports, Inc. **141** Claudio Edinger **144** Courtesy Farrar, Straus & Giroux **145** and **147** Victoria and Albert Museum, London/Art Resource **150** Courtesy the Author **152** Civic Library of Padua/David Harvey/Superstock, Inc. **154** National Gallery, London/Bridgeman Art Library/Superstock **157** Dante Gabriel Rossetti, "*Il Ramoscello,*" 1865. Oil on canvas, 18¾ x 15½ inches. Courtesy of the Fogg Art Museum, Harvard University Art Museums, bequest of Grenville L. Winthrop **162(l)** Bibliotheque Nationale, Paris/E. T. Archives, London/Superstock **162(r)** Composite, "*Brigandine Armor,*" Italian, ca 1400. Steel, brass, velvet; Wt. 41 lbs. Metropolitan Museum of Art, The Bashford Dean Memorial Collection, Gift of Helen Fahnestock Hubbard in memory of her father, Harris O. Fahnestock, 1929.29.154.3 **163(l)** From "*The Book of Samuri: The Warrior Class of Japan,*" by Stephen Turnbull. Copyright © 1992 Bison Books Limited. Published in the U.S. by Arco Publishing, Inc. Photo: Christies. **163(r)** Werner Forman/Art Resource **165** Lloyd Collection/The Manchester Museum **166** Superstock **169** John Morris **170–171** Michael Whelan, "*Weyrworld*" (Cover painting for All The Weyrs of Pern) 1991. Acrylics on watercolor board, 27 x 36 inches., original commissioned by Del Rey Books © 1991, Michael Whelan **174** Walter Velez **179** Michael Whelan, "*Destiny's Road,*" 1991, Acrylics on watercolor board, 30 x 40. Original commissioned by TOR Books © 1991 Michael Whelan **185(t)** Courtesy the Author **185(b)** Trustees of Amherst College **187** Elsie Benally, "*Women's Basketball Team,*" 1991, Sun-dried clay, paint, wool, cardboard, 6 x 2 x 2 inches each. **188** Winslow Homer, "*Mink Pond,*" 1891, Courtesy of Fogg Art Museum, Harvard University Art Museums, bequest of Grenville L. Winthrop **192–193** Romare Bearden, "*The Block,*" 1971. Cut and pasted paper on masonite, three of six panels. Metropolitan Museum of Art, Gift of Mr. and Mrs. Samuel Shore 1978 (1978.61.1-6) **196** Robert Vickrey, "*Seated Negress,*" 1954. Tempera 48 x 21, Courtesy of the Artist **201** Courtesy of Boyds Mills Press **202** Pablo Rivera/Superstock **203** Rene Magritte, "*Le Faux Miroir,*" 1935, Oil on canvas 7½ x 10⅝. © copyright ARS, NY, Private Collection. Herscovici/Art Resource **206(l)** Erich Lessing/Art Resource **206(c)** Erich Lessing/Art Resource

206(r) Ancient Art & Architecture Collection, London
206, 212, 223, 226(icon) Superstock **207(t)** Society S. Giorgio Deqli Sciavone, Venice/Superstock, Inc.
207(c) Stock Montage, Inc., Historical Pictures Service **207(b)** Robert Harding Picture Library **208(t)** Robert Frerck/Odyssey Productions **208(b)** British Museum, London. Bridgeman Art Library/Art Resource **210** Bob Daemmrich/Image Works **211** Mary Kate Denny/PhotoEdit **222-223** *American Liberty, New York*, 1984 © Michael Langenstein, computer graphics created on a Dicomed D38, Collection of the Artist. **223, 277, 304, 312, 318(icon)** Diana Ong, "The Runner," Superstock **225** Myrleen Ferguson/PhotoEdit **227(l)** National Portrait Gallery, London, Gift of daughter Jean Conan Doyle, 1959 **227(r)** Drawing of Sherlock Holmes by John Alan Maxwell for "*The Golden Book*" magazine, December 1930. From *Sherlock Holmes In America* by Bill Blackbeard, published by Harry N. Abrams, Inc. Used with permission **229** from "*Sherlock Holmes London*" by Tsukasa Kobayashi, Akane Higashiyama, and Masaharu Uemura. Copyright © 1984. Used with permission. **233** Fred Strebeigh **235** From "*The Adventure of the Dying Detective*," illustration by Walter Paget in *The Strand Magazine*, 1913 **243** Peter Poulides/Tony Stone Worldwide **245** Colleen Browning, "*Sly's Eye*," 1977. Oil 45¾ x 56½ inches. Art and Law 1986. Copyright 1986 Writ Publishing Corporation **248** AP/Wide World **251** Jeffry Myers/Stock Market **252** Henriette Wyeth, "*Young Peter*." Oil 15¾ x 14¼ inches. Photo Courtesy of Hurd-La Rinconada Gallery, San Patricio, NM. **255(t)** AP/Wide World **255(b)** Courtesy of the Author **257** © Marc Rosenthal **258** © 1993 Peggy Tagel/H.K. Portfolio **262** British Museum, London/Superstock **265** Bridgeman/Art Resource **269, 270, 276(icon)** Superstock **270(t)** North Wind Picture Archives **270(bl)** North Wind Picture Archives **270(br)** North Wind Picture Archives **271(t)** Mary Evans Picture Library **271(c)** UPI/Corbis-Bettmann **271(b)** N.Rowan/Image Works **273** Peter Menzel **274–275** Dale D. Glasgow/National Geographic Society **278(l)** Morris Dollens **278(r)** NASA **280** Courtesy of the Artist **283** Private Collection. Photography courtesy of the Charles Burchfield Archives, Burchfield-Penney Art Center, Buffalo State College, Buffalo, NY **287** New York Post staff photo by William Jacobellis/University of Georgia Press **289** Jacob Lawrence, "*Vaudeville*," 1951. Tempera on gesso. 30 x 20 inches. Hirshhorn Museum and Sculpture Garden, Smithsonian Institution, gift of Joseph H. Hirshhorn, 1966. Photo: Lee Stalsworth. **291** Jacob Lawrence, "*Grand Performance*," 1993. Lithograph on Rives, BFK paper, 26½ x 20¼ inches. Courtesy of the Artist and Francine Seder Gallery, Seattle, WA **301** From "*I Never Saw Another Butterfly: Children's Drawings and Poems from Terezin Concentration Camp*," 1942–1944/State Jewish Museum, Prague **305(b)** Corbis-Bettmann Archive **307** Raymond Lark, "*Society*," oil painting 24 x 30 inches. Collection of Mary Moran, New Jersey. Photo courtesy Edwin Smith & Company, Los Angeles **312(t)** Bibliotheque Royale Albert 1er, Brussels **312(bl)** Corbis-Bettmann Archive **312(br)** North Wind Picture Archives **312(icon)** Diana Ong, "The Runner," Superstock **313(cl)** North Wind Picture Archives **313(cr)** AP/Wide World **313(b)** UPI/Corbis-Bettmann **313(t)** "*Trail of Tears*" by Robert Lindneaux, Woolaroc Museum, Bartesville, Oklahoma **314** David Young-Wolff/PhotoEdit **317** Superstock

328–329 "*In Pursuit of Paradise*" © Kara Szathmary **329(icon)** Superstock **329(icon)** Superstock **330(t)** Greenberg/PhotoEdit **330(b)** Mary Kate Denny/PhotoEdit **331(t)** Bonnie Kamin/PhotoEdit **331(b)** David Young-Wolff/PhotoEdit **332(icon)** Superstock **333** From the Estate of Rod Serling **335** Charles Burchfield, "*Yellow Afterglow*," 1916. Watercolor with pencil on paper, 20 x 14 inches. Collection of the Burchfield Art Center, Buffalo State College, Buffalo, New York, gift of Tony Sisti, 1979:29. **339** Eric Dinyer/Graphistock **345** Robert McCall **348** Corbis-Bettmann Archive **350** Illustration from *The Cremation of Sam McGee* by Robert Service, Introduction by Pierre Berton, Illustrations by Ted Harrison. Illustration copyright © 1986 by Ted Harrison. Reprinted by permission of Greenwillow Books, a division of William Morrow & Company, Inc. **355** Richard McNamee **356** Linda Nelson/Gould Design **361** Laszlo Moholy-Nagy, "*Light-Space Modulator*," 1923–1930. Steel, plastic, wood; height: 4 feet 11½ inches. Courtesy of the Busch-Reisinger Museum, Harvard University Art Museums, Gift of Sibyl Moholy-Nagy, © President and Fellows Harvard College. **365(t)** Courtesy of the Author **365(b)** AP/Wide World **366-367** U. S. Embassy Photo **372(b)** Courtesy, Harper, Collins Publishers **373** Fan Kuan, "*Travelers Among Mountains and Streams*," early 11th century. Hanging scroll, ink on silk, 81¼ inches. National Palace Museum, Taipei, Taiwan **374** Robert Gwathmey, "*Portrait of a Farmer's Wife*," 1951. Oil on canvas, 44¼ x 34 inches. Hirshhorn Museum and Sculpture Garden, Smithsonian Institution, Gift of The Joseph H. Hirshhorn Foundation, 1966. © VAGA (Photo: John Tennant). Museum No. SG66.2304 **377, 378, 383, 384(icon)** Superstock **378** The Granger Collection, New York **379** Jean-Loup Charmet **380(tl)** British Museum **380(tr)** Royal Geographical Society **380(b)** Bridgeman/Art Resource **381** North Wind Picture Archives **382** North Wind Picture Archives **385(t)** Courtesy Scholastic **385(b)** Courtesy Harper, Collins Publishers **387** "*That Gentleman*" 1960 Andrew Wyeth, Egg tempura on board. 23¼" x 47¾". Dallas Museum of Art, Dallas Art Association Purchase. **390** Thomas Eakins, "*The Banjo Player*," study for "*Negro Boy Dancing*," c. 1878. Oil on canvas, 20 x 15¼ inches. National Gallery of Art, Washington, D.C.; collection of Mr. and Mrs. Paul Mellon **396** UPI/Corbis-Bettmann **399** William Vincent, "*Maasai, Masai Mara*." Oil, 48 x 36 inches **403** William Vincent, "*Magestic King*." Oil, 36 x 48 inches. **409** Courtesy the Author **411** Eva Hesse, "*Untitled*," Gouache & collage on paper mounted on board 22 x 22 x 4 inches 1964 © The Estate of Eva Hesse. Courtesy Robert Miller Gallery, New York. **414** Superstock **415** Courtesy Viking Press, Photo: Bonnie Schiffman **417** George Rodrigue, Richard Steiner and Blue Dog Galleries, **420** THE FAR SIDE copyright 1987 FARWORKS, INC. Distributed by Universal Press Syndicate. Reprinted with permission. All rights reserved. **422(t)** Courtesy Prescott Street Press **423** Roxana Villa/Stock Illustration Source, Inc. **428** Photo by K. Yep **431** Edo period, unidentified artist, Sotatsu-Korin School six fold screen: River scene with trees and flowers. Colors on paper H 48 in. W 123 in. Metropolitan Museum of Art, Gift of Horace Havemeyer, 1949 (49.35.2) **434, 435, 440, 451, 454, 486, 494(icon)** Superstock **435** Robert Caputo/Aurora B Boltin Picture Library **436(insert)** National Museum of African Art, Eliot Eliosfon Photographic Archives, Smithsonian

436–437(background) Stock Montage, Inc. 437 Stock Montage, Inc. 438(tl) North Wind Picture Archives 438(tr) UPI/Corbis-Bettmann 438(b) North Wind Picture Archives 439(tl) North Wind Picture Archives 439(tr) Stock Montage, Inc. 439(c) North Wind Picture Archives 439(b) Stock Montage, Inc. 450–451 Christie's, London/Superstock 455 AP/Wide World 456 *"Extra Paper (State Street Scene)"* 1946, watercolor on paper, 17 3/4 x 24 inches, A. J. Motley, Jr./46, DuSable Museum of African American History 461(l) Courtesy, Addison-Wesley, Photo: Spencer Jarnigan 461(r) The Audubon Society 463 Erich Lessing/Art Resource 468, 472 Two illustrations from "Alfred the Sweet-shop Cat" from *James Herriot's Cat Stories* by James Herriot, with illustrations by Lesley Holmes, pages 10-11 and left on page 1. Illustrations © 1994 by Lesley Holmes. Reprinted by permission of St. Martin's Press, Inc. and Harold Ober Associates, Inc. 479 AP/Wide World 481 Jacob Lawrence, *"The Library,"* 1960. Tempera on fiberboard, 30 x 24, National Museum of American Art, gift of S. C. Johnson & Sons, Inc./Art Resource, New York 487 Courtesy, Arte Publico Press, Photo: William Ahrend 488 Lerner Fine Art Colllection/Superstock, Inc. 495 THE FARSIDE © 1990 FARWORKS, INC. Distributed by Universal Press Syndicate. Reprinted with permission. All rights reserved. 496(t) North Wind Picture Archives 496(cl) North Wind Picture Archives 496(cr) North Wind Picture Archives 496(b) Stock Montage, Inc. 497(tl) North Wind Picture Archives 497(tr) Martin/Custom Medical Stock Photo 497(br) Corbis-Bettmann Archive 497(bl) UPI/Corbis-Bettmann 498(t) Art & Science, Inc./Custom Medical Stock Photo 498(c) Custom Medical Stock Photo 498(l) D.Richardson/Custom Medical Stock Photo 499, 500, 510, 550(icon) Superstock 501 Courtesy Harper, Collins, Photo: Zoe Kamitses 503 Private Collection, Courtesy of Hirschl and Adler, NY, Photo: © Zindman/Fremont 505 Christie's, London/Superstock, Inc. 507 Superstock 511 AP/Wide World 513 Private Collection/Romare Howard Bearden, Foundation, Inc. 519 © Gina Carra 524 Private Collection/Robert Vickrey 529 Cornell Capa/Magnum Photos 531 UPI/Corbis-Bettmann 534 Courtesy Pfeifer-Hamilton Publishers 536 Uehlsmann, Jerry 538 Jerry Uehlsmann 541 Courtesy Harper, Collins Publishers 543 Philbrook Museum of Art 546(t) Corbis-Bettmann Archive 546(bl) Library of Congress 546(c) Ancient Art & Architecture Collection/Ronald Sheridan Photo-Library 546–547(br) Library of Congress 546(icon) Superstock 547(t) Smithsonian Institution 547(c) Corbis-Bettmann Archive 549 United Feature Syndicate 560–561 *"Death on the Ridge Road,"* Grant Wood, 1935, Williams College

Museum of Art, Gift of Cole Porter 561, 564, 609, 610, 615(icon) Tom Holton/Superstock 561, 616, 665, 666, 670(icon) Marilee Whitehouse-Holm, International/Superstock 562(t) Carol Hoy 563(b) Illustration by Maurice Wilson from *"The Jungle Book"* by Rudyard Kipling, published by Schocken Books, 1984. © The National Trust, Illustration © Macmillan Publishers Ltd., 1983, All rights reserved. 565 Photo by Sandra L. Swans/Random House 567 Cleveland Museum of Art, 1995, Gift of Mrs. Malcolm L. McBride, CMA 57.432 570–571 Tom Medcalf for Scott, Foresman 576(b) Dartmouth College 579, 581 Peter Adler Collection/From the book *Asafo! African Flags of the Fante,"* published by Thames and Hudson 583 © 1982 Robert Bateman reproduction rights, Courtesy of Boshking, Inc. and Mill Pond Press, Inc. 586 Courtesy of Arte Publico Press 589 Courtesy of the artist, Carol Hoy, Albuquerque, NM, Photo: Bob Wartell 593 National Portrait Gallery, London 595 From *"The Painted Garden,"* Quarto Publishing, painting from Christie's Contemporary Art, London. Reproduced with permission. 600 Victoria & Albert Museum, London/Art Resource 603 Illustration by Maurice Wilson from *"The Jungle Book"* by Rudyard Kipling, published by Schocken Books, 1984, Text © The National Trust, illustrations © Macmillan Publishers Ltd. 1983, All Rights reserved. 609, 610(icon) Superstock 613 Wolfgang Bayer 614 Larry Luxner 619 Museum of Fine Art, Boston/Lerner/Superstock 625 Tretlakov Gallery, Moscow/A. Burkatousky/Superstock, Inc. 631 Private Collection/Superstock 639 AP/Wide World 641 Superstock 646(b) AP/Wide World 646(t) UPI/Corbis-Bettmann 647 Lawrence, Jacob. *"Industries attempted to board their labor in quarters that were oftentimes very unhealthy. Labor camps were numerous."* Panel 46 from *"The Migration Series,"* (1940–41; text and title revised by the artist, 1993). Tempera on gesso on composition board, 18 x 12' (45.7 x 30.5 cm). The Museum of Modern Art, New York. Gift of Mrs. David M. Levy. Photograph © 1995 The Museum of Modern Art, New York. 648 Superstock 653 *"Morning Star Over Cerro Gordo,"* R. Douglas Wiggins, 1993, oil on canvas, 43" x 60", Cline Fine Art Gallery 657 AP/Wide World 659, 660–661 Janet Fleisher Gallery 666(l) Metropolitan Museum of Art, Rogers Fund and Contribution from Edward S. Harkness, (80178B) 666(cl) Sappho/Art Resource 666(cr) Maurice Durand Collection of Vietnamese Art, Southeast Asian Collection, Sterling Library, Yale University 666(r) Museum of Antiquities, Ife 667(l) Folger Shakespeare Library, Washington, D.C. 667(cl) Nevada Historical Society, Reno 667(cr) AP/Wide World 667(r) Sygma 669(c) Kevin Schaefer